# BUSINESS COMMUNICATION FOR THE COMPUTER AGE

M. H. Rader, Ph. D.
Arizona State University

Linda A. Kurth, Ph. D.
Phoenix College

Published by

**E55**  **SOUTH-WESTERN PUBLISHING CO.**

CINCINNATI     WEST CHICAGO, IL     CARROLLTON, TX     LIVERMORE, CA

**ISBN:** 0-538-05550-2

**Library of Congress Catalog Card Number:** 87-60126

1 2 3 4 5 6 7 8 9 D 6 5 4 3 2 1 0 9 8

**Printed in the United States of America**

# PREFACE

Inside the office—from business to business—between states and around the world—information is traveling farther and faster than ever before. Companies are handling *more* information than ever. The "information explosion" means that managers and other business professionals are communicating more than they did in the past.

To succeed in business now and in the future, students must master the communication skills that are necessary in a high-technology business environment. These skills include basic competencies in written and oral communication and, in addition, the ability to use a computer.

## The Need for Change

According to a report in *The Journal of Business Communication*, business communication instruction is lagging in use of computer technology.[1] Companies are presently installing computer-based communication systems at a rapid rate, and business communication instruction is now in a period of transition as we adapt our courses to technological change. A national survey of business communication instructors sponsored by the AACSB revealed that 24 percent were using computers for instructional purposes and 61 percent were considering using them.[2] A research project sponsored by the Association for Business Communication concluded that ". . . business communication instructors need to be able to do more, however, than simply 'tell' their students about computer-based communication systems. They need to be able to practice what they preach."[3] The report strongly recommended that business communication instructors adopt computer-based methods of communication instruction. Additionally, the report concluded that "The future of the Association may well depend on how quickly its members can develop expertise in computer-based forms of communication."

## Meeting the Challenge

This textbook was developed to meet the challenge of integrating traditional business communication skills with modern computer technology. The book builds a foundation of communication skills that students can use throughout their business careers. Students will learn how to plan and write letters, memos, and reports. They will master the oral communication skills that are necessary for meetings, presentations, and interviews. Students also will get the "big picture" of how to manage communication—people, information, and technology—throughout an organization. This foundation, reinforced

---

[1]John M. Penrose, Joel P. Bowman, and Marie E. Flatley, "The Impact of Microcomputers on ABC with Recommendations for Teaching, Writing, and Research," *The Journal of Business Communication* 24, no. 4 (Fall 1987): 88.

[2]Mary Munter, "Using the Computer in Business Communication Courses, *The Journal of Business Communication* 23, no. 1 (Winter 1986): 32.

[3]Penrose et al., 89.

with relevant applications and case studies, will help students to become effective communicators in today's high-technology business world.

## A Contemporary Approach

*Business Communication for the Computer Age* merges traditional business communication instruction with modern technology. The text integrates computer technology and related communication applications throughout the book rather than confining them to one or two chapters. It emphasizes skills that students will need in their business careers and stresses the application of those skills to current business problems.

The text is intended for use in sophomore and junior-level principles of business communication courses, including those in AACSB-accredited institutions. Progressive colleges, universities, and community colleges will find that the book meets the needs of all business students as well as nonbusiness students who take business communication courses. The book is written in a nontechnical style that accommodates students who have not taken a computer course.

## Contents and Organization

The book contains 20 chapters that are organized into the following seven parts:

Part 1 contains two chapters and an eight-page insert of color pictures showing contemporary uses of business communication. The first chapter introduces business communication, discusses its relevance and use of computer technology, and presents an overview of the textbook. The second chapter presents communication theory as a framework for studying business communication and its applications.

Part 2 includes two chapters that cover principles of written communication. Chapter 3 presents the elements of effective business writing—the classic "five C's" of business communication. Chapter 4 discusses how to plan and organize business messages. Both chapters employ a practical "how to" approach and contain many relevant examples.

Part 3 includes three chapters that discuss how to write various types of business letters and memorandums. The chapters contain up-to-date examples of individually prepared and computer-generated messages.

Part 4 contains four chapters that deal with business reports. The first two chapters cover business research methods—planning a research project, writing a research proposal, collecting data, and analyzing data—presented in greater depth than most textbooks. Chapter 10 covers graphic communication and illustrates many examples of computer graphics and related equipment. Chapter 11 discusses writing style, structure, and format of formal and informal reports. Two complete reports—a formal analytical report and an informal memorandum report—are included as examples.

Part 5 includes four chapters devoted to employment communication and other special-purpose messages. Chapter 12 discusses resumes and job-application letters, and Chapter 13 covers employment interviews and other employment communication. Chapter 14 introduces contemporary credit and collection messages and procedures, and Chapter 15 discusses goodwill and personnel messages. The discussion of "Credit and Collection Messages" (Chapter 14), is innovative in its presentation of technological changes that have radically affected how businesses communicate credit and collection information.

Part 6 contains three chapters that present various types of oral and non-verbal communication. This section includes the following topics: listening and nonverbal communication, oral presentations and dictation, and business meetings. These chapters are written from a practical "how to" perspective.

Part 7 presents a view of communication throughout organizations. This section contains two chapters — one about communication technology and the other about the management of organizational communication. Chapter 19 discusses computer-based communication systems and contains eight-pages of color pictures of various systems components. Chapter 20 "wraps up" the text by discussing effective management of organizational communication from a systems perspective.

The book also includes three appendices that contain a review of grammar and mechanics, a review of document formats, and a glossary of computer terms. Appendix A contains rules of grammar and mechanics, including punctuation, capitalization, abbreviation, number style, word division, and proofreaders' marks; it also contains a list of 100 frequently misspelled words. In addition, the appendix provides clear examples of the application of each rule, as well as exercises for students to complete.

Appendix B serves as a reference for document formats. Letter parts and styles, memorandums, and a formal academic-style report are included in this appendix.

Appendix C contains a glossary of 100 computer terms that are related to business communication. The glossary is intended for students to use as a vocabulary reference.

## Special Features

*Business Communication for the Computer Age* contains the following special features to enhance student learning:

1. *Vignettes*. Each chapter opens with a brief conversational-style vignette of a business situation that relates to the chapter topic. The vignettes are designed to add interest, realism, and relevance to the chapters.
2. *Chapter Review*. The review questions included at the end of each chapter may be assigned as homework or used for individual study.
3. *Applications*. Each chapter includes a number of realistic and timely applications that may be used as homework assignments or in-class projects.
4. *Case Studies*. Each chapter contains a case study that relates to the chapter topic. Case studies are designed to stimulate lively class discussions and may be used as group or individual projects.

5. *Suggested Readings*. A brief list of current or classic books is included at the end of each chapter. The suggested readings may be used to supplement the textbook or provide material for students' written or oral reports.

6. *Visual Aids*. The book contains a wealth of visual aids to enhance student learning. The graphics artwork included in Chapter 10 is particularly noteworthy.

## Instructional Supplements

The following supplements are available to accompany the textbook:

1. *Instructor's Manual*. The comprehensive instructor's manual contains teaching tips; transparency masters; tests; and solutions to chapter reviews, applications, case studies, and appendix exercises.

2. *Supplementary Applications Template Diskette*. This up-to-date supplement replaces traditional workbooks and study guides with a computer diskette containing composition and text-editing applications. Versions are available for use with WordStar, WordPerfect, MultiMate, DisplayWrite 3, and AppleWorks.

3. *MicroSWAT Test Bank*. This state-of-the art feature generates chapter tests, unit tests, and examinations. Versions are available for use on the IBM PC and Apple IIe and IIc computers.

## Acknowledgments

The authors are grateful to P. K. Ebert for contributing 11 case studies and writing the sample reports included in Chapter 11. In addition, we wish to thank Lynne McClure for writing six of the case studies.

We also extend our thanks to the following individuals who have shared their ideas, materials, time, and support: Vanessa Dean Arnold, University of Mississippi; Barbara Duel, Motorola, Inc.; Doris Engerrand, Georgia College; Cathryn Friedman, Arizona State University; Clifford J. Hurston, Arizona State University; Charles Kuhn, Central Missouri State University; Thomas Lyon, The Arnold Corporation; Emmett McFarland, Central Missouri State University; Willie Minor, Phoenix College; B. Scot Ober, Central Michigan University; Norman K. Perrill, Arizona State University; Mary Martha Rader, New Times, Inc.; Lois Ripley, Sears, Roebuck & Co.; Lynn Whitman, Broadway Southwest; Al Williams, University of Southern Louisiana.

Also, we appreciate the assistance of the following reviewers who provided many helpful suggestions: Frances G. Chandler, Santa Monica College; Sam Deep, University of Pittsburgh; Doris D. Engerrand, Ph.D., Georgia College; Clinton O. Longenecker, Ph.D., University of Toledo; Jeffery D. Stauffer, Ed.D., Ventura College; Dr. William J. Vaughn, Pan American University, Brownsville.

Finally, we extend a special thanks to our mentors, Wayne M. Baty and Keith Davis, who inspired us to begin, motivated us to continue, and helped us in innumerable ways.

*M.H.R. and L.A.K.*

# CONTENTS

# FOUNDATIONAL COMMUNICATION CONCEPTS

## PART 1

Communication involves people, ideas, and language. Every culture throughout history has developed a system of communication called *language*, which may be written or spoken. Communication is vital to civilization because government and other social institutions and organizations depend on relationships among people and those relationships are based on communication.

In our culture, the economic system functions through business organizations, which rely on various forms of communication to conduct their business activities. Through communication, employees coordinate the interrelated tasks necessary to accomplish company goals, manage the internal structure and systems of the company, and relate to one another on a personal level.

Today's communication systems are extremely complex, as machines have become increasingly involved in the process of communication. The basic components of people, ideas, and language have expanded to include sophisticated machines, electronic signals, and special languages. In business organizations, communication has entered the computer age.

# BUSINESS COMMUNICATION AND COMPUTERS

## CHAPTER 1

Imagine arriving at work in the morning, turning on the computer at your desk, and checking your **electronic mail**. You find three messages that had been sent to you and stored in the memory of your computer after you left the office the day before.

The first message on your computer screen is a memo to you from someone in another department of your company. You compose a reply at your computer keyboard and then send your memo by electronic mail to a computer terminal in the appropriate department.

The second message is a sales report from one of your company's regional offices in another state. You briefly scan the sales report displayed on your computer screen, then store it electronically for later reference.

The third message is a notice about an upcoming **electronic meeting** linking participants at various locations across the country through their computer terminals. You decide to participate in the meeting, so you transfer the notice to your **electronic calendar**, which keeps track of your daily schedule in the computer.

Is this scene part of the distant future? No, this technology is here today and is only a sample of the communication technology you will be exposed to in your business career. Electronic sending and storing of information is part of business communication in the computer age.

This chapter provides a brief discussion of the following topics:

- An introduction to business communication, its role in business organizations, and its importance for various business careers
- The changing technology of the computer age and the implications for business communication
- Goals and objectives for improving your business communication skills
- An introduction to *Business Communication for the Computer Age* and an overview of its contents

## INTRODUCTION TO BUSINESS COMMUNICATION

**Business communication** refers to the process of transmitting business information from one person to another and assessing the effects of that process on people's behavior. Business communication takes place whenever a sender relays business information to a receiver. The information, which deals with a business topic or activity, may be in various forms or media such as meetings, oral and written reports, letters, memorandums, and computer printouts.

Although communication may involve all our senses, we mainly use four basic processes to send and receive business information. We send business information by *speaking* and *writing,* and we receive business information by *listening* and *reading*. As an academic discipline, business communication focuses on the role of the sender, not because the receiver's role is unimportant, but because the sender does most of the work and is primarily responsible for the success or failure of the message. For that reason, effective business communication requires writing and speaking skills, and business communication courses emphasize improving those skills.

### Communication in Business Organizations

Communication is important for every business organization because all business activities depend upon communication in one form or another. To conduct their business, companies must communicate with people (such as employees, customers, suppliers, the media, stockholders, and government agencies) both inside and outside the organization.

Communicating with people outside the company is referred to as **external business communication**. Various types of business letters, advertising campaigns, and public relations activities are examples of external business communications.

**Internal business communications**, which are intended primarily for employees of the company, are necessary for coordinating activities and relationships within the organization. Interoffice memorandums, meetings, interdepartmental reports, computer printouts, bulletin boards, and employee newsletters are examples of internal business communications.

## Communication in Business Careers

Communication plays a vital part in professional-level business careers. People employed in high-level business positions are generally required to spend more of their time communicating than are lower-level employees. Assembly-line workers, for example, usually spend only a small percentage of their working time communicating with others. On the other hand, the major task of business executives is communication. One communication industry expert has reported that business executives spend an average of 94 percent of a typical work day on communication activities. **Oral communication** (mostly meetings and telephone calls) takes up 69 percent of their time. **Written communication** (reading and writing reports, letters, and memos) occupies 25 percent of the average executive's work day (Plotzke, 1982, 8).

Communication is so important for advancement that a manager may be promoted to an executive position primarily because of her or his speaking and writing abilities. In such an instance, the ability to communicate can be more of a significant factor than other qualifications such as technical knowledge, intelligence, and initiative.

Other professional-level business positions also require communication skills. Accountants need to be competent writers because writing reports is one of their most important responsibilities. Likewise, economists, financial analysts, marketing researchers, statisticians, and many middle managers also write reports as a major job responsibility. Computer programmers and systems analysts spend a great deal of time writing reports and manuals as well.

Everyone needs **interpersonal communication skills**, which require the ability to express oneself clearly and relate well to others when carrying on a conversation. Many business people also need to be skilled in giving oral presentations to large or small groups. For example, marketing, public relations, training and development, personnel management, and other business careers specifically require public-speaking skills.

In summary, all professional-level business careers require the ability to communicate oral and written information effectively. Speaking and writing skills are universally important for success in the business world.

# COMPUTER-AGE TECHNOLOGY AND BUSINESS COMMUNICATION

The changing technology of the computer age has increased the importance of communication skills. Today's *information explosion* has made communication even more important than in the past because organizations handle more information every year. Before it can be used, information must be communicated to those who need it. Instead of reducing communication or lessening its importance, computers have changed the communication process by simplifying communication methods and taking the drudgery out of many communication tasks. As a result, business jobs have changed and will continue to change in the next few years.

**Computer literacy,** or familiarity with computers, is now a necessity in the business world. One survey found that 70 percent of employees working in various types of professional-level business positions such as accounting, data processing, marketing, management, and finance were using personal computers on the job (Cerveny and Joseph, 1986, 14-15). A study conducted by the Stanford University Graduate School of Business revealed that senior executives who use computers were using them for planning and decision support (60 percent), office automation (57 percent), and monitoring and control (51 percent). The study also indicated that 55 percent of the executives had a computer at home (Moore, 1986, 7).

In the past, business communication mostly consisted of paper correspondence, telephone calls, and meetings. In today's communication milieu, paper correspondence is being replaced by electronic mail. Telephones are being supplemented by voice and electronic message systems, and meetings are often being conducted through computer conferences and other types of teleconferences.

## Multi-Function Workstations

The **multi-function workstation** (often called an *executive workstation*) has become standard equipment on the desks of many executives, managers, and other business professionals. These workstations may include a personal computer or a computer terminal linked to a larger computer.

With a multi-function workstation, business professionals can use a computer to perform many routine tasks that used to be handled by secretaries and other support personnel. Since the computer is faster, more accurate, and involves a more efficient use of time, many executives are now using computers to compose correspondence rather than dictating them to a secretary.

Multi-function workstations are systems that facilitate communication by applying computer processing and data-storage resources to compiling, interpreting, and analyzing information. A well-designed system can easily provide all of the following workstation functions:

1. Text editing through word-processing packages
2. Spelling and grammar checking
3. Computer-generated graphics
4. Spreadsheet analysis
5. Electronic mail
6. Computer conferencing
7. Electronic scheduling and calendaring

8. Database management and indexing
9. Information tracking

These features will be discussed in more detail in later chapters.

## Computer Software

Computer application packages known as **software** are commercially available for most computers. **User-friendly**—that is, easy-to-operate—software performs one or more applications or functions such as preparing accounts payable, accounts receivable, general ledger, mailing lists, payroll, stock charts, spreadsheets, inventory control records, and production schedules.

**Word Processing**. In simple terms, **word processing** means writing with a computer. Word-processing software tells the computer what to do with your text as you key it in and after you have entered it. Common applications for word processing include writing letters, memos, and reports.

Early versions of word-processing programs (often referred to as *first generation* software) were used mainly by secretarial personnel. Today, integrated management-support software, which is designed for managers, combines several functions such as word processing, database management, spreadsheet analysis, and graphics.

Picture yourself preparing a report on a typewriter for one of your business classes. After spending what seemed to be an eternity writing in longhand, you are ready to type what you hope will be the final copy. However, since you are not an expert typist, you know it might not be your last attempt. After making a couple of mistakes, which you paint over with white-out, you begin to feel anxious and tense about more typos. You are approaching the end of the page, and one more mistake will be the last straw! After all, you already have ten pages to retype because you found errors even after you took the paper out of the typewriter.

The advanced technology of word-processing software now relegates such an experience to the past. Most word-processing packages can perform the following functions:

1. Insert and delete characters, words, lines, or paragraphs
2. Move blocks (groups of lines) of text
3. Search and replace all occurrences of a misspelled or misused word with the correct word
4. Screen format (keyed in instructions tell the printer how the document is to look when it is printed)
5. Set tabs and margins (similar to standard typewriter settings)

Additional features of some word-processing packages include spelling checkers, grammar and punctuation checkers, and **mail merge** (the ability to merge documents with mailing lists). Some software will automatically number pages, format a document, and place footnotes at the bottom of a page.

ILLUSTRATION A    THE MULTI-FUNCTION WORKSTATION IS BECOMING STANDARD EQUIPMENT ON THE DESKS OF EXECUTIVES AND MANAGERS.

ILLUSTRATION B    COMPUTERS HAVE CHANGED THE COMMUNICATION PROCESS BY TAKING THE DRUDGERY OUT OF MANY TASKS.

ILLUSTRATION C    COMPUTER LITERACY OR FAMILIARITY WITH
COMPUTERS IS NOW A NECESSITY.

ILLUSTRATION D    PROFESSIONAL-LEVEL BUSINESS PERSONNEL
ARE USING PERSONAL COMPUTERS FOR VARIOUS TASKS.

ILLUSTRATION E   BY USING COMPUTER-GENERATED GRAPHICS, YOU CAN EASILY CONSTRUCT PROFESSIONAL-LOOKING VISUAL AIDS.

ILLUSTRATION F   THE COMPUTER AGE HAS CHANGED BUSINESS COMMUNICATION METHODS.

ILLUSTRATION G   TODAY, INTEGRATED MANAGEMENT-SUPPORT SOFTWARE COMBINES
FUNCTIONS SUCH AS SPREADSHEET ANALYSIS AND GRAPHICS.

ILLUSTRATION H   USER-FRIENDLY SOFTWARE
PREPARES ACCOUNTS RECEIVABLE AND INVENTORY
CONTROL RECORDS.

ILLUSTRATION I  EVEN THOUGH A COMPUTER IS A POWERFUL TOOL, ITS IQ IS ZERO! YOU STILL NEED TO LEARN PRINCIPLES OF BUSINESS COMMUNICATION.

ILLUSTRATION J  ELECTRONIC MAIL SWIFTLY RELAYS INFORMATION THROUGH TELECOMMUNICATION SYSTEMS.

ILLUSTRATION K   INTEROFFICE MEETINGS ARE ONE FORM OF INTERNAL BUSINESS COMMUNICATION.

ILLUSTRATION L   MANY BUSINESS PEOPLE NEED TO BE SKILLED IN
GIVING ORAL PRESENTATIONS TO LARGE OR SMALL GROUPS.

ILLUSTRATION M    A JOB INTERVIEW TESTS YOUR ORAL COMMUNICATION SKILLS.

ILLUSTRATION N    INTERDEPARTMENTAL REPORTS (COMPUTER PRINTOUTS) ARE NECESSARY FOR COORDINATING ACTIVITIES WITHIN AN ORGANIZATION.

ILLUSTRATION O   MANY COLLEGE STUDENTS OWN
PERSONAL COMPUTERS AND USE THEM FOR
HOMEWORK ASSIGNMENTS.

ILLUSTRATION P   TELEPHONE COMMUNICATION OFTEN PLAYS
A VITAL PART IN BUSINESS TRANSACTIONS.

However, such software does not eliminate the need for those who use it to know and apply the rules of English mechanics. For example, a spelling checker may not be able to determine if a word is spelled correctly in context. In other words, it may not be able to distinguish between "to," "too," or "two."

**Computer Graphics**. Graphics software can create visual displays of various types. By using computer-generated graphics, you can easily construct professional-looking visual aids such as pie charts, line graphs, and drawings to enliven business reports and group presentations. Graphics packages are also used extensively in designing technical illustrations, advertising layouts, and engineering specifications. To use graphics software, a computer must have a CRT terminal (screen) with graphics capability. Some graphics terminals can construct graphics in a variety of colors.

## Electronic Mail

**Electronic mail** swiftly relays computerized information by telecommunication systems. The latter consists of data communication networks that involve one or more channels such as telephone lines, various types of cables, microwave relay stations, or communication satellites to transmit data from one computer to another.

To use a computer-based mail system, you simply key a message on a computer keyboard, and your message will be converted into electronic signals that are transmitted through the telecommunication system. Your message will instantly be sent to the receiver's computer and stored in a special file (sometimes referred to as an *electronic mailbox*) until the message is retrieved.

Electronic mail can be used to send messages to other employees in the same building, to company branch offices, and to other companies across the country or around the world. Organizations can use electronic mail to transmit computer files containing massive amounts of data just as easily as they can use it to send short messages such as memos or letters.

Electronic mail is the fastest and least expensive method of sending large quantities of data across long distances. Some executives use electronic mail as a substitute for transcontinental telephone calls, particularly when the sender and receiver are several time zones apart. For example, an electronics company located in Phoenix, Arizona, communicates regularly with its subsidiaries in France and Germany. However, it is the middle of the night in Europe when it is daytime in Phoenix. Electronic mail solves the problem of time differences because messages sent at any time of the day or night are stored in the receiver's computer until he or she arrives at the office and accesses (retrieves) the information.

One popular option is **certified electronic mail**, which automatically notifies the sender when the message has been received. Another option is **computer conferencing**, which companies use for long-distance meetings and conferences by linking several computers in various locations.

## IMPROVING BUSINESS COMMUNICATION SKILLS

Even though a computer is a powerful tool, its IQ is zero! Therefore, when using a computer to complete assignments in this text or for job-related tasks in the future, you will need to learn and apply principles of business communication. The basic writing concepts, theories, and other principles presented in the chapters of this book provide the firm foundation you will need to become an effective business communicator.

Business-communication principles encompass concepts from a number of related fields such as psychology, English, management, organizational behavior, computer science, speech, marketing, and public relations. To communicate effectively, you also need certain personal attributes such as sensitivity to other people, common sense, and the motivation to learn. Finally, you need to develop certain skills that will help you accomplish your goals in your business courses, in your personal life, and in your future career.

The expertise and skills that this textbook emphasizes are intended to help you achieve the following objectives:

1. To learn about communication theories and processes that apply to business organizations
2. To be able to use communication to convey information and influence people favorably
3. To know how to analyze and solve business communication problems
4. To improve your ability to express yourself in writing
5. To develop your skills in nonwritten communication, including speaking to groups, listening, interviewing, and conducting meetings
6. To learn about communication management and technological innovations in business communication

## OVERVIEW OF THE TEXTBOOK

This textbook is designed to modernize business communication instruction by bringing together business communication theory and modern applications. *Business Communication for the Computer Age* integrates traditional business communication instruction with current communication technology. The textbook emphasizes areas and develops skills that you will need in your future career. The book also stresses the application of these skills to current business situations; and all examples, exercises, and cases are as realistic as possible.

The textbook is divided into the following major sections: Foundational Communication Concepts, Written Communication Principles, Business Letters and Memorandums, Business Reports, Special-Purpose Messages, Nonwritten Communication, Communication Throughout the Organization, and three appendices. The appendices, which are designed to be used as references, include information such as a dictionary of computer terminology, letter and memorandum formats, and a review of English mechanics. Several review exercises are also included.

At the end of each chapter, review questions and applications are provided to help you understand and assimilate the material. Each chapter also contains a case for you to study, individually or with a group of other students. Suggested readings, which include a list of current or classic books about the topics dealt with in each chapter, may be used to supplement the textbook or to provide material for you to use in preparing oral presentations or written reports.

## SUMMARY

Business communication is concerned with the process of sending and receiving business information to and from individuals and organizations. Business information is generally communicated in forms such as meetings, oral and written reports, letters, memorandums, computer messages, etc. Thus, business communication courses emphasize writing and speaking skills.

Communication skills are a requirement for success in any business career. Writing skills are needed in most middle- and upper-level business positions, while interpersonal communication skills are necessary at all levels for the purpose of getting along with other people. Most professional-level business people also conduct or participate in meetings and speak to groups occasionally, and oral communication skills are an important requirement for them as well.

The computer age has changed business communication methods. Instead of writing messages in longhand or dictating them to a secretary, business professionals now use computers to compose messages. With the new technology, one does not have to be an expert typist to write and print perfect letters, memorandums, and reports. Some word-processing software packages help check spelling, grammar, and punctuation. With electronic mail, written messages can be sent instantly from one computer to another, over short or long distances, without the help of a secretary.

By using computer technology, you no longer need to depend on a secretary to set up and type your business messages or proofread and correct your business writing. Since you may be doing these tasks yourself on the computer in your future career, you will need improved business communication skills, including a knowledge of English mechanics, spelling, writing style, and correct formats. Some degree of *computer literacy,* or familiarity with the computer, will also be helpful in your career. This textbook and its supplements are designed to help you improve your communication skills.

## CHAPTER REVIEW

1. Define the term *business communication* and list some of its forms or media.
2. List the four basic processes for sending and receiving business information.
3. Differentiate between *internal* and *external* business communications and give three examples of each.
4. React to the following statement and explain your answer: Computer technology has made business people's jobs more complicated.
5. What is a *multi-function workstation*? Who uses it, and for what purposes?
6. Define *word processing*. Who uses it, and for what purposes?
7. What is *integrated management-support software*? Who uses it, and for what purposes?
8. What is *electronic mail*? Do you think electronic mail will be widely adopted for home use in the future? If your answer is no, why not? If your answer is yes, do you think it will replace home mail delivery someday?
9. Identify your future career. List the various types of communication you will need to use in that career.
10. Business writing has traditionally followed this sequence: dictate, type, proofread, type, mail. What technological innovations have changed that task pattern? What would be a more efficient task pattern for business communicators to use?

## APPLICATIONS

1. Spend an hour or two in your college's personal computer lab. First, become acquainted with the machine. Have the lab instructor or assistant show you how to get started. Second, get acquainted with a word-processing package. Learn to move the cursor around, and practice keying the first lesson or two from the instruction manual. Then print a copy of your practice lessons to submit to your instructor.

2. After completing No. 1 above, answer the following questions:
   a. What is a software *menu*?
   b. What is the purpose of the control key on your computer's keyboard?

3. Write a one- or two-page report about word-processing software for personal computers. Obtain your information from current computer and software magazines. The objective of your report is to recommend an inexpensive

word-processing program that a college student taking business courses might purchase to use for homework assignments. Compare prices and capabilities, including the special features of word-processing software.

4. Review advertisements for computer printers of various types in current data processing magazines. Prepare a short report defining the state of the art in speed, optional features, and cost.

5. Write a two- or three-page description of a typical Monday in your life as you imagine it will be ten years in the future. What kind of work will you be doing? What technology will you be using at work and at home that is not available now? Describe your activities from 7 a.m. until 11 p.m.

## CASE STUDY

"That computer is out to get me! I worked for five hours—for *five hours*—and it ate three pages of my monthly report! I wish we were back in the good old days before everything had to be done on a computer. That machine HATES me!" complained Jerry Curtis to anyone in the office who would listen.

"I know what you mean," agreed Karen Morris. "My workstation always picks the worst possible time to be uncooperative too. Last Friday it would not let me into the Region 3 database so that I could get Mr. Wilson his sales projections when he needed them. Fortunately Tom came by and convinced it that I really needed the Region 3 information. Otherwise, you would all be going to my computer's funeral this morning. One of these days I'm going to smash that machine!"

Tom Steeling smiled to himself as he listened to the two account representatives commiserate. Tom was the office manager for General Products, a wholesaling firm that had grown from a storefront operation to a $5 million-a-year business in only 14 years.

"Yes, those were the good old days, all right," Tom thought to himself. "They should have been here when we started. Each account representative did well to keep track of three or four accounts. On the road, we always wrote the orders not knowing if the inventory was in our warehouse."

"Back in the office, we had to prepare each order with five carbon copies—one for purchasing, one for inventory, one for the customer, one for accounting, one for packaging and shipping, and one for the account file. All six had to be distributed to the right place—and if anything on the order changed, all six had to be corrected."

"The time lag was lengthened by orders through the mail—both from our customers and to our suppliers. And telephone orders were at the mercy of whoever answered the phone—and when he or she decided to file the order."

"We had so much paper to keep track of six years ago (when we went over the $3 million mark) that seven clerks were hired to file papers. And no matter how careful they were, some things were always lost in the filing system, never to be found again. Yes, those were the good old days, all right."

Tom looked around the office with its ten neat workstations. Ten representatives handled all of the General Products accounts—a 400 percent improvement in efficiency over the old noncomputerized system. Even Jerry and Karen (who had been with the company only a few weeks and were still learning how to use their workstations) each handled work that under the old system would have required three people.

"The computerized system isn't hard to use, but you do have to follow the instructions," Tom thought to himself. "The computer didn't lose Jerry's pages. He probably forgot to 'save' them. And last Friday, Karen was using the wrong access code for Region 3. They both need to pay more attention to the directions. When they finally understand how powerful a tool the computer is—and how much easier their jobs are because of it—Jerry and Karen will not complain anymore."

Tom sat thinking a few moments longer about what he could say to Jerry and Karen. When he approached them, Tom had a smile on his face.

1. If you were in Tom Steeling's place, how could you convince Jerry and Karen how valuable their multi-function workstations are?
2. *The Intimate Machine* by Neil Frude discusses people's tendency to assign human characteristics to computers. Why do you suppose Karen and Jerry are reacting in this way to their workstations?
3. Why does the company have each account representative handle her or his own data management rather than delegate this task to a secretary? Since account representatives generally earn higher salaries than secretaries, wouldn't secretarial help for data management actually save the company money?

# REFERENCES

Robert P. Cerveny and Daniel A. Joseph. "Large Business Organizations' Use of PC Technology," *Journal of Systems Management* 37, no. 6 (June 1986): 14-17.

Jeffrey H. Moore. "Senior Executive Computer Use," Unpublished paper, Stanford University Graduate School of Business, July 1986.

George T. Plotzke. "New Technology Creates Office of the Future," *Management Review* 71, no. 2, (February 1982): 8-15.

## SUGGESTED READINGS

Frank, Darlene. *Silicon English: Business Writing Tools for the Computer Age*. San Rafael, CA: Royall Press, 1985.

Frude, Neil. *The Intimate Machine: Close Encounters With Computers and Robots*. New York: New American Library, 1983.

Kenney, Donald P. *Personal Computers in Business*. New York: American Management Associations, 1985.

Shafer, Dan and The Waite Group. *Silicon Visions: The Future of Microcomputer Technology*. New York: Prentice-Hall, 1986.

Williams, Frederick. *The Communications Revolution*. New York: New American Library, 1982.

# COMMUNICATION FOUNDATIONS AND PROCESSES

## CHAPTER 2

Jack Walters, the sales manager of an electronics manufacturing company, has a stack of unread mail six inches high on his desk. He comes into the office at 11 a.m. from a staff meeting which ran longer than scheduled. Two people are waiting for him in the outer office for appointments that had been scheduled for 10:00 and 10:30.

"The president called to find out why the monthly sales report is a week late," his secretary tells Jack. "The president wants you to call him right back."

"Also, two of the sales representatives have a question about the new price list. They need an answer before noon."

Jack Walters' experiences are not unusual. As the work of business organizations has become highly technical and as organizations themselves have become more complex, business managers are flooded with information and requests for information. Both executives and middle managers send and receive information from various communication channels such as scheduled meetings and conferences, unscheduled interruptions from superiors and subordinates, telephone calls, letters, memos, reports, and publications.

Business communication has become an extremely complex process involving people, information, language, and machines. As a framework for studying business communication and its applications in the computer age, you need to be familiar with general communication theory and processes. This chapter introduces communication theory as a basis for understanding the business communication applications in the chapters that follow. We will examine the following topics:

- The relationship between information and communication
- The communication process and its components
- Communication models
- Categories of communication
- One-way and two-way communication
- Purposes of messages in organizations and an introduction to communication networks
- Human relations and its importance for effective communication
- Barriers to communication and some ways to avoid them

## INFORMATION AND COMMUNICATION THEORY

Managers use information to reduce the uncertainty involved in making decisions. Without timely and accurate information, decision making would be uninformed guesswork.

**Information** is a pattern of sounds, numbers, letters, or codes. We usually think of information in the form of spoken or written language. **Communication** occurs when a person sends information that another person receives and finds meaningful. In *Human Behavior at Work*, Davis defines communication as "the transfer of information and understanding from one person to another person" (1981, 399).

In a broader sense, one can argue that machines also communicate with one another, as well as with people. The technological revolution has made it possible for computers to communicate with other machines (such as other computers and assembly-line robots) without direct human intervention. Science-fiction movies such as *War Games* and *2001* have portrayed computers taking over rather than being controlled by humans. In reality, however, computers cannot actually control the entire process of communication; they merely facilitate communication by eliminating much of its drudgery.

### Communication Components

The communication process consists of five basic components: *sender*, *message*, *channel*, *receiver*, and *feedback*. The following paragraphs will discuss each of the five basic components in detail.

**Sender and Receiver**. For communication to occur, the sender must convey information and the receiver must perceive the meaning of the information. This process takes place whether a large number of people are involved (such as in mass communication), or if only one or two individuals are involved.

**Message**. A **message** is information which is transmitted and from which the receiver perceives meaning. In other words, messages relate meaningful information from sender to receiver.

Messages may be either verbal or nonverbal. **Verbal** (linguistic) **messages** use spoken or written language. When composing verbal messages such as conversations, business letters, or memorandums, we are concerned primarily with the choice of words.

**Nonverbal messages** are unspoken, unwritten messages transmitted in the following ways:

1. Body language (smiling or frowning, gesturing, etc.)
2. Physical characteristics (hairstyle, height, weight)
3. Personal space and environment (physical closeness to others, room size, furniture arrangement)
4. Objects (clothing, eyeglasses, briefcase)
5. Time (promptness, length of a meeting)

For example, what messages could be intended by flashing red lights? Some possibilities might be that a fire truck or ambulance is approaching, a train is coming down the railroad tracks, the road is under construction, or the Christmas lights are turned on. Chapter 16 discusses nonverbal messages in more detail.

**Channel**. The **channel** is the physical means used to send the message. Some channels (including face-to-face conversations, meetings, and hand-written notes) use only our individual skills such as speaking, listening, reading, and writing. Printed channels include media such as newspapers, magazines, books, brochures, signs, etc. Electric and electronic channels include machines such as telephones, radios, televisions, movie projectors, and computers.

Many messages involve the use of more than one type of channel. For example, a person giving a group sales presentation might use channels such as a formal speech, printed materials, and a videotape, while the people in the audience use individual channels to listen, read, and view pictures or graphs.

**Feedback**. When communicating with another person face to face, we send and receive messages at the same time. When the receiver responds to the sender's message, this process is called **feedback**. Feedback, like the original message, can be in any form — written, oral, or nonverbal. "Lynn, that's a good suggestion!" is an example of oral feedback. Frowns, smiles, and yawns are all forms of nonverbal feedback. In business organizations, formal evaluations of employee performance are an example of written feedback.

Feedback may be positive, negative, or neutral. Positive feedback gives positive reinforcement to the source — it tells the receiver that he or she is doing a good job. In contrast, negative feedback tells us that problems exist. Negative feedback may be helpful to the communicator by providing information on improvements that can be made. By receiving negative feedback from a supervisor, for example, we may learn how to improve our performance.

Feedback may be direct or indirect as well as intentional or unintentional. The sender of a message may obtain indirect feedback simply by observing the receiver's unintentional nonverbal behavior. Enthusiastic applause is an example of intentional positive feedback that audiences provide to speakers. On the other hand, a speaker might receive indirect negative feedback by observing that the audience has poor eye contact with her or him. Effective speakers are sensitive to feedback and use it constantly to adjust their performance to meet the needs of various audiences. For example, a number of yawns could provide feedback to a speaker that a lecture is boring, and he or she could decide to interject an appropriate joke, increase the volume of her or his voice, or otherwise change the delivery to enliven the presentation. On a personal level, we use feedback as a tool to help us get along with other people.

## Encoding and Decoding

The process of producing messages, speaking and writing for instance, is called **encoding**. By translating our ideas into sound waves or writing the ideas on paper, we are encoding our messages just as telegraphers did when sending messages in Morse code. When someone receives a message and translates the code into ideas, the receiver is **decoding** the message. However, the decoded message may or may not be the sender's intended message. Various communication barriers can cause encoding and decoding problems. For example, loud noises and other distractions can interfere with the decoding process. Communication barriers are discussed in more detail later in this chapter.

## Communication Models

**Communication models** represent basic theories about the process of communication and enable us to make predictions about various communication processes. Most of the early models viewed communication as a one-way process, consisting of a sequence of steps as a person transmitted a message to another person.

Let us look at Shannon and Weaver's *Mathematical Theory of Communication* model (1949, 7) which represents communication as a one-way process proceeding from the left to the right, as shown in Figure 2.1. In this classic model, the information source (for example, a speaker) decides on a message and sends it through a transmitter (for example, a telephone). The electric impulses from the transmitter are then sent by means of a communication channel such as a telephone cable. The electrical impulses are relayed to a receiver (such as the phone receiver at the other end), converted back into an audio message, and perceived by the destination (a person listening). Shannon and Weaver referred to any type of interference with the receiver's perception of the message as **noise**, which included such problems as static on the line and distractions at the destination.

Shannon and Weaver's model included all the components of communication previously discussed except feedback. Later writers added feedback to Shannon and Weaver's model.

## FIGURE 2.1 SHANNON AND WEAVER'S CLASSIC COMMUNICATION MODEL

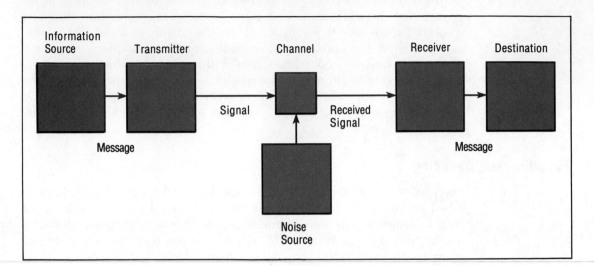

Source: Claude E. Shannon and Warren Weaver, *The Mathematical Theory of Communication and Recent Contributions to the Mathematical Theory of Communication* (Urbana, Ill: University of Illinois Press, 1949), 7. (Reprinted by permission of the Board of Trustees of the University of Illinois.)

Berlo (1960, 51) in *The Process of Communication* questioned the idea that communication is a fixed series of steps with a beginning and an ending. Berlo believed that the entire process was much more complex than it had previously been considered and that individuals *simultaneously* affect one another. According to Berlo's theory, individuals send (encode) and receive (decode) information at the same time.

Figure 2.2 represents communication as an interactive two-way process that includes simultaneous message encoding, decoding, and feedback.

## CATEGORIES OF COMMUNICATION

Communication may be classified according to four categories: administrative, interpersonal, intrapersonal, and mass. Business communication deals mainly with **administrative communication**, which consists of messages relating to the work of a business organization. Letters, memorandums, reports, business meetings, and interviews are common types of administrative communication.

In contrast, **interpersonal communication** relates to nonbusiness issues. In the work setting, interpersonal communication occurs when employees discuss topics that are unrelated to business. However, administrative and interpersonal communication are often difficult to separate, since business topics may be combined with nonbusiness topics. For instance, business deals are sometimes made on the golf course or at social gatherings.

## FIGURE 2.2 TWO-WAY INTERACTIVE COMMUNICATION MODEL

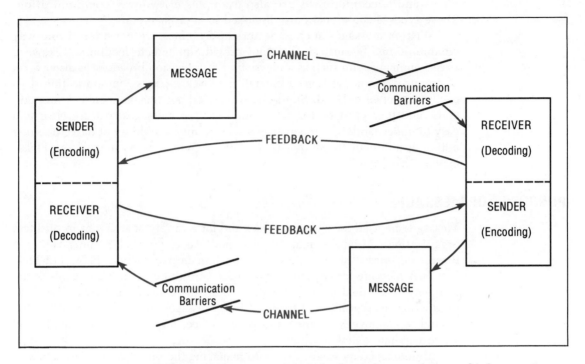

**Intrapersonal communication** takes place in the mind of one person. During intrapersonal communication, the sender and receiver are the same person. Talking to yourself while driving down the freeway or singing to yourself in the shower are obvious examples of intrapersonal communication. However, intrapersonal communication can also occur in organizational settings. Individual decision making and planning are mental processes that are examples of intrapersonal communication. For instance, intrapersonal communication takes place when an executive vice president plans for the future or decides to issue a new company policy.

**Mass communication** deals with messages sent to large numbers of people, usually through media such as television, radio, newspapers, and magazines. Business organizations utilize mass communication when they advertise their products and services to the public. Organizations also utilize mass communication to develop goodwill with the community. For example, an electric power company might place a public relations advertisement in the local newspaper about ways to conserve energy.

## ONE-WAY AND TWO-WAY COMMUNICATION

Conversations are an example of **two-way communication**, with participants sending and receiving messages at the same time and providing immediate feedback to each other. Face-to-face meetings and telephone conversations are the most common examples of two-way communication. Computer conferences and teleconferences are also examples of two-way communication. These types of conferences are discussed in later chapters.

Written messages such as letters and memos are considered **one-way communication** because they do not provide immediate feedback. Likewise, mass communication such as a newspaper or television broadcast is also a form of one-way communication. Although feedback to mass communication does occur, it is often delayed. Similarly, writers do not receive feedback immediately; and they must be careful to send written messages that are clear and easy to understand. The receiver of a written message does not have the same option as a listener to ask questions such as "What do you mean?" or "Please explain that again."

## PURPOSES OF MESSAGES

Messages are used for many purposes and for a variety of activities in business organizations. Messages may be classified according to their purposes into three categories: task, maintenance, and human (Goldhaber, 1974, 112-113).

**Task messages** are concerned with accomplishing the primary goals of the company. They deal with information about the company's activities such as production, marketing, and finance. Task messages transmit information that is vital to employees for their job performance, for example, information on how to operate a new machine.

**Maintenance messages** deal with managing the internal structure and systems of the company. Maintenance messages are concerned with internal activities such as personnel management, union relations, and the operation of company day-care centers and cafeterias. Maintenance messages primarily include policy and procedure information; personnel manuals are an example.

**Human messages** deal with interpersonal relations and employee morale. People need to know that they are appreciated; human messages meet this basic need by conveying a genuine interest in and concern for people. If managers neglect this area, severe morale problems may occur. Human messages create an atmosphere of appreciation and trust. Examples of human messages include recognizing employees for a job well done, inviting them to the annual Christmas party, joking with someone on the elevator, and listening sympathetically to a person who has a problem.

## COMMUNICATION NETWORKS

Within organizations, messages travel from one person to another along various routes or paths called communication **networks**. Networks depend largely upon the relationships between the people involved. **Formal networks** follow the pattern of formal relationships outlined in the company's organization chart. Many messages follow the formal hierarchial network proceeding downward from president to vice president, to division manager, to department head, etc. On the other hand, many messages travel along **informal networks,** which follow various patterns of informal relationships called the *grapevine*. For example, news might travel along the grapevine from a sales representative to a secretary to another secretary and then to a department head.

Messages can flow along formal and informal communication networks in more than one direction. The direction in which a message typically flows is related to the purpose of the message.

**Downward communication** travels down the formal organization chart from superior to subordinate. In downward communication, the superior initiates the message and the subordinate receives it. In organizations with an autocratic (authoritarian) management style, most formal messages flow downward.

**Upward communication** is initiated by the subordinate and sent upward to her or his superior. Managers can promote upward communication with employee committees, suggestion systems, formal grievance procedures, and company-sponsored social events. Informal channels are especially effective in encouraging or discouraging upward communication. The grapevine will inform employees if an *open-door policy* is genuine or merely window dressing. The participative (democratic) style of management encourages upward communication. Policies and procedures that genuinely welcome and encourage upward communication tend to improve both the quality and quantity of information that management receives; but if action is never taken on employees' suggestions or grievances, then worker morale is likely to suffer. Thus, upward communication quickly ceases to exist if it is not taken seriously.

**Horizontal** *(lateral)* **communication** deals with messages that flow between individuals on the same level within a department or in different departments. Formal horizontal communication generally consists of activities such as team efforts to coordinate tasks and share information. Examples include department head meetings, committee meetings, and computer printouts routinely sent from one department to another. Informal messages often play an important role in horizontal communication. The grapevine can be an effective way for new employees to "learn the ropes" and develop good relationships with their peers.

## HUMAN RELATIONS

Business communication as a discipline has its roots in the *human relations* approach to management, which dominated management theory in the 1940's. The human relations movement was pioneered by Elton Mayo and his group of researchers at the Hawthorne Plant of the Western Electric Company near Chicago (Roethlisberger and Dickson, 1939). The human relations approach focused on concern for the individual and emphasized that *people-oriented* participative management was superior to *production-oriented* authoritarian management. Human relations theory, which drew heavily from the behavioral sciences such as psychology and sociology, encouraged upward communication in organizations. Over the years, the human relations school of management has evolved into today's *human resources* approach to organizational behavior (Goldhaber, 1974, 54-55).

In business communication, human relations may be separated into two areas — industrial relations and public relations. **Industrial relations** refers to relations within an organization; for example, relations between management and labor. **Public relations** refers to relations between a company and people outside the company, such as customers, stockholders, and the community.

A pioneer who profoundly influenced the application of human relations theory to business communication was Dale Carnegie. His classic book, *How to Win Friends and Influence People* (1936), was based on the idea that knowing how to relate to people is essential for business success. Carnegie, who was originally a writer of history books, became interested in human relations when writing a biography of Abraham Lincoln. Carnegie studied Lincoln's techniques for handling people and observed that his success in leadership was largely due to his superb ability in the area of human relations. Today we recognize that an understanding of human relations is a requirement for effective communication and, in turn, for effective leadership.

Who does the company promote to head the management information systems department? Do you think the person with the greatest technical knowledge or the person the boss likes the best will be promoted? Of course, technical knowledge is important; but management probably will select the person whom they can work with the best.

Customers are more likely to discontinue doing business with a company because someone hurts their feelings or makes them angry rather than because they are dissatisfied with the company's products. If a salesperson is rude or curt, customers will feel insulted and may take their business elsewhere.

## Communication and Human Relations

In business communication, we attempt to affect people in a certain way. Sometimes we inform people; sometimes we attempt to persuade them. In either case, we want our message to have the desired effect on the receiver — to influence her or him in the way we would like. Therefore, before deciding upon a strategy for achieving the goal of a message, the sender should analyze the receiver's probable reaction to the message. Skilled business communicators develop sensitivity toward others' viewpoints and feelings. This sensitivity, or *empathy*, is developed by listening to and observing people's reactions to various situations.

People usually like a person who brings good news. On the other hand, people tend to dislike someone who delivers bad news. Bad news is the most difficult kind of message to deliver. In ancient times, the bearer of bad tidings was sometimes put to death. If we use the right strategy, however, the receiver of our bad news can accept it and still feel positively toward us and toward the company.

Although feedback is an essential part of human relations, people tend to have difficulty accepting negative feedback. For good public relations, therefore, direct criticism of customers and clients must be avoided. For effective industrial relations, skilled managers give employees negative feedback tactfully.

Most dissatisfied customers do not bother to give negative feedback; they simply discontinue doing business with a company. Usually only a small percentage of dissatisfied customers will take the time to let a company know their problems and those individuals tend to be repeat customers (Zweig, 1986, 27). For that reason, businesses generally welcome customer complaints and attempt to resolve the customers' problems.

## Computers and Human Relations

Just because we communicate more and more with machines rather than in person does not mean that we can neglect the importance of human relations. As business offices become increasingly computerized, workers have started to complain that their jobs are becoming dehumanized. Many business professionals are now spending a major portion of their working day in front of a computer terminal instead of interacting with people as frequently as they did in the past. Such individuals may feel isolated because their social needs are not being met.

Computer conferences are an example of a communication channel that could be criticized for neglecting human relations. In computer conferences, participants do not meet face to face but simply read each other's remarks on their computer screens. In one computer-manufacturing company, managers complained that computer conferences between branch plants have become strained. One manager remarked, "It's easier to tell someone that you think he's stupid when he's separated from you by 2,000 miles of cable."

Although insulting people may be easier if you are not face to face with them, they will have the same reaction as if you had offended them in person. We must take care not to let technology dehumanize our interactions. Human relations are just as important as ever.

## BARRIERS TO COMMUNICATION

To communicate effectively, we must be aware of the common barriers between the sender of the message and the receiver. Some obvious communication barriers are noise (static on the line, loud music, etc.) and printing or typing errors.

Barriers are found both at the individual level and at the organizational level. At the individual level, barriers exist primarily because people have different backgrounds and values and view things in diverse ways. Similarly, organizations differ in their histories and policies (corporate values). Figure 2.3 illustrates some of the common barriers to communication.

## FIGURE 2.3 BARRIERS TO COMMUNICATION

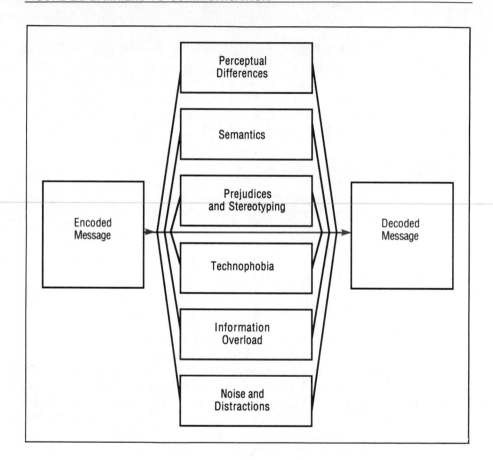

## Perceptual Differences

**Perception** is the process of decoding or interpreting information. People tend to perceive information in a way that is consistent with their beliefs and self-concept. Perceptual differences among individuals and various groups can be largely attributed to the following individual and environmental factors:

1. Age
2. Sex
3. Educational level
4. Cultural background

    5. Socio-economic status
    6. Religious beliefs
    7. Geographic differences
    8. Personality variables
    9. Organizational affiliation

**Selective perception** refers to people's tendency to pay attention to certain communication inputs, while ignoring others. People perceive various stimuli differently, based on their cultural backgrounds, previous experiences, and their interests. People tend to ignore information that conflicts with their personal beliefs, value systems, and expectations. Selective perception occurs when receivers decode information on the basis of their interest in the subject, their opinion of the sender, their own roles in the company, or other personal factors. For example, a worker who distrusts a supervisor would be unlikely to react favorably to that supervisor's constructive suggestions.

## Semantics

The study of word meanings and the way they are used is called **semantics**. A word can have different meanings in different contexts or have various connotations to different people. For instance, what is your reaction to the word *responsibility*? To some people, "responsibility" has a negative connotation—it means a burden. To other people, the word has a positive connotation—it implies power, prestige, and increased pay. Geographic and other cultural differences can create semantic difficulties. The word *union* could provide vastly different reactions, depending on whether an individual is from Pittsburgh (heavily unionized) or Phoenix (nonunion)—or whether that person is an electrician or a manager.

Semantic difficulties are caused also by differences in education and choice of profession. Using long or technical words that may not be in the listener or reader's vocabulary can be a major barrier to communication. **Jargon** is language that is peculiar to a particular occupation or technical area. Using jargon that may be unfamiliar to the audience creates a too-common communication barrier. For example, computer professionals are aware that RAM means *random access memory*. In the accounting profession, everyone knows that LIFO means *last in, first out*. But people outside those professions probably would not be familiar with either term or understand the concepts involved without some explanation.

## Prejudice and Stereotyping

**Prejudice** (bias) and **stereotyping** (generalizing about categories of people) are major barriers to communication. Everyone has prejudices, both for and against certain things and people. We tend to stereotype people on the basis of set opinions we have about age, sex, roles, race, religion, marital status, and so forth. We may unconsciously stereotype what someone says or does because that person is a member of some group—football players, women, teenagers, a minority, etc. Managers tend to stereotype workers and workers tend to stereotype managers. The habit of classifying people into categories creates a major barrier to communication. The only way to avoid stereotyping is to make an effort to keep an open mind. Avoid letting yourself draw generalizations or make judgments about people before you know them well.

## Technophobia

**Technophobia**, or fear of technology, is becoming a commonplace communication barrier. Although technophobia may be associated with all kinds of technology, we are seeing its growing occurrence with the introduction of computers. Technophobia is based on people's resistance to change, which stems largely from their fear of the unknown.

Technophobia is actually based on a number of fears about computers. Some of these are fear of being replaced by computers, fear of losing status and prestige, fear of appearing incompetent, fear of failure or embarrassment, and fear of damaging the equipment.

You may experience some elements of technophobia when you sit down in front of a computer for the first time, if you are used to writing with a pencil or composing at your trusty old portable typewriter. Like most people who use a computer for word processing for the first time, you probably will feel a bit technophobic; but this natural reaction is soon overcome by your increasing confidence in yourself and the machine.

Management can take steps to deal with employees' technophobia. Fear of being replaced by computers can be overcome by dealing openly with the matter from the start. Management can meet with groups of workers to assure them that no one will be replaced by computers and to explain how the computer will simplify their work.

Managers, in particular, tend to fear loss of status. Top management can overcome this barrier by serving as role models. If top managers themselves use computers, then middle managers will soon get over their fear that computer use causes them to lose status and prestige.

Fear of failure or embarrassment can be diminished by providing appropriate training for users of new equipment, while the fear of appearing incompetent can be overcome by permitting employees to take home a computer or terminal. Many companies have purchased portable computers just so that employees may experiment with the machines in the privacy of their homes.

Another management approach to technophobia is simple patience. Eventually group pressure will motivate most technophobics to conform. As more people in the company begin to use computers, the ones who do not may begin to feel left out. Sooner or later, curiosity or need will overcome the fear of technology.

## Information Overload

**Information load** refers to a person's capacity to process information. Business people are constantly bombarded with information inputs (stimuli) such as telephones ringing, customers demanding attention, stacks of paperwork sitting on their desk, and constant interruptions. Jack Walters, the busy sales manager described at the beginning of this chapter, is a typical example of a worker receiving more information than he can effectively handle. This condition is called **information overload**.

Ideally, our information output should be balanced with our input. In other words, we should be able to process information as we receive it. However, when the inputs increase beyond our ability to process them, we begin to experience information overload. High levels of stress are associated with information overload. Sales people in retail stores experience information overload during the Christmas rush, and college students often experience information overload during the week of final exams. In contrast, people such as night security guards who receive little input, experience **information underload**, which is associated with boredom.

Information overload is an almost universal problem for business executives, with some executives becoming too overloaded to return phone calls or answer mail. As a result, subordinates, customers, and clients are likely to find them inaccessible—and human relations may suffer.

People suffering from information overload often cope with the situation by letting all their work pile up, working faster and less accurately, or by ignoring lower-priority items. If resulting errors and omissions affect customers and clients, loss of goodwill is likely to occur.

Constructive techniques for managing information overload include using time productively, delegating routine tasks to subordinates, and conducting meetings efficiently. In addition, managers can help others avoid information overload by sending them only necessary information, keeping written messages short, and condensing long computer printouts in one or two pages.

## Noise and Distractions

Noise and other distractions are common communication barriers, adversely affecting productivity and contributing to information overload. Office work space can be designed to minimize noise from computer printers, copying machines, typewriters, etc. Many computer printers can be fitted with special plastic covers to muffle the noise, and rubber or felt pads can be placed under other office machines to reduce the sound. Acoustical wall and floor coverings, as well as ceiling tiles, can also be extremely effective in noise reduction. Distractions such as people constantly opening doors and walking by can be minimized by placing desks and other furniture away from heavy traffic areas.

## SUMMARY

Communication is a complex process involving a sender, a message, a channel, a receiver, and feedback. Models illustrate various theories of communication; current models depict communication as a two-way process, with the sender and receiver encoding and decoding messages simultaneously.

Communication in organizations involves various types of one-way and two-way messages (administrative, interpersonal, intrapersonal, and mass) traveling downward, upward, and horizontally along both formal and informal networks to meet organizational goals (task messages), keep up the internal structure (maintenance messages), and/or set up employee relationships (human messages).

Business communication theory evolved from the human relations approach to business management. Empathy, which is essential to human relationships, deters potential communication barriers between senders and receivers. Noise and distraction represent common barriers to communication. Differences in individual perceptions, as well as cultural and language differences, often come between the sender and the receiver as well. Within organizations, communication barriers include information overload and technophobia.

## CHAPTER REVIEW

1. Distinguish between *information* and *communication*.
2. List and explain the five components of the communication process. Which component was not included in Shannon and Weaver's classic communication model?
3. List and describe four categories of communication. Give two examples of each.
4. Is a decoded message always identical to the message that was encoded? Why or why not?
5. Define *selective perception* and give an example that you have experienced or observed.
6. What is *semantics*? How is semantics related to communication barriers?
7. Describe an example of prejudice or stereotyping that you have encountered. What problems did it cause for you or for others?
8. Describe three communication barriers (besides perception, semantics, and prejudice or stereotyping) that you have encountered. What problems did they create?
9. What is negative feedback? Should negative feedback be encouraged or discouraged in business organizations? Why?
10. Distinguish between formal and informal communication networks and give an example of each.

## APPLICATIONS

1. Use the following feedback exercise as a class experiment. Make two drawings consisting of several geometric shapes (triangles, rectangles, circles, etc.) superimposed on one another. Give one drawing to Person *A*, who goes to the back of the classroom and faces the wall away from the chalkboard. (1) Person *A* describes the drawing to Person *B*, who will attempt to redraw it on the chalkboard without looking at Person *A* or asking any questions (one-way communication). (2) Now try it with the second drawing. This time *B* may ask questions of Person *A*, but must not face her or him (two-way communication). (3) If *B* still is unsuccessful, increase the feedback from Person *B* to Person *A* by having *A* and *B* face each other as they repeat the exercise. What communication barriers did *A* and *B* encounter? How was feedback related to *B*'s performance.

2. Write a short paragraph summarizing an article you read in a magazine or newspaper. Have someone read the paragraph while three members of the class (*A*, *B*, and *C*) wait outside. First, call in Student *A* and select someone to repeat the paragraph from memory to Student *A*. Second, call in Student *B* and have Student *A* relay the paragraph from memory to Student *B*. Third, call in Student *C* and have Student *B* repeat the story from memory to Student *C*. Finally, have Student *C* repeat the paragraph. Discuss how and why the original message was changed.

3. Write a one-page paper in which you describe a communication problem you have encountered and discuss it in relation to the communication model presented in Figure 2.1 or Figure 2.2.

4. Assume that you are the new president of a company with a poor record of industrial relations. Write a one-page paper that (a) describes likely barriers to upward communication in the company, and (b) suggests ways to overcome these barriers and improve upward communication.

5. Someday robots containing highly developed *artificial intelligence* may be able to perform certain office tasks. List and describe three communication-related tasks that you think robots will be able to do in business offices in the future. Also, list three communication-related office tasks that you think robots never will be able to take over. Defend your position.

## CASE STUDY

Jane Anderson, manager of a technical-support unit at Westlake Manufacturing Company, had just sat down at the table in the executive conference room with the other members of the Employee Grievances Committee. Jane was the newest member of the committee, which was composed of representatives from both management and labor. Over the years, the committee had settled many labor disputes and personnel problems.

When Jane first learned that she had been elected, she was excited and at the same time concerned that she did not know much about the committee except that it arbitrated labor disputes. She was also nervous about serving on the committee when she learned that she would be the first woman to serve on the committee in its twenty-year history. She worried that other committee members might not accept her or perhaps treat her in a condescending manner.

Across the table from Jane sat Harry Wilkerson, who until today had been the newest member on the committee. The job of secretary had always been delegated to the newest member of the committee; thus Harry was in a somewhat jovial mood because he knew that today he would be relieved of the responsibility of taking the minutes.

"Well, we'd better get started," said Dave Taylor, the chair of the committee. "The meeting will come to order."

"First, I'd like to introduce Jane Anderson, who is beginning a three-year term on our committee today."

"Jane, I'd like to start you off by asking you to be secretary of our group. I know you'll do a great job of taking the minutes."

At that point, everyone in the group laughed except Jane."I guess so," Jane replied reluctantly. "Women always get stuck with that job."

After the meeting was over, Dave whispered to Harry, "That Jane Anderson doesn't seem to be very cooperative. I don't think she wants to be on this committee."

1. Why did Dave get the impression that Jane did not want to serve on the committee?
2. What perceptual problems are involved in the communication breakdown between Jane and Dave? Why did they occur?
3. Who was guilty of stereotyping? Why?

# REFERENCES

David K. Berlo, *The Process of Communication: An Introduction to Theory and Practice* (New York: Holt, Rinehart and Winston, 1960).

Dale Carnegie, *How to Win Friends and Influence People* (New York: Simon and Schuster, 1937).

Keith Davis, *Human Behavior at Work: Organizational Behavior*, 6th ed. (New York: McGraw-Hill, 1981).

Gerald M. Goldhaber, *Organizational Communication* (Dubuque, IA: William C. Brown, 1974).

Fritz J. Roethlisberger and W.J. Dickson, *Management and the Worker: An Account of a Research Program Conducted by the Western Electric Company* (Cambridge, MA: Harvard University Press, 1939).

Claude E. Shannon and Warren Weaver, *The Mathematical Theory of Communication and Recent Contributions to the Mathematical Theory of Communication* (Urbana, IL: The University of Illinois Press, 1949).

Phillip L. Zweig, "Banks Stress Resolving Complaints to Win Small Customers' Favors," *The Wall Street Journal*, December 8, 1986, 27.

## SUGGESTED READINGS

Berlo, David K. *The Process of Communication: An Introduction to Theory and Practice*. New York: Holt, Rinehart and Winston, 1960.

Farace, Richard V., et al. *Communicating and Organizing*. Reading, MA: Addison-Wesley, 1977.

Goss, Blaine. *Processing Communication: Information Processing in Intrapersonal Communication*. Belmont, CA: Wadsworth, 1982.

Trenholm, Sarah. *Human Communication Theory: An Introduction*. Englewood Cliffs, NJ: Prentice-Hall, 1986.

Tubbs, Stewart L. and Sylvia Moss. *Human Communication*. 5th ed. NY: Random House, 1986.

# WRITTEN COMMUNICATION PRINCIPLES

## PART 2

Effective business writing creates a good impression and gets results. To be effective, business writing must incorporate five basic qualities — the five C's of business communication: clearness, conciseness, completeness, consideration, and correctness.

A skilled writer begins by analyzing the situation and planning the message carefully. Various types of business messages require different approaches and plans of organization. The writer should select the organization plan best suited to achieving the purpose of the message and then outline the message.

In a well-written message, paragraphs and sentences flow smoothly. To produce a smooth flow of ideas, the writer uses a number of techniques to provide unity, emphasis, parallel construction, and transition.

# FIVE C'S OF BUSINESS COMMUNICATION

## CHAPTER 3

A pharmaceutical company spent more than a million dollars developing a new drug, only to learn that one of its scientists had discovered the same drug several years before. Management had overlooked the earlier discovery because it was hidden in the middle of a long report that no one could wade through.

Good business writing is easy to read and has the desired effect on the reader. Effective business writing gets this type of feedback:

"It makes sense."

"It flows well."

"I liked reading it."

Writing is a skill somewhat like flying an airplane. Although you can learn the basics from classroom instruction, you can become proficient only by actual practice.

Good writing is easy to recognize but not so easy to define. Effective business writing, however, has all of the following characteristics: *clearness*, *conciseness*, *completeness*, *consideration*, and *correctness*. These five components, known as the five C's of business communication, are discussed in Chapter 3.

## CLEARNESS

Because they are easy to understand, clear messages are efficient for organizations. On the other hand, unclear messages waste a reader's time and can cause costly mistakes. When readers have difficulty decoding messages, they must cope with the problem in the following ways:

1. Ask for clarification. This extra effort causes delays, creates unnecessary correspondence, and increases long-distance telephone bills.
2. Look up words in the dictionary. This step also wastes time, and in business, time is money.
3. Guess at the meaning. If the reader makes a wrong guess, expensive mistakes can occur.

To ensure clearness, you should first visualize your reader. Do not attempt to impress your reader with your vocabulary. Use simple, everyday language for business writing rather than a scholarly writing style.

## Impressive Words

After reading the report three times and looking up every other word in the dictionary, I'm still not sure what it means.

Avoid using unnatural and impressive language. Impressive words create a barrier to communication. Writers who use impressive words don't *help*, they *facilitate*; they don't *walk*, they *ambulate*. Do not use an elegant "five-dollar" word when a simple "five-cent" word will do. Simple language does not talk down to a reader—it improves communication.

As an example, here are some impressive words that are not appropriate for most business communication:

| Impressive | Simple |
|---|---|
| • acrimonious | • angry |
| • designation | • choice |
| • endeavor | • try |
| • enigma | • question |
| • remuneration | • pay |
| • soporific | • dull |
| • unpretentious | • simple |
| • utilization | • use |
| • veracity | • truth |

## Jargon

I gave up trying to use that software because I couldn't understand the user manual. You'd have to be a computer expert to read it.

Trade or technical **jargon** is the special language of a particular industry or technical field. Every business area such as accounting, finance, and economics has its own jargon. In the computer area, jargon is sometimes referred to as *computereze*. Can you understand the *computereze* in the following sentence?

Chris booted the system, ran the object module, and dumped the buffer.

Here is a translation:

Chris started the system, ran the program, and printed the data.

Computer jargon is so specialized and extensive that entire dictionaries of computer terms are published. Dictionaries are also published for other technical fields such as science, engineering, and medicine. (Appendix C of this book includes a brief glossary of computer terms.)

Jargon may be either appropriate or inappropriate, depending upon the intended receiver. If your reader is a customer or client who may not be familiar with the jargon, you should either define the terminology or eliminate the jargon altogether.

## Misplaced Modifiers

Place modifiers carefully so that they will have a clear relationship to the words you intend them to describe. Misplaced modifiers obscure your meaning and distract readers.

An example of a frequently misplaced modifier is the *dangling participle*. Participles are verbs used to modify a noun. Introductory participles modify the subject of a sentence, which should immediately follow the participle.

DANGLING: *While baking a batch of Quick-Jif chocolate cookies*, a bug was found in the package.

In this sentence, taken from a letter to a foods manufacturer, the introductory participial phrase is misplaced. The phrase "While baking a batch of Quick-Jif chocolate cookies" dangles because it does not modify the subject of the sentence.

IMPROVED: While baking a batch of Quick-Jif chocolate cookies, Mrs. Brown found a bug in the package.

Take a look at this sentence:

DANGLING: A portable computer was on her desk, *which was never used*.

Is the computer or the desk never used? In this example, the adjective clause "which was never used" is misplaced.

IMPROVED: A portable computer, which was never used, was on her desk.

Now look at this sentence:

MISPLACED: The sales representative approached the client *with self-confidence*.

Does the sales representative or the client have self-confidence? In this sentence, the prepositional phrase "with self-confidence" is probably misplaced.

IMPROVED: With self-confidence, the sales representative approached the client.

## Ambiguous Pronouns

Every pronoun should refer clearly to its antecedent. (The antecedent of a pronoun is the noun it replaces.) Ambiguous pronouns can confuse a reader; therefore, avoid using pronouns that do not refer clearly to an antecedent.

AMBIGUOUS: The office manager told the accountant that *she* could use the new graphics terminal.

Who could use the new graphics terminal—the office manager or the accountant?

IMPROVED: The office manager gave the accountant permission to use the new graphics terminal.

Look at this example:

AMBIGUOUS: Carol called Linda about revising *her* report.

Which report needs revising—Carol's or Linda's?

IMPROVED: Carol called Linda about revising the June sales report.

Avoid using the words *this* and *that* as pronouns with vague antecedents. Instead, use *this* and *that* as demonstrative adjectives to modify a specific noun.

WEAK: Interest rates are expected to rise in the next few months. *This* makes bonds a poor investment.

BETTER: Interest rates are expected to rise in the next few months. This interest increase makes bonds a poor investment.

WEAK: The price of our computer with graphics capability decreased from $3,000 to $2,250 this month. *That* is a 25 percent saving for our customers.

BETTER: The price of our computer with graphics capability decreased from $3,000 to $2,250 this month. The reduced price saves our customers 25 percent.

## Concrete Words

These memos do not say much of anything. They are so boring I usually toss them in the 'round file' without reading them.

Concrete words are the key to an interesting writing style. **Concrete language** is strong, specific, and dynamic. On the other hand, vague, ambiguous wording is weak, colorless, and boring.

Three techniques can help you to develop a concrete writing style:

1. Use objective language.
2. Use active voice.
3. Avoid expletives, especially at the beginning of a sentence.

**Use Objective Language.** Avoid using language that merely conveys your opinion or interpretation; instead, use language that presents specific information. Be particularly careful to use objective adjectives and adverbs rather than vague, subjective modifiers, as shown in the following examples:

SUBJECTIVE: The company had a *terrible* decrease in sales last year.

OBJECTIVE: The company had a 30 percent decrease in sales last year.

SUBJECTIVE: The director of finance makes *a lot* of money.

OBJECTIVE: The director of finance earned a $100,000 salary this year.

SUBJECTIVE: Our Daizee computer printer is *very slow*.

OBJECTIVE: Our Daizee computer printer can only print 20 characters per second.

SUBJECTIVE: The company *very quickly* promoted Christy to sales manager.

OBJECTIVE: After only six months, the company promoted Christy to sales manager.

**Use Active Voice.** In sentences written in the active voice, the subject acts, and the direct object of the sentence receives the action of the verb. Active voice strengthens sentence construction because it is clear and direct.

In passive voice, the subject of the sentence receives the action of the verb. Passive voice is weak and vague; it also deters the use of *action* verbs. Unfortunately, passive voice is often overused in business writing.

Notice that the active-voice versions of the following sentences are more forceful:

PASSIVE: The site for the new building *has been selected* by the president of Acme Company.

ACTIVE: The president of Acme Company selected the site for the new building.

PASSIVE: A new mini-computer *was ordered* by the accounting department.

ACTIVE: The accounting department ordered a new mini-computer.

Writers sometimes deliberately obscure their meaning by using the passive voice. Use this technique sparingly because it weakens your writing style. The next sentences, which are even more vague than the previous examples, intentionally do not identify the *doer* of the action of the verbs:

PASSIVE: The site for the new building *has been selected*.

PASSIVE: A new mini-computer *has been ordered*.

PASSIVE: All expenses *were paid* in advance.

Occasionally, passive voice is appropriate for variety in your writing or when a negative situation calls for tact. In the following examples, the active-voice sentence bluntly blames John for the damage to the computer printer. In contrast, the passive-voice version conveys the information about the machine but avoids blaming a specific individual.

ACTIVE: John damaged the new computer printer because he left it on all Labor Day weekend.

PASSIVE: The new computer printer was damaged because it was left on all Labor Day weekend.

**Avoid Expletive Beginnings**. Expletives are insignificant, meaningless words that frequently occupy the usual position of the subject or direct object of the sentence. Avoid using expletives, particularly at the beginning of a sentence, because they weaken your writing. "*It* is" and "*There* is" and "*There* are" are common expletive beginnings.

The following sentences illustrate expletive beginnings. Notice that eliminating the expletives ("it" and "there") improves each sentence.

POOR: *It* is important to write good reports.

BETTER: Writing good reports is important.

POOR: *There* are many loopholes in the tax laws.

BETTER: The tax laws contain many loopholes.

## CONCISENESS

Every day I get stacks of correspondence and reports. I have no time for all that mail, so I usually avoid reading anything longer than one page.

Concise writing contains essential information in the fewest possible words. Readers appreciate conciseness because it focuses their attention and saves them time. In contrast, wordy writing is tedious for the reader and inefficient for both the writer and the reader.

The following long-winded paragraph needs pruning:

It is essential that the employee should generally be given an opportunity to talk and to explain the problem in her or his own words and present the information relevant to the situation. If necessary, it is important to question the employee to make an evaluation of the facts and information which may not have previously been brought to the attention of the supervisor. If the grievance incident involves or concerns more than one employee, all those who may have been involved in the incident or who can furnish pertinent information should also be given the opportunity to give their information according to specified procedures.

This passage contains 105 words. The following revision condenses the essential information into 23 words:

Be sure to get all the facts. First, interview the employee who filed the grievance. Then interview all others involved in the incident.

Eliminate unnecessary words, phrases, sentences, and entire messages. If you can cut the length of a message by a significant percent, you will improve its efficiency in the same proportion. In the example above, the second paragraph is 22 percent as long as the first and could be read and understood in only 22 percent of the time required for the first paragraph.

As an example of conciseness improving efficiency, an engineering supervisor for the Phoenix city government received a salary bonus for a suggestion to condense a 35-page monthly report to one page. The suggestion saved the city $30,000 in the first year alone.

Use the following techniques to achieve conciseness in your writing:

1. Check the readability level.
2. Prune unnecessary words.
3. Avoid trite expressions.
4. Eliminate redundancies.

## Readability Level

**Readability** is the degree of reading difficulty of written messages. Messages containing long, rambling sentences or many long, unfamiliar words are generally harder to read than messages containing shorter sentences and words.

Readability formulas provide a readability index of written material by measuring such factors as sentence length and word length. A readability index is a grade-level equivalent. An index of 10, for example, indicates that a person who had completed ten years of education would be able to read the material with ease, but a person whose schooling had stopped at the eighth grade would probably find the material difficult to read.

The Gunning Fog Index provides a good estimate of readability. The Fog Index is derived from a formula that involves sentence length and word length. Long words and long sentences will cause the Fog Index to be high. The higher the Fog Index, the less readable is the message.

Business messages, which should be written so that they are easy to understand, usually have a fairly low Fog Index. For example, *The Wall Street Journal* has a Fog Index averaging 11 for all pages; but its front page averages 9 or less.

Letters and short memorandums generally should have a Fog Index between 7 and 11. Formal research papers and technical or scientific reports may have a Fog Index of 14 or 15 because of complex words which are necessary.

If your letter or short memorandum has a Fog Index that exceeds 11, your sentences are probably too long; and you may be using too many long words. When your Fog Index is too high, your writing is neither clear nor concise. To improve the readability of your writing, select short, common words and write few sentences containing more than 20 words.

Readability can be calculated manually or by computer. Some computer programs for writing improvement can generate a readability index. To calculate the Fog Index manually, apply the following formula to a passage containing 100 to 125 words (Gunning, 1968):

$$\left[\left(\frac{\text{Number of words}}{\text{Number of sentences}}\right) + \left(\frac{\text{Number of long words} \times 100}{\text{Number of words}}\right)\right] \times .4$$

Step 1 - Find the average length of sentences in the passage.

a. Count the words in the passage. (If a particular word appears more than once, count it each time.) _____

b. Count the sentences in the passage. (In compound sentences, count each independent clause as a separate sentence.) _____

c. Divide the number of words by the number of sentences to get the *average sentence length*. (Round to the nearest whole number.) _____

Step 2 - Find the percentage of "long" words

a. Underline each word that is *three or more syllables* in length. Do not include capitalized words, compound words (such as *salesperson* and *nevertheless*), or verbs made into three syllables by the addition of "-es" or "-ed" (such as "trespasses" or "created"). Count the number of words you underlined. _____

b. Divide the number of "long" words by the total number of words you counted in Step 1. _____

c. Multiply your result by 100 (simply move the decimal two places to the right and round to the nearest whole number). _____

Step 3 - Apply the Fog Index constant (.4)

a. Add the Step 1 result to the Step 2 result. _____

b. Multiply the sum by .4; disregard any digits following the decimal point. _____

Adapted from *How to Take the Fog out of Writing*, 1985: Dartnell Books © Gunning-Mueller Clear Writing Institute, Santa Barbara, CA 93110. Used with permission.

Now apply the Fog Index to the following passage from a report about computer systems (the "long" words are underlined):

Prior to the development of database management information systems, a company's departments generally maintained separate record systems. With a database system, a company can increase its data-processing efficiency by utilizing a general data-storage approach. The company stores its data in a way that can be accessed by many users for various applications. In order to prevent file duplication, information is grouped and organized into a centralized database which is accessed by several departments. Database systems improve efficiency by preventing redundancy. Files can be brought up to date by making a change only once, and the new information will immediately be available to every department.

Step 1:
a.  Number of words in passage                                                = 110
b.  Number of sentences in passage (6—including one
    compound sentence)                                                         = 7
c.  Number of words divided by number of sentences (110/7)                     = 16
                                                                               (rounded)

Step 2:
a.  Number of "long" words                                                     = 28
    Total number of words in passage                                           = 110
b.  "Long" words divided by total words in passage (28/110)                    = .2545
c.  Multiply by 100 (.2545 × 100) and round                                    = 25

Step 3:
a.  Step 1 result + Step 2 result (16 + 25)                                    = 41
b.  Sum × Fog Index constant (41 × .4); drop digits to right of
    decimal point                                                              = 16

The Fog Index of 16 (college-senior level) is much higher than it should be, even for a formal report. The passage contains too many long words and long sentences to be understood easily. Shorter words and shorter sentences will save time and effort for the reader of this message.

## Unnecessary Words

The St. Louis Chamber of Commerce received the following letter:

My wife and I plan to visit St. Louis in May. We will be attending the Kiwanis convention and visiting my cousin Harold. We plan to be in the area for about a week unless we take a side trip to Kansas City.
    Please send some information about entertainment in the St. Louis area.

To fill the writer's request, does the Chamber of Commerce need all the information included in the first paragraph? Or could the entire first paragraph be eliminated?

Better information is not necessarily more information. To prune unnecessary words, omit details that the reader will not need.

Then examine your writing style. Are your sentences too long and complex? Many writers have the bad habit of using a clause when a phrase will do, or using a phrase when a word will do.

To eliminate unnecessary words, condense subordinate clauses to a phrase or a word:

| Wordy | Concise |
|---|---|
| • people who have computer backgrounds | • people with computer backgrounds |
| • individuals who have ambition | • ambitious people |
| • wildlife which is endangered | • endangered wildlife |
| • a contract that was signed | • a signed contract |

Condense phrases to a word:

| Wordy | Concise |
|---|---|
| • at a fast rate | • fast |
| • at all times | • always |
| • at the present time | • now |
| • at this time | • now |
| • due to the fact that | • because |
| • for the purpose of | • for |
| • in a positive way | • positively |
| • in many cases | • often |
| • in order to | • to |
| • in regard to | • about |
| • with experience | • experienced |

On the other hand, avoid oversimplifying your sentences. Writing that consists only of simple sentences of uniform length is choppy and dull. A Fog Index of less than 7 is an indication that your writing style is too simple.

Another way to eliminate unnecessary words and strengthen your writing is to use action verbs. In the following examples, the phrases containing weak verbs can be replaced by a single action verb:

| Weak Verb Phrases | Action Verbs |
|---|---|
| • arrive at a decision | • decide |
| • conduct a study of | • study |
| • conduct an audit | • audit |
| • give consideration to | • consider |
| • have a disagreement | • disagree |
| • hold a meeting | • meet |
| • make an analysis of | • analyze |
| • make an examination | • examine |
| • make inquiry | • ask |
| • take into consideration | • consider |

## Trite Expressions

**Trite expressions** (cliches) are words and phrases that are overused and have become worn out and monotonous. Today's trite expressions were yesterday's standard usage. In the following examples, the words and phrases in the right column are more concise and up to date than the trite expressions on the left:

| Trite | Improved |
|---|---|
| • advise | • tell |
| • at your earliest convenience | • soon |
| • communication | • letter |
| • contact | • write, call |
| • enclosed, please find | • here is |
| • in accordance with your request | • as you requested |
| • in compliance with your request | • as requested |
| • in the amount of | • for |
| • in the event that | • if |
| • in the near future | • next week |
| • inform | • tell |
| • per your request | • as requested |
| • prior to | • before |
| • this is to acknowledge | • thank you for |
| • under separate cover | • by parcel post |

## Redundancies

**Redundancy** is unnecessary repetition of an idea. Material that contains redundancies is distracting and unnecessarily time consuming to read as the following examples show:

| Redundant | Better |
|---|---|
| • basic fundamentals | • fundamentals |
| • consensus of opinion | • consensus |
| • end result | • result |
| • exact same | • same |
| • few in number | • few |
| • important essentials | • essentials |
| • month of January | • January |
| • necessary requirement | • requirement |
| • new innovation | • innovation |
| • past history | • history |
| • repeat again | • repeat |
| • 3 p.m. in the afternoon | • 3 p.m. |
| • typical example | • example |
| • year of 1988 | • 1988 |

## COMPLETENESS

The employees of an electronic manufacturer received the following memorandum:

---

```
     TO:   All Employees
   FROM:   Terry Wilkins, Personnel Director
   DATE:   November 30, 19--
SUBJECT:   Health Insurance Changes
```

Effective January 1, several major changes will take place in the Metropolis Health Insurance plan.

All employees are invited to attend a one-hour informational program on December 1 concerning these changes. Jack Raymond, Information Officer at Metropolis Insurance Company, will conduct the program and answer any questions you may have about the changes.

---

This message is incomplete because it does not indicate the place or time of the meeting. A message is complete only if it gives readers all the information they need.

To be complete, informative messages must include the following *four W's* — who, what, where, and when. In this memorandum, the *who* and *what* were included, but the *when* was incomplete and the *where* was omitted. After several employees called for additional information, the embarrassed personnel director had to send another memo specifying the location and time of the meeting.

Incomplete messages are usually a result of the writer's carelessness or vagueness. Which of the *four W's* are missing in the following incomplete sentences?

INCOMPLETE: The Colorado Hospital Association is sponsoring a workshop in September.

IMPROVED: The Colorado Hospital Association is sponsoring a conference on September 7 and 8 at the Towers Hotel.

INCOMPLETE: There will be about 40 people attending the meeting.

IMPROVED: About 40 hospital administrators and physicians will attend the meeting.

INCOMPLETE: We would like to invite you to give a talk to our group.

IMPROVED: You are invited to present a 45-minute talk on "Computers and Communication" to the Colorado Hospital Association at 9 a.m. on September 8.

INCOMPLETE: The Education Department has several films available.

IMPROVED: We are enclosing a list of the Education Department films that are available.

## Carelessness

Omitting essential information wastes time and increases personnel costs. To get the needed information, the receiver of an incomplete message must make a telephone call (sometimes a long-distance call) or write another letter. In the case of the health-insurance memorandum you just read, for example, the personnel director had to send a second memo to more than five hundred employees.

An accounting student received the following response to a letter of inquiry she sent to the state board of accountancy:

---

Dear Ms. Haney:

A brochure containing excerpts of the Arizona Accountancy Law and Rules is enclosed. This brochure explains the certification requirements and also describes the CPA examination.

A Directory of Arizona CPA's is available upon request. Please sign and return the enclosed Request for Public Record Form if you wish to receive the Directory.

Sincerely,

Frances A. Simons
Executive Director

bh

Enclosures (2)

---

Unfortunately, the envelope did not contain either of the two enclosures! The student was then forced to write a follow-up letter and wait for another reply. The writer's negligence created time loss and extra expense for both the state agency and the student.

Incomplete messages often have other expensive consequences. When customers receive insufficient information, their goodwill—and their business—may be lost.

Employees sometimes face the problem of not receiving the information they need to do their jobs properly. When employees receive insufficient information, their guesswork may cause costly errors. Incomplete information can cause defective products, machinery breakdowns, safety hazards, and employee morale problems.

To prevent careless mistakes, plan business messages before you write them, check for the four W's, and take the time to read your messages carefully before you sign them. Before sealing the envelope, check to make sure that all the enclosures are included.

## Vagueness

Messages are often incomplete because of the writer's vagueness. Some writers use vague, ambiguous language because of their inexperience or their indifference to the reader's needs.

Although most vagueness in business writing is unintentional, sometimes writers are deliberately vague to avoid commitment or to avoid revealing unfavorable information. Such tactics are seldom effective, particularly in response to a direct inquiry. Regardless of whether the information is omitted deliberately or accidentally, the consequences will be negative. If a customer's questions are not answered satisfactorily because of a writer's vagueness, a loss in goodwill will probably occur.

These vaguely worded sentences need more specific information to make them complete:

VAGUE: Your attention to the matter will be appreciated.

IMPROVED: I will appreciate your planning the Hospital Association staff meeting.

VAGUE: We can offer you a suitable honorarium.

IMPROVED: We can offer you a $100 honorarium.

VAGUE: Mr. Jones responded appropriately.

IMPROVED: Mr. Jones answered all our questions about the insurance policy.

VAGUE: Ms. Anderson was uncooperative.

IMPROVED: Ms. Anderson turned down our offer to purchase the property for $125,000.

Incomplete information can be unethical and even illegal if information is withheld in order to deceive or defraud. The following advertisement was reported to the Consumer Fraud Division of a state Attorney General's office.

When a customer asked to see the $399 sectional sofa, she discovered that the price was actually three times the advertised price, or $1,197 ($399 per section)! Lawsuits and possible prosecution for fraud may result from such unethical business practices.

## FIGURE 3.1 MISLEADING ADVERTISEMENT

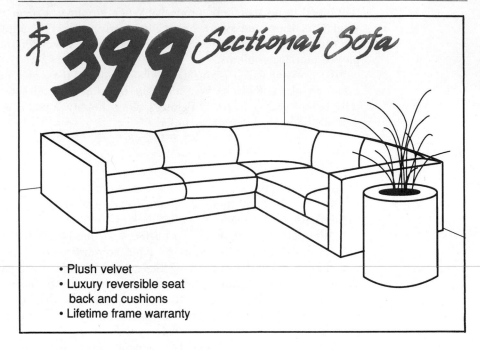

- Plush velvet
- Luxury reversible seat
  back and cushions
- Lifetime frame warranty

## CONSIDERATION

Good human relations depend on consideration for other people. Considerate writers are prompt, tactful, positive, courteous, and fair. Considerate messages build goodwill, but inconsiderate messages annoy or insult the reader.

A job applicant received the following letter:

---

Dear Mr. Gregory:

We have received your application for the position of Training Director.

Unfortunately, after reviewing your credentials, we have determined that you are unqualified for this position.

The position has been filled by Dr. William Holland.

Sincerely,

---

What do you think will be Mr. Gregory's reaction to this letter? How do you think he would feel if he happened to meet Dr. Holland?

The writer of this letter should not have tactlessly revealed the name of the individual who was selected for the position. The word "unqualified" is another indication that the writer had little consideration for the reader's feelings.

The success or failure of a business message depends on the reader's reaction to it. A successful writer develops sensitivity to the reader's feelings and needs. To write messages containing the fourth C, consideration, visualize your reader. Put yourself in the reader's place and imagine that you are the reader. Try to understand your reader's feelings and point of view.

## You Attitude

Messages with the "you" attitude express ideas from the reader's viewpoint. Readers are more interested in ideas that meet *their* needs than in ideas that meet the writer's needs. "We"-attitude messages, which express ideas only from the writer's viewpoint, are usually ineffective. Successful business messages appeal to the reader's interests and needs.

Stress *you* and *your* instead of *I*, *me*, *we*, and *us*. A letter does not have the "you" attitude if it contains more *I*'s and *we*'s than *you*'s.

The following phrases are examples of "we" attitude and "you" attitude:

| We Attitude | You Attitude |
| --- | --- |
| • I am interested in finding out about... | • Please send me some information about... |
| • We have received your letter... | • Thank you for your letter... |
| • We have five models... | • You can select from five models... |
| • To update our files... | • To verify your group insurance benefits... |

## Promptness

A considerate person is conscientious about being on time. Prompt messages convey a positive impression of the sender. In contrast, late messages convey an impression that the sender is indifferent or inefficient.

Replies to routine letters and memos should be sent within three to five business days. More urgent messages should be answered within 24 hours. Prompt responses to orders and inquiries promote sales, and prompt thank-you messages promote goodwill.

If a message cannot be answered promptly with a conventional letter or memorandum, using a short-cut procedure is usually preferable to delaying the message. Many companies use preprinted "speed letter" forms for writing notes in longhand (see Figure 3.2). Some managers occasionally jot a reply in longhand in the margin of the message they received and return it to the sender.

FIGURE 3.2 "SPEED LETTER" FORM

# WILLIS ELECTRONICS, INC.
302 South Central Avenue
Phoenix, AZ  85041-3450

## SPEED LETTER
This speed letter is designed to give you
a FAST reply to your inquiry

Date: _____9/3/--_____

Yes, Atlas circuits are now in stock. We are enclosing a new price list.

R. T. Johnson

## Courtesy

People expect to hear a courteous *please* and *thank you*. Failure to observe these amenities can offend people and damage goodwill. Some business people are courteous to customers but are not always courteous to the employees they supervise. A good manager is careful to build positive relationships with coworkers at all levels.

If you should make an error, do not be afraid to apologize. A courteous apology builds credibility and goodwill.

To add consideration to your business messages, use the following courteous phrases generously:

### Courteous Phrases

- We appreciate . . .
- Thank you for . . .
- We are pleased to . . .
- May I ask you to . . .
- You were nice to . . .
- Please let me know . . .
- I am sorry that . . .
- I apologize for . . .

## Positive Tone

The attitude that a message projects is called its **tone**. A positive tone is cheerful and helpful, while a negative tone is pessimistic and unpleasant, as shown in the following examples:

NEGATIVE: *Unfortunately*, we could not process your insurance claim because you *neglected* to sign the form.

POSITIVE: Please sign the enclosed form so we can process your insurance claim promptly.

NEGATIVE: Your automobile insurance policy has *expired* because you *failed* to pay the bill on time.

POSITIVE: Please send us your check so we can reinstate your automobile insurance policy.

A positive tone reflects courtesy and diplomacy. Experienced writers emphasize the positive aspects of a message and avoid using negative words such as the following examples:

### Negative Words

- unfortunately
- fail
- reject

- deny
- delinquent
- expired
- regret
- unsatisfactory

## Integrity

Writing considerate messages in a positive tone does not imply that you should distort the truth. Integrity (honesty and truthfulness) in business communication is essential for credibility and for maintaining successful human relations. Integrity is the foundation of a sound code of business ethics.

Exaggerations that might be acceptable in social relationships are not appropriate in business communication. For example, when turning down an undesirable social invitation, you might give a not-quite-honest reason such as "I'm busy." On the other hand, concealing or misrepresenting the truth in a business transaction is unethical and possibly illegal. Various federal and state laws protect the public from deceptive business communications, particularly in advertising, credit, and collections.

Of course no one likes to hear unfavorable news such as "Your application for credit is not approved because of your poor credit rating." However, a company that gives a false reason for rejecting a credit application could be subject to a lawsuit. In business messages, always tell the truth in a tactful way.

## Sex-Fair Language

**Sex-fair** (nonsexist) language treats both sexes with equal status and respect. Language that stereotypes or reflects bias against either men or women is referred to as **sexist** language. Sexist language offends many readers.

Avoid references to males and females in stereotyped roles and occupations or with stereotyped characteristics. Also, avoid using the pronoun *he* when referring to a category of people that may include women. Instead, use the plural pronoun *they*, or use *he or she*.

Here are some examples of sexist and sex-fair language:

| Sexist | Sex-Fair |
|---|---|
| • stewardess | • flight attendant |
| • chairman | • chair or chairperson |
| • salesman | • salesperson, sales clerk, or sales representative |
| • policeman | • police officer |
| • authoress | • author |
| • male nurse | • nurse |
| • mankind | • humanity |
| • one-girl office | • one-secretary office |

The following sentences containing sexist pronoun references are rewritten in sex-fair language:

SEXIST: Every employee should check *his* personnel records...

SEX-FAIR: All employees should check their personnel records...

SEXIST: Call a plumber and have *him* repair...

SEX-FAIR: Call a plumber to repair...

# CORRECTNESS

The correctness of business messages depends on factors such as the appropriate format, English mechanics, and keyboarding accuracy. Errors in arrangement, punctuation, and typing, for example, send a message that the writer is careless, uneducated, or lacking intelligence. The reader may conclude that the writer, or even the company, is inefficient or incompetent.

As an example, assume that you wrote to two rival electronics companies for information about their new computers. You receive an attractively typed, error-free letter from Company A. Company B sends you a smudged letter containing several grammatical errors and five misspelled words. What conclusion would you draw about those two companies? Which company's computer would you be more likely to purchase?

Company B may actually manufacture a better computer than Company A's. Perhaps Company B is so overwhelmed with orders that the marketing department hired temporary clerical employees who made the errors. Nevertheless, the company is responsible for the employees' errors, which can tarnish its image.

## English Mechanics

Correctness includes all the elements of English mechanics — spelling, grammar, punctuation, capitalization, and sentence structure. In addition to creating a bad impression, errors in mechanics distract the reader and thus lessen the effectiveness of a message. To ensure that your writing is free of errors in English mechanics, check each message carefully before sending it.

As discussed in Chapter 1, some word-processing software packages include optional features such as spelling, grammar, and punctuation checkers. Although such software is extremely helpful for finding many errors in mechanics, this software cannot detect certain types of errors. For example, spelling checkers will not discover an error when the word *your* is substituted for *you're* since both are actual words. Always have a dictionary and a reference manual handy when you write. (Appendix A of this book contains a review of English grammar and mechanics.)

## Appropriate Format

Experienced business writers generally use standard formats for their business messages. Readers expect business letters, memorandums, and reports to follow recommended styles and formats.

Using a nonstandard format detracts from a message by drawing the reader's attention to its layout rather than to its contents. Sales promotional letters may occasionally have an unusual format as an attention-getting device. Standard styles are essential, however, for most business messages.

Business letters are traditionally single spaced, with double spacing between paragraphs. A double-spaced job application letter, for example, could be rejected on the basis of its nonstandard format. The personnel manager receiving the letter may think that the applicant is inexperienced, naive, and perhaps unqualified for the job.

Recommended formats for business letters, memorandums, and business reports are included in Appendix B.

## Proofreading

Carefully proofread your business messages for content and typographical errors. Always double check facts and figures that represent the four W's discussed on page 45. Billing and other content errors can cause a company to lose customers. Only one zero makes the difference between $1,000 and $10,000; omitting a zero could be a very costly mistake!

Typographical errors create a bad impression. "Typos" can also be expensive errors, particularly when discovered after numerous copies of a message have already been printed and must be discarded.

Office automation has generally improved the accuracy of business communication. However, the computer age has also created certain types of errors in business communication. Computer errors generally occur because the people programming or operating the computer make errors in logic, make careless mistakes, or fail to provide for exceptions.

Problems frequently occur with computer mailing lists. As an example, for printing salutations on a mass mailing of form letters, the computer could be programmed to print the second word in the first line of each mailing address (probably the addressee's first name) after *Dear*. However, this system does not provide for exceptions. For instance, if the mailing list contains only an addressee's initials after her or his courtesy title (for example, *Mr. J. T. Johnson*), the salutation would appear as *Dear J.*

As another example of a problem with mailing lists, a word-processing operator flagged the first and last words in the first line of each mailing address to be printed in the salutation after *Dear*. In other words, the salutation for *Mrs. Alice Smith* would be *Dear Mrs. Smith*. Since a computer was unable to anticipate exceptions, Mr. Robert T. Garwood, Jr., received a letter addressed to *Dear Mr. Jr.*

Can you find a major error in the following letter to a job applicant?

---

Dear Carolyn:

Thank you for your application for our Assistant Buyer position. I appreciate your promptness.

Carolyn, could you please suggest a few tentative dates that would allow you to travel to Houston and visit us. Please send me two or three alternative dates in May.

Again, thank you, first name, and I will look forward to hearing from you soon.

Cordially,

---

To personalize this form letter, the computer program that merged this letter with a mailing list was supposed to print the addressee's first name three times. When someone neglected to "flag" the addressee's name in the last paragraph, several dozen job applicants received letters containing the same error!

People are offended by errors in their names, especially when accompanied by the wrong courtesy title. Gender errors are particularly offensive. Using a mailing list previously taken from the telephone directory yellow pages, a real-estate company mailed a computer-generated sales letter to medical doctors and their spouses. The computer, which had no way of knowing a person's gender by her or his name, was programmed to add *and Mrs.* to each name on the list. In this case, sex stereotyping created a particularly offensive error — Dr. Gloria Williams received a letter addressed to *Dr. and Mrs. Gloria Williams*.

People react to such computer errors in various ways, ranging from indignation to amusement. Occasionally someone will take the time to provide feedback about the error.

An oil company, which had purchased a mailing list from a bank-card company, sent a letter offering a credit card to recipients of the letter and other members of their families. The letter stated: "Please indicate on the enclosed form the names of your family members you would like to receive additional cards."

The mailing list included the names of several companies, which received the same form letter. One letter, which was sent to an elevator manufacturing company, began "Dear Mr. Elevator." The following letter is adapted from a reply composed by an elevator company employee, who had quite a sense of humor:

```
                 EASTERN ELEVATOR COMPANY
                   193 PROSPECT AVENUE
                 NEW HAVEN, CT 06511-2418
                            June 6, 19--

Mr. William G. Paulsen
Vice President, Marketing
Texxon Oil Company
4847 Pendleton Parkway
San Antonio, TX 78228-7899

Dear Mr. Paulsen:

    I couldn't decide whether I should write to you,
to your Public Relations Manager, Mr. Relations, or
directly to Mr. Texxon Oil. But since you were the
one to write to me, I've decided on you.

    Naturally, I hope we become good friends and
possibly the Elevator family and Oil family can get
together in the future. In the meantime, I hope we
will be good enough friends for me to call Mr. Oil -
"Tex." You may call me by my first name, "Eastern."

    The entire Elevator family and I will certainly
use your credit card. I would like additional cards
as listed below:

              Freight Elevator - my son
              Service Elevator - my daughter
              Escalator        - my mother
              Dumb Waiter       - my stepson

    Naturally, I await your prompt response so the
entire Elevator family can put these cards into use.

                            Sincerely,

                            Eastern Elevator
```

No matter who—or what—makes an error, the person whose signature appears on the message is responsible for the consequences of the error. Carefully proofread all your messages before sending them.

## SUMMARY

Poorly written business messages create a bad impression and may be ignored by the receiver. Various types of errors in business writing can have negative consequences that will confuse, distract, or irritate the reader. In contrast, effective business writing has the desired impact on its receiver. Good business writing includes the five basic C's of business communication — clearness, conciseness, completeness, consideration, and correctness.

## CHAPTER REVIEW

1. What problems can occur from using *impressive words* and *jargon*?
2. List three jargon words or expressions in your major field of study.
3. Define *active* and *passive* voice. Give an example of each.
4. What are *expletives*? Give two examples of expletives. Do expletives improve or weaken sentence construction?
5. List three ways to achieve *conciseness* in your writing.
6. Calculate the Gunning Fog Index for a 120-word memorandum containing 8 sentences with 30 "long" words. How would you rate the readability of this memorandum?
7. Define *redundancy*. Give three examples of redundancies.
8. What are some of the consequences of *carelessness* and *vagueness* in business writing?
9. Define the "you" attitude.
10. How promptly should routine business letters be answered?

## APPLICATIONS

1. Compute the Fog Index on a sample of your writing that is 100-200 words long. For example, use your *Day in the Future* composition (Chapter 1, item 4, page 11).
   a. Underline the "long" words and show all calculations.
   b. Is your Fog Index too high or too low for that type of composition? (A range of 7-11 is appropriate for *Day in the Future*; a range of 12-14 is more appropriate for a formal research paper.)
   c. Are your sentences too long or too short?
   d. Did you use too many long words?
2. Evaluate a research paper that you or one of your classmates wrote for another class. Select two pages for analysis and underline all the *impressive words* and *jargon* on those two pages.
3. Indicate the weakness in each of the following sentences; then revise the sentences to make them *clear* and *correct*.
   a. Confirming our telephone conversation, the price of the air conditioner is $1,950.
   b. Upon entering the office, the reorganization was apparent.

    c. Faced with the imminent arrival of a microcomputer to embellish the office furnishings, the accountant was apprehensive about the prospect.

    d. Erudite auctorial pursuits obfuscate business communication.

    e. She sent an order for the service department to insert a null modem between the printer port and the demo end of the fan cable.

    f. After the auditors discussed the problem with the purchasing department, they decided that a number of procedures should be changed.

    g. The service department will repair your car, which we hope is satisfactory.

    h. The local unemployment rate has dropped to 6 percent. This is causing a shortage of workers in several areas.

    i. Although advertising expenses increased a lot, sales of the RX-20 model declined dramatically this year.

    j. It is a good time for investors to consider purchasing real estate.

4. Revise the following sentences to make them concise.

    a. To the best of our knowledge, we have not yet received a full and complete credit report from the Associated Credit Bureau.

    b. We at the Humboldt Company will be more than willing to do our utmost to provide you with low-in-cost office products that are high in quality.

    c. As you are probably aware, firsthand expertise with the very latest and up-to-date computer equipment is a necessary requirement for this job in particular.

    d. Will you please acknowledge receipt of this contract by calling us at 457-2091 at your earliest convenience.

    e. Without a doubt, people who have strength of determination can have success in this commercial enterprise.

    f. If you should be in our neighborhood, stop by and let one of our real estate personnel take you on a tour of these properties that we have available for you to see.

    g. I am writing this letter to you at this time with the idea that this information may be beneficial to you in making major decisions about planning for your future retirement.

    h. It is important that you, as a member of the Central Missouri Credit Union, receive this brochure, which explains the benefits we offer to all members.

    i. I would like to make a request that you sign this form and send it to us by return mail as soon as possible.

    j. Last week, after he had read the report, Mr. French made several positive and complimentary remarks about the new advertising campaign.

5. Change the following sentences from passive to active voice.

    a. New employees were asked by the personnel department to attend an orientation meeting.

    b. A 10 percent raise in salary is anticipated this year.

    c. The accident may have been caused by the carelessness of the maintenance department.

    d. The facts should be checked before action is taken.

    e. The check was not found in the letter by the credit department.

6. What information is incomplete or missing in the following sentences?
   a. Our interest rate on personal loans is very competitive.
   b. Please send us a check for $45.95, plus tax.
   c. We mailed the book you requested today.
   d. The meeting will be held next Thursday on the third floor.
   e. The new XT 400 gets excellent gas mileage.

7. Revise the following sentences to include more consideration for the reader, particularly a better "you" attitude, a positive tone, and sex-fair language.
   a. Your order has been delayed because you failed to include the correct credit information.
   b. We cannot possibly send a repairman until next Monday.
   c. Your delinquent loan payment has finally arrived.
   d. We want to point out that our cash management account is not intended for the naive, small investor.
   e. You damaged the computer by failing to read the directions in the user manual.
   f. Don't forget to call us by Friday, or you will lose this chance to buy the property.
   g. Every city councilman should indicate his views on the zoning ordinance.
   h. Unfortunately, we cannot send you the book until the new edition arrives from the publisher.
   i. We need to elect a new chairman of the personnel committee.
   j. I wish to thank you for the helpful attitude of your salesmen.

8. How many spelling and other errors can you find in the following letter? Proofread it carefully and count the errors. Refer to Appendices A and B for rules about letter style and format, punctuation, abbreviation, capitalization, and writing numbers.

---

October 6, 19--
Kendrick Manufacturing Co.
412 Washington Street
Monroe City, MO 63456-3669
Dear Sir:

   As you requested we have filled out and enclosed the credit form you sent us.

   As we noted on the form, we have done a considerabel ammount of business with the Anderson Co. during the past 2 or 3 years. During that time we never had to send them a reminder that their account was over due. In fact on all but one ocassion they have taken advantage of the 2 percent discount we allow for paying bills within ten days.

If you should extablish a credit relation ship
with the Anderson Co. we are sure you will be
pleased with their cooperetion and eficiency.

If you need any additionel information about this
company be sure sure to right us.

Cordially Yours

Vera James
Credit Manager

ss:VJ

---

## CASE STUDY

Martin Trellis, regional supervisor for TeleWays International (T. W. I. N.)
long-distance telephone company, pointed emphatically at the mimeographed
instructions posted over each service representative's desk as he began the
monthly training meeting.

### PROCEDURES FOR EXPEDITING THE RESOLUTION OF ACCOUNT DISCREPANCIES

1. Check all facts with the data in the computer
   database. If paper and computer records disagree,
   always assume that the computer listings are
   correct.

2. Determine the relavent time accruement of the
   discrepancy. If one month or less, the appropriate
   interpersonal medium is the postal service; if
   greater than one month, a telephone contact
   communicates stronger concern.

3. Using the appropriate medium as described in #2
   above, make the contact. In the communication,
   delicately but firmly apprise the offending
   subscriber of the following information:
   a. who you are
   b. that you represent the telephone company
   c. what account you are inquiring about
   d. the nature of the account discrepancy which
      needs to be corrected

4. Elicit from the offending subscriber the following
   information:
   a. his version of how he became delinquent
   b. an indication of when and how he will correct
      the discrepancy

```
5. If making a postal contact, apprise the offending
   subscriber that you can be reached by phone through
   our central switchboard number, 555-TWIN, and that
   his haste in correcting his discrepancy will lessen
   the likelihood of a blot on his credit record.
```

```
REMEMBER, ladies, you are the companies primary
contact with the customer. Following the above
procedures exactly will solve any discrepancy problem
that arises. We wrote these rules to make your job
easier—DON'T DIVEATE FROM THEM!
```

"I cannot emphasize too strongly the importance of following these instructions exactly," Mr. Trellis began. "They are clear and explicit, and they cover all billing problems you are likely to encounter. So just follow the instructions and you can't go wrong. If you don't follow them, however, the result may be ill-will or even a lost customer."

The following week, a customer received the same message three days in a row on his telephone answering machine. It said: "Hi! This is Steve from the phone company. I need your address. Please call me at five-five-five-ten and tell me what your address is. Thanks."

The customer tried calling five-five-five-one-zero, but the number never rang. So he then tried calling the service numbers listed in the telephone directory, but the customer-service representative from the local phone company told him that the records were correct. Three weeks later, the customer's TeleWays long-distance service was disconnected.

A call to the TeleWays office revealed that the service was disconnected because the customer's last bill had been returned to the office stamped "addressee unknown." The bill had been sent to 4129 West University, but the customer lives at 2149 West University—and has for ten years!

The customer commented, "If you wanted to talk to me, why didn't you leave a number that would ring? And, if you wanted to verify my address, why didn't you just look it up in the telephone directory?"

When the matter was referred to Martin Trellis, he apologized and told the customer that T.W.I.N. would reinstate his long-distance service immediately. Trellis then called Steve Sykes, the service representative who had handled the account in question, into his office. Trellis said, "The instructions clearly cover the appropriate action in this situation. Why didn't you follow them, Steve?"

Sykes replied, "I did."

1. Is Mr. Trellis correct? Did the "Procedures for Expediting the Resolution of Account Discrepancies" give Steve clear instructions for handling this situation? Why or why not?
2. Why was the customer unable to return Steve's call? Was this failure a result of the "Procedures"?

3. Did the "Procedures" communicate consideration for customers? For the TeleWays customer service representatives? Discuss your answer.
4. Evaluate the conciseness and completeness of the "Procedures."
5. Evaluate the correctness of the "Procedures." Based on your evaluation, what is your impression of Mr. Trellis as a supervisor?

## SUGGESTED READINGS

DiGaetani, John L., Jane B. DiGaetani, and Earl N. Harbert. *Writing Out Loud: A Self-Help Guide to Clear Business Writing*. Homewood, IL: Dow Jones-Irwin, 1983.

Flesch, Rudolf. *The Art of Readable Writing*, Rev. ed. New York: Harper and Row, 1974.

Guffey, Mary Ellen. *Business English*, 2nd ed. Boston: Kent Publishing Co., 1986.

Gunning, Robert. *The Technique of Clear Writing*, Rev. ed. New York: McGraw-Hill, 1968.

Strunk, William and E. B. White. *The Elements of Style*, 3rd ed. New York: Macmillan, 1979.

# ORGANIZING WRITTEN COMMUNICATION

## CHAPTER 4

Tom, a college student with a major in management information systems, was having difficulty writing a research paper for one of his courses. When he finally finished writing a rough draft of the paper, he was not satisfied with the results.

Deciding to seek help, Tom showed the paper to his business communication professor. "I know the paper isn't very good," Tom told him, "but I don't know exactly what's wrong with it."

The professor scanned the paper and immediately diagnosed the problem. "Tom, how do you go about starting to write a computer program?" he asked.

Tom replied, "I work from an outline or a flowchart."

The professor suggested, "If you would follow the same procedure when you write a research paper, your ideas would be arranged in a more logical sequence. The problem with your writing is its lack of organization."

A skilled writer begins a message by carefully planning it before writing a word. When you plan the message, you decide how to approach the writing task.

This chapter discusses how to plan messages and organize complete messages, paragraphs, and sentences. The following topics are included:

- Steps in planning business messages
- Procedures for selecting a plan of organization
- Basics of constructing an outline
- Strategies for organizing paragraphs and sentences
- Methods of achieving unity, emphasis, and parallel construction
- Techniques for providing transition

## PLANNING A MESSAGE

Poorly organized messages reflect a lack of planning by wandering aimlessly from one idea or point to another. In a well-organized message, however, the writer has planned a smooth flow of ideas linking the whole message together. A skilled writer plans the organization of a total message, the paragraphs, and the sentences within the paragraphs.

Planning a message includes these steps: (1) determining the objective of the message, (2) visualizing the reader, (3) choosing the message medium and format, (4) selecting a plan of organization and (5) constructing an outline.

The first step in planning is determining the objective of the message. Analyze your specific situation. What do you want your message to accomplish? Are you sending routine information? Are you attempting to persuade someone to buy a product or do you a favor?

Business messages fall into several categories—those that inform (including those that convey favorable, unfavorable, and routine information), those that request routine information, and those that attempt to persuade. Into which of these categories does your message fit?

Second, visualize the reader and put yourself in her or his place. What would be your reaction to the message? Would the reader be pleased to receive your message? Would the reader be disappointed about the message? Or would the reader have a neutral attitude—of being neither pleased nor disappointed?

Next, decide what medium you will use to transmit the message. Will your message be oral or written? Written messages are often slower and more expensive than oral messages such as meetings and telephone calls. Many messages, however, should be in writing. Letters, short memorandums, long memorandum reports, and formal business reports are common media for written business messages. Select the medium and format that are most appropriate for your intended reader or readers.

After choosing the format, select an appropriate plan of organization for your message. Business messages are organized according to several standard patterns. Which one is most likely to achieve your desired results? The following section discusses the advantages of various patterns of organization.

Finally, develop an outline which puts your planning steps on paper. Can you construct and follow a logical outline? If so, your message will be well organized.

## SELECTING A PLAN OF ORGANIZATION

The initial steps in planning a message involve determining the appropriate pattern of organization. The writer should select a plan of organization that is compatible with the objective of the message, its reader, and its format.

Business messages may be classified according to standard patterns of organization. A writer should organize every business message according to one or more of these organization plans.

Short business messages, including letters and short memorandums, generally should be organized in one of two basic ways. Organizing a long message such as a report or a long memorandum is a more complex task because the writer may choose from a wide selection of organization plans.

## Short Business Messages

Business letters and short memorandums fall into the following four categories according to the anticipated reaction of the reader:

| Type of Message | Anticipated Reader's Reaction |
|---|---|
| • Favorable | • Positive |
| • Routine | • Neutral |
| • Unfavorable | • Negative |
| • Persuasive | • Interested ... Indifferent |

**Favorable** messages include many types of business letters and memorandums that the receiver would be pleased to get—her or his reaction will be positive. For example, a letter granting a request or claim, a letter offering someone a job or accepting a job offer, and a memorandum granting a budget request are all favorable messages.

**Routine** messages have a neutral effect on the receiver. Approximately 70 to 75 percent of all business messages fall into this category. Examples of routine messages include requests for information, simple claim letters, and letters and memorandums conveying typical business information.

**Unfavorable** messages include letters and memorandums that will disappoint the receiver—the reaction will be negative. For instance, letters denying a request or claim, a letter turning down a job applicant, and a memorandum turning down an employee's request or application for a promotion are unfavorable messages.

**Persuasive** messages attempt to induce the reader to take some action. The receiver's reaction may range from extreme interest to indifference, depending upon the situation. Sales letters are a typical example of persuasive messages. A reader may be indifferent to an unsolicited sales promotional letter. In contrast, a customer is likely to be enthusiastic about receiving a sales letter responding to her or his inquiry about a product.

**Direct Organization**. In the direct (deductive) plan of organization, the main idea appears at the beginning of the message—preferably in the first sentence. Additional information, including supporting details, appears in subsequent paragraphs.

The direct plan is based on the psychological principles of *primacy* and *recency*. According to these learning principles, people tend to remember best what they saw or heard first (**primacy**) and last (**recency**). Therefore, the beginning of a message generally stands out as its most emphatic part. The ending is the second most emphatic part, and the middle part is least emphatic. The direct plan is recommended for two types of messages—favorable and routine. In favorable messages, the good news stands out if the writer places it in the first sentence. After reading the favorable information first, the reader may be more receptive to the rest of the message.

The following letter accepting an invitation includes the favorable response in the first sentence, and the remaining paragraphs contain the details:

```
Yes, I will gladly judge the Future Business Leaders
of America state competition.

The "Job Interviewing" event is my first preference;
"Public Speaking" is my second choice. However, I am
willing to judge any event listed in your letter.

I am looking forward to working with these outstand-
ing business students.
```

With routine messages, the main idea is presented in the first sentence primarily for efficiency. The reader can comprehend the subject of the letter or memorandum faster when it appears at the beginning.

The details and supporting information appear in one or more subsequent paragraphs. Routine and favorable messages should end on a positive note, as shown in the example, or with a neutral statement. Chapter 5 discusses these types of messages in more detail.

**Indirect Organization**. The indirect (inductive) plan of organization is recommended for unfavorable and persuasive messages. Inductively organized messages have a positive or neutral beginning. The explanation follows in subsequent paragraphs, and the main idea appears between the middle and the end of the message. The closing paragraph contains a positive or neutral statement.

In unfavorable messages, the indirect plan de-emphasizes the bad news by placing it in a nonprominent position. According to the principles of primacy and recency, the middle part of a message will receive little emphasis.

Since the opening sentence sets the tone for the rest of the message, a negative beginning should be avoided. The beginning should establish contact with the reader without hinting that the message is unfavorable. The main idea in the unfavorable message (such as "The job you applied for has already been filled" or "We are unable to refund your money") appears after the writer explains the reasons. The message should end with a positive or neutral sentence that promotes goodwill with the reader.

In the following unfavorable letter, the bad news appears at the end of the second paragraph:

```
Thank you for asking me to serve on the State
Advisory Committee for Vocational Education.

I have always enjoyed working with young people
preparing for careers in business. However, I recently
accepted a one-year position at our Canadian subsid-
```

```
iary. Since I am leaving the country in January,
I will not be able to serve on the advisory committee
this year.

     Please keep me in mind for the future. You have my
best wishes for a successful year.
```

For persuasive messages, the indirect plan provides a more subtle approach than the direct plan allows. In persuasive messages, the main idea (such as "Buy an E-Z microwave oven") should appear after the reasons have been explained. The beginning sentence should contain a positive opening to establish rapport with the reader, and the last sentence should be positive to promote goodwill. Chapters 6 and 7 discuss unfavorable and persuasive messages in more detail.

## Long Business Messages

Messages such as business reports and long memorandums may be organized in several different ways. Long business messages may be organized in a direct or indirect pattern. In addition, other methods of organization include the chronological, geographical, value, importance, simple-to-complex, function or product, and alphabetical plans. Some long business messages combine two or more of these methods, with one primary and one or more secondary organization patterns.

Choosing the best organization plan depends on the individual situation and is much like choosing a set of plans for a new building. The first step is to review all the available blueprints. The second step is to eliminate those that do not fit the situation, and the last step is to choose one of the remaining plans that best meets your primary purpose.

**Chronological**. Time sequence, or chronological order, may be used when time is an important factor. A monthly sales report, for example, may present information in chronological order by week; or a weekly report may present information in order from Monday through Friday. As another example, a Workers' Compensation report may require an accident to be recorded in the order in which the events occurred. Also, procedures for operating a computer or other equipment are best written step-by-step in the order in which the instructions should be followed.

Chronological order is probably somewhat overused in business writing. For instance, when job application letters and resumes are arranged in chronological order, they tend to appear like monotonous autobiographies. Chronological order does not provide the flexibility for the writer to emphasize strengths and to subordinate weaknesses. Moreover, if a major point happens to fall in the middle of the chronological sequence, the reader might easily overlook it. Chronological order works best when all items are equally important. When the material has no logical time sequence, chronological order should be ruled out.

**Geographical**. Geographical order involves organizing material by location. Sales reports, for example, may be arranged by county, state, or region. Geographical arrangement simplifies writing and is easy for the reader to follow. The weaknesses, however, are similar to those inherent in chronological order. Geographical order provides little flexibility or variety, and many business report topics have no logical geographical sequence.

**Value**. Some business reports lend themselves to an arrangement by value. A financial report, for example, might list stock and bond investments in descending order by value or amount of the investments.

A weekly real-estate sales report might also be organized by value. In this case, the largest sale of the week would be listed first. If business is slow on Mondays and most large sales tend to occur later in the week, the writer might prefer to organize the weekly sales report by value rather than in chronological order. The value arrangement allows the writer to emphasize the largest property sale by including it first.

**Importance**. The largest item is not necessarily the most important one. For instance, in a budget request, the highest priority item may not be the most costly one. In that case, the writer may choose to organize the request by importance — generally in descending order. Many organizations attempt to improve performance as part of a management-by-objectives (MBO) program. With this system of management, employees and their supervisors work together to develop objectives for individual job performance. MBO reports are another example of organization by importance. Such reports generally rank objectives in order of their potential effect on organizational goals. MBO reports usually identify problems in order of importance, with the most serious problem first and the least serious problem last.

**Simple to Complex**. The simple-to-complex arrangement is helpful when the message is difficult to understand. Technical or abstract material aimed at readers with a nontechnical background lends itself to this pattern of organization. If a writer were to place the most abstract or complex concept at the beginning of a technical report, a busy manager attempting to read the report would likely become frustrated and stop reading it.

Think about how your last course in a technical subject such as computer programming or business statistics was organized. The instructor probably presented the simplest concepts first and then gradually introduced the more complex topics. You can use the same strategy when organizing business messages that require a great deal of explanation.

**Function or Product**. Many business reports and memorandums are organized into major categories by function (such as production, marketing, and finance) or by product (such as sporting goods, hardware, or automotive supplies). This arrangement works best if the writer intends to emphasize the various functions or products almost equally.

An example of a report organized by function might be the annual report of a business school, in which the major categories would be the various departments (accounting, economics, finance, etc.). In many companies, various reports such as marketing and quality-control reports are arranged by product.

**Alphabetical**. The main advantage of the alphabetical arrangement is that it is an impartial way to arrange information. You can use alphabetical order when you wish to avoid arranging items in any priority. A list of people's names (such as at the beginning of a memorandum sent to several individuals) is one kind of information that lends itself to alphabetical organization.

Alphabetical order is used most effectively as a secondary method of organization. After choosing another primary method of organization — for example, geographical — you might arrange the various cities or states in alphabetical order.

## OUTLINING THE MESSAGE

After you have determined the best plan of organization for your message, make an outline. Outlining is probably the most crucial (and unfortunately the most neglected) step in the process of organizing business messages. Making a detailed outline clarifies your thinking process and almost guarantees that your writing will be well organized. Outlining also helps you to stress important ideas so that your message will have the desired emphasis. Many mediocre writers could become good writers if only they would learn to make an outline first.

## Outlining Short Messages

For letters and short memorandums, your outline may consist of only a few brief items. Simply jot down several points you want to make, and arrange the points in the most effective sequence for achieving your objective.

In the sample of a "favorable message" (page 66), an outline of the letter might include the following items:

Letter Accepting a Speaking Invitation:

1. Accept the invitation
2. Include additional information
   a. Request overhead projector
   b. Enclose resume
3. Close courteously

In the sample of an "unfavorable message" (page 66), an outline of the letter might include the following items:

Letter Declining a Speaking Invitation:

1. Express appreciation for the invitation
2. Explain the situation
   a. Employer limits outside consulting
   b. Schedule is already full

3. Decline the invitation politely
4. Suggest alternative speakers
5. Close courteously

## Outlining Long Messages

An outline for a report several pages long may have three or more levels (degrees) of major divisions and subdivisions. The outline may later provide the actual headings and subheadings in the report.

**Outline Format**. An outline should contain the main ideas you intend to cover in your report. The following example outlines the main parts of a business report written to solve a problem about selecting an office computer.

    I. Introduction
       A. Problem Statement
       B. Research Methods
   II. Findings
       A. Hardware
          1. Memory
          2. Printers
          3. Disk Drives
          4. System Compatibility
       B. Software
          1. Word Processing
          2. Spreadsheets
          3. Databases
       C. Price
       D. Service
  III. Conclusion

Formal outlines often follow the pattern illustrated, which may include the following sequence of numbers and letters:

    I. First-degree topic
       A. Second-degree topic
          1. Third-degree topic
             a. Fourth-degree topic
             b. Fourth-degree topic
                (1) Fifth-degree topic
                (2) Fifth-degree topic
                   (a) Sixth-degree topic
                   (b) Sixth-degree topic
          2. Third-degree topic
       B. Second-degree topic
    II. First-degree topic

This system of outlining does not require you to label the first-degree topics with Roman numerals. You may begin the outline with a capital letter or an Arabic number. However, you should follow the appropriate sequence thereafter.

| Correct | Correct | Incorrect |
|---|---|---|
| A. First major topic | 1. First major topic | 1. First major topic |
|   1. Subtopic |   a. Subtopic |   A. Subtopic |
|   2. Subtopic |   b. Subtopic |   B. Subtopic |
| B. Second major topic | 2. Second major topic | 2. Second major topic |

The Roman numeral system of outlining permits a maximum of six degrees of divisions and subdivisions. Long documents such as policy and procedures manuals may require more subdivisions than the Roman numeral system allows. In such cases, the decimal system of outlining may be used. The decimal system is expandable to an infinite number of divisions.

## The Decimal Outline

1.0  First-degree heading
    1.1  Second-degree heading
        1.1.1  Third-degree heading
        1.1.2  Third-degree heading
            1.1.2.1  Fourth-degree heading
            1.1.2.2  Fourth-degree heading
    1.2  Second-degree heading
2.0  First-degree heading

Whether you use the Roman numeral or decimal system of outlining, you should place the main topics in the first-degree position. First-degree divisions may be subdivided into second-degree divisions, which include supporting information for the related main topic. If necessary, second-degree divisions may be subdivided into third-degree divisions, and so on.

One important outlining rule is that if you subdivide a division, you must include at least two subdivisions. In other words, every "1" must be followed by a "2," and every "A" must be followed by a "B."

**Parallel Construction in Outlining**. In every outline, the same-degree topics must have parallel grammatical construction. For instance, the parallel topics could consist of all noun phrases or all sentences. In the following examples, the nonparallel headings consist of phrases that begin with a gerund, a verb, and a noun. In contrast, the parallel headings all begin with a gerund.

| Nonparallel | Parallel |
|---|---|
| • Purchasing a computer | • Purchasing a computer |
| • Learn to operate a computer | • Learning to operate a computer |
| • Knowledge of programming | • Writing computer programs |

Although same-degree headings should be parallel to one another, they do not necessarily need to be parallel to headings of a different degree. For instance, the first-degree headings may be all phrases and the second-degree headings all sentences, as shown in the following example:

ACME COMPANY USES OF PROPOSED COMPUTER

   I. Accounts Receivable
     A. Computer will keep track of balances.
     B. Printer will generate monthly statements.
  II. Spreadsheet Analysis
     A. Computer will compare projected and actual sales.
     B. Computer will compare budgeted and actual profit margins.
 III. Word Processing

## ORGANIZING PARAGRAPHS AND SENTENCES

After writing an outline of a message, the writer should organize the individual paragraphs and sentences. For a message to achieve the desired effect, the paragraphs and sentences must be planned and organized as carefully as the outline. Skilled writers organize their paragraphs and sentences to provide *unity*, *emphasis*, *parallel construction*, and *transition*.

### Unity

Each paragraph should present and develop one main idea. A paragraph has **unity** if it deals with only one main topic. Unity is important for clear writing. If the writer includes too many different ideas in a paragraph, the reader will have difficulty following the train of thought.

Each paragraph should contain a **topic sentence**, which is the sentence containing the main idea of the paragraph. The topic sentence may be placed anywhere in the paragraph, depending upon the writer's plan of organization. Often the topic sentence is the first sentence of the paragraph; sometimes it is the last sentence. Can you identify the topic sentence in the following paragraph?

The accounting department needs a new copier. The old copier, which was purchased in 1979, has been constantly breaking down. Last year the repairs on that machine cost over $2,000. In the first six months of this year, the repairs have totaled $2,500.

In this example, the first sentence is the topic sentence. As you can see, the other sentences develop the idea presented in the first one. When you construct a paragraph, do not wander away from the central thought, or the reader will become confused.

## Emphasis

Skilled writers know how to use the psychological strategy of stressing important points while de-emphasizing unfavorable ideas and less important details. **Emphasis** is essential for clarity as well as for psychological strategy.

Good writers use the following techniques to emphasize their ideas clearly:

1. Position in the sentence or paragraph
2. Length of sentence or paragraph
3. Grammatical construction
4. Explicit or implicit language
5. Headings and enumerations
6. Special effects

**Position.** As previously discussed, the beginning of a message stands out the most, and the ending receives nearly as much emphasis as the beginning. In contrast, the middle part of a message receives the least amount of attention. The principles of primacy and recency apply to paragraph and sentence construction as well as to the entire message.

To emphasize an important sentence, place it at the beginning or the ending of the paragraph. To de-emphasize a sentence, place it in the middle of the paragraph.

Likewise, the beginning and ending words in a sentence stand out, while the middle words receive less emphasis. Organize your sentences so that the most important words come at the beginning or the end of the sentence. Place words you want to de-emphasize toward the middle of the sentence.

Which of the following three sentences emphasizes the words "Ace lawnmowers" the most? Which sentence places the least emphasis on the words "Ace lawnmowers"?

1. *Ace lawnmowers* are best for quiet operation and low price.
2. For quiet operation and low price, get an *Ace lawnmower.*
3. For quiet operation and low price, *Ace lawnmowers* are best.

The first sentence places the most emphasis on "Ace lawnmowers," and the third sentence places the least. If you bury the main idea in the middle of a sentence, the reader may miss the point.

In business letters, *you* is an example of a word that should be emphasized (to attain the *you attitude*), while the word *I* should be de-emphasized. Avoid placing *I* at the beginning of a sentence, especially if it is the first sentence in a paragraph.

**Length.** Do not make the mistake of attempting to keep your paragraphs the same length. Uniform paragraphs are monotonous to read, and they lack emphasis.

An idea in a short paragraph stands out more than it would if placed in a long paragraph. To emphasize the key idea in a business letter, place it in a short, one-sentence paragraph. If the key idea is unfavorable to the reader, place it in the middle of a long paragraph.

Short sentences are more emphatic than long ones. In long sentences, the main point can easily get lost in all the words.

In which of the following sentences do the words "membership drive" receive more emphasis?

1. After receiving a list of new employees from the personnel department, the Employees Association considered ways to increase the number of members and voted to have a *membership drive* in May.

2. The Employees Association voted to have a *membership drive* in May.

Observe that the second sentence gets right to the point about the membership drive. In contrast, the first sentence buries the membership drive idea among all the other words.

A sentence stands out if it is shorter than the surrounding sentences. When expressing an unfavorable idea, be careful not to place it in a short sentence.

**Grammatical Construction**. Grammatical construction also affects emphasis within sentences. Compound sentences are less emphatic than simple sentences. (A simple sentence contains only one independent clause, and a compound sentence contains two or more independent clauses.) To emphasize a point, place it in a simple sentence. To de-emphasize a point, place it in a compound sentence.

SIMPLE SENTENCE: Mary Robbins is an expert on Lang computers.

COMPOUND SENTENCE: Mary Robbins is an expert on Lang computers, and she is familiar with several other types of computers as well.

Notice that the first sentence places more emphasis on Lang computers than the second sentence does. If the message relates specifically to Lang-brand computers, the first sentence would be preferable.

Complex sentences contain an independent clause and one or more dependent clauses (dependent clauses cannot stand alone without the rest of the sentence). In complex sentences, place the main idea in the independent clause, and place the secondary idea in the dependent clause.

Which sentence places the most emphasis on John's computer purchase?

- Independent Clause:
  - *John bought a new* computer, so we tried out the new software package.
- Dependent Clause:
  - *After John bought a new computer*, we tried out the new software package.
- Dependent Clause:
  - We tried out the new software package that *John bought for his new computer*.

The first sentence emphasizes the computer purchase by including it in an independent clause. The other two sentences place more emphasis on the new software package.

**Explicit or Implicit Language.** To emphasize a point, express it in specific terms. To de-emphasize an idea, express it in implicit (implied) terms. Explicit language is particularly appropriate for positive ideas; implicit language is more appropriate for negative ideas.

Which of these two sentences has a better treatment of the negative idea — Frank's illness?

- Explicit:
- Implicit:

- We were sorry to hear that Frank just had a triple bypass operation.
- We were sorry to hear about Frank.

Which of these two sentences is more positive?

- Explicit:
- Implicit:

- We were glad to hear about your promotion to sales manager.
- We were glad to hear about your career move.

**Headings and Tabulations. Headings** and subheadings are very effective for emphasizing key points in memorandums and reports. Although headings are seldom used in short letters, they may be used occasionally in long business letters.

**Tabulations** are effective for emphasis in all types of business messages. The reader can follow a list of parallel items much more easily than a long narrative. The following example illustrates the advantage of using a tabulation:

NARRATIVE: We recommend installing the computer network because it is more efficient and because it will save money. We also suggest that a network could be used to implement database management.

TABULATION: We recommend installing the computer network because of the following advantages:
1. Efficiency
2. Economy
3. Database management

Tabulated items may be listed vertically, indented, or centered. The items may be prefaced with numbers, letters, or bullets.

| Enumeration | Bullets |
|---|---|
| 1. Studio apartments | • Studio apartments |
| 2. One-bedroom units | • One-bedroom units |
| 3. Two-bedroom units | • Two-bedroom units |

**Special Effects**. Special effects are often used in sales messages and reports, particularly if the message is printed. Advertising copy employs a great variety of special effects to attract readers' attention. Color, graphics, and varied type styles (such as printing in bold letters or all capitals) may be used for emphasis. White space can also be used to emphasize a message. Special effects are discussed in greater detail in Chapter 10.

## Parallel Construction

In addition to unity and emphasis, parallel construction is one of the methods of organizing paragraphs and sentences in a logical way. Parallel construction is a technique used to indicate that two or more ideas are equal by repeating the same grammatical pattern of words, phrases, clauses, or sentences. Writing that lacks parallel construction is difficult to read. The following sentences illustrate nonparallel and parallel construction.

NONPARALLEL: The position is prestigious, challenging, and also the money isn't bad.

PARALLEL: The position offers prestige, challenge, and money.

NONPARALLEL: Mary discussed the capability of the new computer and what it is going to cost.

PARALLEL: Mary discussed the capability and cost of the new computer.

As previously mentioned, tabulations are a good way to emphasize several ideas with equal importance. Tabulations should contain items with parallel grammatical construction, as the following example illustrates:

NONPARALLEL: The office manager recommended replacing the copier for the following reasons:
1. Its age
2. Its slow speed
3. The repair bills are too high.

PARALLEL: The office manager recommended replacing the copier for the following reasons:
1. Its age
2. Its slow speed
3. Its repair bills

PARALLEL: The office manager recommended replacing the copier for the following reasons:
1. Our copier is ten years old.
2. The copier is too slow.
3. Its repair bills are too high.

## Transition

To make your writing flow smoothly, provide cues to help the reader follow your train of thought. These cues should include the various emphasis techniques discussed in this chapter. In addition, use the following techniques to provide for the transition of an idea from one sentence to another:

1. Repeat a key word or phrase
2. Use pronouns and synonyms
3. Include connectives

**Repeat a Key Word or Phrase**. Repetition is an essential component of the reinforcement process which is necessary for learning and remembering information. Repetition is a simple but very effective way to link two or more sentences, as shown below:

GOOD TRANSITION: Lang computers have dominated the market for *office systems* for the past ten years. *Office systems* are one of the fastest growing areas of the industry.

When using this technique, however, be careful not to confuse repetition with redundancy, which is *needless* repetition of a word or idea.

REDUNDANCY: Employees who have a grievance should report the grievance to the grievance committee.

REPETITION: Japanese automobiles, Japanese computers, and Japanese televisions are everywhere.

**Use Synonyms and Pronouns**. One way to achieve transition without becoming redundant is to use a synonym for a word used in the previous sentence. Another technique is to use a pronoun that refers to a noun in the previous sentence.

POOR TRANSITION: *The Commercial Venture* is her favorite magazine. Many people like to read about the stock market and finance.

GOOD TRANSITION: *The Commercial Venture* is her favorite *magazine*. This *publication* contains articles about the stock market and finance.

POOR TRANSITION: The automotive shop employees have complained about a lack of ventilation in the building. Last week fumes and smoke caused widespread illness.

GOOD TRANSITION: The automotive shop *employees* have complained about a lack of ventilation in the building. *They* reported that several *workers* became ill last week from fumes and smoke.

**Include Connectives**. Connectives are words that help to bridge the gap between sentences. They provide transition by signaling the reader that the next sentence contains more related information, a comparison or contrast, an example or result, or a conclusion or summary. Some common connectives are listed:

• Addition                    • and, also, another, besides, equally important, first, second, third, further, furthermore, in addition, last, moreover, next, too

- Comparison or Contrast

- or, but, however, in contrast, more than, nevertheless, on the other hand, still, yet

- Conclusion or Summary

- finally, in conclusion, in short, in summary, to summarize, to conclude

- Example

- for example, for instance, in other words, in particular, that is

- Result

- accordingly, as a result, consequently, therefore, thus

## SUMMARY

Before writing a business letter, memorandum, or report, the writer should carefully plan and organize the message. He or she should begin by determining the objective of the message, visualizing the reader, choosing the medium and format of the message, selecting a plan of organization, and constructing an outline.

Either the direct (deductive) or the indirect (inductive) organization plan is recommended for most business letters and short memorandums. For routine and favorable messages, use a direct plan; for unfavorable and persuasive messages, use an indirect plan.

Business reports and memorandums longer than one page may be organized by a number of different plans, including chronological, geographical, value, importance, simple-to-complex, function or product, and alphabetical patterns. Select the plan of organization best suited to achieving the purpose of the message.

The next step is to construct an outline of the message with proper outlining sequence and parallel construction. Then organize and develop the paragraphs and sentences. Effective writers use various techniques to achieve unity, emphasis, parallel construction, and transition.

## CHAPTER REVIEW

1. What are the four basic categories of short business messages?
2. Describe the direct plan of organization. List two categories of business messages that should have a direct plan of organization.
3. Describe the indirect plan of organization. List two categories of business messages that should have an indirect plan of organization.
4. Recommend the most appropriate plan of organization for each of the following business messages:
   a. A letter turning down a request
   b. A short memorandum offering an employee a promotion
   c. A report describing the layout of a small office building
   d. A three-page memorandum outlining a budget request for the next year
   e. A procedures manual for operating a computer
   f. The annual report of an electronics firm

      g. A utility company public relations report explaining how nuclear power plants work

      h. An inventory of office equipment

      i. An invitation to an office party

      j. A letter informing health insurance policyholders of minor changes in the procedures for filing a claim

5. What is the most emphatic position in a paragraph? The least emphatic?

6. List five techniques to achieve emphasis in paragraphs and sentences.

7. Define *unity*. Does the term apply to sentences or paragraphs?

8. Define *transition*. List three techniques to achieve transition.

# APPLICATIONS

1. Reorganize the following message to improve paragraph unity:

   Welcome to Forrest Manufacturing Company. All of us at Forrest take pride in working for one of the most progressive companies in the state. If you will come by the Personnel Office between the hours of 9 and 12 next Wednesday, March 14, Arlene Kelly will be available to explain our insurance and retirement benefits package.

   She will also brief you about our vacation policy and other fringe benefits. Your supervisor, Bill Oshima, has asked that you drop by his office also, so he can show you around the Management Information Systems Department. He would like to introduce you to the other employees and show you the new computer system. We are confident that you will be a valuable addition to our staff. Best wishes in your new position.

2. Revise the following passage to improve its transition:

   Management by objectives is a popular method of employee evaluation. Companies are using this very effectively.

   Employees and supervisors work together to set goals. Evaluation and feedback motivate individuals, who participate in setting their own objectives. A follow-up meeting takes place after a set time period (for example, six months). It can work well. The supervisors must be trained. Problems may occur when the evaluation is not accurate.

3. Revise the following outline to achieve logical organization and to comply with the rules for outlining:

   ANDERSON'S, INC. MERCHANDISE RETURN POLICY/PROCEDURES

   I. Introduction

  II. Store Policy

 III. Procedures for Customers with a Receipt

     A. Even Exchanges

       1. Exchange merchandise in department

       2. Fill out "Merchandise Exchange" form

       3. Return receipt to customer

      B. Cash Refunds
        1. Fill out "Cash Refund" form
        2. Sending customer to Credit Department
      C. Customers Without a Receipt
        1. Verification of merchandise
          a. Send customer to Credit Department

4. Revise the following sentences to achieve parallel construction:
   a. The Consumer Research Bureau conducted the telephone survey courteously and with efficiency.
   b. Last year Marilyn attempted to sell cars, to work at a bank, and wrapping packages at a department store.
   c. Our company rewards intelligent employees and those who work hard.
   d. In the library, computers are used not only to keep track of the book inventory but also conducting data searches.
   e. Titan Company invited everyone, including factory workers, office employees, management, and those who have retired, to the Christmas party.

5. Revise the following sentences to emphasize the main idea.
   a. I would like to recommend Jane for the promotion because she is our best employee.
   b. He does not want to be a programmer, although he is interested in computers.
   c. The house is fairly new, but it needs to be repainted.
   d. Government bonds postpone tax on interest; they now earn high interest; and the interest is not subject to state or local taxes.
   e. You have been an outstanding employee, and I would like to congratulate you for winning the Employee-of-the-Year award and present you with this certificate.

## CASE STUDY

Paul Ayala shook his head in dismay. "I've read this accident report three times, and I'm still not sure what happened," he confessed to Terri Briggs, another adjuster for Alta Insurance Company, with whom he shared an office.

"I must straighten out this report and get to the facts, or we'll never be able to settle this claim. If Smith, our client, is at fault, we're liable for all claims in the accident. If Jones, the other driver, is at fault, we may not have to pay even court costs.

"Understanding the facts of this accident is worth at least $500,000 to Alta Insurance—but I just can't figure it out!" "Let me see if I can help," Briggs volunteered. "They say two heads are better than one!"

However, a careful reading of the accident report (reproduced below) indicated to Briggs that solving this case might require more than two heads.

### Report of the Investigating Officer

Neither passenger in the Smith vehicle was wearing a seat belt at the time of the accident. Jones was alone in the car. The dog that Jones said she was trying to avoid hitting was killed at the scene of the accident. A pedestrian witness said that the light was still yellow when Smith entered the intersection.

The Smith vehicle hit the Jones vehicle broadside, forcing the Jones vehicle into the two vehicles in the eastbound lanes. All injured parties were taken to County General Hospital by helicopter because of the rush-hour traffic. No tickets were issued at the scene of the accident.

### Jones' Statement

The accident occurred when I was attempting to bring my car out of a skid by steering into the other vehicle. I skidded when I tried to avoid hitting the dog. The dog walked out into the intersection just as the light turned yellow. I thought he would stop, but he didn't, so I had to brake and skid.

### Smith's Statement

The lady was driving all over the road. I had to swerve several times before I hit her. My wife and I were late for a dinner engagement, but we didn't run a red light. When everything had settled, we were sandwiched between her and the other two. I didn't see any dog.

1. Can you determine what happened? Discuss the reasons for your answer.
2. Which plan of organization discussed in this chapter would be appropriate for the accident report? Why?
3. Evaluate the report writer's unity and transition. What transition techniques discussed in this chapter might improve understanding?

## SUGGESTED READINGS

Brusaw, Charles T. et al. *The Business Writer's Handbook*. New York: St. Martin's Press, 1982.

Fielden, John S., Jean D. Fielden, and Ronald E. Dulek. *The Business Writing Style Book*. Englewood Cliffs, NJ: Prentice-Hall, 1984.

Henze, Geraldine. *From Murk to Masterpiece: Style for Business Writing*. Homewood, IL: Richard D. Irwin, 1984. (Chapter 4, "A Guide to Editing for Organization and Structure: The Paragraph," 54-71).

Keenan, John. *Feel Free to Write: A Guide for Business and Professional People*. New York: John Wiley, 1982. (Part Two, "Understanding the Writing Process," 20-83).

Tichy, H. J. *Effective Writing for Engineers, Managers, Scientists*. New York: John Wiley, 1966. (Chapter 4, "Two Dozen Ways to Begin: Their Advantages and Disadvantages," 25-63; Chapter 5, "Effective Organizing," 64-88; Chapter 13, "Style and Sentences," 234-257; Chapter 14, "Style and Paragraphs," 258-283).

# BUSINESS LETTERS AND MEMORANDUMS

## PART 3

Business letters and memorandums are an integral part of the work of every business organization. Every business function (for example, purchasing, marketing, and management) involves business letters and memorandums.

Every consumer and professional-level employee needs to know how to write business letters and memorandums. In the first five years after college, business graduates write an average of 3 to 8 letters and 7 to 13 memorandums each week on the job, according to one survey (Rader and Wunsch, 1980).

Well-written business letters present a positive image of a company to customers and clients. In contrast, poorly written letters present a negative image and may harm the sender's business.

Memorandums carry messages throughout an organization in various directions — downward, upward, and across the organization. An employee's ability to write good memorandums can be an important factor for her or his career advancement.

Business letters and memorandums may be classified in four major categories. *Routine* messages are the most common type. Other categories include *favorable, unfavorable,* and *persuasive.*

▼ ▼ ▼ ▼ ▼ ▼

# ROUTINE AND FAVORABLE MESSAGES

## CHAPTER 5

Leslie Hill, Director of Public Relations for United Electric Company, looked up from a pile of letters on her desk as the office mail clerk pushed a cart into her office.

"Chuck, are you bringing me more letters?" she asked.

"Only 25 or 30 today," he replied as he placed a thick stack of envelopes on her desk.

"I'm so far behind now that I don't know if I'll ever get caught up answering all these letters," she fumed. "The letters take hours to compose because they're all different," she added. "I wish I had a formula for writing letters!"

Although no magic formula exists for writing letters, they are much easier to compose if you use one of the two basic plans introduced in Chapter 4. The direct (deductive) plan is recommended for routine or favorable messages, and the indirect (inductive) plan is recommended for unfavorable or persuasive messages.

This chapter discusses routine and favorable business letters and memorandums, including the following types:

• Requests
• Inquiries
• Orders
• Order acknowledgments

- Simple claims
- Favorable responses
- Favorable announcements
- Favorable offers

## COSTS OF BUSINESS CORRESPONDENCE

The bulk of business correspondence consists of messages that are relatively brief. According to the Dartnell Institute of Business Research (1986), an average business letter contains approximately 185 words. This figure translates to a one-page letter.

Although most business letters are short, they are nevertheless costly to produce. An average business letter dictated to a secretary costs $8.92, as shown in Figure 5.1. Note that labor costs are the largest proportion of expenses.

### FIGURE 5.1 AVERAGE BUSINESS LETTER COSTS $8.92

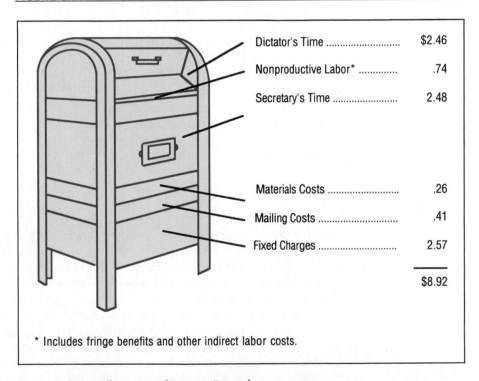

| | |
|---|---|
| Dictator's Time | $2.46 |
| Nonproductive Labor* | .74 |
| Secretary's Time | 2.48 |
| Materials Costs | .26 |
| Mailing Costs | .41 |
| Fixed Charges | 2.57 |
| | $8.92 |

\* Includes fringe benefits and other indirect labor costs.

Courtesy of Dartnell Institute of Business Research

The costs become enormous when these figures are multiplied by the more than 50 billion business letters mailed in the United States in one year (Shurter and Leonard, 1984). Many companies attempt to reduce some of the costs and increase the efficiency of written communication by using computer-generated or preprinted form letters whenever possible.

## DIRECT PLAN OF ORGANIZATION

As discussed in the previous chapter, *routine* business messages are common types of letters and memorandums that are expected to have a neutral impact on the receiver. *Favorable* business messages are those that transmit good news to the receiver.

The direct (deductive) plan of organization is recommended for routine and favorable business letters and short memorandums. In a deductively organized message, the main idea appears at the beginning. Since the beginning of a message stands out more than any other part, the direct plan of organization uses this strategy to emphasize the main point.

### Favorable Messages

**Favorable messages** transmit good news to the receiver. Examples of favorable messages include favorable responses (approving a request for travel funds), favorable announcements (reporting a salary increase), and favorable offers (offering a job).

In favorable messages, the writer should emphasize the good news by placing it at the beginning—preferably in the first sentence. After reading the first sentence, the receiver may be expected to react positively and thus become psychologically more receptive to the details that follow.

A deductively organized favorable message is depicted in Figure 5.2. In this graph, the positive beginning tapers off to the neutral details that follow. Notice that the graph resembles the right half of a bell-shaped curve.

### Routine Messages

According to various estimates, between 70 and 75 percent of all business messages fall in the *routine* category. Inquiries, routine requests, orders, acknowledgments, and simple claims are examples of **routine messages**.

Since people are accustomed to receiving routine messages, their reaction to these messages is generally neutral. They probably will be neither pleased nor disappointed when they receive a routine message.

For routine messages, the direct organization plan should be used primarily because it is the most efficient way to organize information. Efficiency is an important issue because of the large volume of routine messages most business organizations send and receive.

When the main idea appears in the first sentence, the reader can comprehend the message rapidly. He or she can quickly determine the topic of the message by scanning the first line or two rather than having to read every word. Because of its efficient arrangement, the direct plan of organization

FIGURE 5.2 FAVORABLE MESSAGE (DEDUCTIVE ORGANIZATION PLAN)

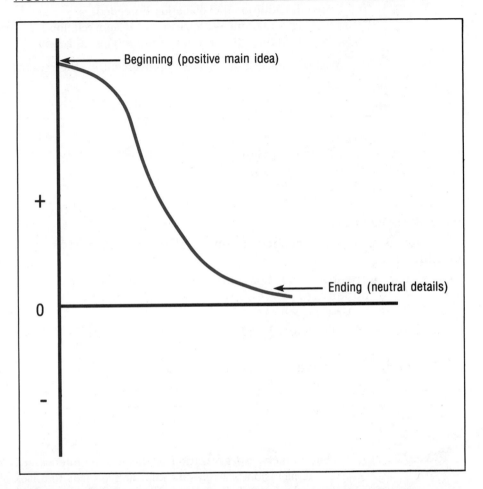

facilitates decision making. Because the direct plan allows the topic of the message to be apprehended quickly, the plan speeds up the delivery of messages to the correct departments and expedites records management.

## Routine Requests

The direct plan of organization for **routine request messages** is based on an assumption that the reader will be willing to comply with the request. Therefore, persuasion is unnecessary.

Place the main idea of the letter or memorandum at the beginning, followed by the explanation and details. The following outline summarizes the parts of a routine request:

1. Beginning paragraph — Requests the specific action you want

2. Middle paragraph(s) — Gives a brief reason for making the request and provides additional explanation if needed
3. Ending paragraph — Expresses your appreciation and contains an optional "action ending" that reiterates the requested action

This request letter needs improvement for the reasons noted at the right:

---

Mr. Ron Harrison
Director of Public Relations
Eastern Electronics Corporation
105 Allison Wells Parkway
Plainsboro, NJ 08535-2953

Dear Mr. Harrison:

    I am doing some research on Eastern Electronics Company.

    Postpones the main point

    On the surface, the company seems to be doing well. As a potential investor, I am interested in finding out more about it.

    Includes irrelevant details

    Please send me a copy of your latest annual report.

    Finally gets to the point

    Thank you in advance for your cooperation.

Cordially,

    Ends with a trite expression

---

The inductive organization of the letter unnecessarily delays the main idea. The inclusion of irrelevant information leads to a lack of conciseness. In addition, the letter has a trite ending rather than an action ending.

The following revision is deductively organized and concise:

---

    Please send me a copy of the latest Eastern Electronics annual report.

    Main idea

    As a potential investor, I am interested in finding out more about your company.

    Explanation

    I will appreciate your sending the report.

    Action ending

---

This memorandum is another good example of a routine request:

```
     TO:   Helen Adams                          Main idea
   FROM:   Jack Meredith
   DATE:   October 10, 19--
SUBJECT:   REQUEST FOR MONTHLY SALES REPORT

   Please add my name to the list of people who
receive the monthly sales report.

   My name has been omitted from the distribution      Explanation
list. I need the monthly sales figures to calcu-
late the quarterly budget for the Quality Control
Department.

Thanks!                                                Appreciation
```

Another type of routine request is a letter asking for a reservation. Notice that the following example uses this same basic pattern:

```
   Please reserve a single room for June 11 and        Main Idea
12.

   If possible, I would prefer a room on the           Details
ground floor. My arrival time will be approximately
5 p.m.

   I will appreciate a prompt confirmation.            Action ending
```

## Inquiries

**Routine inquiries** are requests for specific information that do not require persuasion.

Include the main idea at the beginning of the message, followed by the explanation and details. The following outline summarizes the parts of a typical inquiry:

1. Beginning paragraph
   a. Requests the information you need
   b. If necessary, gives a brief reason for wanting the information
2. Middle paragraph(s)
   a. Provides additional explanation, if needed, to help the reader understand exactly what information you want
   b. Asks specific question(s)
3. Ending paragraph
   a. Specifies the action you would like the reader to take
   b. Expresses your appreciation

Vague wording such as "Please send some information" may cause the reader to send the wrong kind of information. You will be more likely to get the specific information you need if you ask specific questions.

If you ask two or more questions, number them. Numbering the questions encourages the reader to answer each one. When preparing each question, be sure to use parallel construction; never mix questions with statements. Word the questions carefully to ensure clearness. Be concise and avoid redundancy.

If you are asking several questions, begin with the easiest to answer and end with the most difficult. Using the simple-to-complex plan of organization for each question will make the letter seem easier to answer.

This letter of inquiry needs improvement as indicated on the right:

---

| | |
|---|---|
| In December, my sister sent me a Slow Cooker manufactured by your company. So far, I have been very pleased with it. | Postpones the main point |
| I am wondering how much electricity it uses and how expensive it is to operate. | Asks vague question |
| I am also concerned about what effect it may have on the vitamin content of foods. | Includes too many "I's" |
| Can you answer my questions? I would appreciate this information. | Finally gets to the main point |
| Thank you for your cooperation. | Has a trite ending |

---

This letter needlessly postpones the main idea because of its inductive organization. Another weakness is that the vaguely worded indirect questions do not encourage the reader to provide specific answers. Furthermore, the letter lacks the "you" attitude; two successive paragraphs begin with *I*. Finally, the trite ending thanks the reader in advance for cooperating. The following revision is a better inquiry:

---

| | |
|---|---|
| Please answer the following questions about the Model 86 Slow Cooker: | Main idea |
| 1. How many watts of electricity does it use? | Specific numbered questions |
| 2. How much does it cost to operate? | Parallel construction |
| 3. What effect does it have on the vitamin content of foods? | |
| I will appreciate your sending me this information about my Slow Cooker. | Courteous ending |

---

In the improved version, the main idea receives emphasis because it appears in the first sentence. The numbered questions are clear and their grammatical construction is parallel. Notice that all three numbered items are complete sentences ending with question marks.

Avoid ending a message with enumerated items. You will need to include a closing sentence. In this letter, the enumeration is followed by a closing sentence that courteously expresses appreciation. The ending sentence should not contain trite expressions such as *thank you in advance* or *thank you for your cooperation* if the reader has not yet cooperated. To avoid a trite ending, use a verb in the *future* tense ("I *shall* appreciate," "I *will* appreciate," or "your cooperation *would be* appreciated").

## Orders

Large companies frequently place orders by using preprinted **purchase order forms**. An example of a purchase order form is shown in Figure 5.3. Small businesses typically place orders by writing **order letters**.

FIGURE 5.3 PURCHASE ORDER FORM

Texscan MSI

TEXSCAN MSI CORPORATION
3855 SOUTH 500 WEST, SUITE "S"
SALT LAKE CITY, UTAH 84115
PHONE: (801) 262-8475

PURCHASE ORDER

PURCHASE ORDER NUMBER | CHANGE ORDER | DATE

↑ THIS NUMBER INDICATES A CHANGE TO THE ORIGINAL ORDER NOT A NEW PURCHASE ORDER

VENDOR NAME

☐ CONFIRMING - DO NOT DUPLICATE

☐ ACKNOWLEDGEMENT REQUIRED | TERMS

☐ NON-TAXABLE THIS MATERIAL FOR RESALE / EXEMPT FROM SALES AND USE TAXES UTAH RESALE PERMIT #X-1858 | SHIP VIA - CHEAPEST WAY UNLESS OTHERWISE SPECIFIED

☐ TAXABLE THIS ORDER SUBJECT TO APPLICABLE SALES AND USE TAXES | TRANSPORTATION CHARGES TO BE PAID BY ☐ SELLER ☐ PURCHASER

VENDOR PHONE | VENDOR CODE | ACCOUNT NUMBER | DELIVER TO

| ITEM | TEXSCAN MSI PART NUMBER | REV. | DESCRIPTION | | PRICE | PER | QUANTITY | UM | DELIVERY DATE |
|---|---|---|---|---|---|---|---|---|---|
| | | | | | | | | | |

SAMPLE

REMARKS | BUYER'S SIGNATURE

ABOVE PURCHASE ORDER NUMBER MUST APPEAR ON ALL ACKNOWLEDGMENTS, PACKING LISTS, BILLS OF LADING, PACKAGES, INVOICES AND CORRESPONDENCE RELATED TO THIS ORDER. ADDRESS ALL INQUIRIES AND CORRESPONDENCE REGARDING THIS PURCHASE ORDER TO BUYER.

THIS PURCHASE ORDER IS SUBJECT TO THE TERMS AND CONDITIONS ON THE FACE AND REVERSE SIDE HEREOF. ALL TERMS AND CONDITIONS OF THIS AGREEMENT BECOME BINDING ON THE TENTH DAY AFTER RECEIPT OF THIS ORDER UNLESS SELLER ADVISES BUYER IN WRITING OF ANY EXCEPTIONS TO THIS ORDER. TERMS AND OR CONDITIONS OF PURCHASE

Courtesy of Texscan MSI Corporation

Order letters must be particularly clear, correct, concise, and complete. If an order contains several items, the listed items should be numbered and tabulated. A typical order letter should follow this outline:

1. Courteously asks the reader to fill the order
2. Includes complete information about the merchandise
   a. Item number, model, color, size, etc.
   b. Quantity and price of each item
3. Includes shipping directions and any special considerations
4. Specifies the terms of payment

The following order letter includes all the necessary information. Notice that the main point of the letter is in the first sentence, followed by the details:

---

```
285 West 27 Avenue
Ann Arbor, MI 48109-1830
September 15, 19--

Alta Vista Computer Products
1609 East Fremont Street
Denver, CO 80202-2425

MERCHANDISE ORDER

Please send the following software for the RT-90
Model 10A computer:
```

| Item No. | Description | Quantity | Price | Total |
|----------|-------------|----------|--------|---------|
| 243 | Super Taxprep | 2 | $ 89.95 | $179.90 |
| 407 | Graphmaster | 1 | 249.95 | 249.95 |
| 598 | Stock Manager | 1 | 124.95 | 124.95 |
| | | | | $554.80 |

```
Please charge the $567.30 total ($554.80 plus $12.50
postage) to my American Bankcard. The account number
is 134-9008; expiration date, 12/89.

I will appreciate your sending this software by
first-class mail to the above address.

Lee J. Coury
```

---

## Order Acknowledgments

Many companies send a postcard or letter to acknowledge that an order is being filled. However, with the cost of an average business letter now exceeding $8, most companies cannot afford to acknowledge every order with an individualized letter. To reduce communication costs, many companies use preprinted forms or computer-generated form letters to acknowledge routine orders. An example of a computer-generated order acknowledgment form is shown in Figure 5.4. Other preprinted order acknowledgment forms can be filled in with a pen or typewriter.

## FIGURE 5.4 A COMPUTER-GENERATED ORDER ACKNOWLEDGMENT FORM

**L.L. Bean, Inc.**
Main Street
Freeport, Maine 04033-0001
*Outdoor Sporting Specialities since 1912*

ORDER NUMBER 41220 2980 661      DATE 12/01/--

| | STOCK NUMBER | COLOR | QTY. | SIZE | DESCRIPTION | AMOUNT |
|---|---|---|---|---|---|---|
| | 421650006M | GREEN | 1 | M | BAXTER STATE PARKA, MEN'S | $ 66.00 |
| | | | | | TOTAL | $ 66.00 |
| | | | | | THANK YOU FOR YOUR GIFT TO J. WILSON | |

MS. MARY HOCKER
P.O. BOX 2305
NEW ORLEANS, LA   70125-7611

| MDSE. VALUE | TAX | POSTAGE/HANDLING CHARGES | TOTAL AMOUNT | AMOUNT SENT | CREDIT CARD NUMBER |
|---|---|---|---|---|---|
| $66.00 | | FREE | $66.00 | $66.00 MC | 1234 0000 0000 0000 MC |

Courtesy of L.L. Bean, Inc.

Companies send order acknowledgment letters primarily to create customer goodwill and to encourage future orders. The following outline summarizes the parts of an order acknowledgment letter:

1. Notifies the customer that the order is being filled
2. Confirms shipping information, if necessary
   a. May specify date and method of shipment
   b. May explain payment terms
3. Expresses appreciation for the order
4. Encourages future orders

An example of a typical computer-generated acknowledgment letter appears in Figure 5.5. When the company processes an incoming order, the computer initiates an acknowledgment letter. The computer printer automatically fills in the correct information about each order, including the customer's name and address.

## Claim Letters

Customers often write claim letters when they are dissatisfied with a product or service. **Claim letters** request an adjustment for unsatisfactory merchandise, poor service, billing errors, and other problems.

## FIGURE 5.5 A COMPUTER-GENERATED ACKNOWLEDGMENT LETTER

*SAVECO Co.*
P.O. Box 1354
Dallas, TX 75228-3351


October 10, 19--


Mrs. Anna Jenkins
301 Poplar Street
Austin, TX 78705-2935

Dear Mrs. Jenkins:

Thank you for your application for SAVECO Insurance.
You should receive your new SAVECO automobile
insurance policy within the next ten days.

By letting SAVECO insure your car, you'll save at
least 20 percent on your automobile insurance pre-
miums.  Despite its low cost, however, our service is
second to none.  I think you'll be impressed, right
from the start, with SAVECO'S concern for our
policyholders.

We are at the end of a toll-free number (1-800-555-
2387) not just during business hours, but 24 hours a
day, including Christmas, New Year's, and the Fourth
of July.  Any time you have a question, just give us
a call.

Welcome to SAVECO!

Cordially,

*Ted Elliott*

Ted Elliott
Customer Representative

ve

Unfortunately, only a small percentage of dissatisfied customers ever take the time to tell a company about such problems. The majority of people who experience a problem with a product or service simply take their business elsewhere. To prevent such loss of customers, most companies are usually glad to make adjustments. Another reason why companies welcome claims is that they provide a source of feedback about product reliability and quality control.

Claim letters fall into two categories: (1) *simple claims* and (2) *persuasive claims*. Simple claims should be organized deductively, and persuasive claims should be organized inductively.

Simple claims are requests for adjustments when the problem is routine and covered by company policy; for example, defective merchandise under warranty provides an occasion for the writing of a simple claim letter. Simple claim letters should be organized deductively because persuasion is unnecessary.

Persuasive claim letters are appropriate if the problem does not clearly fall into a routine adjustment category or if the problem requires a complicated explanation. (Chapter 7 discusses persuasive claim letters in more detail.)

Claim letters should reflect all five C's of business communication, especially courtesy. A polite letter that states the facts objectively is very likely to get good results. Unfortunately, many claim letters are rude, sarcastic, and insulting. Such letters offend the reader and cause the writer to lose credibility. Discourteous letters are ineffective because they antagonize the reader.

Too many claim letters are similar to this one:

---

It's a wonder we have any customers left after selling your crummy brand of dog food!

Beginning insults the reader

Your smooth-talking sales representative talked us into ordering 20 cases of your new brand of so-called Super Dog Diet. After getting several complaints from customers, I decided to check it out myself. When I opened three 10-pound bags, I discovered black hairs in the dog food, along with a moldy, musty odor.

Details are sarcastic

How disgusting! Our customers and their pets should not have been subjected to such an awful experience.

The writer exaggerates

If you do not send us a full refund for $240 immediately, you will be hearing from our attorney.

Main idea threatens the reader

We are storing the rest of the dog food in our garage. If you want it to be returned, you'll have to come and pick it up.

Ending is negative

---

If you received this discourteous letter, what would be your reaction? Of course, most people will be more likely to cooperate if they receive a courteous, objective letter instead of an angry and insulting one. The following revised claim should get better results:

---

Please send us a $240 refund for 20 cases of
Super Dog Diet.

*Courteously requests adjustment*

On February 3, our store received 20 cases of
your dog food. After several of our customers
returned the Super Dog Diet they had purchased, we
discovered that the bags had a musty, moldy odor. The
dog food also appeared to be contaminated with black
hairs.

*Objectively states the facts*

We sent you a check for the dog food on
February 28. A copy of the invoice is enclosed.

*Includes necessary details*

Please send us a prompt refund and let us know
if you want us to return the remaining six cases of
Super Dog Diet to you C.O.D.

*Has action ending*

---

Simple claim letters should begin by asking for an adjustment in the first paragraph. Avoid wasting the reader's time by telling an involved story before getting to the point. State what specific action you would like the company to take. For example, you might want the company to repair the merchandise without charge, exchange the merchandise, or refund your money. The middle paragraph explains the problem, and the ending courteously refers again to the action that you are requesting. The following outline summarizes the parts of a simple claim letter:

1. Beginning paragraph—Requests the specific adjustment the writer wants
2. Middle paragraph(s)—Explains the facts clearly and objectively
   a. Includes exact or approximate date of purchase
   b. Provides essential details (model number, size, color, etc.)
   c. If available, encloses evidence of purchase
   d. If necessary, returns or offers to return the merchandise
3. Ending paragraph—Expresses appreciation and includes an action ending

In the following example, the writer encloses the sales receipt and returns the merchandise in a package attached to the letter:

---

Please send a white king-size fitted sheet to
replace the blue one in the attached package.

*Requests the adjustment*

The sheets and pillowcases you sent are very
nice, but the fitted sheet is blue. The other sheets

*Explains the facts*
*Includes the details*

```
and pillowcases are white, as I ordered on November 5.
The enclosed sales receipt was attached to the order.

    If no white king-size fitted sheets are              Suggests an
available, I will return the entire set for a            alternative
a refund.

    I would appreciate an exchange or a refund.          Includes an action
                                                         ending
```

If you enclose a sales receipt, make a copy to serve as a record of the purchase. However, sometimes no sales receipt is available—for instance, when the merchandise was received as a gift.

In the following example, the writer had no sales receipt because she received the dishes as a wedding gift. She did not return the damaged merchandise because the broken dishes had no resale value. Offering to return the dishes was as effective as returning the dishes would have been. Moreover, the writer saved money for postage by not returning the broken merchandise. As a result, the company accepted the writer's word and promptly replaced the merchandise.

```
Briarwood, Inc.
1902 Los Feliz Boulevard
Los Angeles, CA 90039-2540

ADJUSTMENT REQUEST

Please send me a new 16-inch platter and two dinner    Requests the
plates in the "Jentilly" pattern of Briarwood          adjustment
Earthenware.

Your brochure states that Briarwood Earthenware        Explains the facts
can be used in the oven if put in when the oven is
first turned on and if the earthenware is at room
temperature. Although I was very careful to comply,
the plates and platter were cracked when I removed
them from the oven.

Shall I mail the plates to you or discard them?        Offers to provide
                                                       proof
I would appreciate your replacing the earthenware
as soon as possible.                                   Includes an action
                                                       ending
Mary Ann Scott
```

## Favorable Responses

As previously discussed, favorable responses to claims and other requests should be organized deductively. The writer should emphasize the good news by placing it at the beginning of the message. The following outline summarizes the recommended organization for favorable response messages:

1. Beginning paragraph—Announces the favorable news
2. Middle paragraph(s)—Expresses appreciation and includes any additional information
3. Ending paragraph—Closes courteously

**Adjustment letters** are favorable responses to customer claim letters. Because adjustment letters are opportunities to build customer goodwill, the letters must not seem to condescend or to blame the customer. The writer's tone should be helpful and positive.

This adjustment letter is a favorable response to the previous claim letter:

---

Dear Ms. Scott:

Two new Briarwood Earthenware dinner plates and one platter in our "Jentilly" pattern are being mailed to you today.

*Introduces the good news*

Thank you for taking the time to tell us about your experience with our Earthenware. We are certainly concerned about this incident and sincerely appreciate being notified.

*Expresses appreciation*

Although our product development and quality-control standards are stringent, occasionally errors do occur. The information you provided will be most helpful to our quality-control staff in analyzing and improving our manufacturing processes.

*Provides an explanation*

We will take every step possible to ensure that your future purchases of Briarwood Earthenware are perfect in every way.

*Includes a positive ending*

Cordially,

Bonnie Vasquez, Assistant Director
Consumer Relations Department

---

This memorandum provides a favorable response to a special request:

---

TO: Charles Luckett
FROM: Andrea Washington
DATE: February 10, 19—
SUBJECT: EMPLOYEE GRIEVANCES COUNCIL

Yes, I accept the nomination to serve on the Employee Grievances Council next year.

*Favorable response*

I want to thank the nominating committee for considering me. If elected, I will do my best to be a fair and impartial member of the Council.

Expression of appreciation

As you requested, I am enclosing a copy of my resume.

Additional information

If you need anything else, call me at Extension 244.

Courteous ending

---

Favorable responses to inquiries should build goodwill for the company. Many companies also use responses to inquiries as an opportunity to sell their products. (Sales letters are discussed further in Chapter 7.) The following letter responds favorably to a letter of inquiry:

---

Dear Mrs. Morales:

We appreciate your interest in Top-Point coffee and are glad to answer your questions, as follows:

Responds favorably and courteously

1. Yes, Top-Point 97 percent decaffeinated coffee can be included in a caffeine-restricted diet.

Answers specific questions

2. Our Top-Point brand contains only 2 to 4 milligrams of caffeine per 6-ounce cup. This negligible amount is only 3 percent of the 60 to 99 milligrams of caffeine in a 6-ounce cup of regular coffee.

Includes important facts

An article entitled "How Much Caffeine Is in the Cup?" is enclosed.

Encloses additional information

Thank you for your interest in United Foods products. Please let us know any time we can be of assistance.

Closes courteously

Cordially,

---

## Favorable Announcements

Favorable announcements should follow a pattern similar to that of favorable responses by stating the good news in the opening paragraph. This type of message should be organized according to the following outline:

1. Beginning paragraph—Announces the good news
2. Middle paragraph(s)—Includes additional details
3. Ending paragraph—Closes courteously

This letter informs a contestant that she has won a prize:

Dear Mrs. Lovett:

Congratulations! You have won a major prize in our Tastee-Fresh Ice Cream national sweepstakes! | Announces the good news

To verify that you are in compliance with the rules of our sweepstakes, please sign the enclosed affidavit to confirm that no member of your family is an employee of Consolidated Dairy Products. Also, please fill out and sign the enclosed Form 4591, as required by the Internal Revenue Service. Be sure to include your Social Security number and your telephone number. | Includes details

Please mail these forms to us in the enclosed envelope within the next seven days. Shortly after we receive these documents, we will call you to provide additional details about your prize. | Provides additional information

Your entry was one of only three selected as a national grand-prize winner. Again, congratulations! | Closes courteously

Cordially,

This memorandum is another example of a favorable announcement:

TO:      All Employees
FROM:    Alvin Labens, President
DATE:    May 28, 19--
SUBJECT:    INCREASE IN INSURANCE BENEFITS

On behalf of the Board of Directors, I am pleased to announce two major additions to the fringe benefits package for all employees: | Announces favorable news

1. The Washington Mutual life insurance coverage is being increased from $15,000 to $25,000 at no cost to the employee. | Provides facts

2. Free dental insurance for employees and their dependents is being added to the Olympian Health Insurance plan.

The attached brochures provide further details about these new benefits, which become effective July 1. | Includes details

If you would like more information, please call             Closes courteously
Marty Adler in Personnel Services at Extension
838. He will be glad to answer your questions.

## Favorable Offers

**Favorable offers** are based on the presumption that the reader will be pleased with the offer. Therefore, the writer should present the main idea—the offer—in the first paragraph. Examples of favorable offer letters include those containing offers for various business transactions (such as offers to purchase property) and letters offering job applicants a position. (Chapter 13 discusses job-offer letters in more detail.) Some favorable offers are put in memorandum form. The following memo offers an employee a promotion:

TO:     Amy Hillstead
FROM:   Charlene Schwartz, Sales Manager
DATE:   October 10, 19--
SUBJECT:    PROMOTION TO ASSISTANT BUYER POSITION

As one of our most outstanding salespersons,              Main idea
you have been selected for promotion to assistant
buyer.

You were chosen for this position from over 30            Details
eligible employees. The assistant buyer position is
a management-level assignment.

Congratulations, Amy! Please stop by my office            Action ending
to let me know if you accept the promotion.

## SUMMARY

Most of the letters and memorandums that managers and other business professionals write may be classified as routine or favorable messages. Routine messages have a neutral impact on the receiver, while favorable messages have a positive impact.

Examples of routine messages include requests, inquiries, orders, acknowledgments, and simple claims. Examples of favorable messages include favorable responses, announcements, and offers.

Routine and favorable business letters and short memorandums should have the direct plan of organization. In favorable messages, the writer should emphasize the good news by placing it at the beginning. In routine messages, the writer should place the main idea at the beginning primarily because of reading efficiency.

## CHAPTER REVIEW

1. List five examples of routine messages.
2. Outline and explain the plan of organization for routine business messages.
3. List five examples of favorable messages.
4. Why do favorable and routine messages have the same plan of organization?
5. Identify the two types of claim letters and explain the difference between them.
6. Do most companies order merchandise by writing order letters? Explain your answer.
7. Many retail companies abide by the policy, "The customer is always right." How could this old saying relate to customer claims? Why?
8. What are the advantages of computer-generated order acknowledgment forms and letters? Can you think of any disadvantages?
9. What are purchase order forms? How are they used?
10. What effect do a manager's written communication skills have on her or his productivity? Justify your response.

## APPLICATIONS

1. Point out the weaknesses of the following *opening* sentences for the types of letters indicated and then revise each one:
   a. I would like to purchase a carrying case for my ST-86 portable computer. (Order letter)
   b. Your Axletic jogging shoes are the worst quality I've ever seen! (Simple claim letter)
   c. Last week I purchased a Word Compatible software package from Mercury CompuStore. (Simple claim letter)
   d. I apologize for the defective Word Compatible software you received. (Letter granting a claim)
   e. I am a student at the University of Virginia. (Letter of inquiry about the "Summer at Sea" program)

2. After receiving poor service and cold food at an expensive restaurant, Tracy Rymer wrote a claim letter asking for a full refund. She received the following letter in reply:

Dear Ms. Rymar:

I am sorry for the bad experience you had at our restaurante. We offer specials for $9.95, which include chose of pototes or rice, hot bread, and our salad bar. Our food costs are high, but we provide an excellent special which are customers come in for.

    Enclosed is a gift certificate for $10.95, you
may use at your next visit.
    Hoping to hear from you again, I am.
Yours truly,

a. What reaction would you expect Tracy to have to this letter?
b. How many typographical, English mechanics, and other errors can you find?
c. Does the letter use the appropriate organization plan? Justify your response.
d. Are the opening and closing paragraphs appropriate? Why did you reach that conclusion?
e. Revise the letter and correct the errors.

3. During your senior year, you consider applying for admission to the MBA (Master of Business Administration) program at a university in your state. Write a letter of inquiry to its Graduate Business Admissions office and ask specific questions about admission requirements [grade-point average and GMAT (Graduate Management Admissions Test) scores and costs]. Also inquire about the possibility of financial aid.

4. Write a letter to a company or government agency in which you inquire about its products or services. Do not ask for just "some information." Ask specific, pertinent questions — at least three. Make sure your enumerated questions have parallel construction. Because your letter actually will be mailed, prepare a stamped, addressed envelope. Also, make an extra copy of the letter for your instructor to use for writing comments and grading.

5. Write a simple claim letter for a real situation in which you have received an unsatisfactory product or service within the past year. Because your letter actually will be mailed, prepare the original, an extra copy of the letter, and a stamped envelope.

6. You are the office manager for Greene Chemicals Company. You are researching the possibility of replacing all the typewriters at Greene with electronic typewriters that can double as computer printers. To double as a printer, a typewriter must be connected to the computer with a device called an "interface." Your company also has a substantial investment in more than 30 Lang-brand microcomputers. Write a letter of inquiry to Janis Typewriters, Inc., 9324 Ravenswood Avenue, Chicago, IL 60640-0590 to find out if a Janis interface is available for Lang microcomputers. If so, which models of Janis electronic typewriters does it fit? You should also inquire about the cost of the interface and the typewriters.

7. You are assistant district sales manager for Metropolis Insurance Co. Jim Oliver, your boss, is district sales manager. For the past several years, Jim and you have exchanged Christmas presents. This year, you would like to give Jim something that he can use for his favorite hobbies — hunting and fishing.

However, Jim has started talking about giving up his hobbies because his feet hurt too much from the cold. You want to surprise him this Christmas with a pair of battery-powered electric socks, but you do not know if such a product really exists or where to find it. You vaguely remember seeing an ad for electric socks in a sports magazine several years ago. Write a letter of inquiry to Sportsman's Paradise (a large sporting goods supply company), 102 East Second Avenue, Moonachie, NJ 07074-7871. If Sportsman's Paradise does not stock such an item, perhaps someone in the marketing department could suggest another company that might.

8. You are public relations officer for Atlas Spa and Fitness Centers. You answer a letter of inquiry from Mrs. Rene Sherman, 750 Oxford Drive, Gardena, CA 90247-7991. She saw a sign that Atlas is opening a fitness center in her city and requested information about (1) exercise programs, (2) programs for weight loss, and (3) the date when the facility will open. Write a letter explaining that the new Center will be a large facility with a complete diet and exercise program, including a swimming pool, exercise equipment, whirlpool, sauna, steam rooms, locker room, nursery, aerobics programs, and classes on nutrition. Programs are designed exclusively for women every Monday, Wednesday, and Friday, with co-ed programs on evenings and weekends. Costs vary from a $30 monthly membership to a $750 lifetime membership. The Center opens in six weeks. Since she took the time to write, you send her a one-week free membership certificate so she can try out the new facilities.

9. You are chief accountant for Lomax Shoes, a family-owned chain of three shoe stores located in El Paso, Texas. Last night you saw an ad in *Accounting World* magazine for an inexpensive computerized accounting system that might be just what your company needs. The ad said that for just $60 you can order a complete set of Accounting Pro manuals and demonstration disks to try out the system. If you decide to buy the system, the $60 will apply toward your purchase. If you decide against the system, you can return the demo package for a complete refund. Your firm does not use purchase order forms for anything except shoes. Write an order letter to Northeast Software, Inc., P. O. Box 392, East Hartford, CT 06118-6056. Be sure to mention the brand of microcomputer in your office and to enclose a check for $60.

10. During a routine checkup, your doctor discovered that your cholesterol level is above normal. Although the doctor prescribed a low-fat diet, you have had difficulty following the advice because you do not have all the information you need about the fat content of foods. Write an order letter for a *Lifesaver Calorie and Fat Guide* to Center for Public Health, 1701 North Street, Washington, DC 20009-8199. Enclose a check for $7.50.

11. You are supervisor of the mail-order department at Continental Coin Company in St. Louis, Missouri. Most of your customers are wealthy coin collectors and precious metal investors. These individuals usually expect their orders to be filled on the day you receive them. However, your department sometimes runs behind schedule when the volume of business is heavier than usual. Design

an order acknowledgment form letter that can be generated automatically by the computer. The letter should inform a customer that the order is being filled, build customer goodwill, and promote coins as a good investment.

12. You recently purchased a box of 12 Randolf double-sided, double-density floppy computer disks from a large discount department store. When you attempted to format the disks, your computer would not accept four of them. The screen displayed a message that track 2 was defective on each disk. You took the disks back to the store where you purchased them, but the customer-service specialist told you that the store could not exchange just the four disks. You would have to return the entire box of disks. Since you have already used some of the other disks, you are unable to return all of them. "Defective disks may be returned to the manufacturer" is printed on the box. Write a claim letter to Randolf, Inc., Computer Products Division, P. O. Box 5012, Spring Valley, NY 10977-4625.

13. You recently bought a one-acre lot for a vacation home in the mountains. After seeing an ad in *Better Vacations* magazine, you are considering buying a log-cabin kit. Write a letter to Associated Log Home Builders of America, P.O. Box 1990, Houlton, Maine 04730-3761. Ask for a copy of their free booklet, *Everything You Want to Know About Log Homes.* Also, ask them for the names of log home builders in your state.

14. Six months ago you purchased a $75 Superior digital watch. It has many features, including a calendar, light, stopwatch, and alarm. However, last week the light stopped working. You replaced the battery twice, but the light still did not work. A watch repair person suggested that you return it to the factory. The watch has a one-year warranty on parts and labor. Write a claim letter to Superior Electronic Company, 9314 Hermosa Avenue, San Francisco, CA 94122-7871.

15. Three months ago the owner of your apartment building sent you a letter stating that several repairs, including painting the interior and installing new carpets, were scheduled for your apartment. For those repairs, the rent would be raised $25 per month. Although you have paid the increased rent for the past three months, no repairs have been made. You have called the owner three times and left messages on his answering machine, but he has failed to return your calls. Write a claim letter to Mr. Dave Littrell, 307 South Adams Street, Warrensburg, MO 64093-1149. Ask him to make the repairs promptly or send you a $75 refund for the extra rent you paid for the past three months.

16. You recently purchased a pair of Mustang 405 jeans (32-inch waist, 38-inch length) that cost $24.95. The first time you washed the jeans, a seam unraveled and left a hole in the right leg just above the knee. Write a claim letter to Mustang, Inc., 3400 Los Cabellos Avenue, San Francisco, CA 94104-0561, and ask for a replacement or a refund. Enclose a copy of the sales receipt and offer to mail the jeans if necessary.

17. Last Christmas you received a Quasaire telephone-answering machine as a gift from your brother. Upon installing the answering system, you discovered that the announcement tape was defective. Since the tape inside the cartridge was broken, you were unable to record a message. Write a simple claim letter to Quasaire, Inc., Service Department, 1561 16th Street, Miami, FL 33139-6153. Ask for a replacement tape.

18. You are customer relations director for Randolf, Inc., Computer Products Division. Write a favorable response to the claim letter in Item 12. Address the letter to Ms. Cindy Hwang, 1602 Lakeview Avenue, Apartment 204, Houston, TX 77040-7091. Enclose four replacement disks, plus two extra free disks. Be sure to include an explanation and an apology for the problem she encountered.

19. You are president of Rochester Insurance Co. Write a memorandum announcing an office party for all employees on Friday, May 17, at 4 p.m. The office will close one hour early for the party, which is being held to celebrate the company's golden anniversary.

20. You are human resources director for the Florida Department of Revenue. Write a memorandum addressed to Ann DeCastro, Administrative Assistant I, informing her that she is eligible to take a promotional exam. Although the state exam for Administrative Assistant II has not been given for two years, it will be offered next month because several Administrative Assistant II's are expected to retire at the end of the year. Invite her to come by your office to fill out an application if she is interested.

# CASE STUDY

"Well, do we have many alumni signed up for the banquet, yet?" asked Marlene Stimpson, president of the spring pledge class to Epsilon Gamma chapter of Alpha Alpha Alpha business society.

"No, only four alums have responded so far," replied Cheryl Crandell, a member of the pledge class. "I wrote to over 100 alums in the Chicago area and most of them haven't even bothered to respond."

"The banquet is only two weeks away. If we don't have a good alumni turnout, we'll never hear the end of it from the actives—not to mention the other business clubs on campus," moaned Jerry Shore, another pledge. "You'd better get moving on this, Cheryl, or we may never be actives!"

"It's not my fault. I wrote to everyone over a month ago. They just haven't written back," sighed Cheryl. "I suppose we could try calling some of them to see if they got the letter."

A copy of the form letter Cheryl Crandell sent to the Tri-Alpha alumni is reproduced below. As you read it, try to determine why so few people responded.

Mr. Eldon Jones
Kay and Gorkey Importers
1101 South Madison Street
Chicago, IL 60602-1162

Dear Mr. Jones:

   My name is Cheryl Crandell, and I'm a new pledge to
Alpha Alpha Alpha business society. As you know, our
society is one of the oldest and largest in the United
States with 74 chapters in business schools all over
the country. Business leaders such as the presidents
of IBM, DuPont, and General Electric were Tri-Alphas
when they were in college. So, being a Tri-Alpha makes
us part of the "cream of the crop," and we should
maintain and be proud of our ties with the society.

   Epsilon Gamma (our chapter here at Tindall College)
is having its spring banquet next month, and I am in
charge of contacting the chapter alums. The members
told me to make sure that all alums in the Chicago
area know about the banquet because we normally have a
good alumni turnout. We really want you at the
banquet.

   Thanks, in advance, for your quick response!

Fraternally,

Pledge Cheryl Crandell

1. Does the letter follow a direct plan of organization? Explain your answer.
2. Is the letter clear and complete? Justify your response.
3. Does the letter make a response easy for the alumni? Why or why not?
4. If you were a member of Cheryl Crandell's pledge class, what suggestions might you make to her for improving the letter?

## REFERENCES

*Dartnell Target Survey*, The Dartnell Institute of Business Research (Chicago: The Dartnell Corporation, 1986).

M.H. Rader and A.P. Wunsch, "A Survey of Communication Practices of Business School Graduates by Job Category and Undergraduate Major," *The Journal of Business Communication* 17, no. 4, (Summer 1980), 33-41.

Robert L. Shurter and Donald J. Leonard, *Effective Letters in Business*, 3rd ed. (New York: McGraw-Hill, 1984), 3.

## SUGGESTED READINGS

Fielden, John S. and Ronald E. Dulek. *Bottom-Line Business Writing*. Englewood Cliffs, NJ: Prentice-Hall, 1984.

Geil, Lloyd H. *Executive's Desk Manual of Modern Model Business Letters*. Englewood Cliffs, NJ: Executive Reports Corporation, 1981. (Chapter 2, "Letters Granting Customer Requests," 201-218).

Markel, Michael H. and R. J. Lucier. *Make Your Point: A Guide to Improving Your Business and Technical Writing*. Englewood Cliffs, NJ: Prentice-Hall, 1983.

Murphy, Herta A. and Herbert W. Hildebrandt. *Effective Business Communications*, 4th ed. New York: McGraw-Hill, 1984. (Chapter 7, "Direct Requests," 151-187; Chapter 8, "Good-News and Neutral Messages," 189-221).

Wilkinson, C. W., Dorothy C. Wilkinson, and Gretchen N. Vik. *Communicating Through Writing and Speaking in Business*, 9th ed. Homewood, IL: Richard D. Irwin, Inc., 1986. (Chapter 6, "Good News and Goodwill Messages," 142-185).

# UNFAVORABLE MESSAGES

## CHAPTER 6

Frank Williams, purchasing agent for Mid-State Metals Company, came out of his office and threw up his hands.

"I don't believe it!" he exclaimed.

"What's the matter?" asked Marge Phillips, his assistant.

"We've been doing business with Linville Copper Company for ten years, and listen to this letter they sent us":

Dear Mr. Williams:

We received your letter about the shipment of No. 12 copper wire that you claim is defective.

We have sold many shipments of this wire and no one else has ever complained. We believe that our wire is of the highest quality.

Unfortunately, your claim must be refused.

If you have further questions, do not hesitate to write.

Cordially,

Pat Kelso

Frank continued, "Who does that Kelso think he is anyway? His company has just lost several hundred thousand dollars worth of our business over this $200 claim."

Delivering bad news while maintaining goodwill is not an easy task. Unfavorable messages require more careful planning and a higher degree of diplomacy than routine or favorable messages because the main idea is disappointing to the reader.

This chapter discusses the indirect plan of organization, which is recommended for unfavorable messages, and presents the following types of letters and memorandums:

- Denials of requests for information, favors, and funds
- Customer claim denials
- Unfavorable order acknowledgments
- Disappointing announcements

## INDIRECT PLAN OF ORGANIZATION

The indirect (inductive) plan of organization is recommended for messages that are expected to disappoint the reader. The direct (deductive) approach is inappropriate for unfavorable messages because it emphasizes the bad news at the beginning. After receiving disappointing news, the reader is not likely to be receptive to the rest of the message.

As discussed in Chapter 4, the beginning and ending of a message receive the most emphasis while the middle receives the least emphasis. Thus, the indirect plan of organization softens the impact of bad news by placing it in the middle of the message.

An inductively organized unfavorable message is depicted in Figure 6.1 as an inverted bell-shaped curve.

With the indirect plan of organization, the message begins with a positive or neutral statement. The writer then includes a tactful explanation before stating the unfavorable news, which is de-emphasized because of its position in the middle of the message. One advantage of this arrangement is that the explanation receives more emphasis than the unfavorable main idea. Another advantage of indirect arrangement is that the reader becomes aware of the reasons before being turned down. If the reasons are presented in a fair and logical way, the reader is more likely to accept the unfavorable news without feeling rejected or insulted. On the other hand, if clients or customers feel that they are being treated unfairly, a natural reaction is for them to take their business elsewhere. Effective business messages, of course, do not evoke this type of response.

Notice in Figure 6.1 that the main idea (the negative statement) comprises only a small part of the message. The negative statement should be as short as possible, and an unfavorable message should close with a positive or neutral statement. Business messages should never have a negative ending.

The following general outline is recommended for various types of unfavorable messages:

1. Opening—Begins with a positive or neutral paragraph acknowledging the receiver

## FIGURE 6.1 UNFAVORABLE MESSAGE (INDUCTIVE ORGANIZATION PLAN)

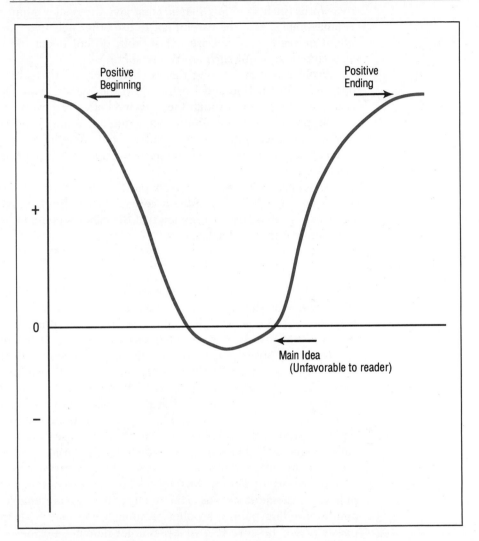

2. Explanation—Describes the reasons for the decision that follows
3. Main idea—Tactfully presents the unfavorable news
4. Ending—Suggests alternative solution(s), if possible, and closes on a positive note

## Opening

The opening paragraph of an unfavorable message should politely acknowledge the reader and mention the subject of the letter or memorandum in a positive or neutral way. Avoid making a negative situation worse by restating the reader's problem in detail. Eliminate from the opening paragraph negative words (such as *unfortunately*) that give the reader a hint that the message is unfavorable. Also, be careful not to use other negative words (such as *complaint* or *regret*). If you are not at fault, do not begin the message with an apologetic statement such as *We are sorry*.

Avoid using an opening that is completely off the subject. An irrelevant opening is distracting and frustrating to the reader, who should not have to read part of the way through the message before discovering what it is about.

Be positive in the opening statement. For example, express appreciation to the reader, compliment the reader about something, or grant part of the request. The tone of the beginning paragraph should be that of sympathetic consideration.

Avoid beginning with an overly positive statement that may imply a favorable decision. For example, a refusal letter beginning with "Yes, we agree . . ." gives a false impression that the claim is going to be approved, only to disappoint the reader later on.

## Explanation

The next paragraph or paragraphs of an unfavorable message should explain the reasons for the decision. Be careful to present the facts in an objective way so that the reader understands that the decision is not being made arbitrarily or unfairly. If possible, give reasons that benefit the reader.

One good strategy is to arrange the facts in order from the most positive to the least positive. Tactfully bring up the negative information after you have discussed the positive aspects of the situation.

If you need to convey the idea that your company is not at fault, make sure that you do not appear to blame or accuse the customer. A better strategy is to present the idea in general terms and to use passive voice and impersonal language. For example, instead of bluntly stating "You made an error," a more tactful sentence would be "Apparently an error has been made."

An important rule in business communication is: Don't hide behind a policy. A statement such as "Due to our policy, we are unable to . . ." is an example of hiding behind a policy. Although you may wish to state the company's policy, be sure to give a reason for denying a claim or turning down a request. If possible, explain the policy in terms of how it benefits the reader.

## Main Idea

An unfavorable decision should be presented as a logical conclusion drawn from your explanation of the facts. Be sure to tie the negative decision to your explanation by using a transitional word or phrase (such as *therefore* or *as a result*).

Try to de-emphasize the refusal statement as much as possible by not placing it in a separate one-sentence paragraph or in the first sentence of a longer paragraph. Instead, try placing it in the middle or at the end of the explanatory paragraph or in a paragraph suggesting an alternative solution.

De-emphasize the negative statement by using one or more of the techniques discussed in Chapter 4. For example, you might include it in a subordinate clause or use the passive voice.

If a refusal is not likely to offend the reader, the main point may be stated explicitly. For example, you might say in a refusal letter, "Therefore, we will not be able to send you information about our advertising budget." However, if you think the reader is likely to take a refusal personally, a better strategy may be to imply the refusal rather than stating it explicitly. Try something like, "Since advertising is so highly competitive, we must keep our budget confidential," and then suggest an alternative solution.

Keep your sentences as positive as possible under the circumstances. Instead of using negative words such as "reject," "deny," or "refuse," use a positive word or phrase with the word "not." As an example, "Your application has not been approved" is more positive than "Your application has been refused."

## Ending

The ending of an unfavorable message should be aimed at rebuilding goodwill with the reader. Do not dwell on the disappointing news by discussing it any more than necessary. Shift your ending quickly from the unfavorable main idea to a more positive note.

One good way to end a message positively is to suggest an alternative solution to the reader's problem. After denying a request for information, for example, you might send the reader some related material or suggest another source of information. Be as helpful as you can by including specifics such as the address and phone number of the information source.

Focus on the positive rather than the negative aspects of the message. Avoid using negative words and apologies such as "I regret" or "We are sorry" in your closing. Never include a statement such as "I hope you will continue to do business with us," which suggests that the customer might not be inclined to do so in the future.

The ending of an unfavorable message should include a courteous offer to provide additional assistance to the reader if needed. Be careful not to end with a trite or negative expression such as "do not hesitate to ask" or "please contact me."

If appropriate, briefly promote the company's products or services at the end of a message. If a sale is mentioned, you may enclose a sales-promotional brochure or other printed information about products in which you think the reader might be interested. However, use a low-key approach and incorporate the "you" attitude rather than the "we" attitude discussed in Chapter 3.

## REQUEST DENIALS

Companies receive countless requests of various types from customers, clients, salespeople, and the public. Many of these requests must be turned down because they are unreasonable or against company policy. This section discusses denials of requests for information, requests for favors, and solicitations for donations. Claim denials are included in the next section of this chapter; denials of specialized requests such as credit applications and letters of reference are discussed in later chapters.

Every request, whether reasonable or not, should be answered politely. A blunt, tactless response damages human relations and may cause the loss of a customer. In contrast, a carefully constructed request-denial message not only avoids offending the reader but also actually builds goodwill by dealing with the request in a positive way.

Request denials nearly always should have the indirect plan of organization. On rare occasions, the direct plan of organization may be appropriate as a last resort when you must respond to a persistent and unreasonable individual who refuses to take no for an answer.

## Denying Requests for Information

Business organizations receive many requests for information from investors, students, customers, and clients. Companies usually grant most of these requests if they are reasonable. However, some requests must be denied for legal reasons or to protect confidential information from competitors. Other requests for information are denied because the information is not readily available and would be too expensive to collect.

The following message denies a request for confidential information. If you had made the request, what would be your reaction to the letter?

---

Your request of March 21 has been received. | States the obvious

Unfortunately, we are forced to refuse your request for information. Company policy prevents us from releasing confidential information. | Uses negative words
Lacks indirect organization
Hides behind a policy

Do not hesitate to write if we can be of service in any other way. | Ends with trite, sarcastic statement

---

The following letter is more positive and courteous:

---

Thank you for requesting information about United Computer Company and its products. | Courteous opening

As you may know, the computer industry is very competitive. Because of this competition, our | Objective explanation

marketing strategy falls under the heading of "clas-       Good transition
sified" information. Consequently, we are unable to        Tactful denial
provide students with information about our adver-
tising budget.

Perhaps the enclosed literature will give you              Alternative solution
some alternative information you can use in writing
your paper. The four-color brochure is an example of
our latest advertising campaign for the FS-88
computer. We are also enclosing an article entitled        Additional
"Advertising Personal Computers" that appeared in the      information
August issue of Advertising World.

Best wishes for the success of your research               Positive ending
paper.

---

Notice that the second letter gives a good explanation of the reason before denying the request. The explanation is presented in an objective way so the reader will not feel that the decision is being made arbitrarily.

The improved version also emphasizes the alternative solution rather than the denial statement. Even though the writer turns down the request, the tone of the letter is more positive than that of the first version. The writer builds goodwill by attempting to help the student who requested the information.

## Declining Requests for Favors

Companies often receive requests for favors from customers, from other organizations, and from their own employees. Many of these favors, which may involve requests for special discounts and other special treatment, cannot be granted.

Every request, whether reasonable or unreasonable, deserves a courteous response. The following memorandum tactfully denies an employee's request to use the company cafeteria for weekly meetings of a local political action group:

---

TO:      Diane Mullins, Management Analyst
FROM:    William J. Simpson
         Vice President of Operations
DATE:    May 12, 19--
SUBJECT:    USE OF TRI-STATE CAFETERIA

Congratulations on your election to the presi-             Opens positively
dency of North Valley Young Republicans! We are

always pleased when Tri-State Manufacturing employees assume leadership roles in local organizations.

We appreciate your interest in holding meetings of the Young Republicans group in our cafeteria. The management of Tri-State Manufacturing is usually willing to assist civic groups by providing facilities after working hours.

Expresses appreciation

Since a large part of Tri-State's business depends on government contracts, we have a policy not to endorse political groups. Although providing facilities would not technically be an endorsement of a political party, we must avoid even the appearance of involvement in partisan politics.

Explains company policy

Denies the request diplomatically

Let me suggest that you ask Marianne Johnson at Sullivan Sheet Metals or Louis Henderson at First State Bank. I mentioned your group to Marianne and Louis, and both of them indicated that they could probably work something out. Sullivan Sheet Metals has a cafeteria, and the bank has a large meeting room.

Suggests an alternative solution

Provides additional information

Best wishes to you and your group.

Ends on a positive note

## Turning Down Requests for Funds

Although many companies routinely donate money to charity and other worthy causes, business organizations usually receive many more requests than they are able to grant. Most form-letter solicitations do not require a reply. Individualized requests for solicitations from charitable and other nonprofit groups, however, deserve a response.

The following letter tactfully denies a request for a contribution:

State University is to be congratulated for its efforts to establish a Center for Engineering Excellence. The Center should be an asset to the business community of our state.

Courteous opening

Our firm receives numerous requests for financial support from many worthy organizations and institutions. Once a year, our Philanthropy Committee meets to evaluate requests and to determine which ones to fund. However, the funds have already been allocated for the next year.

Tactful explanation

Polite refusal

```
    Your efforts to establish the Center are to be          "You" attitude
commended. Best wishes for the success of the Center.       Positive closing
```

Without offending the reader, this letter politely turns down the request for funds. To avoid giving the reader false hope, the letter does not suggest an alternative. However, the writer is careful to end on a positive note.

## CUSTOMER CLAIM DENIALS

Customer claims include those asking for a refund, an exchange, or free repair. Customers seek adjustments for merchandise that is defective or that differs in quality, size, or function from the customer's expectations.

Some large retail firms have very liberal adjustment policies; such companies grant nearly every claim whether or not it is justified. Such policies are based on the premise that favorable adjustments are worth the cost because they build customer goodwill.

Other companies have more conservative adjustment policies because of the high cost involved in granting claims. Discount stores often require merchandise to be returned within 30 days after purchase and usually demand a receipt. Companies with high-cost, low-volume products (such as automobile dealers or home builders) rarely allow returns or exchanges and seldom grant claims after a customer's warranty has expired.

Adjustment denials are difficult to write because the writer and the customer have different points of view. The writer believes that the claim is unjustified, while the customer believes that the claim is reasonable. When you write a claim-denial letter, your goal is to turn down a customer's claim while maintaining goodwill. If you use the right approach and your letter is well written, the customer will be more likely to accept the negative decision.

Perhaps the best way to build goodwill is to suggest an alternative solution to the customer's problem. For instance, if you cannot repair an item free of charge, you could perhaps offer to repair it at a reduced rate. As another example, if you cannot refund a customer's money for a product with an expired warranty, you might offer a special discount on a new purchase.

In either of these situations, you may wish to include sales promotional information in your letter. Every interaction with a customer can have a direct or indirect effect on future sales. Your letter provides an opportunity to keep the customer "sold" on your product and your company even though you are turning down the claim.

Promoting a product that the customer has previously purchased is called **resale**. The following paragraph, which could be included in a claim-denial letter, is an example of resale:

Your Nikad cordless telephone is a versatile, high-frequency speaker phone. Its tiny receiver contains intricate components that are controlled by a single computer chip. This patented system provides a range and quality of sound that are unsurpassed by much larger telephones.

The following claim-denial letter needs to be revised:

---

Dear Mrs. Edwards:

    Thank you for your letter of October 21.      Has a trite opening

    Our service department reports that the heating   Is blunt and tactless
coils of your Sunshine Slow Cooker are rusty. The
only way this type of damage can occur is by the   Uses negative words
customer's failure to follow the directions printed  Blames the
on the warning label. The label, which is located on  customer
the base of the cooker, states "Caution: Do Not
Immerse in Water."

    Unfortunately, we must deny your claim and are  Uses more negative
returning your Slow Cooker.    words

    We hope that you will understand our point of  Closes with "we"
view and that you will continue to do business  attitude
with us.

Sincerely,

---

This letter is sure to antagonize the reader. The writer tactlessly blames the customer and fails to suggest an alternative solution. In addition, the letter overemphasizes the denial statement by including it in a separate paragraph and by using negative words. The ending lacks the "you" attitude and implies that the writer's only concern is to keep the customer's business. In fact, the ending is likely to give the customer the idea that she *should* discontinue doing business with the company.

The following letter is an improvement:

---

Dear Mrs. Edwards:

    Thank you for writing to us about your Sunshine  Positive, courteous
Slow Cooker. We are always glad to get feedback from  opening
our customers.

    The Sunshine Slow Cooker is one of the most popu-  Resale
lar appliances made because of its versatility and
reliability. To ensure customer satisfaction, our  Explanation of
company offers a one-year warranty covering any  warranty policy

defects of materials or workmanship in all the
appliances we manufacture.

During a thorough inspection of your Slow Cooker,      Objective discussion
our technicians found that the heating coils are       of the reasons
rusty. To prevent this type of damage from occurring,
we place a label stating "Caution: Do Not Immerse in
Water" on the base of every Slow Cooker. Therefore,
water damage is not covered by warranty.               Refusal

We can, however, send you a brand-new base for         Alternative solution
your Slow Cooker at our wholesale cost of only $6.95.
Since the retail price of a Slow Cooker is $24.95,
the new base is a bargain.

To order a new base, simply fill out and mail          Easy action
the enclosed card. In a few days, you can again be
enjoying a meal that cooked itself!                    "You"attitude
Cordially,

---

This letter has a more positive tone than the first version. The writer includes positive statements at the beginning and end of the letter and states the reason for the denial in an impersonal way. Instead of bluntly telling the customer that she caused the damage, the letter gets the point across indirectly but objectively. This approach prevents the customer from thinking that she was treated unfairly.

The letter also uses resale effectively. The writer takes the opportunity to promote the product in the second paragraph and at the end of the letter. However, be careful in your use of the "resale" technique. For example, stressing product reliability would not be appropriate if the product has been damaged or if it does not work. The reader would be likely to interpret such statements as sarcasm.

## UNFAVORABLE ORDER ACKNOWLEDGMENTS

Companies sometimes are unable to fill a customer's order promptly because of problems with the merchandise or with the order itself. In such cases, the company must send the customer a message explaining why the order has not been filled. Occasionally an order cannot be filled and must be declined. Other orders may be delayed for various reasons; sometimes the delay is due to the customer's error.

### Declined Orders

Companies sometimes must decline to fill orders. For example, a customer may order merchandise that is not in season or no longer available. Manufacturers or wholesale companies occasionally receive retail orders they cannot fill because the company accepts only commercial orders.

The following letter from a mail-order nursery denies a customer's order in a positive way. Notice that the letter de-emphasizes the refusal of the order and stresses the alternative suggestion.

---

Dear Mr. Perez

Thank you for your February 28 order for two dozen bare-root Owens pecan trees. We appreciate your interest in Whitmire Nursery products, which are famous for their quality and value.

*Courteous opening*

*Resale*

Our company is always careful to ensure that our customers get the best results possible with our trees and other nursery products. In your area of northern Michigan, trees must be able to survive sub-zero temperatures. Owens is a paper-shell variety of southern pecan tree that cannot tolerate a cold climate.

*"You" attitude*

*Explanation*

*Implied refusal*

As an alternative, let me suggest the Northern Hardy pecan tree. The Northern Hardy pecan is a beautiful shade tree that grows well in the cold climate in your area. These trees produce a large pecan nut similar to the Owens but with a harder shell. Our bare-root Northern Hardy trees are the same price as the Owens.

*Alternative solution*

*Additional information*

Our nursery also stocks several varieties of hickory and walnut trees that you may wish to consider. We offer a six-month unconditional guarantee on all our trees, which are among the finest grown in the country.

*Another suggestion*

*Resale*

A new catalog and price list are enclosed. To place another order, simply call us at 404-629-3164. Now is the time to do your spring planting!

Sincerely

*Action ending*

---

## Incorrect or Incomplete Orders

Companies occasionally receive orders they cannot fill because the customer has neglected to include the correct information. In such situations, the company must tactfully request additional information.

The following letter reveals the writer's lack of tact:

We are unable to fill your order for five dozen RS-34 computer ribbons because you failed to include all the information.

You neglected to include the correct model number, and you did not specify what color ribbon you want. The ribbons come in black, navy blue, and green.

Because of your error, we are holding the order. Please send us the correct information by return mail.

> Blunt, deductive opening
>
> Criticism of customer
>
> Negative language
>
> Customer blame
>
> Trite expression

The following version has a more positive tone and avoids blaming the customer. Notice that it also does a good job of selling the company's products.

Thank you for your order for three dozen Compu-Print ribbons. CompuPrint offers the most popular and versatile line of discount computer supplies on the market today.

We stock more than 50 different types and sizes of ribbons for various brands and models of computer printers. You may wish to refer to the enclosed catalog for additional information about our complete line of computer products.

So that we can fill your order accurately, please send us some additional information about the ribbons you ordered. Please indicate on the enclosed postcard the ribbon color you prefer (black, navy blue, or green) and the model number of your Oshika printer. You should receive the ribbons within two weeks after we receive the postcard.

An announcement about the annual CompuPrint spring sale is also enclosed. From April 15 to May 30, we are offering many special values on office supplies and computer furniture marked down 25 percent from the regular discount price. Be sure to take advantage of these special once-a-year values!

> Positive opening
>
> Resale
>
> Transition
>
> Additional information
>
> Tactful reason
> Main idea
>
> Polite request
>
> "You" attitude
>
> Sales promotion
>
> Positive ending

## Backordered Merchandise

If a customer orders goods that are out of stock, the company should inform the customer that the merchandise is backordered. Letters acknowledging delayed shipments are classified as unfavorable because the message is disappointing to the customer.

Many companies use preprinted postcards or computer-generated forms or form letters for this type of correspondence. If the order is a large one, an individualized letter may be more appropriate.

When notifying the customer that the shipment is delayed, concentrate on the positive aspects of the message. Avoid using negative language such as "We are sorry that we are unable to send . . . " or "Shipment of your order will be delayed due to circumstances beyond our control." Instead of emphasizing what you *cannot* do, the letter should stress what you *can* do. However, be sure to give the customer a reason for the delay (stated in positive terms).

The following letter from a furniture manufacturer tells a retail store that a delivery will be delayed:

| | |
|---|---|
| Thank you for your order for three dozen O'Malley L-shaped computer desks. | Appreciation for the order |
| This new line of office furniture has been extremely popular ever since we introduced it six months ago. In fact, we have received so many orders for these computer desks that our factory is now operating on a 24-hour, seven-day schedule to keep up with the demand. | Resale<br><br>Explanation (in positive terms) |
| We will be able to ship your desks in approximately four weeks. You can be sure that these popular desks will arrive at your store by November 15, in plenty of time for the Christmas rush. | Main idea<br>Resale<br><br>"You" attitude |

## UNFAVORABLE ANNOUNCEMENTS

Companies sometimes must announce news that is unfavorable to customers or employees. Such announcements may be concerned with disappointing news such as price increases, reduced services, or new rules and regulations. Such announcements should follow the basic indirect plan of organization for unfavorable messages.

The following memorandum announces unfavorable news about an important employee fringe benefit:

```
      TO:    All Employees
    FROM:    Evelyn Mayfield, Personnel Manager
    DATE:    November 25, 19--
 SUBJECT:    CHANGES IN ATLANTIC HEALTH INSURANCE
```

As you know, Mid-States Technology offers one of the best fringe-benefit packages of any comparable company in this state. We provide excellent insurance and retirement benefits for all our employees.    | Positive opening

However, for the past several years, health-care costs have been increasing rapidly. The cost of our Atlantic health-insurance group policy has been escalating at an alarming rate. If Mid-States Technology were to continue to maintain the present health insurance coverage for each employee's family, the increased cost would exceed anticipated salary raises.    | Explanation / Further details

We have examined various ways to reduce health-insurance costs so that we may continue to give our employees their annual raises in salary. After lengthy negotiations with the Atlantic Health Company, we have reached an agreement.    | "You" attitude

Effective January 1, the following changes will take place in your Atlantic health-insurance plan:    | Decision

1. The deductible amount for each family will be increased to $250 per year.
2. The 80 percent insurance will apply to the first $5,000 per family. After $5,000, 100 percent coverage will apply.    | Details

Most employees will not be greatly affected by these changes. The costs we save will go directly into your salary raise next July.    | "You" attitude

A booklet explaining the provisions of your Atlantic Health Insurance plan will be enclosed with your next paycheck. If you have any questions, please stop by the personnel department.    | Additional information / Courteous ending

## SUMMARY

Letters and memorandums that are expected to disappoint the receiver are classified as *unfavorable* messages. Unfavorable messages include denials of various types of requests, refusals of customer claims, unfavorable order acknowledgments, and unfavorable announcements.

The indirect (inductive) plan of organization is recommended for unfavorable messages. This plan de-emphasizes the bad news by placing it in the middle of the message.

The beginning of an unfavorable message should acknowledge the reader in a positive way. The middle paragraphs should present an explanation and then tactfully give the unfavorable news. Finally, you may suggest an alternative and then close on a positive note.

## CHAPTER REVIEW

1. Identify advantages of using the indirect rather than the direct plan of organization for unfavorable messages.
2. Explain how the principles of primacy and recency apply to unfavorable messages.
3. Name the four parts of an unfavorable message.
4. Defend this statement: "Every letter is a sales letter." How does the statement apply to unfavorable messages?
5. What is the goal of a claim-denial letter?
6. Should claim-denial letters contain an apology for denying the claim? Explain your answer.
7. When writing a claim-denial letter, how would you attempt to keep a customer's goodwill?
8. Define *resale*. Under what circumstances would resale be appropriate in claim-denial letters?
9. Evaluate each of the following opening sentences for a letter informing a customer that a shipment of merchandise will be delayed.
   a. Your order of June 15 for a Sonar mobile telephone has been received.
   b. I am sorry to inform you that your order will be delayed.
   c. Unfortunately, we have been overwhelmed with many orders for Sonar mobile telephones.
   d. Thank you for ordering a Sonar mobile telephone, the most exciting innovation in communication since Alexander Graham Bell invented the telephone.
10. Evaluate the following sentences. Which one would you prefer for the last sentence of a claim-denial letter, and why?
    a. We hope you will continue to do business with us.
    b. I trust you will understand this policy.
    c. To receive your 10 percent discount, simply bring this letter to our nearest store.
    d. Do not hesitate to contact us if we can help you in any other way.

## APPLICATIONS

1. You are public relations director of the Atwood Cheese Company. Mary Maxwell, a student at Lakewood Community College, sends you a letter re-

questing a copy of your firm's annual report. She would like to use the information contained in the report for a research paper she is writing about the dairy industry. However, you cannot grant her request because Atwood is a privately owned company and does not publish an annual report. The firm's financial reports are confidential. Write a letter that denies her request and enclose a U. S. Department of Agriculture booklet about the cheese industry.

2. You are general manager of Vasco Foods International, a small manufacturer of specialty foods, P. O. Box 234, Helena, AR 72342-0071. You receive a letter from Fred Hendricks, 108 Elm Street, Canton, MA 02021-3751. Fred had used your famous southern-style Shady Table barbecue sauce for many years when he lived in Texas. However, he has moved to Massachusetts, where Shady Table sauce is not available. He asks you to send him the recipe for Shady Table so he can make his own barbecue sauce.

The recipe for Shady Table is, however, a company secret. Write Fred a letter refusing his request. To keep Fred's goodwill, send him a free quart-sized bottle of Shady Table. Suggest that he order Shady Table directly from the factory in the future, since your company does fill retail orders from out-of-state customers. Include a Vasco price list with your letter.

3. You are plant manager of the Consolidated Electronics plant in Poway, California. You receive a letter from Mrs. Frances Martinez, who is a third-grade teacher at Del Oro Elementary School, 426 El Rancho Avenue, Poway, CA 92064-6511. She requests that her third graders be permitted to tour the plant and see computer chips being made.

You cannot comply with her request because your entire plant operates in a sterile, dust-free environment. One particle of dust would ruin a computer chip. Your employees must take a shower and wear special protective clothing, including overalls, hat, boots, and rubber gloves, before entering the inner "clean" part of the plant. No one is allowed to enter the plant without taking these special precautions. Children cannot be accommodated because the protective suits are available only in adult sizes. Try to offer an alternative.

4. You are owner/manager of the Valley Computer Warehouse, a discount computer store. You sell computers and computer supplies at "rock-bottom" prices. Approximately half your business is wholesale mail order (you advertise in a leading computer magazine), and the other half of your business is retail.

You receive a letter from Robert Greenstein, purchasing agent for Rifkin Equipment Co., a manufacturer of heavy construction equipment. Greenstein wants to order 50 Calcstar FX-70 microcomputers for Rifkin's entire staff of upper-level and middle managers. He requests a 20 percent discount for placing such a large order.

Although Valley Computer Warehouse frequently receives large orders, your policy is never to give customers a special discount. The advertised price for the FX-70, and all the other computers you carry, is already wholesale. Write Greenstein a letter denying the discount but keeping his goodwill (as well as the order).

5. You are managing partner of Sands and Johnson, a local public accounting firm. Today you received a letter from Dr. Diane Murphy, Professor of Accounting at McClellan State University. As sponsor of the campus accounting club, she asks you to send a representative to speak to the club next month about accounting careers.

   Unfortunately, the next two months are the busiest time of the year for your firm. With the tax season and year-end closings approaching, your C.P.A.'s are all working a 60- to 80-hour week. Write Dr. Murphy a letter that tactfully refuses her request. Offer to send one of your senior-level accountants after the busy season is over.

6. You are general manager of Robinson's, a local chain of four grocery stores. Rev. Richard Hannan, St. Augustine's Center for the Homeless, 101 Fifth Street, Memphis, TN 38105-6029, writes you a letter requesting a donation of unsalable food. He asks your company to contribute damaged cans of food and overripe vegetables to his organization, which feeds nearly a hundred indigent people two meals each day.

   Because of the state health laws, you will not be able to grant his request. The damaged cans and overripe foods are a health hazard. Write him a courteous letter denying his request. As an alternative, send him a $500 donation.

7. You are public relations director of the First United Bank. Many people seem to have the erroneous idea that banks are a good place to ask for money for charitable causes. Although the bank has a small budget for community-service projects, the Board of Directors must approve any contributions in advance. This year the funds have already been allocated. After receiving ten requests for financial donations from various organizations this week, you decide that a form letter can be used. The letter will be stored in the computer and individualized by adding appropriate information such as the name of the receiver and the name of her or his charitable project. Design an appropriate letter, leaving blanks for information to be filled in for each individual situation.

8. You are a customer service representative for Computron Electronics Company, the California-based manufacturer of the popular Computron portable computer. The Computron IV is a lightweight model with a keyboard that snaps onto the computer screen for easy carrying. You receive a claim letter from Allen J. Hansen, P. O. Box 905, Akron, OH 44321-0655, about the latches fastening the keyboard onto the computer. He complains that the plastic latches are too flimsy and have broken from frequent use. He asks your company to repair his computer free of charge.

Your company offers a 90-day warranty on the Computron. This type of warranty is standard throughout the computer industry. Since he purchased his computer 18 months ago, you will not be able to grant his claim.

Write Mr. Hansen a claim-denial letter. Suggest that he order a new pair of latches from your company for only $7.95. Since the latches can be easily installed with a screwdriver, he can replace them himself.

9. You are customer service manager of Edgeway Furniture Manufacturing Company, which makes fine leather-upholstered furniture. You receive a letter from Mr. William Cooper, 355 Waterford Road, Austin, TX 78759-6089, who claims that a sofa he purchased three months ago is falling apart. His letter contained a 6" square of leather that had several rips and holes in it. His letter states:

At the price I paid, I never expected that your company would use defective leather. The entire right side of the sofa is falling to pieces. Please refund my $3,500.

Rhonda Tanner, the plant quality-control supervisor, examined the leather sample and reported to you that the leather is not defective but appears to have been damaged by puncturing and tearing. She thinks the damage was probably done by a cat sharpening its claws. This problem is a common one since animals love the smell of fine leather.

Write a letter to Mr. Cooper. Deny his claim but keep his goodwill by offering to reupholster the right side of the sofa at cost, which will be approximately $75 plus shipping charges. Tactfully suggest that he get a scratching post for the cat. He might also try breaking his cat's habit by taping a cloth sprayed with Pet-Away cat repellent to the right side of the sofa.

10. As manager of Popular TV and Appliance Store, you receive a letter from Major Robert Tsai, 1905 East Golf Avenue, Lowry Air Force Base, Colorado 80220-2957. Major Tsai complains that his Model TX30 Explorer video cassette recorder works fine on the four standard broadcast channels, but it does not work on the cable television channels. He purchased the VCR nearly a year ago, just before he left for an overseas assignment. At that time, he did not have cable TV. Since he wants to record cable TV movies, he is extremely disappointed in the VCR and wants a full refund of the $495 that he paid for it.

Write a letter denying the request. Model TX30 is not designed for cable TV. Suggest that he can solve the problem by purchasing a "block converter" for $59.95. This device, which attaches to the VCR, receives cable signals and converts them to UHF signals, which all VCRs can receive.

11. You are owner/manager of the Goodland Auto Service Store. You receive the following letter from F. T. Willingham, 3824 Sunland Lane, Orlando, FL 32806-2683:

Please refund the $79.95 that I paid for a Goodland heavy-duty car battery which I purchased from you last summer.

The battery became defective recently when I was towing my travel trailer on a trip to North Carolina. Since the battery operates the entire electrical system of the trailer, I was forced to purchase a new battery. Since no Goodland dealers were located in that part of North Carolina, I had to purchase a different brand.

Although the Goodland battery I purchased from you had a five-year warranty, the battery only lasted five months. Please send me the refund as soon as possible.

Write Mr. Willingham a letter tactfully denying his claim. The battery he purchased is not intended to be used in a travel trailer. The instructions accompanying the battery state that such use voids the warranty. Recreational vehicles and boats should have a deep-cycle battery, which can be recharged many times without damage. He purchased the battery on sale and did not tell you that he planned to use it in a trailer. You had assumed he intended to use it in an automobile.

12. You are general manager of Walton Carpet Company, a manufacturer of industrial-grade carpeting. The minister of a small local church sends you an order for 2,000 square feet of tan carpeting for the education building and 1,500 feet of blue carpeting for the chapel.

Your factory does not sell direct to the public. In fact, the smallest roll of carpeting your factory produces contains 5,000 square feet. Write a letter that tactfully declines the order. Suggest that the minister order it from Carpet Town, a local store that carries the Walton line. Send the letter to Rev. Daniel Martin, First Community Church, 411 Oakhurst Street, Calhoun, GA 30701-3983.

13. You are office manager of Harris Nursery, a large specialty mail-order nursery located in Florida. You receive an order from Mrs. Harriet Wilson, 811 La Paz Boulevard, Tucson, AZ 85718-3299, for six "cocktail" trees. (Cocktail trees bear Valencia oranges, ruby-red grapefruit, and lemons grafted on the same tree.) Unfortunately, Arizona has banned the shipment of citrus trees from Florida because of an outbreak of citrus canker disease. Write a letter turning down the order.

14. You are sales manager of Wesley Glass Company, a large manufacturer of glass windows. Two months ago you received an order from James T. Heider, Purchasing Agent for Eagle Construction Company, 1456 Wisconsin Avenue, Milwaukee, WI 53218-2152, for 350 custom-made window panels 1/4 inch thick. At that time, you had written him that your company would be unable to

fill orders for 1/4-inch glass until after your new tempering machine would be installed in two months. Mr. Heider had responded that the delay would not be a major problem. Today you received a call from the plant manager that the tempering machine will not be installed on time—it will be approximately five weeks later than originally planned. Write Mr. Heider a letter informing him of the additional delay and giving him the option to cancel the order.

15. You are sales manager of Courtesy Recreation Vehicles. Today you receive a letter from a dissatisfied customer, George Miller, 302 Jefferson Street, Anaheim, CA 92806-0988. Mr. Miller, who purchased a Matador travel trailer from you six months ago, wants to return the trailer and asks for full refund of the $12,500 he paid for it. His letter protests:

> The trailer is too hard to hitch up, and I can't back it at all. You should never have sold a travel trailer to a man my age.

Write a letter tactfully denying his request. Although your company does offer a 30-day guarantee, it does not apply in his situation because he purchased the trailer six months ago. If he purchases a new motor home from you, however, you will give him a $12,500 trade-in allowance for the trailer. Motor homes do not have to be hitched to another vehicle, and they are easy to back. Enclose a brochure on Trailaway Motor Homes.

16. You are director of the accounting department at Blackwell Pharmaceuticals Co. Your firm employs 25 sales representatives who call on drugstores throughout the four-state region. Your department processes the paperwork for the sales representatives' expense accounts. Every month, the sales reps turn in a "Travel Expense Reimbursement" form itemizing their travel expenses. The accounting department is responsible for checking the forms and issuing reimbursement checks.

The sales reps travel throughout the region most of the time and return to the office during the last three days of each month. They turn in their expense forms on their first day back in the office, and your department always processes the forms immediately so that the reps can pick up their reimbursement checks within 24 hours.

Beginning next week, however, your department must process travel reimbursements manually because a new computer system is being installed. For the next two months, travel reimbursement checks will be available one week, instead of 24 hours, after a rep turns in an expense form. Write a memo informing the sales staff about the delay and telling them that the checks will be mailed to their home addresses.

17. You are director of data processing at Ellis Technologies, Inc. You receive a memo from Henry Jackson, vice president of sales, in which he complains about the accuracy of the weekly sales report. Jackson wants to know when the new Archtype RA-410 database management system will come online.

Since the RA-410 is somewhat incompatible with the present system, you are going to wait until the new Lang XZ-600 is available. The Lang system is less expensive but will have more capabilities than the Archtype system. The XZ-600, which can interface with the present system, has been ordered but will not be in operation until next July. Write Jackson a memo explaining that the proposed database management system has been postponed for several months.

18. You are the assistant administrator of Good Samaritan General Hospital. The director of medical records sends you the following memorandum:

> TO:    Jim Guthrie
>
> FROM:  Lucy Patterson
>
> DATE:  October 10, 19—
>
> SUBJECT:   REQUEST FOR COMPUTER TERMINALS
>
> Several of the computer terminals in the Medical Records Department need to be replaced. Our old RT-70 terminals should be phased out, not only because they are in poor condition, but also because they are obsolete.
>
> I believe new equipment is overdue for our department. As a result, I am requesting authorization to order ten new SJ-90 terminals, which will cost approximately $1,200 each.
>
> If you would like additional information about the SJ-90, please let me know.

To control costs, the hospital is now attempting to slash its entire operating budget by 6 percent. Two weeks ago, the Board of Directors directed the administration to defer major purchases until after December 31, the end of the fiscal year. Write Ms. Patterson a memorandum denying her request.

19. Your firm (Amtek Chemicals, Inc.) is opening a new branch in Anchorage, Alaska, in January. Last week your boss (Ed Richards, the vice president) called you into his office and offered you a promotion to the job of sales manager for the new branch. The position pays $10,000 a year more than you presently earn. You told Mr. Richards that you would let him know your decision in a few days.

You discuss the matter with your family, but they do not want to move to Alaska because of the cold weather. Write Ed Richards a memorandum turning down the offer.

20. You are business manager for the county planning commission. Today you received travel requests from Mary Earnhardt, one of the planning commissioners, to attend a convention in Chicago. The Commission's total travel budget for the year was $39,000. However, travel expenditures already total $41,500

this year. Write her a memorandum diplomatically turning down her travel request.

## CASE STUDY

"P. T., you did it again!" sighed Connie Chow, supervisor of customer relations for Gaffer's Department Store.

Connie had just spent 20 minutes listening to an unhappy customer express her irritation with Gaffer's Department Store, in general, and with P. T. Worthington, in particular.

"I gave you a simple assignment, P. T. All you had to do was tell Mrs. Champion clearly, but sympathetically, that personal items cannot be returned or exchanged because of the state health department regulations. You should have suggested that Gaffer's would restyle her new wig so she would be happy with it."

"According to Mrs. Champion, the letter you sent first insulted and demeaned her and then tried to sell her a fortune in 'worthless products to go with that equally worthless wig'!"

"The company paid for you to take that writing class at the university. Haven't you learned anything there that would help you in this situation?"

P. T. answered, "I'm glad you mentioned that class. Everything that we've covered in class on writing unfavorable messages was in the letter I sent to Mrs. Champion. It had an *indirect* organization plan. It *opened* politely and brought up the subject in a neutral way. Then it *explained* why she couldn't return the wig. It used the *"you" attitude* to reinforce how much we value her as a customer. It suggested a practical *solution* to her problem, and it *closed* on a positive note. My business communication instructor would be proud of that letter. Here's a copy of the letter. You explain why Mrs. Champion is so upset."

Mrs. George Champion
423 Hayes Street
Gary, Indiana 46404-7199

My Dear Mrs. Champion:

No, Mrs. Champion, we cannot refund your money for the styled wig that you purchased. Much as I, personally, would like to see you get your money back, company policy forbids returns or refunds on hair pieces—particularly those that have been cut and styled as yours was. Signs around the wig department clearly state this "no return/no refund" policy. Surely you noticed them when you were in last week to purchase the wig in question!

I agree with you that the synthetic wig is difficult to style with materials normally used for one's own hair. For this reason, we also sell wig spray and metal brushes for synthetic wigs. Though the $12 price of the spray and the $15 price of the brush are slightly higher than you normally would pay for a regular hair brush and hair spray, that's the price you have to pay for owning a wig.

If you had thought to buy a wig block for only $12.50 when you went home with the wig, you might have found the experience of attempting to set the hair piece less frustrating. That's why we have the wig blocks right next to the cash register, so that inexperienced ladies will remember to buy them.

If, after purchasing these little necessities, you still cannot handle the wig, why don't you just resign yourself to having it set by our excellent beauticians every two weeks. It's worth the $25, don't you think?

I am really sorry that you are unhappy with your wig. We're used to having happy and satisfied customers, and I assure you that none of us here at Gaffer's will rest easily until you settle your problem.

Most cordially yours,

P. T. Worthington, Adjuster

1. Is P. T. correct in saying that the letter has an indirect organization plan with a neutral beginning? Why?
2. Does the letter suggest a practical solution to Mrs. Champion's problem? Explain your answer.
3. P. T. maintains that the letter closes on a positive note. Is the ending positive? Sincere? Believable? Why or why not? Identify any attitude or tone problems in other parts of the letter.
4. If you were P. T.'s business communication instructor, how would you evaluate this letter? What suggestions might you make to P. T. for writing future unfavorable messages?

## SUGGESTED READINGS

Geil, Lloyd H. *Executive's Desk Manual of Modern Model Business Letters*. Englewood Cliffs, NJ: Executive Reports Corporation, 1981. (Chapter 3, "Letters Refusing Requests - While Keeping Goodwill," 301-322).

Himstreet, William C. and Wayne Murlin Baty. *Business Communications: Principles and Methods*, 8th ed. Boston: Kent Publishing Company, 1987. (Chapter 7, "Writing About the Unpleasant," 159-180).

Huseman, Richard C., James M. Lahiff, John M. Penrose, and John D. Hatfield. *Business Communication: Strategies and Skills*, 2nd ed. Hinsdale, IL: The Dryden Press, 1985. (Chapter 6, "Bad-News Letters," 145-174).

Poe, Roy W. *The McGraw-Hill Handbook of Business Letters*. New York: McGraw-Hill, 1983.

Sharp, Deborah Whittlesey. *Writing Business Letters with a Personal Touch*. Belmont, CA: Lifetime Learning Publications, 1984.

# PERSUASIVE MESSAGES

## CHAPTER 7

Evelyn James sat down with Bill Gallagher at a table in the company cafeteria and asked, "Bill, did you get my memo about contributing to the Employee Courtesy Fund?"

"I think I received it a couple of weeks ago," replied Bill. "Was that the memo about money for sending flowers to hospitalized employees?"

"Yes, that's the one. Do you have any idea why no one has contributed?" asked Evelyn.

"I think so," said Bill. "First of all, your memo wasn't persuasive. The memo should have been able to sell the idea that the fund is a worthy cause," said Bill.

"Secondly, people tend to procrastinate. Your memo should have encouraged them to contribute right away," he added.

"Will you help me write another memo?" asked Evelyn.

"I'll be glad to," replied Bill. "Let's work on it this afternoon."

As discussed in Chapter 5, the direct plan of organization for *routine* messages is based on the assumption that persuasion is unnecessary. However, some business messages do require persuasion; for example, Evelyn James' memo.

The strategy for persuasive messages presumes that the reader will initially resist or oppose an idea. The writer anticipates that the reader may be unwilling to cooperate unless logical explanations and convincing reasons for cooperating are provided. For example, attempting to sell someone a product or asking management to increase a department's budget would require convincing explanations.

Persuasive messages are designed to influence readers to take action such as when buying a product or accepting an idea. The objective is to overcome anticipated barriers such as the reader's lack of interest or resistance to change.

The indirect organization plan is recommended for persuasive messages. When taking an indirect approach, the writer introduces the main idea (buy this product or grant this request) after first capturing the reader's interest and presenting persuasive evidence.

This chapter presents the following kinds of persuasive business letters and memos:

• Sales letters
• Persuasive claim letters
• Requests for favors
• Requests for donations
• Other persuasive requests

Later chapters introduce other specialized persuasive messages. Chapter 12 presents job-application letters and resumes, and Chapter 14 includes collection letters.

## SALES LETTERS

Sales letters are an important advertising medium. For some organizations, **sales letters** (direct-mail advertising) are the primary means of persuading the public to purchase products and services.

Sometimes a company may send sales letters to prepare prospective customers for a sales representative's visit. Sales letters also are used to persuade customers to visit a store or an exhibition at a trade show.

Companies frequently send sales letters in response to a customer's inquiry. This type of letter, called a **solicited sales letter**, may be partially or completely individualized for each customer.

Many organizations send **unsolicited sales letters** (sales promotion letters) to everyone on a large mailing list. Some sales promotion letters are printed form letters addressed to "Dear Homeowner," "Dear Consumer," or "Dear Physician." In other sales promotion letters, a computer may individualize the message by adding the receiver's name and address and including the name in the salutation (e.g., "Dear Mrs. Smith").

Unsolicited sales letters may be mailed either by first class or third class (bulk mail). However, personalized form letters with first-class postage are much more effective than third-class letters. Individualized messages help to overcome consumers' resistance to form letters.

## Planning Sales Letters

Effective sales letters require more planning and preliminary work than do most other business letters. Before you begin writing a sales letter, you should follow these preliminary steps:

1. Learn about the product or service.
2. Know the reader.
3. Select the appeal.
4. Outline the message.

**Learn About the Product**. Successful salespeople must know a great deal about their product or service. In the following example, one salesperson who lacks product information loses a customer, while another uses product knowledge to make a sale.

Marie Anderson, owner of Sun Florist Shop, has just purchased a Toyota pickup truck for flower deliveries. Shopping for a camper shell to cover the truck bed, she stops at a recreation vehicle dealer whose sign advertises camper shells.

When she inquires about purchasing a camper shell, the salesperson points to a pile of various types of truck-bed covers and says nonchalantly, "Help yourself."

Marie notices that some of the shells seem to be constructed of metal, while others appear to be made of fiberglass or wood. "What's the difference?" she asks.

"Some of them are aluminum," the salesperson replies, "but I really don't know much about them."

In frustration, Marie leaves and drives her pickup to another company. "What kinds of pickup shells do you have for a Toyota?" she asks the salesperson.

"Aluminum, fiberglass, and wood," the salesperson replies. "What do you plan to carry in your truck?"

When Marie explains about the flower deliveries, the salesperson recommends a shell made of plastic-coated insulated plywood. "This model will help protect the flowers from extreme temperatures."

"You're an excellent salesperson," says Marie. "I'll take it."

Before you attempt to persuade someone to purchase a product, whether you are communicating orally or in writing, learn the facts about the product, the market, and the competition. Carefully research the subject, including reading any sales promotional literature that may be available from your competitors or from other sources such as *Consumer Reports*. Use the product yourself and ask for feedback from other people who have used it. Learn about all the features of the product. Find out how it is constructed and from what materials. If possible, visit the factory that makes the product and observe the manufacturing or assembly process. You should also become familiar with the price, warranty, maintenance procedures, and the most common repair problems.

If time and budget permit, conduct research that compares your product with other competitive products. Product and market research may involve laboratory tests, experiments, and public-opinion surveys.

**Know the Reader**. Customers have different interests and needs; therefore, your sales message will be effective the more you know about the reader. When you write *solicited sales letters*, your best source of information may be the customer's letter of inquiry or telephone call.

You can do a better job of tailoring your sales letter to a reader's needs if you can get some information about her or him. Is the reader representing a company or is the reader a consumer? Do you know the reader's approximate age, level of education, and knowledge of the product? What is the reader's motive for her or his interest in the product?

For example, if you were answering an inquiry about a portable computer, you would need to know how much the customer knows about computers. Is the customer a professional computer programmer, a business executive, or a high-school student who likes to play video games? Is the customer paying for the computer, or is the customer's employer paying for it? If you know the answer to these questions, your letter will have a better chance of success because you can design it to appeal to the customer.

When writing *unsolicited sales letters*, you may have little or no information about the readers. To help overcome this problem, many companies purchase special mailing lists to target potential customers. **Mailing-list companies** sell mailing lists of names and addresses of consumers of a particular age, income level, marital status, geographic location, occupation, etc. To advertise a retirement community in Florida, for example, a home builder might purchase a mailing list of senior citizens residing in the Southeast. On the other hand, a computer dating service might purchase a mailing list of single men and women between the ages of 25 and 35 who live in the local area.

Some companies compile their own mailing lists from sources such as records of previous customers, telephone directories, city directories, school directories, membership lists, automobile registrations, and contest entries. Local newspapers also provide a source of names and addresses; for example, marriage and birth announcements, lists of high school and college graduates, and notices of real-estate transfers.

To disseminate sales letters effectively, a company should use a mailing list that is accurate and up to date. Addresses, including ZIP codes, must be correct for your message to be delivered to the right place on time. The name must be spelled correctly, and courtesy or professional titles (Mr., Ms., Mrs., Miss, Dr.) must be correct. If not, prospective customers will be annoyed.

Since mailing lists rapidly become outdated, using an old mailing list can be a costly mistake. Advertising specialists estimate that approximately 28 percent of the names and addresses on a mailing list will become obsolete within one year (Bovée and Arens, 1982, 589). Purchasing a mailing list may be more cost effective than compiling your own list because professionally prepared lists usually have a guaranteed accuracy rate of 90 to 95 percent.

You should not rely on the post office to forward mail to a prospective customer who has moved. In any case, first-class mail is forwarded for only six months; third-class mail is not forwarded unless the addressee specifically agrees to pay forwarding postage.

A strategy for keeping mailing lists current is to stamp "Return postage guaranteed" on envelopes. If a message bearing this stamp is undeliverable, the post office will return it to the sender. Many companies use this strategy to eliminate names from a mailing list and reduce the cost of future mailings.

To evaluate the effectiveness of a mailing list, send the letter to a small sample of the names on the mailing list. The test mailing can reveal many problems that should be corrected before you send the entire mailing.

**Select the Appeal**. After analyzing the prospective reader or readers, you should carefully select a sales appeal by determining how your product best meets the reader's individual needs. Psychologist Abraham H. Maslow (1954) developed a widely accepted approach to understanding how needs motivate human behavior. Maslow proposed the following hierarchical classification (levels) of human needs:

1. Physiological needs (water, food, sleep, shelter, etc.)
2. Safety and security (freedom from danger and fear of the unknown)
3. Social needs (love, friendship)
4. Esteem and status (self-respect and other people's respect)
5. Self-actualization (fulfillment of one's ambitions, creativity, etc.)

Since lower-order (physical) needs are basic to survival, people will attempt to meet those needs before they become motivated to satisfy their higher-order (emotional) needs. For example, people who are hungry and cold will not be concerned about social needs, self-esteem, or self-actualization.

Although human needs are primarily hierarchical, Maslow also recognized that people are sometimes motivated by more than one category of needs at the same time. According to his theory, however, the unsatisfied lower-order needs will influence an individual's behavior more strongly than will the higher-order needs.

Even though a sales message cannot create needs, it can increase people's awareness of existing needs. Sales messages attempt to influence buyer behavior by pointing out a need and illustrating how a product can meet that need.

For instance, sales appeals for insurance can be based on each of the needs identified by Maslow, as shown in the following examples:

---

### Physiological Needs

Descriptors: Food, health, home, pain, warmth, cold
Examples: The best health care.... Your home will be covered.... Out in the cold....

### Safety and Security

Descriptors: Assurance, guarantee, protection, safety
Examples: Guaranteed income.... Protect your assets.... You're safe from intruders....

### Social Needs

Descriptors: Caring, concern, family, friendship, love, popularity
Examples: Your loved ones.... You are part of the Metropolis family.... We care about you....

### Esteem and Status

Descriptors: Expensive, important, prestigious, respected, successful
Examples: Successful executives choose.... The most prestigious company.... People will respect your good judgment....

### Self-Actualization

Descriptors: Achieving, exciting, fulfilling, enjoyable
Examples: This plan will help you achieve your goals.... Your fondest dreams will come true.... Enjoy your retirement....

---

Promotional appeals may be classified in two categories—functional appeals and psychological appeals. These two types of appeals are based on the notion that some products satisfy consumers' functional (physical and practical) needs, while other products satisfy their psychological (emotional) needs. **Functional appeals** involve a description of the physical features of the product, while **psychological appeals** are based on the buyer's feelings as a result of owning or using the product.

For instance, when you describe an automobile, a functional appeal might stress gas mileage, safety, or repair record. In contrast, a psychological appeal might stress prestige, popularity, or glamour. You should carefully select your appeal by determining how your product best meets the reader's individual needs. Some of the most common advertising appeals are classified in the following lists:

### Functional Appeals

- Comfort
- Convenience
- Durability
- Economy
- Efficiency

### Psychological Appeals

- Adventure
- Affection
- Excitement
- Glamour
- Nostalgia

- Entertainment
- Health
- Profit
- Safety
- Security
- Self-improvement
- Time saving

- Parental love
- Popularity
- Praise
- Recognition
- Respect
- Status
- Sex appeal

Although a product may have several advantages, the primary emphasis of a sales letter should be on the **major selling point**, which is the main appeal. Select for your sales message a major selling point that you think will best appeal to your customer's needs. For instance, if the customer is a college student, the major selling point for a computer might be the low price. On the other hand, if the customer is a business executive, your major selling point might be user friendliness or brand prestige.

**Outline the Message.** The last step in planning a sales letter is to make an outline. Carefully organize your outline to emphasize the major selling point, incorporate the appeals you selected, and include all the necessary information about the product or service. Remember that the objective of your sales letter is to persuade the customer to purchase what you are promoting. Every topic included in your outline should have a specific purpose that is part of the plan of organization. Finally, review your outline and omit any point that does not make a positive contribution to your sales message.

Effective sales letters generally follow this basic outline:

1. Opening paragraph — Establishes contact with your reader
2. Middle paragraph(s) —
   a. Generates interest and desire
   b. Convinces the reader
3. Ending paragraph — Provides incentive for action

## Writing Sales Letters

Sales letters are a specialized form of persuasive messages requiring creativity and excellent communication skills. When writing a sales letter, make sure that all parts of the letter fit together logically. Your letter should be clear but concise, using appropriate language for the reader. Use short sentences, active voice, and action verbs. Carefully avoid subjective statements, a negative tone, and unpleasant ideas that might offend the reader.

The "you" attitude is probably the most important quality of an effective sales letter. The writer should acquire the background for incorporating the "you" attitude in the planning stage by learning about the customer's needs. Because customers' individual needs motivate them to buy, you should select an appeal that addresses the reader's unconscious question about the message, "What's in it for me?"

Buyers are usually more interested in *benefits* than in facts. To be persuasive, your letter should translate facts about your product or service into benefits to the reader. Here is an example of a fact-oriented statement:

Our computer-products company carries six brands of computers and over 200 software packages.

This fact-oriented statement probably would be more effective if it were revised to stress the reader's benefits, as illustrated by the following sentence:

You will find everything you need here in our wide selection of six brands of computers and over 200 software packages.

**Establish Contact with the Reader**. The opening paragraph of a sales letter should be positive, interesting, and short. It should introduce the major selling point in a way that appeals to the reader's needs.

When you receive a customer inquiry, you know that the person is already interested in your product. Therefore, the opening sentence of a solicited sales letter does not require a striking attention-getter.

A solicited sales letter should begin by expressing appreciation for the customer's inquiry and introducing the major selling point, as shown in the following examples:

1. Thank you for asking about our money-saving "Call Home" long-distance plan that is based on time, not distance.

2. We're glad you're interested in discovering the difference between frustration and success—our new Plain and Simple spreadsheet software.

In an unsolicited sales letter, the first sentence must capture the reader's attention. If the writer is unable to win the reader's attention in the first sentence, the message will be ineffective. The opening must be striking enough to induce an indifferent receiver to read the rest of the letter. Advertisers often use the following types of openings in sales letters:

1. Announce a sweepstakes or other contest.

You may already be a winner in our $25,000 sweepstakes!

2. Use an unusual salutation.

Dear Big Spender:
The chances are that you're spending too much money on car insurance.

3. Offer a bargain.

Get a 50 percent discount on top brand-name computer furniture!

4. State an unusual fact.

Today ten Americans became millionaires!

5. Use an "if" opening.

If you like to s-t-r-e-t-c-h every dollar, check around and you'll discover that our savings accounts pay the highest interest rates in town!

6. Ask an interesting question.

Do you want your money to grow more money?

7. Offer the reader a gift.

A free television set is yours!

8. Print the reader's name.

Here's some good news for you, Mr. Sanchez!

9. Report a startling news headline.

PATIENT SUES GOOD SAMARITAN DOCTOR FOR $5 MILLION

10. Challenge the reader.

Find a lower health-club rate than ours, and we'll give you double your money back!

Present your opening in terms of benefits to the reader, and use vocabulary that is appropriate for the reader. Avoid trite or negative opening statements. Make sure that the opening paragraph is short (only one or two sentences) and related to the major selling point, because an irrelevant opening may confuse or irritate the reader. The opening should be a logical introduction to the information contained in the second paragraph.

**Generate Interest and Desire**. After your opening has captured the reader's attention, generate interest in your product or service by describing it in terms of benefits to the reader. Expand the product description and use the appeal selected during planning to concentrate on how the merchandise meets the reader's needs. Focus on the major selling point, which should be introduced in the first paragraph.

The following paragraph, taken from a letter promoting a magazine, appeals to the reader's need to save money on home improvements:

Save thousands of dollars by letting *you* be the expert instead of paying one. DO-IT-YOURSELF magazine is packed with great ideas and expert step-by-step guidance you can use to make valuable improvements on your home. Soon you'll be building walls...tiling a floor...installing a modern, elegant kitchen.

Use clear but vivid language that excites the reader's imagination. Use action verbs, graphic nouns, and adjectives that appeal to the reader's five senses, as shown in the following examples:

1. Cruise the legendary Rhine River, dance to a melodious Viennese Waltz, and taste the world-famous Austrian pastries...

2. See a wild Flamenco Show in Spain and toast in the sun on the jet-set beaches of the French Riviera...

3. Sink into your Moonbeam waterbed and feel the ecstasy of floating on a cloud.

4. See the admiring glances and heads turning as you zoom into view in your flashy new RX-34 convertible.

The product description, which is generally the longest part of a sales letter, may contain several paragraphs. Organize your description so that it leads your reader from interest in the product to a desire to buy it.

**Convince the Reader.** The best strategy for establishing conviction is to include evidence that your statements about the product are true. Try to increase your credibility by backing up your claims with proof.

Your evidence should be factual, accurate, and specific. As you describe the product, use objective language rather than vague generalities. Establish your credibility by quoting specific facts, figures, and prices, as shown in the following examples:

1. You will stay only at first-class European hotels, NO YOUTH HOSTELS. You will have an outstanding tour guide because all our tour guides are graduate students at the University of Vienna.

2. Compare and save. One full year of WEEKLY NEWS regularly by subscription costs $32.00, newsstand value $78.00. OUR PRICE—$20.00!

However, be cautious about emphasizing the price of the merchandise unless low price is your major selling point. If possible, quote prices in terms of small amounts such as dollars or cents per week or per unit (for example, 38 cents per magazine).

You can use various kinds of evidence to convince the reader, including one or more of the following techniques:

1. Report independent performance test results.
2. Quote recognized literature (such as trade or consumer magazines).
3. Include government statistics.
4. Use the names of satisfied customers or include their testimonials.
5. Offer a free trial period.
6. Provide a money-back guarantee of satisfaction.
7. Send a free sample.
8. Enclose additional information, such as a brochure or individualized computer printout.

Enclosures can be an extremely effective way to convince the reader, especially if they accompany a strong sales letter. Your letter should mention any enclosure or separate mailing such as a catalog, brochure, or free sample. However, avoid using trite expressions such as "Enclosed is" or "under separate cover."

**Provide Incentive for Action**. Every sales letter should motivate the reader to specific action, such as filling out an order form, visiting a store, or placing a telephone order. The ending of your letter should reinforce the major selling point and stimulate the reader to act.

Effective sales letters provide a stimulus to overcome people's tendency to procrastinate. An excellent way to close the sale is to offer an incentive for immediate action. Use one or more of the following strategies to show your reader that immediate action is to her or his advantage. To maintain a sound code of business ethics, of course, such statements must be accurate.

1. Indicate that the price is going to increase soon.

**Buy now before the scheduled January price increase.**

2. Point out that the sale is scheduled for only a short time.

**This special sale price is effective for only two weeks.**

3. Mention a limited supply of the product.

**We have only five of these models left—call us today before our supply is gone.**

4. Give the customer a discount.

**If your Christmas order arrives before November 30, we will give you a 20 percent discount from the regular price.**

5. Offer a premium.

**If you purchase a Porta-Com computer within the next ten days, you will receive $500 worth of free software.**

Make the suggested action, including paying the bill, easy for the customer. For example, enclose a postcard or order form to facilitate the ordering process. In addition, paying the bill will seem easier if the customer can use a credit card number rather than mailing a check.

Your closing should be concise and emphatic as well as courteous. The final sentence should clearly request the action you want the customer to take and briefly reinforce your major selling point, as shown in the following examples of action endings:

1. **Call us toll free at 800-555-4111 today to take advantage of this special price, which will never again be this low!**

2. **Mail this reply card today to order your magazine subscription and find out if you have won our $25,000 sweepstakes!**

Many sales letters contain a postscript to reinforce the action ending, as shown in this example:

**P.S. REPLY TODAY. If you call within 72 hours, you will receive a bonus gift valued at $25!**

## Seeing the Complete Package

Persuasive messages are usually longer than most routine, favorable, or unfavorable business messages because they require more explanation and detail. Sales letters frequently require two pages because of a lengthy description of the product. The following examples of a solicited and an unsolicited sales letter are considerably longer than the messages illustrated in Chapters 5 and 6.

**A Solicited Sales Letter**. The following sales letter was sent in response to a customer's inquiry about a microwave oven. An attention-getting opening was unnecessary in this letter because the reader had already expressed an interest in the product.

---

Dear Mrs. Hale:

Thank you for your interest in Stapana's Micro-Range, the microwave oven that is the greatest cooking discovery since fire.

*Establishes contact with the reader; hints at major selling point*

Being a career woman as well as a homemaker, you probably find that the amount of leisure time you have is limited. The Micro-Range can help you solve this problem by greatly reducing the amount of time you spend in the kitchen. This oven allows you to prepare a complete meal in just minutes. For example, you can prepare a hamburger in 60 seconds, a baked potato in 4 minutes, or a ham in 25 minutes. You save 75 percent of actual cooking time.

*Introduces major selling point*

*Describes the product*

The Micro-Range also helps reduce clean-up time to almost nothing. You can cook food on paper plates and then just throw them away, or you can cook right in the serving bowls and take them directly to the table. You'll never have to wash another pot or pan. The oven itself is also easy to clean. The sides, top, and bottom of the unit do not get hot, so splatters can't burn on. You simply wipe out the oven with a damp cloth. You'll be able to get out of the kitchen fast and have much more time to spend with your family.

*Appeals to reader's needs*

Food prepared in your Micro-Range oven tastes better than when it is prepared by conventional cooking methods. When you place food in the oven, it absorbs the microwave energy and turns it into heat that cooks the food inside and out at the same time. Therefore, foods have less dehydration and loss of

*Describes further advantages*

natural juices. Cooking in the Micro-Range is also greaseless and fat-free, so it is better for your health.

The Micro-Range oven by Stapana is the first portable all-electronic 115-volt cooking unit ever developed for the home. It was the first microwave oven to meet the Consumer Product Safety Standards of the U.S. Government. It also has the exclusive electronic safety lock developed by Stapana that automatically locks the door as soon as the Start switch is pushed so that the oven cannot be opened while in operation.

*Convinces the reader*

The Micro-Range oven is the only microwave oven that has an exclusive five-year warranty including five full years of coverage on parts and labor. Our quality is backed by the strongest warranty on any electronic appliance you have in your home.

*Describes the warranty*

A brochure describing the three models of the Micro-Range oven in more detail is enclosed. It includes the prices, explains the basic differences between the three models, and describes the features that you will not find on any other microwave oven.

*Presents additional evidence*

During April, the Micro-Range ovens are on sale at a 10 percent discount; and with the purchase of an oven, you get a free browning tray and ten free cooking lessons. So stop by and take advantage of this excellent chance to find out what it is like to have extra leisure time.

*Provides incentive to action*

*Reinforces major selling point*

Cordially,

---

**An Unsolicited Sales Letter**. The following unsolicited sales letter promotes subscriptions to *BARRON'S*. Notice the personalized salutation, the opening that attracts the reader's attention by asking a question, the use of paragraph headings as a special effect, and the postscript that reinforces the action ending:

---

Dear Mr. Harrington:

Would you be surprised to know that you are the type of person for whom BARRON'S is written and edited?

*Attracts attention*

*Hints at major selling point*

You are. And you can prove it by answering three simple questions:

1. Do you have any money invested--or to invest?
2. Do you want to protect that money?
3. Do you want that money to earn more money...to grow?

If you answered <u>yes</u> to these questions, you owe it to yourself to read BARRON'S every week.

BARRON'S isn't just for professional investors or for individuals who spend a great deal of time supervising their portfolios and participating in active trading. BARRON'S is for busy people like you--men and women who would like to know more about all the investment opportunities open to them, who are smart enough to seize those opportunities, but who don't have all the time in the world to spend on it.

### Every week in BARRON'S: a world of investments...a world of opportunities

BARRON'S can open your eyes to investment opportunities you never imagined. BARRON'S reports in depth, not just on the stock market, but on every investment area from futures to bonds to precious metals to foreign markets to mutual funds...even real estate and art. Anywhere and everywhere you can put your money to work to earn more money.

### Expert opinions in clear, simple English

Every week, some of the country's best-known and most widely respected investment experts talk to you in the pages of BARRON'S. They tell you what's happening in specific companies and industries, why it's happening, and what it means to investors like you. Every issue gives you 40 pages of investment information written in plain, non-technical English.

### A special introductory offer

Do you know how little a weekly subscription costs? Only $19 for 13 weekly issues is a bargain all by itself. And when you compare it with what some people pay for investment information, BARRON'S is an unbelievable bargain.

What's more, we'll give you a money-back guarantee; if you are disappointed in any way with BARRON'S, just let us know and we'll return the unused

---

*Margin annotations:*

- Generates interest
- Promotes "you" attitude
- Major selling point
- Converts interest to desire
- Includes additional details
- Convinces the reader
- Mentions the price as an additional advantage
- Establishes conviction

portion of your subscription price—no questions asked.

> You owe it to yourself to read
> BARRON'S every single week.

Reiterates "You" attitude

To take advantage of our special introductory offer, simply fill out and mail the enclosed order card today.

Provides incentive for action

Sincerely,

Robert M. Bleiberg
Editorial Director and Publisher

Enclosures

P.S. If you use BARRON'S in connection with your investments—or in your business—your entire subscription may be tax deductible.

Additional reinforcement

(Courtesy of Dow Jones & Company, Inc.)

---

## PERSUASIVE CLAIM LETTERS

Claim letters request an adjustment for unsatisfactory merchandise, poor service, billing errors, and other problems. As discussed in Chapter 5, claim letters fall into two categories: *simple claims* and *persuasive claims*. Simple claims, which request an adjustment when a problem is routine (covered by company policy) should follow the direct organization plan because persuasion is unnecessary.

A persuasive claim letter is appropriate, however, if the problem does not clearly fall into a routine adjustment category or requires a complicated explanation. A persuasive claim letter is also warranted if you previously sent a simple claim letter that the receiver denied or disregarded. To persuade an unwilling reader, use the indirect plan of organization, as shown in the following outline:

1. Opening paragraph — Begins with a positive or neutral statement with which the reader is likely to agree
2. Middle paragraph(s) —
   a. Describes the reasons for the request
   b. Requests a specific remedy
3. Ending paragraph — Ends with a positive statement expressing optimism

A persuasive claim letter should open with a positive or neutral statement related to the claim. Next, present the facts that provide the basis for the claim. Then ask for a specific adjustment (for example, refund of money or replacement of defective merchandise). The request for an adjustment should be assertive but polite. Finally, end the letter with a positive statement. The writer of a good persuasive claim letter should be objective, avoid exaggeration, and refrain from sarcasm.

The writer of this negative, subjective, and sarcastic claim letter antagonizes the reader:

---

Dear Mr. Nelson:

On March 3, I complained to your service manager about the slipshod repair jobs your company did on my car.

*Negative opening*

It has been over a month, and nothing has been done to correct the problem. Perhaps as owner of Nelson Motor Co., you will be willing to take some action.

*Expletive beginning*
*Vague (what action?)*

The unfortunate incidents began on the morning of February 16, when I first brought my 1985 XZ4 to your service department. Since my car had begun to stall when I stopped at traffic lights, I told the service advisor that the carburetor needed to be fixed. That afternoon I paid the $67 bill and picked up the car.

*Negative word*

The next afternoon on my way home from work, the car stalled right in the middle of the street and refused to start. Another motorist pushed me around the corner and out of the way of traffic, and I called a tow truck to take the car back to Nelson Motor Co. The towing cost me $25. Needless to say, I was furious. I am a busy person and need this aggravation like a hole in the head.

*Incident description*

*Exaggeration*
*Sarcastic tone*

Your mechanics supposedly fixed the car again, and I paid the bill (this time $132) and picked up the car again on February 18. The car ran okay until three days later, when it stalled in the middle of the freeway.  This time the towing cost $55.

*More sarcasm*

Since I no longer had confidence in your company, I had the tow truck take the car to Westside Motor Company. Their bill was only $10 to replace a dirty fuel filter, which they said was the only problem. Since that time, the car has run perfectly.

*Too negative*

Your mechanics should have discovered that the problem was only a dirty fuel filter. Because of your mechanics' ineptness, I have spent $199 for unnecessary repair work, plus $80 in towing bills.

*Accusing*

*Negative*

Fair is fair. I insist on a $279 refund from your company. All receipts are enclosed.
Sincerely,

|                                    | Too forceful |

The following improved version of the letter contains a more positive beginning and ending:

Dear Mr. Nelson:

For the last five years, I have been a loyal customer of Nelson Motor Company. Until recently, I have been pleased with the efficiency of your service department.

Positive opening

On February 16, I brought my 1986 XZ4 to your service department. Since my car had begun to stall when I stopped at traffic lights, I told the service advisor that the carburetor needed to be repaired. That afternoon I paid the $67 bill and picked up the car.

Description of events

The next afternoon on my way home from work, the car stalled right in the middle of the street and would not start. Another motorist pushed me around the corner and out of the way of traffic, and I called a tow truck to take the car back to Nelson Motor Company. The towing bill was $25.

Further description

Your mechanics worked on the car again, and I paid the $132 bill and picked up the car on February 18. The car ran okay until February 21, when it stalled in the middle of the freeway. This time the towing cost $55.

Additional facts

Since your service department had been unable to solve the problem, I had the tow truck take the car to Westside Motor Company. Their bill was only $10 to replace a dirty fuel filter, which their mechanic said was the only problem. Since that time, the car has run perfectly.

Explanation

Because your service department did not find and repair the problem, I have spent $199 for unnecessary repair work, plus $80 in towing bills, in addition to my inconvenience. The receipts for these bills are enclosed.

Conviction

|  |  |
|---|---|
| I believe any company can occasionally make a mistake and that you are fair and will want to rectify the situation. Therefore, please send me $279 reimbursement for your unsatisfactory repair work and for the towing expenses that I incurred. | Positive statement<br><br>Request for action |
| By making this adjustment, you will restore my confidence in Nelson Motors as a fair and honest company. I will then be able to look forward to doing business with you in the future.<br>Sincerely, | Optimistic ending<br><br>Positive tone |

## REQUESTS FOR FAVORS AND DONATIONS

When writing a letter or memorandum asking someone to do a favor or donate money to a worthy cause, you should follow the basic outline for persuasive letters. The message should follow the indirect plan of organization with your request following the explanation.

Requests for favors and donations appeal primarily to the receiver's good nature and goodwill. To be effective, however, such messages should also point out indirect benefits for the reader, such as recognition, loyalty, reciprocal favors, publicity, and tax advantages. The "you" attitude is especially important. Anticipate the reader's objections and include in your discussion a thorough explanation designed to overcome the reader's expected resistance.

The following letter, which recruits volunteers for a worthy cause, tactfully avoids explicit mention of fund raising:

|  |  |
|---|---|
| Dear Mrs. Pennington:<br>   MARK YOUR CALENDAR! | Attracts attention |
|    Remember Saturday, April 12, because that day many people are helping to conquer cancer by climbing South Mountain. | Has positive tone |
|    Those who join us will do their part to fight cancer, meet interesting people, and have an exciting time. Only one day is required. | Stresses reader benefits |
|    We are currently organizing a committee of dynamic people who have these qualifications: | Generates interest |
| * Good organizers<br>* Detail-oriented people<br>* People with good business contacts<br>* Sales-oriented people (for recruiting volunteers)<br>* People to help with publicity | Includes details |

Do you and your friends have any of these
qualifications? We also need people to register
climbers and staff water stops.

So mark your calendar and give us a call at
555-1685 to join our team and do your part!
Sincerely,

| | Presents main idea |

Promotes action
ending

## OTHER PERSUASIVE REQUESTS

The indirect plan of organization is also recommended for other messages to which the writer expects initial opposition or resistance. For example, a suggestion for a change in policy or request for a budget increase might require persuasion to convince management.

When writing a persuasive request to someone higher up in an organization, be assertive but tactful. To be effective, your message should clearly document a problem or need *before* making the request.

The steps in planning a persuasive memo are similar to the steps recommended for planning sales letters. First, gather information about the subject and research the topic carefully. Second, analyze the reader's interests and concerns. Third, select a rationale that will appeal to the reader. Finally, make an outline of your message.

The following memorandum requests the purchase of a new copying machine:

---

TO:      Helen C. Birkins, Director
         Administrative Management
FROM:    Lee J. Meredith, Office Manager
DATE:    March 21, 19--
SUBJECT: COPYING MACHINE

So far this year, the repair bills for our
high-speed Model 2300 GTJ copier have totaled over
$1,200.

*Attracts attention*

The copier, which is six years old, seems to
be breaking down almost weekly. At this rate, by the
end of the year we could almost buy a new copier for
the amount we will spend on repairs.

*Generates interest*

A new Model 5400 GTJ copier would cost approximately $5,000. I believe we would save money in the
long run by replacing the old copier now. Therefore,
I am requesting that an additional $5,000 be added to

*Convinces the reader*

*Presents main idea*

```
this year's equipment budget to replace the Model
2300 copier.
     I am attaching a brochure about the Model 5400.     Includes additional
If you would like additional information, please let    information
me know.                                                 Encourages action
```

Notice that the writer attracted his boss's attention by discussing over-spending—a topic he knew she was particularly concerned about. The memo develops the idea to its logical conclusion—saving money (by buying the new copier) instead of spending more money for repairs. Observe also that the memo follows the same pattern as a sales letter. The message attracts the reader's attention, generates interest in the topic, convinces the reader, and encourages action. Since the writer does not have the authority to make the decision suggested in the memo, the writer carefully avoids an overly strong approach and tactfully suggests action.

## SUMMARY

Persuasive messages are intended to convince a reader to act; for example, to buy a product or to accept an idea. The indirect plan of organization is recommended for persuasive messages. When using this strategy, the writer attracts the reader's interest, presents the evidence, and then introduces the main idea.

Solicited and unsolicited sales letters, which follow the same basic outline, differ primarily in the opening paragraphs. Unsolicited sales letters (direct-mail advertising) require an attention-getting opening, while solicited sales letters do not.

Effective sales letters require extensive planning and other preliminary work. The writer should know the product well and understand the reader. The appeal and the major selling point should be tailored to meet the reader's needs. A sales letter should establish contact with the reader, generate interest and desire, convince the reader, and provide incentive for action.

Other persuasive messages include persuasive claim letters, requests for favors and donations, and persuasive memos. Persuasive memos may include requests for change and employee suggestions to management.

The indirect organization plan and the "you" attitude are essential for these various types of persuasive messages. The writer should anticipate the reader's objections and include a thorough explanation designed to overcome expected resistance.

## CHAPTER REVIEW

1. Are persuasive messages more nearly similar to routine or to unfavorable messages? Why?

2. Are persuasive messages usually shorter or longer than routine messages? Explain your answer.
3. What are the two categories of sales letters? How do they differ?
4. Summarize the four steps in planning a sales letter.
5. Identify Maslow's five levels of human needs and give an example of each.
6. What are the two categories of advertising appeals? Describe five examples of each, and match each of your examples with a product that might fit that advertising appeal.
7. Describe the basic outline for a sales letter.
8. What is the "major selling point" of a sales letter? Which parts of a sales letter should mention the major selling point?
9. Select a major selling point and one supporting selling point that could be used in a sales letter for each of the following products:
   a. A four-wheel drive pickup truck
   b. A fiberglass swimming pool
   c. An automatic garage-door opener
   d. A cruise to Tahiti
   e. Membership in an exercise/health club
10. Identify the two categories of claim letters and describe the difference between them.

## APPLICATIONS

1. You are assistant sales manager of the Electronic Mart, a discount mail-order electronics company. Today you received a letter from Ann Gladstone, the marketing director of Top-Notch Motor Company. Ms. Gladstone would like to know your lowest price for an order for 200 walk-around stereo tape players, which Top-Notch plans to give customers as a sales promotion.

   Write Ms. Gladstone a sales letter quoting your best wholesale price of $39.95 each for the Model 3400 Hoshiwa which runs on either two alkaline AA batteries or on AC house current. This compact model, which doubles as an FM radio, gives the listener a *super stereo* effect (the sense of being surrounded by musical instruments). The 3400 also has a noise-reduction feature that eliminates the hiss without affecting the quality of the music.

2. You are the sales manager of Pro-Tect Company, which manufactures burglar alarms. The Pro-Tect system uses a unique patented infrared sensor system, which is less prone to receiving false alarms than older models. The Pro-Tect system is easy to install, inexpensive, and includes several special features. When the alarm sounds, the lights automatically come on. As an optional feature, the system can be connected to a monitoring service. The lower half of the infrared beam can be turned off to prevent pets from triggering the alarm. The wholesale price of this system is only $149.95. Write a sales letter to be sent to hardware stores throughout your state.

3. You are planning to sell your house because your employer, Aimes Manufacturing Co., is transferring you to another state. The layout of the house is convenient and it is well-built—good reasons to think you can sell it easily. To avoid paying a realty commission, you decide to sell it yourself. The house is a three-bedroom, two-bath, semi-custom brick model. Your asking price is $80,000.

   Since your house is located close to the Aimes plant, you decide to advertise it first to Aimes employees. Write a form sales letter to distribute to all employees of Aimes Manufacturing. In your description of the house, make any assumptions you wish.

4. You are customer relations specialist for Delmar Electronics, Inc. Each week you receive several letters inquiring about the features of your new Delmar video cassette recorder. Until now, you have answered each inquiry with a personal letter. To save time and increase efficiency, you have decided to prepare a form sales letter to answer the inquiries.

   The Delmar VCR is a combination TV receiver and recorder/player. Since the VCR has a built-in tuner, it can tape a program no matter which channel the TV is set on. The Delmar uses a VHS format, which has more capability than the Beta tapes. The Delmar has automatic rewind, remote control, frame advance, and search. Delmar is the only VCR on the market with all-channel cable capability. The picture and sound quality are rated excellent by *Consumer Reports*. Design a form sales letter for answering inquiries about the Delmar VCR.

5. You are sales manager for QualiChem Construction Company, which installs hot tubs and spas. Write an unsolicited sales letter advertising a Jet-Swirl water spa. This fiberglass model soothes and relaxes you with its swirling luxury and warm bubbles of hydro-therapy. Your letter should use psychological appeals, and your major selling point should be the luxurious feeling of using a Jet-Swirl water spa. The Jet-Swirl is available in a choice of nine colors to coordinate with home decors.

6. Two weeks ago Popular Electronics installed an AM/FM radio-cassette player in your new car. While installing the unit, the mechanic must have damaged your car's wiring, because the brake lights and windshield wipers do not work now. Since the car is under warranty, you took it back to the car dealer, who reported that the wires were apparently damaged when the stereo was installed. The car dealer charged you $95 to repair the wiring. Write a persuasive claim letter to Popular Electronics, 3345 East Broadway, Del Mar, CA 92014-7736.

7. Last Saturday you had dinner at the Villa Italia, an expensive Italian restaurant. You ordered a veal scallopini dinner, which was fairly good. However, when you took a bite of the accompanying roll (which was stale and hard as concrete), you cracked a molar. Your dinner companion heard the "crunch"

and saw you grimace from the injury to the tooth. Today your dentist verified that the tooth needs to be crowned—a procedure that will cost $325.

The owner of the restaurant is legally responsible for the injury since the tooth was perfectly sound before you damaged it on the roll. The restaurant's liability insurance should pay for your dental work. Write a persuasive claim letter to Ms. Anna DeGrazia, owner of the Villa Italia Restaurant, 1225 East Fremont Avenue, New Orleans, LA 70115-2638.

8. On December 1, you ordered a $39.95 gift box of assorted cheeses and smoked sausage from the Wisconsin Cheesery, P.O. Box 203, Monroe, WI 53566-5698, as a Christmas gift for your friend Kristen Murray, 356 Boxwood Lane, Winchester, TN 37398-4199. However, she never received it. The Wisconsin Cheesery sent you a postcard on January 21 stating that the cheese was returned to the factory because the post office could not find such an address. However, the Murrays have lived at 356 Boxwood Lane for the past 12 years. On January 24, you wrote the Cheesery a letter asking them to send another box of cheese and sausage to your friend.

Today (March 30) you called Kristen about the package, and she told you that it just arrived yesterday. The cheese is fine, but the sausage does not taste fresh. You advised Kristen to keep the cheese but throw away the sausage. She should not have to return the sausage—she's been inconvenienced enough already. Write the Wisconsin Cheesery a persuasive claim letter asking for a full refund.

9. Last Monday, you took your car to Craig's Auto Repair for a front brake job. You paid the bill and picked up your car at five o'clock that afternoon. The new brakes seemed to work fine. However, on the way home you heard a clanging noise. When you reached home, you noticed that one of your expensive wheel covers (the front right) was missing. Apparently the garage did not put it back on properly. A replacement wheel cover will cost $75. Write a persuasive claim letter to Craig Johnson, Owner, Craig's Auto Repair, 486 Fourth Street, Tulsa, OK 74128-7690.

10. Two months ago, you had minor surgery and then sent the doctor's bill for $480 to Atlas, your health insurance company. Atlas is supposed to pay 80 percent of all "reasonable" medical fees. Today you received a letter from the insurance company stating that since a reasonable fee for that type of surgery is $320, your doctor overcharged you $160 for the surgery. Atlas will reimburse only 80 percent of $320, and you are liable for the difference. You called your doctor's office to determine if the charges were an error, but the receptionist told you that the bill was correct and that you had to pay the difference. Write a persuasive letter requesting an adjustment to Dr. Phyllis Rice, Broadview Medical Center, 411 18th Avenue, Cleveland, OH 44130-3397.

11. You are volunteer area coordinator of Food for World Hunger, an international charitable organization that sends food to starving people in foreign countries.

To raise money for the annual fund drive, the volunteers set up information booths in local shopping centers. Write a persuasive letter asking permission to set up booths outside all the Dallas-area Archway grocery stores during the week of November 15-22. Address your letter to A. J. Wilkinson, President of Archway Stores, Inc., 1355 Industrial Boulevard, Dallas, TX 75253-2972.

12. You are leader of a troop of 25 eleven- and twelve-year old Scouts. The Scouts are interested in touring a dairy products plant to see milk, butter, and cheese being processed and packaged. Write a persuasive letter asking for a plant tour to be arranged for the Scouts. Address the letter to James R. McPherson, Plant Manager, Sunshine Dairy Products, 1806 Industrial Boulevard, Memphis, TN 38128-3467.

13. You are vice president and program chair of a student professional organization related to your major (such as the Accounting Club or Marketing Club). Your organization needs a speaker for the next monthly meeting. Write a persuasive letter inviting a local business leader to speak to your group about a specific topic. Although your club has no funds to pay an honorarium, you invite the prospective speaker to be your club's guest at dinner before the meeting.

14. Your firm is sponsoring two co-ed exercise groups — an aerobics group and a jogging group. Both groups meet for 30 minutes during the noon hour. As an incentive to participate, the company is extending the lunch hour an extra 15 minutes for those who join either group. The director of human resources has asked you to be in charge of promoting the new exercise groups to all employees. Both groups will tailor the exercise program to meet each employee's needs. No one is too old or out of shape to join. Write a persuasive memo urging all employees to join an exercise group.

15. You are the owner of a four-plex apartment. Yesterday one of your renters called you to complain that the air conditioning would not shut off. The air conditioner is a roof-mounted electric heat pump that doubles as a furnace in the winter. You call Graber's Air Conditioning Service and explain the problem. The service representative on the phone tells you that the problem may be due to a bad relay on the fan motor and that someone will be out right away to repair it.

   You then drive to the apartments to wait for the Graber truck which arrives 30 minutes later. The repairperson gets out of the truck, looks at the roof of the building, and exclaims, "I can't repair that heat pump — it's been raining, and the roof is wet. The dispatcher said that the unit was inside the building. We don't work on air conditioners in the rain because of the danger of electrocution. I'll have to come back tomorrow."

   Two weeks later, you receive a $122 bill for two service calls ($45 each), plus a $32 fan-motor relay. You don't think you should be charged for the first service call, since the service representative who took the order never asked you if the heat pump was mounted on the roof. Write a persuasive letter requesting an adjustment. Address the letter to Graber's Air Conditioning Service, 3002 Jersey Street, St. Louis, MO 63133-4282.

16. Yesterday one of your friends and you had lunch at the Campus Inn, your favorite local restaurant. Unfortunately, your table was next to two tables of cigarette smokers. The smoke was so thick that you were unable to enjoy your meal. Write a letter attempting to persuade the owner, Annette Furillo, Campus Inn, 306 East College Avenue, Birmingham, AL 35217-0993, to set aside an area for nonsmoking customers.

17. Write a letter indicating your opinion about a current event, a controversial topic, or a problem at your college or university (for example, lack of parking spaces). Address the letter to the editor of your college's student newspaper or to the dean of students. Using the indirect plan of organization, write a letter suggesting a solution to the problem.

18. You are manager of the Home Furnishings Department at Clark's Department Store. Write a memo to Louise Patton, general manager of the store, and request two more sales clerks for your understaffed department. Last month, the overtime totaled more than $3,000 in your department. Hiring two additional employees will cut overtime and actually save money in the long run.

19. As accounting manager at Acme Insurance Company, you write a memo to the director of finance. Your memo suggests abolishing the policy of not allowing employees to take equipment home and recommends a new policy allowing employees to check out the company's new Portacom computers overnight and on weekends. The change in policy would improve the productivity of employees who wish to do work on their own time. The computers are light weight and easy to carry.

20. You are data processing manager for Andrews Insurance Company. Next month, a national computer trade fair is going to be held in Atlanta, Georgia. The latest computer hardware and software will be demonstrated at this three-day trade fair. Your job requires you to be familiar with state-of-the-art computer equipment and software, which will be available in one location at the national trade fair. Unfortunately, you exhausted your travel budget for the year when you attended a week-long computer seminar in Philadelphia. Write a memorandum persuading your boss, Kenneth G. Martin, vice president of administration, to provide an additional $900 in travel funds so that you can attend the conference.

# CASE STUDY

"Well, we finally heard from the other dude ranch in Arizona," announced Risa Gonzales as she greeted her husband at the door. "The letter from Circle C came in today's mail."

Carlos Gonzales read the letter his wife handed him. Then as he slowly looked up, he asked, "What do you think? Where shall we go for Christmas?"

Risa Gonzales had written to two dude ranches in Arizona for specific information on facilities and expenses.

Can you comfortably and affordably house a family of five for two weeks? Do you have someone to care for our two-year-old daughter Nell while the rest of the family goes sightseeing? Is transportation available? Will we have to eat all our meals in the restaurant (with three children)?

The two ranches — Wrangler's Ranch and Circle C — each responded by mail. The letters are reproduced below. As you read the letters, think about the Gonzales family's needs.

---

(Letter A)

Mr. Risa Gonzales
3210 Watline Place
Laurel, MD 20708-0391

Dear Mr. Gonzales:

We're so pleased to receive your letter asking about the <u>Circle C Dude Ranch</u>. We're just as sure as can be that <u>you</u>, Mr. Gonzales, will love visiting Phoenix, Arizona. All of us like it here, and we're sure you will too!

Imagine yourself sitting around the pool sharing small talk with a bevy of BEAUTIFUL GIRLS—or dancing 'til dawn under the clear Arizona moon. Sounds too good to be true? But there's more!

We organize tours to all the interesting parts of the Valley of the Sun. The price of a tour includes admission to points of interest, meals, and all the BEER you can drink on the bus ride to and from the tour site.

I've enclosed a brochure describing all the other interesting and exciting things about <u>Circle C Dude Ranch</u>.

When you've made a decision, write to us again and we'll make the arrangements.

Looking forward to hearing from you, I remain,

Yours truly,

Joe Pilcher, Manager

---

(Letter B)

Mrs. Risa Gonzales
3210 Watline Place
Laurel, MD 20708-0391

YOUR CHRISTMAS VACATION IN THE VALLEY OF THE SUN

Thank you for writing us about Wrangler's Ranch--the real Western family fun vacation ranch.

At Wrangler's Ranch your family can:

* Ride through the desert on horseback
* Go on a hayride on a horse-drawn wagon
* Enjoy a cowboy cookout of steaks grilled over a mesquite-wood fire
* Go on a jeep trip to an authentic ghost town
* Visit the Papago Indian reservation and visitors' center
* Attend an old-time barn dance
* Swim in our Olympic-sized heated pool
* Relax in our soothing hydro-spa
* Take a luxurious steam bath
* Play 18 holes of golf
* Take a sunbath in the warm Arizona sun

Yes, all of the accommodations you asked about in your letter are available at Wrangler's Ranch. Because Wrangler's Ranch has hosted family vacations for 25 years, we have anticipated--and met--the needs of the Gonzales family; specifically:

1. Our family bunkhouses have two bedrooms, each with twin beds, and the living room sofa opens into a queen-size bed. The kitchen is fully equipped with all cooking utensils and dinnerware. If you don't wish to cook, you can enjoy delicious home-style meals in the Ranch dining room. A family of five will feel right at home at Wrangler's Ranch.

2. Nursery facilities are available for our younger guests, age 0 through 6 years old. The nursery is open seven days a week from 7:30 a.m. to 8 p.m. Supervised activities available for older children include horseback riding lessons, arts and crafts, swimming lessons, and junior rodeo.

3. Wrangler's Ranch provides limousine service to and from the airport. Simply call us at 555-8946 when

```
      you arrive. If you wish to rent a car at the
      airport, rates vary from $14.95 to $25 per day.
```

Additional information and photos of our 800-acre
guest ranch are included in the enclosed brochure. All
these facilities are provided for $85 per day for a
family of five, plus moderately-priced meals in the
Ranch dining room.

Since Christmas is our most popular season, you will
need to make your reservations very soon. Call the
Ranch today at 602-555-8946 to make sure we will have
accommodations available for your family.

We look forward to having the Gonzales family at
Wrangler's Ranch this Christmas!

John R. "Spunky" Riden, Trail Boss

---

1. Do both letters follow the plan of organization for persuasive messages (establish contact, generate interest and desire, convince, and provide incentive to action)? Explain your answer.
2. Did the writers of both letters plan the message carefully (know the product, know the reader, select the appropriate appeal)? Why or why not?
3. If you were Carlos and Risa Gonzales, which ranch would you select? Why?

## REFERENCES

Courtland L. Bovée and William F. Arens, *Contemporary Advertising* (Homewood, IL: Richard D. Irwin, 1982).

Abraham H. Maslow, *Motivation and Personality* (New York: Harper and Row, 1954).

## SUGGESTED READINGS

Holtz, Herman. *Persuasive Writing*. New York: McGraw-Hill, 1983.

Karlins, Marvin and Herbert I. Abelson. *Persuasion: How Opinions and Attitudes Are Changed*. 2nd ed. New York: Springer Publishing Co., 1970.

Kobs, Jim. *Profitable Direct Marketing: How to Start, Improve, or Expand any Direct Marketing Operation*. Lincolnwood, IL: Crain Books, 1979.

Nash, Edward L., ed. *The Direct Marketing Handbook*. New York: McGraw-Hill, 1984.

Stone, Bob. *Successful Direct Marketing Methods*. 3rd ed. Lincolnwood, IL: Crain Books, 1984.

# BUSINESS REPORTS

## PART 4

People in the business disciplines such as accounting, advertising, computer information systems, finance, management, marketing, and so forth are responsible for preparing various kinds of oral and written reports. As a business student, you undoubtedly will be required to write one or more reports (term papers) each semester as assignments for your business classes.

Business managers rely on written and oral reports for the information they need in making decisions. Reports are used for transmitting routine data as well as for presenting solutions to specific business problems. Written reports are discussed in Chapters 8-11; oral reports are discussed in Chapter 17.

Planning a written report involves identifying the problem, collecting preliminary information, and selecting one or more research methods that utilize secondary or primary sources of data. The researcher then develops a written plan or proposal for management approval.

After collecting the relevant information, the researcher organizes, analyzes, and interprets the data and then writes the report. The writer must select an appropriate level of formality for the report. The report may include various types of relevant graphic aids.

# PLANNING THE REPORT

## CHAPTER 8

"Here's another request for a research proposal!" exclaimed Jeff Hillstrom, a young engineer at Tech-Lex Electronics.

"I don't understand why we plan so many research projects when the Executive Committee turns down half of the proposals we write," he complained.

"You would be surprised just how important our proposals actually are," replied Marsha Weeks, the section manager.

"When one of our proposals is approved, the company invests a great deal of money for research and development. Over $2 million was invested in a research project last year, and two people were promoted because of it," Marsha explained. "One of them developed the proposal and the other one wrote the final report."

As Jeff discovered, reports can be essential to success in one's career. In large organizations, executives and managers rely on internally generated reports as a major source of information for making business decisions. With the advent of computers, small businesses are also able to analyze complex data and prepare business reports.

This chapter discusses different types of business reports and focuses on the planning stage of business research. The following topics are included:

• Purposes and classification of business reports
• Secondary research methods
• Primary research methods
• Outline of the research plan or proposal

## PURPOSE OF REPORTS

The purpose of most business reports is to present objective information relating to a specific business topic or problem. Business reports are used primarily to transmit essential information from one person to another or from one organizational unit to another. Reports give managers the information they need to make business decisions.

## Classification of Reports

Business reports may be either written or oral. Written reports generally have a more complex structure than other written business messages such as letters, while oral reports provide more detailed information than most other forms of oral communication such as meetings. This chapter focuses primarily on written business reports; oral reports are discussed in Chapter 17.

Written business reports differ in subject matter, purpose, destination, length, and format. To meet their needs, organizations use many different kinds of reports which are categorized according to four main classifications: *flow*, *function*, *frequency*, and *formality*.

## Flow

**Flow** refers to the direction in which reports travel within the structure of the organization, from the source to the final destination. Four classifications of reports by directional flow are *upward*, *downward*, *horizontal*, and *external*.

Upward and downward reports flow vertically within the organization. **Upward-directed reports**, which originate at lower levels, are directed to individuals at a higher level. The majority of all business reports flow in an upward direction and are important in the decision-making process. A financial report prepared by the accounting department for the vice president of finance is an example of an upward-directed report.

In contrast, **downward-directed reports** originate at a higher level and are directed to employees at a lower level in the organization. For example, the vice president of marketing might send a sales report to the director of marketing research. Staff assistants of higher-level managers often prepare such downward-directed reports.

**Horizontal reports**, which travel between individuals or departments on the same level in the organization, are essential for coordinating activities among departments. For instance, the accounting department might prepare budgets or financial reports for the production department.

Although the three types of reports described are internal, some reports are directed to individuals outside the company or to other organizations. Examples of external reports include statistical, financial, or other reports to the state or federal government, stockholders, contractors, suppliers, etc.

## Function

**Function** refers to the overall purpose of a report. The two primary functional classifications of reports are *informational* and *analytical*.

**Informational reports** present objective statistical, financial, or other descriptive data. Common examples of informational reports include balance sheets, income statements, budgets, credit reports, sales and other activity reports, project status reports, and annual reports. Informational reports contain objective facts but omit the writer's opinions and subjective interpretations. The writer presents data without analyzing or evaluating, drawing conclusions, or making recommendations.

**Analytical reports** are intended to help solve a specific business problem. An analytical report not only presents objective data but also analyzes and interprets the data, and recommends a solution to the problem. Examples of analytical reports include feasibility studies, investment analyses, market analyses, cost-reduction proposals, and sales proposals.

## Frequency

Two major classifications of frequent reports include *periodic* and *special reports*. **Periodic reports** are issued at regular intervals (such as weekly, monthly, quarterly, semiannually, or annually). Since periodic reports are routine, they often appear as computer printouts that are automatically generated from the company's database. **Special reports**, on the other hand, are usually prepared in response to a specific request by management. A special report may evolve into a periodic report if management requests it more than once.

## Formality

**Formality** is another basis for classifying reports and relates mainly to the format, writing style, and length of the report. The varying degrees of formality are shown in the following diagram:

**informal**    ⟨ - - - - - - - | - - - - - - - | - - - - - - - | - - - - - - - | - - - - - - - ⟩    **formal**
(casual-style                                                                              (academic-
memo/letter reports)                                                                       style reports)

Extremely **informal reports** may appear in the form of a short memorandum or business letter written in a casual style.

At the opposite end of the formality continuum are **formal reports**, which follow a standardized structure and format specified in a style manual. Academic-style reports are prepared in *manuscript* (double-spaced) format. Prescribed parts generally include title page, table of contents, summary or abstract, body, bibliography, and appendices.

In business organizations, many formal reports follow a less standardized format than academic-style reports. If the report is prepared from internally generated sources of data, no bibliography is necessary; other parts may also be omitted. The report may be single spaced, and the writing style, too, may differ from that of academic-style reports.

Formal reports are generally longer, more tightly organized, more objective, and more impersonal than informal reports. Both formal and informal reports are discussed in greater detail in Chapter 11.

## SOURCES OF BUSINESS INFORMATION

The information contained in a business report may come from various sources. In some cases, no research is necessary. For example, a computer might automatically generate a routine monthly sales or inventory report from the company's database. Special reports, however, require the writer to collect data by conducting some type of research.

Although sources of data for business research vary widely, they may be categorized as either *secondary* or *primary*. **Secondary data** come from published materials such as books, newspaper and magazine articles, and government documents. **Primary data** are generated from original sources such as company records, surveys, or experiments.

Business reports often contain both primary and secondary data. To avoid unnecessary duplication of effort, the researcher should first review any available literature on the research subject. If relevant information has already been published, it may provide sufficient data for the report. If the published material is not entirely satisfactory, the researcher may be able to use it for background information or as a model for designing primary research. Secondary data can be used to help the researcher understand the problem, evaluate alternative methods of solution, plan the study, and write a proposal for primary research.

### Secondary Research

A search for secondary data should begin in a business library. Business libraries or business departments of public or academic libraries are available in most cities. Many large companies have their own specialized libraries to serve various departments and employees.

Business libraries specialize in current information on business and economic topics such as finance, investments, tax, marketing, and manufacturing. A business librarian can help locate information relating to various business topics, even if the publications you need are not available in that library. Almost unlimited sources of information are available, usually free of charge, from other libraries throughout the country through the *interlibrary loan services*. By using this cooperative library network, a librarian can locate and obtain just about any type of publication, including books, periodicals, and government documents, usually within two or three weeks.

**Book Indexes.** To find out if the library has books pertaining to a particular topic, first consult the library catalog system. The library will have either a card catalog, microfiche file, or computer terminal in which books are listed alphabetically by subject as well as by title and author. The catalog system will list a Library of Congress or Dewey decimal number for each book in the library. The books are arranged on the shelves by the Library of Congress (LC) or Dewey decimal number. To find the appropriate LC subject heading for your research topic, refer to the reference book entitled *Library of Congress Subject Headings: Principles and Application*. This dictionary-like volume is usually located near the card catalog or terminal.

To find other books on the topic that are not in that particular business library, use *Books in Print* or *Cumulative Book Index*. *Books in Print*, a comprehensive index to all books that are currently published in the United States, includes volumes listing books by subject (*Subject Guide to Books in Print*) as well as by title and author. For books that currently may not be in print, use the *Cumulative Book Index*, which indexes all English-language books that have been published since 1912 by author, title, and subject.

**Periodical Indexes.** To locate newspaper and magazine articles about your topic, use one or more of the business periodical indexes and abstracting services. Abstracting services publish abstracts (short summaries) of articles. *Ulrich's International Periodicals Directory* provides a complete listing of all indexing and abstracting services. The major printed business indexes and abstracting services are listed below:

1. *Business Index* is a subject index of over 800 business publications, including *The Wall Street Journal* and the business section of the *New York Times*, on microfilm. It is the most comprehensive and up-to-date index of business literature available.
2. *Business Periodicals Index*, which is one of the best general indexes to business articles, includes thorough coverage of 350 business periodicals by subject of article. It is more convenient than *Business Index*, which requires the use of a microfilm reader.
3. *Business Publications Index and Abstracts* is a newer service that became available in 1983. It indexes 700 English-language business periodicals by subject and author; it also includes a one-paragraph abstract for each article.
4. *Predicasts F & S Index United States* is probably the best index for finding articles about a specific company, industry, or product. It indexes over 750 business periodicals. *Predicasts* also publishes two similar indexes of articles about foreign businesses and companies (*Predicasts F & S Index Europe* and *Predicasts F & S Index International*).
5. *Predicasts Overview of Markets and Technology (PROMT)* provides abstracts of articles about industries and companies. It focuses primarily on trade journals and is less comprehensive than the *F & S Index*.
6. *The Wall Street Journal Index* is a good source of company information, listed by company name. It contains two sections on general news and

corporate news. For general articles published in *The Wall Street Journal*, the *Business Index* provides more information than *The Wall Street Journal Index*.

**Government Publication Indexes.** The federal government is the largest publisher in the United States. Many of its publications provide statistical, economic, and other information that is valuable to business and industry. The following catalogs and indexes list federal and state government publications:

1. *Index to U.S. Government Periodicals* lists approximately 180 United States government periodicals by subject. Although this index is not specifically business related, it has good coverage of industry and economic information.
2. *Monthly Catalog of United States Government Publications*, published by the United States Superintendent of Documents, lists publications of the federal government.
3. *Commerce Publications Update*, which is printed biweekly, lists titles of the most recent publications of the Department of Commerce. The Department of Commerce also prints an annual *Publications Catalog* that includes a subject index.
4. *American Statistics Index: A Comprehensive Guide to the Statistical Publications of the United States Government* specializes in statistical publications of the government. It has two volumes — an index volume (listing subject, category, and title) and a volume containing abstracts.
5. *Statistical Reference Index Annual* lists statistical publications of state governments and private organizations such as trade associations. It includes an index volume and an abstract volume.

**Computer-Based Search Services.** Computer technology has greatly simplified the process of searching for various kinds of business and economic information. Many libraries, research service companies, and corporations have computer terminals that can access various commercial information services.

A **database** is an organized collection of related information that is stored in computer-readable form. Information service systems can search hundreds of databases and print out a list of relevant publications and abstracts in a few minutes.

Libraries typically pay a monthly fee to gain *online* access to various databases from information service vendors. The term **online** means that a library's computer terminals have direct access to the vendor's central computer. The equipment includes a computer terminal (including keyboard and screen), a **modem** (a device that connects the terminal to the system through a telephone), and a printer. Major information service vendors are DIALOG Information Services, Inc., Bibliographic Retrieval Services (BRS), and ORBIT® (from SDC® Information Services).

A database search can save 90 percent of the time involved in a manual search for sources of relevant information. In only a few minutes, you can obtain a complete up-to-date bibliography and an abstract for each publication listed.

The cost of a computer-based search depends upon the policy of the library conducting the search. Some libraries charge a flat fee, while others charge a fee that varies according to the length of the search. An *average* search takes 15 minutes and costs about $32 (*Directory of Online Databases*, 9). However, a search may cost only a few dollars if the bibliography contains only a few citations. If time is not a crucial factor, you can cut the cost by having the search-service company print the bibliography *offline*, (where the search-service computer is located) and mail it to you. An average offline bibliography takes three to five days and costs about 34 cents per item.

A librarian who is trained in using the system will conduct the computer search. Make an appointment with the librarian to discuss the **search strategy**, which involves choosing an appropriate database and selecting specific **descriptors** (words) to be entered into the computer. If the descriptors are not specific enough, you will receive irrelevant information, and the cost of the search will increase unnecessarily.

Information service vendors offer access to various databases of business and economic information, including indexes, abstracts, directories of companies, and numeric databanks which contain financial and statistical information. Complete descriptions of various databases are found in the *Directory of Online Databases*.

The following bibliographic databases of business and economic information are available from the major information service vendors:

1. *ABI/INFORM* indexes and contains abstracts of over 650 American and international business and management periodicals. Besides using descriptors, ABI/Inform has a classification system which permits users to arrange descriptors in subsets before searching for the specific terms. For example, to search for articles about computer artificial intelligence, the primary descriptor would be "computer"; "artificial intelligence" would be a subset of that category.

2. *Management Contents* is the online version of *Business Publications Index and Abstracts*. It includes citations and abstracts of over 700 international periodicals, books, research reports, proceedings, and other sources of business and economic information.

3. Predicasts *(PTS) F & S Indexes* are the online version of the *Predicasts F & S* indexes. This database encompasses more than 2,500 American and international business publications, including investment advisory services, trade journals, newspapers, government reports, and international agency publications.

**Corporate and Industry Directories.** You can find a wealth of financial and other information about specific American and international companies and industries in the business library. Many comprehensive corporate and industry directories, investment services, and specialized bulletins provide timely reference material for business research.

The following directories and other publications are excellent sources of financial, corporate, and industry information:

1. *Dun and Bradstreet's Million Dollar Directory* is a four-volume annual directory that provides basic information about more than 160,000 privately and publicly owned American companies. It lists each company's address, type of business, approximate sales, other financial data and information on top executives. The volumes are divided alphabetically by company name, with Volume 4 listing firms geographically and by federal Standard Industrial Classification (SIC) code.

2. *Moody's Industrial Manual* includes detailed financial and other information about all companies listed on the major stock exchanges. Annual volumes and weekly reports are available. Moody's also publishes *Moody's Transportation Manual*, *Moody's OTC Industrial Manual* (for unlisted "over the counter" companies), *Moody's Public Utility Manual*, *Moody's Bank and Finance Manual*, *Moody's Municipal and Government Manual*, *Moody's Bond Record*, *Moody's Handbook of Common Stocks*, and various other investment services.

3. *Standard Directory of Advertisers* lists advertising and other information about 17,000 companies. The directory, arranged by industry, includes approximate sales, products, trade names, and advertising costs.

4. *Standard and Poor's Register of Corporations, Directors and Executives* is an annual directory containing information about 45,000 companies. It consists of three volumes, including (1) general information about corporations, listed alphabetically; (2) biographical information of officers and executives; (3) a listing of firms by geographical location and by Standard Industrial Classification (SIC) code.

5. *Thomas Register of American Manufacturers* and *Thomas Register Catalog File* are published annually in 19 volumes. The various volumes contain indexes to cover information on more than 123,000 manufacturers, specific products, and trade names. The catalog file contains copies of company product catalogs.

**Other Information Sources.** To find additional sources of information in the business library, consult *Business Information Sources* or *Encyclopedia of Business Information Sources*. Other sources of secondary data not available in libraries are provided through special financial, investment, tax, and other services such as *Dun and Bradstreet's Credit Service*. The *Directory of Business and Financial Services* is a good reference guide that lists various types of special subscription services.

The process of searching for secondary sources of business information is summarized in Figure 8.1.

## Primary Research

When the information you need is not available from secondary sources, consider conducting *primary (original) research*. **Primary research** involves the

## FIGURE 8.1 SECONDARY RESEARCH SOURCES

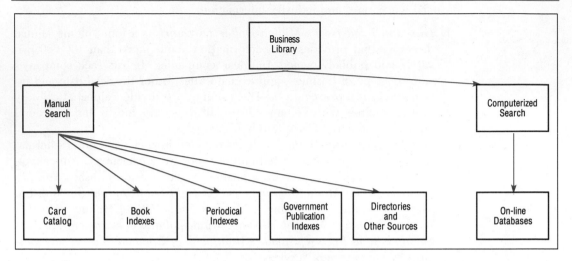

use of one or more of the following methods of obtaining information:

1. Observational (passive) research
2. Survey research
3. Experimental research

Research methods are not mutually exclusive. Many researchers use more than one method of collecting data for a single project.

**Observational Research.** **Observation** involves *passive* methods of data collection; that is, the individuals or groups that are being studied do not actively participate in the research process. Data are collected in ways other than involving people in experiments, surveys, or interviews.

Two types of passive research are (1) direct or indirect observation and (2) correlational studies.

**Direct or Indirect Observation** is a means of collecting data by systematically observing and recording events as they occur. These methods are often used to collect marketing and sales data. For instance, consider a research project evaluating consumer acceptance of a new product being test marketed in a grocery store. An example of direct observation would be to stand by the store display and count the number of people who put the product in their grocery carts.

An indirect method of observation might involve calculating the number of items sold by recording the inventory at the beginning and the end of the day, and by noting the difference. A computerized checkout system could be used as an alternative to provide a method of indirect observation. By scanning the Universal Product Code (UPC) on each item when groceries are checked out, the system automatically enters data into the computer for each item that is sold. The system can instantly indicate the total number of a product sold in a day.

The most important advantage of both direct and indirect observation are objectivity, accuracy, and simplicity. Costs, however, can be great for large-scale studies such as those conducted on a national scale. Another disadvantage is that many kinds of data such as attitudes, intelligence, etc., cannot easily be observed, while some types of information cannot be observed without invading people's privacy.

**Correlational studies** are another method of observational research. With this method, no new information is actually collected. This technique utilizes existing data (from secondary sources) and analyzes the data statistically to discover new information. *Correlation* is a statistical value that shows the relationship between separate variables (existing factors). Researchers use this technique to analyze an existing database, such as company records or government and industry statistics, to discover new relationships between the variables contained in that data. Various statistical techniques such as correlation coefficients and regression analyses are used to determine the relationship between variables and to make predictions for the future.

For example, a company might need to identify factors characterizing good and bad credit risks to develop guidelines for evaluating credit applications. The best source of information for this project probably would be the existing database of company credit records. A statistical computer program could be used to calculate the relationship between customers' credit records and various factors such as occupation, income, and previous credit rating. This information would be used to develop a statistical profile of customers who are likely to pay their bills on time.

Insurance companies also use correlational studies to calculate risk factors such as age, gender, and cigarette smoking. Economists use similar techniques for economic forecasting, and market researchers use these methods for determining projected sales and optimum prices.

Correlational studies generally have the advantage of being objective and accurate. However, a major problem is that the results are only as accurate as the database. The results will not be valid if the database is outdated or contains errors and omissions. Therefore, the researcher should consider using correlational methods only if the accuracy of the database can be verified.

Another potential problem is that the results of correlational studies can be, and often are, misinterpreted. Although this type of research can identify relationships between variables, those relationships do not necessarily indicate cause and effect.

We have no way to determine if variable $A$ caused variable $B$, or if variable $B$ caused variable $A$. For instance, an insurance company might study factors related to poor health and identify low income as a related variable. However, the researcher has no way of determining whether low income causes poor health or if poor health causes low income. The possibility also exists that $C$, an unidentified factor, might cause both low income and poor health.

**Survey Research**. Researchers use the **survey** technique to obtain data by asking people for information. Surveys used for business research are generally conducted by interviews that are either face to face, over the telephone, or by questionnaires.

If a firm conducted a telephone survey to determine if a television advertising campaign was effective, they probably would not have enough time or money resources to call every household in the city. Instead, they would probably select a smaller group of people (the *sample*) who would fairly represent all television viewers in the area (the *population* they wish to study). **Sampling**, which is used in conducting nearly all surveys, is based on the mathematical probability (chance) that the sample will have characteristics similar to those of the population that the researcher wants to study.

Public opinion polls such as the Harris and Gallup polls use sampling techniques to collect political and other kinds of data from small groups of people who are representative of the public. Marketing researchers use sampling techniques extensively when surveying consumers about various products. Quality-control researchers rely on sampling because they could not possibly open every can or package to examine and test products. Similarly, auditors use sampling techniques because examining every financial transaction would be too time consuming and expensive.

A systematic means of sample selection is an important consideration in conducting surveys. Common sample-selection techniques include (1) random sampling, (2) sequential random sampling, (3) stratified random sampling, and (4) convenience sampling.

**Random sampling** is the most scientific method of sample selection. With this method, every member of a population has an equal chance of being included in the sample. For example, a firm conducting a survey of its customers might manually select a 10 percent sample by printing the name of each customer on a card, mixing the cards in a box, and randomly drawing 10 percent of the cards. Today, however, a company would be more likely to choose the random sample by using a computer to match customers' account numbers with *random numbers* selected by the computer.

**Sequential random sampling** is a method commonly used when the population to be surveyed is not classified numerically. If an alphabetized list of customers contains no identifying numbers, a researcher might randomly draw a number between one and ten (for example, seven), select the seventh name on the list and every tenth name after that. In other words, he or she would select the seventh name, the seventeenth name, the twenty-seventh name, and so on until the end of the list.

**Stratified random sampling** is a technique frequently used for sampling subgroups within a population. Marketing researchers often employ this method when they need to sample groups by predetermined criteria other than random selection (for instance, age, income, gender). First the researcher systematically divides the population into subgroups and then randomly draws samples from each of the subgroups. For example, a firm might conduct a survey of the reactions of four major ethnic groups to a television commerical. For this particular study, the research design might specify the selection of 25 subjects from each of the four groups, even though the ethnic groups may not actually be dispersed equally throughout the population. The researcher would then randomly select a sample of 25 subjects from each of the four ethnic groups.

**Convenience sampling**, which is the least scientific method of sampling, uses nonrandom means of selecting subjects to be surveyed. Sample selection is based on convenience rather than mathematical probability. Convenience sampling is used in business research when low cost and fast results are more important considerations than precision. Handing out questionnaires to people who happen to be in a shopping mall and interviewing people walking down the street are common examples of convenience sampling.

The major drawback to convenience sampling is that the sample may not be representative of the population. For example, if you wanted to find out consumers' spending patterns on groceries in your city, you might decide to use a convenience sample of shoppers in a suburban grocery store between 10 a.m. and 2 p.m. on a Wednesday. From the sample of shoppers surveyed, you might conclude that the average grocery bill in your city is $75 per week. However, the average found in the survey might not be representative of the population (i.e., grocery shoppers throughout the city) because of other variables that may have affected the selection of your sample. The time of day, day of the week, average income level of people in that particular neighborhood, and nature of the store you selected might all have some influence on the composition of your sample. Because of the day and time in which you conducted the survey, perhaps nonworking people (retirees, homemakers, etc.) are over-represented in your sample. Or, perhaps the store you selected might be located in an area of people who have lower- or higher-than-average incomes. An additional factor could be that cost-conscious people tend to shop on Wednesdays because the grocery sale advertisements are printed in the local paper on that day. Or, perhaps the store you selected has higher-than-average prices, and thus low-income people might seldom shop there. All of these factors might affect the results of your research.

Surveys rely on either *interviews* or *questionnaires* as a means of collecting data. **Interviewing** is a common data-collection technique in small-sample research. **Mailed questionnaires** are usually preferred in large-scale research projects because they are more cost effective. In comparison to mailed questionnaires, **personal interviews** are an extremely labor-intensive, time-consuming, and expensive method of data collection.

Interviews may be conducted in person or over the telephone. Although telephone interviews are less expensive to conduct than face-to-face interviews, personal or confidential information generally cannot be elicited effectively over the telephone. To obtain meaningful information, the interviewer must be able to gain the respondent's trust. If not, the respondents may be unwilling to provide honest answers. Interviewers should identify themselves, briefly explain the purpose of the interview, and assure the respondent that her or his answers are confidential.

The interview questions, as well as the interviewer's behavior, should be neutral, unbiased, consistent, and should in no way influence the respondents' answers. To prevent such problems, interviewers should be trained in appropriate interviewing techniques, which are discussed in greater detail in Chapter 13.

Mail surveys have several practical advantages such as objectivity, cost, and ease of distribution. A carefully worded questionnaire can be more objective than an interview because it lessens the possibility of human error on the part of the interviewer. By using a well-designed printed questionnaire, the researcher can ensure that respondents are asked identical questions. Because of their low cost and ease of distribution, mailed questionnaires are particularly advantageous for surveys encompassing a wide geographic area.

Questions should be easy to understand and answer and should not be vague or too personal. Avoid "leading" questions that give a cue to the respondent. For example, "What is your favorite brand of ice cream?" would be preferable to "Is Woody's your favorite brand of ice cream?"

If a questionnaire is poorly designed, it may not produce reliable results. **Reliability**, a term applied to various kinds of research, means consistency of results. For instance, a questionnaire that is ambiguously worded would be unreliable because individuals could interpret the questions differently. Chapter 9 includes a more detailed discussion of questionnaire design.

An important issue often overlooked in mail surveys is the problem of low response rates. People who respond tend to have stronger feelings (either positively or negatively) about the survey topic than people who do not respond. Therefore, a low rate of response is an indication that the respondents may not be representative of the sample.

Researchers use various methods to increase the rate of response to mail surveys. Using first-class postage, attaching a persuasive cover letter to the questionnaire, handwriting the letter signature, sending reminder letters, following up with telephone calls, and providing incentives such as free samples or coupons are common techniques for improving the rate of response.

**Experimental Research**. Although experimental research has been traditionally used in the sciences, it is also becoming popular in business. In experiments, the variables are carefully controlled and measured. The researcher selects two or more sample groups and then exposes them to one or more *treatments* while holding other factors constant. In a typical experiment, the researcher randomly divides the subjects into two groups of equal size. One group is the *experimental* group that receives some special treatment, and the other group is a *control* group that receives no treatment or a different type of treatment.

For example, a medical researcher might test the effectiveness of a new flu vaccine by assigning a group of volunteers to one of two test groups by drawing their names randomly out of a hat. Random assignment to treatments will ensure that the two groups are equivalent. One group receives an injection of the vaccine, and the other group receives an injection of saline solution. Later, after both groups are exposed to a flu virus, the researcher can determine whether the experimental group remained healthier than the control group.

In business research, experiments are usually conducted in the *field* (natural environment) rather than in the laboratory. Experiments are used to test the effectiveness of variables such as different types of training programs, marketing strategies, price changes, and product designs. In field as well as laboratory experiments, however, subjects must be randomly assigned to the experimental or the control group rather than being allowed to choose the type of treatment they receive. If the groups are not randomly assigned to treatments, then the results might be caused by prior differences between the groups rather than by the difference in treatment that they received.

Field experiments are somewhat limited by the difficulty of controlling variables in the business environment. For example, if the experimental and control groups work together, the research results might not be valid if the subjects discuss their treatments and share information with one another. If the two groups are physically separated, other *nuisance* (uncontrolled) variables might affect one group and not the other group, or affect one group differently than the other group. For instance, one group might have a supportive supervisor and the other group might have a supervisor who is opposed to the research; this nuisance variable might affect their attitudes or performance in some way.

The research method (observation, survey, or experiment) chosen for a particular business problem depends on factors such as the nature of the problem, the budget, and time constraints. The method of research should be valid for the problem that has to be solved. Research **validity** means that (1) the research measures what it is supposed to measure and (2) the results can be generalized from the sample or experimental group to the entire population of interest.

## OUTLINE OF THE PLAN

After determining what information is needed and selecting a method of research, the researcher must develop a plan for the research. The written plan for a routine business report might consist of a simple outline if the information is already available in the company's database. The following example outlines the plan for a simple periodic report:

ADMINISTRATIVE SERVICES DEPARTMENT
QUARTERLY BUDGET-ANALYSIS REPORT

1. Obtain sources of data
   A. "Annual Department Budget" report
   B. "Monthly Personnel Costs" reports for the quarter
   C. Monthly printouts from the purchasing department
   D. Monthly telephone bills for the quarter

2. Analyze data
   A. Insert spreadsheet disk into microcomputer Drive A
   B. Insert disk labeled "Budget Analysis Report" into Drive B
   C. Open file and enter data
3. Print five copies
4. Distribute copies to departments
   A. Purchasing
   B. Accounting
   C. Personnel
5. Retain two copies for department files

Analytical reports that present solutions to special business problems generally require a more complex research plan. A research plan that has not yet been approved by management is called a **research proposal**. Some organizations submit proposals for externally funded research projects to government agencies or other organizations. Because of its complexity, however, this type of proposal is not discussed in this chapter.

Before attempting to write a research proposal, a researcher should clearly define the specific business problem that he or she wishes to solve. The first step in designing a research project is to identify the main issues and determine what information is already available and what is not. Next the researcher designates the purpose and objectives of the study, gathers background information, and identifies limiting factors. Then the researcher selects specific research methods and procedures and finally writes a research proposal.

The following outline shows the parts of a typical plan or proposal for an analytical report:

RESEARCH PROPOSAL

1. Identifying information
   A. Title and topic of project
   B. Authorization for project
   C. Name, title, and department of researcher
2. Purpose of research
   A. Background information
   B. Problem statement
   C. Scope of project
3. Procedures
   A. Sources of secondary data
   B. Description of primary research methods
      (1) Data collection
      (2) Data analysis
   C. Research limitations
4. Description of report format
5. Personnel and time schedule
6. Budget

Although the information included in a research plan or proposal may differ from this outline, these sections are fairly typical of detailed proposals. However, many proposals likely will contain fewer parts and less detail.

## Identifying Information

The written research plan should begin with a brief identification section or cover page. This section should include the four w's (who, what, where, and when). The authorization states for whom the report is prepared. For example:

RESEARCH PLAN

Testing Consumer Acceptance of Proposed Packaging
for Hansen's Frozen Dinners
in Selected Los Angeles Supermarkets
Prepared for
Harry B. Dalton, Vice President of Marketing
Prepared by
Kristen C. Ayala, Assistant Director of Research
October 15, 19--

## Purpose of Research

This part of the proposal discusses the *what* and *why* of the research project. The **introduction** or **background information** section provides a general discussion of the research topic and explains why the research is necessary. The **problem statement** summarizes the objectives of the study, for example:

To test market a new styrofoam container for Ryan's Frozen Dinners, the research department will conduct a survey of consumers' reactions and report the research results.

The **scope** of the project is what the study will include and what it will not include, for example:

The study will include factors related only to the appearance of the packaging. Other considerations such as durability and cost of the packaging will not be evaluated.

## Procedures

The procedures section outlines the *how* or the proposed research methods, including the sources of secondary data. Some proposals also include a complete bibliography.

The proposal should clearly outline the design of primary research projects and present the anticipated methods of *data collection*. Some research proposals include copies of questionnaires or list specific questions to be asked in interviews. The validity and reliability of specific research techniques may be discussed along with a description of methods of *data analysis* which will be used, including the use of statistical tests.

The research *limitations* identify and discuss constraints, such as lack of funding, time, or trained personnel. Restricting a study to three stores in the Los Angeles area instead of conducting a national survey is an example of a limitation.

## Description of Report Format

The plan briefly describes the report format. Will it be in the form of a computer printout, memorandum, or a formal printed report?

## Personnel and Time Schedule

The personnel section outlines the specific responsibilities of the various personnel who will be involved in the research. The time schedule indicates the tentative dates on which the various phases of the research project will be completed.

## Budget

Finally, the plan should include an itemized budget for the entire research project, including cost of materials, personnel, consultants, equipment, printing, postage, travel, and so forth. Many cost-conscious managers believe that the budget is the most important part of a research proposal.

An example of a research proposal is shown in Figure 8.2.

### FIGURE 8.2 RESEARCH PROPOSAL

PROPOSAL FOR A STUDY OF THE USE
OF THE APEX ELECTRONIC MAIL SYSTEM

Prepared for
Mary C. Nadorff, Director of Administrative Management
Prepared by
Karen Layton, Management Analyst
June 1, 19—

Background Information

Based on company projections and information provided to us last year by Tang, Inc., our firm estimated that a Tang Electronic Mail System would

increase the productivity of our internal communications. As a result of those projections, a Tang
system was purchased and installed last January. To
date, the effectiveness of the system has not been
evaluated.

## Problem Statement

The proposed research project will determine the
level of utilization and effectiveness of the new Tang
Electronic Mail System.

## Scope of Project

The project will involve determining the current
level of employee use of the electronic mail system
and comparing that level with previous projections.
The study will evaluate both quantitative and
qualitative factors but not costs.

## Data Collection and Analysis

Quantitative data will be obtained by accessing
relevant records in the company's database. Qualitative data will be obtained by conducting a survey of
company employees and by analyzing the results of that
survey.

## Limitations

The survey will be limited to a random sample of 100
of the 500 employees who are presently authorized to
use the electronic mail system.

## Report Format

Ten copies of a formal typewritten report will be
prepared and submitted to Mary Nadorff by September 1
for presentation at the next Executive Committee
meeting.

## Personnel and Time Schedule

| Date | Personnel | Activity |
|------|-----------|----------|
| July 1-14 | Anne Weatherly | Develop a computer program to generate frequency-of-use data on the electronic mail system since its installation. |

| July 15–21 | Joyce Hughes | Compare the actual system use with last year's projections. |
| July 22–31 | Joyce Hughes | Design and pretest a questionnaire to measure company employees' evaluations of the quality of the system. |
| Aug. 1–6 | Mark Ortega | Collect data from a random sample of 100 managers, supervisors, and administrative support staff. |
| Aug. 7–15 | Joyce Hughes Mark Ortega | Code, edit, and analyze data. |
| Aug. 6–31 | Joyce Hughes | Write the report. |
| Sept. 1 | Joyce Hughes | Submit the report to M. Nadorff. |

Budget

| Salaries (Hughes, Ortega, Weatherly) | $10,500 |
| Supplies | 250 |
| Printing | 450 |
| Total costs | $11,200 |

## SUMMARY

Business reports are an important way of transmitting objective information from one organizational unit to another. Both written and oral reports provide managers with the information they need for solving business problems and for making appropriate decisions. Various types of written business reports are classified according to flow, function, frequency, and formality.

The sources of data used to prepare business reports may be categorized as either secondary or primary. Secondary research uses published materials as the sources of data; primary research uses data collected first hand.

Conducting secondary research requires a knowledge of the sources of information available in the business library. Business students should be able to use the various business indexes, computer-based search services, directories, and other sources of business information.

Primary research methods include observational, survey, and experimental research. A carefully designed study should be valid and the measurement techniques should be reliable.

The final step in planning a research project is to develop a written outline of the plan or to write a formal proposal. A proposal should include identifying information, purpose of research, procedures, description of report, personnel and time schedule, and budget for the project.

## CHAPTER REVIEW

1. Identify and discuss the four classifications of business reports.
2. Describe the directional flow of business reports in organizations.
3. Distinguish between *informational* and *analytical* reports.
4. How do *formal* and *informal* reports differ?
5. How could you find and obtain current books that are not in the library you are using?
6. How can computer technology be used in searching for *secondary sources* of business information? Describe a typical system.
7. How expensive is a computer search for a term report? Explain your answer.
8. Describe the procedures you would use to find articles about *fiber optics*.
9. What are *correlational studies*? Discuss how they are used in business research.
10. Define *random sampling* and discuss its advantages.
11. Discuss the advantages and limitations of *convenience sampling*.
12. Discuss the advantages and disadvantages of *surveys* as a method of data collection.
13. Describe the characteristics of *experimental research*.
14. Define the following terms:
    a. *database*
    b. *observational research*
    c. *stratified random sampling*
    d. *reliability*
    e. *validity*
15. Differentiate between the terms *scope* and *limitations* in a research proposal.

## APPLICATIONS

1. In each of the following cases, which type of primary research (observational, survey, or experimental) would be best? Defend your answer.
   a. Measuring consumers' brand preference for peanut butter.
   b. Determining the need for a day-care center for employees' children.
   c. Counting the number of people who apply for a credit card during the grand opening of a new store.
   d. Determining the relationship between employee age and absenteeism from work at Darvex Company.
   e. Comparing the effectiveness of two unsolicited sales letters that a direct-mail company is considering using.

2. Identify which of the following indexes are available in your college library. List the call number and describe the location of each index (floor, reference section, shelf or table, etc.):
   a. *Subject Guide to Books in Print*

  b. *Cumulative Book Index*
  c. Card catalog or terminal
  d. *Business Periodicals Index*
  e. *Business Index*
  f. *Predicasts F & S Index United States*
  g. *Reader's Guide to Periodical Literature*
  h. *The Wall Street Journal Index*

3. Develop a bibliography of at least two books and ten articles on one of the following subjects. Your bibliography should include (for books) author, title of book, place of publication, name of publishing company, and date of publication. For articles, the bibliography should include author, title of article, name of magazine or newspaper, volume and number, date, and page numbers.
  a. Advertising laws and regulations
  b. Artificial intelligence
  c. Business cycles
  d. Business ethics
  e. Computer graphics

4. What company manufactures each of the following brands? (Use *Thomas Register Company Profiles*.)
  a. Camut surface grinders
  b. Saran wrap
  c. Blue Bonnet margarine
  d. Flurostone concrete floor hardener
  e. Compu-Stick pressure-sensitive labels
  f. Heros bubble gum

5. Using *Thomas Register Products and Services*, identify three companies that manufacture the following products:
  a. Computer decks
  b. Magnesium acetate
  c. Welding temperature indicators
  d. Digital filters

6. Look up the following companies in *Moody's Industrial Manual* and find the following information: (1) mailing address, (2) year of incorporation, (3) number of shareholders, (4) dividends per share last year (end of year).
  a. Coca-Cola Company
  b. General Electric Company

7. Look up the following information in *Standard & Poor's Corporation Records*:
  a. How much long-term debt does ABS Industries, Inc., have?
  b. What is the primary business of Cetus Corp.?
  c. Where and when was Vector Graphic, Inc., incorporated?
  d. What famous hotel, ship, and airplane does Wrather Corp. own?

8. Construct a one- or two-page proposal for one of the following research projects. The proposal should contain identifying information, purpose of study

(including background information, problem statement, and scope), and procedures (including research methods and limitations). Be practical but creative in briefly supplying necessary details or background information. Do not include a budget.

a. You are director of marketing research at Olson Cosmetics Company. Ms. Charlene Taylor, president of the company, wants to know the extent of the non-infant market for Olson's Baby Shampoo. She asks you to find out what percent of the consumers who purchase the baby shampoo use it for alternate purposes such as shampooing adults' hair, bathing pets, washing lingerie, etc.

b. You are a research analyst for American Drug Products, Inc., a manufacturer of nonprescription drug products such as eye drops, headache tablets, and cold remedies. The company is preparing to test market a new allergy remedy called "Drialine" in six locations throughout the country. George Farnsworth, the director of research, wants you to design a study comparing the effectiveness of two advertising media — magazine versus television ads.

c. You are personnel director for Kahn, Canter, and Burns (a large local public accounting firm). Harriet Kahn, one of the managing partners, is concerned that stress from working long hours during tax season may be causing employees to become physically ill. (This year several accountants developed serious illnesses such as ulcers and heart disease.) She would like you to conduct a study to find out if such a correlation actually exists. The information you need (hours worked per week and rate of employee absenteeism) is already available in the computer database.

d. You are personnel manager for Cactus Software Development, Inc. Recently you have become concerned about the high rate of turnover among Cactus' computer programmers in the past six months. You decide that some type of research should be undertaken to determine why this group is leaving. You believe that the data should be collected from employees who resign or who have already left the company. Your proposal should be directed to Arlene Hunter, vice president.

9. Last January your company purchased 175 microcomputers for its employees. As manager of operations, you want to find out to what extent the computers are being used and for what purposes. You have a hunch that many computers are merely collecting dust on people's desks. Write a memorandum to Mary Rose Wilcox, the director of research. The memo should request an appropriate study of computer usage and results should be available one month from today. Your memo should contain the following information: title, authorization, background information, problem statement, scope, procedures (data collection and analysis methods, limitations), description of report format, and time schedule. Give Ms. Wilcox the authority to make decisions about the budget and assignment of personnel to the project.

10. Orally present the above proposal to the class and have the members of the class discuss the strengths and weaknesses of your proposal, particularly the research methods.

## CASE STUDY

Glenda James, a training coordinator at Gas and Electric Utilities, Inc., sat with her co-workers during a coffee break.

"I'm really disappointed," she told them. "Do you remember the research proposal I submitted last week? Well, it was turned down."

"That's too bad," Chuck Baker said. "You had some terrific ideas for a research project."

"Yes, we need to learn more about the effectiveness of our training programs," Karen Sareno agreed. "Why was the proposal rejected?"

"I don't know," Glenda replied. "Let's look it over when we get back to the office. Perhaps you can give me some feedback."

After the break, the group looked at Glenda's proposal:

RESEARCH PROPOSAL:
MEASURING THE EFFECTIVENESS OF THE TRAINING PROGRAMS
AT GAS & ELECTRIC UTILITIES, INC.

### Purpose of Proposed Project

Gas and Electric Utilities, Inc., has a policy of promoting its own employees to management positions rather than hiring managers from outside the organization. For this reason, the training department is responsible for preparing and implementing effective management development programs for potential managers.

In keeping with this philosophy, the training department attempts to use state-of-the-art methods in these programs. Therefore, the training department proposes research to identify the effectiveness of current training methods.

The objectives of the proposed project are as follows:

1. To identify the methods now being used in the training department;

2. To evaluate the effectiveness of various methods in teaching management skills;

3. To recommend ways to improve the current training program.

## Procedures

An experiment will be conducted that will use the following methods of data collection:

1. Trainees under age 40 will be assigned to Group A. Trainees who are 40 and over will be assigned to Group B. One group will receive an experimental type of training, and the control group will receive a traditional (lecture) type of training.
2. To assure randomization, a coin will be flipped to determine which group (A or B) is the experimental group and which is the control group.
3. Effectiveness of each training method will be determined by the trainees' evaluation of these methods.

## Budget

| | |
|---|---:|
| Identification of new teaching methods | $2,000 |
| Purchase of training materials | 3,500 |
| Printing of questionnaires to measure trainees' ratings of teaching methods | 500 |
| Statistical analysis | 1,500 |
| TOTAL | $7,500 |

1. What information did Glenda omit or fail to explain fully in her proposal?
2. Identify weaknesses in the research methods outlined in the proposal and discuss how the design of the experiment could be improved.

# REFERENCES

*Directory of Online Databases*, 6, no. 3, Spring 1985, 9.

# SUGGESTED READINGS

Daniells, Lorna M. *Business Information Sources*, Rev. ed. Berkeley: University of California Press, 1985.

Davis, Duane and Robert Cosenza. *Business Research for Decision Making*. Boston: Kent Publishing Company, 1985.

Johnson, H. Webster, Anthony J. Faria, and Ernest L. Maier. *How to Use the Business Library with Sources of Business Information*, 5th ed. Cincinnati: South-Western, 1984.

Wasserman, Paul, Charlotte George, and James Woy, eds. *Encyclopedia of Business Information Sources*, 5th ed. Detroit: Gale Research Co., 1983.

# COLLECTING AND ANALYZING DATA

## CHAPTER 9

Joan Gibbons, accounting manager at Carlisle Electronics Company, was deeply engrossed in thought as she drove out of the company parking lot. She was on her way home from work after attending a stressful meeting chaired by the company's controller.

"What information do I need?" she asked herself as she drove toward the freeway.

Dan Ortega, the controller, had delegated to Joan the responsibility of finding out whether the company's recently leased long-distance telephone lines were cost effective.

Before Joan reached home, she had decided to look for answers to the following questions:

1. Have other companies found leased long-distance phone lines to be cost effective?
2. Has the service increased the number and length of long-distance calls at Carlisle?
3. Are employees abusing the service by making personal calls?
4. What are the projected overall cost savings or increases at Carlisle since the lines were installed?

"I just have to figure out how to get all that information," Joan said to herself.

Joan Gibbons knew that collecting and analyzing research data are complex processes. She was aware that a researcher can obtain data from a variety of internal and external sources to solve a business problem.

This chapter, which focuses on methods of collecting and analyzing business research data, discusses the following topics:

- Searching the company database
- Gathering secondary data
- Collecting primary data
- Designing questionnaires
- Conducting survey interviews
- Selecting other methods of collecting data
- Classifying and coding data
- Editing data
- Analyzing data

## SEARCHING THE COMPANY DATABASE

Many business organizations routinely collect, analyze, and store tremendous amounts of internal information. Much of the research that takes place in large companies uses information from an existing database within the company. Before collecting data from external sources, you should determine if the desired information for a research project already exists in the company's database.

To ensure confidentiality of information, many companies require the employees to have a security clearance before certain information in the database is made available to them. The company will usually provide the necessary security clearance for an employee who needs the information for a legitimate purpose.

Most large companies have a **data dictionary**, which is a directory of the contents of the company database. To search for information in the company's database, first consult the data dictionary, which identifies each file name and record layout. The record layout identifies the *fields*, which indicate where the data are located in particular records.

For example, if you were conducting research for a manufacturing company, you might need to forecast seasonal demand for a particular product. By accessing marketing and inventory information contained in the database, such as part numbers, quantity on hand, work in process, and history of previous orders from customers, you could calculate projections of inventory that the company should carry at various times of the year.

As part of the research project, you might need to search the database to find the quantity of a particular product that the company currently has in stock. To find that information, you could look first in the data dictionary to find the file name, for example, "Finished Goods Inventory." In addition, the data dictionary should indicate that in the file each record representing a product that the company manufactures contains these fields: "item number," "description," and "quantity on hand." Therefore, to find the quantity of the item in inventory, you would simply access the "Finished Goods Inventory" file in the database, find the appropriate record, and read the "quantity on hand" field.

## COLLECTING SECONDARY DATA

External sources of business information include both secondary and primary data. As discussed in Chapter 8, **secondary sources of data** include books, periodicals, government documents, and other published materials. **Primary sources of data** include original research such as surveys, experiments, and observational studies.

When you conduct secondary research, the first step is to develop a comprehensive bibliography of secondary sources that pertain to your research topic. Your search should include sources of information available in the business library such as book and periodical indexes, government publication indexes, or computer-based search services.

After you develop a preliminary bibliography of possible sources, your next step is to obtain a copy of the publications listed in the bibliography. Beginning with the most recent sources, look up the publications included in your bibliography. The library may have a hard (printed) copy of a publication or a copy stored on microfilm or microfiche. If not, order the publication through the interlibrary loan services.

Briefly scan the books, articles, and other publications to determine whether they are relevant to the topic. Eliminate irrelevant, outdated, or repetitious publications from the final bibliography.

Copy or photocopy passages in books and articles that you intend to use as references. Some researchers copy information on data (note) cards, which can easily be sorted by category or subject area. Using data cards to record information can expedite the writing of the report. Each data card should have a corresponding bibliography card containing the complete bibliographic reference (author's name, title of article or book, etc.). The format for entries in a bibliography is discussed in Chapter 11. Indicate on the bibliography cards and the data card the relevant page numbers that have been cited. Data cards should contain page numbers but not the complete bibliographic reference.

## COLLECTING PRIMARY DATA

When conducting primary research, review the procedures outlined in the research proposal before beginning to collect research data. If management approves the entire proposal, few, if any, changes in the research design may be necessary. However, management may alter the focus or budget of a research proposal and require a change in the design and/or scope of the project. A budget reduction, for example, might require consideration of a less expensive method of data collection using mailed questionnaires rather than telephone interviews, reducing the size of the sample, or limiting the study to a smaller geographic area than originally proposed.

Research design is nearly always influenced by costs, time, and other practical considerations. However, a researcher should always ensure that the research design is adequate for obtaining valid results. No matter how well written it may be, a business report has little value if the research design is weak. As discussed in Chapter 8, common weaknesses in research design include nonrandom or nonrepresentative sample selection, insufficient sample size, lack of random assignment of subjects to experimental groups, and inappropriate or inaccurate statistical analysis. Such problems may occur if the researcher does not have a strong background in business research methodology, including quantitative/statistical analysis.

## Questionnaire Design

Surveys are one of the most common methods of collecting business research data, particularly from consumers. Survey research involves using personal interviews or questionnaires to collect data from a sample of subjects who are representative of the population that is being studied.

In mail surveys, which are used frequently in business research because of their low cost, the design of the questionnaire is essential to the reliability and validity of the results. A badly designed questionnaire will not produce high-quality data.

Before designing a questionnaire, first refer to the problem statement in the research proposal. The questionnaire should elicit the specific information needed to answer the questions or meet the objectives outlined in the problem statement. Exclude questions that are irrelevant to the purpose of the study.

Determining the structure and format of the questionnaire depends upon the type of research conducted. Some questionnaires contain **open-ended questions** that allow the respondent to write a short answer or description. In contrast, **closed-ended questions** restrict the answer to a specific type or range of responses. Closed-ended questions are usually multiple choice or dichotomous (two-choice answers, such as true-false, yes-no, male-female). The following items are examples of closed-ended and open-ended questions:

**Closed Ended:** The service you received at the restaurant was: (check one)

           _____ Excellent

           _____ Good

           _____ Average

           _____ Poor

           _____ Unsatisfactory

**Open Ended:** Please comment about the quality of service you received at the restaurant.

**Closed-Ended Questions**. Closed-ended questions simplify data coding and analysis because the responses are classified into prearranged categories. Closed-ended questions are also usually easier to analyze statistically than open-ended questions. As an example, an analysis of the responses to the previous closed-ended question might reveal the following range of responses:

22% Excellent

45% Good

20% Average

8% Poor

5% Unsatisfactory

These answers would provide management with important statistical information; namely, that 67 percent of the respondents rated the service at the restaurant as better than average. However, this format does not allow room for details or for the expression of specific problems.

Closed-ended questions are especially useful for eliciting sensitive or controversial data such as age, income, or information about an employer or supervisor. People are generally more willing to answer such questions if they are asked to choose a range rather than to provide an exact figure, as shown in the following example:

What was the total income of your immediate family last year? (check one):

_____ Below $10,000

_____ $10,000 - $19,999

_____ $20,000 - $29,999

_____ $30,000 - $39,999

_____ $40,000 - $49,999

_____ $50,000 or above

When designing closed-ended questions, be sure to provide sufficient categories for the responses and determine that the categories do not overlap. The following example contains insufficient response categories and overlapping categories.

_____ Under 21

_____ 21-30

_____ 30-40

_____ 40-50

_____ 50-60

Three ages (30, 40, and 50) appear in two categories. Also, no category is provided for individuals over 60.

This response format is better:

_____ Under 21

_____ 21-29

_____ 30-39

_____ 40-49

_____ 50-59

_____ 60 or over

When composing multiple-choice questions, make sure that the response format allows for all possible choices, including categories such as *other*, *no opinion*, and *don't know*. The use of too-narrow categories that force respondents to select an inappropriate answer often yields inaccurate data. The following question does not allow for all possible choices:

Which type of milk do you usually purchase? (Check one)

_____ Whole milk

_____ 2 percent butterfat

_____ 1 percent butterfat

_____ Skim milk

The selections provided do not include an appropriate response for a consumer who does not purchase milk or who purchases more than one type of milk. Another problem is that a category is not provided for other kinds of milk, such as buttermilk or powdered milk. In addition, the word "usually" is vague and can be interpreted in several ways. The following question is better:

Which types of milk do you usually purchase at least once a week? (Check one or more responses.)

_____ Whole milk

_____ 2 percent butterfat

_____ 1 percent butterfat

_____ Skim milk

_____ None

_____ Other (please specify) _____

Notice that the last response is open ended. Many questionnaires contain both open-ended and closed-ended questions.

**Open-Ended Questions**. Although closed-ended questions are valuable for revealing general kinds of information, open-ended questions are better for eliciting details. The open-ended version of the question evaluating the restaurant service might elicit the following responses:

The food was marvelous, except for the stale bread.

Excellent service.

Robert, our waiter, was rude and overbearing.

Nonsmoking section was too small.

Rest room was not clean.

The detailed information provided by the open-ended format can be extremely beneficial. However, a statistical analysis of open-ended questions is difficult because the researcher must determine how to categorize a wide variety of answers in a meaningful way. For statistical analysis, the data must be categorized manually and coded before it can be interpreted.

**Organizing and Writing the Questionnaire**. Questionnaire items should be carefully worded so that they are clear, concise, and easy to read. To ensure readability, use simple, concrete language, short sentences, and correct English mechanics. An effective questionnaire should reflect courtesy, a positive tone, the "you" attitude, and sex-fair language. In addition, the questionnaire should contain clear directions for completing each section.

To make the questionnaire seem easier to answer, arrange questions in the most advantageous order. Easy-to-answer items should appear first; difficult or controversial items should appear toward the end of the questionnaire.

Reduce the questionnaire to the shortest form possible for achieving your objective. The simpler the questionnaire appears to be, the more likely people will be to respond. To keep the number of pages to a minimum, print the questionnaire on both sides of the paper and use a fairly small (but readable) typeface.

The questionnaire should include instructions for mailing or submitting the questionnaire, such as depositing it in a collection box or sending it by interoffice mail.

The following questionnaire was designed to collect marketing data from a sample of cable television subscribers:

## SURVEY OF CABLE TV SUBSCRIBERS

DIRECTIONS:    Please answer <u>all</u> the following questions and mail the questionnaire today in the enclosed postage-free envelope.

For each of the following questions, check (√) the most appropriate response.

---

1. What is your age?

(1) _____ Under 21
(2) _____ 21-29
(3) _____ 30-39
(4) _____ 40-49
(5) _____ 50-59
(6) _____ 60 or over

---

2. What is your favorite type of TV program?

(1) _____ Comedy
(2) _____ Action Drama
(3) _____ Other Drama
(4) _____ Game Show
(5) _____ Sports
(6) _____ News
(7) _____ Other (please specify) _____

---

3. On the average, how many hours per week do you personally watch TV?

(1) _____ 5 or less
(2) _____ 6-9
(3) _____ 10-19
(4) _____ 20-29
(5) _____ 30-39
(6) _____ 40 or over

---

4. On the average, how many different channels do you watch in a week?

(1) _____ 1 or 2
(2) _____ 3 or 4
(3) _____ 5 or 6
(4) _____ over 6

---

5. Have you ever recorded cable TV programs on a VCR (video cassette recorder)?

(1) _____ Yes
(2) _____ No

For each of the following statements, please circle the number for the response that most closely indicates your opinion.

| | Strongly Agree | Mildly Agree | No Opinion | Mildly Disagree | Strongly Disagree |
|---|---|---|---|---|---|
| 6. Most TV ads are helpful to consumers. | 1 | 2 | 3 | 4 | 5 |
| 7. Most TV news is biased. | 1 | 2 | 3 | 4 | 5 |
| 8. Movies are the best programs on TV. | 1 | 2 | 3 | 4 | 5 |
| 9. I seldom watch sports on TV. | 1 | 2 | 3 | 4 | 5 |
| 10. I am pleased with the ARTA cable TV service I receive. | 1 | 2 | 3 | 4 | 5 |

11. My favorite current TV program is (please specify):

Do not write in this space.

_____

12. The brand of TV I watch most frequently is (please specify):

Do not write in this space.

_____

Stamp or print the recipient's name on the mailing list and on that person's questionnaire with the same identifying number. As each completed questionnaire is received, you will be able to check off the respondent's name on the mailing list. This procedure enables the researcher to identify nonrespondents and to send them one or more follow-up mailings.

**Pretesting.** To produce a well-designed questionnaire, develop a draft, pretest it, and then make revisions. One or more pretests will be necessary to identify inconsistencies, errors, omissions, ambiguous wording, and unclear directions.

If possible, pretesting should include individuals who are part of the target population or who have characteristics similar to those of the target population. If the intended population of the study consists of assembly-line workers, for example, then the pretest should not be administered to accounting-department employees. The researcher should take care, however, to separate the pretest group in some way from the actual sample selection. In one study, the design of the questionnaire and its pretesting were handled according to the following procedures:

1. Develop a draft of the questionnaire.
2. Have several assembly-line workers in Plant A critique the questionnaire.
3. Revise the questionnaire.
4. Pretest the second draft with a sample of Plant B assembly-line workers.
5. Develop the final draft.
6. Administer the questionnaire to the target group (a sample of assembly-line workers in Plant C).

Ideally the assembly-line workers in all three plants should have had similar characteristics (age, sex, education, work experience, etc.). These factors could be easily determined by collecting the appropriate information from all three groups and comparing them.

**Cover Letter.** A persuasive cover letter should accompany each questionnaire. To be effective, a cover letter should be as well planned and carefully worded as a sales letter. As a persuasive letter, the cover letter should have an inductive (indirect) plan of organization. The "you" attitude, discussed in Chapter 3, is especially important.

For best results, personalize the cover letter as much as the budget permits. Various techniques to increase the rate of response include the use of individualized rather than printed form letters, first-class postage, and handwritten rather than printed signatures. Some researchers use incentives such as coupons and free samples to increase the rate of response. A stamped and addressed or business-reply envelope should always be enclosed.

A cover letter should include the following points:

1. Briefly explain the research project, its significance, and the importance of the respondent's opinion.
2. Emphasize any benefits to the respondent.

3. Mention that the questionnaire will take only a few minutes to complete.
4. Stress that her or his response will be confidential.
5. Ask the respondent to fill out the questionnaire.
6. Express appreciation to the respondent.

The following letter is an example:

---

Dear _____ :

    Would you like to help choose the type of programs that are shown on cable TV?

    You have been selected as one of a group of cable TV subscribers who will have an opportunity to comment on the programs and services that we offer on ARTA Cable Network. By participating in this survey, you will help us provide the type of high-quality entertainment that you enjoy.

    The questionnaire takes only a few minutes to complete. Your answers, of course, will be confidential.

    Please help us plan next year's programs by filling out the enclosed questionnaire and mailing it to us today in the enclosed postage-free envelope. Your assistance will be greatly appreciated.

Cordially,

---

**Follow-Up Messages.** Since a low rate of response is likely to bias the results of a survey, the researcher should send one or more **follow-up messages** to individuals who did not return their questionnaires. Follow-up messages may consist of letters, postcards, or telephone calls. These messages briefly remind the recipient about the research project, stress its importance, and ask her or him to return the questionnaire promptly. Many researchers send two, three, or even four follow-up messages to those who fail to return their questionnaires. Follow-up letters may also include another copy of the questionnaire.

The following letters are examples of survey follow-ups:

---

(First reminder)

Dear _____ :

    Here's a chance to have a say in the programs that are offered on ARTA Cable TV.

Recently you were selected to participate in an important research project on cable television. If you have completed the questionnaire and returned it to us, please accept our sincere thanks.

If you have not, please fill it out and mail it today. The questionnaire takes only a few minutes to complete, and your answers will be strictly confidential.

If you did not receive the questionnaire or if you misplaced it, please let us know. We will make sure that you get another copy right away.

Cordially,

_____

_____

(Second reminder)

Dear _____ :

We value your opinion and want you to be happy with your cable TV service.

Recently we invited you to participate in a research project about cable television. On May 9, we mailed you a questionnaire. If you have already completed it and mailed it, please accept our sincere thanks.

Don't miss this opportunity to "vote" on programs and services that will be available on ARTA. If you have not yet completed your questionnaire, please do it today. We must receive your questionnaire no later than June 15.

We are enclosing another questionnaire in case you didn't receive the first one. The questionnaire takes only a few minutes to fill out, and your answers will be kept confidential.

Cordially,

_____

## Survey Interviews

**Personal interviews**, including face-to-face and telephone interviews, are another method of collecting primary data for business research. Although more expensive than mailed questionnaires, interviews are often used in marketing research, particularly for evaluating consumer acceptance of products being test marketed.

For good results, interview questions must be carefully worded, and the interviewers should be well trained and closely supervised. If not, several problems are likely to develop that might bias the data and invalidate the research.

**Planning Survey Interviews.** The process of developing an interview-type survey is similar to that used in developing a questionnaire. Survey interviews should be more carefully planned and more tightly structured than most other kinds of interviews. (Other types of interviews are discussed in Chapter 13.)

In survey interviews, every interviewee should be asked the same questions, in the same way, and in the same order. Interviews can include either open-ended or closed-ended questions or a combination of both types, all of which should be worded just as carefully as the items in a printed questionnaire. Questions should not lead the interviewee to give a particular response; instead, questions should be neutral.

**Training the Interviewers.** Interviewers should have certain minimum qualifications such as the ability to enunciate clearly, acceptable personal appearance (for face-to-face interviews), good interpersonal skills, and a positive attitude. These qualities are necessary for developing rapport with the subjects who might not be willing to cooperate fully unless they like and trust the interviewer.

Interviewers should be provided with an *interview guide* that includes a sample "script" listing all the questions to be asked in the interview. In addition, they should also be supplied with interview-response forms on which to record the interviewees' answers.

Training the interviewers is essential; training sessions often include the following topics:

1. *How to select the subjects.* Techniques may include procedures for systematically selecting interviewees in stores or shopping malls, appropriate hours to call or visit subjects at home or office, random dialing procedures for telephone interviews, and follow-up procedures.
2. *How to approach the subject.* Procedures should include introducing themselves; identifying the company; and explaining the purpose of the interview, its importance, and the amount of time it requires.
3. *How to develop trust.* Topics that should be discussed are privacy, confidentiality, and respect for subjects' rights.
4. *How to be considerate.* Consideration for the respondent involves courtesy, tact, avoidance of sensitive or embarrassing issues, and expressing appreciation after the interview.
5. *How to be objective.* Objectivity includes following the interview guide meticulously, avoiding giving nonverbal cues or biased feedback to the respondent, and accurately filling out an interview-response form.

Training sessions usually involve role playing, in which the prospective interviewers practice by interviewing one another. Videotaping is an excellent way to give feedback to those participating in the role-playing process.

**Supervising the Interviewers.** Close supervision of personnel is necessary for ensuring the accuracy of the data, particularly when the interviewers are part-time or temporary employees. Some companies routinely survey a sub-sample of interviewees to verify that the interviews actually took place, that the information was recorded accurately, and that the interviewer made a favorable impression.

## Other Methods of Collecting Data

Business researchers sometimes use other means of data collection such as direct observation, and electronic instruments or mechanical devices such as counters. Trained observers are often used in observational and experimental research; the observers unobtrusively watch and record people's behavior.

In experimental research, the observers may be located behind a one-way mirror so that the subjects do not see them. In field studies, the observers may be disguised as maintenance or security personnel. For legal and ethical reasons, however, researchers using such methods should take care not to invade people's privacy or betray their trust.

Electronic or mechanical instruments are a good way of collecting relatively simple data such as counting numbers of people, amounts of money, purchase totals, number of automobiles driving down a street, etc. Turnstiles, electronic door openers, cash registers, and various types of scanning devices are examples of data-collection instruments.

# PROCESSING DATA

When collecting secondary data for a research project, you may begin to sort and analyze the data while collecting it. For example, as you read publications on business applications software, you may make notes on index cards and sort the cards into various categories such as "word processing," "spread-sheets," "database management." Then as you continue reading, you may add cards in these categories and new categories.

In primary research projects, the data must be sorted, checked for accuracy, and analyzed in some way. The steps in processing primary data are classifying, coding, editing, and analyzing.

## Classifying and Coding Data

The data collected from an individual, such as one respondent to a question-naire, make up a *record*. Each record is comprised of individual data items (responses) called *fields*. Collectively the data records of all respondents are entered into a computer to become a *file*. Before questionnaire or interview data can be entered into a file, the data must be in a form that the computer can analyze (sort, count, etc.). First the data must be classified; then, coded.

Classifying involves separating data into categories. In the survey of cable TV subscribers on pages 195-196, for Question 5, only two responses, "yes" or "no," are possible; thus, these data are classified when the respondent checks a response. Question 11, which asks for the respondent's favorite television program, has many possible responses. You may in effect reduce the number of different responses by grouping the responses by type of program or time of the broadcast or by names of program sponsors. Similarly, Question 12, which asks respondents to list the brand names of their television sets, has many possible responses. The responses may be more meaningful if the data are classified in some way such as the manufacturers' location in "domestic" or "foreign" markets.

Coding data involves assigning a code to each possible response. Consider the following item from the cable TV survey:

2. What is your favorite type of TV program? (check one)

_____ (1) Comedy

_____ (2) Action Drama

_____ (3) Other Drama

_____ (4) Game Show

_____ (5) Sports

_____ (6) News

_____ (7) Other (please specify _____ )

Suppose a respondent checks "Comedy" in the example above, while another respondent checks "Game Show" and a third checks "Sports." "Comedy," "Game Show," and "Sports" cannot be entered into the data file because nothing allows these "raw" data to be analyzed. Therefore, a code must be assigned to each possible response; the code, rather than the raw data, is entered into the file. If a respondent to this question checked "Sports," then a "5" would be entered into the data field reserved for responses to Question 2. Numerical codes, rather than alphabetic codes, should be assigned to facilitate analysis of the data.

Responses to open-ended questions also may be coded. For example, in coding the "other" responses to the preceding example, you might assign an "8" to documentaries, "9" to talk shows, "10" to holiday specials, and so on.

Coding also involves assigning the location of each field within a data record. Location codes show the exact positions in the record that a particular response code will occupy and reveal how many digits make up each response code. For the following questions, codes indicating data fields are printed to the right of each item.

Social security number ..................... _____ (1-9)

Age .......................................... _____ years   (10-11)

Sex ....................................... (1) _____ (male)
                                          (2) _____ (female) (12)

Marital status ........................... (1) _____ (married)
                                          (2) _____ (unmarried) (13)

Formal education ............................ _____ years   (14-15)

These location codes show that the data field for social security number will contain nine digits and occupy positions 1 through 9 of the data record, while the field for the age and education items each will contain two digits and occupy positions 10 and 11, and 14 and 15, respectively. The sex and marital status fields consist of one digit each and occupy positions 12 and 13, respectively, in the record.

The first positions in a record may be reserved for codes identifying the particular survey and respondent, in which case the first data field may occupy positions 7-15, for example. Consecutive data fields should be reserved for items in the order listed on the questionnaire or interview-response form.

A researcher should consider the need for coding data while designing questionnaires and interview-response forms. To facilitate data entry, the codes assigned to response categories should be printed on the questionnaire to the left of the corresponding responses. Codes for open-ended items usually are not printed on questionnaires; for smooth data entry, the response codes may be written in the margin beside the item. The location codes should be printed to the right of each item, especially if the data fields vary in the number of digits contained. To facilitate quantitative analysis of the data, the coding must be compatible with the computer software used. For example, the researcher must know how the software will deal with multiple-response items (questions for which respondents are to check all applicable responses). Therefore, the researcher should discuss the research project with the computer specialist who will eventually analyze the data.

## Editing Data

Good researchers are meticulous about the accuracy of their work. To ensure accuracy, carefully check all research data for apparent inconsistencies and errors. Before entering the data, carefully check all questionnaire responses and other raw data for missing information and inaccuracies. In some research projects, you might simply insert a code for "no response" and eliminate that part of the record from the analysis. In research projects that require greater precision, you might need to call the respondent for the missing data.

After entering the data, obtain a frequency distribution for that data; that is, tabulate the number of different responses to each item. This process of editing a second time will identify data-entry and other errors that might have been missed in the initial editing.

For example, the following frequency distribution might summarize the responses to a true-false question:

Question 2:

| Response | Frequency |
| --- | --- |
| 0 | 3 |
| 1 | 35 |
| 2 | 10 |
| 8 | 1 |

Under the "Response" column in this tabulation, "0" is the code for "no response"; "1" is the code for "true"; and "2" is the code for "false." The "Frequency" column indicates that 3 respondents left the item blank, 35 respondents answered "true," and 10 respondents answered "false." However, the "8" entered in the response field for this question probably indicates a data-entry or coding error in one record. By checking the individual records, you can find and correct the mistake.

## Quantitative Analysis

After a researcher edits the data and corrects any errors, the next step in conducting quantitative research is to analyze the data statistically. Before using data to draw a conclusion, the researcher must summarize and interpret the data in a meaningful way. A numerical summary that describes a set of data is called **descriptive statistics**. Three common descriptive statistics are *frequency distribution*, *central tendency*, and *dispersion*.

**Frequency Distribution**. As previously described, **frequency distributions** tabulate the number of different responses to each item. As an example, suppose that the vice president of human resources at Atlas Insurance Company is considering the possibility of offering a writing-skills workshop for the company's insurance agents. To determine if the workshop is needed, the training department administers a short standardized English mechanics test to a sample of 50 insurance agents selected at random from a directory of the company's employees.

After the 50 employees take the ten-item test, a training department employee grades the test and tabulates a summary of the results. Tabulation provides the researcher with a frequency count that reveals how the data are distributed. Although hand tabulation is sometimes satisfactory for small samples, computer tabulation of data is generally a more efficient method for large samples.

The frequency distribution table shown in Figure 9.1 shows the number of correct answers the agents scored (out of ten questions).

## FIGURE 9.1 FREQUENCY DISTRIBUTION

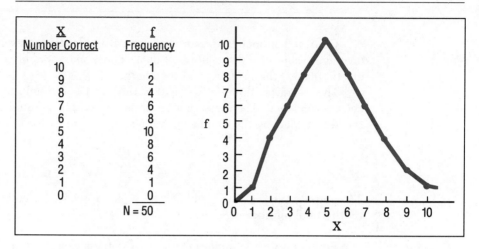

| X Number Correct | f Frequency |
|---|---|
| 10 | 1 |
| 9 | 2 |
| 8 | 4 |
| 7 | 6 |
| 6 | 8 |
| 5 | 10 |
| 4 | 8 |
| 3 | 6 |
| 2 | 4 |
| 1 | 1 |
| 0 | 0 |
| | N = 50 |

The test scores (number of correct answers) are represented by a capital "X." The frequency column (labeled "f") shows the number of agents who earned each score on the test. "N" represents the total number of **observations** (agents who took the test), which is also the *sum* of the *frequency* column.

Figure 9.1 also represents the same data in the form of a graph. The data points, which are plotted on the graph as dots, connect to form a *normal frequency distribution*. This distribution is shaped in the form of a bell curve and is typical of data collected from large samples.

Frequency distributions are commonly translated into percentages. Distributions of sample data are often shown in this form because the same percentages can be applied to the population. To calculate percentages, simply divide the frequency (f) of responses in each category by the total number of respondents (N).

Figure 9.2 shows a distribution of respondents' ages as percent of responses to a survey:

## FIGURE 9.2 PERCENTAGE DISTRIBUTION OF AGES

| Respondent's Age | Frequency (f) | Percent of Total |
|---|---|---|
| Under 21 | 0 | 0 |
| 21-29 | 8 | 16.0 |
| 30-39 | 15 | 30.0 |
| 40-49 | 18 | 36.0 |

| | | | |
|---|---|---|---|
| 50-59 | | 7 | 14.0 |
| 60 or over | | 2 | 4.0 |
| | Total | 50 | 100.0% |

---

**Central Tendency.** Measures of **central tendency** represent the "typical" (average) value of a distribution of data. Three measures of central tendency are the *mean*, the *median*, and the *mode*.

The mean (arithmetic average) is the most commonly used measure of central tendency. The **mean** of a set of data is simply the sum of the values in the set divided by the number of values. The formula for the mean is represented by

$$\overline{X} = \frac{\Sigma X}{N}.$$

To compute the mean ($\overline{X}$), add ($\Sigma$) the separate scores (X) and divide this sum by the total number of scores (N).

For example, a sample of ten real-estate salespersons sold the following number of houses and commercial properties in one year:

| Realtor | No. of Properties Sold (X) |
|---|---|
| 1 | 60 |
| 2 | 45 |
| 3 | 31 |
| 4 | 28 |
| 5 | 20 |
| 6 | 16 |
| 7 | 16 |
| 8 | 14 |
| 9 | 12 |
| 10 | 8 |
| | 250 |

$$\overline{X} = \frac{\Sigma X}{N} = 250/10 = 25$$

In this example, the mean is calculated by dividing 250 (total number of properties sold) by 10 (total number of realtors). Thus, the mean number of properties sold per realtor is 25.

Most statistical procedures involve calculation of the mean. One disadvantage of the mean as a measure of central tendency, however, is that a few very high or very low scores will distort the mean as representative of the entire distribution. For example, a realtor sold the following properties (one large commercial property and nine moderately priced houses) in one year:

Selling Prices (X)

$3,400,000
90,000
82,000
75,000
68,000
66,000
61,000
55,000
53,000
50,000
───────────
$4,000,000

$$\overline{X} = \frac{4,000,000}{10} = \$400,000$$

In this case the one commercial property distorted the mean ($400,000), which was not "typical" of any of the properties.

The **median** is another measure of central tendency. When the set of data is arranged from high to low or vice versa, the median is the midpoint. If the distribution contains a few extremely high or low values, the median is a better measure of central tendency than the mean.

What is the median of the following distribution of salaries?

$75,000
56,000
45,000
45,000
38,000
33,000
31,000
30,000
28,000

When the distribution contains an *odd* number of observations, the median is the middle observation. Here the median salary is $38,000 because four salaries are higher and four salaries are lower.

When the distribution contains an *even* number of observations, calculate the median by taking the midpoint between the two middle observations. In the real-estate example on this page, N = 10. Thus, you could calculate the median by taking the midpoint between the fifth and sixth observations ($68,000 and $66,000). Simply add the two middle observations together and divide by two.

$$\frac{68,000 + 66,000}{2} = 67,000$$

The result is a mean of $67,000.

The **mode** is the most frequently occurring observation in a distribution of data. Although the mode is usually not as satisfactory a measure of central tendency as the mean or median, researchers sometimes use the mode for special types of descriptive statistics.

What is the mode of the responses to the following question?

**How many television sets do you own?**

| Response | Frequency |
|----------|-----------|
| 0 | 2 |
| 1 | 6 |
| 2 | 12 |
| 3 | 8 |
| 4 | 5 |
| 5 | 1 |
| 6 | 1 |

The mode of this distribution of data is "2" because it is the most frequently occurring response (12 responses).

**Dispersion.** Measures of central tendency describe the typical value in a distribution. Measures of **dispersion** describe how the data vary. Three of the most common measures of dispersion are the *range*, the *variance*, and the *standard deviation*.

The **range**, which is the simplest measure of dispersion, is the difference between the largest and the smallest values in a distribution of data. For example, if the highest score anyone earned on a real-estate licensing exam was 95 and the lowest score was 45, then the range is 50 (95 minus 45). The range is a somewhat biased statistical measure because it is affected by the size of the sample. (Large samples tend to have larger ranges than do small samples.)

The **variance** is used primarily as a measure of dispersion when sample data are used to estimate a population. The variance is the mean of the squared deviations from the overall mean of a data distribution.

To calculate the variance, follow these steps:

1. Compute the mean of the distribution by the formula $\overline{X} = \Sigma X/N$.
2. Subtract the mean value from each score in the distribution.
3. Square each item in the results of Step 2.
4. Add the squared differences.
5. Divide this sum by the number of values in the distribution.

In the following example, "X" represents each individual score and "$\overline{X}$" represents the mean of the distribution.

$$(\text{Step 1}) \quad \overline{X} = \frac{\Sigma X}{N} = \frac{220}{5} = 44.$$

|              |          | (Step 2)                    | (Step 3)                    |
|--------------|----------|-----------------------------|-----------------------------|
| Employee     | Age (X)  | $X - \overline{X}$          | $(X - \overline{X})^2$      |
| Frank        | 25       | $-19$                       | 361                         |
| Mary         | 33       | $-11$                       | 121                         |
| Helen        | 46       | $+ 2$                       | 4                           |
| Patty        | 52       | $+ 8$                       | 64                          |
| Thomas       | 64       | $+20$                       | 400                         |
|              | 220      |                (Step 4)     | 950                         |

(Step 5) 950 divided by 5 = 190

The **standard deviation** is the square root of the variance. The standard deviation is generally more convenient to use than the variance because the standard deviation is expressed in terms similar to those of the original distribution of data (such as employees' ages). In the previous example, the standard deviation is calculated by finding the square root of 190, or 13.78 *years*.

The preceding examples demonstrate how various measures of dispersion and central tendency may be calculated. In business organizations, researchers generally calculate these measures on a computer by using appropriate statistical software.

**Statistical Inference.** Researchers analyze data in many ways, depending on factors such as the type of data, the research design, and the size of the sample. Because most business research data are obtained from samples, the researcher must have some degree of confidence that the sample data are actually representative of the population and that the research results did not occur simply by chance. The concept of drawing inferences from research data is called **statistical inference**.

By using various statistical techniques, researchers can rule out the possibility that results were obtained by fluctuations in measurements. Some of the more common statistical techniques available are *t-tests*, *analysis of variance*, *analysis of covariance*, *chi-square test*, *correlation coefficients*, and *regression analysis*. Detailed description of these methods of quantitative analysis is beyond the scope of this textbook; however, these techniques are discussed in most business statistics books. Researchers use standard statistical software packages to calculate these statistical tests on the computer.

## SUMMARY

Business researchers use a variety of methods to collect and analyze data. When attempting to solve a business problem, a researcher may obtain information from various sources such as the company's database, secondary research, or primary research.

When collecting primary data, researchers often design questionnaires or interview-type surveys. Both kinds of surveys should be carefully planned, organized, and pretested.

After collecting data, the researcher should sort it, check it for accuracy, and analyze it. These procedures are data classification, coding, editing, and quantitative analysis.

When analyzing data, researchers typically begin by obtaining descriptive statistics such as frequency distributions, central tendency, and dispersion. Researchers use computers to calculate various statistical tests, depending on the type of data, the research design, and the sample size.

## CHAPTER REVIEW

1. Describe how an employee can search for and obtain information in a company's database.
2. Distinguish between *open-ended* and *closed-ended* survey questions; describe the advantages and disadvantages of each.
3. Explain how a researcher can determine which questionnaires are returned in a mail survey.
4. Discuss how a researcher can obtain a high rate of return in a mail survey.
5. Describe how you would develop and pretest a questionnaire to measure customers' evaluations of the effectiveness of sales clerks in a department store.
6. Why do survey interviewers need formal training? What information should be presented in interviewer training sessions?
7. In addition to surveys, what other external methods of collecting data are used in business research?
8. Distinguish between *classifying* and *coding* data.
9. Define *descriptive statistics*. List three types of descriptive statistics.
10. Describe three forms that a *frequency distribution* can take.
11. List and describe three measures of central tendency.
12. Distinguish between *central tendency* and *dispersion*.
13. Define the following terms:
    a. *Range*
    b. *Variance*
    c. *Standard deviation*
14. Define *statistical inference* and discuss its use in business research.
15. How can a business researcher conduct complex statistical tests accurately?

## APPLICATIONS

1. Arlene Miller, management analyst at Ocotillo Software Company, needs to determine the reasons for employee turnover in the company. Outline the procedures she might follow to collect the data she needs.

2. Interview someone in the data-processing department of a local company about the organization's procedures for database management. In advance, prepare a list of open-ended and closed-ended questions that you wish to ask in the interview. Take careful notes and present a short report of your findings to the class.

3. Design a short mail questionnaire to elicit consumer preferences for ice cream and frozen yogurt.

4. Design a short mail questionnaire to evaluate consumers' reaction to a new brand of toothpaste called Placquegard. Assume that two weeks ago your company sent a free sample of Placquegard to every household included in the survey.

5. Write a cover letter for the questionnaire described in Item 4.

6. Write a follow-up letter to individuals who did not return the questionnaire described in Item 4.

7. Write a second follow-up letter to individuals who did not return the questionnaire described in Item 4.

8. Compose a list of three open-ended and three closed-ended questions to be used in a telephone survey to determine customer satisfaction with the service department of a local Chevrolet dealer.

9. Ten car salespersons each sold the following number of cars in one week:

| Salesperson | No. of Cars Sold |
|---|---|
| 1 | 13 |
| 2 | 9 |
| 3 | 8 |
| 4 | 6 |
| 5 | 5 |
| 6 | 4 |
| 7 | 2 |
| 8 | 2 |
| 9 | 1 |
| 10 | 0 |

a. Calculate the mean number of cars sold.
b. Determine the mode.
c. Determine the median.

10. Ten people in a mall were asked the following question: "Approximately how many times on an average do you shop at a Hi-Top grocery store per month?" The question yielded the following responses:

0, 1, 2, 4, 5, 6, 7, 8, 8, 9

a. Calculate the range.
b. Calculate the variance.
c. Calculate the standard deviation.

# CASE STUDY

John Osaru is the marketing director for Nature-Way Cosmetics, Inc., a cosmetic manufacturing company. The company needs to develop new products, and John's major responsibility right now is to conduct a survey to find out what new products Nature-Ways' customers would like to have.

Because the budget is limited, John decides to save money by surveying a small group of local women instead of using a sample of consumers throughout the nation. He checks the mailing lists in his department and identifies twenty women who live in his area. "Twenty should be a large enough group," he estimates.

John designs a questionnaire that asks for various kinds of input from respondents. He decides to include a stamped, addressed envelope to ensure that all twenty will return their questionnaires promptly.

When planning the questionnaire, John considers the kinds of comments that customers have made in letters and phone calls. After a great deal of thought, John prepares the following questionnaire:

---

### NATURE—WAY COSMETICS, INC.
### Survey of Customers and Potential Customers

*Instructions:* Please fill in this form and return it to us promptly. Thank you.

Name _____

1. What do you like about Nature—Way products?

2. What do you *not* like about Nature—Way products?

3. What Nature—Way products do you (or would you like to) use?

4. Can you suggest other products that you would like to use if Nature—Way developed and produced them?

5. What is your age?

6. What price range seems appropriate for cosmetics?

7. Your family income is:
   under $10,000 a year _____
   $10,000 to $20,000 a year _____
   $20,000 to $40,000 a year _____
   $40,000 or over a year _____

8. Where do you see most of our ads?

                    THANK YOU

---

1. Will John's questionnaire produce the information he needs? Defend your answer.
2. How can John classify, code, and analyze the responses to this questionnaire?
3. Identify the weaknesses in the overall research design.
4. Identify the weaknesses in the questionnaire design.
5. What steps could John have taken to develop a better questionnaire?

## SUGGESTED READINGS

Clark, Charles T. and Eleanor W. Jordan. *Introduction to Business and Economic Statistics*. 7th ed. Cincinnati: South-Western, 1985.

Dillman, Don A. *Mail and Telephone Surveys: The Total Design Method*. New York: Wiley, 1978.

Emory, C. William. *Business Research Methods*. 3rd ed. Homewood, IL: Richard D. Irwin, Inc., 1985.

Sekaran, Uma. *Research Methods for Managers: A Skill-Building Approach*. New York: Wiley, 1984.

Zikmund, William G. *Business Research Methods*. Hinsdale, IL: Dryden Press, 1984.

▼ ▼ ▼ ▼ ▼ ▼

# GRAPHIC COMMUNICATION

## CHAPTER 10

Product managers of a large beverage company recently faced the dilemma of introducing a new soft-drink flavor that was similar to that of two competing brands. They also needed to know which bottling companies were available to bottle the new product.

Instead of examining a large number of statistical computer printouts, the managers found the answer in a picture. Using graphics software, a computer quickly "pulled" information from the company's database. These data indicated which beverage companies were producing a similar competitive product, as well as names of independent bottling companies in various areas of the country.

Within minutes, a sharp color-coded map of the United States appeared on their computer screen showing the relevant data. With this information, the managers were able to select their market and introduce the product.

The type of situation just described, in which companies are using computer-generated graphics to speed up and to improve corporate decision-making, is becoming common. Managers and other business professionals are using the power of computer technology to create illustrative graphics easily and accurately. Report writers, however, often need some background knowledge of graphics; this chapter provides information on the following topics related to graphic communication:

- Guidelines for placement, size, numbering, titles, documentation, and interpretation of graphics
- Formal and informal tables
- Bar charts, including simple, multiple, subdivided, and bilateral bar charts
- Pie charts

- Line graphs, including single, multiple, and component-part line graphs
- Miscellaneous figures, including pictograms, maps, flow charts, organizational charts, schematics, diagrams, drawings, and photographs
- Computer graphics, including software, input devices, and output devices

## INTRODUCTION TO GRAPHICS

The term **graphics** refers to any illustration or "picture" containing data. Many informal and formal reports use graphics in company annual reports. Examples are shown in Figures 10.1 to 10.4 on pages 215–217. Although not a true "picture," **tables** (data arranged in columns and rows) also are considered a part of graphic communication and are discussed in this chapter.

The purpose of graphics is to enhance written communication by simplifying complex information, interpreting detailed material, and emphasizing special points. Graphics can also provide supplementary data that are not discussed in the written report. In addition, well-constructed, attractive graphics improve the overall format and appearance of a report.

### Placement in Reports

The placement of a graphic in a report should be as close as possible to the paragraph that introduces the graphic. Do not include a figure or table in the body of a report without referring to it in the narrative. When introducing a graphic, emphasize its content rather than just the graphic number. The sentence just before the figure or table may end in one of the following ways:

..., as shown in Figure 2.
..., indicated in Table 12-3.
... (see Figure 8-9).

## FIGURE 10.1 SUBDIVIDED BAR CHART FROM ANNUAL REPORT

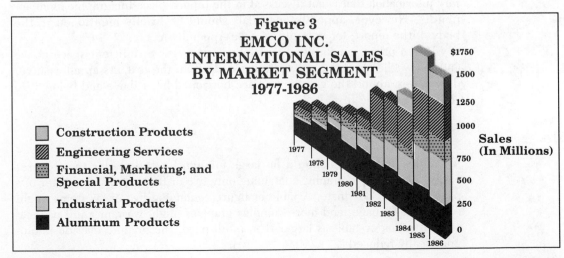

Figure 3
EMCO INC.
INTERNATIONAL SALES
BY MARKET SEGMENT
1977-1986

- Construction Products
- Engineering Services
- Financial, Marketing, and Special Products
- Industrial Products
- Aluminum Products

Sales (In Millions)

### FIGURE 10.2 MULTIPLE LINE GRAPH FROM ANNUAL REPORT

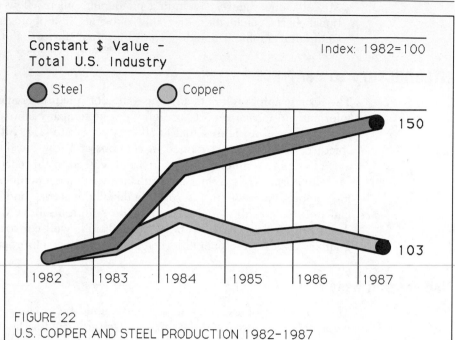

FIGURE 22
U.S. COPPER AND STEEL PRODUCTION 1982–1987

The size of the graphic will determine its exact location on a page. If the graphic is small, place it on a page surrounded by text. If a graphic is introduced near the bottom of a page, you may place it at the top of the next page. If the figure or table takes up a full page, place it on the first page following its introduction. If the information shown in the graphic illustrates supplementary information that is not discussed in the report, place the graphic in an appendix. However, appendix materials should be briefly mentioned in the body of the report; for example, . . . (see Appendix A).

When preparing the final draft of a report, leave sufficient space above and below the graphic to separate it clearly from the text. As an alternative, draw a box around the graphic or place horizontal lines above and below it to set it off from the text.

## Size

All tables and figures should be large enough for the reader to interpret easily. For a simple graphic containing only two or three items, a quarter of a page is usually adequate. A table or figure containing five or six items might require half a page, and more complex graphics might warrant a full page. If an illustration or table is larger than a full page, the graphic may be photographically reduced.

FIGURE 10.3 SINGLE LINE GRAPH FROM ANNUAL REPORT

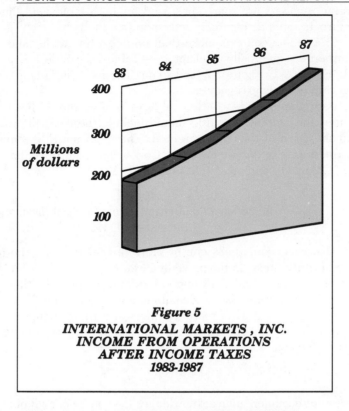

*Figure 5*
***INTERNATIONAL MARKETS , INC.***
***INCOME FROM OPERATIONS***
***AFTER INCOME TAXES***
***1983-1987***

FIGURE 10.4 PIE CHART FROM ANNUAL REPORT

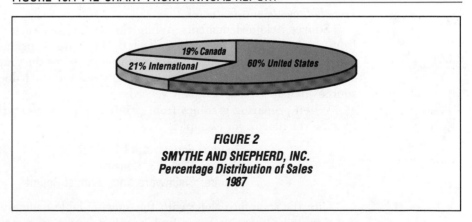

*FIGURE 2*
*SMYTHE AND SHEPHERD, INC.*
*Percentage Distribution of Sales*
*1987*

## Numbering and Titles

Except for minor tables which are part of a paragraph, all graphics should be numbered. Traditionally, tables have been numbered consecutively with Roman numerals—Table I, Table II, and so on. All other graphics are numbered consecutively with Arabic numbers—Figure 1, Figure 2, and so on. Arabic numbers are sometimes used for both tables and figures—Table 1, Figure 1, Table 2, Figure 2, and so on.

If a report contains more than one chapter, tables and figures may be numbered sequentially by chapters—Table 1-1, Table 1-2, Figure 1-1, Table 2-1, Figure 2-1, Figure 2-2, and so on. The most important factor in numbering graphics is consistency.

Any graphic aid, whether table or figure, should have a title that describes the content. The title should include the *who*, the *what*, the *where*, and the *when* of the data presented. The following title conveys information on the four w's; *who* (Acme Paint Co.), *what* (paint inventory), *where* (Denver, Colorado), and *when* (December 31, 1987).

Table I
Acme Paint Co., Denver, Colorado, Paint Inventory
December 31, 1987

However, sometimes one or more of the "w's" may be omitted for the sake of conciseness. In the preceding example, the "where" might be omitted.

The numbers and titles of graphics may be placed either above or below the graphic in uppercase or a combination of upper and lowercase letters. An increasing practice is to place numbers and titles at the left margin, either above or below the graphic. Again, consistency in placement throughout a report is essential.

## Documentation

Pertinent documentation acknowledges the source of a graphic aid or provides explanatory information about it. Two forms of documentation are *source acknowledgments* and *footnotes*.

**Source Acknowledgments**. When the writer constructs a table or figure from original data that he or she collected, the source is **primary**. In this case, the writer may either indicate *Source: Primary* below the graphic or omit the source note altogether. Business firms generally do not document internal sources of data such as company records.

When preparing graphics from printed sources, the writer should cite specific references; for example:

Source: *Forbes*, April 14, 1987, 39
Source: 1980 U.S. Census
Source: Smithware, Inc., Annual Report

Cite the reference along with the specific table or figure number if you use a table or figure verbatim from another source. If the source is a copyrighted book or periodical, you should obtain and document permission from the publisher to reproduce it, as follows:

Source: *The Wall Street Journal*, October 20, 1986, 21, Table 1
(Used by permission)

Cite the situation, the location(s), the date(s), and other pertinent information if sources are personal correspondence, interviews, conversations, and so on, for example:

Source: Personal interview with John P. Kane, Jr., Vice President,
Kane & Sons, Inc., Chicago, Illinois, September 30, 1987.

**Footnotes.** Place footnotes, which provide explanations of parts of tables or figures, below the graphic aid. Key footnotes with a superscript (raised) letter or an asterisk. Avoid using numbers for footnoting graphics because numbers may be confused with data given in the table or figure.

## Interpretation

The discussion or interpretation of a graphic aid should briefly summarize the illustration rather than merely repeat all the data shown in that table or figure, as shown in the following examples:

Total sales increased each year for the past five years, as shown in Table 1.

TV ads constituted the largest percentage of the 1988 advertising budget (see Figure 6).

The writer should include enough information to help the reader understand the graphic. If the graphic is very simple, the writer may omit the interpretation.

## TABLES

**Tables** present data arranged in rows and columns (rows are horizontal; columns are vertical). Tables may range from short informal listings without identifying numbers and titles to long formal reference tables.

## Informal Tables

The following examples illustrate informal tables that might appear as part of a paragraph in a report.

Computer speed can be stated in the following units of time:

| | |
|---|---|
| Milliseconds | One-thousandth of a second |
| Microseconds | One-millionth of a second |
| Nanoseconds | One-billionth of a second |
| Picoseconds | One-trillionth of a second |

Informal tables may have column and row headings but omit *identifying numbers* (such as Table 3) and titles, as shown in the following example:

Sales of microcomputers increased in each division from the previous month as these figures show:

| Division | November Sales | December Sales | Percent Increase |
|----------|----------------|----------------|------------------|
| 1 | $89,261 | $120,429 | 34.9% |
| 2 | 75,893 | 84,671 | 11.6 |
| 3 | 63,578 | 78,436 | 23.4 |

## Formal Tables

Formal tables may include identifying numbers, titles, headings, rows and columns of data, footnotes, and sources. A formal table is illustrated in Table 10.1.

### TABLE 10.1 EXAMPLE OF A RULED FORMAL TABLE

Table 13-3
PECAN, WALNUT, AND ALMOND CONSUMPTION PER CAPITA[a]

| Year | Pecans | Walnuts | Almonds |
|------|--------|---------|---------|
| 1981 | .38 | .43 | .35 |
| 1982 | .38 | .40 | .35 |
| 1983 | .36 | .43 | .26 |
| 1984 | .34 | .49 | .27 |
| 1985 | .34 | .53 | .35 |
| AVG.[b] | .36 | .46 | .32 |

[a]pounds per person
[b]5-year average

Source: *U.S.D.A. Crop Production Bulletin, 1980-85 Annual Summary*

## Additional Guidelines

A few additional guidelines for constructing tables are as follows:

1. A subtitle may be used below the main title for further explanation.
2. Fractions should be stated in decimals and aligned at the decimal point.
3. Whole numbers in numerical columns should be aligned on the right. Items in the non-numerical column are aligned on the left.
4. A standard unit of measure (feet, thousands of dollars, etc.) should be used and may be explained in a footnote as necessary.
5. Data not available should be shown by a dash (—) or the abbreviation for "not available" (N.A.) rather than by using a zero.

## Table Formats

Table 10.1 shows a ruled format where lines divide major sections of the table. An open (table with no lines) or boxed (table with lines around it) format may also be used. An open-table format is shown in Table 10.2, and a boxed-table format in Table 10.3.

### TABLE 10.2 EXAMPLE OF AN OPEN-TABLE FORMAT

Table 5-1
America's Highest Average Annual
Per Capita Income Areas

| Area | Income |
|------|--------|
| Anchorage, Alaska | $11,366 |
| Bridgeport/Stamford/<br>    Norwalk/Danbury, Connecticut | 10,412 |
| Washington, D.C. | 10,295 |
| Midland, Texas | 10,084 |
| San Francisco/Oakland, California | 9,650 |

Source: U.S. Census Bureau, 1984

### TABLE 10.3 EXAMPLE OF A BOXED-TABLE FORMAT

Table 4
Leading Spreadsheet Software

| Brand<br>Name | Percent of<br>Market |
|---------------|----------------------|
| Lotus 1-2-3 | 47% |
| VisiCalc | 22 |
| SuperCalc II | 12 |
| Other | 19 |

Source: *USA Today*, October 18,
    1984, 3B

Informal tables generally provide qualitative information such as checklists, guidelines, rankings, listings, or instructions. However, this type of information also can be shown in formal tables, as illustrated in Table 10.4.

## TABLE 10.4 EXAMPLE OF FORMAL TABLE WITH QUALITATIVE INFORMATION

### Table 3.4
### Items That May Be Omitted From Resumes*

High school educational data

Previous employment addresses and supervisor names

Offices held in professional organizations

Personal information that violates EEOC regulations

References upon request

*According to survey of personnel administrators.

Source: Kevin L. Hutchinson, "Personnel Administrators' Preferences for Resume Content: A Survey and Review of Empirically Based Conclusions," *The Journal of Business Communication*, 21, no. 4, (Fall 1984): 11

## FIGURES

Any graphic aid other than a table is usually referred to as a **figure**. Various types of figures include bar charts, pie charts, line graphs, and other miscellaneous graphic aids.

## Bar Charts

Bar charts are useful for comparing one quantity with another. The length or height of bars represent differences in quantities.

The bars are placed on a grid containing a horizontal (x) axis and a vertical (y) axis. Four common types of bar charts are simple, multiple, subdivided, and bilateral charts.

**Simple Bar Charts. Simple bar charts** are used to compare various quantities by the lengths of vertical or horizontal bars of equal widths. Figure 10.5 is an example of a vertical simple bar chart where time (years, months, etc.) is indicated along a horizontal axis, and quantitative units are indicated along a vertical axis.

If time is not a variable, a horizontal simple bar chart is appropriate (see Figure 10.6 on page 224). In horizontal bar charts, the horizontal axis contains scale values, and the vertical axis contains the titles of categories of data.

Scale values for simple bar charts should be equal and begin at zero. Bars of equal width should be placed at equal intervals along the vertical or horizontal axis. If these conditions are not met, data distortion and false interpretations may occur.

## FIGURE 10.5 SIMPLE VERTICAL BAR CHART

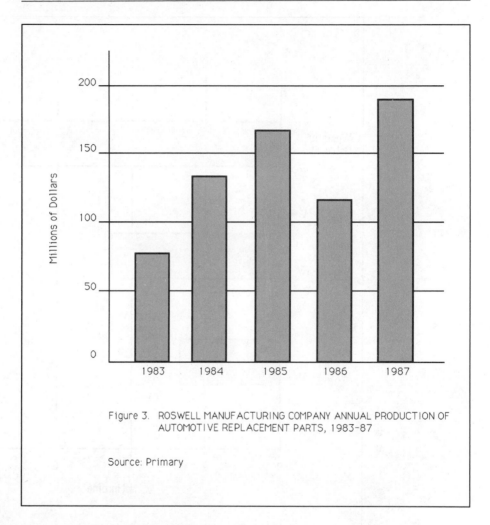

Figure 3.   ROSWELL MANUFACTURING COMPANY ANNUAL PRODUCTION OF
AUTOMOTIVE REPLACEMENT PARTS, 1983–87

Source: Primary

    Although not necessary, exact quantities may appear at the end or inside of each bar (see Figure 10.7 on page 225). This optional technique reflects quantities more precisely and accurately. Color, shading, and cross-hatching (stripes) can be used for emphasis as well.

    When one or two bars are disproportionately larger than the others (i.e. several million compared to a few thousand dollars), a **scale break** may be used to indicate that the scale does not apply to one or two items. The scale break may be represented by two straight or jagged parallel lines (see Figure 10.7). Use scale breaks only when necessary; identify scale breaks prominently to prevent misreading of data.

## FIGURE 10.6 SIMPLE HORIZONTAL BAR CHART

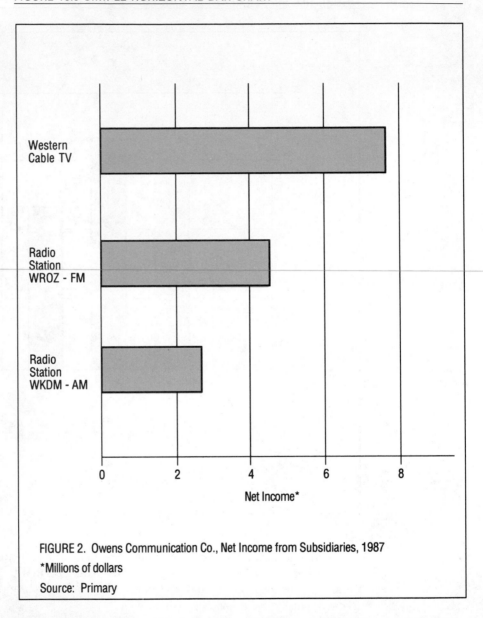

FIGURE 2.  Owens Communication Co., Net Income from Subsidiaries, 1987

*Millions of dollars

Source:  Primary

**Multiple Bar Charts**. A **multiple bar chart** is used to compare two or three different amounts for a particular category or time period. For example, a company's annual report might contain a multiple bar chart showing both net earnings and dividends for five years. The total for each primary category (year) does not appear in a multiple bar chart. Secondary categories (earnings and dividends) do not have to be additive (add up to a meaningful total).

## FIGURE 10.7 SIMPLE HORIZONTAL BAR CHART WITH SCALE BREAK

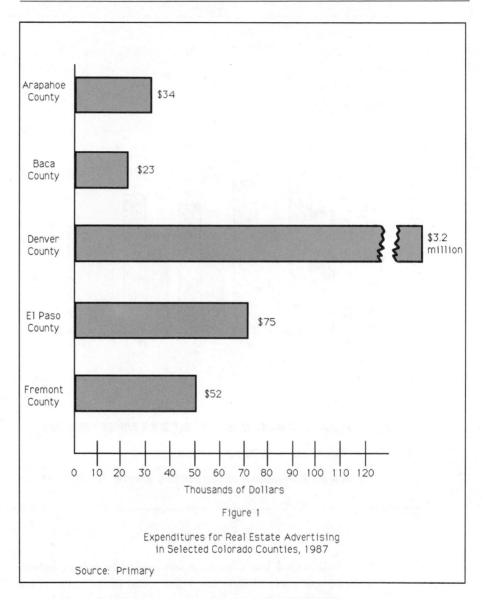

Figure 1

Expenditures for Real Estate Advertising
in Selected Colorado Counties, 1987

Source: Primary

To avoid confusion, no more than three secondary categories should be compared for each primary category in one chart. Use color, shading, or cross-hatching to differentiate between different items being compared, and also include a key to the coloring as part of the chart. A multiple bar chart is shown in Figure 10.8.

## FIGURE 10.8 MULTIPLE BAR CHART

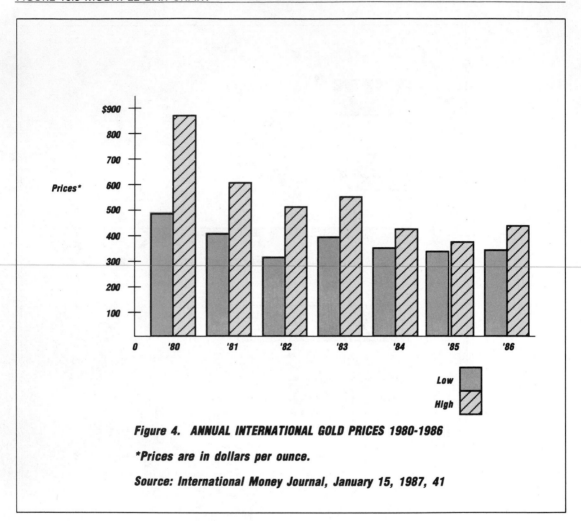

Figure 4.  **ANNUAL INTERNATIONAL GOLD PRICES 1980-1986**

*Prices are in dollars per ounce.*

Source: International Money Journal, January 15, 1987, 41

**Subdivided Bar Charts**. A **subdivided bar chart** breaks a single bar into component parts to show the relationship of the parts to the whole. The secondary categories must be additive. Use color, shading, or cross-hatching to distinguish between the parts; include a key to differentiate between the colors. A subdivided bar chart is shown in Figure 10.9.

**Bilateral Bar Charts**. A **bilateral bar chart** illustrates both positive and negative numbers on the vertical axis. The negative figures are shown below a central reference point (usually zero). Bilateral bar charts are frequently used to show a company's profit and loss history, with the loss figures often pictured in red ink. An example of a bilateral bar chart is shown in Figure 10.10 on page 228.

FIGURE 10.9 SUBDIVIDED BAR CHART

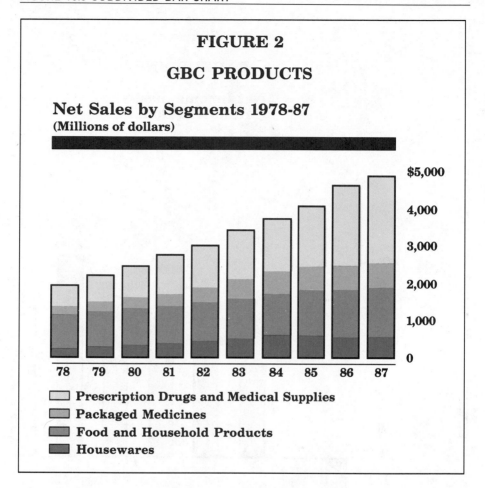

**FIGURE 2**

**GBC PRODUCTS**

**Net Sales by Segments 1978-87**
**(Millions of dollars)**

Legend:
- ▢ Prescription Drugs and Medical Supplies
- ▨ Packaged Medicines
- ▨ Food and Household Products
- ▧ Housewares

## Pie Charts

A **pie chart** is a circle or "pie" divided into sections or "slices" (see Figure 10.11 on page 229). Pie charts show the percentage that component parts (slices) represent of a whole circle (pie). The following guidelines should be followed in constructing a pie chart:

1. Compute the percentage of the whole that each part represents. All parts must total 100 percent. Since the "pie" or circle consists of 360 degrees, multiply each percentage by 360 degrees. For example, a "slice" representing 25 percent of the whole is 90 degrees (360 degrees x .25 = 90 degrees).

2. Measure with a protractor and draw the largest part or "slice" of the pie beginning at the 12 o'clock position.

FIGURE 10.10 BILATERAL BAR CHART

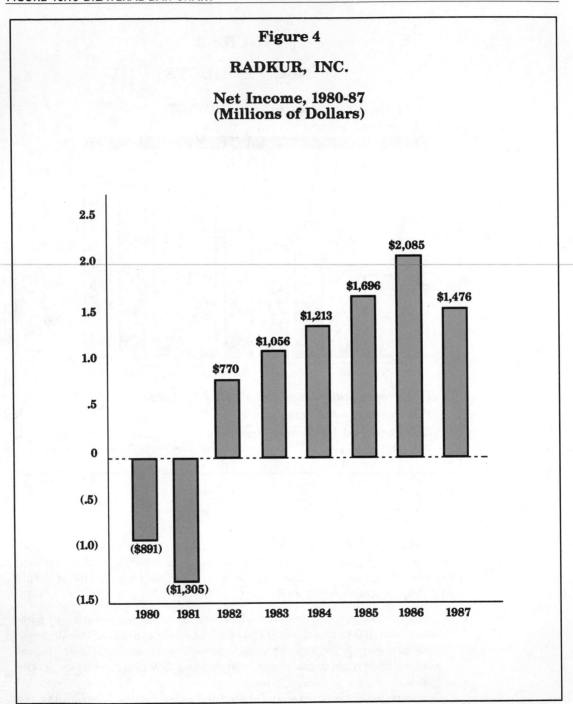

**Figure 4**

**RADKUR, INC.**

**Net Income, 1980-87**
**(Millions of Dollars)**

## FIGURE 10.11 PIE CHART

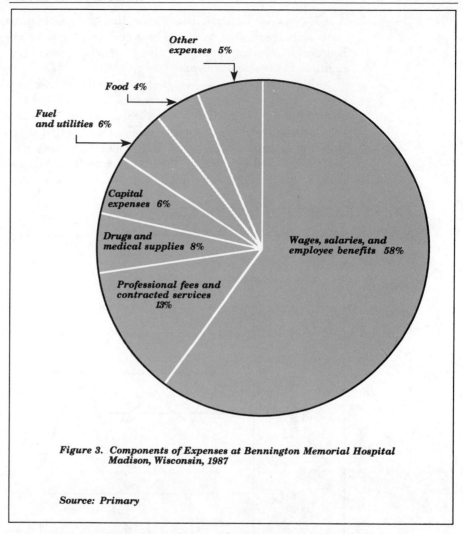

Other
expenses  5%

Food  4%

Fuel
and utilities  6%

Capital
expenses  6%

Drugs and
medical supplies  8%

Professional fees and
contracted services
13%

Wages, salaries, and
employee benefits  58%

*Figure 3.  Components of Expenses at Bennington Memorial Hospital
Madison, Wisconsin, 1987*

*Source: Primary*

3. Move clockwise in descending order from largest to smallest. The only exception to this guideline is the miscellaneous category. This part should be the last "slice" of the pie even if its percentage is larger than that of other parts of the pie.

4. Label each "slice" or part and the percentage it represents unless the "slice" is too small; in that case, draw an arrow from the part to a label. Parts may be emphasized by using color, shading, or cross-hatching.

5. When using two or more pie charts in the same figure, the "pies" or circles should be the same size. Although pie charts are good for comparing the parts of a whole for a particular point in time, they are not effective for comparing two or more periods if the numeric totals are more important than the percentage breakdown.

## Line Graphs

A line graph, as illustrated in Figure 10.12, shows both trends and comparisons. Data are plotted on points on a grid over a given time period, and a line is drawn to connect the points. Three common types of line graphs are single, multiple, and component-part line graphs.

**Single Line Graphs.** When showing only one series of continuous data, such as total monthly sales for one year, use a single line graph. As with bar charts, this type of graph has a horizontal and a vertical axis. Time is shown on the horizontal axis, and quantity changes are plotted on the vertical axis. All scale intervals should be equal. Each value along with its corresponding time period is plotted on the grid; then the plotted points connect to show the continuous movement of the data. At least ten points should be plotted. For

### FIGURE 10.12 SINGLE LINE GRAPH

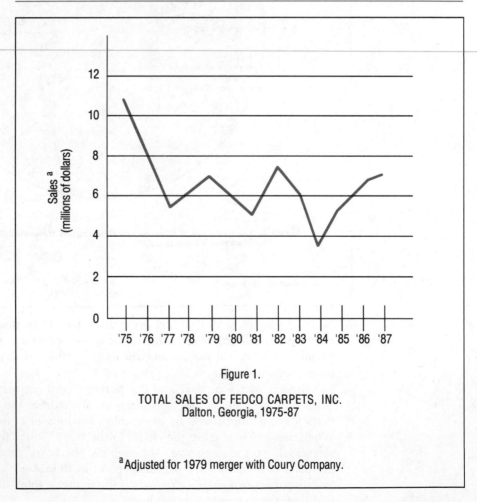

Figure 1.

TOTAL SALES OF FEDCO CARPETS, INC.
Dalton, Georgia, 1975-87

[a] Adjusted for 1979 merger with Coury Company.

fewer than ten points, a vertical bar chart is more appropriate. A single line graph is shown in Figure 10.12.

**Multiple Line Graphs**. When comparing two or more series of values (such as primary and secondary users of personal computers) on the same graph, use a multiple line graph (see Figure 10.13). The lines contained in this type of graphic presentation should be clearly differentiated. Using different colored lines or varying the lines from solid to dots, dashes, or a combination of dots and dashes is helpful. A key identifying the variations in lines is also necessary. To avoid confusion, limit the number of lines used in one graph to three or four.

**Component-Part Line Graphs**. To show component parts of a series of data by use of a line graph, use a component-part line graph or cumulative line graph (see Figure 10.14). This type of line graph can show only one series of data and is constructed with a top line indicating the total of the series.

## FIGURE 10.13 MULTIPLE LINE GRAPH

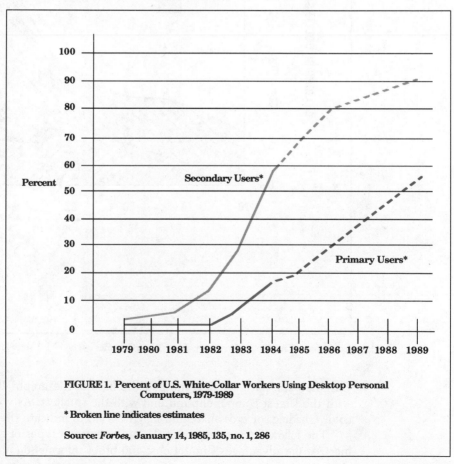

FIGURE 1. Percent of U.S. White-Collar Workers Using Desktop Personal Computers, 1979-1989

* Broken line indicates estimates

Source: *Forbes*, January 14, 1985, 135, no. 1, 286

Courtesy of Forbes, Inc.

## FIGURE 10.14 COMPONENT-PART LINE GRAPH

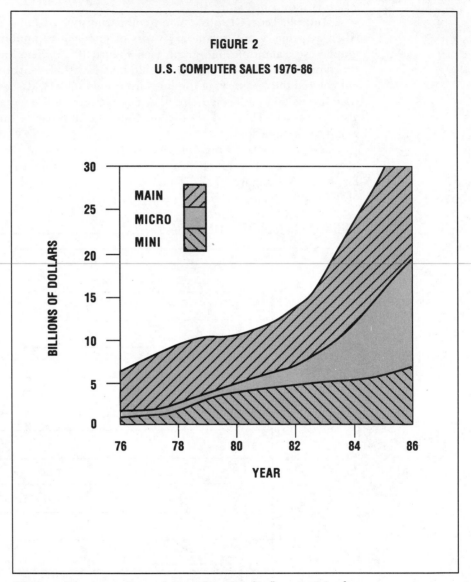

**FIGURE 2**

**U.S. COMPUTER SALES 1976-86**

Courtesy of Enertronics Research, Inc., "EnerGraphics" version 1.3 software

Cumulate the parts by beginning at the base of the graph. If possible, begin with the largest component and end with the smallest. As with other figures, color, shading, or cross-hatching may be used to indicate the separate parts.

The following comparison of the most common types of graphic aids summarizes the advantages, limitations, and other information about each type of aid.

## COMPARISON OF COMMON GRAPHIC AIDS

| Graphic Aid | Advantages | Limitations | Comments |
|---|---|---|---|
| Table | Most versatile graphic aid. Shows exact quantities. | Does not emphasize trends. Is less interesting than other formats; can become mono-tonous to the reader. | Totals may appear at top, bottom, left margin, right margin, or be omitted. |
| Pie Chart | Shows percentage breakdown. | Cannot represent absolute quantities. Shows only one point in time. Cannot show secondary categories. Components must total 100 percent. | For comparison of two time periods, use two pies in one figure. |
| Simple Bar Chart | Compares absolute quantities over time or at one point in time. Does not require continuous data. Compared quantities do not have to be additive. | Not recommended for percentages. Cannot show secondary categories. | Use vertical bars if time is a factor. Use horizontal bars to compare quantities at one point in time. |
| Multiple Bar Chart | Compares component values over time or at one point in time. Does not require continuous data. Primary categories do not have to be additive. Recommended when secondary categories consist of two or three variables. | Not recommended for percentages. Categories do not have to be additive. Not recommended if secondary categories consist of more than three variables. Does not show totals. Requires color, shading, or cross-hatching. | Use vertical bars if time is a factor. Use horizontal bars to compare quantities at one point in time. |

COMPARISON OF COMMON GRAPHIC AIDS

| Graphic Aid | Advantages | Limitations | Comments |
|---|---|---|---|
| Subdivided Bar Chart | Compares component values over time or at one point in time. Does not require continuous data. Primary categories do not have to be additive. Shows totals. Number of secondary categories is unlimited. | Not recommended for percentages. Secondary categories must be additive. Requires color, shading, or cross-hatching. | Use vertical bars if time is a factor. Use horizontal bars to compare quantities at one point in time. Label small amounts outside bars by using brackets or a straight line as leaders. |
| Bilaterial Bar Chart | Used to show positive and negative changes. Compared quantities do not have to be additive. Usually compares values over time. | Bars should be vertical. Negative quantities may be colored red. | Often used to show a loss. |
| Single Line Graph | Compares quantities over time. | Requires continuous data. Must plot a minimum of ten points. | Plot time on the horizontal (X) axis; plot quantities on the vertical (Y) axis. Other types include multiple line graphs and component-part line graphs. |

## Miscellaneous Figures

To enhance the narrative, business reports may incorporate other less common types of figures. Pictograms, maps, flow charts, organizational charts, schematics, diagrams, drawings, and photographs are all examples of such figures.

**Pictograms**. Instead of vertical or horizontal bars as in simple bar charts, **pictograms** feature pictorial symbols to represent data. Magazines and newspapers often use pictograms to appeal to the public. An example of a pictorial symbol is a stack of coins or bills representing expenses or savings. Cars, trucks, ships, or houses might be used to indicate the number sold or built. Symbols representing either males or females might be used to indicate populations by sex. Any pictorial symbol may be used as long as it clearly represents the data.

In constructing pictograms, follow the same guidelines used for developing bar charts. In addition, make all pictorial symbols of equal size. A comparison should be based entirely on the number of symbols used rather than the size of the symbol. Making some symbols larger than others may be misleading. A pictogram is shown in Figure 10.15.

### FIGURE 10.15 PICTOGRAM

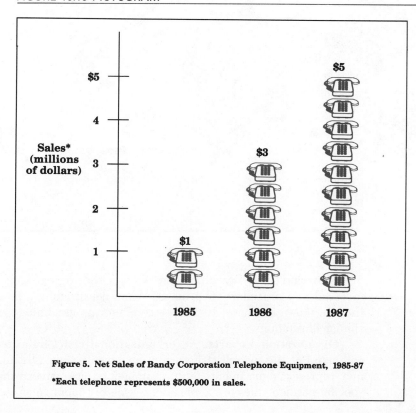

Figure 5.  Net Sales of Bandy Corporation Telephone Equipment, 1985-87

*Each telephone represents $500,000 in sales.

**Maps**. Business reports sometimes contain maps of geographic areas. A special type of map that compares quantitative information by geographic area is called a **statistical map**, as shown in Figure 10.16. Various graphic techniques such as color, shading, cross-hatching, or dots and symbols representing data can be used effectively.

## FIGURE 10.16 STATISTICAL MAP

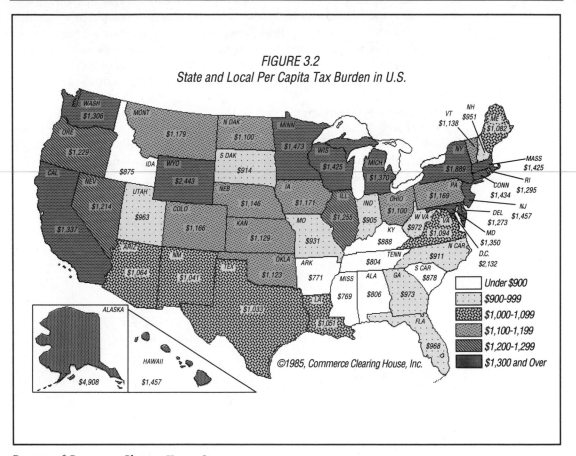

FIGURE 3.2
State and Local Per Capita Tax Burden in U.S.

©1985, Commerce Clearing House, Inc.

Courtesy of Commerce Clearing House, Inc.

**Flowcharts**. A **flowchart** represents the logical sequence of steps involved in a procedure or process. When constructing a flowchart, such as the one shown in Figure 10.17, use computer programming symbols or other similar illustrations.

**Organizational charts**. An **organizational chart** indicates the chain of command or the overall structure of an organization. Organizational charts may represent departments (e.g., customer service, advertising, accounting), specific position titles (e.g., president, vice president, manager), or function

## FIGURE 10.17 FLOWCHART

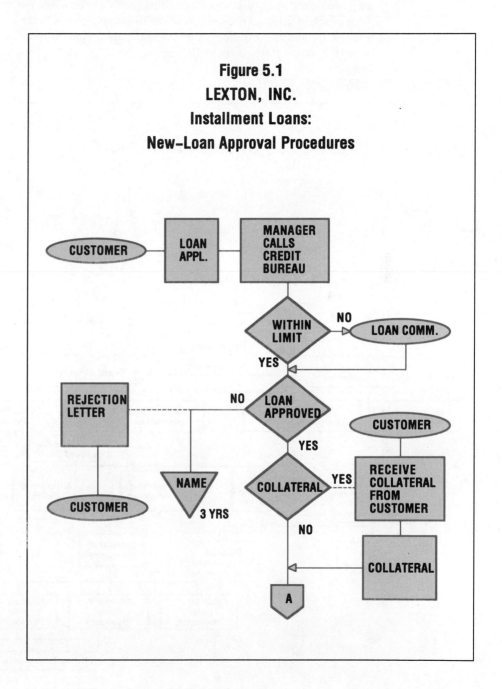

Courtesy of Micrografx, Inc., PC-Draw Software

(e.g., product development, marketing, human resources). Solid lines generally indicate direct or line relationships, and broken lines indicate indirect or staff relationships. An example of an organizational chart is shown in Figure 10.18; another example of an organizational chart from a company annual report is shown in Figure 10.19.

## FIGURE 10.18 ORGANIZATIONAL CHART

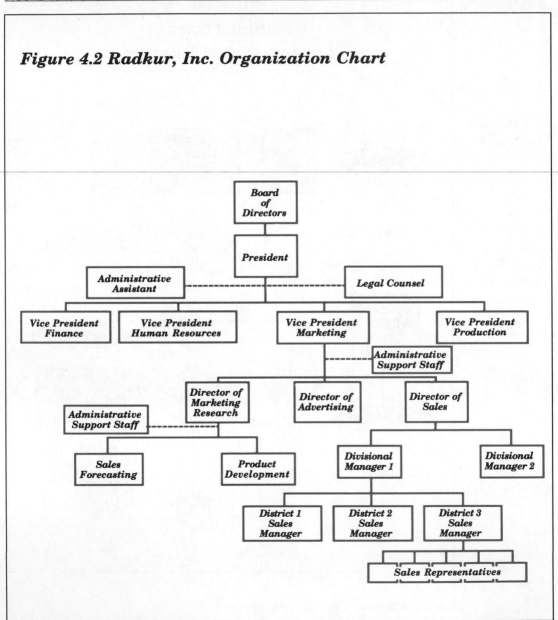

*Figure 4.2 Radkur, Inc. Organization Chart*

## FIGURE 10.19 ORGANIZATIONAL CHART

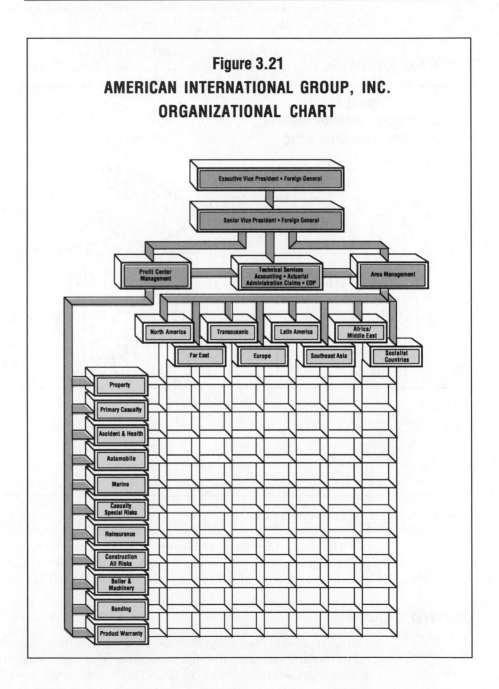

Courtesy of American International Group, Inc.

**Schematics**. **Schematics** (cutaway drawings) are used to show component parts of an object or subsurface sections. An example of a schematic is shown in Figure 10.20.

## FIGURE 10.20 SCHEMATIC

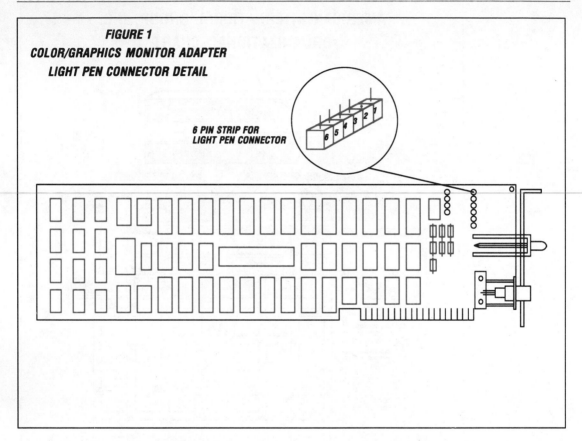

Courtesy of Micrografx, Inc., PC-Draw Software

**Diagrams, Drawings, or Photographs**. To represent an object accurately, use a diagram, drawing, or photograph. All three are excellent for showing details. An example of a diagram is shown in Figure 10.21.

## COMPUTER GRAPHICS

Just as technology has simplified the creation of letters, memorandums, and other business messages through word processing and computers, it has made computer-generated graphics an important business tool as well. Today computers can produce line graphs, bar and pie charts, maps, flowcharts, scatter diagrams, and even three-dimensional images in a variety of different colors.

## FIGURE 10.21 DIAGRAM

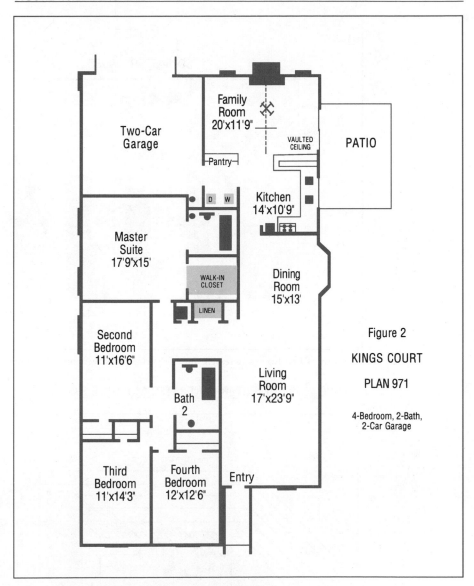

Courtesy of Micrografx, Inc., PC-Draw Software

Several examples of graphics produced by computers have been shown throughout this chapter. Additional examples are shown in Figures 10.22 through Figure 10.26 on pages 242-245.

## FIGURE 10.22 COMPUTER-GENERATED MULTIPLE BAR CHART

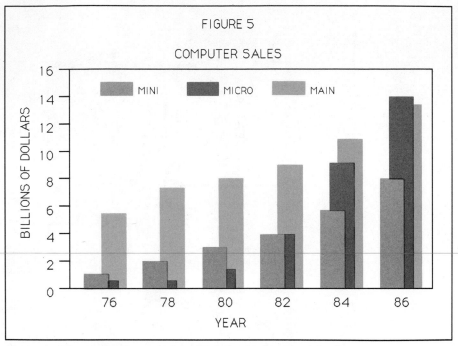

Courtesy of Enertronics Research, Inc., "EnerGraphics" version 1.3 software

## FIGURE 10.23 COMPUTER-GENERATED MULTIPLE BAR CHART

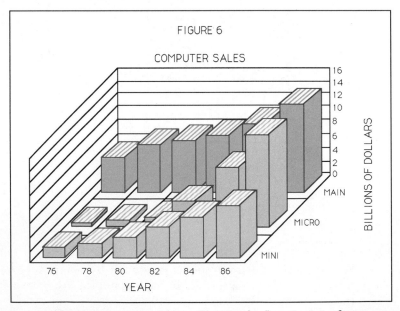

Courtesy of Enertronics Research, Inc., "EnerGraphics" version 1.3 software

## FIGURE 10.24 COMPUTER-GENERATED SUBDIVIDED BAR CHART

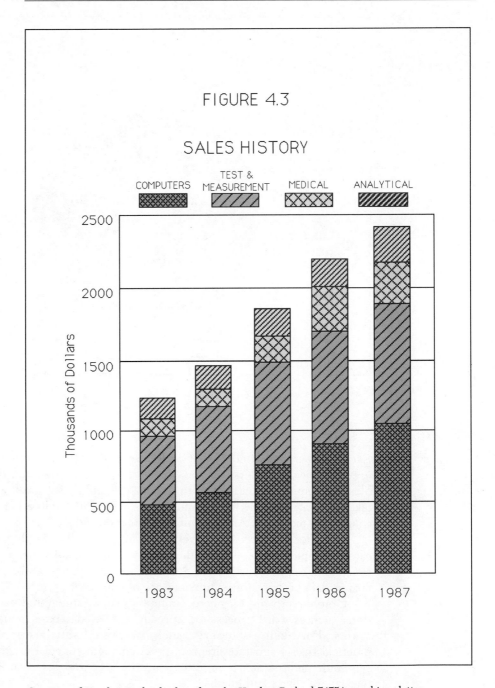

Courtesy of Hewlett-Packard, plotted on the Hewlett-Packard 7475A graphics plotter

## FIGURE 10.25 COMPUTER-GENERATED PIE CHART

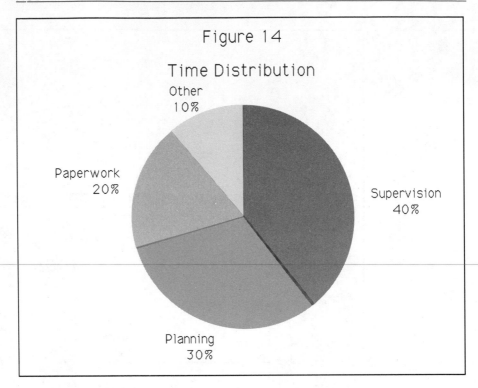

Figure 14

Time Distribution

Courtesy of Hewlett-Packard

## Software

Executives are now finding that a report containing multi-colored graphic figures is easier to understand and interpret than long rows and columns of tables in computer printouts. With the use of graphics software, a manager can
take raw data in table format and change it instantly into a line graph, a bar
chart, or a pie chart. Artistic ability is not required.

Graphics software that is available ranges from the simple to the sophisticated. Simple programs limit the variety of line graphs, bar charts, and pie
charts that can be constructed. Software may also limit the ability to label and
format data because these functions are often preset.

Graphic software for microcomputers may be integrated with other functions such as word processing, spreadsheet, or database management programs. For business reports, such integrated software is usually more
practical than a separate graphics program. Some special graphics programs
can "pull" information from an organization's central database (files) and format it into charts and graphs.

With other graphics software, a computer can keep a set of frequently
used charts and graphs current by automatically generating new charts and

graphs as the database changes. Graphics software in the future may be able to select the most effective graph for a particular set of data. Researchers predict that artificial intelligence technology will make such developments possible.

## FIGURE 10.26 COMPUTER-GENERATED MULTIPLE LINE GRAPH

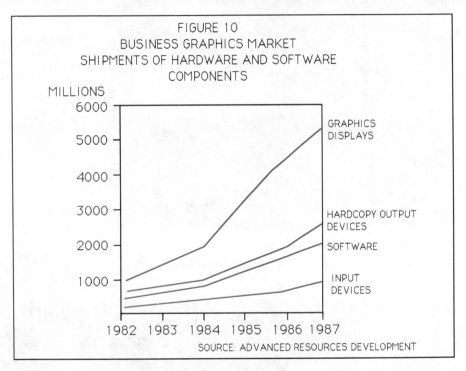

Courtesy of Micrografx, Inc., PC-Draw Software

## Input Devices

Many input devices, in addition to the usual computer keyboard, are available for computer graphics. A hand-held puck called a *mouse* or a *joy stick* that controls the movement of a *cursor* (the position indicator that is displayed on a computer screen) are other means of creating graphics. An *electronic stylus* or *pen* or a *mouse* are used to construct graphics on a *tablet*. *Light pens* that are pointed directly at a computer display are also used to create graphics. An example of a computer keyboard as a device for creating graphics is shown in Figure 10.27A. A hand-held cursor used on an electronic tablet is shown in Figure 10.27B; an electronic stylus used on an electronic tablet is shown in Figure 10.28.

## FIGURE 10.27 COMPUTER GRAPHICS INPUT DEVICES

**A—KEYBOARD**
Courtesy of Sperry Corporation, Sperry™ Personal Computer

**B—HAND-HELD CURSOR**
Courtesy of Sperry Corporation, SPERRY Computer-Integrated Manufacturing/Mechanical Engineering (CIM/ME) System

## FIGURE 10.28 COMPUTER GRAPHICS INPUT DEVICE (ELECTRONIC STYLUS AND TABLET)

Courtesy of Hewlett-Packard

## Output Devices

Output can be displayed on a computer screen, on paper, transparencies, slides, or on large room-sized screens. The image on a computer screen permits the user to see a table or figure as it is being created. Once the desired graphic is completed, the output device such as a daisy-wheel, dot-matrix, laser, or ink-jet printer can produce a hard (paper) copy (see Figure 10.29A). Plotters, which use pens to draw graphics, are also popular output devices (see Figure 10.29B).

## FIGURE 10.29 COMPUTER GRAPHICS OUTPUT DEVICE

**A—PRINTER**

Courtesy of Software Publishing Corporation, PFS: Graph on IBM PC

**B—PLOTTER**

Courtesy of Hewlett-Packard, Hewlett-Packard 7550A Plotter

Transparencies can be made directly from computer screen images. Black and white or color 35mm slides are produced by a camera filming the graphic displayed on a computer screen. Projection of graphics onto large room-sized screens is accomplished by attaching a light-wave projector to a computer. This on-site projection allows the user to make forecasts or changes and immediately display the effects.

## SUMMARY

Graphics are informative, powerful means of conveying information. When properly selected and formatted, graphics can enhance any business report.

Guidelines for constructing graphics are discussed in the sections on placement, size, numbering, titles, documentation, and interpretation.

Two broad categories of graphics are tables and figures. Tables consist of data arranged in rows and columns. Figures include all other graphics such as bar and pie charts, line graphs, maps, pictograms, flowcharts, and so on.

Bar charts compare one value to another by the length of equal-width bars. Four types of bar charts are simple, multiple, subdivided, and bilateral charts. Pie charts show the relationship of the parts or "slices" to the whole circle or "pie." Line graphs illustrate trends and comparisons over time. Three common types of line graphs are single, multiple, and component-part line graphs.

Computer graphics have become an important tool in businesses today because of the availability of graphics software for personal computers, as well as the improvement of input and output devices used in creating graphics. Because of the increased speed and ease with which computer graphics can be created, computer-generated graphics have become a major force in the decision-making process in today's business environment.

## CHAPTER REVIEW

1. Define the term *graphics* and explain why they are important in business communication.
2. What is the difference between a *figure* and a *table*?
3. Describe where graphics should be placed in business reports.
4. What criteria would you use to determine how large a graphic should be?
5. Explain how graphics should be numbered.
6. Briefly describe two different forms of documentation used with graphics and give an example of each.
7. How do informal and formal tables differ?
8. Define the term *scale break* and explain how it is used.
9. Describe the use of bilateral bar charts.
10. What is the difference between a multiple line graph and a component-part line graph?

## APPLICATIONS

1. Which specific type of graphic aid would you use for each of the following situations? Defend your answer.
   a. The percentage breakdown of how an average middle-income family of four spends a dollar
   b. The total annual sales of the Kurrad Corporation for the past ten years
   c. A comparison of the monthly number of flights for the past year of each of three leading airline companies
   d. The percentage of last year's graduating class at your college who have obtained full-time employment
   e. The total sales of Westwood Motor Co. by product (cars, trucks, vans) for the current year
   f. The number of pieces of first-, second-, third-, and fourth-class mail handled each month by the United States Postal Service for the current year
   g. The total sales for the three major divisions of the Kurrad Corporation for the week of July 12, 1987
   h. The total income, including operating and nonoperating income, of the Kurrad Corporation for the past 15 years
   i. The sales revenue of the Kurrad Corporation for the past three years, including cost of goods sold, expenses, and profit
   j. The number of credit customers for the Kurrad Corporation from 1970 to 1987

2. Select at least six examples of graphics (three tables and three figures) from newspapers and magazines and critique the use and format of each example.

3. Construct a multiple bar chart from the following data for three major divisions of Radkur, Inc.

| Year | Division 1 | Division 2 | Division 3 |
|------|-----------|-----------|-----------|
| 1986 | 9 million | 4 million | 2 million |
| 1987 | 12 million | 6 million | 4 million |

4. Construct a subdivided bar chart representing the number and sex of employees of Radkur, Inc.

| Year | Males | Females |
|------|-------|---------|
| 1980 | 192 | 224 |
| 1981 | 215 | 256 |
| 1982 | 231 | 278 |
| 1983 | 227 | 269 |
| 1984 | 303 | 320 |
| 1985 | 319 | 357 |
| 1986 | 322 | 361 |
| 1987 | 320 | 355 |

5. From the following data, construct a bilateral bar chart of the net profit of Radkur, Inc.

| 1980 | + 15.2 million |
|------|---------------|
| 1981 | + 9.0 million |
| 1982 | - 3.1 million |
| 1983 | - 12.5 million |
| 1984 | + 5.3 million |
| 1985 | + 10.8 million |
| 1986 | + 12.1 million |
| 1987 | + 9.9 million |

6. From the following data, construct a pie chart of the distribution of Radkur, Inc., products (in units) worldwide.

| Australia | 65,000 |
|-----------|--------|
| Canada | 739,000 |
| Europe | 517,000 |
| South America | 228,000 |
| United States | 3,456,000 |
| Other countries | 29,000 |
| TOTAL | 5,034,000 |

7. Construct a line graph from the following production data (in units) of Radkur, Inc., for the past year.

| January | 927,000 | July | 358,000 |
|---------|---------|------|---------|
| February | 879,000 | August | 419,000 |
| March | 803,000 | September | 621,000 |
| April | 567,000 | October | 504,000 |
| May | 746,000 | November | 752,000 |
| June | 301,000 | December | 908,000 |

8. From the following data, construct a multiple line graph for net sales for two subsidiaries of Radkur, Inc.

| Year | Subsidiary 1 | Subsidiary 2 |
|------|--------------|--------------|
| 1978 | 3.1 million | 2.4 million |
| 1979 | 4.6 million | 4.0 million |
| 1980 | 5.8 million | 3.2 million |
| 1981 | 12.3 million | 8.1 million |
| 1982 | 9.4 million | 6.5 million |
| 1983 | 6.7 million | 3.8 million |
| 1984 | 10.1 million | 8.0 million |
| 1985 | 15.2 million | 12.3 million |
| 1986 | 9.0 million | 10.7 million |
| 1987 | 12.5 million | 9.5 million |

9. Construct a component-part line graph representing sales (in millions) for O'Leary's Home Center for the following departments.

| Year | Hardware | Gardening | Plumbing |
|------|----------|-----------|----------|
| 1978 | 20.4 | 1.4 | 12.3 |
| 1979 | 23.3 | 1.2 | 14.6 |
| 1980 | 25.8 | 1.6 | 18.0 |

| | | | |
|---|---|---|---|
| 1981 | 27.3 | 1.8 | 23.2 |
| 1982 | 26.1 | 2.0 | 28.4 |
| 1983 | 28.9 | 2.3 | 30.1 |
| 1984 | 29.2 | 2.9 | 36.5 |
| 1985 | 31.3 | 3.5 | 39.2 |
| 1986 | 32.5 | 4.2 | 40.3 |
| 1987 | 34.9 | 5.5 | 40.8 |

10. With the following data, construct a pictogram showing the number of housing units built each year in the city of Troy. Each symbol should represent 100 units.

| | |
|---|---|
| 1980 | 123 |
| 1981 | 245 |
| 1982 | 304 |
| 1983 | 452 |
| 1984 | 225 |
| 1985 | 356 |
| 1986 | 480 |
| 1987 | 622 |

## CASE STUDY

"If we want to prevent employee turnover," insisted Joan Rivera, "we'll have to start paying our people higher salaries."

"Nonsense!" retorted Henry Tiede. "Look at the statistics in Higgins' cost analysis report. We're matching industry norms — and have for over 15 years."

"Where did you get the idea that we were matching industry norms?" asked Rivera. "I don't recall any national statistics being included in that report."

"Well, even if our people are below industry norms," added Rhonda Mattling, "we can't afford to increase salaries by much. Salaries already make up the bulk of our operating expenses. If we increase salaries, we'll have to raise our prices, and the company can't afford to do that in today's economy."

"Wait a minute," spoke up Gerry Tims. "I looked at Higgins' report. As I recall, a big chunk of our operating budget goes to training and development. Our employees don't need to spend so much time in T & D classes. Why don't we just cut the T & D budget and add to salaries the money we save?"

"You must have been reading a different report than the one I received," answered Rivera. "As I recall, T & D was a small part of the operating budget, something like 10 percent. Even if we cut all of the T & D budget and add it to salaries, we'd still be below average for the industry. Our people need training. If we cut the training budget, we'll only create other problems."

"I don't know what you're all so worried about," said Tiede. "The figures in the report clearly indicate that our blue-collar workers have been consistently earning higher than the national average for our industry since 1970.

And as of 1987, our white-collar employees will beat the national average as well. Although I agree with Gerry Tims that too big a chunk of our operating costs has been going to training and development, I don't see any reason to increase salaries at this time."

As the executive committee continued the discussion of income at Silvers Manufacturing, Carl Higgins looked puzzled. "I wonder where all the confusion is coming from," he thought to himself. "My report is perfectly clear. They didn't even have to read the report—the graphic aids tell the whole story."

Two of the graphic aids from Higgins' report, both of which present information being discussed by the executive committee, are reproduced in the following figures.

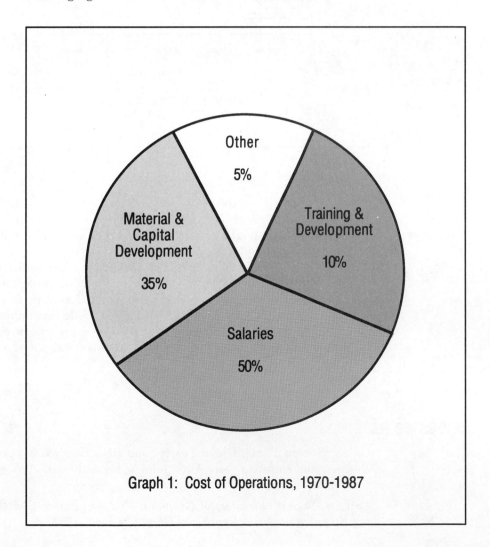

Graph 1:  Cost of Operations, 1970-1987

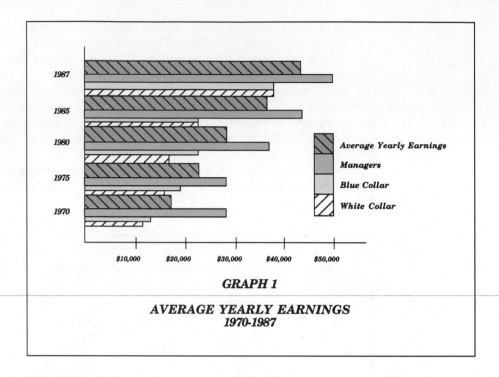

**GRAPH 1**

**AVERAGE YEARLY EARNINGS**
**1970-1987**

1. Is Rivera or Tims right about the amount that training and development represents in operating costs? Why do they have different impressions about the meaning of the pie chart?
2. Is Tiede correct in thinking that the company's blue-collar workers have been earning higher than the industry national average since 1970? Are white-collar employees exceeding the national average in income? How might the graphics in the report have given Tiede that impression?
3. If Higgins asked your advice on how to improve his graphic aids, what suggestions would you give? Identify at least three ways in which each of the graphic aids could be improved.

## SUGGESTED READINGS

Golen, Steven P., C. Glenn Pearce, and Ross Figgins. *Report Writing for Business and Industry*. New York: John Wiley and Sons, 1985. (Chapters 5 & 6, 89-135).

Lefferts, Robert. *Elements of Graphics: How to Prepare Charts and Graphs for Effective Reports*. New York: Harper & Row, 1981.

Lesikar, Raymond V. and Mary P. Lyons. *Report Writing for Business*, 7th ed. Homewood, IL: Richard D. Irwin, 1986. (Chapter 14, 215-240).

Lewell, John. *Computer Graphics: A Survey of Current Techniques and Applications*. New York: Van Nostrand Reinhold, 1985.

Treece, Malra. *Effective Reports*, 2nd ed., Boston: Allyn & Bacon, 1985. (Chapter 11, 221-254).

# WRITING THE REPORT

## CHAPTER 11

"I'm leaving next Tuesday to recruit accounting majors at three state universities," said Ellen Jeffers, the personnel director of Benjamin, Gurrerra, and Klock, a public accounting firm. "Do you have any particular instructions for me?" she asked Walter Klock, one of the managing partners.

"Yes, Ellen, recruit only the accounting graduates who can write reports," he replied. "This year we've had to fire several staff accountants who couldn't do a decent job of writing audit reports."

"In fact," Walter continued, "I'd like you to ask each interviewee for a copy of a research report he or she wrote as a course assignment. Before we invite candidates for a second interview, I want to see their reports myself."

If you were one of the applicants, would you have a well-written report for Walter Klock to examine? In many business careers, report-writing skills are critical to success. This chapter will discuss the following topics as they relate to writing reports:

- The writing style and structure of both informal and formal reports
- The parts of a formal report, including the preliminary parts, the body, and the supplementary parts
- The format of reports, including headings, spacing, page numbering, margins, and documentation

## INFORMAL REPORTS

**Informal reports**, the most common type of report used in business today, are often written in memorandum format. As discussed in Part III, memorandums convey internal information within an organization. Many routine informal reports consist of computer printouts that may have various formats.

External reports (i.e., those sent to people outside the organization) are usually more formal. However, some companies occasionally use *letter reports*, which are informal external reports written in the form of a long business letter.

Business organizations use many kinds of informal reports. Although most informal business reports contain routine information, some informal reports are analytical and based on research.

Most of the principles of written communication discussed in Chapters 3 and 4 apply to both informal and formal reports. However, informal and formal reports differ somewhat in writing style and structure.

## Informal Writing Style

Informal reports are written in an **informal** (*conversational*) **style**. This style of writing is characterized by the use of *personal pronouns* and *contractions*.

Writing as one talks—in a casual and natural style—can convey a personal touch. Personal pronouns (such as *I*, *me*, *we*, *us*, and *you*) should be used. Contractions (such as *he'll*, *she'll*, *I'll*, *aren't*, *isn't*, and *won't*) are also acceptable.

EXAMPLES: As *you* requested, *I've* analyzed the Winchell proposal.

*We'll* compare several alternatives to the Blackwell inventory system that *you* suggested last week.

## Structure

Informal reports have the same basic *structure* as other memorandums. However, memorandum reports differ from short nonreport memorandums primarily in *length* and in *organization*. Informal reports usually are longer than other memorandums and should be organized more tightly by employing headings, subheadings, and enumerations.

Three characteristics related to the structure of informal reports are *the use of deductive order; the use of few or no preliminary and supplementary parts; and the use of an abbreviated, concise layout*.

**Deductive Order**. Since the **deductive** (*direct*) **plan of organization** presents the main idea first, the reader can obtain the information necessary with which to make decisions quickly. Because many reports contain routine information, deductive arrangement is logical and helpful to a busy executive. Other ways of organizing routine reports are as chronological order, geographical location, value, importance, simple to complex, function or product, and alphabetical order, as discussed in Chapter 4. However, if time is a consideration in the decision-making process, a deductive approach can achieve goals within the most efficient time frame and with the least amount of effort.

**Few or No Preliminary and Supplementary Parts**. Informal reports usually deal with day-to-day information that needs little preliminary explanation, for example, a weekly sales report. Determining what introductory material is needed depends upon the reader's background knowledge of the subject.

Supplementary parts at the end of an informal report consist of attachments that are added for clarification or for later review. Again, the needs of the reader determine what information should be included at the end of the report.

**Abbreviated, Concise Layout**. Informal reports usually contain headings and enumerations to enhance organization. Tables and figures may be included. These techniques aid conciseness by eliminating long narrative descriptions.

An example of an informal report is shown in Figure 11.1 on pages 271-272.

## FORMAL REPORTS

A formal report usually is concerned with a major investigation. Because a formal report normally deals with a complex subject and is longer than most informal reports, more time and effort go into its preparation. Since management uses the information contained in formal reports for making major decisions, these reports are more detailed and thorough in scope than informal reports. Formal reports are written in manuscript format, containing certain preliminary and supplementary parts. These parts assist the reader in understanding the results of the study.

### Formal Writing Style

Formal reports should have a **formal** (*impersonal*) **writing style**. This style is characterized by the use of the *third person* throughout the report. Avoiding use of first- or second-person pronouns shifts the emphasis from the writer(s) and reader(s) of the report to the facts and results of the research. An objective, impersonal tone can be achieved by eliminating personal pronouns such as *I*, *me*, *we*, *you*, and *us* or possessive pronouns such as *my*, *your*, *our*, particularly in referring to the reader and the writer. Likewise, referring to people by their first names should also be avoided.

Formal reports should omit contractions and avoid the use of one-sentence paragraphs, except as a transition sentence before headings, figures, and tabulations.

The following example of a sentence from an informal report contains both personal pronouns and contractions. For the writing style to be appropriate for a formal report, the sentence should be revised:

INFORMAL: As you requested, I've analyzed the Winchell proposal.

FORMAL: This report, which the Executive Committee requested, presents an analysis of the Winchell proposal.

Notice that the formal version eliminates the contractions and personal pronouns. Because the writer does not speak of herself or himself, the formal version seems more objective.

Objectivity is essential in writing a formal report and the writer should omit personal observations, emotional language that tends to pass judgment, and biases. The report should emphasize facts rather than the writer's opinions. However, opinions, may be presented if they are labeled as such and if they come from a credible source, such as a recognized expert. An objective report should clearly state what the facts are without judging them as good or bad.

## Structure

Academic-style formal reports are typewritten in manuscript style, which is double spaced with paragraph indentions. However, many companies use a single-spaced format with indented or blocked paragraphs and double spacing between paragraphs for formal reports.

Two other features characterize formal reports: *inductive order* and the addition of *preliminary and supplementary parts*.

**Inductive Order**. Formal reports may be written using the deductive plan of organization or any of the other plans of organization outlined in Chapter 4. However, many formal analytical reports use the **inductive** (*indirect*) **plan of organization**.

Inductive arrangement follows the traditional order of presenting the introduction, body, and ending. The introductory material prepares the reader for the report. The body presents the facts along with an analysis of the facts. Finally, the ending may summarize the information, state conclusions based on the findings, and suggest recommendations based on the conclusions.

**Preliminary and Supplementary Parts**. A formal report contains both preliminary and supplementary parts. The **preliminary parts** consist of the letter or memorandum of transmittal, the title page, the contents page and list of illustrations, and the summary. **Supplementary parts** include the bibliography and the appendix materials.

## Formal Report Parts

The **parts** of a **formal report** may be divided into three major divisions — the *preliminary parts*, the *body of the report*, and the *supplementary parts*. The following outline lists these parts:

I.  Preliminary Parts
    A.  Letter or Memorandum of Transmittal
    B.  Title Page
    C.  Contents Page and List of Illustrations
    D.  Summary

II. The Body of the Report
   A. Introduction
   B. Findings/Discussion
   C. Report Ending
III. Supplementary Parts
   A. Bibliography or References
   B. Appendix Materials

**Preliminary Parts.** Parts of a report that appear before the actual text or body of the report are the **preliminary parts**. These parts provide the reader with information about the body of the report.

*Letter or Memorandum of Transmittal.* A **letter** or **memorandum of transmittal** is a message that transmits the report from the writer to the reader. If the report is sent within an organization, the writer attaches a **memorandum of transmittal** to the report. If the report is sent outside the organization, a **letter of transmittal** is used.

The direct plan of writing is appropriate for the transmittal message, as in the following outline:

1. Begin the message with its goal, which is transmitting the report to the reader. "Here is the report you requested about . . . " is a suitable opening.
2. Follow the opening with a brief statement of the purpose or goal of the report. You may also include a summary of the report at this point, but this overview should be brief.
3. Acknowledge the help of people who assisted with the research, if appropriate.
4. Close the message courteously. Thank the person who requested the study, express willingness to do additional research, or suggest future actions which might be necessary.

The writing style of the message of transmittal is usually informal (personal). Characteristics of this type of writing include the use of the active voice and personal pronouns (I, we, you). A sample memorandum of transmittal is shown in Figure 11.2 on page 273.

*Title Page.* This page is the second part of the preliminary section in a report. The **title** of a report should immediately tell the reader what the report is about and, as applicable, should answer the questions *who*, *what*, *where*, *when*, and *why*. Even though conciseness is important, a brief title may be too general or vague. Compare the following titles for completeness:

BUYING A MICROCOMPUTER

AN ANALYSIS OF MIDWESTERN UNIVERSITY STUDENTS'
PREFERENCES WHEN BUYING A MICROCOMPUTER
FOR HOME AND SCHOOL USE

The first title leaves questions unanswered as to the *who* and *where* of the report, while the second title is more comprehensive and descriptive.

The **title page** should also identify the name, title, and firm (if different from that of the writer) of the person(s) requesting the report or to whom the report is to be sent. The name, title, and company of the writer or writers of the report also should be included. In addition, the date of the report should appear on the title page. A sample title page is shown in Figure 11.3 on page 274.

*Contents Page and List of Illustrations.* A guide to the contents of a formal report appears on the **contents page**. This page indicates the organization of the report and outlines it with page numbers. The outline corresponds to the actual headings in the body of the text. A listing of these headings on the contents page helps readers locate various parts of a report and is particularly helpful if a reader wishes to save time by reading only certain key parts. In addition, the contents page may also list preliminary and supplementary parts of the report.

If the report contains several tables and figures, a "list of illustrations" may be prepared and placed below the table of contents or on the page after the contents page.

A contents page may be formatted in various ways. Outline symbols may be used to indicate various divisions. Capitalizing, indenting, and connecting dots (leaders) provide clarity. A sample contents page and a list of illustrations page are shown in Figure 11.3 on page 274.

*Summary.* A brief, condensed description of the contents of the report is called the **summary** or *executive summary*. In academic reports, this section may also be called an *abstract*. The purpose of the summary is to provide the reader with a shorter, more compact version of the report. For a busy executive, the summary may provide enough information for decision making, with the contents page directing the reader to other essential parts for further study.

All important items, including the introduction, the findings/discussion section, and the ending of a report, should be included in the summary. Writing the summary means reducing these important parts to key points. A formal analytical report and its summary are often organized in the following indirect order: purpose, research methods, findings, and report ending. However, a direct plan enables the reader to know the results of the study immediately. The direct plan simply places the conclusions at the beginning of the report, followed by the purpose, the research methods, and the findings. A sample summary is shown in Figure 11.3 on page 274.

**Body of the Report**. The major section of any report is the **body**. In formal analytical reports, the body is divided into three parts: the *introduction*, the *findings/discussion section*, and the *report ending*.

*The Introduction.* The purpose of the **introduction** is to provide the reader with enough background about the report so as to know (1) what the report is about, (2) why the report was written, and (3) how the research was conducted.

Since the first paragraph or paragraphs of the report body are obviously introductory, a heading labeled *Introduction* is unnecessary if the title of the report is at the top of the first page. However, the word *Introduction* is appropriate if the title is omitted from the first page of the body of the report (See Figure 11.4 on page 275).

The introduction may include a statement of authorization, background information, the scope of the report, definition of terms, and the research limitations. These parts are optional and should be used as necessary. However, two parts are essential—the problem statement and a description of the research methods.

The *problem statement* tells the reader what the report is about. Other common names for this introductory part are the *objective*, *purpose*, or *goal* of the report. The problem statement is usually worded in the infinitive form (to + a verb), as in the following examples:

The purpose of this study is *to compare* the effectiveness of....

The purpose of this report is *to review* the procedures used in....

The purpose of this study is *to determine* the appropriate way of....

Some research proposals ask *research questions* that the study will attempt to answer or include *hypotheses* that state expected outcomes, as follows:

RESEARCH QUESTION: Do consumers prefer styrofoam or foil containers for frozen T.V. dinners?

or

HYPOTHESIS: Consumers will prefer styrofoam to aluminum-foil containers for frozen T.V. dinners.

*Research methods* include the ways in which the information for the report was collected. This section identifies the type of **research** used—primary and/or secondary—and describes the **methodology**. The writer should discuss the research design, which includes all the steps in the data-collection process. Enough information should be provided to convince the reader of the researcher's ability to accomplish the research objective.

An example of the introductory paragraphs of a report is shown in Figure 11.4 on page 275.

*Findings/Discussion.* The **findings/discussion** part of the report presents, analyses, and interprets the information that was collected. The writer should use a heading for this section that describes the specific findings (rather than use the word *Findings* or *Discussion*). In the sample report, the headings for the findings/discussion section are *Cost of Alternatives* and *Effects of Government Legislation*.

Sample pages of the findings/discussion section of this report are shown in Figure 11.5 on pages 276-280.

*Report Ending.* As discussed in Chapter 9, the type of report written will determine whether its ending should contain a summary, conclusion(s), a section on recommendations, or a combination of all three.

A *summary* of the major points of the findings/discussion section is frequently used in informational reports and differs from the preliminary summary. While the preliminary summary reviews the entire report, the **summary** at the end of the report is an overview of the research findings. The following examples are sample summary statements:

Office managers perceive the lack of incentives as a serious productivity problem.

As the previous timetable indicates, all phases of the project are on schedule.

The *conclusion(s)* section is used at the end of analytical reports. Information must not only be presented but also interpreted in analytical reports. In addition, this analysis may include an evaluation of the causes or reasons behind the findings and conclusion(s), based on the findings. All evidence for conclusions should be included in the report. The following statements are examples of conclusions of reports:

On the basis of preliminary test findings, the installation of the X590 system could save Deltar, Ltd. $45,000 a year.

Survey results indicate that First State Bank is weak in the convenience-conscious and upscale white-collar target market.

A *recommendations* section is used when a course of action is required. **Recommendations** are drawn from appropriate conclusions and may be a separate part of the report or may be included in the conclusions section. The following statements are sample recommendations:

Based on additional research of costs and locations of automatic teller (AT) services, the first recommendation is to expand the AT system of First State Bank.

The recommendation is made to add additional physical fitness equipment to aid employees in their efforts to improve their overall health.

An example of a report ending is shown in Figure 11.6 on pages 281-282.

**Supplementary Parts**. Information that is not essential in the body of a report but that may be helpful to a reader should be included in the **supplementary parts** of a report. These parts are placed at the end of a report as separate, added-on sections. Two major supplementary parts are the bibliography (or references) and the appendix.

*Bibliography or References.* This section lists all secondary sources used in preparing a report. It contains not only sources cited within a report as references but may include other sources reviewed for informational purposes as well. The bibliography or references section generally appears before the appendix, but some style manuals recommend its placement after the appendix.

No major divisions are necessary if the bibliography is short. A main heading of *Bibliography* or *References* followed by an alphabetical list of the sources is sufficient. However, if many sources are to be included, the bibliography or references section may be separated into major divisions of published sources such as books, periodicals, government documents, and other miscellaneous publications such as yearbooks and bulletins. Unpublished sources such as dissertations, manuscripts, interviews, surveys, and personal letters may be listed in one or more separate divisions as well. All sources in each division must be alphabetized.

Style manuals differ somewhat in the format that they recommend for bibliographies. However, no matter what style manual you use, the basic bibliographical information is similar.

For publications with one or two authors, arrange the entries alphabetically, with the primary author's last name first. Generally, publications with three or more authors should include the first author's name, followed by the Latin abbreviation *et al.*, which means *and others* (for example, Weatherby, Samuel, et al.). As an alternative, simply use *and others* after the first author's name (for example, Weatherby, Samuel, and others).

For book entries, the bibliography or references section should list the author(s) (last name first), title of the book (underlined), place of publication, publisher, and copyright year. For periodicals, the bibliography entry should include the author(s), title of the article (usually in quotation marks), name of publication (usually underlined), volume and issue numbers, issue date, and page number(s).

The first line of a bibliography or references entry should be blocked with the left margin, with following lines indented from the left margin. This indented style emphasizes the alphabetized format. Most style manuals recommend single spacing within each entry and double spacing between entries. Periods or commas separate the items in an entry. A sample bibliography is shown in Figure 11.7 on page 283.

*Appendix*. Place supplementary information in the appendix. This information is provided for the reader's additional study, if necessary. Include each item as a separate appendix and give it a title, as shown in the following examples:

Appendix A: Cover Letter

Appendix B: Questionnaire

Appendix C: Follow-Up Letter

## FORMAT OF REPORTS

The **format** or arrangement of a report involves *headings*, *spacing*, *page numbering*, *margins*, and *methods of documentation*. Numerous style manuals are available to assist a writer in determining an appropriate format for a report. Some of these manuals are as follows:

Brusaw, Charles T., Gerald J. Alred, and Walter E. Oliu. *The Business Writer's Handbook*, 2nd ed. New York: St. Martin's Press, 1982.

Campbell, Williams Giles, and Steven Vaughan Ballou. *Form and Style: Theses, Reports, Term Papers*, 6th ed. Boston: Houghton Mifflin, 1981.

Achtert, Walter S. and Joseph Gibaldi. *The MLA Style Manual*. New York: Modern Language Association, 1985.

*Publication Manual of the American Psychological Association*, 3rd ed. Washington, D.C.: American Psychological Association, 1983.

*The Chicago Manual of Style*, 13th ed. Chicago: University of Chicago Press, 1982.

Turabian, Kate L. *A Manual for Writers of Term Papers, Theses, and Dissertations*, 5th ed. Chicago: Univers'.y of Chicago Press, 1987.

## Headings

**Headings,** which serve as directional signals in a report, lead both the writer and reader through a report in the same way that road signs lead a driver on a highway. Headings improve readability by signaling the end of one section and the beginning of another. Headings also serve as attention getters by directing the reader to sections of a report that are of particular interest.

**Content of Headings.** Since headings help the reader to locate key points in a report, the headings should be informative and descriptive. Headings may consist of a word, a few words, or a complete sentence. The most common format for headings is that of a few words or a phrase. One-word headings may be too broad, and complete sentences may be too lengthy. Compare the following headings in a section of a report that defines voice processing systems:

TWO WORDS: Voice Processing

SENTENCE: Voice Processing Systems Include Two Different Types of Systems.

PHRASE: Defining Voice Processing Systems

The first heading, *Voice Processing*, may be too general for the content of the section that it describes. Many other topics besides a definition of voice processing systems could be included under such a heading. Although the second heading, *Voice Processing Systems Include Two Different Types of Systems*, is informative, it is too long and cumbersome. The third heading, *Defining Voice Processing Systems*, clearly focuses on the subject matter to be discussed.

**Origin of Headings.** As discussed in Chapter 8, always make an outline of the plan for a research project. When you begin to write the report, the items in that outline become the headings in the report. The relationship of headings to a partial outline of a report is shown in Figure 11.A on page 266.

## FIGURE 11.A ORIGIN OF HEADINGS FROM REPORT OUTLINE

SELECTING A MICROCOMPUTER

I.   Overview of the Problem

II.  Guidelines for Selection

    A.   Determine the Intended Use

    B.   Choose Hardware

        1.   Selecting a Microprocessor
        2.   Selecting Secondary Storage

           a.   Floppy Disk
           b.   Hard Disk

SELECTING A MICROCOMPUTER

- - - - - - - - - - - - - - - - - - - - - - - - -
- - - - - - - -.  - - - - - - - - - -.  - - -
- - - - - - - - - - - - - -.

### Overview of the Problem

- - - - - - - - - - - - - -.  - - - - - - - -
- - - - - - - - - - - - - - - -.  - - - - - - - - - -
- - - - - - - -.

### Guidelines for Selection

- - - - - - - - - - - - - - - - - - -.  - - - - - - - - -
- - - - - - - - - - - - - - - - - -.  - - - - - - - -.

### Determine the Intended Use

- - - - - - - - - - - - - - - - - - - - - - -
- - - - - - -.  - - - - - - -.

### Choose Hardware

- - - - - - - - - - - - - - - - -.  - - - - - - - -
- - - - - - - - -.  - - - - -.

Selecting a Microprocessor.  - - - - - - -
- - - - - - - - - - - - - -.  - - - - - - - - - - - - -
- - - - - - - - -.

Selecting Secondary Storage.  - - - - - -
- - - - - - - - - - - - - - - -.  - - - - - - - - - -
- - - - - - - - -.

### Floppy disk
- - - - - - - - - - - - -.  - - -
- - - - - - - - - - -.

### Hard disk
- - - - - - - - - - - - - -.  -
- - - - - - - - - - - - - - - - - - - -.

**Parallelism of Headings.** Headings of the same degree should have parallel grammatical construction. In Figure 11.A the following headings are parallel to each other:

I and II
II-A and II-B
II-B-1 and II-B-2
II-B-2-a and II-B-2-b

Compare the following headings:

| Nonparallel Headings | Parallel Headings |
| --- | --- |
| Looking at the Company's History | History of the Company |
| Company Sales | Sales of the Company |
| Consideration of Company Expenses | Expenses of the Company |

**Placement and Style of Headings.** The importance or rank of various degrees of headings may be indicated by the **placement and style of headings** within a report. A writer may use various combinations of placement and style, as long as the chosen combination is consistent throughout the report.

The traditional style of triple spacing before a heading is inconvenient for computer usage because most printers are pre-set for double spacing. As a result, some companies have eliminated triple spacing and are now using double or quadruple spacing before headings. A heading style that is compatible with pre-set double spacing is shown in Figure 11.B.

## FIGURE 11.B PLACEMENT AND STYLE OF HEADINGS

### FIRST—DEGREE HEADING (TITLE)

The title of a report, which is a first—degree heading, should be centered, typed in capital letters, and not underlined. A quadruple space follows the title before the first line of the body of the report. The title or first—degree heading should not be immediately followed by a second—degree heading; some narrative should separate the two types of headings.

#### Second—Degree Headings

Major sections of a report (that correspond to the Roman numerals of a report) are outlined as second—degree headings. Center, underline, and capitalize the first letters of important words of second-degree headings. Use a double space above and below this type of heading.

Third—Degree Headings

Starting at the left margin, third—degree headings correspond to the A, B, C, and following letters in a report outline. Underline third—degree headings and capitalize all important words. Use a double space above and below this type of heading.

Fourth—Degree Headings. Indent from the left margin and type the fourth—degree heading, underline it, and end it with a period. A fourth—degree heading corresponds to 1, 2, 3, and following numerals in a report outline. The paragraph begins on the same line as the heading. Use a double space above this type of heading.

A fifth—degree heading is part of the first sentence of a para—graph. Underline only the first word or key words and capitalize only the first word. Use a double space above this type of heading.

All topics of equal importance should have the same type of heading throughout the report. For a short informal report, one or two degrees of headings may be sufficient. For longer and more complex reports, the writer may use several degrees of headings, as shown in Figure 11.B.

## Spacing, Page Numbering, and Margins

Although most academic-style formal reports are double-spaced, some business organizations use single spacing in formal reports. In either case, quotations of more than four lines are single spaced, usually indented from both margins, but not enclosed in quotation marks. An example of a long quotation is shown in Figure 11.5 on page 276.

Traditionally, page numbers on preliminary parts of a formal report are in small Roman numerals (i, ii, iii, iv, etc.) placed near the bottom of the page, as shown in Figures 11.3 on page 274. Other page numbers appear in Arabic numbers at the top right corner (See Appendix B). When using word processing software, you may have to place page numbers at the bottom of a page, usually at the center. This placement is acceptable as long as page numbers are placed consistently.

Some reports contain a *running title*, which is a shortened version of the main title of a report (approximately three or four words), at the top of each page. The running title and the page numbers should appear on the same line at opposite margins (see Figure 11.1 or 11.5 on pages 272 and 276).

The top, side, and bottom margins of a formal report should be at least one inch in width. Reports that are bound on the left should contain a 1 1/2-inch left margin to accommodate the binding.

Informal reports, discussed earlier in this chapter, are generally single spaced, with double spacing between paragraphs. Page numbering and margins are similar to that of formal reports.

## Documentation

Secondary sources of data are protected by copyright laws. If you are quoting directly from another author or authors, you must acknowledge your source. If you are **paraphrasing** (stating someone else's ideas in your own words), you must also acknowledge your source. Giving credit where credit is due is very important. Not to do so is **plagiarism**, which is a form of theft and is a serious violation of ethics. However, information that is considered general knowledge and is not quoted directly does not need to be documented.

Appropriate **documentation** increases a writer's credibility. Citing recognized authors helps to convince your reader that your statements are based upon facts and supported by authorities.

Report writers may select one of various acceptable methods of documentation. Three basic types of documentation are *author-date references*, *endnote references*, and *footnote references*.

**Author-Date References**. Placing the author's name and publication date in parentheses, after the cited work, is used in **author-date references** (often referred to as *internal citations*), for example:

Performance budgets allow government agencies more flexibility than traditional line-item budgets (Pierce, 1985).

Specific page numbers may also be included, as follows:

Standardized UPC codes have enabled retailers to improve the accuracy and productivity of inventory-control procedures by 40 to 50 percent (Ross, 1987, 281).

Additional variations of author-date references appear in the following paragraph:

Little difference between the two computerized accounting methods was noted. Sanchez (1985, 281) firmly believes, however, that the first method is more efficient. Several other experts concur with Sanchez (Ho, 1984; Gordon, 1985; Smith and Taylor, 1983; Minor et al., 1982). Davis stated the importance of this methodology as early as 1975. Even governmental agencies have taken a stand in favor of this procedure (Federal Reserve Bank, 1984; FDIC, 1982).

In the second sentence of the previous paragraph, the author's name is used as part of the text. In the third sentence, multiple references are separated by semicolons, and a reference with three or more authors uses the first author's name and *et al*. The fourth sentence places the author's name and publication date within the text. Finally, the last sentence refers to two government agencies. Full documentation of each reference should be provided at the end of the report in alphabetical order on a bibliography or reference page. An *Endnotes* section is unnecessary when this reference style is used.

Another method of internal citation that is becoming increasingly popular uses a number to refer to each cited source; the number cross references the citation to a corresponding item in the bibliography. With this method, each entry in the bibliography must be numbered as well as alphabetized. In the following example, the *7:28* refers to entry number 7 in the bibliography, page 28; the *3:102* refers to entry number 3 in the bibliography, page 102.

**Imports to Eastern-European countries increased 35 percent from 1980 to 1985 (7:28). In the next two years, however, imports decreased by 8 percent (3:102).**

When using this method of internal citation, the writer must number each item in the alphabetized bibliography, as follows:

1. Adams, M. J. *The Polish Economy, 1975-1985*. New York: Political Economic Press, 1987.

2. Blakemore, Andrew. "The Balance of Payments in Soviet-Bloc Countries," *European Financial Journal*, (October 12, 1987): 1-10.

3. Carelli, Mary. *The Eastern European Farm Crisis*. Chicago: University of Chicago Press, 1986.

**Endnote References**. **Endnotes** are references placed at the end of a report with the use of key numbers. Documentation appears at the end of a citation either as a raised number (superscript) or as a number in parentheses. The numbers appear in sequential order throughout the report. In addition to the bibliography or reference list, a section entitled *Endnotes* also appears at the end of the report. Citations are listed in numerical order in this section.

**Footnote References**. Placing references at the bottom of the page on which the citation occurs is an older method of documentation that is becoming less popular. Superscript (raised) numbers are keyed to **footnotes** at the bottom of the page.

Use the style of documentation that your instructor or employer recommends, and use that style consistently. Style manuals provide specific guidelines for consistent documentation.

## FIGURE 11.1 MEMORANDUM REPORT

# MILLER MANUFACTURING COMPANY

**INTEROFFICE MEMORANDUM**

TO:    Robert Elston, Director of Finance

FROM:  Sara George, Financial Analyst  *SG*

DATE:  July 31, 19--

SUBJECT:  PROGRESS ON H2X SUPPLY STUDY

Our study of the various alternatives for supplying H2X generic doll-body components is progressing on schedule and is now approximately 25 percent complete.

### Description of Alternatives

The following alternatives are being considered for generating sufficient components to meet the requirements of our ten-year contract with Cornucopia Vending:

1. Buying all units for the first five years and manufacturing the units ourselves for the next five years

2. Manufacturing 1 million units per year and buying the shortfall (any additional units we'll need over the 1 million number)

3. Manufacturing 1 million units per year for the first five years (we'll buy the shortfall during those years); then retooling to manufacture 2 million units per year for the next five years

### Work Completed

The previously established bases of comparison for our study were present value of alternative costs (at a 15 percent opportunity cost) and potential impact of government legislation. I've completed my analysis of both factors for Alternative 1.

### Costs of Alternative 1

Only four suppliers manufacture units that are compatibile with our needs. Of the four, Timmons, Inc., in Boise, Idaho, has the lowest price. The average total cost per H2X unit from Timmons is $1. Weaverly and Clamper both offer the next-lowest costs per unit ($1.05). Costs of purchasing the units are summarized in Table I.

## MEMORANDUM REPORT (CONTINUED)

PROGRESS ON H2X SUPPLY STUDY                                      2

TABLE I

### COST COMPARISON OF FOUR SUPPLIERS OF H2X COMPONENTS
(per 1 million units)

|                        | Timmons     | Weaverly    | Clamper     | Kroeger     |
|------------------------|-------------|-------------|-------------|-------------|
| Material Costs         | $  850,000  | $  903,000  | $  898,000  | $  956,000  |
| Shipping Costs         | 150,000     | 149,000     | 155,000     | 143,000     |
| TOTAL COSTS            | $1,000,000  | $1,052,000  | $1,053,000  | $1,099,000  |
| TOTAL COSTS PER UNIT   | $1.00       | $1.05       | $1.05       | $1.10       |

### Government Impact of Alternative 1

Since Alternative 1 doesn't require the immediate purchase of additional machinery, we wouldn't be directly affected by changes in Federal OSHA requirements for the first five years. However, we might be affected indirectly if our supplier has to retool present operations to meet stricter noise-pollution regulations. The price per unit would then undoubtedly increase to cover any additional costs of pollution-control equipment.

### Work Schedule

Additional research is scheduled for August, as follows:

1.  The cost of purchasing production equipment is being assessed, and a comparative report should be completed by August 15.

2.  An evaluation of the impact of proposed OSHA regulations began two days ago. Staff in the offices of Senators Wilson and Dearing have agreed to send us documents summarizing the recent hearings on noise pollution. As soon as this material arrives, we can proceed with this part of the study.

A draft of the final report will be ready for you by August 31.

lak

## FIGURE 11.2 MEMORANDUM OF TRANSMITTAL

# MILLER MANUFACTURING COMPANY

**INTEROFFICE
MEMORANDUM**

**TO:**     Karl Jenkins, General Manager

**FROM:**   Robert Elston, Director of Finance *re*

**DATE:**   September 1, 19--

**SUBJECT:**   REPORT COMPARING H2X SUPPLY ALTERNATIVES

Here is the report you requested that compares H2X supplternatives for meeting the manufacturing contract with Cornucopia Vending.

The report shows that purchasing H2X components for the first five years and manufacturing the units the next five years is our best option.  As you requested, we compared each alternative on the basis of both present value of projected costs and the potential impact of federal noise-pollution legislation.

If you need additional information, please call me.

lak

Attachment

## FIGURE 11.3 TITLE PAGE/CONTENTS/ILLUSTRATIONS/SUMMARY PAGE

COMPARISON OF H2X COMPONENTS SUPPLY ALTERNATIVES

AT MILLER MANUFACTURING COMPANY

FOR THE NEXT TEN YEARS

Prepared for

Karl Jenkins

General Manager

Prepared by

Robert Elston

Director of Finance

September 1, 19--

---

CONTENTS

ii

---

LIST OF ILLUSTRATIONS

iii

---

SUMMARY

The best option for supplying H2X components for the contract with Cornucopia Vending is to purchase the units for the first five years of the ten-year contract and then install the equipment necessary to manufacture the components for the years six through ten.

Three purchasing versus manufacturing alternatives were compared according to the cumulative net present value of costs. Alternative 1 was nearly $1.2 million less costly than the next best alternative.

The potential effects of federal OSHA noise-pollution legislation were also considered for each of the three alternatives. Under Alternative 1, federal regulations would have no immediate effect on Miller Manufacturing because equipment purchases would be deferred for five years.

iv

## FIGURE 11.4 INTRODUCTORY MATERIAL OF A REPORT

<u>Introduction</u>

Miller Manufacturing recently negotiated a long-term contract with Cornucopia Vending to provide "Tutti Tots," a popular toy sold in vending machines. The terms of the contract specify that Miller Manufacturing will supply Cornucopia with this product for ten years, according to the following schedule:

| | |
|---|---|
| Year 1: | 1.2 million units |
| Year 2: | 1.4 million units |
| Year 3: | 1.6 million units |
| Year 4: | 1.8 million units |
| Years 5-10: | 2.0 million units per year |

Over the life of the contract, the price will be fixed at $200 per gross. Consequently, Miller seeks to produce "Tutti Tots" at the lowest possible cost per unit.

A key component of each "Tutti Tot" is the H2X generic doll body. This study analyzes and compares alternative methods for generating sufficient H2X components to meet the needs of the Cornucopia contract.

**Problem Statement**

The purpose of this study is to compare three alternatives available to Miller Manufacturing for acquiring adequate supplies of H2X components during the next ten years.

**Research Methods**

Preliminary analysis of economic conditions (Association for Better Business, 1986, 15-18) indicates that Miller has three feasible alternatives:

1.  Buy all units needed for five years; then purchase the necessary equipment and begin manufacturing the units internally.

2.  Purchase equipment sufficient to manufacture 1 million H2X units per year and buy additional units needed over the 1 million number for the duration of the contract.

3.  Purchase equipment sufficient to manufacture 1 million H2X units per year for the first five years and buy additional units needed over the 1 million number; in the sixth year, purchase the rest of the equipment necessary to produce 2 million units per year for the next five years.

# FIGURE 11.5 BODY OF A REPORT

H2X SUPPLY ALTERNATIVES                                              2

The three alternatives will be compared according to the following factors:

1. The present value of the costs of the alternatives (given a 15 percent opportunity cost)

2. The impact of potential government legislation related to stricter noise-pollution regulations in manufacturing plants

### Costs of Alternatives

The three alternatives were analyzed through use of a Cactus spreadsheet program, as follows:

### Alternative 1

An investment of $3 million at the end of the fifth year would be required under Alternative 1. This investment would have to be written off during the last five years of the Cornucopia contract. As Karl Jenkins, General Manager of Miller Manufacturing, noted in a recent interview:

> One of the secrets of Miller Manufacturing's success is our policy of allocating the cost of equipment to the first major job for which it was purchased. Any "leftover" life then becomes a "gift" in our budget for small contracts. This policy gives Miller a real competitive edge (television interview, May 23, 1987).

Costs of Alternative 1 are shown in Table 1.

As shown in Table 1, purchasing costs are greatly reduced under Alternative 1, and the tax advantage of depreciating (using straight-line depreciation) the production equipment is substantial. However, production costs associated with making the H2X are also substantial. Because Miller personnel will be learning to operate the new equipment during the sixth year of the contract, operating costs during that year can be expected to be higher than in subsequent years. Industry averages (Keene, 1986, 73-80) suggest that Miller has a 20 percent chance of sixth-year operating costs being as high as $2 million, and an 80 percent chance of $1.2 million. Operating costs during the last four years of the contract can be expected to level out at $600,000 per year.

The cumulative net present value of the cost of Alternative 1 (calculated at a 15 percent opportunity cost) is $7,471,400 over the ten years of the contract.

## BODY OF A REPORT (CONTINUED)

H2X SUPPLY ALTERNATIVES                                                                    3

TABLE 1

PROJECTED COSTS OF MILLER MANUFACTURING FOR ALTERNATIVE 1 *
FOR THE TEN-YEAR CORNUCOPIA CONTRACT

| | Year 1 | Year 2 | Year 3 | Year 4 | Year 5 | Year 6 | Year 7 | Year 8 | Year 9 | Year 10 |
|---|---|---|---|---|---|---|---|---|---|---|
| Production Units (in 1,000's) | 1,200 | 1,400 | 1,600 | 1,800 | 2,000 | | | | | |
| Equipment Cost (in $1,000's) | | | | | 3,000 | | | | | |
| Production Cost (in $1,000's) | | | | | | 1,300 | 600 | 600 | 600 | 600 |
| Depreciation (in -$1,000's) | | | | | | (300) | (300) | (300) | (300) | (300) |
| Net Cost (in $1,000's) | 1,200 | 1,400 | 1,600 | 1,800 | 5,000 | 1,000 | 300 | 300 | 300 | 300 |
| Present Value Factor | .870 | .756 | .657 | .572 | .497 | .432 | .376 | .327 | .284 | .247 |
| Net Present Value of Cost ($1,000) | 1,044 | 1,058 | 1,051 | 1,026 | 2,485 | 432 | 112 | 98 | 85 | 74 |
| Cumulative Net Present Value of Cost ($1,000) | 1,044 | 2,102 | 3,154 | 4,183 | 6,668 | 7,001 | 7,214 | 7,312 | 7,397 | 7,471 |

* Alternative 1 = Purchasing all H2X units each year for five years from a supplier and then manufacturing internally all units each year for the next five years

## BODY OF A REPORT (CONTINUED)

H2X SUPPLY ALTERNATIVES                                              4

### Alternative 2

The immediate purchase of $2 million worth of equipment (depreciated over ten years) would be required under Alternative 2. Because Miller Manufacturing personnel would be learning how to operate the new equipment during its first year of operation, operating costs during the first year are expected to be higher than in subsequent years of the contract.

Industry averages (Keene, 1986, 73-80) indicate that Miller has a 75 percent chance of first year costs equaling $1.5 million and a 25 percent chance that the costs will be only $1.2 million. A 75 percent chance exists that subsequent operating costs will be $700,000 per year, and a 25 percent chance that the operating costs will be $600,000 per year.

Alternative 2 combines purchasing and producing the H2X as a means of minimizing the capital expenditure while still gaining some of the benefits of producing. The cumulative net present value of the costs of Alternative 2 is $9,029,050, as shown in Table 2.

### Alternative 3

Alternative 3 differs from Alternative 2 by using income generated during the first five years of the contract to fund the purchase of the remaining production equipment in the sixth year. Operating the new equipment during the last five years should generate a consistent increment in operating costs.

Industry averages (Keene, 1986, 73-80) indicate a 60 percent probability of additional costs totaling $700,000 per year during the last five years of the contract under this alternative. Costs totaling $500,000 per year have a 40 percent probability.

The cumulative net present value of the costs of Alternative 3 is $8,661,370, as shown in Table 3.

### Effects of Government Legislation

A key consideration in any decision involving the use of heavy industrial equipment is the effect of present and potential government legislation. Since the Keeter Law of 1970, 117 pieces of federal legislation regarding the effects of manufacturing industries on the environment have become law. The trend is ". . . toward even more stringent governmentally imposed restrictions on private industry. By the year 2000, freedom in industrial choice will be but a foggy memory of times gone by" (Samuels, 1986, 83).

Noise-pollution limits, as defined by the federal government, are a critical concern in purchasing equipment for the H2X

## BODY OF A REPORT (CONTINUED)

H2X SUPPLY ALTERNATIVES    5

TABLE 2

PROJECTED COSTS OF MILLER MANUFACTURING FOR ALTERNATIVE 2[*]
FOR THE TEN-YEAR CORNUCOPIA CONTRACT

| | Year 1 | Year 2 | Year 3 | Year 4 | Year 5 | Year 6 | Year 7 | Year 8 | Year 9 | Year 10 |
|---|---|---|---|---|---|---|---|---|---|---|
| Production Units (in 1,000's) | 200 | 400 | 600 | 800 | 1,000 | 1,000 | 1,000 | 1,000 | 1,000 | 1,000 |
| Equipment Cost (in $1,000's) | (NOTE: $2,000,000 purchase previous year to first year of Cornucopia Contract) | | | | | | | | | |
| Production Cost (in $1,000's) | 1,425 | 675 | 675 | 675 | 675 | 675 | 675 | 675 | 675 | 675 |
| Depreciation (in -$1,000's) | (100) | (100) | (100) | (100) | (100) | (100) | (100) | (100) | (100) | (100) |
| Net Cost (in $1,000) | 1,525 | 975 | 1,175 | 1,375 | 1,575 | 1,575 | 1,575 | 1,575 | 1,575 | 1,575 |
| Present Value Factor | .870 | .756 | .657 | .572 | .497 | .432 | .376 | .327 | .284 | .247 |
| Net Present Value of Cost ($1,000) | 1,327 | 737 | 772 | 787 | 783 | 680 | 592 | 515 | 447 | 389 |
| Cumulative Net Present Value of Cost ($1,000) | 3,327 | 4,064 | 4,836 | 5,622 | 6,405 | 7,086 | 7,678 | 8,193 | 8,640 | 9,029 |

[*]Alternative 2 = Manufacturing 1 million H2X units per year and buying any additional units over 1 million each year from a supplier

# BODY OF A REPORT (CONTINUED)

TABLE 3

PROJECTED COSTS OF MILLER MANUFACTURING FOR ALTERNATIVE 3*
FOR THE TEN-YEAR CORNUCOPIA CONTRACT

| | Year 1 | Year 2 | Year 3 | Year 4 | Year 5 | Year 6 | Year 7 | Year 8 | Year 9 | Year 10 |
|---|---|---|---|---|---|---|---|---|---|---|
| Production Units (in 1,000's) | 200 | 400 | 600 | 800 | 1,000 | | | | | |
| Equipment Cost (in $1,000's) | (NOTE: $2,000,000 purchase previous year to first year of Cornucopia Contract) | | | | 1,000 | | | | | |
| Production Cost (in $1,000's) | 1,425 | 675 | 675 | 675 | 675 | 1,295 | 1,295 | 1,295 | 1,295 | 1,295 |
| Depreciation (in -$1,000's) | (100) | (100) | (100) | (100) | (100) | (200) | (200) | (200) | (200) | (200) |
| Net Cost (in $1,000's) | 1,525 | 975 | 1,175 | 1,375 | 1,575 | 2,095 | 1,095 | 1,095 | 1,095 | 1,095 |
| Present Value Factor | .870 | .756 | .657 | .572 | .497 | .432 | .376 | .327 | .284 | .247 |
| Net Present Value Of Cost ($1,000) | 1,327 | 737 | 772 | 787 | 783 | 905 | 412 | 358 | 311 | 270 |
| Cumulative Net Present Value of Cost ($1,000) | 3,327 | 4,064 | 4,836 | 5,622 | 6,405 | 7,310 | 7,722 | 8,080 | 8,391 | 8,661 |

*Alternative 3 = Manufacturing 1 million H2X units per year and buying any additional units over 1 million for the first five years and manufacturing 2 million units per year for the next five years

## FIGURE 11.6 ENDING MATERIAL OF A REPORT

H2X SUPPLY ALTERNATIVES                                                                    7

components.  The trend in controlling noise pollution is toward lower decibel levels ("Noise Pollution Limits," 1987, 12).

If the trend toward lower decibel levels continues, industrial equipment that **operates** at a decibel level over 80 will require specialized modifications for operation (Higgins, 1987, 102).  Industrial equipment that operates above an 80 decibel level may even be banned.

The press that creates the generic H2X components currently operates at an 85-decibel level.  Because all three of the alternatives under consideration involve purchasing an H2X press, the effects of government legislation must be considered for each alternative.

Alternative 1

Although Alternative 1 requires the purchasing of an H2X press, the purchase would be made five years from now.  The new presses available at that time would more than likely meet the government requirements for allowable decibel levels.

Alternative 2

An H2X press would have to be purchased for the coming year for Alternative 2.  Because presses currently available operate at an 85-decibel level, a newly acquired press may need costly modification in the near future.  If such modifications cannot be made, the press may become obsolete.

Alternative 3

Although Alternative 3 would require the purchase of some of the equipment five years from now, most of the required equipment is to be purchased in the coming year.  As with Alternative 2, the equipment may require modifications to meet allowable decibel levels or may become useless if modifications are not possible.

Conclusions

Clearly, both monetary investment and government regulations limit the choices to three feasible alternatives available to Miller Manufacturing for acquiring adequate supplies of H2X components in the next ten years for the Cornucopia contract. From the perspective of government restrictions, Alternative 1 has far less risk than either Alternatives 2 or 3.  From a cost viewpoint, Alternative 1 is the most cost efficient.  The costs of the three alternatives are summarized in Figure 1.

## ENDING MATERIAL OF A REPORT (CONTINUED)

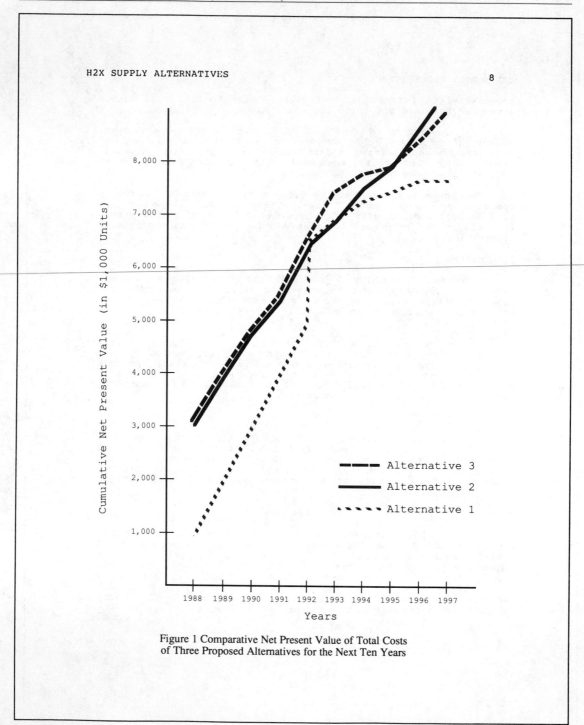

H2X SUPPLY ALTERNATIVES                                    8

Figure 1 Comparative Net Present Value of Total Costs
of Three Proposed Alternatives for the Next Ten Years

## FIGURE 11.7 BIBLIOGRAPHY PAGE

H2X SUPPLY ALTERNATIVES                                              9

<u>Recommendation</u>

Alternative 1 is the least costly of the three alternatives and also is relatively less risky in terms of government sanctions. Therefore, the recommendation is made that Miller Manufacturing purchase H2X components for the first five years of the Cornucopia contract, buy the H2X press in the sixth year, and manufacture the components during the last five years of the contract.

H2X SUPPLY ALTERNATIVES                                             10

REFERENCES

Association for Better Business. <u>Survey of Buying Power, 1975-1980</u>. Great Neck, NJ: Association for Better Business, 1986, 15-18.

Chelsey Area Chamber of Commerce. <u>Economic Growth: Will We See It in Our Time</u>? New York: Chelsey Area Chamber of Commerce, 1985.

Higgins, Allayn. <u>The Federal Government and You, the Business Manager</u>. New York: Scrimshaw Publishers, 1987.

Jenkins, Karl. Interview with Tom Prentice, commentator of WKTV-3 "Meet the Economic Community," May 23, 1987.

Johnson, Horace. "Government Projections on Noise Pollution." <u>Our Nation</u>, 4, no. 8 (September 1985): 823-901.

Keene, Jonathon. "Projecting the Economy Through the Year 2000." <u>Business Interface</u>, 2, no. 1 (January 1986): 73-80.

Occupational Safety and Health Administration. "Noise Pollution Limits in Manufacturing Plants." <u>OSHA Publication No. LGA 87-201</u>. Washington, DC: United States Government: Printing Office, 1987.

Samuels, T. T. <u>The Death of Private Industry</u>. Washington, DC: Middledown Publishing, 1986.

## SUMMARY

The two major differences between informal and formal reports are in writing style and structure. An informal, personal writing style characterizes informal reports, while formal reports have a formal or impersonal writing style. In terms of structure, informal reports contain few or no preliminary and supplementary parts, while formal reports contain both.

The preliminary parts of a formal report may include a letter or memorandum of transmittal, a title page, a contents page, list of illustrations, and a summary. The body of a report contains an introduction, a findings/discussion section, and the ending of the report. The supplementary parts of a report consist of a bibliography and appendix.

The format of a report incorporates the appropriate headings, spacing, page numbering, and margins. The use of an accepted style manual can aid the report writer in these areas as well as in the methods of correct documentation.

## CHAPTER REVIEW

1. What are the differences in writing style between an informal and formal report?
2. Explain why a direct plan of organization is often used for informal reports and why an indirect plan of organization is generally used for formal reports.
3. Identify whether the following sentences are examples of formal or informal writing styles and explain why.
   a. I've attached additional cost data for you to examine.
   b. Appendix B contains monthly inventory reports for the past two years.
   c. For further information, call Hal, who will direct the next phase of this project.
   d. According to personnel department statistics, our affirmative action program is not having the anticipated results.
4. Identify the four preliminary parts of a formal report and explain the purpose of each part.
5. Identify two parts that are essential to the introduction of a formal report and indicate why they are important.
6. What should be included in the findings/discussion part of a formal report?
7. Identify each of the following statements as report findings, conclusions, or recommendations.
   a. Acme Company should consolidate the operations of the two Denver plants.
   b. Eighty-five percent of Acme employees are opposed to the proposed merger with Bafus, Inc.
   c. Acme employees are not complying with minimum OSHA safety requirements because they have not received adequate training.
   d. We have concluded that Acme should lease rather than purchase an ABC computer.
   e. The results of the consumer attitude survey are summarized in Table I.

8. Identify the two supplementary parts discussed in the chapter. Should every report contain these parts? Why?

9. Defend the statement "Report headings should be informative and descriptive."

10. Explain the purpose of documentation and briefly describe three methods of documentation.


# APPLICATIONS

## Informal Reports

1. The Collection Agency

You are assistant to Vivian Henderson, vice president of finance at Windward, Inc., a chain of six department stores located in the Kansas City area. Ms. Henderson tells you that Grace Washington, the company's credit and collection manager, has suggested that Windward may be able to save money by discontinuing its present contract with Godell Collection Agency. She thinks that Windward could handle the entire collection process internally by hiring a salaried attorney and by expanding the responsibilities of the collection department. Henderson wants you to study the topic and report your findings to her.

Grace Washington tells you that she believes the collection agency charges too much for doing very little work. The Godell Agency charges a 50 percent fee for collecting accounts that are 120 days overdue. The agency sends one certified letter to delinquent customers and then files a suit against them two weeks later if the bill is still unpaid. By using this method, the agency recovers about 25 percent of the delinquent accounts. She tells you that her department could handle the increased workload by hiring two additional collectors and one additional accounts receivable clerk.

You next talk with Hal Ortega, the personnel director. Ortega tells you that credit department collectors cost the company an average of $17,000 each in salary and fringe benefits, and accounts receivable clerks cost the company $16,000 each.

Ortega also thinks that hiring an attorney could be a problem. Since some of the company's customers live in Missouri and some in Kansas, the attorney would need to be a member of both state bars. As an alternative, the company could hire two half-time attorneys, one for each state (the two courthouses are only ten miles apart). A full-time attorney would require a salary of around $50,000 (including fringe benefits), and two half-time attorneys would earn about $20,000 each. (According to company policy, part-time employees do not receive fringe benefits.)

The controller's office gives you the following information:

a. Overdue accounts turned over to Godell Collection Agency in the past 12 months totaled $2,500,000 ($1,750,000 owed by Missouri residents and $750,000 by Kansas residents). The agency collected $420,000 in Missouri and $202,500 in Kansas; after the agency deducted the usual 50 percent fee, the company received $311,250.

b. A 5 percent increase in overdue accounts is projected for the next 12 months.

c. If the contract with the collection agency is discontinued, court costs (in addition to attorneys' salaries) would be approximately $40,000 ($30,000 in Missouri and $10,000 in Kansas).

After reading some industry statistics, you determine that an in-house system probably would collect at least 80 percent as much as the collection agency.

Be creative in your analysis of the information. Write an informal report of your findings to Vivian Henderson.

## 2. Comparing Insurance Rates

You are a staff accountant for Giantco Interiors, a large wholesale company specializing in floor coverings (carpet and tile) for commercial buildings and apartment complexes. Anne Larson, chief accountant for the company, asks you to look into the possibility of finding a less expensive insurance carrier for Giantco's fleet of nine trucks and five cars. After making several phone calls, you obtain the following information:

5 Lancer station wagons (last year's model):

|  | 1 | 2 | 3 | 4 | 5 |
|---|---|---|---|---|---|
| $200,000/$300,000 liability | $255 | $220 | $238 | $225 | $245 |
| $10,000 medical payment | 20 | 18 | 22 | 17 | 25 |
| $50 deductible comprehensive | 90 | 95 | 80 | 105 | 98 |
| $250 deductible collision | 195 | 205 | 190 | 220 | 215 |
| $25,000/$50,000 uninsured motor vehicle | 25 | 20 | 30 | 45 | 40 |

9 Cavalcade 3/4-ton trucks (current year's model):

|  | 1 | 2 | 3 | 4 | 5 |
|---|---|---|---|---|---|
| $200,000/$300,000 liability | $352 | $325 | $298 | $335 | $332 |
| $10,000 medical payment | 38 | 40 | 42 | 45 | 35 |
| $50 deductible comprehensive | 202 | 198 | 200 | 190 | 215 |
| $250 deductible collision | 302 | 310 | 325 | 295 | 298 |
| $25,000/$50,000 uninsured motor vehicle | 45 | 40 | 52 | 48 | 43 |

Number 1 is the carrier that is presently insuring the company's fleet. Compare rates for the five companies and write an informal report of your findings to Ms. Larson.

## 3. The New Word-Processing System

You are assistant director of human resources at Boettcher Electronics, Inc. Jack Ross, the director of human resources, informs you that next month the company is purchasing a new word-processing system. The company's 42 office employees will each have a computer terminal and letter-quality printer linked to a central minicomputer.

Since the office employees are unfamiliar with this system, they will need to be trained. The manufacturer recommends 12 hours of training for an operator to become familiar with the system.

Mr. Ross tells you to look into various ways in which the 42 office employees can be trained. By checking around, you identify the following possibilities:

a. Hiring a consultant to train the office employees. P and D Consulting can train them at their own workstations, three at a time, for a total fee of $10 an hour per person, or $30 per hour.
b. Arranging for the local community college to train the office employees in a series of workshops on campus. Each individual would attend three half-day seminars at the college campus. The seminars would each accommodate 10-12 people at the same time, at a total cost of $95 per participant.

The second option would involve reimbursing travel expenses (at 23 cents per mile) to those who drive their own cars (the distance is 10 miles one way). By carpooling, four or five people could travel together. Another expense would be the additional salaries for the one hour per trip that participants would be away from their regular assignments (average office employees' salaries are $7 per hour).

Compare the two options and recommend the better solution. Report your findings and recommendation in an informal report to Mr. Ross.

4. The Telephone System
You are business manager of Rothwell Memorial Hospital, a 500-bed nonprofit health-care facility. As part of a major cost-cutting campaign, you are presently investigating various ways to reduce overhead expenses.

The hospital leases its PBX system and telephones from the local phone company for $240,000 per year, including maintenance. As an alternative, you decide to look into the possibility of purchasing a complete system from Phone-Net Company. Phone-Net produces a multiline microprocessor-based private branch-exchange digital switching network that can handle up to 1,000 telephones.

The Phone-Net system costs $1.5 million, including installation; the system could be depreciated over five years. The system comes with a full one-year warranty. After the first year, a service contract could be purchased from Phone-Net for $55,000 per year.

Analyze the facts and present your findings in an informal report to Dr. Arthur Kuhn, the hospital administrator.

5. The Landscaping Problem

You are assistant to Henrietta Morgan, the vice president of finance at W. R. Schwartz, Inc., a corporation specializing in real-estate investment and property management. Having recently constructed a new 1,200-unit luxury apartment complex, the company has sent you to the site to meet with the new manager to negotiate financial management plans for the complex.

One of your major tasks is the problem of grounds maintenance. You plan to investigate and recommend whether the company should employ its own grounds-maintenance crew or hire a landscape company on a contract basis.

You determine that if the company employs its own crew, the following expenses will be incurred per month:

| | |
|---|---|
| Wages (3 gardeners) | $4,420 |
| Supplies (fertilizer, pesticides, etc.) | 150 |
| Other (equipment repairs, etc.) | 100 |
| Total | $4,670 |

The company would also need to purchase the following equipment which could be written off as an expense in the first year:

| | |
|---|---|
| Commercial lawnmowers (3 @ $450) | $1,350 |
| Edgers (2 @ $115) | 230 |
| Power rake | 650 |
| Total | $2,230 |

You obtain bids from three commercial landscape-maintenance companies as follows:

a. A & G Landscaping - $54,000 per year for a three-year grounds and lawn-maintenance contract.

b. Ritter Landscaping & Maintenance - $5,000 per month (one-year contract for complete grounds and lawn care).

c. Southern Landscape - $65,000 per year (two-year contract with a one-year renewal option at the same rate).

Write an informal report of your findings to Ms. Morgan. The report should contain your recommendation.

# Formal Reports

1. Voice Technology

Write a formal informational report about voice-communication technology. The report should focus on business applications such as voice mail, voice-recognition and voice-verification units, speech synthesis equipment, electronic speech compressors, etc. All sources should be no more than two years old.

2. Computer Graphics

Write a formal informational report about computer-generated graphics. Include a discussion of available software and related graphics hardware such as graphics display terminals, printers, plotters, etc. All your sources should be no more than two years old.

3. Buying a Microcomputer

Write a formal analytical report about the most important characteristics and/ or functions of microcomputers (personal computers) to be considered when buying such equipment. For background information, include data from at least five secondary sources no more than two years old. Also, include a survey of one or more vendors. Your report should present findings, draw conclusions, and make recommendations on the most salient characteristics and/or functions of microcomputers.

4. Student Usage of Microcomputers

Write a formal analytical report about the use of microcomputers by students at your college. Obtain primary data from a survey of 35 to 50 students. Develop a questionnaire to determine what percentage of the students do not use computers off campus; determine the reasons for not using them. Your sample should be representative of the student body. Survey students in the cafeteria, union, etc. (not just students in business classes). Include at least five recent articles about college students' use of microcomputers in your paper as background information. Your report should present findings, draw conclusions, and make recommendations on how to increase computer usage among college students.

5. Student Evaluations of Microcomputer Qualities

Write a formal analytical report about the factors college students consider when buying a microcomputer (personal computer). Obtain primary data from a survey of college students. Design a questionnaire that elicits information about factors such as cost, ease of use, portability, available software, simplicity of the user manual, etc. Instruct survey participants to rate each factor in terms of importance on a scale of 1 to 5 (from most important to least important). Your sample should be made as representative as possible by surveying students in the cafeteria, union, etc. (not just students in business classes). Your results should be based on 35 to 50 responses. Include at least five recent library sources in your paper as background information. Your report should present findings, draw conclusions, and make recommendations on the factors one should consider when buying a microcomputer.

6. Direct-Mail Versus Television Advertising

Write a formal analytical report comparing the advantages and disadvantages of direct-mail versus television advertising for a particular product that you would like to market. Your sources of data should include at least ten books or current business articles. Your report ending should contain specific conclusions and recommendations.

7. Renting Versus Buying a House

Write a formal analytical report comparing the advantages of renting versus buying a house. Collect both primary and secondary data. Surveys of renters and/or realtors would be appropriate means of obtaining primary data. Secondary sources should include at least ten relevant articles or books. Analyze cost factors such as amount of down payment, monthly payments, current interest rates, tax advantages, and comparable rents. In your report state the problem, present an analysis of data, state one or more conclusions, and recommend renting or buying a home.

8. Automobile Insurance Rates

Conduct a study of current automobile insurance rates for a person (of your age, marital status, and driving record) who needs to insure a particular make and model of car. Collect primary data from a telephone survey of at least five major insurance companies. In addition, collect secondary data from sources such as *Best's Insurance Reports*, *Consumer Reports*, *Consumers' Research*, including at least three current articles on the subject. Write a formal analytical report that includes a problem statement, findings, conclusion(s), and recommendation(s).

9. Investing a $20,000 Inheritance

Assume that you have just inherited $20,000 from your uncle, whose will specified that the money must be invested in a trust fund to be administered by the trust department of the Eastern State Bank. You cannot withdraw the money from the trust fund for ten years. The will states that you have the option of choosing any three stocks listed on the New York Stock Exchange and determining in what amounts you wish to purchase shares totaling $20,000. All dividends will be reinvested in the same stocks, and in ten years the stock will be sold and you will receive the proceeds. To comply with the terms of the will, you must conduct an analysis of the companies you select and write a formal analytical report of your findings, conclusions, and recommendations for the executor of your uncle's estate, Mr. Wayne Winter, manager of the trust department of Eastern State Bank. Collect your data from secondary sources such as *Moody's Industrial Manual*, company annual reports and 10-K reports, financial periodicals, and subscription investment services such as *Value Line*.

10. Problem on Campus

Write a formal analytical report on one of the following topics related to your college or university:
a. food service
b. parking
c. housing

Conduct a survey of students and review at least five pertinent articles or books. Include objective facts to support your findings, conclusions, and recommendations.

## CASE STUDY

You are the vice president of human resources for CompoTec, a medium-size electronics firm. Jane Blakely, the personnel director, reports to you. Because of increased demand for the firm's products, you have asked Blakely to investigate two alternatives: (1) hiring more employees during the current day shift, and (2) hiring employees for a newly created night shift.

Blakely assigned the project to Hal Winters, an employee specialist. She asked Winters to investigate the pros and cons of each alternative and to write an informal report, including the following items:

a. A brief description of each alternative
b. A list of factors, based on expert opinion, to be considered when comparing the alternatives
c. A discussion of the advantages and disadvantages of each alternative
d. A recommendation based on the findings

Winters wrote the following memorandum:


MEMORANDUM

TO:    Jane Blakely, Director of Personnel

FROM:    Hal Winters, Employee Specialist

DATE:    August 31, 19—

SUBJECT:    ALTERNATIVES REGARDING HIRING DECISIONS

The better of the two alternatives considered for hiring new employees is to increase the number working on the current day shift, rather than to start a new night shift.

### Description of Alternatives

The two alternatives considered for hiring new employees are as follows:

1. Hire additional employees for the current day shift
2. Hire employees for a new night shift

### Expert Opinion about Factors to Consider

According to experts in the field and on the basis of this writer's experience, the issues to be considered are as follows:

1. Cost of each alternative

2. Effects of productivity

3. Effects on morale

### Pros and Cons of Each Alternative

#### Pros of Alternative 1

* Increased cost would result from a greater number of machines needed, new employees' salaries and benefits, and training. Costs of running the plant facilities would increase only by the amount of energy needed by additional machines.

* Productivity would increase according to the number of new employees. Training time would be minimized, because new workers could learn from those currently on day shift.

#### Cons of Alternative 1

* Buying additional machines would be very costly because new machines cost $5,000 to $8,000 each and used machines are hard to find. I know from experience that used machines break down frequently; therefore, I recommend that we buy new ones.

* Morale would be affected negatively. Hiring new employees during the day shift would mean more crowded conditions than at present, and this problem will result in conflict among employees. I learned in a recent seminar that employees need their own space at work. Our present employees would definitely resent new workers.

#### Pros of Alternative 2

* Morale would be higher, since day shift and night shift employees would not have to work together and each would have more room.

* Costs would be lower because no additional machines would be needed.

* Productivity would increase once new employees learned how to do the work. I am not sure how to compare the productivity of employees working during the night shift with productivity under conditions in Alternative 1.

Cons of Alternative 2

   \* Morale would suffer somewhat because the employees on each shift would not know one another. I have seen this problem occur at work in other places.

   \* Costs of running the plant would increase since all power, etc., would have to be on twice as long as usual. I don't know exactly what the amount would be.

   \* Several articles I've read say that new shifts are not a good idea for most businesses.

   \* I have a strong hunch that this is a poor idea.

Summary

   Alternative 1 is the better for our company. See Table 1 for details.

TABLE 1

| Alternative | Pros | Cons |
|:-----------:|:-----|:-----|
| 1 | Strong | Weak |
| 2 | Weak | Strong |

1. If you were the vice president, how would you react to this report?
2. If you were Jane Blakely, what suggestions for improving the study and report would you give Hal Winters?

## SUGGESTED READINGS

Baxter, Carol McFarland. *Business Report Writing: A Practical Approach*. Boston: Kent, 1983.

Golen, Steven P., C. Glenn Pearce, and Ross Figgins. *Report Writing for Business and Industry*. New York: John Wiley & Sons, 1985.

Lesikar, Raymond V. and Mary P. Lyons. *Report Writing for Business*, 7th ed. Homewood, IL: Richard D. Irwin, 1986.

Lewis, Phillip V. and William H. Baker. *Business Report Writing*, 2nd ed. Columbus, OH: Grid, 1983.

Treece, Malra. *Effective Reports*, 2nd ed. Boston: Allyn & Bacon, 1985.

Wilkinson, C. W., Dorothy C. Wilkinson, and Gretchen N. Vik. *Communicating Through Writing and Speaking in Business*, 9th ed. Homewood, IL: Richard D. Irwin, 1986.

# SPECIAL-PURPOSE
# MESSAGES

PART 5

Business communication includes various categories of employment-related and other special-purpose messages. Employment communication includes resumes, job-application and other letters written by applicants and employers, and interviews.

Job applicants who have expertise in written and oral communication have a decided advantage over applicants who do not. Similarly, employers need good communication skills with which to recruit and hire qualified individuals.

Other specialized messages that are essential for the daily operations of any business organization include credit and collection messages; goodwill messages; and personnel messages such as recommendation letters, employee appraisals, and policy and procedure statements.

# RESUMES AND JOB APPLICATION LETTERS

## CHAPTER 12

A newspaper article featured a story about outlandish blunders in resumes that hindered job applicants' chances of employment (Linscott, 1984, 6). A few examples of these blunders follow:

- A bookkeeper wrote, "I am very conscientius and accurite."
- A computer operator was "proud to win the Gregg Typting Award."
- One individual wrote that she worked for a "firm that currently employs twenty odd people."
- Under hobbies, "golf and bride" were listed.
- Another individual left his last job because "the sales manager was a dummy."
- Under job objective, an assistant treasurer wrote: "My objective is money. If two jobs are available, one as corporate treasurer and the other shoveling...I'll pick up the shovel if it pays more."

Undoubtedly, these blunders *did* attract some attention to the resumes, but they probably *did not* secure the writers a job. To be successful in obtaining a desired career, you need to sharpen your communication skills and put your abilities into action. Some *special messages* related to employment are highlighted in this chapter and the next chapter. Specifically, this chapter includes the following topics:

- **Job-search process**, including (a) self-analysis, which determines your goals and assesses your qualifications and (b) job-market analysis, which comprises a study of job sources and job appraisals

- **Resumes**, including content, appearance and mechanics, and styles (traditional, functional, and modified-traditional)
- **Application letters**, including solicited and unsolicited letters and how to write them

## THE JOB-SEARCH PROCESS

One of the major decisions you will make in your lifetime will be in your choice of a career. In obtaining that career, you will demonstrate the written and oral communication skills that you have developed. Your resume, application letters, interviews, and job follow-up messages will reflect your communication skills. Although your education and work experiences will be important in obtaining the job you want, the way in which you present yourself to the prospective employer is even more critical. In other words, the job-search process involves "selling" yourself to a prospective employer. More specifically, the job search process involves five components:

1. *Self-analysis* — determining your career goals and assessing your qualifications for a particular job
2. *Job-market analysis* — seeking possible job sources and appraising jobs available to you
3. *Resume and application letter preparation* — convincing a prospective employer that you are the right person for a particular job
4. *Interview preparation* — validating your interest in a particular job and producing a need or a desire on the part of a prospective employer to hire you
5. *Follow-up and other job-related letter preparation* — reinforcing your interest in a particular job and supporting your employment search

This chapter includes the first three topics. Chapter 13 contains the last two items.

## Self-Analysis

If you wish to find a job that is right for you, you need to understand your career goals and employment qualifications. Ask yourself the following questions to determine your career goals:

1. What kind of work would I really enjoy doing?
2. Where do I want to do this job? Where do I want to live?
3. What can I reasonably expect to earn?
4. Do I want to work with others or by myself? If with others, what type of people?
5. Do I want to work indoors or outdoors? Do I like physical work or sedentary work?
6. Do I want a routine job or one with advancement opportunities? Can I handle pressure and deadlines?

7. Do I want to be part of a large organization or a small one?
8. Do I want to be my own boss or to work under someone else's supervision? Do I need structure, or can I work independently?
9. Do I want to work an eight-hour day with set hours, or am I willing to work varied hours and possibly overtime, including nights and weekends?
10. Am I more interested in job security, or in a job that offers more challenge and possibly less security?
11. Am I willing to move to another area or to travel as part of my job?
12. What fringe benefits do I need now and in the future?

After examining your career goals and placing your emphasis on what you want, turn the tables and think in terms of what a prospective employer might want from you. Which of the following qualifications do you have to offer an employer?

- Accuracy
- Adequate education
- Ambition
- A sense of humor
- Communication skills
- Cooperativeness
- Decision-making skills
- Dependability
- Determination
- Enthusiasm
- Good judgment

- Initiative
- Integrity
- Leadership skills
- Neatness
- Objectivity
- Punctuality
- Related work experience
- Responsibility
- Self-confidence
- Tactfulness

After completing this brief but helpful self-analysis, you should consider where to find jobs and how to appraise them.

## Job-Market Analysis

Perhaps you have heard of individuals who obtained jobs by "being at the right place at the right time" or because "they knew the right person." These advantages sometimes do help people get jobs. However, knowing where to look for jobs is also important.

**Job Sources.** You can obtain information about broad occupational areas at your campus career placement center or campus library. Here are a number of references for job seekers:

The Career Guide: Dun's Employment Opportunities Directory. Describes employment opportunities, locations, and benefits in companies with 1,000 or more employees. Published by Dun's Marketing Services.

CPC Annual. Contains three volumes. Volume one contains articles on career planning and the job search; volumes two and three provide information on hundreds of employers seeking college graduates for administrative, business, and technical jobs. Published by the College Placement Council.

Dictionary of Occupational Titles. Contains descriptions of approximately 20,000 occupations. Published by the United States Department of Labor.

The Encyclopedia of Associations. Contains information about trade associations and organizations.

Million Dollar Directory. Contains names, addresses, and other information about 160,000 firms worth over $500,000. Published by Dun & Bradstreet Corporation.

National Business Employment Weekly. Contains information about career-advancement positions in organizations throughout the United States. Published by *The Wall Street Journal* on Sundays.

Occupational Outlook for College Graduates. Contains employment information for jobs requiring post-high school degrees. Published by the United States Bureau of Labor Statistics.

Occupational Outlook Handbook. Contains detailed information and summaries of employment information about 400 occupations covering about 80 percent of the jobs in the United States. Describes job duties, working conditions, education and/or training requirements, job outlook, and earnings. Published by the United States Bureau of Labor Statistics.

Occupations in Demand at Job Service Offices. Describes job openings listed with the public employment service. Published monthly by the United States Department of Labor.

Standard & Poor's Register of Corporations, Directors, and Executives. Contains financial and other information about 45,000 companies. Published by Standard & Poor's Corporation.

Thomas Register of American Manufacturers. Contains a listing of 123,000 American manufacturing firms organized by type of product and brand name. Published by Thomas Publishing Company.

---

Business magazines such as *Business Week*, *Fortune*, and *Forbes* provide valuable information about many companies. Professional journals, newspapers such as *The Wall Street Journal*, and local newspapers contain hundreds of job advertisements. Company annual reports, brochures, and house organs (company publications) also provide insight into job possibilities.

Be sure to take advantage of the services offered by the career placement center and guidance/counseling department on campus. Employment agencies, both private and state operated, are also good sources of discovering job openings in local firms. Often these agencies and school facilities have access to databases which not only describe careers but also list openings nationwide. Some agencies allow employers to receive application letters and resumes electronically and to conduct initial screening for job openings without conducting person-to-person interviews.

The following online career databases are available in many libraries, college placement offices, and state employment agencies:

*Discover for Schools* and *Discover for Adults* are produced by American College Testing (ACT). This career-planning system has the following parts: self-information, strategies for identifying occupations, occupational information, and searches for educational institutions. The adult version includes a section about resumes.

*Guidance Information System (GIS)* provides information that can assist in making career choices. GIS is a national network cooperatively developed by the United States Labor Department and various state employment services. Its files include occupations in the armed services and in private organizations; information on colleges, graduate and professional schools; and sources of scholarships and financial aid.

*SIGI* and *SIGI Plus (Systems of Interactive Guidance and Information)* are published by Educational Testing Services. (*SIGI* is intended for high-school and college students, and the *SIGI Plus* system is for adults seeking a career change.) This online career-development system provides lists of occupations that meet the user's specifications and qualifications and predicts the user's probabilities for success. It contains six interrelated systems (Values, Locate, Compare, Prediction, Planning, and Strategy).

Effective sources of information may be provided by professors and instructors you have for classes, people who actually work in the area of your chosen career, and friends and relatives. Seek out these people for job leads and opportunities. Equally helpful, but often neglected sources, are college alumni and members of civic groups and professional associations.

Another way of finding information about jobs is by directly approaching company personnel departments. Many college graduates assume that after they have finished their education, jobs will "fall into their laps." This stroke of luck is *extremely* rare — job opportunities rarely come "knocking at your door." As a potential employee, you need to do the knocking on doors. Studies indicate that the majority of jobs are not advertised in local newspapers or listed with employment agencies. Instead, most applicants get their information about job openings by asking friends and relatives or by contacting employers directly.

**Job Appraisal**. Once you have one or more leads to possible jobs and have determined that your qualifications match the job requirements, you need to appraise these job possibilities. Instead of asking yourself what you have to offer the employer, ask yourself what the job will offer you. Consider specific factors such as potential for advancement, fringe benefits, salary, and additional training. Also include general factors such as the firm's status within the industry, its financial condition, its objectives for the future, its capacity for expansion, and its use of new technology.

Questions related to your own personal concerns about what responsibilities the job will entail, the benefits it will offer, and so forth can be answered by talking with individuals in the human resources or personnel department or to other employees of the company. You can find the answers to many questions about the company's status, product line, etc., in annual reports and company brochures.

## RESUMES

After your job appraisal, you will need to prepare a resume. The purpose of your resume is not to get you a job but to obtain an interview for a job. Often the first impression an employer will have of an applicant is from her or his **resume**, which is an advertisement or marketing tool highlighting an applicant's qualifications. You should sell yourself and your qualifications in your resume so as to convince an employer to meet you in person for an interview. Therefore, significant time and effort should go into its development before you write the accompanying application letter.

No one style of a resume is correct. An important rule to remember is that your resume should be concise. It should emphasize your best qualifications as they relate to the job for which you are applying. Employers reviewing resumes will initially take only a few seconds to scan them while looking for key qualifications. Do not understate your qualifications—but do not misrepresent them either.

A one-page resume will generally suffice and is usually preferable to a longer one. However, two pages may be acceptable, as long as the content of a resume emphasizes early the relationship of qualifications and job requirements and continues to show this relationship. Two-page resumes are common for individuals who have a great deal of work experience. However, all information should be pertinent to the position for which you are applying.

## Resume Content

The content of a resume will vary from person to person. Since everyone has different talents, experiences, and skills to offer an employer, you should design your resume to highlight your unique qualifications.

Although resumes may contain various kinds of information, you do not need to include everything. The order in which you present the information may vary, depending upon which qualifications you wish to emphasize. Omit irrelevant information; for example, details that have no relationship to the job for which you are applying. Tailoring your resume to a specific job usually is better than preparing a general one that could be used for almost any position.

**Identification.** This section of the resume includes the name, address, and telephone number of the applicant. You may use a descriptive heading such as *Resume of* or *Qualifications of* followed by your name. In most cases, just your name typed at the top of a page will suffice. Emphasize your name by typing it in capital letters or by printing it in bold letters centered near the top of the page.

Your complete address should appear after your name. If you have a temporary school address and a permanent home address, be sure to indicate both addresses and the dates on which you can be reached at each address.

Include your telephone number and area code. If you cannot answer your telephone during the day, provide a telephone number where messages may be left and indicate that it is a message phone.

If you are graduating, include a date of availability in the identification section of your resume. You should start your job search prior to graduation and, therefore, should indicate when you will be available to start work, as shown in the following examples:

AVAILABLE: May 15, 19—

-or-

AVAILABLE: Immediately

As an alternative, place your availability date under "Personal Information," which is discussed later in this chapter.

Today most employers discourage the use of photographs on resumes. Federal regulations prohibit employers from using criteria such as age and race, which pictures reveal, as bases for hiring. Only in cases where appearance is a bona fide occupational qualification (a necessary requirement for the normal operation of a business), such as modeling or theatrical positions, should a job applicant include a photograph as part of a resume.

Here is an example of an identification section:

SALLY A. MORGAN

| Temporary Address (until May 15, 19—) | Permanent Address (after May 15, 19—) |
|---|---|
| 153 West Palo Verde Lane Tempe, Arizona 85281-6711 (602) 965-7420 Messages: (602) 820-3841 | 482 North Circle Drive Columbus, Ohio 43210-3561 (415) 238-6682 |

AVAILABLE: June 15, 19—

**Job/Career Objective.** A brief statement of your **job/career objective** specifies the type of position that you are seeking. A resume may include both short-term and long-term career goals.

A job/career objective is beneficial but optional. This part of a resume suggests to a prospective employer that you have given serious consideration to your career plans. In addition, a clearly stated objective helps the employer to sort out resumes according to various categories of job openings.

Your career objective should be neither too broad nor too specific. Being too specific may exclude you from being considered for similar or related job opportunities. On the other hand, being too broad may indicate that you do not have a clear career goal or do not know what employment opportunities are available within a particular company.

You should also avoid being "I-centered" in writing your objective. Instead, emphasize what you have to offer the employer. Compare the following examples of job/career objectives from the resumes of recent college graduates:

OBJECTIVE: I am seeking a challenging position with an accounting firm.

OBJECTIVE: Internal auditor with a large accounting firm.

OBJECTIVE: A responsible entry-level staff accounting position with a leading public-accounting firm. Desire employment that includes training and opportunities for advancement to senior-level accountant.

The first objective is too broad because the individual fails to indicate the type of accounting position desired. In contrast, the second example is too specific. A recent graduate probably would be underqualified for the position; furthermore, such a specialized position may not be available. The third example allows some flexibility as to the type of entry-level position and reflects the applicant's maturity in her or his choice of words. In addition, the applicant compliments the company by referring to it as a "leading public accounting firm" and suggests her or his ambition by mentioning desire for training and advancement.

**Qualifications Summary**. Another optional part of a resume is a **qualifications summary**, which is a brief description of your overall qualifications. Highlight your most important and pertinent qualifications in this section in a one- or two-sentence summary. Although used infrequently, this summary is worth including in any resume because it quickly tells a prospective employer why you should be considered for an interview. Details supporting this summary follow in additional parts of your resume. As an alternative, you may combine a condensed statement of your qualifications with the job/career objective.

Here is an example of a combined objective and qualifications summary in the resume of an individual applying for a trust officer position with a large urban bank:

QUALIFICATIONS SUMMARY: Have six years experience as a competent assistant trust officer in a medium-sized bank. Am knowledgeable in the use of computers in banking and have an MBA in finance. Am seeking a position of trust officer in a progressive bank where advancement depends on productivity and performance.

**Education.** The education section generally lists information such as degrees earned, names of schools attended, dates of attendance or graduation, and grade-point average. You may also include additional information such as academic honors, other specialized training, extracurricular activities, and offices held in organizations. Omit high school information from this section unless you received specialized training in high school that is related to the type of job you are seeking.

The kind of degree or certificate that you last earned should appear first because it is usually more important to a prospective employer than the name of the school and the dates attended. Use your own judgment about what is most relevant to the position.

If space permits, list specific courses related to the position you are seeking. Employers may not be familiar with courses required for all degree and certificate programs, and the type of courses that you took may not be apparent. For example, a B.S. degree in business administration with a major in general business does not tell an employer what areas of business were emphasized. Specify particular courses if they are closely related to the job for which you are applying.

Unless your grade point average (GPA) is a "B" or higher, do not include it on the resume. If you do include it, be sure to indicate the appropriate scale; for example, GPA = 3.74 (4-point scale).

If you worked to pay for all or part of your education, include this information. If your graduation is sometime in the future (more than two to three months away), use an appropriate phrase such as "Will be graduating with a B.S. in . . ." or "Pending graduation with an A.A. in . . ." as part of the education section of your resume.

Here is an example of how information might be organized in the education section:

## EDUCATION

B.S. in Business Administration. Computer Information Systems Major, Southern University, Little Grove, Alabama, May 1988. Major GPA 3.29 (4-point scale).

| Computer Courses: | Other Related Courses: |
|---|---|
| Basic Programming I & II | Business Communication |
| Business Databases | Business Policies |
| Cobol Programming I & II | Human Relations in Business |
| Interactive Business Programming | Management Principles |
| Introduction to Computer Information Systems | |
| Systems Analysis & Design | |

Worked 20 to 30 hours a week to finance 75 percent of education expenses.

Associate Science Degree in Accounting, Athens Junior College, Athens, Georgia, May 1986. Dean's List for four semesters.

**Experience**. If you have had significant work experience that relates to the job for which you are applying, list this experience before the education section. Work experience traditionally has been listed in reverse chronological order with the most recent job listed first. However, if a previous job relates better than a recent one to your present job search, list that position first.

Grouping work experience according to different areas of specialty is also appropriate. For example, you might list all marketing jobs under "Marketing Experience" and all computer jobs under "Computer Experience." As with all other sections on your resume, be sure to emphasize your best qualifications first in the experience section. You may list military experience that relates to the job for which you are applying, either under the experience section or in a separate section.

If you lack related work experience, list any previous jobs you may have had. For example, if you have had several part-time jobs while in school, you might want to summarize them as follows:

**Part-time jobs as gas station attendant, sales clerk, and grocery store stocker and bagger while attending college.**

If you have no paid work experience but have done volunteer work, include that experience in this section. Even though the experience may seem insignificant to you, any work experience, paid or unpaid, demonstrates to a potential employer that you have assumed responsibility and exhibited ambition.

The work experience section usually emphasizes your job title or type of work performed. In some cases, however, you may wish to stress where you worked or your dates of employment rather than your job title. Use whatever arrangement that reflects your qualifications best.

You also may include the name and location of your past employer(s) and dates of employment (these do not need to be exact: month and year, summer and year, or Christmas vacation and year will suffice). Indicate whether the employment was full time, part time, or seasonal; the responsibilities you assumed; any promotions you received; or special accomplishments that were recognized. In stating responsibilities, use action verbs such as those in the following list. Use the present tense when describing current job duties; use the past tense when describing a previous job.

| | | |
|---|---|---|
| accomplished | designed | planned |
| achieved | developed | prepared |
| administered | directed | presented |
| allocated | evaluated | produced |
| analyzed | guided | researched |
| arranged | initiated | reviewed |
| compiled | implemented | scheduled |
| completed | improved | sold |
| constructed | installed | supervised |
| coordinated | managed | trained |
| created | organized | wrote |

Describe important accomplishments such as promotions, supervisory experiences, implementation of a new idea or project you suggested, or being named "top salesperson of the week."

You may include licenses or certificates you hold either in the experience section or in a separate section. Special credentials such as certified public accountant, certified administrative manager, certified life underwriter, or licensed real-estate agent may be very positive selling points in obtaining a job. Here is an example of an item in the experience section of a resume:

## EXPERIENCE

Credit Manager, Stross Manufacturing Co., Baltimore, Maryland, full time 1981-1988.

Responsibilities: Coordinated and managed accounts-receivable department. Supervised ten employees. Was responsible for installing and developing procedures for new R200 computer system.

**Personal Information**. The personal information section in your resume is optional and is less common today than in the past. Under Title VII of the Civil Rights Act of 1964 and its 1972 and 1978 amendments, employers cannot discriminate against an individual based upon age, sex, national origin, marital status, handicap, or religion. Therefore, many employers advise job applicants not to include such personal information. The only exception would be when an employer proves that disclosure of personal information is a requirement for employment.

You may list certain personal information if you believe that it might be helpful to you in obtaining a job. For example, if you are applying for a position as an assistant to a senator of a particular political party, you should state your affiliation with that organization. If affirmative action is a positive consideration, you might wish to indicate indirectly that you have a minority ethnic background (for example, "member of Hispanic Business Students' Association").

Some individuals think that stating that you are single indicates your availability to travel or relocate. This assumption, however, may not be true. List only personal information that will help you obtain a job. If you are in doubt about listing any information, do not list it.

A better title than "Personal Information" is "Personal Interests and Skills." Under this title, you can list your willingness to travel or relocate, your fluency with specific computer or foreign languages, your artistic talents, and other information that may be important. In addition, you can list membership in professional or student organizations, recognitions and/or awards, and job-related hobbies. Be sure that all of these items convey a positive image.

**References**. The names, addresses, and telephone numbers of individuals who are willing to give an employer an opinion of your qualifications are called **references**. Past employers and teachers are usually best because they are in a position to provide an accurate and unbiased evaluation of your character, skills, and work habits. Avoid using family members, close friends, and neighbors as references because employers are likely to consider them to be biased in your favor.

Some resumes include the names and addresses of three to five individuals as references. Today most resumes mention references with one of the following techniques:

References               -or-               References

Available upon request.                    Available at:

                                           Career & Placement Center
                                           Phoenix College
                                           1202 West Thomas Road
                                           Phoenix, AZ 85013-6529
                                           (602) 555-2492, Ext. 602

-or-

References will be furnished upon request.

If saving space is an important consideration, use one of the above techniques rather than listing specific references. Stating "References will be furnished upon request" may also prevent many employers from going out of their way to get more information about you.

When listing references, include a courtesy or professional title (such as Mrs., Mr., Miss, Ms., or Dr.), the individual's position title, the name of her or his company or affiliation, complete mailing address, and telephone number, including the area code. For a local reference, you may omit the mailing address because the employer probably will call rather than write to the reference.

Here are two examples of how to list references on a resume. The second example does not include the mailing address because the reference is local. To save space, the second example appears on one line.

Dr. Samuel O. Morgenstein, Chair
Management Department
Southern Florida University
Miami Beach, Florida 33161-7811
(943) 163-0428

-or-

Mr. Thomas Chow, Manager, Ace Appliances, (601) 482-3517

## Resume Appearance and Mechanics

Your resume should be typewritten or professionally typeset. If possible, use a word processor or a computer with a word-processing software package to prepare an error-free resume. Keeping a copy of your resume on a diskette will enable you to revise it easily with each job you apply for or to update it for later use as your career opportunities change.

Use underlining, capital letters, indenting, bold type, hyphens, bullets, dashes, asterisks, and other means of highlighting to make headings and other items stand out. Headings and even spacing between and within sections will make your resume easy to read. If your resume extends to two pages with only a small amount of information on the second page, redesign the layout so that all items are distributed evenly on the two pages.

Place the headings at the center of the page or flush with the left margin. Headings may consist of one or two words such as "Education" or "Academic Preparation," "Experience" or "Work Experience." Headings may be more descriptive as well; for example, "Supervisory Training and Experience" or "Auditing and Tax Experience."

As much as possible, avoid using personal pronouns (such as *I*, *you*, *we*) in the resume. Use clear, action verb phrases and active-voice statements. Keep all listings and headings on the same level of importance and maintain parallel construction.

Your resume must be free of typographical, grammatical, and punctuation errors. If possible, have someone knowledgeable in English mechanics review your resume. Your business communication professor, an English professor, or other instructors may be willing to help you. If such help is not readily available, have a friend or relative proofread your resume. Do not give a prospective employer any reason to discard your resume during the initial screening of applicants, particularly for something so easily corrected as a keyboarding error.

If you do not prepare each resume individually, have additional copies printed professionally or use a high-quality method of duplication. Be sure that no lines, smudges, or unevenness in copy are visible. If you use a computer to prepare your resume, use a letter-quality printer or a correspondence-quality dot-matrix printer. A little extra effort and cost in producing a professional-looking resume will be to your benefit.

Use bond paper that is identical to that used for your application letter. White paper is preferable for both items; some experts, however, suggest using beige, off-white, or a light gray to help your resume stand out from most of the others. Do not use brightly colored paper that would distract from the content of your resume.

## Resume Styles

Three basic styles are generally used for resumes—the traditional, the functional, and the modified traditional.

**Traditional**. The **traditional** (*non-narrative*) **resume style** is advantageous for individuals with extensive, uninterrupted work experience that is related to the position being applied for. Traditional-style resumes are usually divided into sections in this sequence: identification, objective, education, experience, personal, and references. The information contained in the education and experience sections is generally in reverse chronological order, with the most recent experiences listed first. The work-experience section contains job titles, dates of employment, and duties performed in each job. A traditional resume of a graduating college senior is shown in Figure 12.1.

## FIGURE 12.1 TRADITIONAL RESUME

```
                         BRIAN T. GONZALEZ

---------------------------------------------------------------

           304 East Los Amigos Drive, Austin, TX  78712-4411
                         (204) 753-1093
---------------------------------------------------------------

OBJECTIVE:   Graduate in business with knowledge of accounting,
             personnel, and finance.  Seeking position as as-
             sistant to hospital administrator in large urban
             hospital.

EDUCATION:

      * Bachelor of Science in Business Administration,
             University of Texas, Austin, May 1988, Summa
             cum laude.

      * Courses:

        - Accounting I and II       - Introduction to Hospital
        - Administrative Procedures    Administration
        - Business Communication    - Personnel Procedures
        - Introduction to Finance   - Survey of Data Processing

      * President of Senior Class, 1987-1988.
      * Recipient of Rotary Club scholarship, 1986-1988.

EXPERIENCE:

      * Assistant Manager, Taco Delite, Austin, part time 1985-
          1987.

        - Evening assistant manager, supervising ten people.

      * Sales Clerk, Taco Delite, Austin, part time 1984-1985.

        - Counter-help position, dealing with the public.

      * Swimming Instructor, YMCA, Austin, part time 1980-1984.

        - Instructor of beginning, intermediate, and advanced
          classes for children ages 6 to 14.

PERSONAL:

      * Available for employment May 19, 1988.
      * Fluent in Spanish.

REFERENCES:

      * Dr. Carlos J. Ortiz, Chair, Finance Department,
        University of Texas, Austin, (204) 753-4958.

      * Mr. Rick Anderson, Manager, Taco Delite, Austin,
        (204) 753-7401.

      * Mrs. Alice Yang, Director, YMCA, Austin, (204) 753-6289.
```

**Functional**. The **functional** (*narrative*) **resume style** emphasizes specific skills, abilities, or personal characteristics without using the headings of a traditional resume. This style is recommended for individuals with limited or no work experience because it emphasizes capabilities rather than experience. This type of resume is also advantageous for individuals who have had numerous jobs not specifically related to the positions they are seeking. Because of highly flexible organization, the functional style allows a resume to be adapted specifically to each job being sought.

The functional or narrative style emphasizes an applicant's skills and abilities such as those in the following list. These skills and characteristics may be substituted for traditional headings in a resume.

- Artistic
- Communication
- Interpersonal
- Language
- Leadership
- Management
- Mechanical
- Organizational
- Office
- Technical

Personal traits such as the following examples also may be used as headings:

- Accuracy
- Ambition
- Cooperativeness
- Dependability
- Enthusiasm
- Industriousness
- Initiative
- Integrity
- Intelligence
- Motivation
- Personality
- Self-confidence

In the functional style, your education and work experiences may be presented in a way that indicates particular job skills and competencies, wherever they were developed. A listing of job titles and dates of employment may or may not be a part of a functional-style resume. Functional-style resumes contain a narrative description written in complete sentences, relating specific skills and personal characteristics. A functional resume of a community-college student with no related work experience is illustrated in Figure 12.2.

## FIGURE 12.2 FUNCTIONAL RESUME

RESUME OF

AYAKO (SUSIE) MATSUMI                              --OBJECTIVE--

824 Maple Drive                          A hotel management trainee
Philadelphia, PA  19123-7615             position

Phone:  215-890-2361


**Qualifications that are offered to an employer:**

--INTELLIGENT--        Earned grade point average (G.P.A.) is
                       4.68 on 5-point scale with one
                       semester of study remaining toward an
                       Associate of Arts degree in hotel-
                       restaurant management.  Dean's List in
                       all three semesters completed at
                       Oakridge Community College.

--PERSONABLE--         Outgoing personality demonstrated by
                       being selected "Miss Congeniality" for
                       the Miss Pennsylvania competition this
                       last summer.  Was chosen as captain of
                       college women's softball team three
                       consecutive semesters.  Was highly
                       recommended as work-study student for
                       chemistry lab on college campus by
                       peers and faculty.  Am active Big
                       Sister in local community.

--DEPENDABLE--         Always punctual for classes and work.
                       Have been absent from class only three
                       times in three semesters.  Occasion-
                       ally am in charge of supervising and
                       closing chemistry lab on campus.
                       Often am responsible for family of
                       three younger brothers and two younger
                       sisters while parents travel on
                       business.

--INDUSTRIOUS--        Work 20 hours a week under student
                       work-study program on campus.  Have
                       taken full class load of 15 hours each
                       semester.  Work as a volunteer in
                       local hospital pediatrics ward on
                       weekends.

--REFERENCES WILL BE PROVIDED UPON REQUEST--

**Modified Traditional.** The **modified-traditional style** is a combination of the traditional and the functional resumes. This style emphasizes key job requirements, while maintaining some of the categories of a traditional resume. Either traditional or functional headings may be listed in any order, and a narrative, non-narrative, or a combination of these formats may be used. This style stresses important qualifications evidenced by skills or characteristics. A modified-traditional resume with emphasis on work experience is shown in Figure 12.3.

A two-page modified-traditional resume of an individual with specialized experience with computers is shown in Figure 12.4 on pages 314-315.

## Application Letters

The **application** or **cover letter** which accompanies your resume is a persuasive letter that continues the task of "selling" yourself to a prospective employer as part of the job-getting process. Coupled with a resume, an application letter is designed to create enough interest in the applicant's qualifications to win an interview.

An application letter should be clear and concise, and should use language that is meaningful to the reader. The "you" attitude is essential in writing an effective application letter because the employer will evaluate it in terms of "Why should I consider hiring this individual?"

Although the same resume may be copied and sent to many companies, application letters should be individually prepared. Personalize each letter by sending it to a specific individual. This person generally will be the personnel manager or a department head. Ask your college placement office for information or simply call or write to a company and ask for the names and job titles of the individuals who screen job applicants. Sending a letter "To Whom It May Concern" or "Director of Personnel" may result in your letter never getting to the person responsible for reviewing applications. An exception to personalizing each letter occurs when you are writing in response to an advertisement giving only a newspaper box number as an address. In this situation you may need to use the salutation "Dear Director of Personnel."

Use a standard letter style (see the examples that follow in this chapter), and limit your letter to one page. Never use the letterhead of a present employer when you are applying for a job with another firm. Be sure to use the same color and quality of paper that you used for the resume and envelope.

## FIGURE 12.3 MODIFIED-TRADITIONAL RESUME

* * *   Qualifications of STEVEN R. BRONSTON for   * * *
Sales Representative with Lawson Enterprises, Inc.

1004-B South Ve Ella Circle    Home Phone:        (305)821-2905
Tacoma, WA  98497-0611         Answering Service: (305)821-8927

* * * QUALIFICATIONS SUMMARY * * *

Can offer valuable experience in sales techniques.  Have
developed a professional business attitude and find sales to be
enjoyable and a highly challenging and rewarding career.

* * * RELATED WORK EXPERIENCE * * *

**Direct Sales**       Sales Representative with Kirby vacuums for
                       five years.  Was promoted within four months
                       from sales trainee to senior sales repre-
                       sentative.  Received valuable experience in
                       cold calls, sales psychology, and closing
                       techniques.  Won sales awards and left the
                       company as the top sales representative.

**Retail Sales**       Sales Clerk for Wood's Outfitting and Roth's,
                       both clothing stores.  Wood's was my initial
                       employment; was selected for the Roth's
                       position as one of seven people hired out of
                       400 applicants.  Gained experience in
                       approaching people with a positive selling
                       attitude and in suggestive selling techniques.

**Supervision and**
**Public Contact**     Youth Coordinator for Attorney General
                       candidate in Washington.  Supervised a staff
                       of six assistants and approximately 150
                       volunteers.  Duties included giving speeches,
                       recruiting volunteers, and working as an aide
                       to the candidate.  Was in charge of training
                       volunteers on how to approach the public and
                       was responsible for volunteers in designated
                       areas throughout the state.

* * * ACADEMIC PREPARATION * * *

B. S. in Business Administration, Personnel Management,
   Washington State University, Tacoma, Washington, summer
   1980.

* * * PERSONAL INTERESTS AND ACTIVITIES * * *

Member of American Society of Personnel Administration and
   Professional Activities Board for the College of Business,
   Washington State University; Chair for local United Way.
   Hobbies:  golf, tennis, handball, and cooking.

* * * REFERENCES WILL BE FURNISHED UPON REQUEST * * *

FIGURE 12.4 TWO-PAGE MODIFIED-TRADITIONAL RESUME

JENNIFER S. ADAMS

241 East LaSalle
Tempe, AZ  85282-7691
Home Phone:  (602) 982-7646
Office Phone:  (602) 424-5027

EDUCATION

Bachelor of Science - Computer Information Systems, Arizona
State University, May, 1983; GPA 3.25 (4.0 scale).

COMPUTER SKILLS

| | |
|---|---|
| Languages: | COBOL, TAL, FORTRAN, BASIC |
| Tandax Proficiency: | Pathway, Enform, Enable, Data Communication (2780/ 3780 and X25), Exchange |
| ITM Proficiency: | TSO, SPF, Panvalet, IMS, SDSF, Mark IV, IMS, CMS, Quickjob |

COMPUTER EXPERIENCE

Programmer/Analyst

Watcom, Inc.
6384 East McGordon Road
Phoenix, AZ  85043-0761
June, 1983, to present

Was selected and promoted out of 40 Programmer/ Analysts
to install a Tandax computer system in Taunnustein,
Germany.  This system is used as a communication node
between the Watcom European distributors' computers and
Watcom's mainframe computers in Phoenix.  Developed
telecommunication network linking Watcom's distributors in
Germany, England, Finland, France, the Netherlands, and
Italy.  Performed System Management duties, including
resource management, system security, disk file maintenance, and sysgens.  Disassembled and reassembled Tandax

## TWO-PAGE MODIFIED-TRADITIONAL RESUME (CONTINUED)

J. S. Adams, page 2

computer.  Designed and developed 2780/3780 and X25
communication handler.  Performed trouble shooting on
German Bundespost modems.

Designed and developed modules used domestically for the
transfer of data between domestic Watcom distributors and
Watcom's mainframe computer in Phoenix.  Implemented a
computer-to-computer Direct Order Entry System using a
Tandax as the interface between Watcom and domestic
distributors.  Designed and developed IMS modules to
display data received from distributors.  Wrote TAL
modules for Technical Support group, including a JES
console process.

### MANAGEMENT EXPERIENCE

State of Arizona
Department of Economic Security
Phoenix, AZ  85013-6729
December, 1974, to July, 1981

#### Assistance Programs Manager

Managed 180 individuals at the largest Department of
Economics Security office in Arizona.  Developed personnel
and policy procedures.  Conducted personnel evaluations.
Was in charge of monitoring compliance with state and
federal policies and procedures.  Implemented policies
that resulted in a 10 percent increase in productivity and
a decrease from 14 percent to 4 percent error rate, while
reducing staff by one sixth.

#### Program and Project Specialist

Was responsible for the administration of the Assistance
Payments Programs in Maricopa County.  Wrote policy
clarifications and ensured that local offices were meeting
state and federal requirements.

### REFERENCES WILL BE PROVIDED UPON REQUEST

Avoid personal pronouns (such as *I*, *me*, and *my*) at the beginning of sentences by using phrases or clauses to introduce sentences. Be original in your wording and avoid the following weak and overused openings:

"This is my application for...."

"I am writing to inquire about the possibility of obtaining a position with your company."

"This resume is to apply for...."

"I feel I am well qualified for...."

Your application letter is an example of your written communication skills. Present an image of yourself as a capable applicant who is worthy of being interviewed. Be honest and sincere, and at the same time indicate modest confidence in your abilities. Remember to relate your experiences and qualifications to the specific needs of the reader.

## Solicited Application Letters

**Solicited application letters** are letters sent to a prospective employer in response to a written request, "help wanted" advertisement, or an oral invitation to apply for a job. When a specific position is advertised, tailor your application letter and resume to that specific job.

Your response to an advertisement may be one of dozens or hundreds of applications that the company receives. To obtain an interview, you must write an application letter and resume that will stand out from the rest.

A sample solicited application letter to accompany the resume shown in Figure 12.2 is shown in Figure 12.5.

## Unsolicited Application Letters

**Unsolicited application letters**, which are also known as *prospecting* letters, are written to employers who have not advertised a job opening. Aggressive job seekers should seriously consider using this strategy. Because companies do not always advertise every job opening, job applicants should not limit their search to advertised positions.

Unsolicited application letters have the following advantages: (1) they receive less competition than responses to an advertised position, and (2) they may lead to the creation of a new position. For the latter to occur, an applicant must persuade a prospective employer that the company needs someone with her or his qualifications.

Major disadvantages are (1) wasting time in writing to companies that have no openings and (2) attempting to attract attention to specific qualifications without tailoring the letter and resume to a particular opening.

## FIGURE 12.5 SOLICITED APPLICATION LETTER

824 Maple Drive
Philadelphia, PA  19123-7615
May 10, 19--


Mr. Paul C. Smythe, Manager
Eastern and Western Hotels
283 Concord Lane
Philadelphia, PA  19123-8023

Dear Mr. Smythe:

The job requirements listed in your ad in Sunday's <u>Herald</u> for a
hotel management trainee who is "intelligent, personable,
dependable, and industrious" match my qualifications.

On June 1, I will be available for full-time employment with
your hotel.  I am knowledgeable about all aspects of hotel
management--budgeting, accounting, communication, personnel
management, and customer relations.

Competing in the Miss Pennsylvania contest and on the college
women's softball team has taught me the benefits of team
spirit.  I have a friendly, outgoing personality and enjoy
working with people very much.

My dependability is evidenced by my having responsibility in
both my work and home life.  Working 20 hours a week, carrying
a full load of classes each semester, and doing volunteer work
on weekends indicate my industriousness.

After you have reviewed the enclosed resume, please call me to
arrange a time that we might meet.  I certainly would like to
become a part of the Eastern and Western team.

Sincerely,


Ms. Susie Matsumi

Enclosure

An unsolicited application letter that could accompany the resume in Figure 12.1 is shown in Figure 12.6.

## FIGURE 12.6 UNSOLICITED APPLICATION LETTER

Do you need an assistant hospital administrator with supervisory experience and a degree in business administration? If so, please consider me for the position.

Your recent expansion to 600 beds will increase the workload of your hospital administrator, Mr. Peter Steinberg. My knowledge of accounting, finance, and personnel would be helpful to him.

My ability to learn easily and quickly--4.25 on a 5-point scale and a promotion from sales clerk to assistant manager within six months--should make my transition into your organization rather smooth. In addition, my fluency in Spanish would be helpful in dealing with the Hispanic population in Austin.

May we arrange a visit to talk about how I might be able to contribute to your staff as an assistant hospital administrator. I will call next week to set up a mutually convenient time to meet, or you may call me at 753-1093. I look forward to our meeting.

Sincerely,

## Writing the Application Letter

Whether you write a solicited or unsolicited application letter, you should use the same basic outline presented in Chapter 7 for writing a sales letter:

1. Opening Paragraph — establish contact with the reader
2. Middle Paragraph(s)
   a. Generate interest and desire
   b. Convince the reader
3. Ending Paragraph — provide incentive for action

**Opening Paragraph.** When you write an *unsolicited* application letter, your purpose in the opening paragraph is to get the reader's attention. To arouse the interest of the reader, use one of the following techniques:

1.  Summarize two or three of your major qualifications.

Five years of experience working with minicomputers, proficiency in four computer languages, and knowledge of domestic and international network systems are competencies that I can offer your company as a programmer specialist.

A college degree in management, four years of part-time work experience supervising evening employees in a local department store, and a sincere desire to work hard may contribute to your management training program.

2.  Start with a question that indicates a desire on your part to fill the reader's need.

Can your company use a word-processing specialist who accurately types 85 words per minute? If so, please consider me for such a position.

Do you need someone who speaks Spanish fluently, has a mechanical engineering degree, and two years of work experience as part of a company engineering team in New Mexico? If you do, I believe I can help your company at the new branch office at Santa Fe.

3.  Recognize by name an individual who suggested that you apply.

Dr. Samuel Ortega, chair of the Marketing Department at Eastern State University, informed me that your company normally hires one or two graduates each year as marketing researchers.

Ms. Matsu Homoshi of your staff suggested that I submit a resume directly to you for consideration as a sales representative.

4.  Mention a recently reported news item about a company's expansion, new product, or some other achievement.

Congratulations on your new contract with Divisional Bell as outlined in the *Daily Gazette*. My skills as a systems analyst could help to ease your increased workload.

Now that Westco has expanded its operations to the East Coast, perhaps you can use a highly motivated individual with a degree in finance as part of your executive financial training program.

The opening sentence of a *solicited* application letter does not require an attention-getting technique. The opening should refer to your source of information for the position you are seeking and discuss your major qualifications. Here are some examples of possible beginning paragraphs:

Charles Dexter, your representative on campus, asked me to apply for your sales representative opening at Youngstown.

Your ad in Sunday's *Tribune* for a department store manager who is "aggressive but fair and experienced in hiring, evaluating, scheduling, and buying" matches my qualifications quite closely.

As you requested when you spoke with me yesterday, I am submitting my resume, which outlines my experience and educational training in office administration.

Keep in mind that your first sentence is the first impression you make as an applicant for employment. Be positive and original but businesslike in your approach. Write an opening paragraph appropriate for the job for which you are applying. No one paragraph is ideal for every position; use whatever strategy you believe will work best for your situation.

**Middle Paragraphs.** The middle paragraphs convince the reader to consider you for the position. This part of the letter should describe your qualifications as they relate to a particular job. Discuss your major qualifications in specific language rather than in general terms. The person reviewing your letter and resume may not discover your strong points if you do not emphasize them. However, the letter should emphasize relevant points in your resume rather than repeat them.

As in sales letters, choose one or two of your strongest points and describe them. Your emphasis of certain information about your education, work experience, and personal qualities should provide the necessary evidence to convince a prospective employer to interview you.

If education is an important job qualification, emphasize it and point out what you learned and what you can do as a result, instead of merely listing the titles of courses. Rather than the following weak statement:

**"I took Principles of Marketing, Marketing Research, and Marketing Management"**

Focus on specific skills such as in the following example:

**"In my marketing courses, I learned the theoretical background and practical skills needed to write and use questionnaires, to create promotional strategies, and to solve problems through applied quantitative analysis."**

If work experience is a strong selling point, explain your responsibilities in the job(s) you have held, the tasks you performed, and your specific accomplishments. Rather than

**"I worked as an information systems manager"**

write

**"My responsibilities as an information systems manager included supervising six programmers, designing and implementing a computerized inventory control system, and developing policies and procedures for systems operations."**

Highlight personal qualities to show the reader that you know what the job requires in the way of personal traits. Rather than

**"I have good leadership skills"**

add emphasis with

"I have developed my leadership skills by participating in our local civic group as both a member and an officer, by leading the new hospital fund drive in my community, and by organizing a neighborhood security watch campaign."

Use two or three paragraphs to present supporting evidence that you are qualified for the job. To avoid distracting your reader from the content of your letter, refrain from referring to an enclosed resume until nearer the end.

**Ending Paragraph.** The last paragraph should promote the action that you want the reader to take, such as asking for an invitation for an interview or requesting additional information such as a list of references. Be positive and direct in requesting action without being overly demanding. Instead of using the worn statement "May I have an interview at your convenience," be creative in your closing paragraph. The following examples may be adapted to various application letters:

"I would appreciate an opportunity to discuss in more detail my qualifications. After you have reviewed my enclosed resume, will you please call me at 444-3609 to arrange a meeting."

If you are available only at certain times of the day, say:

"Please call me at 555-2187 after 3 p.m. any weekday to arrange a mutually convenient time to meet."

If the job opening is out of town, you might write:

"I will be in Denver the week of July 15. May we arrange a meeting for sometime during that week. I could visit with you then to talk about how I might be able to contribute to your firm as an assistant buyer. Please call me at 802-934-1212 or write to arrange a date and time for our meeting."

If you are not available every day for an interview, say:

"May I have an interview to answer any questions you may have about my qualifications. I am available every day except Tuesdays and Thursdays because of my classes. Please call me at 332-4097.

If you want to convey your confidence in your abilities, you might word your closing paragraph in the following way:

"May I have an interview so that I might discuss my qualifications and desire to be a part of your management training program. I am enthusiastic about starting soon."

If you want to take the initiative in the desired action, mention that you will call to confirm an appointment for an interview. The following technique may cause the reader to make special note of your name because you will be calling her or him:

"To arrange a meeting with you to discuss my qualifications in more detail, I will call you next week. Or, you may call me before then at 492-3058. I look forward to our meeting."

A final sample application letter is shown in Figure 12.7. This letter accompanies the resume shown in Figure 12.4.

## FIGURE 12.7 SOLICITED APPLICATION LETTER

Mary Jo Harper of Tandax Enterprises suggested that I write to you about a programming consultant opening with your company. She mentioned that you are looking for someone with extensive experience with Tandax computers.

Five years of working with Tandax computers both in Arizona and in Taunnustein, Germany, have given me valuable experience. I was selected and promoted from 40 programmer/analysts to install a Tandax computer system in Germany. In addition, I have developed a telecommunication network linking my present employer in Arizona with five other foreign countries.

Additional experience with Tandax and ITM application software is outlined in my enclosed resume. Please take a few moments to review the other qualifications I have listed.

If my experience with Tandax computers fills your needs, please call or write me to arrange an interview. I will be glad to provide you with a list of references, if needed.

Sincerely,

## SUMMARY

The job-search process involves self-analysis, job-market analysis, resume and application letter preparation, interview preparation, and follow-up letter preparation.

Self-analysis includes determining your career goals and assessing your qualifications for a particular job. Job-market analysis encompasses seeking possible job sources and appraising jobs that are available.

The purpose of an application letter and resume is to obtain an interview. Major qualifications should be emphasized in both. How well you promote yourself to a prospective employer will determine your success in securing an interview.

Resume content, which differs for each person, depends upon an individual's qualifications. One of three resume styles—traditional, functional, and modified traditional—may be used.

Application letters, either solicited or unsolicited, are written according to the same basic outline as sales letters. In an application letter, you are selling your qualifications to a prospective employer.

## CHAPTER REVIEW

1. Identify the five components of the *job-search process.*
2. Summarize why *self-analysis* is important in securing a job.
3. Identify sources of information about job openings and decide which would be most helpful to you in obtaining job leads.
4. Justify the importance of *job appraisal.*
5. Identify the purpose of a *resume* and explain why no one style is correct.
6. Defend the inclusion of a *job/career objective* and/or *qualifications summary* in a resume.
7. Explain when the *education section* of a resume should precede the *experience section* and vice versa.
8. Should *personal information* be included in a resume? Why or why not?
9. Identify some advantages and disadvantages of including *references* in a resume.
10. Compare and contrast the three resume styles presented in this chapter. List several distinquishing features for each style.
11. Support the use of the "you" attitude in an application letter.
12. Differentiate between *solicited* and *unsolicited application letters.*

## APPLICATIONS

1. Conduct your own self-analysis by answering the twelve questions in this chapter on pages 297-298. Then write a brief description of your career goals as well as qualifications you have to offer an employer.

2. Choose an occupational area of interest to you. Then using the *Dictionary of Occupational Titles* (D.O.T.) found in the reference section of your college library, write a description of an occupation in your chosen area for which you are or will be qualified. In addition, consult other career publications listed on pages 298-299 of this chapter and list the names and addresses of five companies that might have openings in the occupation you selected.

3. Assume that you are applying for a job in your chosen field. Write a sample paragraph for each of the four techniques for the opening paragraph of application letters that differ from the examples given in the chapter.

4. Write a closing paragraph for an application letter. Make the sample paragraph reflect your qualifications and personality.

5. As your instructor directs, either write suggestions for improving the following application letter and resume, or rewrite both of them. Correct typographical and other errors in content, mechanics, word use, letter format, and writing style.

---

July 31, 19--


309 West McKilleps
Apt. #G-115
Randallstown, Maryland  21133-7891

Attention:  Personnel Director

This is in response to your ad for a GTL Management position appearing in the July 30, 19-- Maryland Herald.

My prior four years of management experience with the Morgan Corporation, should enable me to deal effectively with the responsibilities of finance, marketing, personnel, purchasing, and public relations outlined in your ad.

When you need additional information such as transcripts or references, please call.  I can be reached at 555-3401.

                    Cordially yours,


                    Tracy Toffenetti

**Tracy H. Toffenetti**

---

309 W. McKilleps Apt. G-115, Randallstown, Maryland  21133-7891
(301) 555-9876

---

| | |
|---|---|
| **OBJECTIVE** | Seeking a management position |
| **EXPERIENCE** | While attending school, I worked for four years as a manager for a Morgan Service Station.  This offered me opportunities to act in areas of personnel, finance, purchasing, sales, public relations, marketing, and advertising. |
| Personnel | It was my responsibility to hire all sales staff, motivate, promote, and fire those who did not live up to the quality of performance expected by the Morgan Company. |
| Finance, Sales, Purchasing | I was expected to manage all wages and payroll, tally the days receipts, make required banking arrangements, purchase automotive and general sales merchandise, and maintain inventory control. |
| Public Relations | Any controversy between employee and customer were under my range of responsibilities, and required following up every episode to its satisfactory conclusion. Reports had to be filed with the local Mobil representative. |
| Marketing and Advertising | I was expected also to prepare initial rough copy for sales and marketing campaigns local to our area, and submit a draft for newspaper advertising and other marketing vehicles. |
| **EDUCATION** | B.S. Business Administration, Western University, June 19--. |
| **HOBBIES AND INTERESTS** | Tennis, Golf, Boating, Music, Computers, Camping. |
| **SCHOOL RELATED ACTIVITIES** | Member of the debating team, Speech 101. Big Brother (Worked with disadvantaged youth.) |

6. Critique and/or rewrite the following application letter and resume according to your instructor's directions. Correct typographical and other errors in content, mechanics, word use, format, and writing style.

```
                                7715 North 18th Avenue
                                Redwood City, CA  94062-0714
                                April 29, 19--


Inter-Federal Company
2833 N. Central Street
Oakland, California  94612-3691

Ladies and Gentlemen:

If you need a person to plan, organize, and controll an opera-
tion; I am he.  If you need a person to train, audit, and
manage people; I am he.  If you are in need of a Production Op-
erations Manager; I am he.

The management related courses being taken in order to achieve
a Bacholors degree, along with the on the job experience I have
received, has given me a solid background in Production Opera-
tions Management.

The first-hand experience of working for United Parcel Service,
as listed in the enclosed resume, has given me a keen sense for
the parcel post business.  Working as a supervisor also gave me
an understanding for working with people along with the
knowledge to organize and controll an operation.

I feel that I can perform for you, and get the job done.  Can
we get together to discuss the possibility of a future rela-
tionship with Inter-Federal Company and myself.  I may be
reached at 830-5539, I shall appreciate hearing from you.

                        Confidently yours,



                        Dennis L. Morganworth

enc.
```

**Dennis L. Morganworth**
Applicant for Production Operations Manager
with
Inter-Federal Company

Address: 7715 North 18th Avenue    Telephone:  830-5539
Redwood City, CA  94062-0714  Area Code: (901)

Job Objectives: To become a first-line productions operations manager.
Excell into a higher management position

## Employment Related Experience

Service Assistant             Primary Unload Supervisor
(dock running)                United Parcel Service
Price Corporation             (19-- - 19--)
(present)

## Education for Production Management

Pacific State University
B.S., Production Operations Management
Expected Graduation, Spring, 19--

## Activities

Student Union Representative
Administrative Managment Society

## Personal Information

Marital Status: Single                Health: Excellent
Recreation: Weight Lifting, Reading, Golf

## References

References will be supplied upon request.

*  *  *

Find an employment advertisement (in a newspaper, posted announcement, or other source) for a position that fits your present qualifications for Items 7-9.

7. Prepare a traditional-style resume that you might send in response to the ad.

8. Prepare a functional-style resume in response to the ad.

9. Write a solicited application letter to accompany the resume in numbers 7 or 8.

10. Choose a company you would like to work for and write an unsolicited application letter as though you were actually applying for employment after graduation. Be sure to find out the name and title of the person to whom you should write. Attach your resume to the letter.

## CASE STUDY

"... so, I decided to take the job. On July 1, I officially become a member of the Wesco team. My title will be 'Financial Analyst Trainee.' And in six months—if I do well—I'll be promoted to 'Financial Analyst I.' I'm so excited that I can hardly wait for graduation!"

Tony finished his story with a big smile and hurried down the hall. Bill turned to his friend Sylvia with a puzzled look on his face. "He sure is lucky! I've written to over 20 firms and haven't received any positive responses. Tony and I have the same qualifications—we're both finance majors, and neither of us has any work experience. I used the same cover letter that Tony sent, and my resume is almost identical to his. I wonder why I haven't had any results."

"Where did you send them?" Sylvia asked.

"Since I want a well-paying job with opportunities for advancement, I chose ads from *The Wall Street Journal* that seemed to fit my career goals. Here are copies of several of the ads that I answered." Bill produced five ads from his book bag and showed them to Sylvia.

Reading over the ads carefully, Sylvia finally replied, "I think I see the problem."

1. Study carefully the job ads on page 329. What key part of the job-search process has Bill overlooked? Defend your answer.
2. From Bill's comments, how do you think he selected these particular advertisements?
3. If you were in Sylvia's place, what specific advice would you give Bill?

SR. COST ANALYST.  TGC is growing... and needs an aggressive, hands-on accounting professional for an excellent career opportunity. Develop and maintain cost systems and reporting. Grow to Manager. Requires BA and 3+ years electronics job-cost experience.

Senior Fiscal Analyst responsible for analysis of federal funds received in state. Should have a minimum of Master's degree in public finance, economics, or related field, and at least four years' experience in budgeting or fiscal research. Salary commensurate with experience.

Director of Finance/Controller. Our high-tech electronics company is offering a unique opportunity for an individual to design and implement control systems for our Solid-State Products Division. Responsibilities include all aspects of general accounting, balance sheets, and SEC reports for public audit. This position reports to the president of the division. If you are a high-energy, creative person with a strong cost-accounting background, send us your resume.

SENIOR FINANCIAL ANALYST.  We offer an opportunity to work with many of the most imaginative people in the mining and construction systems industry. Expansion of our operations has created an immediate need for an individual with the following qualifications: Proven track record in financial analysis, business planning, and development. Requires strong skills in finance and accounting. Degree in Business Administration required; MBA in Finance preferred.

Multi-million dollar corporation seeks Chief Financial Officer. Retail background helpful, but not required. Salary six figures +. All replies strictly confidential.

## REFERENCES

Judy Linscott, "Bizarre Gaffes in Resumes Hamper Applicants' Employment Chances," *The Arizona Republic* (August 15, 1984): 6.

## SUGGESTED READINGS

Bolles, Richard N. *What Color Is Your Parachute? A Practical Manual for Job Hunters and Career Changers*, 2nd ed. Berkeley, CA: Ten Speed Press, 1984.

Bostwick, Burdette E. *Resume Writing: A Comprehensive How-To-Do-It Guide*, 3rd ed. New York: Wiley, 1985.

Foxman, Loretta D. and Walter L. Polsky. *Resumes That Work: How to Sell Yourself on Paper*. New York: Wiley, 1985.

Jackson, Tom. *The Perfect Resume*. New York: Doubleday and Co., 1981.

Powell, C. Randall. *Career Planning Today*. Dubuque, IA: Kendall-Hunt, 1981.

Shykind, Maury. *Resumes for Executives and Professionals*, 3rd ed. New York: Arco Publishing Co., 1984.

# INTERVIEWS AND OTHER EMPLOYMENT COMMUNICATION

## CHAPTER 13

Todd Cunningham sat in the reception area outside the personnel office of Racoa International. He was waiting to be interviewed for the position of marketing representative. Another applicant sat across the room from him waiting to be interviewed for the same position. Todd noticed that the other applicant was several years older than he.

Todd asked, "How long have you been waiting?"

"Not too long," answered the other applicant, avoiding eye contact.

Todd thought, "He's not too friendly."

Just then the door of the conference room opened and Todd heard the personnel manager say to a well-dressed young woman, "Thanks for coming. We'll let you know the decision in a few days."

As she left the room, Todd tried to determine from her expression if she appeared to be confident or ill at ease.

As he waited nervously for his name to be called, the following thoughts flashed through his mind:

"I wonder how I compare to these other two applicants? Is my tie crooked?"

Then Todd heard someone call his name, and he thought, "Well, here's my chance."

Todd Cunningham's anxiety is a common occurrence among job seekers on the verge of an interview because the interview leads to the culmination of the job-search process.

This chapter discusses job interviews from two perspectives — the role of the applicant and that of the interviewer. The chapter also includes a discussion of employment-related written communication. Messages to employers include filling out application forms and writing various letters related to the job-search process. In addition to job interviews, the chapter illustrates the employer's role in conducting other personnel-related interviews and writing employment-related letters.

## COMMUNICATION BY THE APPLICANT

In the process of searching for an appropriate position, job applicants communicate with employers in various ways. Applicants generally must participate in job interviews and send various types of written messages in addition to resumes and job-application letters (which are discussed in Chapter 12). This section discusses job interviewing skills — the role of the applicant in participating in a successful job interview. A discussion of various types of written messages that job applicants often must prepare and send to employers is also included.

### Interview — the Applicant's Role

An **interview** is a two-way exchange of information, when participants send and receive information and feedback at the same time. Interviews are characterized by definite roles, purpose, and structure. The two *roles* that interact in interviews are that of interviewer and interviewee. Various kinds of interviews have different *purposes*, such as to gather or convey information, to screen and select individuals, to counsel employees, to review performance, and to influence behavior and attitudes. The *structure* of interviews entails planning, beginning, conducting, and concluding the interview. The interviewing process might involve the usual one-to-one interaction but may also include one-to-group interaction in some situations.

In business organizations, a manager or supervisor usually occupies the role of interviewer, and an employee or job applicant that of the interviewee. Applicants for employment are primarily concerned with job interviews, while employees may participate in other types of interviews such as performance, discipline, and exit interviews.

From the applicant's perspective, the job interview is the most important type of interview. Two types of job interviews are screening interviews and selection interviews. **Screening interviews** are initial interviews of many applicants; **selection interviews** usually involve only a few finalists for a position. For both types of job interviews, an applicant should be equally well prepared.

In **job interviews**, the applicant and the interviewer exchange employment-related information. The interviewee provides information about her or his education, work experience, personality, and other qualifications. The interviewer gives the applicant information about the company, job responsibilities, and other aspects of the position. Based on the information exchanged, the result of the interview may be a job offer and the acceptance of a position.

As a potential job interviewee, you should have two major goals: to sell yourself and to determine if the job will suit your needs. To achieve these goals, you must be well prepared for the interview. The first few minutes are the most important part of the interview. Remember, a first impression tends to be a lasting one.

Make sure that you look professional. Dressing in a conservative business-like manner or as other employees in the company dress will project an image of success and belonging. Be sure your hair, shoes, nails, and accessories are neat. Arrive at least 10 to 15 minutes early so that you have time to comb your hair, to relax, or to collect your thoughts. Have an extra resume in case you are asked for another, and bring a pen and notebook. If the job requires it, bring samples of your work.

You should take time to prepare answers to anticipated interview questions. Interviewers frequently cite poor communication skills and vague answers as weaknesses of job applicants. The following list includes some of the questions that interviewers often ask job applicants. When preparing for a job interview, think about these questions and develop appropriate answers. You might try having a friend ask you some of the questions on page 334 in a practice interview.

When preparing for an interview, you should do some research on the company that you are interviewing with. Learn something about its size, financial status, products, executive officers, position in the industry, potential growth, and so on. Your knowledge of the company will indicate that you are seriously interested in working for that organization. You can find information in sources such as the company's annual report or in such publications as *Moody's Industrial Manual*; *Standard and Poor's Register of Corporations, Directors and Executives*; *Dun and Bradstreet's Million Dollar Directory*; or *Thomas Register of American Manufacturers*.

A general knowledge of the job for which you are interviewing is also important. Try to find out something about specific job requirements and prospects for advancement. Also, do some research on salary ranges for the

---

## INTERVIEW QUESTIONS

1. Why are you seeking a position with this company?
2. What extracurricular activities did you participate in while in school?
3. Which of your courses did you like best? Least? Why?
4. How did you finance your education? What percentage was your contribution?
5. What do you know about our company?
6. What personal characteristics are important for success in your field of work?
7. What did you enjoy most about college? What did you enjoy least?
8. What are your assets or strengths? What are your liabilities or weaknesses?
9. Do you plan on continuing your education? How? When?
10. Are you willing to travel? Relocate?
11. How do you feel about working overtime?
12. How would you describe yourself?
13. What does success mean to you?
14. In what ways have you been successful in your life? How did you achieve this success?
15. What leadership skills do you have?
16. What constructive criticism have you received?
17. Why should I hire you?
18. Which of your accomplishments have given you the most satisfaction and why?
19. What short-term and long-term goals have you set for yourself?
20. Do you think your grades are a good indication of your academic achievement?
21. What was the best job you ever had? The worst job? Why?
22. How can you make a contribution to this company?
23. What is most important to you about a job?
24. Describe your relationship with your last two supervisors.
25. What do you do in your spare time? Do you have any hobbies?

Source: Items 1-11 are adapted from *The Northwestern Endicott-Lindquist Report* by Frank S. Endicott and Victor R. Lindquist, Northwestern University, Evanston, IL (by permission).

---

job in which you are interested so that you can answer questions on what salary you expect.

Prepare questions that you can ask the interviewer as your final step in preparation. Do not dominate or control the interview but have a few intelligent questions ready. Listen carefully to avoid asking a question the interviewer previously answered. The following examples are questions you might ask:

- Would you please describe the duties of this position for me?
- Is this a new position?
- Could you please tell me about the people I would be working with?
- May I see your facilities?
- What are the prospects for advancement?
- What type of orientation or training do you have for new employees?
- Is there anything else I can tell you about my qualifications?
- Can you give me an idea about when you expect to make your decision?

Your confidence in your own ability will be reflected during your participation in the interview. Use the following suggestions as guidelines for your behavior during an interview.

1. *Be yourself.* Assume a friendly, courteous, and confident air, but do not put on a show. View the interview as an opportunity to exchange information and not as if you were on the witness stand. Be enthusiastic and maintain a positive attitude throughout the interview.
2. *Be alert.* Show a genuine interest in the position through your firm handshake, erect posture, good eye contact, and prepared questions.
3. *Follow the interviewer's lead.* Allow the interviewer to control the interview. Listen carefully for cues indicating that the question has been adequately answered, that you may ask questions, or that the interview is drawing to a close.
4. *Stress your potential as a qualified candidate.* Be honest and sincere in your responses, but stress your positive attributes and downplay any negatives. Provide more than *yes* or *no* answers.
5. *Do not criticize former professors or employers.* This criticism only indicates a lack of personal integrity.
6. *Use good judgment in answering what appear to be discriminatory questions.* If the question is not too offensive, answer it. Asking the purpose of the question may reveal that no discrimination is intended.
7. *Express your appreciation.* A simple thank you for the interviewer's time at the end of an interview will enhance your image as a courteous individual.
8. *Follow up the interview with a thank-you letter.* This simple but often overlooked step will provide a strong signal that you are seriously interested in the position. This type of letter is discussed later in the chapter.

You can increase your chances for a successful interview if you are aware of all the factors that the interviewer will consider. Many applicants are rejected because they are not adequately prepared and, therefore, display negative traits during the interview. Some of the negative factors which frequently lead to the rejection of the interviewee are indicated on the following list:

## NEGATIVE FACTORS EVALUATED DURING THE JOB INTERVIEW WHICH MAY LEAD TO REJECTION OF THE APPLICANT

- Poor personal appearance
- Overbearing, overaggressive, know-it-all attitude
- Inability to articulate self clearly; poor voice, diction, and grammar
- Lack of planning for career; no purpose or goals
- Lack of interest and enthusiasm; passive and indifferent
- Lack of confidence and poise; nervousness; ill at ease
- Failure to participate in activities
- Overemphasis on money; interest only in best dollar offer
- Poor scholastic record, just got by
- Unwilling to start at the bottom; expects too much
- Makes excuses, evasiveness, hedges on unfavorable factors in record
- Lack of tact
- Lack of maturity
- Lack of courtesy, ill mannered
- Condemnation of past employers
- Fails to look interviewer in the eye

- Limp, fishy handshake
- High pressure type
- Indefinite response to questions
- Sloppy application blank
- Merely shopping around
- Wants job only for short time
- Little sense of humor
- Lack of knowledge of field of specialization
- No interest in company or in industry
- Too much name dropping
- Unwillingness to relocate
- Cynical or radical attitudes
- Unconventional moral standards
- Intolerant; strong prejudices
- Narrow interests
- Poor handling of personal finances
- No interest in community activities
- Inability to take criticism
- Late to interview without good reason
- Never heard of company
- Failure to express appreciation for interviewer's time

Source: Adapted from the *Northwestern Endicott-Lindquist Report* by Frank S. Endicott and Victor R. Lindquist, Northwestern University, Evanston, IL (by permission).

## Written Messages to Employers

In addition to the writing of the application letter and resume discussed in Chapter 12, a job applicant may need to prepare one or more written messages to prospective employers as part of the job-search process. These additional messages include responses to questions on application forms, various types of follow-up letters, thank-you letters, and replies to job offers.

**Application Forms**. Job applicants often must fill out an application form prior to or after an interview. When you fill out an **application form**, follow these suggestions:

1. Use a black pen if you fill out the application form in longhand. Application forms are usually photocopied, and black ink photocopies better than blue.
2. Read the directions BEFORE you start filling in the blanks. Two common errors on application forms are printing when you are asked to write and starting with your first name when you are instructed to give your last name first, and vice versa.
3. Print or write legibly, spell items correctly, and use proper grammar and punctuation. Since many application forms may be reviewed, the reader probably will screen out those that are illegible or incorrect, no matter how qualified the applicants may be.
4. Fill in all the blanks. If an item does not apply to you, either draw a line through the space or write NA (not applicable) in that space.
5. Have handy a list of dates of employment and schooling; names, titles, addresses, and phone numbers of individuals who will provide references; names of supervisors; previous salary amounts either by the hour, week, month, or year; and other pertinent information. Some of this information will appear on your resume; carry a copy of it with you.
6. State positive or neutral reasons for leaving previous positions. Negative comments such as "didn't like the hours," or "couldn't get along with the boss" will only discredit you. Instead, give positive or neutral responses such as "wanted opportunity for advancement," "better job offer," "seasonal position," or "continued education."
7. Indicate the word "open" for your expectation of salary or enter an appropriate high and low salary range for the particular position for which you are applying. If you list a high salary, you may be asking too much. If you list a low salary, you may be selling yourself short.
8. Summarize your outstanding qualifications if an "Additional Information" section is provided. Leaving this section blank may indicate to a prospective employer that you have no confidence in your qualifications or are unsure of what they are.
9. Sign rather than print your name on the line which is provided for your signature.
10. Proofread the application form when you have completed it. Fill it out just as carefully as you prepared your resume and application letter because the application form also reflects your communication skills.

**Application Follow-up Inquiry**. If you have not received a response to your application letter and resume after two or three weeks, send an inquiry letter. Such an inquiry, which asks about the status of your application, should have a direct (deductive) plan of organization (discussed in Chapter 5). This letter indicates your sincere interest in the company and your determination to obtain a position. More recent information may be included, such as additional classes completed, promotions acquired, new or additional work experience, or other related job information that has occurred since you applied. Here is an example of an application follow-up inquiry.

---

On May 1, I sent my application letter and resume to you for a position as a sales representative. May I please ask the status of my application.

Since applying, I have completed my degree in marketing at Northern University and am continuing my part-time employment as a sales clerk in an athletic shoe store. Because of your excellent reputation, your organization is still my first choice.

If you need additional information or would like me to come in for an interview, please call me at 555-6083 at any time. I will appreciate hearing from you soon.

---

Two precautions about writing this type of letter are that you should neither accuse the employer or insinuate that your materials were lost, nor should you indicate any disappointment or amazement in not being asked for an interview. Be positive and tactful in your inquiry.

**Interview Invitation Acceptance**. Responding to an invitation for an interview, of course, is an easy letter to write. Use a favorable-message (direct) plan of organization in writing this letter.

---

Thank you for inviting me for an interview. Monday, August 17, at 2 p.m. is fine.

I look forward to meeting with you at that time and discussing my qualifications in greater detail.

---

**Interview Thank You**. Assume that you have just completed an interview. An expression of gratitude for the interviewer's time is appropriate even if you think that the interview did not go well, that you will not be considered seriously for a position, or that you no longer are interested in a position with that company. The following letter expresses appreciation for such an interview:

---

    Talking with you yesterday about your organization was very pleasant and informative. I appreciate the friendliness and courtesy shown to me.

    I intend to follow your suggestion about continuing my education during the summer months. Possibly Acme Products will have an opening again that we might discuss in the near future.

---

If you feel particularly good about the interview or received some indication that you would be seriously considered for a position, sending a thank-you letter on the same day or the day after your interview may influence a decision to turn in your favor. Few individuals take the time to write a thank-you letter for a preliminary (screening) interview. A letter of appreciation is more crucial if you are a finalist for the position and received an on-site interview. Employers are often impressed by those who write a prompt, courteous thank-you letter.

Keep your letter courteous, short, and sincere. Include the following items:

1. Opening Paragraph — express your appreciation for the interview.
2. Middle Paragraph
     Emphasize something you learned about the company either during the interview or from reading materials provided after the interview.

-or-

Provide any additional information.

-or-

Review your qualifications briefly.

3. Ending Paragraph
     Indicate your willingness to participate in another interview.

-or-

Express your sincere interest in the position.

-or-

Convey confidence that you are looking forward to a favorable decision because your qualifications meet the job requirements.

Thank you for taking the time today to talk with me about working for your company. I was very impressed with the overall atmosphere of your company as we toured the facilities.

Your discussion of your company's need for a computerized inventory control system was very intriguing. As I mentioned during our talk, the inventory control system that I designed for my present employer was very challenging and successful. Possibly this system could work for your company.

(Name), please consider this experience as you make your choice. I look forward to your decision.

**Interview Follow-up Inquiry.** In most job interviews, you will be told how and when a decision will be made about the position advertised. If you have not been notified by the stated decision date, a brief inquiry such as the following letter is appropriate. Notice that the message is tactful but straightforward.

Two weeks have passed since my interview with you about your management trainee position. You indicated a decision date on August 15.

Since I must continue my pursuit of an acceptable position as soon as possible, I would appreciate knowing if I am to receive an offer from your company. I am still interested in employment with your company and would like to know your decision within the next few days.

**Additional Information Reply.** An employer may occasionally ask for additional information after receiving your application letter and resume or after an interview. For example, this request may be for more details about your qualifications or for a list of references. In replying, be sure to provide the requested information specifically and accurately. Follow this outline:

1. Opening Paragraph—express your willingness to provide the desired information. If after an initial interview, thank the individual for the interview first and then express your willingness.
2. Middle Paragraph—provide information requested. If referring to additional qualifications, give supporting facts.
3. Ending Paragraph—indicate your availability for a first or second interview.

---

    As you requested, I am enclosing a list of
individuals who can speak of my education and work
experience.

    After you have had an opportunity to talk with
these people, please call me about arranging a time
so that we might discuss my qualifications in more
detail. Call me any time at 555-8761. I look forward
to hearing from you soon.

---

**Reply to a Denial**. A company may not have an opening or may have selected someone else for the position for which you applied. No reply is required from you if you are turned down for a job. However, if you wish to be
considered for future openings within that same company, keep the lines of
communication open by responding to the company's denial letter.

You may receive a form letter stating that no position is presently available or, after an interview, a form letter that states that other candidates'
qualifications are more acceptable. Along with the refusal, however, may be
an offer to keep your application on file. If you wish to be considered for
future openings, you should respond accordingly. Include the following information in your letter:

1. Opening Paragraph—express appreciation for considering your qualifications.
2. Middle Paragraph—indicate your desire to keep your application on file
   or your appreciation for the interview learning experience.
3. Ending Paragraph—state future employment possibilities.

---

    Although no position as an internal auditor is
available with your company now, I appreciate your
reviewing my application.

Please keep my application on file for future consideration.

_____

-or-

_____

Thank you for considering my qualifications as an internal auditor with your company.

I appreciate having had the opportunity to interview with you. Such an opportunity is always a valuable learning experience.

Possibly my qualifications will better match your requirements in the future. I will consider reapplying then.

_____

**Job Offer Acceptance.** Since a letter accepting a job offer is a favorable message, it should convey your acceptance of the job offer in your beginning sentence. Follow this opening with necessary information such as confirmation of the starting date and job location. Finally, close with an expression of your enthusiasm to begin work.

_____

Yes, I accept your offer of a management—trainee position. Thank you for your confidence in my ability to do the job.

As you indicated in your letter, I will report to your office on Monday at 9 a.m. for an orientation meeting with other members of the department.

I am eager to start what I anticipate will be a rewarding and satisfying career with Stannell Corporation.

_____

**Job Offer Denial.** If you have the good fortune to receive more than one job offer at a time, you will need to write a job offer denial for those that you do not accept. Because of the time and effort extended to you during your job search with a company, write your denial to that company as soon as possible after accepting a position elsewhere.

Be positive and tactful in writing denial letters, and leave the door open for future possibilities. As an unfavorable message, a letter denying a job offer should have an indirect (inductive) plan of organization. Begin your letter by expressing your appreciation for the offer. Explain your reason for denying the offer. Finally, end the letter with a positive closing.

---

```
     Thank you for your offer of an administrative
assistant position with your company.
     As I indicated during our discussion, I am
interested in working for a large company that can
offer me opportunities for advancement in the
paralegal field. Since being a legal assistant is my
primary goal, I have accepted a position with a large
law firm in Philadelphia.
     Thank you again, (name). Your courteousness and
interest in me as an employee is appreciated.
```

---

**Resignation Letters.** When leaving a position, an employee should write a resignation letter to provide a permanent record of the fact that he or she resigned rather than being laid off or fired. This information may be important later in your career if you need a recommendation from a former employer as you change jobs. Therefore, a resignation letter should be tactful, discreet, and follow an indirect plan of organization. The following information should be included in such a letter:

1. A pleasant opening statement
2. An expression of appreciation and/or a statement of regret
3. A reason for leaving (advancement opportunity, transfer of spouse, change in health, etc.)
4. A date of resignation
5. A courteous closing

A sample resignation letter is shown in the following example:

---

```
   Working for Belldon Company for the past two        Pleasant opening
years has given me invaluable experience as an assis-
tant manager. I appreciate the many opportunities I   Expression of
have had and the friends I have made.                 appreciation
```

Recently, however, I have been offered a position of assistant personnel manager of Heers, Inc., which is a large industrial supply company. Since this position is a career advancement opportunity, I have accepted the offer. Therefore, I am submitting my resignation effective November 1.

Reason for resignation

Resignation and date

I have enjoyed working for the Belldon Company and wish everyone my best.

Courteous closing

# COMMUNICATION BY THE EMPLOYER

Employers communicate with job applicants during job interviews and through written messages such as application acknowledgments, interview invitations, job offers, and job denials. In addition, other personnel-related interviews such as performance interviews, discipline interviews, and exit interviews may be part of an employer's role. This section discusses the employer's role in various types of employment communication.

## Interviews—the Employer's Role

As discussed at the beginning of this chapter, a manager or supervisor generally occupies the role of interviewer. The interviewer is responsible for developing the structure of an interview which consists of planning, starting, conducting, and concluding the interview.

**Planning the Interview.** The planning stage should include the following steps:

1. Determine what the interviewer hopes to accomplish from the interview; for example, screening qualified and unqualified job applicants.
2. Gather appropriate background information about the interviewee.
3. Develop an outline of preliminary questions that will fulfill the purpose of the interview.
4. Decide on the physical setting according to the purpose of the interview—the interviewer's office to reinforce authority or a neutral location such as a lounge or conference room to make the interviewee feel more at ease.

**Starting the Interview**. The beginning of an interview should include one or more of the following strategies:

1. *Establish a rapport, if necessary*. Most interviewees and even some interviewers are nervous at the beginning of an interview. Establishing rapport involves creating a sense of agreement and pleasantness between the interviewer and the interviewee. An enthusiastic verbal welcome along with a smile and a handshake, a brief discussion of the weather, or a comment about some current event of mutual interest are all ways of establishing rapport. However, in some interviews (for example, discipline interviews), "small talk" may not be an appropriate way to begin because it can increase the interviewee's feelings of anxiety. In such a case, getting to the point is preferable.
2. *State the purpose of the interview to the interviewee*. An interviewer should not assume that the interviewee knows the purpose of the interview (for example, evaluating an employee's performance). Simply telling the interviewee what the interview is all about will avoid any confusion and generate a more relaxed atmosphere.
3. *Motivate the interviewee to participate*. Many factors can serve as motivation for interviewees. Depending on the type of interview, motivation can involve factors such as a promotion or raise, a sense of importance, or a feeling of being needed.

**Conducting the Interview**. The main part of an interview consists of asking questions, listening to responses, answering questions, and providing transition from one topic to another during the interview. Types of questions and their purposes are presented later in this chapter, and the topic of effective listening is examined in Chapter 16.

Transition from one topic to another can be achieved by informing the interviewee of the next topic of discussion. A simple summary statement can provide this sense of direction. For example, a personnel interviewer might say to a job applicant, "Now that we have talked about your education, I would like to ask you some questions about your work experience." Such a statement alerts the interviewee that one topic has been completed and the interview process is moving on to another topic. This transition will help ease the interviewee's feelings of not knowing what to expect.

**Concluding the Interview**. Many interviews, unfortunately, end abruptly because of interruptions or because time runs out. Some type of ending is essential to the interview. A brief summary of what took place during the interview gives a sense of completion to all participants and provides a natural conclusion to the interview. Equally significant to the feeling of accomplishment is knowing what actions will follow the interview, such as an additional interview, a job offer, a raise or promotion, a change in position, a written evaluation, and so on.

**Interview Questions**. Interviews may be either structured or unstructured. A structured plan of questioning basically relies on a set of prepared questions. An unstructured plan of questioning, on the other hand, includes no specific prepared questions.

The structured plan of questioning is best in situations where the same questions must be asked in the same sequence to all interviewees. Job interviews are often conducted in this way to ensure that the interview is fair and unbiased in accordance with Equal Employment Opportunity guidelines. In addition, this plan of questioning aids the inexperienced interviewer by providing direction to ensure that relevant and valid information is collected. A disadvantage of this plan, however, is that it does not allow flexibility in asking different questions as needed.

The advantage of the unstructured plan of questioning is that it allows for maximum flexibility in seeking out desired information. With this plan, the interviewer starts the interview with an appropriate question and asks additional questions based on the interviewee's responses. A disadvantage to this plan of questioning is that the interviewer may deviate too far from her or his original objective and fail to obtain all the desired information.

A semi-structured plan of questioning may be the most effective plan for most interviewers. Having some prepared key questions to initiate and keep the discussion flowing, along with questions which are based on the interviewee's responses, will ensure that all areas are covered and yet allow flexibility as needed.

Interview questions may be classified according to the following four types:

*Open and Closed Questions*. **Open questions** allow the interviewee to say as much or as little as he or she wishes in response to a question. In contrast, **closed questions** restrict the interviewee's response to a more specific, direct answer. Consider the possible responses for the following examples of both types of questions:

| Open | Closed |
|---|---|
| • Tell me about any supervisory experience you may have. | • Have you ever had supervisory experience? |
| • What could we change to improve the department's safety record? | • Does the department have a good safety record? |
| • How would you feel about being transferred? | • Would you be willing to be transferred? |

Closed questions can be answered in a word—*yes* or *no*. Open questions, on the other hand, take more time and thought; they require a longer response.

Open questions have the following advantages:

1. They are easier to respond to and have no right or wrong answer; therefore, they put the interviewee more at ease.
2. They indicate how well individuals can think out loud and express themselves.

3. They reveal an individual's knowledge and/or attitude about a subject as well as her or his priorities.
4. They can provide more information than closed questions because they allow the interviewee more flexibility.

Open questions have the following disadvantages:

1. Recording answers is difficult because answers are long and complex.
2. Controlling the direction of the interview may be difficult because interviewees may digress in their responses.
3. The interviewee may take a great deal of time in responding to questions.
4. The interviewee may say much without providing the necessary information.

Closed questions have the following advantages:

1. Answers are easy to record because answers are short.
2. The interviewer can easily maintain control because the interviewee does not have a chance to ramble off the subject.
3. Time is saved because answers are shorter.
4. Reluctant talkers respond more readily because the questions are easy to answer.
5. The interviewee can provide exact information without digressions.

Closed questions have the following disadvantages:

1. They do not allow the interviewee to explain her or his response.
2. They limit the information that can be obtained from the interviewee.

*Direct and Indirect Questions.* A **direct question** does exactly what its name implies—*directs* or leads the interviewee in a particular direction. Two types of direct questions are leading and loaded questions.

**Leading questions** are worded in such a way that the expected response is implied. For example, "Would you be opposed to traveling?" The interviewee's response will probably be "No, I don't mind traveling" even though travel may not be her or his preference.

**Loaded questions** in effect ask and answer the interviewer's question. For example, "Of course you are opposed to that kind of policy." The expected answer is clearly implied. Loaded questions generally trigger emotions or strong feelings and are, therefore, not recommended. Some interviewers, however, do use them if they wish to see how an interviewee will react under stress.

**Indirect questions**, on the other hand, do not direct the interviewee's response. The loaded question previously given might be changed to the indirect question, "How do you feel about that policy?" The revised question does not imply a correct response.

*Hypothetical Questions.* These questions provide a description of an actual situation to which the interviewee must respond. The following question is hypothetical: "If one of your sales reps did not make her or his monthly quota, what would you do?" Hypothetical questions are valuable because they are as close as an interviewer will get to observing actual behavior of the interviewee.

*Probing Questions*. The **probing question** is probably one of the most effective types of questions, motivating the interviewee to provide more detail about what he or she is saying. Such comments as "Please elaborate," "What do you mean?", "Why?", or "Go on" elicit additional discussion.

A good technique that will not bias or direct a response is to repeat part of what the interviewee just said. For example:

INTERVIEWEE: I didn't like all the red tape on my last job.
INTERVIEWER: Red tape?
INTERVIEWEE: Yes, every time a new procedure was needed, I would have
              to fill out a. . . .

An equally effective technique is the use of silence, for silent pause could indicate to the interviewee that he or she may elaborate. If the interviewee does not continue, the interviewer should ask another question to prevent the silence from becoming threatening to the interviewee because he or she does not know what is expected. Nonverbal cues such as a nod of the head in agreement or a smile will also indicate to the interviewee that he or she should continue.

**Job Interviews**. In **job interviews**, the interviewer has two major purposes: to gather information about the interviewee in order to predict whether that individual will be successful on the job, and to convey information to the interviewee about specific job responsibilities and the company as a whole.

Keeping questions relevant to the job will help achieve the first purpose of job interviews. Because each job has specific characteristics that are unique to that position, no all-inclusive list of questions exists.

The second purpose, to convey information about the company and the job to the interviewee, might address any or all of the following areas:

• Specific job responsibilities
• Orientation to fellow workers
• Opportunities for advancement
• Management policies
• Work hours, salary, and fringe benefits

As part of her or his role, an interviewer should be aware of certain legal considerations related to interviewing. The United States Department of Labor and Equal Employment Opportunity Commission guidelines prohibit discriminatory hiring based on race, creed, color, sex, national origin, handicap, or age. Questions related to any of these areas should be avoided because they might be considered discriminatory. The following are examples of questions that should be avoided.

- Where were you born?
- May I see your birth certificate?
- Are you handicapped in any way?
- What religious holidays will keep you from work?
- Have you ever been arrested and for what?
- What is your ethnic background?
- Are you married?
- Do you plan to have children? How many?

Personal questions may be asked only if they refer to a criterion which fulfills a specific job requirement. For example, health-related questions can be asked of applicants for certain jobs (such as airline pilots and air-traffic controllers) for safety reasons.

Interviewers often take brief notes during a job interview to aid in their evaluation of interviewees. Notetaking is an acceptable practice as long as the interviewee is aware of what the interviewer is doing, and if it does not interfere with the interviewer's ability to listen. The interviewer should later review the notes and evaluate the recorded responses to questions according to the specifications of the job and avoid allowing personal biases to enter into the evaluation.

**Performance Interviews.** A **performance interview** is a periodic review, usually quarterly, semi-annually, or annually, in which a supervisor examines and evaluates a subordinate's work performance. The formal appraisal process consists of two phases: a formal written appraisal of the subordinate and an oral feedback session (interview) with the subordinate. Formal written appraisals are discussed in Chapter 15.

The feedback session with the subordinate should involve two-way communication. The supervisor may either evaluate the subordinate first, or allow the subordinate to start the discussion based on her or his self-evaluation or pre-study of the formal appraisal form. In either case, the subordinate should participate in every aspect of the interview. Increased participation may result in a better working relationship with the superior, a greater sense of overall job satisfaction, and better motivation.

Guidelines for performance interviews are as follows:

1. Select a neutral location. Using a supervisor's office can accent the status difference between superior and subordinate. Use of a private conference room may create a more open atmosphere.
2. Discuss both positive and negative performances. Dwelling only on areas that need improvement can make the entire interview session a negative experience for the subordinate. The interview will be ineffective if the supervisor merely dictates a solution that he or she believes is appropriate. The interview will be more of a positive experience and will have better results if both parties can arrive at a mutual solution to problem areas.
3. Set specific, obtainable goals that have been mutually agreed upon. Establish a date of achievement and criteria for achieving these goals.

4. Conclude the feedback session on a positive note. The supervisor should make certain that the subordinate knows exactly what is expected as a result of the performance interview.

**Discipline Interviews.** A **discipline interview** takes place when a manager or supervisor must confront an employee with her or his negative behavior (for example, poor work performance, repeated tardiness, or excessive absenteeism). The purpose of a discipline interview is to change unaccepted employee work behavior to acceptable habits.

No set procedures are recommended for discipline interviews because they may be adapted to different management styles. The following suggestions are general guidelines:

1. Postpone a discipline interview until you know all the facts. Reacting too quickly and losing one's temper may be more harmful to all involved than the infraction. However, do not delay the interview too long for the undesirable behavior may be repeated, lessening the effectiveness of the discipline interview.
2. Conduct the interview privately. Public reprimand only creates additional resentment.
3. Focus on the incorrect behavior rather than on the person. Avoid sounding as though you are overreacting to the situation; for example, refrain from telling an employee who made a mistake that he or she is *always* wrong.
4. Allow the subordinate to explain her or his side of the story. When appropriate, allow the subordinate to suggest corrective action. This participation will demonstrate the supervisor's fairness and concern for the subordinate's feelings.
5. If necessary, administer discipline (such as transfer or demotion) according to the severity of the undesired behavior. Being reasonable in disciplinary action will lessen feelings of resentment.
6. Document the discipline interview for future reference and for legal protection. Include a copy of a description in the employee's personnel file. Some companies have special forms for this purpose and require the employee to sign the form after a discipline interview.

**Exit Interview.** The primary purpose of an **exit interview** is to find out why employees voluntarily leave their jobs. Since recruiting and training new employees is very expensive, many companies interview departing employees to determine if they are leaving because of organizational problems that might be remedied. A routine analysis of information collected from exit interviews may reveal any of the following internal reasons for employee turnover: inadequate supervision, poor working conditions, low pay, little opportunity for advancement, unsatisfactory working relationships, and so on. Some of these conditions could possibly be changed to improve morale and lessen employee turnover.

The secondary purpose of the exit interview is to provide the employee who is leaving with information about final pay, pension and insurance benefits, recommendation letters, and checkout procedures such as turning in keys and equipment. Starting the exit interview with this information helps to relieve any nervousness the interviewee may have and creates a more open atmosphere for discussing the reasons for leaving.

Some exit interviews do not provide reliable information. If the interview is conducted by an immediate supervisor, the true reason for leaving may not be revealed, particularly if the supervisor has provided the reason for leaving. Employees often conceal their real motives for leaving and state other reasons such as better offers or family problems. A skilled interviewer, though, can still obtain valuable information that can be used to improve the organization.

Consider the following guidelines when conducting an exit interview:

1. Persuade the departing employee to be open by explaining your need for her or his help in improving the organization.
2. Conduct a structured interview with prepared questions that cover specific points such as wages, promotion opportunities, positive and negative factors about the job, working conditions, training, supervision, and so on. Use primarily open questions (such as "Why are you leaving Acme?") and probing questions (such as "Tell me more about the problems you just mentioned") to obtain desired information. Avoid loaded questions such as "You must be leaving because you didn't get promoted." Leading questions are occasionally appropriate if the interviewee does not provide relevant information in answers to open questions. In such cases, a leading question may trigger a candid response (for example, "Are you leaving because of problems with your supervisor?").
3. Refrain from agreeing or disagreeing with the departing employee. Collect your information and verify inconsistencies later. Do not let the exit interview become a "gripe session" that puts you on the defensive.
4. Record the interview information for later analysis. Use a prepared questionnaire with adequate space for additional information as the interview proceeds.

This chapter has presented the major types of interviews that occur between employers and employees or job applicants. Other interviews collect survey information for business research from customers or the public. Survey interviews are discussed in Chapter 9.

## Written Messages to Job Applicants

Some day you may be responsible for hiring employees and will need to communicate with job applicants. Employers write various kinds of letters to job applicants such as application acknowledgments, interview invitations, job offers, and job denials.

**Application Acknowledgment**. As a courtesy to applicants, an employer should acknowledge receiving application letters and resumes. Such acknowledgments are commonly form letters, as shown in the following example:

---

(Name)
(Address)
(City, State, ZIP)
APPLICATION ACKNOWLEDGMENT

Your application papers have been received and are being processed. Upon completion of this screening, you will be notified of any positions available that appear to match your qualifications. You should receive notification within the next two to three weeks.

If no positions are available, your papers will be kept on file for six months. You will be notified of any available positions during that time.

Thank you for your interest in our company.

---

**Interview Invitation**. The goal of the job seeker's application letter and resume is to receive an invitation for an interview. Consequently, interview invitations are favorable messages and should be organized deductively.

An employer writing such an invitation should outline all details clearly, including dates, times, location, and any expenses that will be covered by the company. For example:

---

You are invited to our firm for an interview for our management trainee position. Would Wednesday, April 9, at 4 p.m. in my office be convenient? If not, please call to arrange a more convenient time.

Your travel expenses will be reimbursed; therefore, please keep a record of your mileage.

We look forward to talking with you and showing you our facilities.

---

**Job Offer**. A job offer is favorable news. Therefore, organize the letter by the direct plan and begin with the actual job offer. Follow with appropriate details such as a deadline for accepting the offer and other information that might be helpful to the applicant. Invite questions and close with a sincere expression of interest in the applicant, for example:

---

We are pleased to offer you the position of staff accountant with our firm. With your background and experience, you will have an excellent opportunity for advancement with Meyers and James.

We have enclosed a statement of your starting salary and a description of our flexible fringe benefits program. Please give us your decision by October 15 so that we might make the necessary arrangements.

We are very impressed with your qualifications and hope you accept a position with our firm. If you have any questions, please call me collect at (204) 555-0317.

---

**Job Denial**. Receiving a job denial letter is a disheartening experience for any applicant. However, honest but tactful denial messages indicate that the applicant was given fair consideration.

Begin the unfavorable message with a positive or neutral opening; for example, thank the applicant for being interested in your company or for interviewing with you. Follow with a tactful reason for the denial and then state the denial as positively as you can. End with a courteous and friendly closing sentence. An example of a job denial letter follows.

---

Thank you for spending time with us last week, discussing the assistant manager position for our east-side branch.

Many well-qualified individuals applied for this position, and you were one of the finalists. Although the personnel committee had a difficult time selecting only one individual from so many excellent applicants, they have finally made the decision to hire another candidate.

Your interest in our company is appreciated. We will keep your application on file in case a similar opening occurs.

---

## SUMMARY

An interview is a two-way exchange of information between two or more individuals. The interview process is characterized by definite roles, purpose, and structure. Interviews are conducted for the purpose of gathering and conveying information; screening, selecting, and counseling individuals; reviewing performance; and influencing behavior and attitudes.

To a job applicant, a job interview is the most important type of interview. Adequate preparation as well as stressing relevant qualifications by the applicant may result in a successful interview—a job offer.

For an interview to be successful from the employer's perspective, careful consideration must be given by the interviewer to the structure of the interview—planning, starting, conducting, and concluding the interview. Interview questions may follow a structured or unstructured plan of organization and may use any or all of the four categories of questions—open or closed, direct or indirect, hypothetical, and probing. Job, performance, discipline, and exit interviews are common types of interviews occurring in business organizations.

Other written communications related to employment are application forms, applicant-initiated letters, resignation letters, and employer-initiated letters. A carefully filled out application form demonstrates an applicant's communication skills. In addition to preparing a resume and writing application letters, a job applicant may need to write follow-up letters, thank-you letters, and job-offer acceptance or denial letters. Upon leaving a job, an employee should write a resignation letter to terminate her or his position formally. Employers, on the other hand, will communicate with applicants by writing letters such as application acknowledgments, interview invitations, and job offers or denials.

## CHAPTER REVIEW

1. Describe how a job applicant can obtain information about a company prior to an interview.
2. Do you agree or disagree with the following statement: "The first few minutes are the most important part of a job interview." Defend your answer.
3. React to the following statement: "A job applicant should 'sell' herself or himself by dominating the interview."
4. Give three examples of "discriminatory" job-interview questions. If an interviewer asks one of these questions, how should the applicant respond?
5. Justify the importance of sending an expression of appreciation after an interview.
6. React to the following statement: "Letters of resignation are favorable to the sender; therefore, they should have a direct plan of organization."
7. Differentiate between *open* and *closed interview questions*. Discuss when one or the other would be more appropriate.

8. Explain the difference between *leading, loaded,* and *probing questions.* Give an example of each.
9. List and describe four types of interviews.
10. Give an example of an *open* and a *closed question* for each of the four types of interviews that you listed above.

## APPLICATIONS

1. Team up with one of your classmates and select five questions from page 334 and ask each other the questions in a practice job interview.

2. Team up with one of your classmates and conduct a 15-minute simulated job interview. One should play the role of the interviewer and the other the role of the job applicant. Dress appropriately for the interview. The interviewer should prepare a list of questions, and the applicant should supply the interviewer with her or his resume. After the interview, the other members of the class will write a critique of the interview.

3. Obtain a job application form from a local company, fill it out, and turn it in to your instructor for evaluation.

4. Interview someone at a local company who is responsible for interviewing job applicants. Find out how a typical interview is structured and how applicants are evaluated. Write a short report of your findings.

5. Interview someone at a local company who conducts performance interviews as part of the employee-appraisal process. Find out how often performance interviews take place, how they are structured, and how employees are evaluated. Write a short report of your findings.

6. Assume that you are personnel director of a local company that has an opening for an experienced bookkeeper (no college degree required). Company policy requires that all applicants be asked the same questions. After narrowing down the applicants to the top five candidates, you invite the five finalists to a selection interview. Prepare a list of 12 questions to ask each applicant. Include both open and closed questions.

7. Write a job-offer letter to the candidate who was selected for the position described above (Mr. Ron Mendoza, 4135 19th Avenue, El Paso, TX 79902-7681). Offer him a salary of $21,000 per year. The job starts three weeks from the date of the letter.

8. Write a form letter tactfully informing the other four finalists that they were not selected for the position described in number 6.

9. Write a form letter tactfully informing the other 25 applicants (who did not receive an interview) that they were not selected for the position described in number 6.

10. You have just received an offer of employment in your chosen field of work from Ms. Dorothy Ballard, Personnel Director of HML Corporation, 1406 Murray Hill Parkway, East Rutherford, NJ 07073-3669. Write a letter accepting the offer.

11. You have been employed in the position described in number 10 for the past two years. You just received a job offer from the Symington Company, and the new position (in your chosen field of work) is a promotion for you. Write a letter of resignation to Ms. Ballard.

12. Ms. Ballard would like you to stay at HML (see numbers 10 and 11 above). When she offers you a promotion and a salary matching the amount offered you by the Symington Company, you decide to stay at HML. Write a letter turning down the Symington position to Mr. Earl Brady, Vice President, Symington Company, 335 Sandy Springs Road, West Orange, NJ 07051-5991.

## CASE STUDY

Susan Jenkins was applying for her first full-time job. She sat in the personnel office at Elwin Corporation, where she hoped to find work that eventually would lead to a management position. As a new college graduate with part-time sales experience, she felt nervous when Ms. Pennington, the personnel director, called her in for an interview.

Susan picked up her large purse and walked into Ms. Pennington's office. She sat down in the only available chair, which was over in the far corner of the room, put the purse in her lap, and folded her hands on top of the purse. She wondered if Ms. Pennington would be able to hear her from the corner spot. Ms. Pennington's dark blue jacket and white blouse looked very professional as she sat behind the oak desk.

"I see you've done some work before," Ms. Pennington said, looking at Susan's resume. "We like to see even part-time work experience, because it means you understand something about the business world. What kind of work did you do?"

"Oh, it was in sales," Susan said in a loud voice. She crossed one leg and fidgeted with the cuff on her slacks. "But I don't want to go into sales," she said very quickly. "I want something that leads to management."

Ms. Pennington looked at her and smiled. She put the resume down, got up from her desk, and brought her chair around so that she sat near her. Susan played with a loose strand of her long hair and looked at the painting on the wall behind Ms. Pennington.

"All work experience is valuable," Ms. Pennington said. "I'm interested in hearing what you learned from your work experience."

Susan looked down at her shoes and noticed that the right one was scuffed at the toe. "Well," she said, shifting her weight in the chair, "I was a part-time clerk in a department store." She shrugged her shoulders. "I learned that I don't want to have to do that sort of thing. I want to manage people."

Ms. Pennington stood up and shook hands with Susan Jenkins. "Thank you for coming in," Ms. Pennington said. "I don't think we have anything right now, but you are welcome to check back another time."

Susan left the office. "I must not have said what she wanted to hear," she thought. "Perhaps I should have taken a course in public speaking."

1. What mistakes did Susan make in the interview? What suggestions for improvement would you give her?
2. Did Ms. Pennington make mistakes in the interview? What suggestions would you give Ms. Pennington for improving her skills as an interviewer?

## SUGGESTED READINGS

Bruce, Stephen D. *Face to Face: Every Manager's Guide to Better Interviewing*. Madison, CT: Business & Legal Reports, 1984.

Einhorn, Lois J., Patricia Hayes Bradley, and John E. Baird, Jr. *Effective Employment Interviewing: Unlocking Human Potential*. Glenview, IL: Scott, Foresman and Co., 1982.

Fear, Richard A. *The Evaluation Interview*, 3rd ed. New York: McGraw-Hill, 1984.

Richetto, Gary M., and Joseph P. Zima. *Interviewing*, 2nd ed. Chicago: Science Research Associates, 1982.

Stano, Michael E. and N. L. Reinsch, Jr. *Communication in Interviews*. Englewood Cliffs, NJ: Prentice-Hall, 1982.

Stewart, Charles J., and William B. Cash. *Interviewing: Principles and Practices*, 3rd ed. Dubuque, IA: William C. Brown, 1982.

# CREDIT AND COLLECTION MESSAGES

## CHAPTER 14

J. T. Henderson, vice president of Finance at Reston Manufacturing, called Diane Simmons, the company's credit manager, into his office.

"Diane," he said, "you've done an outstanding job with our credit and collection procedures."

Henderson continued, "The computerized credit and collections system you designed has certainly proved its worth. Our slow receivables have improved so much that the company no longer has a cash-flow problem."

Henderson smiled and offered her his hand. "The Executive Committee has approved a promotion and a raise for you. Congratulations!"

As a well-informed consumer, you should have an understanding of the credit process. As a business person, if you work in marketing, retailing, banking, finance, purchasing, small business administration, or other fields concerned with credit, you should have an in-depth comprehension of the concepts, laws, and common business practices that are involved in credit and collections.

This chapter presents a discussion of the following points:

- An introduction to credit and its importance to business organizations and to the economy
- A description of the credit process, including credit approval and denial messages
- An explanation of each stage of the collection process, including a discussion of collection messages
- An overview of the laws that regulate credit and collection procedures and messages

## CREDIT FUNDAMENTALS

The United States economy depends heavily on the use of credit. In fact, over 90 percent of all transactions between industrial and commercial firms are conducted on a credit basis (Cole, 1984, 14), and consumer credit amounts to approximately 60 percent of total personal income in the United States (Cole, 1984, 24). To give you some idea of the enormous amount of money involved, the total amount of outstanding credit card debt in the United States amounts to over a trillion dollars (*The Predicasts Basebook*, November 1986, 85). Credit is so important that if for some reason it suddenly stopped being available, our economy would almost certainly collapse.

Credit transactions between manufacturers, wholesalers, and retailers are commonly referred to as **commercial credit**. Business firms use commercial credit when they purchase merchandise and raw materials from one another. Many companies rely on commercial credit for short-term financing of their production and marketing activities.

**Consumer credit** is important to retail companies because of the volume of business it generates. Various types of consumer credit are charge accounts, credit cards, bank cards, installment sales, personal installment loans, and service credit (for services such as medical care and utilities). We use consumer credit to acquire goods and services now and pay for them later out of our future earnings. Retail firms must evaluate charge-account applicants carefully, however, to prevent problems with people who fail to pay their bills on time.

### Five C's of Credit

When a customer applies for credit, companies traditionally evaluate five factors known as the *five C's of credit* relating to the applicant. The *five C's* are as follows:

1. *Character*. Is the applicant honest and responsible?
2. *Capital*. Does the applicant have financial resources? What is the applicant's net worth (assets minus liabilities)?
3. *Capacity*. Does the applicant have the ability to pay (steady income)? Does he or she have the legal capacity to enter into a binding contract (age 18 or 21, depending on the state)?
4. *Collateral*. Does the applicant have tangible assets (property) that can be pledged to guarantee payment?
5. *Conditions*. Could economic conditions affect the applicant's ability to pay? For example, is he or she likely to be laid off from work because of the economy?

A number of years ago, lenders tended to evaluate the five C's for credit applicants rather subjectively. Today, however, many retail companies evaluate credit applications with a point system based on a *behavioral scoring model* of borrowers most likely to pay their debts. With such a system, the lender assigns points for factors such as the number of years the customer has worked in the same job, owned a home or rented the same apartment, had a checking account, had a good credit rating, etc.

Some companies have credit-evaluation systems that are totally computerized. With such a system, an employee simply places the applicant's credit application form face down on the screen of an optical scanner that "reads" the information into a computer. The computer automatically locates the applicant's credit bureau report and assigns point values to the variables to be scored. Then the computer actually makes the decision, sets a credit limit if the decision is positive, and automatically sends either a credit card or an *adverse action letter* that turns down the application for credit.

## Consumer Credit Bureaus

Most lenders are members of a credit bureau. **Credit bureaus** are membership organizations that keep a computerized file of credit information about people who live in the area. Credit bureaus do not assign credit ratings to people; they simply collect and report information about people's loans and charge accounts, including how quickly people pay their bills. Credit bureaus also report information about legal actions such as wage assignments, tax liens, bankruptcies, judgments awarded to creditors, foreclosures, divorces, and criminal cases. Credit bureaus get their information from the companies that are members of their associations, from public records, and from other credit bureaus. Large retail firms routinely send computer tapes of their credit records once or twice a month to the credit bureau for merging with its computer files.

Many companies have special computer terminals for receiving access to credit bureau files. To obtain a credit report, an employee simply enters a credit applicant's social security number or name and address on the special terminal, and the credit report instantly appears on the screen. A copy can be printed if needed.

A computerized credit report generally covers the following areas for each person's credit account:

1. The customer's account number
2. The date a particular account was opened
3. The date of the most recent transaction on the account
4. The maximum amount the customer ever owed on that account, or the credit limit for that account
5. How much the customer currently owes
6. The amount past due
7. The type of loan
8. The terms of installment loans
9. How promptly the customer pays

For the last item, codes on a scale of 1 to 9 are frequently used in conjunction with a letter code indicating the type of account. For example, an

*R-1* code might indicate that a customer with a revolving charge account pays within 30 days; an *R-5* revolving account might be 120 days past due; and an *R-9* account might have been charged off as uncollectible.

If you want to see your credit record, just ask your bank or a store which credit bureau it uses; simply call the bureau and request a credit report. A printout of your credit record usually will cost about $5. However, the credit bureau is required by law to give it to you without charge if you have been turned down for credit because of information contained in its report.

## Consumer Credit Protection Act

The most important federal law regulating consumer credit is the Consumer Credit Protection Act. The original law, which became effective in 1969, has been amended several times. Highlights of the law and how its titles and amendments affect credit communication are summarized as follows:

1. Title I, known as the *Truth in Lending Act* (1969), specifies that all lenders must disclose the total amount of finance charges and the annual percentage rate to credit customers.
2. Title V, the *Credit Card Issuance Act* (1970), specifies that credit cards may not be issued without the customer's request or application. This law also limits a cardholder's liability to $50 when the card is stolen or otherwise used without permission.
3. Title VI, the *Fair Credit Reporting Act* (1971), requires businesses to inform credit applicants if they are denied credit, insurance, or employment because of information received from a credit bureau. The law also stipulates that if a business denies an applicant credit for reasons other than a credit report, the firm must reveal that information at the customer's request. In addition, the law outlines the procedures for disputing the information in credit reports.
4. The *Fair Credit Billing Act* (1975) is an amendment to the Truth in Lending Act. This law specifies the procedures for correcting billing errors in credit accounts, as follows:
   a. If a customer notifies a company of an error within 60 days of mailing the bill, he or she does not have to pay the bill or any finance charges while waiting for the matter to be resolved.
   b. The firm must acknowledge the customer's letter within 30 days and within 90 days must either correct the error or tell the customer why the bill is correct.
   c. In cases of billing disputes the company may not threaten to harm the customer's credit rating or give out negative information to credit bureaus or other creditors.
   d. The customer does not have to pay finance charges on the disputed amount if the creditor made an error in the bill.
5. Title VII, the *Equal Credit Opportunity Act* (effective in 1975 and amended in 1977), includes the following regulations:

     a. This law prohibits discrimination against a credit applicant on the basis of sex, marital status, race, color, religion, national origin, age, and receipt of income from public assistance programs.

     b. Creditors may not ask about applicants' birth-control practices or childbearing intentions.

     c. Creditors must notify applicants of the actions taken on their applications and provide reasons for denying credit either automatically or on request.

     d. Creditors may ask about age but may not use age as a negative factor for elderly applicants.

     e. Businesses must notify credit applicants of the decision taken on their application within 30 days.

     f. The following information must be given to credit applicants in writing (generally on the application form): "The Federal Equal Credit Opportunity Act prohibits creditors from discriminating against credit applicants on the basis of race, color, religion, national origin, sex, marital status, age (provided that the applicant has the capacity to enter into a binding contract); because all or part of the applicant's income derives from a public assistance program; or because the applicant has in good faith exercised any right under the Consumer Credit Protection Act. The federal agency that administers compliance with this law concerning this creditor is (name and address of the Federal Trade Commission)."

6. Title VIII, the *Fair Debt Collection Practices Act* (1978), regulates the procedures of debt-collection agencies. Examples of prohibitions under the law are listed on page 367.

## Credit Approvals

Credit messages consist primarily of application approvals and denials. **Credit approvals** fit into the category of favorable messages. Instead of sending a credit approval letter, however, some retail companies simply send the customer a credit card inserted in a form that explains the credit terms. Seasonal advertising inserts and other sales promotional materials frequently are enclosed with the credit card.

Many companies, particularly those granting commercial credit, do send letters to their new credit customers. Letters typically follow the basic direct plan for a favorable message (see Chapter 5) — the good news first, followed by the details. The details generally include sales promotional material, credit terms (required by law), expression of appreciation, and resale.

A typical credit-approval letter follows:

Mrs. Georgia Goode
309 Palm Lane
Novato, CA 94948-3619

Dear Mrs. Goode:

   The Mastercraft drapery materials you ordered          Favorable news
are being shipped to your store by Red Lion Freight
Systems.

   Thank you for choosing our line of the finest          Expression of
drapery fabrics in the West to stock in your new          appreciation
decorating center. We welcome your firm as a new
credit customer. The enclosed invoice itemizes your       Explanation of terms
purchases and explains our credit terms.

   We are also sending you a packet of advertising         Sales promotion
materials for you to use in promoting our fabrics.
You will notice that the new Mastercraft line has          Resale
many advantages for a sunny climate and casual
life-style. No lining is needed, and Mastercraft
fabrics are guaranteed for five years against the
fading effects of the sun.

   To place additional orders, simply send us a            Action ending
purchase requisition form or call us at
1-800-555-3164.

Cordially,

## Credit Denials

The 1977 Equal Credit Opportunity Act Amendment requires that when a firm denies credit to an applicant, he or she must be notified of the decision in writing within 30 days. The law also specifies that applicants either must be given the reason for the denial or told that they are entitled to an explanation if they request it.

Credit denial messages, which are frequently referred to as *adverse action* messages, are usually either standardized forms or form letters. The adverse action form on page 364 is typical.

Companies that send adverse action notices in letter format usually include very similar information, in order to comply with the Fair Credit Reporting Act and the Equal Credit Opportunity Act. The federally approved

Mayfield Department Store
552 North Ironwood Avenue
Albuquerque, NM  87107-7478

STATEMENT OF CREDIT DENIAL, TERMINATION, OR CHANGE

Date:  10/10/88

Applicant's name:  Melvin J. Underwood

Applicant's address:  235 Oakhurst Street, Albuquerque, NM  87123-7355

Description of account, transaction, or
    requested credit:  Application for credit card

Description of adverse action taken: Credit denial

PRINCIPAL REASON(S) FOR ADVERSE ACTION CONCERNING CREDIT

1 _____ Credit application incomplete
2 _____ Insufficient credit references
3 _____ Unable to verify credit references
4 _____ Temporary or irregular employment
5 _____ Unable to verify employment
6 _____ Length of employment
7 ___X___ Insufficient income
8 ___X___ Excessive obligations
9 _____ Unable to verify income
10 _____ Inadequate collateral
11 _____ Too short a period of residence
12 _____ Temporary residence
13 _____ Unable to verify residence
14 _____ No credit file
15 _____ Insufficient credit file
16 _____ Delinquent credit obligations
17 _____ Garnishment, attachment, foreclosure, repossession, or suit
18 _____ Bankruptcy
19 _____ We do not grant credit to any applicant on the terms and conditions you request
20 _____ Other, specify: ─────────────────────────────────────────────

Under the law, you have the right to know that our decision was at least in part based on
information, or the lack of information, in a  credit report from:

Associated Credit of New Mexico
300 North Fifth Street
Albuquerque, NM  87165-8096

reasons for credit denial are also generally stated in adverse-action form letters. Such letters usually have an opening that precedes the list of reasons, as follows:

---

```
Dear Customer:
    Thank you for your application for a credit ac-
count at Mayfield's Department Store.
    All credit applications are carefully evaluated.
However, we will not be able to approve the transac-
tion now. The reason(s) are listed below.
```

---

You will notice that this letter differs from the usual indirect plan of organization for unfavorable messages (discussed in Chapter 6) since the decision is given *before* the reasons are listed. In the case of an adverse-action letter, however, the lengthy list of reasons would seem awkward if given before the decision to deny credit.

## COLLECTION MANAGEMENT

Collection is the last stage of the credit process. When customers borrow money or purchase merchandise on credit, they have an obligation to pay on time. Prompt collections are important to any business that extends credit to its customers. Slow collections drain away working capital and can create cash-flow problems for a company. Although a strict credit policy can help prevent collection problems, all companies that extend credit to customers can expect to have some problem accounts.

### Collection Departments

The primary goal of a collection department is to keep accounts up to date, while at the same time promoting goodwill with customers. A collection department usually is supervised by a collection manager or a collection supervisor.

The employees who deal directly with the overdue accounts are called *collectors* or *collection correspondents*. The job of the collector is to communicate with customers whose accounts are past due and persuade them to pay the money they owe. Collectors communicate with late-paying customers mainly by telephone calls and computer-generated letters.

Collection department personnel should have good interpersonal communication skills similar to those of sales personnel. Collectors need to be helpful but persuasive; tactful and polite but firm. They must also be resourceful and assertive, as well as good judges of human nature. Sometimes collectors must also be detectives. If a debtor has disappeared with no forwarding address, the collector will need to do some detective work to locate the missing person, called a *skip*. The job of collector also requires a knowledge of the credit laws, adherence to company policy, and skill in operating a computer terminal.

## Retail Accounts Receivable

Most retail customers pay their bills on time. Some customers fail to do so because they are out of town, they are absent-minded, or because for one reason or another they never received a bill. Occasionally these individuals will need to be reminded about their bills. They will usually pay a bill after receiving a reminder message.

Other retail accounts may go to a collection department for a variety of reasons that may affect how a collector handles the account. Some of the common reasons are listed below:

1. The customer has a temporary financial problem, such as being ill, going on strike, or being laid off from work.
2. The customer has a problem with the merchandise he or she purchased. In this situation, the account should be referred to the customer-service department for immediate action.
3. The customer has not received a bill because he or she has moved. In this case, a tracer form should be sent to the post office. Also, the customer can be called at home or at work. As a last resort, a collector can call the references listed on the credit application. (But the law prevents a collector from telling anyone, even a relative, that the customer's bill is past due.)
4. The customer has not learned how to handle money. The family may be buying too many things they cannot afford.
5. The customer is having marital problems. In some divorce cases, the husband and wife may be hostile to each other and refuse to pay their joint accounts.
6. The customer is deceased. In this situation, the bill should be submitted to the executor of the estate, usually a relative or a bank.

## Commercial Accounts Receivable

Business firms such as manufacturers, wholesalers, and retailers use commercial credit when they purchase merchandise and raw materials from one another. When the economy is in a period of recession, business slows down for these firms; and when business is poor, companies tend to slow down their payments to creditors. This practice creates accounts receivable problems, which can be very serious for a company. In fact, accounts receivable difficulties are ranked as one of the major causes of business failures.

The commercial credit manager must secure the safety of the company's assets with effective collection policies and procedures. Commercial accounts receivable differ from retail accounts receivable in both size and number. Although commercial credit managers usually deal with fewer accounts receivable than do retail credit managers, the commercial accounts are generally much larger than retail accounts. Therefore, the collection procedures for commercial accounts tend to be more individualized than for retail accounts.

## Fair Debt Collection Practices Act

Collection procedures are regulated by the 1970 Federal Fair Debt Collection Practices Act. This law applies specifically to collection agencies rather than to in-house (intracompany) collection departments. However, the Federal Trade Commission requires all in-house collection departments to comply with its rulings.

The Fair Debt Collection Practices Act protects the public from unethical collection procedures. Examples follow:

1. Debtors may not be subjected to harassment, oppressive tactics, or abusive treatment. The law prohibits the collector from making any false statements to a debtor, such as claiming to be an attorney or a government agency.
2. Debtors may not be called at work if the employer or the debtor objects and requests no calls.
3. Debtors may not be called at inconvenient places or times, such as before 8 a.m. or after 9 p.m.
4. No one except the debtors themselves may be told that they are behind on their bills.

The act specifies penalties for violating the law. Debt collectors can be fined up to $1,000, plus actual damages, for violating provisions of the law. **Class-action suits** (those filed on behalf of groups rather than individuals) can be brought against violators, and the penalty is the lesser of $500,000, or 1 percent of the net worth of the collector.

## Computerized Collection Procedures

The collection process today is handled primarily by computerized procedures. Most large companies use an online collection system (OCS). A variety of form letters tailored for many possible situations is stored in the computer.

As a typical example, in a particular department store chain we'll call XYZ Company, the collection department uses more than 50 different form letters.

When a customer's account becomes 60 days past due, the computer automatically refers it to the collection department where the account is assigned to a collector. At XYZ Company, each collector handles between 70-120 accounts per day.

The collectors use a desk-top computer terminal to communicate a variety of information about each account. The information on the computer terminal screen appears in codes. The collection codes in the following list are typical of those used throughout the industry.

## COLLECTION CODES
### (A through C)

| | | | |
|---|---|---|---|
| Acknowledge | ACK | Call back | CB |
| Amount | AMT | Check | CK |
| Application | APP | Checked | CKD |
| Attorney | ATTY | Collector | COL |
| Balance | BAL | Credit | CR |
| Bankruptcy | BKCY | Credit bureau report | CBR |
| Broken promise | BKPRM | Customer phoned us | CP |
| Business phone | BP | Customer will call back | CWCB |

Collectors also use standardized *action and results* codes for data input.

## COLLECTION ACTION AND RESULTS CODES

| Action Codes | | Results Codes | |
|---|---|---|---|
| Telephoned customer | T O/C | Talked to Mr. | TT MR |
| Telephoned nearby | T N/B | Talked to Mrs. | TT MRS |
| Telephoned relative | T REL | Talked to child | TT KID |
| Telephoned reference | T REF | Talked to relative | TT REL |
| Phoned credit counselor | T CCC | Talked to roommate | TT RM |
| Telephoned Mr. | T MR | Talked to landlord | TT LL |
| Telephoned Mrs. | T MRS | Sent letter | SL |
| Phoned directory asst. | DA | Promise to pay | PTP |
| Telephoned attorney | T ATTY | Line busy | BZ |
| Telephoned home phone | T HP | Cancel promise to pay | CANPTP |
| Skip traced | S/T | Left message | LM |
| Telephoned court | T CT | No new information | NO INFO |
| Telephoned bank | T BK | Pending fraud | PND FRD |
| Telephoned prev. employer | T PR POE | Disputed charge | DISP |
| Talked to store | TT ST | Credit pending | CR PND |
| Received letter | REC LTR | Bankrupt account | BKR |

| | | | |
|---|---|---|---|
| Returned check | RT/CK | Unemployed | UNEMP |
| Reviewed account | REV ACCT | Credit counseling | CCC |
| Received payment | REC PMT | Payment in mail | PIM |
| Customer telephoned | O/C T | Paid at store | PD ST |
| Mr. telephoned | MR T | Received payment | REC PMT |
| Mrs. telephoned | MRS T | Request credit report | CBR |
| Attorney telephoned | ATTY T | Req. attorney letter | REQ LL |
| Reference telephoned | REF T | See notes | NOTES |
| Relative telephoned | REL T | No answer | NA |

Collectors record all actions on each account by using these codes online. The computer system is programmed to accept only these codes. For instance, if a collector entered "sent letter" instead of "SL," the computer would show an error message on the screen.

The computer keeps a record of all actions taken by the collection department for each customer's account. The collector determines which actions to take, such as when and how often to call. The collector also makes the decisions about which letters to send the debtor and at what intervals to send the letters. The action and results codes the collector enters into the computer terminal are used to keep a record of all account activities, such as the code number for each letter sent and the date on which it was sent.

In the example on page 370, the information printed in capital letters shows a typical account as it would appear on a computer terminal in a collection department. You can follow the sequence of events by reading the translation, which is printed in parentheses to the right of the code.

The computer record of actions and results codes will show a progression of events. The collector uses this information to make a decision about which action to take next. The computer record also increases efficiency by preventing duplication of effort, such as sending the same message twice. In addition, the record will show all phone calls made to the debtor, including even unanswered telephone calls and busy signals.

A pattern of unanswered daytime phone calls probably would result in assigning the account to a collector who works in the evening. At XYZ Company, the collection department personnel often work until 9 p.m. in order to reach customers who work during the day. No calls are made after that time, however, since the Fair Debt Collection Practices Act prohibits calling debtors between 9 p.m. and 8 a.m.

Although some letters are sent at the discretion of the collector, other letters are initiated automatically by the computer. At many companies, a computer automatically generates reminder notices and the first collection letters when an account becomes past due. A retail company or a bank might use a series of computer-generated reminder notices automatically sent at specified intervals—for example, 30 days, 45 days, and 60 days past due— before assigning an account to a collector. At XYZ Company, the different

```
ACCOUNT  #09-76929-450-1
NAME:  D. LYNN QUINT
ADR:  701 VERA CRUZ BLVD                      (address)
CSZ:  LAS VEGAS   NV   89110                  (city, state, zip)


DATE                  EMP # (employee       TEXT            (action and results)
                            number)

9/22                  0532                   SCL R002        (sent customer letter
                                                             No. R-2)

9/27                  0532                   T HP NA         (telephoned Mrs. Quint;
                                                             she did not answer)

9/28                  0532                   T HP BZ         (telephoned Mrs. Quint;
                                                             line was busy)

9/28                  0532                   T HP PTP 25     (telephoned Mrs. Quint;
                                                             she promised to pay $25)

9/31                  0472                   REC PMT 25      (received $25 payment)
```

computer letters include collection letters for many possible situations. Specialized collection letters include a number of *skip-trace* letters for customers who have left no forwarding address. The computer bank also includes a series of *promise-to-pay* letters.

If a collector enters the result code *PTP* into the terminal, the code automatically generates a series of *promise-to-pay letters* to the individual who promised to pay a certain amount on the overdue account. For instance, if Mrs. Quint promised to pay $25 *per month* on her overdue account, the collector would enter *PTP 25 M* into the computer terminal. That code would activate the promise-to-pay function, which would automatically trigger a series of *promise-to-pay* letters. The computer would issue these letters to Mrs. Quint at specified intervals (weekly, biweekly, or monthly) until the account was paid. The various letters would remind her of her promise to pay $25 per month and thank her for making the last payment or inform her that she did not keep her promise to pay. The following letter is an example of a typical *promise-to-pay* letter. Notice that firmness is a more significant characteristic than "you attitude" in this letter.

---

September 30, 19—

Mrs. D. Lynn Quint
701 Vera Cruz Blvd
Las Vegas, NV 89110—6983

Dear Mrs. Quint:

   The extension of time granted on your account is about to expire. Therefore, we must remind you that on September 28 you promised to pay $25.00 per month on this account.

   You may pay this amount at our store or send it to us by mail in the enclosed envelope.

                    Account No. 09—76929—450—1
                    Balance $456.35
                    Now Due $25.00

Sincerely,

I. M. Fair
Collection Department

---

For the Denver branch of the XYZ Company, all collection letters are sent out from a large computer center located in California. To send a particular letter, the collector in Denver enters a four-digit code for that letter into her or his computer terminal. A computer in California receives the message by electronic mail. Then a computer printer automatically prints the letter and personalizes it by printing the customer's name and address as the letter address and the customer's name in the salutation. The computer printer also automatically fills in the account number, amount owed, and the date the payment was due. Next a machine stuffs the letter into a window envelope, seals the envelope, and meters the postage. Then the letter is mailed to the customer.

## Collection Stages

After a customer purchases merchandise on credit, the company mails out a statement itemizing the transactions, the amount owed, and the date the payment is due. Most companies have several billing cycles per month and mail out statements nearly every day. If payment is not received on time, the collection process begins. The collection process follows a series of stages that progress from impersonal, low-key messages to those with a more personal and forceful tone. This progression is designed to collect most of the accounts by using courteous, low-cost methods which maintain goodwill. The more strident messages are restricted to debtors who have failed to respond to the initial low-key messages.

The four stages are as follows:

1. Reminder
2. Inquiry and discussion
3. Urgency
4. Ultimatum

**First Collection Stage: Reminder**. Most customers who haven't paid their bill on time will do so after one or two reminders. When an account becomes overdue, a computer will automatically generate a reminder notice. The first reminder notice often is printed on the next regular monthly statement, and subsequent reminders may be mailed separately or included with another bill.

Reminder notices are intended to prompt good customers who have simply forgotten to pay their bills on time. A reminder should be one of two or three impersonal form messages. To avoid antagonizing a customer, you should *not* send a collection letter, or any type of personalized letter, at this stage. The reminder, which is usually a computer-generated form message, should be a short, routine-type message with an impersonal tone. Although humor is sometimes used for overdue commercial accounts, humor is not recommended for retail accounts because it may antagonize customers.

At XYZ Company, when a customer's account is 30 days past due, the customer automatically receives another monthly bill with a reminder message generated by the computer.

## FIGURE 14.1 REMINDER MESSAGE

```
               XYZ, INC.

     Previous  Balance            $253.45
     Purchases                      77.88
     Interest  Charge                3.75
     Total  Balance               $335.08
     Minimum  Payment  Due         $75.00


  A  REMINDER  THAT  YOUR  ACCOUNT  IS  30  DAYS  PAST  DUE
```

If the bill is still not paid 15 days later, XYZ sends the customer a second reminder—in a separate envelope. This second notice, which is also generated automatically by the computer, includes a name and a phone number that the customer can call in case of a billing error or an adjustment problem.

## FIGURE 14.2 SECOND REMINDER MESSAGE

```
                        XYZ, INC.
May we remind you of your account balance of $335.08. Your $75
payment is 45 days past due. Please send your remittance today.

If you have already mailed payment, please disregard this notice.

M. A. Goodman
Accounts Receivable Department
Phone 234-3146
```

**Second Collection Stage: Inquiry and Discussion**. When the customer has still not paid the bill after receiving two or three reminder notices and the account has reached a certain *age* (number of days past due — generally around 60 days late), the account goes to the collection department. At this point, the inquiry and discussion stage of the collection process begins.

The purpose of the inquiry and discussion stage is to determine the customer's problem and attempt to persuade her or him to arrange to pay the account. The tone of the message should indicate sympathetic consideration for the customer and a genuine concern for whatever the problem may be. If the customer can't afford to pay the entire amount, then try to extend the payment terms or transfer the customer to a different type of account with smaller payments that the customer can afford. Even when people have financial problems, they can usually make small payments on their accounts. Many companies require at least one full payment in a six-month period to keep the account from being classified as defaulted.

Some companies begin the inquiry and discussion stage with a personalized form letter. Other companies begin with a telephone call or a combination of form letters and telephone calls.

One large retail firm we'll call Robertsons uses an automated telecommunication system. Each past-due customer receives a recorded message when her or his account reaches 60 days past due. A clerical employee without collection experience dials the customer's number, asks to speak to Mr. Frank Lee Late, and then says, "Mr. Late, I have a telecommunication message for you." Then he or she pushes a button, and the customer receives the following recorded message:

Hello, this is Robertsons Collection Department calling about your past-due account. You will have a chance to respond in a moment, and your response will be recorded. Your account is 60 days delinquent. If you have recently made a payment to us, at the sound of the tone tell us the amount and when your payment was made. On the other hand, if you are experiencing a payment problem, please call us at 543-2300. This number, again, is 543-2300. If you do not respond to the tone or we do not receive the call from you that we have requested, we will expect within five days a payment equal to the amount due on your last statement. We will appreciate your cooperation. Please respond at the sound of the tone.

Mr. Late's answer is recorded, and later another clerical employee listens to it and records online the appropriate action and results codes for Mr. Late's response.

Some companies begin the inquiry and discussion stage with a personal phone call to a customer rather than using a recording. Other companies begin this stage with personalized form letters. Inquiry and discussion letters are usually persuasive-type letters, similar to the following one:

---

Dear Mr. Late:

Last month we reminded you of the now—due amount     Establishes contact
of your Robertsons credit account.

Since your account is now 60 days past due, we     Suggests reasons
are wondering if you are experiencing a problem, or
if perhaps we have made an error. Therefore, this
letter is being sent to find out the reason.

If you will tell us about the problem, we will     Appeals to fairness
make every effort to work with you for a fair and
satisfactory solution to whatever the problem may be.

Please send your check immediately or call us     Requests action
at 444—1212 to discuss the situation with us.

Sincerely,

---

If Mr. Late does not respond to this letter and the collector has not been able to reach him by telephone, the next step may be to prevent him from making further purchases to the account in question. Robertsons uses this stronger inquiry letter five days after sending the first inquiry letter.

---

Dear Mr. Late:

Some time ago, we reminded you of the now—due     Establishes contact
amount of your Robertsons credit account. This
account is now more than 60 days past due.

So that you may continue to use your charge     Mentions
privilege, please send us your check by return mail.     consequences

If you are experiencing a payment problem, we          Offers alternative
will try to work out some type of arrangement for      solution
bringing the account up to date.

The amount now due on your account is shown            Requests action
below. Please pay this amount at once or call us at
444-1212.

Sincerely,

---

**Third Collection Stage: Urgency.** Sometimes the debtor will fail to respond to one or two inquiry letters and the collector cannot reach her or him by telephone. At this point, collection letters should become more persuasive and urgent. Many companies also may close a customer's account so he or she cannot make additional purchases. Robertsons sends the following letter before closing an account.

---

Dear Mr. Late:

As you know, your account at Robertsons is past      Establishes contact
due.

Further purchases cannot be authorized until        States the facts
your account is up to date. Although we have no
desire to withdraw your charge privilege, unless you
contact us immediately with a satisfactory
arrangement to pay your account, your credit card    States the
will be canceled.                                     consequences

Please pay the amount listed below at once or call   Requests action
444-1212 for definite arrangements.

Sincerely,

---

At this stage, the telephone calls also become more frequent and urgent in tone. A telephone call should attempt to impress the customer with the seriousness of the situation. Some companies assign accounts at this stage to their more experienced collectors. The collector should probe for information about the customer's personal finances and press for a solution to the payment problem. A typical collection call would include the following points:

1. Identify self and           "This is I. M. Fair of Robertsons."
   company.

2. Give the reason for         "Mr. Late, I am calling about your past-
   the call.                   due account."

| | |
|---|---|
| 3. Wait five seconds. | (Strategic pause) |
| 4. Ask fact-finding questions. | a. "When can we expect this payment, Mr. Late?" |
| | b. "What can we do to help you bring your account up to date?" |
| | c. "What sources of income do you have at this time, Mr. Late?" |
| 5. Arrange payment plan. | If customer's suggestion is not reasonable, insist upon your minimum payment schedule. Establish definite payment date. |
| 6. Overcome objections. | a. Determine specifically what the customer is objecting to. |
| | b. Work out the parts he or she objects to. |
| 7. Reinforce payment plan. | Repeat the payment arrangements agreed to. State amount of payment and date customer will pay. |
| 8. Close. | Express your appreciation for the customer's business, her or his cooperation, and your desire to be of service. |

Keep in mind that you can never antagonize people and influence them favorably at the same time. Use a positive rather than a negative or critical approach. Give the customer the benefit of any doubt, and allow her or him to "save face" whenever possible. Be courteous, considerate, and helpful to the customer, but assume leadership in suggesting and finding a solution to the payment problem.

Never preach, moralize, judge, or argue. However, at the urgency stage the collector often must confront the customer with her or his failure to keep a promise to pay. In that case, the conversation might go as follows:

Mr. Late, you promised to pay last Tuesday, and you promised to pay two weeks ago. But you did not keep either arrangement. We want to work with you; but if you do not keep your arrangements, we won't be able to give you more time....

All telephone calls must be followed by a letter confirming the conversation. At the urgency stage, assertiveness is more important than a positive tone. One company uses the following confirmation letter. Notice the explicit language that calls attention to the customer's negative actions.

Dear Mr. Late:

    We are disappointed that you did not make a payment on your account. Surely you did not intentionally ignore our request, especially when we offered to help you if only you would meet us half way.

    Perhaps there would be a better and clearer understanding if we tell you frankly that no account is permitted to remain at a standstill. You must do something about this obligation now.

    What we are forced to do will depend upon your cooperation. To avoid further complications, we urge you to bring the payment to the credit department at our store nearest you or immediately send it by mail using the enclosed envelope.

Sincerely,

*Problem summary*

*Explicit language*

*Warning of consequences*

*Demand for action*

**Fourth Collection Stage: Ultimatum.** When a customer has failed to respond to all the messages sent so far, a company has no choice but to confront the debtor with an ultimatum. However, most companies are careful to avoid statements that could be interpreted as threats or as attempts to harass debtors. You should refrain from referring directly to lawsuits, attorneys, or collection agencies unless you intend to follow through. Instead, you may use statements such as *take further action* or *use other means to enforce collection*.

You should send only one ultimatum letter, which should specify a deadline date for the debtor to pay the account. Many companies send the ultimatum message by certified mail with a return receipt requested to prove that they mailed the letter and that the debtor received it.

Robertsons sends the following ultimatum message to debtors who have not cooperated in the previous stages of the collection process. Notice that this letter has a very serious tone and prepares the debtor for the unpleasant consequences of her or his failure to pay the account.

Dear Mr. Late:

    We must have your cooperation to settle the long past-due balance owed on your account. Please notify us immediately of your plans for bringing this matter to a conclusion.

*Firm demand*

```
    If we do not hear from you or receive payment in          Deadline
full within ten days from the date of this letter,
then we shall be forced to assume that you do not
intend to cooperate with us to bring about a
voluntary settlement. We shall then be obliged to use        Serious
other means of enforcing collection.                         consequences
Sincerely,
```

If payment is not received by that date, then the company should immediately turn the account over to an attorney or to a collection agency. Many retail companies use collection agencies or attorneys on a contract basis for collecting past-due accounts. Industrial and commercial firms commonly use either in-house or contract attorneys to pursue debtors through the legal system. If a customer goes bankrupt, the account usually must be written off as a loss.

## SUMMARY

Commercial and consumer credit is critically important to business firms as well as to the entire economy. Many business careers require a knowledge of credit practices and an awareness of the laws regulating credit and collections.

Most companies evaluate credit applications carefully to prevent problems with their accounts receivable. Companies evaluate factors known as the "five C's of credit" (character, capital, capacity, collateral, and conditions) when considering credit applications. Credit bureaus play an important part in providing information to lenders, and their computer records are an integral part of retail credit evaluation systems. Various provisions of the Federal Consumer Credit Protection Act have had a major effect on retailers' credit policies and procedures.

Credit approval letters generally should fit the direct plan of organization for favorable messages. Credit denials are commonly referred to as *adverse-action* letters or forms. According to provisions of the Equal Credit Opportunity Act Amendment, adverse-action notices must either include the reason for the denial or state that the receiver has the right to request an explanation.

Provisions of the Federal Fair Debt Collection Practices Act, which regulates collection agencies, also influence the procedures of in-house collection departments. Collection departments are generally staffed by collectors who use a combination of computer-generated collection letters and telephone calls.

Most companies use a series of fairly standard messages at regular intervals when attempting to collect overdue accounts. Form letters appropriate for nearly every conceivable situation are stored in the computer and can either be generated automatically according to the *age* of the account, or be initiated by a collector's entering a code into the computer terminal. Collection procedures generally involve four stages: reminder, inquiry and discussion, urgency, and ultimatum. Reminder notices generally follow the plan of organization for routine messages, while the other three stages fall within the category of persuasive messages and are each progressively stronger in tone. If these procedures fail, the last step is to turn over the account to an attorney or a collection agency.

## CHAPTER REVIEW

1. Identify the major federal law that regulates credit procedures. What act of that law regulates collection agencies?
2. How can a consumer get a copy of her or his own credit record? How much, if anything, does it cost?
3. List and describe the *five C's of credit*. How do modern retail firms evaluate the *five C's* for credit applicants?
4. Describe the role and functions of consumer credit bureaus.
5. What is a *behavioral scoring model* for evaluating credit applications? Name the factors such a system might take into consideration?
6. React to this statement: "Never tell a credit applicant the reason why he or she was turned down for credit." Explain your answer.
7. Why do people's credit accounts go to a collection department? List five common reasons.
8. List the four stages of collection. Recommend a plan of organization that would be most appropriate for written messages in each stage. Defend your recommendations.
9. Explain the importance of goodwill and positive tone in collection letters.
10. Translate the following information from a collector's computer terminal screen:

| | |
|---|---|
| 3/15 | SCL R14 |
| 3/17 | T HP TTKID LM |
| 3/18 | O/C T PTP $50 |
| 3/18 | SCL R22 |
| 3/20 | PD ST $50 |

## APPLICATIONS

1. Find the name and address of a local credit bureau. Write a letter to the credit bureau to inquire about the cost and procedures for obtaining a copy of your credit file.

2. Refer to question number 1. Write a letter ordering a copy of your credit file and send the letter to the credit bureau. If the credit bureau charges a fee, enclose a check for that amount. When the credit file arrives, check it for

errors. If you find any errors, write the credit bureau a letter asking that the errors be corrected.

3. Analyze the following adverse-action letter that was sent to a credit applicant. Identify its weaknesses and point out ways in which it may violate federal credit laws.

Dear Mrs. Johnson:

   Thank you for your interest in a credit account at our store.

   Unfortunately, we will not be able to issue you a Gobel's credit card at this time. This decision should not be considered a reflection on you, as we have established certain minimum requirements for credit accounts.

   Again, thank you for your interest in our store.

Cordially,

4. Analyze the following collection letter which was sent to a retail customer whose account was 60 days past due. Identify its weaknesses.

Dear Customer:

   Kindly communicate with us immediately about your delinquent account of $155.

   This matter is very serious and could have many detrimental consequences.

   If you do not advise us as to this matter or if we do not receive payment of this account in arrears, we shall be forced to consider using legal means at our disposal.

   Enclosed is an envelope for your convenience.

Very truly yours,

5. You are the new credit manager for Nielson's Department Store, 439 College Avenue, Appleton, WI 54911-3999. In the past, the former credit manager used credit letters that did not comply with federal law. The letters were poorly written and contained many trite expressions. You are in the process of designing a point-scoring system for the store's new minicomputer, and you decide to overhaul the credit letters. The letters will be generated and printed by the new computer system. Two letters are needed: a credit approval letter and an adverse-action letter. The letters should create goodwill for the store and promote its business, as well as comply with the law. Write the two letters.

6. You are manager of the Accounts Receivable Department at O'Keefe's Paint Company, 932 Orange Avenue, Los Angeles, CA 90099-8265. O'Keefe's does a

large volume of business with paint contractors, who are usually extended a 30-day line of credit for purchases of paint in large quantities. In the past, O'Keefe's hasn't done a very good job of screening credit applicants; you have had to write off a number of uncollectible accounts. To correct this problem, O'Keefe's has just joined a credit bureau; and you have begun to implement new procedures for objectively evaluating credit applicants. Now you need to develop a tactful form letter for denying credit to contractors who are poor risks. The letter should attempt to keep the customers' goodwill. Stress the advantages of paying cash, which entitles them to a 3 percent discount. Invite the applicant to reapply when the company's financial situation becomes more stable.

7. You are the office manager for Briarwood Office Furniture Co., 1309 Glenridge Drive, Savannah, GA 31410-1622. Last month Dr. Arthur Hanley, a prominent local physician, came into your store and ordered $8,500 worth of office furniture for his new medical clinic. The store manager (your boss) personally took the order and told Dr. Hanley that your store would deliver the furniture to his new clinic (421 North Anderson Blvd., Savannah, GA 31402-7981) and mail the bill to the same address. According to long-standing store policy, all credit customers at Briarwood's use either their MasterCard or Visa for smaller purchases; for larger purchases, they sign a contract that the store later sells to a finance company. Because of this policy, Briarwood's doesn't usually handle collections. Dr. Hanley, however, didn't sign a finance contract. When you didn't receive payment of your bill within 30 days, you then sent him a second bill with a reminder notice printed at the bottom; but he did not respond. The account has now become 60 days past due. Write Dr. Hanley a "reminder" letter.

8. Refer to number 7. Dr. Hanley's account has now become 90 days past due. You call his office several times and leave messages for him to call you, but he doesn't return your calls. Write Dr. Hanley an "inquiry and discussion" letter.

9. Refer to number 7. Dr. Hanley's account is now 120 days past due, and he has not responded to your letter. He has not returned your calls to his office, and his home phone is unlisted. Write Dr. Hanley an "urgency" letter.

10. Refer to number 7. Dr. Hanley's account is now five months (150 days) past due, and still you have received no response. You consult the store's attorney, who agrees to sue Dr. Hanley for the $8,500 if necessary. Write Dr. Hanley an "ultimatum" letter.

## CASE STUDY

"Please tell us in your own words, Miss Stockley, just what happened," Judge Ogden told the plaintiff, who had brought suit against Bilton's Department Store for unfair debt-collection practices.

Lydia Stockley began, "It all started when I bought a new washer and dryer during Bilton's year-end sale six months ago. With an outstanding balance of $600 already on my credit account—and an assigned credit limit of only $1,000—I wondered whether they would let me charge another $640. But, when I told the salesman that I could buy the washer and dryer only if I could charge them to my account, he said that would be no problem.

"My January statement said I must pay $300 on the account—a $50 monthly payment, plus $250 to reinstate my line of credit. But I couldn't afford a $300 payment to Bilton's because I take home only $800 a month. I decided that if they had extended me too much credit, it was their own fault. But I did pay the $50 monthly payment that they had a right to get.

"In February, March, and April, I paid $50 per month on the bill; but they kept harassing me about the amount over my assigned line of credit and wouldn't let me charge anything else at the store. Every month I got a letter telling me I would have to pay more on the bill.

"Then last month (May), someone from Bilton's called me three different times about the bill. She always called during dinner—and last time my date answered the phone. After I finished talking to the woman from Bilton's, he wanted to know what the call was about. Then I had to tell him, and I was so embarrassed.

"That's when I decided that I wasn't going to put up with such treatment any more. I stopped paying on my Bilton's bill and filed this suit in Justice Court against the store for unfair debt-collection practices."

In response to the Judge's questions, Lydia revealed the following facts:

- The telephone caller always identified herself as "Joan Miller from Bilton's Credit Department."
- All three telephone calls were made to Lydia's home between 6:30 p.m. and 8:00 p.m.
- The collection letters all "looked as though they had been written by a computer."
- The original credit approval that came with her credit card specified that her credit line was $1,000 and stated that any charges over this limit would be due on the first billing after the overdraft.

1. Does Lydia have a good case against Bilton's? Should Judge Ogden award damages to her and fine Bilton's for unfair collection practices? Why or why not?
2. If you were the credit manager at Bilton's, what changes, if any, would you make in the store's credit policies and collection procedures? Discuss the reasons why.

## REFERENCES

Robert H. Cole, *Consumer and Commercial Credit Management*, 7th ed. (Homewood, IL: Richard D. Irwin, Inc., 1984), 14, 24.

*The Predicasts Basebook*, November 1986, 85.

## SUGGESTED READINGS

Barzman, Sol, *Everyday Credit Checking: A Practical Guide*. rev. ed. New York: National Association of Credit Management Publications, 1980.

Barzman, Sol. *The Complete Guide for Credit and Collection Letters*. New York: National Association of Credit Management Publications, 1983.

Cole, Robert H. *Consumer and Commercial Credit Management*. 7th ed. Homewood, IL: Richard D. Irwin, Inc., 1984.

Kitzing, Donald R. *Credit and Collections for Small Business*. New York: McGraw-Hill, 1981.

# GOODWILL AND PERSONNEL MESSAGES

## CHAPTER 15

"How is everything going at work?" Charlie Bradley asked his friend Ken Martinsen as they drove into the parking lot of the bowling alley.

"Terrible," replied Ken. "I'm looking for a job with another company."

"Didn't you get your promotion?" asked Charlie.

"Yes, but that didn't solve the problem," Ken answered. "Wedgeworth is such a big, impersonal company that I feel like a nobody."

He continued, "Although I finally received my promotion to senior level, nobody even noticed. I've decided to look for a job at a company that pays more attention to its employees."

Goodwill and personnel messages are two special categories of business communications. Goodwill messages promote public relations with customers and potential customers, and personnel messages support industrial relations with company employees.

Goodwill messages include congratulatory, seasonal, and thank-you letters and memorandums; letters of sympathy; and invitations. Personnel messages include (in addition to messages to job applicants, which are discussed in Chapter 13) recommendation letters, job descriptions, policy and procedure statements, and employee appraisals.

## GOODWILL MESSAGES

*Goodwill* is a word that has several meanings. In the accounting profession, *goodwill* is jargon for an intangible asset representing the value of a company's reputation and clientele. In business communication, the word is used in a more general sense; it simply refers to positive human relations in a business environment.

Because goodwill is intangible, it is difficult to measure. However, maintaining good human relations with customers, clients, and employees is crucial to the success of every business firm.

Although goodwill should be one of the goals of every business message, some messages have goodwill as the primary goal. Goodwill messages are not directly concerned with selling a product or making a profit. The purpose of a **goodwill message** is to build positive human relations and promote a positive, friendly image of the company to its customers and employees.

An effective goodwill message should not directly promote a company's goods and services in any way. Some sales letters attempt to masquerade as goodwill messages; however, such messages are usually ineffective in developing goodwill.

Since goodwill messages affect business only indirectly, the actual value of a goodwill message is difficult to determine. If other factors (price, quality, service, etc.) are equal, however, people often prefer to do business with a firm with which they have a good relationship.

Internal goodwill messages promote positive human relations between management and employees. As discussed in Chapter 2, managers need to be just as concerned about human relations as they are about workers' tasks.

As early as the 1930's, the human relations movement in management theory began to focus on the importance of meeting individual workers' needs rather than merely organizational needs. Today managers recognize that subordinates will generally do a good job if they have high morale and are satisfied with their jobs. To motivate employees to do a good job, they should be made to feel appreciated and that they are part of a group. Appropriate goodwill messages from management can be an important part of this process.

## Congratulatory Messages

Significant accomplishments provide an opportunity to congratulate an individual about her or his achievements. **Congratulatory messages** may be sent to an individual for an important event such as winning an honor or award, completing a college degree, receiving a promotion, getting married, having a baby, celebrating an anniversary, being elected to an office, retiring from the company, and so on. People appreciate receiving prompt, sincere congratulatory messages, which are an excellent way of building goodwill.

Depending on the intended receiver and the desired degree of formality, a congratulatory message may be in the form of a handwritten note, a typewritten business letter, or a memorandum. Because the reader is expected to experience a favorable reaction, such messages should follow the direct (deductive) plan of organization, as discussed in Chapter 4.

The following letter congratulates an employee for an appointment to public office:

Congratulations for your appointment to the State Corporation Commission!

I have always admired your many accomplishments, as well as your personal integrity. The Governor certainly made a wise decision when he selected you for the position.

Best wishes for a successful year.

The following memorandum congratulates an employee for receiving an M.B.A. degree:

Congratulations for receiving your M.B.A.! I was delighted to hear about your latest achievement.

You have done an outstanding job here, as well as in graduate school. Your hard work deserves to be rewarded. Your M.B.A. will be an important factor in your next employee evaluation.

I'm looking forward to seeing you rise in our company. Best wishes for the future.

The following personal note extends congratulations to a colleague and her husband, who have become new parents:

Dear Helen and Mark:

Congratulations to both of you on this proud occasion.

I hear that little Mark is a beautiful baby. In a few days, I'll drop by to see him myself.

In the meantime, if you need a free babysitter, give me a call!

Printed *congratulations cards* are also an appropriate way to convey your interest in someone's success or good fortune. However, a card is more effective if you add a handwritten message.

## Seasonal Messages

Special occasions such as Christmas and other religious holidays, New Year's, Thanksgiving, and birthdays are appropriate times to send goodwill messages. **Seasonal messages** may be used to express greetings and good wishes to customers, clients, and employees. Some companies build goodwill by also sending seasonal gifts such as calendars or ashtrays to their customers. To encourage good industrial relations, many organizations give their employees seasonal gifts such as turkeys, hams, or theater tickets.

Most seasonal messages are printed cards or form messages. However, if time permits, the addition of an original signature or short handwritten note can increase the effectiveness of a form message.

A real estate broker sent the following message to some clients. Notice that sales promotion is tactfully excluded from the message.

In the bustle of our busy lives, we must stop for a moment to recall the real meaning of Thanksgiving.

One of the blessings that I am counting this year is the cordial relationship that we have shared. I consider you to be a good friend as well as a client.

Best wishes to you and your family for a happy Thanksgiving holiday!

A hospital sent the following memorandum to its employees:

    TO:    All Our Employees
    FROM:  Roy T. Stevens, Administrator
    DATE:  December 10, 19—
SUBJECT:   HAPPY HOLIDAYS

May you and your families have a joyous holiday season! On behalf of the Board of Directors, I wish you the very best for the coming New Year.

As a small token of our appreciation for your spirit, enthusiasm, and hard work, we are enclosing a certificate redeemable for a free turkey at any El Rancho Market.

Happy holidays!

## Thank-You Messages

Everyone likes to get positive feedback, especially if it is in writing. Although many people tend to be quick to criticize, few individuals take the time to express their appreciation. **Thank-you messages** are appropriate whenever someone does an especially good job or does you a favor.

The following letter thanks a former employer for helping the writer secure a job. The letter is especially effective because of its positive tone and obvious sincerity.

Thanks to you, I am now the Assistant Manager of Kelly Graphics Company!

Your helpful suggestions, along with the outstanding recommendation letter you wrote about me, were largely responsible for my being hired. I will always be grateful to you for your help and support.

Thank you from the bottom of my heart.

The following note was printed in a company's employee newsletter:

Thank you for your supportive cards, letters, and phone calls. Mary and I are grateful for the concern that all of you have expressed.

Mary is now out of the hospital and is recovering nicely. She is looking forward to next week, when the doctor says she will be able to take the cast off her arm and write to each of you individually.

Your thoughtfulness has meant so much to us––thanks to all of you!

The following form letter thanks contributors to a local charity:

Thank you for your generous contribution to the West Memphis Children's Fund.

Because of caring citizens like you, this year's campaign has been an outstanding success. Your gift means so much to the disadvantaged and handicapped children in our community.

On behalf of the Children's Fund, I extend my sincerest appreciation to you.

A personal thank-you note is, of course, more effective than a form letter. The following note expresses appreciation to an employee:

Dear Bob:

You did an outstanding job as chair of the Employee Social Committee this year.

Because of your hard work, the annual picnic was the best ever. The food was excellent, the games were fun, and we all had a wonderful time.

Thank you for a job well done.

One of the most effective goodwill strategies is to send a letter to an individual's supervisor, as follows:

One of your employees, Evelyn Martinez, is an outstanding account executive.

> She did a fine job of helping me select a portfolio
> of stocks and bonds. I am very impressed with her
> knowledge and helpful attitude. When a computer error
> caused a mistake in my account, she cheerfully stayed
> in the office until 9 p.m. to identify the cause of
> the problem and correct the error.
>
> Thank you for assigning my account to such a
> competent individual.

Appreciation letters from satisfied customers and clients are a positive addition to an employee's personnel file. As evidence of outstanding performance, such letters convey recognition for employees' contributions to an organization.

## Sympathy Letters

When a customer, colleague, or friend is seriously ill or experiences the death of a loved one, the situation calls for a sympathy message. **Sympathy messages** let people know that others are concerned about them.

Sympathy messages consist of two types: get-well letters and condolence letters. In either case, a handwritten note is more effective than a printed card or typewritten letter because it conveys a more personal impression.

The following get-well note was sent to an employee who was hospitalized because of an automobile accident:

> Dear Ralph:
>
> We were sorry to hear about your accident and hope
> you're feeling better.
>
> Although we miss you here at work, everything is
> under control. We're all pitching in to take care of
> everything and are glad to fill in for you. Don't
> worry about a thing.
>
> Best wishes to you, and get well soon.
> Sincerely,

Condolence letters express sympathy to someone who has lost a close relative. The message should be prompt, simple, and sincere. Avoid using blunt, explicit language, including negative words such as "shocked," "tragedy," and "death." On the other extreme, avoid using flowery euphemisms such as "passed on to his reward" or "departure from this life."

The following outline is recommended for condolence letters:

1. Offer your sympathy to the reader.
2. Briefly make a positive comment about the deceased.
3. Close with a warm, comforting expression of your feelings.

The following letter is both considerate and in good taste:

I extend my sympathy to you and your family.

Jim was one of our favorite customers as well as a valued friend for the past fifteen years. He was also an outstanding leader in our community.

We will all miss him very much.

## Invitations

**Invitations** to business or social functions vary widely in the degree of formality. Formal functions require formal invitations, while invitations to informal functions generally have an informal format and writing style. Both kinds of invitations should be brief and follow a direct plan of organization.

**Informal Invitations.** Informal invitations to business-related functions may be either typewritten in usual business-letter format, or they may be printed if the function is a large one. The following informal invitation to a business-related function is typewritten in business-letter format:

Dear Hector:

You are invited to a luncheon honoring the members of the Mayor's Task Force on Employment of the Handicapped.

The luncheon will be held at the Blue Room of the Jefferson Hotel on Wednesday, October 10, at noon. Our speaker will be Dr. Dwayne Harrison of the Rehabilitation Department at the University of Toledo. The topic of his presentation will be "Breaking Down the Barriers."

Please call me at 555-2934 before October 1 to let me know if you will attend.

I'm looking forward to seeing you at the luncheon.

Cordially,

Informal invitations to functions that are primarily social rather than business related are usually handwritten on personal stationery or note paper. A bank branch manager's wife sent a handwritten informal social invitation to her husband's employees and their spouses, as shown in Figure 15.1.

Notice that the writer places her return address at the end rather than at the beginning of the letter in Figure 15.1. This letter style is appropriate for handwritten personal notes.

FIGURE 15.1 SAMPLE HANDWRITTEN INFORMAL INVITATION

December 2, 19 _ _

Dear Frank and Louise:

You are invited to a holiday eggnog party at our house on Friday evening, December 22, at 8.

To get in the holiday spirit, we will play games and draw names for joke gifts. Please bring one inexpensive humorous gift (maximum cost $5) to the party.

Please call me at 555-1928 to let me know if you can come.

I'm looking forward to seeing you. Happy holidays!

Cordially,

Mary Albrecht

334 Birchwood Drive
Kansas City, MO  64141-1195

**Formal Invitations**. Formal invitations are printed on small cards or note paper, as shown in Figure 15.2. A formal invitation contains no heading, inside address, salutation, complimentary close, or signature. Each line is centered. Formal invitations are traditionally written in third person; therefore, the writer should avoid using personal pronouns such as *I*, *we*, and *you*.

FIGURE 15.2 PRINTED FORMAL INVITATION

The Executive Committee

of the Arizona Commission on the Arts

Requests the company of

Mrs. Elisabeth Oliver

at dinner on Saturday, February third, at eight o'clock

at the Grand Ballroom, North Side Country Club

1204 North Desert Lane

Scottsdale, Arizona

R.S.V.P. to
201 Central Avenue
Suite 234
Phoenix, AZ 85032-2212

Black Tie

**Replies to Invitations**. The reply to an invitation should have the same degree of formality as the invitation itself. Informal invitations may be answered with a phone call or an informal note. Formal invitations should be answered with a handwritten note patterned after the format and style of the invitation, as follows:

*Mrs. Elisabeth Oliver accepts with pleasure the invitation of the Executive Committee of the Arizona Commission on the Arts to a dinner on Saturday, February third, at eight o'clock.*

Notice that the reply contains none of the usual parts of a letter such as the heading, inside address, salutation, complimentary close, or signature. Each line should preferably be centered, and verbs should be in the present tense.

A note turning down a formal invitation should follow the same pattern:

> *Mrs. Elizabeth Oliver regrets that, due to a previous engagement, she is unable to accept the invitation of the Executive Committee of the Arizona Commission on the Arts to a dinner on Saturday, February third, at eight o'clock.*

## PERSONNEL MESSAGES

Personnel management encompasses many more activities than selecting and hiring job applicants. After a newly hired employee starts to work for a company, management must help that individual develop into a productive employee who is satisfied with her or his job. Communication activities related to hiring employees are discussed in Chapter 13. This section introduces other personnel messages such as recommendation letters, job descriptions, policy and procedure statements, and employee appraisals.

### Recommendation Letters

The objective of a **recommendation letter** is to provide information about a job applicant to a company that is considering hiring that individual. Recommendation letters are generally written in response to a specific request from the prospective employer. Few employers are willing to accept *To Whom It May Concern* letters in the possession of an applicant because of the possibility of forgery.

As a matter of courtesy, applicants should ask permission first, before listing someone as a reference. Present employers, former employers, and college professors may be listed as references. However, references from present or previous employers tend to carry the most weight because the employer is in a position to provide an unbiased evaluation of the applicant's skills, work habits, and character.

A person writing a recommendation letter has an obligation to be fair and honest. If a recommendation letter includes false statements about a job applicant, he or she can sue the letter writer for libel. **Libel** (written defamation) is the intentional or negligent communication of false information that injures someone's reputation or character.

Confidentiality is an important legal and ethical issue surrounding the use of recommendation letters. Some companies do not require recommendation letters for job applicants because their employees have the right to see their own personnel records. Thus, the company cannot ensure confidentiality of recommendation letters because they are part of the personnel record that an employee is entitled to see. In addition, some companies have policies against providing recommendations for their present or future employees due to the potential for libel suits.

The 1974 Family Education Rights and Privacy Act has also tended to diminish the use and importance of recommendation letters. This act allows a student over 18 and her or his parents to review files kept by public schools, including those of student placement offices in colleges and universities. However, a student may waive the right to see her or his placement file by signing a release form.

The various legal considerations may influence writers of recommendation letters to convey only positive information. However, a well-written recommendation letter provides important details about an applicant's education, work experience, skills, career potential, and personal traits that can help that individual get a job.

Depending on whether its contents are primarily favorable, neutral, or unfavorable, a recommendation letter may have either a direct or an indirect plan of organization. The direct plan is a very effective way to present an entirely favorable recommendation. If the recommendation contains a neutral or negative evaluation, the indirect plan is more appropriate.

**Favorable Recommendations**. When writing a favorable recommendation for a job applicant, you should include the following information:

1. Opening paragraph
   a. Your willingness to write the letter
   b. The applicant's name
   c. A complimentary statement about the applicant
2. Middle paragraph(s)
   a. The length and nature of the association (part-time sales representative, student last semester, etc.)
   b. Facts about the applicant's job responsibilities, job performance, and job-related personality traits
   c. Favorable answers to specific questions
   d. Additional information about outstanding achievements or other qualifications

3.  Ending paragraph
    a.  A summary statement about the applicant's qualifications
    b.  A positive statement indicating your support of the applicant for the position

A sample recommendation letter that supports an applicant is shown in the following example:

---

| | |
|---|---|
| In response to your request for information about Kathy Ross, I am pleased to recommend her as an outstanding employee. | Applicant's name<br>Writer's willingness<br>Complimentary statement |
| Ms. Ross has worked as a teller in our branch bank for the past four years. As her supervisor, I am happy to say that her job performance has been excellent. | Position<br>Length of employment<br>Relationship |
| Her accuracy in handling money and her ability to relate well with customers have made her an invaluable asset to our bank. Her promotion to head teller after only two years supports her capabilities as an outstanding employee. She is an intelligent and dependable worker. Her attendance record is also above average; in four years, she missed only three days due to illness. | Answers to inquiries<br><br>Supporting facts |
| Because of her outstanding work performance, her pleasing personality, and her dependability, I highly recommend Ms. Ross. We are sorry to see her leave but wish her our best. | Summary<br><br>Recommendation<br>Courteous ending |

---

**Neutral or Unfavorable Recommendation Letters**. If you are asked to write a recommendation letter for an individual that you cannot evaluate favorably, you can choose one of these strategies:

1.  Fail to respond to the request for a recommendation letter
2.  Reply with a refusal to write the recommendation
3.  Write a noncommittal letter
4.  Invite the person requesting the recommendation to call you to discuss the applicant
5.  Write a factual letter discussing both positive and negative qualities

The first two options, nonresponse and written refusal, are detrimental to goodwill. The other three options are much better for public relations. However, from a legal standpoint, the first three options are better than the last two. Be very cautious about communicating negative information about an applicant, either orally or in writing.

**Noncommittal letters** simply state the dates of employment (starting and ending) and functions carried out, without any discussion of performance and character. A noncommittal letter may also include an offer to discuss the applicant's qualifications over the telephone. However, to preclude the possibility of being sued for **slander** (oral defamation of character), make sure that your statements can be substantiated.

The following noncommittal letter provides limited information and invites the prospective employer to discuss an applicant's qualifications over the telephone:

| | |
|---|---|
| In response to your inquiry about Betty Robertson, I am glad to provide you with the following information: | Applicant's name<br>Writer's willingness |
| 1. Ms. Robertson was employed at R. B. Interiors, Inc. from April to December, 19––. | Dates of employment |
| 2. She worked as a furniture salesperson part-time while she attended college. | Position |
| If you have specific questions about her, you may call me at 555-6140. | Invitation for telephone call |
| Cordially, | |

If the applicant has good qualities and only minor weaknesses that may not adversely affect her or his performance on the job, you may write a factual letter discussing both strengths and weaknesses that are pertinent to the job. Negative points should be mentioned only if they are deterrents to job performance and can be substantiated by facts. Shortcomings can be subordinated by embedding them between positive qualifications. Whenever making negative statements, be truthful and discreet to safeguard against any possible legal action by the applicant.

The following recommendation letter discusses the qualifications of a former employee who was unsuccessful as a computer programmer. Notice that the letter emphasizes strengths but leaves weaknesses to implication:

In response to your inquiry, I am glad to
provide some information about Henry T. Fredericks,
who has applied for a position with your company as a
sales trainee.

Writer's cooperation
Applicant's name

I was Mr. Fredericks' supervisor when he worked
for Elton Manufacturing as a computer programmer from
May to November last year. At the time we hired him,
he had just received his degree in management information systems from State University.

Relationship
Length of
employment
Additional
information

Mr. Fredericks is a very intelligent, outgoing
individual with an engaging personality. Although he
began his job with us enthusiastically, he was unable
to adjust to a sedentary occupation such as computer
programming. I believe that he will be happier in a
job that offers more interaction with people.

Positive qualities

Subordinated
negatives

Optimistic projection

As a computer sales trainee, Mr. Fredericks'
technical background will be an advantage. With his
outgoing personality, he could be a successful
salesperson.

Positive ending

When writing a recommendation letter, be generous in helping the applicant obtain an appropriate position. At the same time, be fair to prospective
employers so that they will be able to hire someone qualified for the job.

## Job Descriptions

A **job description** is a written summary of the responsibilities, working conditions, and requirements of a specific job. Job descriptions help employees to
understand their own and other people's roles and responsibilities in an organization. Specific, accurate job descriptions are necessary for various personnel activities such as recruiting and orienting new employees, conducting
training programs, and supervising employees.

Personnel specialists obtain necessary information through a process
called *job analysis*, in which data about jobs are collected primarily from interviews and written surveys. The information about a particular job is analyzed and presented in the form of a job description, as shown in the following
example:

### RADKUR, INC.
Job Description

Job Title:        Occupational Safety Inspector

Department:       Safety Engineering

Job Code:         168.167-062

Job Grade:        038

Supervisor:       Director of Safety Engineering

Overtime Status:  Exempt

Date:             July 1, 1987

Job Summary:

Inspects the workplace for health and safety hazards.    Investigates
industrial accidents and writes safety reports.

Job Duties:

Conducts surveys, investigations, and monitoring programs for
    discovering conditions that contribute to hazards in the working
    environment.
Inspects for mechanical, electrical, and chemical hazards such as
    unguarded machinery, improperly insulated or grounded electrical
    equipment, and toxic gases or fumes.
Reviews facilities and inspects fire protection equipment, sanitation
    systems, and utilities.
Conducts accident and injury investigations and maintains follow-up
    records.
Writes safety, accident, and injury reports.
Works with personnel specialists, supervisors, and safety engineer to
    organize and conduct safety-training sessions.

Working Conditions:

Works mostly in office.    Inspections and investigations require work
in factory, warehouse, equipment yard, and motor pool.    Occasionally
may be exposed to hazardous conditions or toxic substances.    Works
primarily 8 a.m. to 5 p.m. shift.    In case of accidents or other
emergencies, may be called in at any time, including nights and
weekends.

Qualifications:

Bachelor's degree in Industrial or Occupational Safety.
Five years' related work experience.
Average physical health is required.
Some climbing, stooping, and moderate lifting is necessary.
Color blindness is not acceptable because of color-coded wiring and
    piping systems.
Writing skills should be above average.
Must be a good teamworker and be able to communicate effectively with
    supervisors, union representatives, and employees.

The job identification section generally includes the following information:

1. *Job Title* — Indicates name of the described position. The name might not be unique to a particular job. For example, an Administrative Assistant I in the marketing department may have different duties than those specified for an Administrative Assistant I position in the accounting department.
2. *Department* — Specifies name of the department to which the position is assigned.
3. *Job Code* — Classifies jobs by numeric code, which is often from the *Dictionary of Occupational Titles* published by the United States Department of Labor.
4. *Job Grade* — Identifies the pay level of the job.
5. *Supervisor* — Identifies the title of immediate supervisor.
6. *Overtime Status* — Specifies whether the job is exempt from federal overtime regulations. Most jobs fall under the provisions of the Fair Labor Standards Act of 1938, which requires overtime pay for employees who work more than 40 hours a week. However, executive, administrative, and professional-level jobs are exempt from overtime regulations.
7. *Date* — Indicates when the description was written. (Old job descriptions are likely to be outdated.)
8. *Job Summary* — Briefly summarizes the major job responsibilities.
9. *Job Duties* — Lists the tasks performed by the jobholder. The tasks should be listed in order of importance, from the most important to the least important. Note that statements are parallel in construction.
10. *Working Conditions* — Describes the physical environment of the job, including negative factors such as noise, heat, hazards, etc. Also outlines special demands such as heavy workload, travel, long working hours, etc.
11. *Qualifications* — Describes minimum qualifications for the job. Qualifications should include relevant requirements such as education, experience, special skills, licenses or certification, and physical requirements, if any.

When writing a job description, avoid vague wording such as "performs administrative work as required." A job description should contain specific, objective information about the position.

Every job should be reviewed periodically to ensure that the description is up to date. When revising a job description, the jobholder, as well as the supervisor, should be included in the analysis.

## Policy and Procedure Statements

Company **policies** are written or unwritten rules or guidelines that set standards for organizational behavior. Companies set policies to help accomplish organizational goals and provide structure for decision making. Clearly stated policies can simplify managers' jobs and lessen the potential for conflict in the organization.

**Procedures**, which may be written or unwritten, are more specific than the policies on which they are based. Companies develop procedures to standardize the way that policies are carried out. Procedures define patterns of behavior that employees are supposed to follow in accomplishing specific tasks.

Small businesses often have no written policies and procedures. Large companies, however, generally do have formal personnel policy and procedures manuals or handbooks that govern employee behavior. As new policies and procedures are developed, executives often transmit them in the form of a memorandum to employees. At a later date, the new policy is added to the personnel handbook.

Policies and procedures statements should be particularly clear and concise. If a new employee receives a six-inch thick policy and procedures handbook, he or she will most likely not read it. A concise manual written in simple language is preferable to a long one that is full of impressive words and bureaucratic jargon.

The following example of a policy and procedures statement is taken from an employee handbook:

---

### Vacation Policy

Vacation time accrues at the rate of one day per month. Employees may take vacation time after their first six months with the company.

### Procedures

1. Employees should submit requests for vacation time to their supervisors in writing at least four weeks in advance.
2. If too many employees ask to go on vacation at the same time, requests will be given priority on the basis of seniority.
3. Two weeks before the requested vacation date, the supervisor should notify the employee if a request has been approved.

---

Notice that the specific procedures are based on the more general policy, which is stated first. Procedures should be worded in very specific, objective language, with parallel construction.

## Employee Appraisals

**Employee appraisals**, often referred to as *performance evaluations* or *performance appraisals*, are the primary means by which an organization obtains feedback about employees' job performance. Companies use employee appraisals as input for important personnel decisions such as employee retention, job assignment, merit pay, promotion, and evaluation of training effectiveness. Employees also benefit from the appraisal process because they receive feedback that can help their morale and motivate them to improve their job performance.

The personnel or human-resource department generally designs the formal appraisal procedures and forms. However, managers and supervisors usually are responsible for filling out appraisal forms, writing open-format appraisals, and conducting appraisal interviews.

Supervisors should be fair and impartial in evaluating the relevant aspects of each employee's work. To ensure consistent application of the appraisal process, organizations commonly use *employee rating forms*. Such forms are used to measure individual work behaviors such as job knowledge, attendance, punctuality, quality of work, quantity of work, cooperation, dependability, and initiative.

Although an employee's immediate supervisor usually completes the appraisal form, many organizations allow employees (and sometimes a group of the employees' peers) to participate in the process. As part of the appraisal process, an employee may complete a *self-appraisal checklist*, which is a form containing a list of questions that relate to her or his job accomplishments and problem areas.

Companies use various techniques for evaluating employees. Common employee appraisal techniques include rating scales, rankings, weighted checklists, forced-choice forms, behaviorally anchored rating scales, open-format appraisals, and management by objectives methods. Some appraisal forms combine two or more evaluation techniques.

**Rating Scales**. Using a **rating scale appraisal**, the rater subjectively evaluates the employee's performance on a scale from low to high. The following example of an item taken from a typical employee appraisal form contains a rating scale ranging from 1 (unsatisfactory) to 5 (outstanding) for various job dimensions. The rater simply circles the number most closely corresponding to her or his evaluation of the employee's performance on each dimension being measured.

ATTENDANCE

| 1 | 2 | 3 | 4 | 5 |
|---|---|---|---|---|
| Unsatisfactory | | Average | | Outstanding |

With this type of employee appraisal, raters should be careful to avoid a type of bias known as the *halo effect*. The **halo effect** occurs when a rater does not evaluate an employee on each dimension but gives the employee similar scores on all items. This problem may occur if the rater does not take sufficient time to consider each item objectively or if the rater has a biased opinion of the employee's worth.

**Rankings**. The **ranking technique** requires the evaluator to compare the employees with one another and rank them from best to worst. For example, a supervisor might assign a rank of 1 to the best employee, a rank of 2 to the second-best employee, and so forth. Employees may be ranked either overall or separately on several items identifying various work behaviors. The ranking method is not practical when large numbers of employees must be evaluated. Another problem is that ranking is not as accurate as other employee appraisal techniques because it provides relative rather than absolute information. For example, the ranking technique would not reveal how much better one employee is than another or if the employees were all excellent or all average.

**Weighted Checklists**. A **weighted checklist** contains a list of statements describing numerous positive and negative job behaviors, as follows:

|  | Check applicable statements | Weights |
|---|---|---|
| 1.  Employee is never late to work. | _____ | _____ |
| 2.  Employee keeps workstation well organized. | _____ | _____ |
| 3.  Employee sometimes fails to follow required safety procedures. | _____ | _____ |

To evaluate an employee's performance, a supervisor checks the statements that are applicable. To arrive at a numerical score, the personnel department simply totals the assigned weights of the checked statements. Because the raters are not given the values of the weights, weighted checklists generally contain less rater bias than rating scales.

**Forced-Choice Technique**. An appraisal form containing groups of two or more work-related statements is used for the **forced-choice technique** of performance appraisal. The rater must select the statement in each group that is most applicable, as shown in the following example:

(Circle a or b)

1. (a)  Usually makes the right decision
   (b)  Often uses poor judgment

2. (a)  Works well with others
   (b)  Has some difficulty getting along with other people

This type of appraisal form usually involves many groups of statements to offset the limited number of choices in each group. The rater often may be forced to select a statement that is not entirely accurate. However, the halo effect is not usually a problem with this technique.

**Behaviorally Anchored Rating Scales.** Another appraisal technique uses scales that are *anchored* by specific statements representing the range of *behaviors* from most desirable to least desirable on a particular job, as follows:

Behaviorally Anchored Rating Scale
for a Sales Representative's
Weekly Expense Reports

(Circle one)

| | | |
|---|---|---|
| Outstanding | 5 | You can expect reports to be 100 percent accurate and always submitted on time. |
| Above Average | 4 | You can expect reports to be 90 percent accurate and submitted on time. |
| Average | 3 | You can expect reports to be reasonably accurate and occasionally one day late. |
| Below Average | 2 | You can expect reports to contain errors and be two or more days late. |
| Unsatisfactory | 1 | You can expect reports to be inaccurate and always turned in one week or more past the deadline. |

Behaviorally anchored rating scales are more accurate but are much more expensive than most other appraisal techniques because the same appraisal form cannot be used for different jobs. Specific scales must be developed for every individual job.

**Open-Format Appraisals.** In **open-format appraisals**, no pre-printed form is used. An employee's supervisor simply writes a description of the employee's strengths and weaknesses. This technique is more flexible but is less objective than other employee appraisal methods.

Many printed appraisal forms include an open-format section in which a space is provided for the rater to write comments about the employee. The comments should contain relevant and objective facts that illustrate and substantiate the rating being given to the employee, as shown in the following example:

COMMENTS: Although Ms. McCain has been with us for only six months, she already has achieved an above—average sales record. The monthly sales have risen from $60,000 to nearly $80,000——a 30 percent increase since she took over the southeastern district. We have gained several new accounts as a direct result of Ms. McCain's efforts.

**Management by Objectives (MBO)**. In the **MBO technique**, each employee and her or his supervisor agree upon measurable performance objectives the employee should reach by a certain time. The objectives target specific behaviors toward which the employee directs her or his efforts. The following example is taken from an annual MBO plan developed for a sales representative. The "Results" column will be completed at the end of the year.

| Objectives for 19— | Results and Explanation |
|---|---|
| 1. To achieve a 5 percent increase in average sales to $44,000 per month by December 31, 19—. | 1. |
| 2. To submit all weekly sales reports on time to meet 5 p.m deadline each Friday. | 2. |
| 3. To achieve a 95 percent average rate of accuracy in sales reports submitted during the year, as reported by accounting department. | 3. |

Formal appraisals generally take place at regularly scheduled intervals. Employees who have been with a company longer than one year may have their performance appraised only once a year. Recently hired employees, however, may be evaluated more frequently; for example, at one-month, three-month, six-month, and one-year intervals after they begin work.

Whichever written methods are used, the written appraisal should be accompanied by a formal appraisal interview between the employee and her or his supervisor. Appraisal interviews are discussed in Chapter 13.

## SUMMARY

Goodwill messages are intended primarily to promote good human relations and develop a positive image of a company. Such messages should not advertise a company's goods and services in a direct way. Examples of goodwill messages include congratulatory, seasonal, and thank-you letters and memorandums. Other examples include sympathy letters and invitations to social functions.

Organizations also communicate with and about their employees by using various personnel messages. These messages include recommendation letters, job descriptions, policy and procedure statements, and employee appraisals.

As a reciprocal courtesy, recommendation letters provide information about a job applicant to a business organization that is considering hiring that individual. Three issues surrounding recommendation letters are honesty, confidentiality, and legality.

Job descriptions summarize the duties and working conditions of jobs and the qualifications required. The information necessary for writing a job description comes from a job analysis.

Policy and procedures statements are written guidelines expressing a company's standards for employee behavior. Policies are general rules, while procedures are steps for accomplishing specific tasks. Policy and procedures statements may be in the form of a memorandum or included in an employee manual or handbook.

Employee appraisals provide input for major personnel decisions such as retention, promotion, and merit pay. An employees's supervisor usually completes a written appraisal, which usually consists of filling out an appraisal form and writing a description of the employee's strengths and areas that need improvement. Written appraisals should be accompanied by an appraisal interview with the employee.

## CHAPTER REVIEW

1. "Congratulatory letters, sales letters, and thank-you letters are all examples of goodwill messages." Is this statement true or false? Defend your answer.
2. On what occasions are thank-you messages appropriate? Are thank-you messages more effective if they are written or oral?
3. Should recommendation letters have a direct or an indirect plan of organization? Defend your answer.
4. Describe the purpose and contents of job descriptions.
5. Should sympathy letters have a direct or an indirect plan of organization? Defend your answer.
6. What are employee rating forms? What do they measure?
7. In what ways do formal and informal invitations differ?
8. What are policy statements? How do they differ from procedure statements?
9. Identify and describe three techniques for written employee appraisals.
10. Define the *halo effect*. With which type of employee appraisal technique is the halo effect usually associated?

## APPLICATIONS

1. You are vice president of the Tolliver Advertising Agency. You just learned that Marie Guzman, a free-lance graphic designer who sometimes does work for your agency, has won a prestigious award. A poster design that she submitted to the Northeast Association of Graphic Designers annual competition has won first place. Write a letter congratulating Ms. Guzman for her outstanding accomplishment.

2. You are vice president of the First National Bank. Marie Garcia, who has been a systems analyst with the bank for the past three years, was recently elected president of the State Data Processing Association. Write a congratulatory memorandum to her.

3. You are a financial analyst for West Broadcasting, Inc., a California-based company that owns several television stations. You have just returned from a much-needed two-week vacation. While you were out of town, Chris Wilson (one of the other analysts) filled in for you. Write a memorandum thanking her for doing much of your work in addition to her usual responsibilities.

4. You are vice president of finance for Global Development Corporation, which has just completed a merger with another real-estate development firm. Write a memo expressing your appreciation to the accounting department employees for their hard work. They all worked ten- and twelve-hour days for the past six weeks to complete all the year-end financial reports that were required before the merger could take place.

5. Write a form birthday message to be sent to each employee on her or his birthday.

6. Write a letter of sympathy to Carol Reiss, one of your subordinates, whose father died yesterday after a lengthy illness.

7. You are head agent for the Bartlesville, Oklahoma, office of Interstate Insurance Company. Write a letter of recommendation for Rhonda Lawler, who has applied for a transfer to the Grandview, Missouri office. Rhonda has worked for you as an associate agent for the past three years. She wants to return to Missouri because she wants to be near her parents, who are both in poor health. You think Rhonda is a good insurance salesperson. She is thorough but not too pushy with clients, who have given you positive feedback about her. Rhonda is a good judge of character and rarely makes mistakes. Everyone seems to like her. Send the letter to T.J. Dalton, Head Agent, Interstate Insurance Company, 32442 Summit Avenue, Grandview, MO 64030-4627.

8. You are purchasing agent for Tri-City Manufacturing. Dennis Ryan, sales representative for Merrill Chemicals Co., took you to dinner last night at the Windmill Restaurant. Write a thank-you letter to Dennis at Merrill Chemicals Co., 3442 Orange Avenue, San Diego, CA 92129-7586.

9. You are production manager of the Ridge Electronics Company. Write a memorandum expressing your appreciation to Vera Ballard-Smith, an employee whose cost-saving suggestion to recycle wasted copper pipe has saved the company $4,000 per month.

10. You are the assistant administrator of Olympic Health Labs, a small company that specializes in laboratory services for hospitals. Write a letter of appreciation to Jay Hannan, an independent insurance agent, 105 Buena Vista Drive, Suite 233, Virginia Beach, VA 23429-6911. Mr. Hannan did a free insurance analysis for your company, and his suggestions have so far saved your company $18,000 in liability insurance costs.

11. You are office manager for Metro Realty Company. Write an appraisal (in memorandum format) of Phil Lamson, who has worked for Metro for the past

six months as a word-processing specialist. Phil set up the new word-processing system for the office and even installed the computers himself. He has excellent technical skills and has trained two word-processing operators on the new system. Address the memorandum to Marcus Benchley, personnel director.

12. You are personnel manager of Prentiss Foods, Inc., a manufacturer of specialty baked goods. Karen Olson, a human relations specialist whom you supervise, tells you that she wants to take evening classes toward a Master of Business Administration degree at State University. She confides that she would like to progress to a management-level position in the company, but that she presently lacks the specific skills to do so (her undergraduate major was psychology). Her application to the program requires a letter of recommendation from her employer. Write a letter strongly supporting her application; address the letter to the Director of Graduate Programs, University of Missouri-Kansas City, Kansas City, MO 64036-1181. You may make any necessary assumptions about her specific qualifications.

13. You are managing partner of the local office of Boswell, Sims, and Merrill, a stock brokerage company. Develop a letter combining Christmas greetings with an informal invitation to the employees' annual Christmas dinner, which will be held at the Riata Steak House, 1096 North 18th Avenue, Seattle, WA 98155-3096, at 7:30 p.m. on Friday, December 22. The letter will be duplicated and mailed to each of the firm's 26 employees.

14. Write a note accepting the following formal invitation:

---

The Board of Directors of the Thunderbird Bank

Requests the company of (your name)

at a groundbreaking ceremony and cocktail reception

commemorating the new Corporate Office Building

on Friday afternoon, October 10, at four o'clock

at 2041 North Alameda Boulevard

Denver, Colorado

R.S.V.P.

15. Write a note declining the invitation in number 14.

16. Visit the personnel department of a local company. Interview a personnel specialist about the company's procedures for employee appraisals. If possible, obtain a blank employee-appraisal form. Present a short oral or written report of your findings to the class.

17. Obtain a copy of a job description for a professional-level and a non-professional-level job from the personnel department of a local company or from other sources. Evaluate the adequacy of the job description; base your analysis on the information presented in the chapter. Prepare a short written report of your findings.

18. Obtain a copy of an employee handbook from the personnel department of a local company or from some other source. Examine its contents and writing style and present a brief oral report of your findings to the class.

# CASE STUDY

"I don't believe it!" exclaimed Bob Lawson, manager of the Tennessee branch office of Timler Electronics, Inc., to Betty Lewis, one of his sales representatives, as he scanned a letter that had just arrived in the afternoon mail.

"Mary Wellington has applied for a job with the state, and the State Personnel Department wants me to write a recommendation letter for her," Bob continued.

Betty asked, "Isn't she the one with the drinking problem?"

"Yes," replied Bob, "she was my secretary two years ago, but I had to fire her for excessive absenteeism. When she started drinking heavily, she wouldn't show up for work for days. Her attendance became very erratic, and she finally admitted that she had a drinking problem."

"I had to fire her," he continued, "and I've heard nothing from her since that day."

1. What are Bob's options for responding to the request for a recommendation?
2. Discuss the advantages and disadvantages (including legal and ethical issues) surrounding each option.
3. If you were Bob, how would you handle the situation?

## SUGGESTED READINGS

King, Patricia. *Performance Planning and Appraisal: A How-To Book for Managers*. New York: McGraw-Hill, l984.

Patten, Thomas H. *A Manager's Guide to Performance Appraisal: Pride, Prejudice, and the Law of Equal Opportunity*. New York: Macmillan Publishing Co, 1982.

Poe, Roy W. *The McGraw-Hill Handbook of Business Letters*. New York: McGraw-Hill, 1983.

Schell, John and John Stratton. *Writing on the Job: A Handbook for Business and Government*. New York: New American Library, l984. (Chapter 21, "Policies and Procedures," 274-278).

Werther, William B. and Keith Davis. *Personnel Management and Human Resources*, 2nd ed. New York: McGraw-Hill, 1985.

# NONWRITTEN COMMUNICATION

## PART 6

To be an effective business communicator, you will need to develop a variety of skills. Those skills include not only proficiency in writing, but also in listening, nonverbal communication, speaking, and conducting meetings.

Listening is an active mental process that involves more than hearing the message. Effective listening requires attention, understanding, and remembering.

Nonverbal communication is an essential component of organizational behavior. Nonverbal communication, which is closely interwoven with verbal communication, reflects various cultural norms.

Oral communication skills, including one-to-one interactions, group presentations, and meetings, are essential for business success. Managers rely on oral communication for tasks such as giving instructions to subordinates, interacting with clients, and presenting ideas to superiors. Most business professionals give oral presentations occasionally or frequently. Another form of oral communication is dictation, which is used in preparing written messages.

Meetings are an important vehicle for decision making in business organizations. Throughout your professional career, you will be involved in many meetings, either as a leader or a participant.

# LISTENING AND NONVERBAL COMMUNICATION

## CHAPTER 16

A manager experiencing difficulty with a sales representative attempts to discuss the matter with the vice president.

Manager: "Bill just never gets his reports in on time. The procedure for filling them out isn't that hard. I've shown him at least a dozen times. The other sales reps never have any problems with them. I just don't understand why he's so...."

(The phone rings, and the VP answers it. The call is about playing golf with a client after lunch. He finally hangs up the phone.)

VP: "Okay, you were saying something about—who was that again? Charlie?"

(The VP glances at his watch and murmurs something about 15 minutes.)

Manager (rolling his eyes): "No, Bill is the sales rep who never gets his reports in on time and...."

(The VP's administrative assistant enters with a report just delivered from the accounting department.)

VP: (The VP starts flipping through pages of the report.) "Well, it's probably no big deal. See what you can do about it." (He gets up from his seat.) "Say, I have to run. I'll help you any time you have a problem. My office door is always open to you." (The VP puts his hand on the phone and starts dialing.)

Manager (shrugging his shoulders): "Sure."

In this scenario, the VP's nonverbal cues and failure to listen contradicted his verbal offer of help. Listening and nonverbal communication are essential skills for effective management.

This chapter discusses the following topics dealing with listening and nonverbal communication:

- Types and levels of listening
- Importance of listening
- Barriers to listening
- Ways to improve listening
- A definition of nonverbal communication
- Nonverbal communication related to the body, the voice, and the environment

## LISTENING

Most of us can hear, but we don't always listen. How true this statement often is! Many of us can recall our parents saying, "If I've told you once, I've told you a thousand times...." Why didn't we do what we were told? Didn't we hear the words? Of course, but we may not have listened.

Hearing is the receiving of sound waves with our ears. Hearing (the auditory sense) is a passive, physical process that occurs with little or no effort. Although we may hear the police siren blow, the thunder crack, the dog bark, or the motorcycle roar, we may not listen to them.

Although listening involves hearing, the two processes are not the same. **Listening** is an active, mental process that occurs not only with our ears but also through a concentrated effort of our minds and eyes as well. Through listening, we attach meaning to the sounds we hear. Listening is a rather intricate process that involves four elements: *attention*, *hearing*, *understanding*, and *remembering*.

**Attention**. Although our ears are steadily bombarded by various noises, we cannot possibly sort out all the sounds we hear and direct our attention to them individually. The process of choosing one sound over another is called **selective attention**. For example, selective attention takes place in a noisy office when an employee listens to someone explain how to do something and ignores other conversations or phones ringing.

**Hearing**. When our ears receive sound waves, **hearing** takes place. Three things happen when hearing occurs. First, we discriminate among and between different sounds of speech—an "e" and an "i" or a "p" and a "b." Second, we put these sounds into meaningful patterns which become words. Third, we place words into meaningful patterns which become language.

**Understanding**. The third element of the listening process, **understanding**, is the process of assigning meaning to the sounds or words we hear. Often the receiver's understanding agrees closely with the meaning the speaker had in mind when sending the message. However, since understanding is based largely on past experiences, people may interpret information differently.

**Remembering**. The final element of the listening process is **remembering**, which is the storage of information for later use. We use our **short-term memory** when we remember as many as five to seven items simultaneously for up to 30 seconds (Atwater, 1981, 89, 95). A very common example of short-term memory occurs when a directory assistance operator gives you a telephone number. Usually we can remember a telephone number long enough to dial it. To be retained, however, information must be repeated. To remember that phone number five minutes later, you probably would need to repeat it several times. The retention of information for longer than 30 seconds is called **long-term memory**.

## Types and Levels of Listening

Types of listening are active and interactive listening. **Active** (*formal*) **listening** occurs when the listener has little or no occasion to interact either verbally or nonverbally with the speaker. Examples of active listening include watching TV or a home video movie, listening to the radio, attending a college lecture, or sitting in as a nonparticipant during a court trial or a company board meeting. **Interactive** (*informal*) **listening** takes place when the listener has the occasion to interact either verbally or nonverbally with the speaker, such as in a one-to-one conversation or in a group discussion.

Levels of listening depend on the importance or the relevance of the message conveyed by the speaker to the listener. The three levels of listening include *casual*, *attentive*, and *empathetic listening*.

**Casual Listening**. **Casual listening** takes place primarily for enjoyment or to fulfill social needs. Examples of casual listening include listening to music on radio or television, talking about the weather before your class starts, discussing sports beside the water fountain, and chatting about fashions during the coffee break.

**Attentive Listening**. At the **attentive** level of **listening**, the receiver absorbs information that he or she will most likely need to act upon. Obtaining feedback, asking questions for clarification, evaluating comments, and remembering details are all essential at this level. Attentive listening occurs in business meetings or conferences, small-group training seminars, or teacher-student conferences.

More specifically, attentive listening can be classified as discriminative or critical listening. *Discriminative listening* is used in situations requiring complete understanding and memorization of specific information. A new assembly-line worker listening to a supervisor explaining how to run a particular piece of machinery provides an example of discriminative listening.

*Critical listening* is used in situations where we need to evaluate the accuracy and "reasonableness" of information. Cases where we suspect that we might be listening to a biased source of information call for critical listening.

For example, when a personnel manager interviews a prospective job applicant, the interviewer listens critically to what the applicant says to assess the applicant's suitability for employment.

**Empathetic Listening**. Another level of listening requires us to listen "between the lines." We use **empathetic listening** when we listen *with* the person or, in other words, from the speaker's internal frame of reference rather than from our own point of view. Empathetic listening is difficult because most of us have a tendency to relate our own experiences or to give advice. For empathetic listening, although you may not agree with the speaker's point of view, you should attempt to understand it.

Equally important at this level of listening is "hearing" omitted words ("I'm upset") and nonverbal cues (facial expression that indicates anxiety). The listener should convey verbally or nonverbally her or his sensitivity to the speaker through such phrases as "I understand," "What you are saying is . . . ," "I follow you," or nodding the head in agreement.

## Importance of Listening

A classic study found that white-collar workers spent about 70 percent of their work time communicating (reading, writing, and listening), and 45 percent of the workers' time was spent in listening (Rankin, 1920, 177-179, 414-420). More current research indicates that executives spend 45 to 63 percent of their working time listening (Keefe, 1971, 10; Maidment, 1984, 18; Montgomery, 1981, 16).

If listening is the most frequently used communication skill, what advantages will result from effective listening? Although the desire to be heard and to be part of an organization is a common human need, business people at all levels frequently complain that others fail to listen. Listening is critical for maintaining the morale of subordinates. For harmonious labor relations, not only do employees need to listen to their supervisors, but also supervisors need to listen to their employees.

Much of the work in a business environment is that of decision making, and decisions are made from information. Costly mistakes can occur if one does not listen to information or receive it completely and accurately. Listening is important to individuals because it enables them to gain essential information, to be more effective in interpersonal relations, to gather data to make sound decisions, and to respond appropriately to messages they hear (Hunt, 1980, 79-81).

Effective listening also improves feedback. If the listener is receptive to the speaker's point of view, the speaker will likewise tend to listen more effectively to the listener's point of view. This empathetic listening provides greater understanding of others and leads to better overall communication.

## Barriers to Listening

Many obstacles and barriers may interfere with our listening ability. The reasons why people do not listen can be divided into two basic types of barriers—*physical* and *psychological barriers*.

**Physical Barriers.** Listening may be impaired by the following physical barriers:

1. *Physical limitations*. Complete or partial deafness will, of course, hinder listening ability. Ear infections or head colds may also restrict effective listening, at least temporarily.
2. *Internal competition for attention*. The mind wandering to other matters (for example, worrying about business or personal problems) is a major reason for inefficient listening. Also, being tired, hungry, or in pain due to a headache or a sore back directs our attention to a more pressing physical need than listening.
3. *External competition for attention*. Noise, excessive cold or heat, or being overloaded with too many environmental stimuli or things to do are factors that compete externally for the listener's attention and thus impair effective listening.
4. *Mental laziness*. Listening requires effort because people have the ability to think four times faster than the average speaker can talk. If a topic being discussed is too complex, long, or unfamiliar to a listener's understanding, he or she may fail to concentrate and "tune out" the speaker. Excessive relaxation may also cause mental laziness. Effective listening takes work!
5. *Physical distractions*. A speaker's body language, speech patterns, accent, grammar, or manner and style of dress may distract us from listening. The listener may be inclined to pay more attention to such distractions than to the primary message.
6. *Excessive notetaking*. Attempting to write down every word a speaker says rather than concentrating on main ideas or concepts may cause us to miss the overall meaning of the message. In some cases, however, just the opposite might be true. We may be concerned only with hearing the main ideas and consequently may lose out on some very important supporting details. When taking notes, the listener should attempt to sort out the main ideas and write down only the essential information.

**Psychological Barriers.** Five typical psychological barriers to listening include the following factors:

1. *Selective perception*. People are conditioned not to listen to something that does not agree with their preconceived notions. Our personal biases sometimes prevent us from hearing the total message, and we hear only what we want to hear. For example, an irate customer who is upset about poor service or defective merchandise is likely to hear only her or his own side of the story. Our negative feelings about the subject may even cause

us to plan our rebuttal while the speaker is talking rather than to listen to the other person's point of view.

2. *Emotions.* Certain words may trigger ideas or provoke feelings that may interfere with listening. These emotions may overpower the content of the message. For example, what feelings might the following message evoke? "All computer programmers think alike!" This statement might be interpreted by some listeners as meaning that computer programmers have tunnel vision. However, the message might have been completed as follows: "All computer programmers are alike! They think very logically."

3. *Lack of motivation.* Listeners may not pay attention to a speaker unless they consciously or subconsciously perceive a need to do so. As one example of motivation to listen, think of your own situation. How carefully do you listen to a class presentation by fellow students if you know that you will not be tested on it and that you do not have to evaluate the material?

4. *Speaker-listener relationship.* If a supervisor (such as the vice president in the scenario at the beginning of this chapter) says that he or she is always available to help a subordinate but never follows through to provide assistance or advice, how long will subordinates be willing to confide in that individual? Credibility and respect for one another are important considerations in keeping lines of communication open for both listening and speaking.

5. *Unwillingness to listen.* Lack of willingness to listen is an attitude that is formed *before* listening takes place. A few reasons why people may not have a desire to listen are as follows: 1) people do not want to hear negative information; 2) listeners may feel that a speaker has nothing of value to say; and 3) most people would rather talk than listen.

Many of these barriers are factors that we cannot control or do much about. However, awareness of such factors can enable us to adjust our listening habits accordingly and lead us to look at ways of improving our listening skills.

## Ways to Improve Listening

A pioneer in listening research found that individuals function at 25 percent efficiency when listening (Nichols, 1957, ix). In other words, 75 percent of what we hear is not retained. Another study found that almost 60 percent of communication problems in business are due to poor listening (Montgomery, 1981, 6). Poor listening skills may result in needless misunderstanding and errors. To improve your listening skills, follow these guidelines:

**Attempt Both Physical and Mental Alertness in Listening.** Listening is an active rather than passive activity. How alert are you during a professor's lecture if you have had very little sleep the night before? You need to be physically rested to be an effective listener. Try to maintain eye contact with the speaker and to sit up in an attentive position. Although you may be able to listen in a sprawled-out position, poor posture gives negative feedback to the speaker.

Mental alertness is as important as physical alertness. Since you as a listener are in a more passive role than the speaker, paying attention requires motivation. Try not to tune out the speaker.

When the topic is difficult to comprehend, you may need to do some prior research so that you will be mentally prepared to listen. For example, if you are going to hear a lecture about computerized voice technology, you may need to become familiar with terminology such as "digitized format," "synthesized speech," or "voice compression."

Remove as many distractions as possible. This procedure may be as simple as closing a door or a window, turning off piped-in music, or moving away from a window seat. Even though many individuals prefer to sit toward the back of the room in a formal listening situation, you can focus your attention better if you are seated close to a speaker.

**Evaluate the Subject Matter, Not the Speaker's Style**. Sometimes the listener is more concerned with the speaker's clothes, style of hair, gestures, or a monotonous voice than with what is being said. As a listener, your attention should be directed to the message and not to the speaker's eloquence or lack of eloquence.

**Focus on Main Points**. Avoid dwelling on every bit of information presented. You should screen facts from opinions and essential information from nonessential detail. An effective strategy is to determine the speaker's primary purpose and then focus on the specific topics or areas that are of use to you. This technique will make a seemingly uninteresting topic more interesting and help you want to listen.

This same focus on main points is essential in taking notes. Your methods of notetaking may vary from speaker to speaker. For a very complex and technical presentation, you may need to tape the speaker. In this case, be sure to obtain permission first. In less formal situations, however, a simple outline of main points or key ideas probably will be sufficient. If you attempt to record a speaker's comments verbatim, you probably will miss most of that speaker's important points. While you are still jotting down every word of the first topic, the speaker may already be on the next topic.

**Evaluate and Respond Only When Understanding is Complete**. Although everyone has preconceived ideas about many topics, try to keep an open mind when listening. Make an effort to maintain a listening atmosphere that is objective and free of personal bias. Refrain from becoming defensive as soon as you hear an emotionally sensitive word or phrase. For example, words and phrases such as "staff reduction," "sexual harassment," or "computer phase-in and job elimination" may have emotion-laden meanings. Also, you may miss part or all of the message if you are thinking about what you are going to say when the other person stops talking or how you are going to refute her or his comments.

**Look for Nonverbal Messages**. When you listen, be aware of the speaker's nonverbal cues. Use not only your ears but also your eyes. Often the nonverbal signals and omitted words may be more convincing than what is actually said. For example, a sweaty brow and shaky hands may raise questions in your mind about the speaker's confidence.

**Be Courteous to the Speaker**. The courtesy you extend to a speaker during her or his talk will enable that individual to be more enthusiastic about the presentation. A simple nod of your head or a smile is an appropriate form of positive feedback. Maintain eye contact both as a means of feedback to the speaker and as a way of maintaining your level of attention. Avoid annoying the speaker with distractions such as yawning, tapping your finger or pen on the table, or flipping through a newspaper or magazine. Ask questions when appropriate to show interest as well as to clarify main points and ideas you may have missed during the presentation.

**Expand Your Listening Experience**. Any skill requires practice, whether it be serving in tennis, playing a musical instrument, learning computer keyboarding, or listening. To perfect your listening skill, you need to experience new and different listening situations. For instance, you might perfect your listening skill by attending lectures about unfamiliar topics.

**Use Spare Thinking Time**. The human brain can process information much faster than an individual can speak. Although a person's average speaking rate is between 100-150 words per minute, the mind can comprehend an average rate of 400-500 words per minute (Goss, 1982, 91). To avoid daydreaming, use the spare time to think about what the speaker is saying. Summarizing ideas presented, interpreting and analyzing remarks, or anticipating comments yet to come are a few suggestions for use of this spare thinking time.

# NONVERBAL COMMUNICATION

**Nonverbal communication** can be defined as the part of a message that is not in words. These nonverbal cues may be conscious or subconscious on the speaker's part. If any discrepancy between the spoken word and the nonverbal behavior occurs, the nonverbal cues usually outweigh the verbal cues.

A major study of nonverbal communication revealed that only about 7 percent of most messages are transmitted by words and 93 percent by nonverbal language (Mehrabian, 1968, 53-55). Of that 93 percent, 55 percent consists of facial expression, body position, and gestures; and 38 percent is tone and inflection of the voice.

Nonverbal and verbal communication are interrelated. Nonverbal behavior can either reinforce or contradict verbal signals (Knapp, 1978, 21-26). A person who points east while giving directions for reaching a specific location is an example of nonverbal communication supporting or reinforcing verbal communication. A speaker claiming, "I wasn't the least bit nervous," after talking in a trembling voice and gesturing with shaking hands provides an example of nonverbal cues that contradict the verbal signal.

Differences in cultural norms may contribute to nonverbal communication problems, particularly in international communication. For example, in the Middle East, people are more comfortable conversing when they are only a few inches away from each other. In other cultures, such close proximity would be a violation of *personal space*. In the United States, the "okay" sign is made by making a circle with the thumb and forefinger and extending the other fingers. In South America, this same gesture is a sign of contempt. In Thailand, pointing one's foot at someone else is considered to be a serious insult. Visitors to Thailand, therefore, should sit with both feet firmly on the floor rather than crossing their legs.

## Nonverbal Communication Related to the Body

Which of the following actions would you generally recognize as examples of attentive behavior?

- Cleaning one's fingernails
- Nodding the head
- Looking directly at the speaker
- Cracking knuckles
- Looking away from the speaker
- Moving toward the speaker

Nodding the head in agreement, good eye contact, and moving toward the speaker are all examples of attentive behavior. The remaining three are examples of inattentive behavior.

We use our bodies to convey our attitudes and emotions. This nonverbal communication may be through facial expressions, gestures and body movements, touching, or even body shape and appearance. In communication, the study of body movements is called **kinesics**. A pioneer researcher found that over 700,000 nonverbal cues may be sent through body movements of one kind or another (Birdwhistell, 1952, 3).

**Facial Expressions**. The face is the most expressive part of the body. Eye contact, which is probably the most important facial expression, can be classified in terms of various functions: seeking information, expressing feelings, regulating conversation, and attempting to influence someone's behavior (Druckman et al., 1982, 74).

Generally, people unconsciously use eye contact for the following reasons:

1. To seek feedback about the reactions of another person
2. To signal that the communication channel is open
3. To indicate a need to be included in or be a "part of the action"
4. To cause anxiety or stress in another person
5. To signal interest in another person

Conversely, people seldom use eye contact in the following instances:

1. If they wish to hide something
2. When they compete with one another
3. If they feel dislike, tension, or fear of deception
4. When they begin a long recitation or when a listener expects a long recitation
5. If they do not want to maintain social contact (McCrosky, 1971, 112-114)

Eye contact increases between two people if they like each other or if they are separated by greater distances. On the other hand, eye contact diminishes when people are physically close and do not have a strong bond of liking for each other. Women tend to use eye contact more than men. Also, high-status people generally receive greater eye contact from subordinates than vice versa.

**Gestures and Body Movements**. You are probably familiar with people who "talk" with their hands. Gestures generally supplement, substitute for, or contradict the spoken word. Examples are many—showing the "V" for victory sign, crossing the fingers to indicate good luck, blowing a kiss to show affection, clenching a fist to display anger, thumbing a ride, or tapping the fingers to demonstrate impatience.

Body movements, including posture, are another type of nonverbal communication. For example, leaning towards the person you are talking with and relaxing your arms at your sides or on the arm rests generally indicate interest and openness. In contrast, leaning back and folding your arms across your chest demonstrates a lack of interest or being closed to the present conversation.

Studies conducted in organizations show that people relax most with persons of lower status, a little less with peers, and least of all with higher status individuals (Mehrabian, 1968, 53-55). In groups, people sitting facing each other in a circle may indicate that no one else is welcome to join the group. What unspoken message is clear at a party when a small group of people talking turn their backs to an approaching individual?

**Touching**. Although considered extremely important in the development of children, physical touching is usually replaced by verbal and other nonverbal cues as a child approaches adulthood. The handshake is one of the few acceptable means of touching in our culture. A limp handshake communicates weakness or a lack of interest and carries a negative interpretation. A moist or damp handshake indicates nervousness or fear. A firm handshake demonstrates strength and self-confidence and is interpreted positively by the other person. In contrast, a painful handshake may give an overly aggressive impression and threaten the receiver.

**Body Shape and Appearance**. Consider the emphasis that society places on a person's appearance. Television, radio, newspapers, and magazines are dominated by advertisements for toothpaste, deodorants, makeup, hair products, and clothing.

Stylish clothing and slim, youthful bodies are admired in our culture. Appearance is particularly important for the sake of making a positive first impression, and first impressions tend to be lasting ones.

## Nonverbal Communication Related to the Voice

"Don't use that tone of voice with me!" Has anyone ever said that to you? The issue in the example is not so much *what* was said but *how* it was said. The study of how language is articulated is designated as **paralanguage** (Trager, 1958, 1-12) and has two basic parts: vocalization, such as laughing, crying, clearing the throat, "ums," or pauses; and voice qualities, such as pitch, volume, and rate.

Repeat the following sentences emphasizing the italicized words:

1. I would like *you* to finish the report today.
2. I would like you to *finish* the report today.
3. I would like you to finish the *report* today.
4. I would like you to finish the report *today*.

Note that the emphasis on the italicized word changes the meaning of each sentence, as follows:

1. Emphasizes the receiver of the message
2. Implies that the receiver doesn't finish what he or she starts
3. Places emphasis on the task
4. Implies that the receiver failed to meet a deadline

Generally, words of anger are accompanied by a loud voice. A person talking rapidly may be nervous or excited. Talking slowly may indicate sorrow or discouragement. A constant use of "ums," "ahs," or long pauses indicates anxiety, tension, or lack of credibility. However, brief pauses at properly placed intervals in a speech may enhance the message being delivered.

## Nonverbal Communication Related to the Environment

How would you feel if after several class meetings you arrived a little late to class and found someone else sitting in your usual seat? You might feel somewhat annoyed, as though someone had invaded your territory. Where we sit, how close we sit or stand while talking with another person, or how large or where our office is located are all nonverbal cues related to the environment. Environmental messages, include factors such as territory and space, physical arrangement, objects, color, and time.

**Territory and Space.** People tend to be concerned about the amount of space or territory they control. You may be familiar with the psychological advantage in a football game of playing on the home field, for example.

The following space and territory "rules" are common in the business environment:

1. Higher status individuals have more and better space than those with lower status.
2. Meetings usually occur in the territory (office) of higher status individuals (superiors) than in that of subordinates.
3. Higher status individuals can invade the territory (come in without an appointment or sit down without an invitation) of lower status individuals more easily than vice versa.

The head of a corporation generally has the largest office on the top floor, plush furniture, carpeting, and large windows. Personnel at lower levels in the organizational hierarchy occupy smaller, less elaborate offices than those of individuals at the level above them.

A study of office space utilization in the corporate headquarters of a major American corporation revealed that the chief executive officer's private office on the top floor was 875 square feet. Depending on their rank, other employees worked on lower floors in offices that were 375, 300, 225, 150, or 100 square feet in size (*Science 86*, 1986, 18-19).

In certain other cultures, space is less important than in American corporations. For example, in Japanese companies, offices are usually the same size, without regard to an employee's rank or status.

Lower ranking individuals generally need permission (such as an appointment) to invade the territory of a higher ranking individual. However, higher ranking individuals are free to call on subordinates at any time ("John, would you please come over to my office right away.") or to enter a subordinate's office at any time and sit down without an invitation.

Space is closely related to the concept of territory. The study of personal space is called **proxemics**. Four distances, which reflect degrees of liking or preference, are used by most Americans in their business and social interactions, as follows (Hall, 1966, 111-129):

1. *Intimate Distance*. From touching to 18 inches is usually reserved for loving, protecting, comforting, telling secrets, and ironically, fighting. However, if this distance is trespassed upon or forced, automatic defenses such as looking away, appearing embarrassed, becoming rigid, or remaining silent will surface. For example, note what happens in a very crowded elevator when too many people attempt to squeeze in.
2. *Personal Distance*. From one and a half to four feet is the imaginary "bubble" space around us. Usually this distance is reserved for close friends. The distance during conversation is actually determined by the relationship and feelings between the people involved. Violation of our "bubble" will result in negative reactions similar to those for violating the intimate distance.
3. *Social Distance*. From four feet to twelve feet is the distance used most often in business. Short distances are maintained in informal meetings and longer distances for formal meetings.

4. *Public Distance*. For public speaking, the distances are usually greater than twelve feet. In this setting, communication is primarily one way from a speaker or entertainer to an audience. Figure 16.1 illustrates intimate, personal, social, and public distances.

## FIGURE 16.1 PROXEMIC DISTANCES

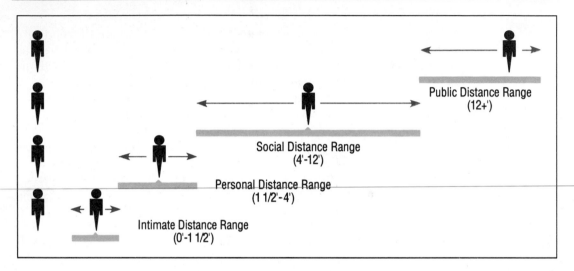

**Physical Arrangement**. Some buildings, rooms, and furniture arrangements can facilitate communication. Rooms with high ceilings, few windows, and wide-open areas are not conducive to communication because they seem cold and impersonal. In contrast, smaller rooms tend to encourage interaction among occupants.

A round table normally promotes discussion, while a rectangular table encourages participants to take sides, to focus on the head of the table as the leader, and to talk with individuals across the table. The same is true of rows of chairs. Parallel rows discourage participation, while circular patterns encourage participation.

Do you feel more comfortable talking to a professor while sitting in front of the desk with the professor behind it, or sitting beside the desk next to the professor? Depending on its arrangement, furniture can either serve as a barrier or can facilitate interaction.

**Objects**. Paintings, plants, carpeting, drapes, colorful partitions, upholstered furniture, and family photos all add warmth to office surroundings. As long as these items are not distractions, they can enhance communication.

**Color**. The color of clothing and room furnishings may affect communication by establishing a mood or tone. Yellow, red, and orange, which are "warm" colors, are associated with creativity and extroverted behavior. Gray, green, and blue are "cool" colors which are associated with analytical thinking and introverted behavior (Fabun, 1968, 20-25).

**Time**. Our culture values time, which determines when we eat, sleep, work, and play. Being on time communicates responsibility and efficiency, while tardiness communicates lack of interest, disrespect, and irresponsibility.

Time may also reflect status. A person with lower status is generally expected to wait for the higher ranking person. For example, colleges have informal rules governing how long students should wait for a professor to appear for class. However, professors generally do not wait for late students. Persons of equal status may have an unwritten rule of waiting five minutes for each other. Persons of higher status are also allotted more time with superiors and have less difficulty securing earlier appointments with them than do lower status individuals. Higher status people such as managers usually do not "punch a clock" and are allowed more flexible hours than lower status employees such as production workers.

All nonverbal cues should be considered in relation to verbal cues and not as separate entities having no relationship to the context in which they occur. As a sender, use nonverbal communication to strengthen and reinforce your verbal messages.

## SUMMARY

Listening is a mental process which involves attentiveness, hearing, understanding, and remembering. Two types of listening, active and interactive, are conducted on three levels: casual, attentive, and empathetic listening. Although effective listening is vital to professional success and a sense of self-esteem, both physical and psychological barriers may exist. Suggested guidelines for improving listening by overcoming these barriers can help to strengthen management skills.

Nonverbal communication is that part of a message not conveyed in words but mixed, deliberately or unintentionally, with verbal communication. Nonverbal communication may be classified as it relates to the body, to the voice, and to the environment. Facial expression, gestures and body movement, touching, and body shape and appearance are nonverbal cues related to the body. Paralanguage, the study of how language is articulated, includes both vocalization and voice qualities. Nonverbal communication related to the environment includes messages conveyed by territory and space, physical arrangement, accessories, and uses of time. Differences in nonverbal communication cues exist among various cultures.

## CHAPTER REVIEW

1. Describe the four elements of the listening process.
2. How does hearing differ from listening?
3. Name the types and levels of listening. Give examples of the two types of listening and the three levels of listening other than the examples given in this chapter.

4. Give four reasons why listening is important and provide an example of each.
5. List three examples of both physical and psychological barriers to listening.
6. Describe how listening skills can be improved.
7. How are nonverbal and verbal cues interrelated?
8. List and describe the three classifications of nonverbal communication and give two examples of each type.
9. Define the terms *proxemics* and *paralanguage*.
10. Explain the importance and implications of time as a factor in nonverbal communication.

## APPLICATIONS

1. Carefully observe an office on or off campus and identify five barriers to listening (distractions) in that office. Write a memorandum to your instructor that recommends changes that would make the office more conducive to effective listening.

2. Find an executive who is willing to have you observe her or him on the job for a few hours. Observe the executive's activities and note the nature of each activity and the time spent on each. Then write a short report indicating how much and what percent of her or his time this individual spent in talking, reading, writing, and listening. Include a graphic representation of your findings.

3. Write a one- or two-page paper about a listening problem you have encountered.

4. Keep a diary of all your communication activities including reading, writing, listening, and speaking, for one weekday and a Saturday or Sunday. Write a memorandum report to your instructor in which you present the results, including the proportion of time each day spent on each of the four communication activities. Include at least one graphic aid such as a table or chart.

5. Conduct a conversation with a friend about a controversial topic. While talking, put your hands behind your back to avoid gesturing. Have a third friend observe changes in facial expressions; in upper body movement; and in voice pitch, tone, etc. Once these changes have been recorded, write a description of the nonverbal communication that was used other than gesturing.

6. Record all the examples of nonverbal communication you see during five minutes of a television program, a teacher's lecture, a conversation between two people, or some similar situation. Be sure you are not able to hear what is being said. Upon completion of your observation, write a short informal report about your findings. Be sure to include an analysis of the classifications of nonverbal communication you saw, as well as how these behaviors might have affected communication.

7. Evaluate an example of a business letter you received recently. Identify at least three nonverbal cues contained in the letter and envelope.

8. Observe the reception area of either a bus terminal, a doctor's office, or a corporate headquarters and note the nonverbal cues in the environment. Write a short report describing the cues and discuss whether these cues were appropriate or inappropriate for that environment.

9. Choose a friend to complete this exercise with you. While sitting with your back to each other, convey the following emotions to each other by repeating one letter of the alphabet in a different way: fear, love, disappointment, anger, joy, sadness.

10. Find a frequently used elevator and ride it a number of times. While the elevator is very crowded, talk to someone, move closer to someone, and face the back of the elevator. While the elevator is less crowded, talk to someone, move closer to someone, and face the back of the elevator. Note the reactions you receive. Write a description of your findings.

## CASE STUDY

Although Dan Miller's day was as hectic as usual, he was able to maintain a calm demeanor. Dan prided himself on being able to handle stress, being open, and having a good relationship with his employees.

As he wrote a rough draft for a report, Ellie Watson appeared at his office doorway. "May I see you for a minute?" she asked, somewhat timidly. "I have an appointment with you."

"Sure, Ellie, come in," Dan said, moving his arm in a sweeping movement. Ellie looked around the room. One chair faced Dan's desk, but it was about four feet away from the desk. Ellie moved the chair closer to Dan's desk and sat down.

Dan leaned back in his chair and folded his arms across his chest. "What's the problem?" he asked, with a furrowed brow.

"Well," Ellie said, looking at her hands and then up at Dan, "it's not really a problem. It's just that, well...."

Dan looked at the clock on his desk and then tapped his finger on his appointment book. He leaned forward and looked at Ellie. "It's just what?" he asked.

"Well," Ellie said, "I've been here about a year now and have pretty much learned all the aspects of my job, and...."

"Oh," Dan said, raising both hands in front of him with the palms facing Ellie. "You want a raise! Well, right now we've had some budget cuts, and...."

"No, no," Ellie interrupted, leaning forward, "it's not a raise." Dan dropped his hands in his lap and leaned against the back of the chair. He looked at the ceiling. "Good," he said, "then what?"

"Well," Ellie said, "I wondered if I could talk to you about future plans for me here."

Dan gathered up his appointment book and papers on his desk. "Sure, Ellie," he said, standing up behind his desk. "Let's schedule some time to talk about it. I back all of my employees."

1. How did Dan's self-image compare with how he actually treated Ellie?
2. What nonverbal behaviors on Dan's part alienated Ellie?
3. If you were in Ellie's place, how would Dan's behavior have affected you?

## REFERENCES

Eastwood Atwater, *I Hear You—Listening Skills to Make You a Better Manager* (Englewood Cliffs, NJ: Prentice-Hall, 1981).

Ray L. Birdwhistell, *Introduction to Kinesics* (Louisville, KY: University of Louisville Press, 1952).

Daniel Druckman, Richard M. Rozelle, and James C. Baxter, *Nonverbal Communication: Survey, Theory, and Research* (Beverly Hills, CA: Sage Publications, 1982).

Don Fabun, *Communications: The Transfer of Meaning* (New York: Macmillan, 1968).

Blain Goss, *Processing Communication: Information Processing in Intrapersonal Communication* (Belmont, CA: Wadsworth, 1982).

Edward T. Hall, *The Hidden Dimension* (Garden City, NY: Doubleday, 1966).

Gary T. Hunt, *Communication Skills in the Organization* (Englewood Cliffs, NJ: Prentice-Hall, 1980).

William Ford Keefe, *Listen, Management! Creative Listening for Better Managing* (New York: McGraw-Hill, 1971).

Mark L. Knapp, *Nonverbal Communication in Human Interaction*, 2nd ed. (New York: Holt, Rinehart and Winston, 1978).

Robert Maidment, *Tuning In: A Guide to Effective Listening* (Gretna, LA: Pelican Publishing Company, Inc., 1984).

James McCroskey, Carl E. Larson, and Mark L. Knapp, *An Introduction to Interpersonal Communication* (Englewood Cliffs, NJ: Prentice-Hall, 1971).

Albert Mehrabian, "Communication Without Words," *Psychology Today* 2, no. 4 (September 1968): 53-55.

Robert L. Montgomery, *Listening Made Easy—How to Improve Listening on the Job, at Home, and in the Community* (New York: American Management Associations, 1981).

Ralph Nichols and Leonard Stevens, *Are You Listening?* (New York: McGraw-Hill, 1957).

Paul T. Rankin, "Listening Ability: Its Importance, Measurement and Development," *Chicago Schools Journal* 12, no. 10 (June 1930): 177-179, 414-420.

"Science of Business," *Science 86* 7, no. 2 (March 1986): 18-19.

George L. Trager, "Paralanguage: A First Approximation," *Studies in Linguistics* 13, (1958): 1-12.

## SUGGESTED READINGS

Beattie, Geoffrey. *Talk: An Analysis of Speech and Non-Verbal Behaviour in Conversation*. Milton Keynes, England: Open University Press, 1983.

Glatthorn, Allan A. and Herbert R. Adams. *Listening Your Way to Management Success*. Glenview, IL: Scott, Foresman and Company, 1983.

Poyatos, Fernando. *New Perspectives on Nonverbal Communication: Studies in Cultural Anthropology, Social Psychology, Linguistics, and Semiotics*. Oxford, England: Pergamon Press, 1983.

Reed, Warren H. *Positive Listening: Learning to Hear What People Are Really Saying*. New York: F. Watts, 1985.

Steil, Lyman K., Larry L. Barker, and Kittie W. Watson. *Effective Listening — Key to Your Success*. Reading, MA: Addison-Wesley, 1983.

Wiemann, John M., and Randall P. Harrison, eds. *Nonverbal Interaction*. Beverly Hills, CA: Sage Publications, 1983.

# ORAL PRESENTATIONS AND DICTATION

## CHAPTER 17

"Mac" McClain is sales manager of the Kansas and Missouri division of an electronics distributing company. Mac is a large, affable man with an engaging personality. He is the mainstay of the division sales office and supervises a staff of fifteen people, including six sales representatives. Mac has been with the company for ten years and was promoted to sales manager six months ago when the firm opened a new branch in Kansas City.

Mac has an excellent record of dealing with individual clients. His new position as sales manager, however, requires him to give sales presentations to groups of people about once a month. Unfortunately, Mac has always had a problem speaking in front of groups.

The night before Mac has to give a sales presentation to a large group, he suffers from headaches and insomnia. He often gets an upset stomach just before giving his presentation.

Since Mac is embarrassed about his fear of public speaking, he has never admitted it to anyone in the company. In fact, no one knows about the problem except Mac's wife.

As Mac discovered, business managers must communicate orally with people not only on a one-to-one basis but also in groups. Oral presentations are an important form of communication in business organizations. Dictation is another mode of oral communication that is the responsibility of many business managers. Through dictation, managers express ideas orally for written communication. This chapter includes the following topics as they relate to oral presentations and dictation:

- Oral presentations vs. written messages
- Purpose of oral presentations
- Speaker credibility and audience analysis
- Preparation and delivery of oral presentations
- Dictation methods
- Proper dictation techniques

## ORAL PRESENTATIONS VS. WRITTEN MESSAGES

Many of the principles of written communication discussed in previous chapters also pertain to oral presentations. However, some differences do exist. Written messages and oral presentations have the following basic differences:

- Control of the audience
- Timeliness of the feedback
- Use of visual cues

### Control of the Audience

In written messages, the reader is your audience, over whom you have little control. In fact, you do not know if the message will actually be read! Since the reader controls the pace, he or she can re-read difficult sections of the message, stop and make notes, or think more about particular concepts.

In an oral presentation, the speaker has more control of the audience. The speaker's inflection, gestures and other nonverbal cues, and additional speech dynamics all affect audience control. If the speaker talks in a monotone or too rapidly, the audience is likely to take mental sidetrips; and the speaker may lose control of the audience. On the other hand, if the speaker develops an interesting presentation and has a good delivery, the audience will be more likely to listen.

### Timeliness of the Feedback

Feedback from memos, letters, and reports may not come to the sender for days or weeks. Often such a delay can be helpful because it allows the receiver more time to develop a carefully planned and organized response to the message. Of course, much feedback from oral presentations is immediate. After receiving verbal and nonverbal reactions from the audience, the speaker can clarify ideas to assure that effective communication takes place.

### Use of Visual Cues

In written messages, visual cues such as paragraphing can be used to provide unity and structure. Punctuation and underlining can be used to show emphasis, relationship, and transition.

In oral presentations, visual cues generally complement the oral message by providing additional information to the audience. Visual cues may include the speaker's expression, gestures, and use of graphic aids.

## PURPOSE OF ORAL PRESENTATIONS

In business, **oral presentations** may be used to persuade individuals to undertake a particular action, to raise issues for consideration, to explain policies and procedures, to provide basic information, to suggest possible solutions to a problem, to recommend a plan or course of action, or to stimulate thought about a particular situation. One or a combination of any of these purposes are all reasons for making an oral presentation.

For all types of oral presentations, the ultimate goal is to influence the behavior or attitude of your listeners in some way. This change may be immediate, such as in a persuasive presentation asking for a prompt decision. Or the results may be delayed, such as in an informational presentation where the behavior change may take place in the future. Everything you do from preparation to delivery of your oral presentation should be aimed at influencing your audience. This influence may be as subtle as sparking an emotion or triggering a thought, or as direct as actually requesting a desired action.

## CREDIBILITY OF THE SPEAKER

At one time or another, you may have jokingly stated "Consider the source!" when referring to the believability of someone's comments. Indeed, your perception of what you believed that individual to be was very important in influencing your acceptance of that person's message.

**Speaker credibility** depends upon how an audience perceives a speaker's command of or expertise in a subject area; overall objectivity, trustworthiness, and goodwill; and enthusiasm in giving a speech. Each speaker has some credibility before giving an oral presentation. For example, a person considered to be an expert in a particular field because of her or his previous competence and authority carries this credibility along to a speaking engagement.

When you present a speech, your truthfulness, goodwill, and overall reputation will influence an audience's evaluation of your presentation. Of course every time you speak, that particular presentation enhances or diminishes credibility. Your poise and diction in delivery and presentation of facts in an organized, convincing manner will help to establish audience rapport. This rapport leads to increased credibility. Therefore, your total credibility is influenced both by how the audience perceives you prior to the presentation as well as by the impressions you create during the presentation.

## ANALYSIS OF THE AUDIENCE

Since the goal of an oral presentation is to change the behavior or attitude of the audience, a presentation must focus on their interests and attitudes. When analyzing these factors, you should consider the *demographics* and *size* of the group.

## Demographics

Such characteristics as age, sex, occupation, education, religious preference, and geographical background are all characteristics that provide clues about an audience's values, beliefs, and attitudes. These clues help the speaker adjust the message to the interests and level of the audience.

In predicting attitudes, two factors are essential—why people are attending a particular oral presentation and what views they are likely to have about the topic. In business, people generally attend presentations because they are required to do so or possibly because they are interested in the subject matter and wish to learn more about it.

The audience's willingness to attend a presentation affects how well they receive it. However, attendance does not guarantee a positive attitude toward the topic of the presentation. The more opposition a group may have toward the topic, the harder the speaker needs to work to persuade them or to win their approval.

The group's background, education, and knowledge of the subject will have a direct effect on the language chosen and the content of the presentation. Because listeners do not have the opportunity to review or repeat portions of an oral presentation as they could re-read a written message, the ideas and language need to be especially appropriate for the level of the audience.

If you use language that is too simple, you may bore or offend the listeners. On the other hand, jargon or overly difficult language will frustrate the audience. A level of difficulty and detail that is intended for the "average" members of an audience is probably best. More well-informed individuals generally will not mind the detail and background explanation.

## Size

The larger the audience, the more formal the presentation should be. Larger audiences are more difficult to communicate with because the listeners' knowledge of the topic, attitudes, and educational background are likely to vary widely. Since a small audience is generally more homogeneous and cohesive, the presentation can be less formal for small groups. The size of the group will also affect such factors as audiovisual aids and means of delivery, as discussed in Chapter 18. The presenter must ensure that all members of an audience can hear and see the presentation.

# STEPS OF PREPARATION

Once you have determined the purpose of your oral presentation and have analyzed the prospective audience, eight important steps remain in preparing for your presentation. These steps are as follows:

1. Determine the objective(s).
2. Research the subject.
3. Consider the time allotment.
4. Outline the presentation.
5. Use transitional aids.
6. Plan the use of audiovisual aids.
7. Control nervousness.
8. Rehearse the presentation.

## Determine the Objective(s)

The first step in planning an oral presentation is to determine the objective or objectives of the presentation. The objectives, which are based on the results that the speaker has achieved or would like to achieve, should be stated in specific terms. The following examples show a specific objective derived from the general purpose of each planned presentation:

GENERAL PURPOSE: to inform
SPECIFIC OBJECTIVE: to explain the exact steps in using a new electronic mail system

GENERAL PURPOSE: to persuade
SPECIFIC OBJECTIVE: to convince the production department to convert to the use of a networked computer system for inventory control

## Research the Subject

In researching a subject, you may use a number of sources. Many companies have their own specialized libraries; public, college, and university libraries are also good sources of information. Individuals having years of experience in a particular area may draw on their own knowledge and expertise. In addition, you can consult fellow workers and outside experts. When using outside sources or consultants, remember to give credit to those sources, or your credibility as a speaker may suffer.

## Consider the Time Allotment

Before making an outline, consider the time allotment for the presentation. In most cases, the speaker will have a time limit. Going beyond the allotted time will do nothing to achieve your goal of changing your audience's behavior or way of thinking. In fact, being insensitive to other people's time is likely to alienate the audience.

Keep your presentation as short as possible if no time has been allotted. Holding an audience's attention beyond 15 to 20 minutes is difficult without the use of questions or visual aids. Keep a wrist watch on the lectern and observe the audience for nonverbal cues (yawns, lack of eye contact, nodding heads) while you are giving an oral presentation. Because a preceding speaker may have used part of your allotted time, be prepared to adjust your presentation to the time you actually have when you address the audience. An effective speaker knows when to stop talking.

## Outline the Presentation

The outline of an oral presentation consists of three parts — the *introduction*, the *body*, and the *conclusion*. The next three sections discuss each of these parts in detail.

**The Introduction**. The first few moments of a presentation should be devoted to the introduction. If you have not been formally introduced, you need to tell the audience who you are and give a brief self-description to establish credibility.

Next, you need to capture the attention of your audience. A number of techniques can be used such as showing an eye-catching visual aid.

---

```
    Marilyn Green is a public relations specialist for a
large university. Her primary responsibility is vis-
iting high schools and community colleges to recruit
business majors for the university.

    Marilyn is a very popular speaker, and her presen-
tations are always interesting. When Marilyn gives her
standard recruiting speech, she begins the presenta-
tion by asking the question, "Why would you want to be
a business major at State University?" She then pulls
a bundle of dollar bills from her coat pocket and
shows it to the audience. From that point on, she
holds the audience spellbound.

    The University's Director of Public Relations plans
to retire at the end of the year. He is seriously
considering recommending Marilyn for his job.
```

---

Other ways to attract interest include the following techniques:

1. Tell a story that makes an appropriate point.
2. Quote a recognized expert.
3. Ask a question or questions to stimulate interest.

4. Make an astonishing statement that may be either factual or hypothetical in nature.
5. State the benefits of your presentation as they relate to your audience.
6. Refer to a current event that relates to your purpose.
7. Use humor only if it is relevant to your topic. Remember that a business presentation is not for entertainment but for serious undertaking of business to be accomplished.

Once you have captured the attention of your audience, give the purpose of your presentation. This step is very important, for it allows your audience to focus on this theme and to follow your presentation more effectively.

Finally, establish rapport with your audience. You need to win your listeners over immediately by your friendliness, your sincerity and honesty, and your confidence in the importance of your presentation.

A final note about the introduction is to remember that the psychological principles of primacy and recency (discussed in Chapter 4) also apply to oral presentations. First impressions are essential. The extent to which your audience is supportive of your ideas will be affected by those first few critical moments.

**The Body**. The **body** is the core of your presentation and consists of main ideas and supporting ideas. Main ideas, which are based on your general purpose and specific objective, are points you want your audience to remember. Since listeners are not able to grasp and retain many ideas during an oral presentation, one or two main ideas are best, with probably no more than three or four supporting points.

Supporting points verify, substantiate, or reinforce the main idea or ideas. To make your presentation more understandable, use any or all of the following forms of supporting evidence:

1. *Analogies*. When drawing an analogy, a speaker compares two different things by stressing the similarities. An example might be to compare the development of a flowchart for a computer program to following exit signs on a freeway.
2. *Examples*. Using examples or representations of particular situations can support the speaker's points. Examples generally help to clarify statements. The important point in using examples is to make sure that the example is representative of the point being made and is understandable to the audience.
3. *Quotations*. The use of quotations or testimonials (citing opinions or statements of other individuals) may also support the speaker's points. When quoting someone, be certain that the audience considers the source credible and that the quoted passage relates to your purpose. People who are not famous may be cited so long as you establish who they are and why their words can be considered authoritative.
4. *Statistics*. An effective way to present quantitative information is by using statistics. In contrast, too many statistics can be boring or difficult to

understand; and sometimes they can be misleading. However, appropriate statistics can vividly show the relationship between items and can accurately indicate trends.

Organize main ideas and supporting points in a logical and consistent sequence. (Chapter 4 "Organizing Written Communication" contains a discussion of various organization plans.) The most effective plan depends upon the purpose of your presentation.

**The Conclusion**. The **conclusion** or ending is the last impression you will make. This impression, which will remain with your audience, will help influence the change in behavior or attitude in your audience that occurs because of your presentation. When concluding, be forceful and positive. Give your listeners some indication that you are ending by using one or a combination of the following techniques:

1. Summarize the main idea(s) and supporting points.
2. If appropriate, suggest or challenge the audience to take a definite course of action.
3. Propose a solution or solutions.
4. Ask for approval of a request.
5. Quote a pertinent source.

An example of a hypothetical outline is shown as follows:

TENTATIVE PRESENTATION OUTLINE

  I.  Introduction
     A.  Introduce self (if necessary)
     B.  Capture audience attention
     C.  State purpose of presentation
     D.  Establish rapport with audience
  II.  Body
     A.  Present first main idea
        1.  Supporting point
        2.  Supporting point
     B.  Present second main idea
        1.  Supporting point
        2.  Supporting point
 III.  Conclusion

## Use Transitional Aids

Integrating the introduction with the body and the conclusion requires good transition. This transition can be accomplished in part by tone of voice, voice inflection, pauses, gestures, and audiovisual aids. Even more important are transitional words that help the listener move smoothly from one point to the next, that show the relationship between parts and ideas, and that unify the development of the parts into the whole. (See Chapter 4, pages 77–78, for a list of transitional words.)

## Plan the Use of Audiovisual Aids

Speakers use audiovisual aids effectively in oral presentations for one or a combination of the following purposes:

1. To provide variation and to maintain interest during the presentation
2. To facilitate the direction of the presentation
3. To clarify, interpret, confirm, represent, and define critical ideas presented

The type of audiovisual aid used depends upon the purpose of the oral presentation. Visual aids such as charts, graphs, and tables are good for emphasizing specific points, are fairly inexpensive, and may employ color effectively. Flip charts or easel pads are two other ways to introduce data visually during the presentation. Chalk boards or felt-tip boards are useful in presenting material that does not need to be retained. However, writing on the board does require an interruption of a presentation and takes up time as well. Overhead-projector transparencies can project printed or graphic material. Additional information can be marked on the transparencies with special pens.

Videotapes, audiotapes, films, slides, and filmstrips provide a highly professional touch to presentations. However, cost and time may be deterring factors in the development of original audiovisual productions. Computer graphics are discussed in Chapter 10.

The following points are helpful hints for using audiovisual aids during oral presentations:

1. Preview all commercially prepared materials such as tapes and films for defects.
2. *Prior* to your presentation, check your audiovisual equipment to make sure it is working properly.
3. Keep the line of sight of members of your audience open. Do not block vision by poor arrangement of equipment or room layout — everyone must be able to see.
4. Make sure visual aids are large enough for everyone in the group to see. To avoid distracting your audience, keep audiovisual aids out of sight until needed.
5. Provide a summary handout, including visual aids, if you want participants focusing their full attention on your presentation rather than concentrating on taking notes. Do not distribute the handout in advance, however, or the audience may read the handout instead of listening to you.

6. Keep all audiovisual aids simple. Present only one idea or concept at a time. Do not "overload" your audience by straining both their visual and auditory channels.
7. Talk to your audience and not to your audiovisual aids.

All these considerations are important. However, the primary criterion in determining the usefulness of an audiovisual aid is whether it will help to achieve the purpose of your oral presentation.

## Control Nervousness

If in the opening vignette Mac had simply attempted to "psych" himself to eliminate anxiety before his presentations, he probably would have failed to do so. The confidence and poise he needs can result only from systematic training and practice (Rogers, 1982, 17).

Stage fright is a perfectly normal reaction to a stressful situation. Speaking before a group singles out the speaker as the leader. The speaker is expected to be in charge and to have everything under control. Eliminating nervousness in a high-pressure situation is difficult because the body automatically responds to stress by increasing the production of adrenalin, which is a stimulant to the central nervous system. However, some speakers actually use this biological impulse as a source of energy to give a more enthusiastic, animated presentation.

Here are a few helpful ways to deal with stage fright:

1. Set a realistic goal. Do not expect perfection. Visualize a speaking situation as a positive effort and not as a battle of "you against them." Concentrate on your topic and not on what the audience might be thinking of you.
2. Breathe to release excess energy and relieve tension. Make a conscious effort to pause and breathe at moments of nervousness. Focusing on breathing will slow down your reflexes, give you more control, and allow you time to think as you speak.
3. Channel the remaining nervous energy into your talk. Your excited inner feelings can convey your enthusiasm for your topic to your audience. Thus, a state of excitement can become a positive source of energy that adds to your effectiveness as a speaker.
4. Practice, practice, practice. Every successful presentation will make the next one easier.

## Rehearse the Presentation

Rehearsing a presentation or going through a dry run is often a neglected step in preparing for an oral presentation. However, rehearsing is necessary to ensure a polished delivery.

Depending upon your experience as a speaker, the amount of practice you need may vary. A novice may want to begin practicing with a cassette recorder to check the time, speed of delivery, and overall flow of ideas. Next, practice facial expressions and gestures in front of a mirror. Rehearsing before a colleague can provide constructive criticism and suggestions for improvement. Finally, duplicate the conditions of your actual presentation as much as possible. This strategy will eliminate most surprises during your actual presentation and will familiarize you with the room arrangement and the audiovisual equipment.

Rehearsing can boost your confidence in addition to helping you improve the wording, identify flaws, and check out audiovisual aids and equipment. Through repeated rehearsals, your material becomes part of your stored memory and reduces the fear of "going blank." If making a presentation seems to be an awkward role for you, repeated rehearsals will help you to feel more comfortable in the role of presenter. Having doubts about your capabilities will more than likely be conveyed to your audience and do little for your credibility.

A word of caution—do not over-rehearse. Striving for perfection in delivery may make your presentation stiff, mechanical, and headed straight for failure. An occasional "um" will make your delivery sound more natural.

## DELIVERY OF THE PRESENTATION

Delivery is the final task in oral presentation after determining the purpose, analyzing the prospective audience, and preparing the presentation. Delivery of a presentation includes the following factors:

1. Modes of delivery
2. Use of visual and vocal cues
3. Audience participation

### Modes of Delivery

Two basic modes of delivery exist for making oral presentations—*unplanned* and *planned*. Each type of delivery has its advantages and disadvantages.

**Unplanned**. When you are asked to speak on the spur of the moment with little or no preparation, you are giving an **unplanned** (*impromptu*) **delivery**. The major advantage of this type of delivery is its spontaneity. Its major disadvantage is that unplanned presentations are usually poorly organized. Impromptu delivery occurs most often in conferences as a direct result of some question or issue arising out of the discussion. Because of their experience, executives often may be called upon to say a few words on such occasions. However, if an individual has nothing to contribute on a subject, he or she should decline the invitation to speak.

**Planned**. Three types of planned modes of delivery are the memorized, the textual, and the extemporaneous delivery.

1. *Memorized delivery*, which is probably the least effective of the three types of planned delivery, has several limitations. Since the entire text is memorized, the speaker runs the risk of forgetting something. Memorized delivery tends to become very mechanical and unnatural because it lacks spontaneity. The only advantage this mode offers is that it allows for precise wording and use of eye contact, gestures, and movement.

2. *Textual delivery*, or reading from a manuscript, is effective for complex presentations and for presentations having statistics or other vital information that must be conveyed accurately. A major disadvantage of this type of delivery is that it tends to be boring. If a presenter is merely standing before an audience and reading a paper without any eye contact, voice inflection, or gestures, the paper might just as well have been duplicated and sent to the members of the audience. With sufficient rehearsal and an informal delivery and writing style, this mode can be acceptable. However, the presenter should be careful not to allow the manuscript to become a barrier between her or him and the audience.

3. *Extemporaneous delivery* is used most often in business settings. This mode of delivery requires careful thought and planning but little or no memorizing. Extemporaneous delivery allows the speaker to have great spontaneity and be flexible in adapting to audience feedback.

    The speaker generally uses notes, and the format of these notes depends upon the speaker's choice. Some speakers use simple note cards (4" x 6" or 5" x 7"), while others prefer full-sized sheets of paper. A well-organized outline typed on note cards is easy to hold and allows for details to be filled in from memory. The speaker should avoid reading word for word. The outline format provides enough structure to aid delivery but still allows enough flexibility to make minor changes if necessary.

    You can personalize the notes by writing cue words such as "pause," "more emphasis here," or "smile" in the margin. Try using color and underlining to highlight important points. Jot insertions in the margins about use of visual aids and gestures. Remember to number your cards in case you should accidentally shuffle or drop them. If the cards get out of sequence, you can quickly rearrange them and continue.

## Visual and Vocal Cues

The actual delivery of an oral presentation should enhance the content of the message. Delivery that does not distract from content involves a number of visual and vocal cues, as follows:

**Eye Contact and Facial Expression**. Eye contact is probably the most important nonverbal cue used in oral presentations. Maintaining eye contact with your audience keeps the audience involved. Attempt to make eye contact as naturally as possible, as if you were talking with the individuals. Instead of glancing at just a few people in front, try to make all the members of the audience a part of your presentation. However, you will not be able to establish eye contact with many people in very large audiences.

Facial expressions can also complement verbal messages. A delivery with a variety of facial expressions is more favorable than one that lacks expression.

**Posture, Gestures, and Body Movement.** To convey alertness and to command attention, keep your body erect without appearing stiff. Try to appear relaxed without slouching. Natural-looking gestures can reinforce and emphasize points or aid in transition of ideas or parts. However, if gestures are not natural, they may be distracting.

Movement can add variety to a presentation. For example, moving from one spot to another can be used for transition. Moving forward can be used to emphasize a point. Pacing back and forth, however, draws attention to the movement rather than to what is being said. A fixed microphone, on the other hand, restricts the speaker's movement too much.

**Rate of Delivery.** If you speak too rapidly, the audience may have difficulty following your presentation. On the other hand, speaking too slowly may cause an audience to become bored. To avoid both problems, vary the rate of delivery. Important points or difficult concepts should be spoken at a slower rate, while ideas that are easy to understand should be spoken at a faster rate. Pauses can also add variety, as long as they are not filled with "you know" and "ah." Too long a pause can also break a listener's concentration.

**Volume and Pitch.** The volume should be loud enough so that everyone can hear. You can indicate emphasis through variations in volume. Talking at a consistent pitch or in a monotone will divert your audience's interest. Varying the pitch is a key to using your voice effectively.

**Pronunciation.** Listeners react to the speaker's grammar and word pronunciation and tend to make negative judgments about a speaker's intelligence, education, and expertise if he or she does not speak precisely. Some common mispronunciations that undermine good delivery are "yeah" for "yes," "shouda" for "should have," or "kin" for "can."

## Audience Feedback

Speakers receive two forms of audience feedback—*indirect feedback* and *questions*. The next two sections discuss these forms of feedback.

**Indirect Feedback.** This type of audience feedback occurs during a presentation. An experienced speaker is alert to **indirect feedback**, most of which is nonverbal. Puzzled looks or blank stares are cues that the audience may not be following the presentation. Nodding heads, smiles, and applause tell the speaker that the audience is reacting positively. Depending upon the audience's reactions, a speaker should attempt to adjust the presentation accordingly. In addition, indirect feedback can help the speaker to improve the presentation for the next time he or she needs to deliver it.

**Questions.** The appropriate time for questions from the audience is left to the discretion of the speaker, who should let the audience know at the beginning when questions can be asked. Questions can provide necessary clarification and assure understanding. You should plan time for answering questions from the audience, but be direct and brief in answering so that your presentation does not extend past its allotted time. Avoid getting off the subject, whether questions are answered during or after a presentation.

Keep the following points in mind when handling questions:

1. Repeat the question so that everyone can hear it.
2. Be sure that you and your audience understand the question before you answer it.
3. Direct your response to the entire audience and not just to the person asking the question.
4. If you cannot answer a question, say so and offer to do further research about the question.
5. Stop incoming questions by asking for only one or two more questions.

In summary, speaker credibility and audience analysis are necessary for successful oral presentations. An effective delivery results from thorough preparation and rehearsal of the presentation, which will improve with practice.

# DICTATION

Dictation, either into a machine or directly to a secretary, is one of the many forms of oral business communication. **Dictation** is the process of transmitting information orally for the preparation of written business messages.

Although letters, memos, and reports sometimes are still written in longhand and given to a secretary to key on a typewriter or computer, writing in longhand is an inefficient method of producing business messages. Although an individual can write at about 20 words a minute, he or she can dictate the same information at about 80 to 100 words a minute. Dictation is generally a faster and, therefore, less expensive method than longhand for originating written business messages. Machine dictation is generally more convenient and faster than live dictation. Because it does not require a secretary to be present during dictation, machine dictation is also less expensive.

## Dictation Methods

Business writers generally use one of two methods of dictation—*"live"* or *machine dictation*. The method depends on the message being dictated and the equipment and office staff available.

**"Live" Dictation.** Dictating directly to a typist while the words are being typed is one form of "live" dictation. This technique is used primarily for short rush messages. However, this method is costly because it involves two people's time. The dictator must speak clearly and slowly enough for the keyboard operator to type the message. The first draft is generally a rough draft, which is later corrected and retyped.

Another method of "live" dictation is dictating to a secretary who uses shorthand to record the message. However, individuals who are capable of writing shorthand are becoming increasingly rare. In today's business environment, top-level executives usually have a personal secretary; but when starting out in business, you cannot expect this convenience. As with direct dictation, dictating to a secretary is costly because two salaries are involved at the same time. In addition, live dictation tends to become more time consuming because of interruptions such as important telephone calls. The major advantages, however, are immediate feedback in restating previously dictated material and instantaneous clarification and corrections.

**Machine Dictation.** Microphones and telephones are usual media for machine dictation, where information is recorded electronically on belts, tapes, disks, or cassettes. Dictation may be transcribed immediately or later. Machine dictation equipment can be either a portable hand-held unit, a desktop unit, or part of a centralized unit.

Portable dictation equipment, such as a battery-operated unit, is particularly useful when the dictator is away from the office. With portable equipment, a writer can dictate at home, in a car, in a hotel room, or almost anywhere. (See Figure 17.1.)

Desk-top units differ according to function. Some units only record messages; others only play back recorded messages for transcribing; and some perform both functions. A microphone is used and the dictated message is recorded on cassettes, tapes, disks, or belts. (See Figure 17.2.)

### FIGURE 17.1 PORTABLE DICTATION EQUIPMENT

Courtesy of Dictaphone Corporation

## FIGURE 17.2 MACHINE DICTATION EQUIPMENT

A—DESK-TOP UNIT

B—PLAY-BACK UNIT

A centralized dictation system uses telecommunication techniques and sophisticated word processing for convenience and efficiency. The dictator simply accesses the system with a telephone. The message is then immediately transcribed or recorded for later transcribing.

A machine dictation method still under development is voice-recognition equipment. This equipment "recognizes" an originator's spoken words and displays the message on a computer screen. Words not recognized or incorrectly displayed are keyed in either by the dictator or a secretary. Voice recognition is discussed in further detail in Chapter 19.

## Proper Dictation Techniques

Dictation is a process that should involve three phases — *preparing to dictate*, *dictating the message*, and *checking the transcribed message*. All three phases involve skills that a dictator can develop.

**Preparing to Dictate**. Efficient dictators must be well organized. Just as you need to prepare before writing a message, you need to prepare to dictate a message. Preparing to dictate involves four important steps, as follows:

1. *Gather the information*. Have the correspondence you are answering — a letter, a memo, or a report — available. In addition, you may need files containing previous correspondence or other pertinent materials.
2. *Visualize the reader*. Form a mental picture of the receiver either from previous correspondence or by inferences. This process will make your dictation more natural. The mental picture may also help reduce any reluctance you may have about talking to a machine or dictating to a secretary.
3. *Plan the message*. For an experienced dictator, planning the message may simply require making a few mental notes. A less experienced dictator may either write a few notes on the correspondence received or make an outline of the message. An important consideration in planning dictation is to determine the purpose of the message. Organize the message according to that purpose.
4. *Prepare for the actual dictation session*. Preparation for dictating includes setting a specific time for dictation. Some executives prefer morning hours after they have reviewed their mail. If you are using the "live" dictation method, you need to schedule a time when the dictation likely will not be interrupted. When using machine dictation, be sure that you have an extra cassette or disk and that your equipment is in proper working order.

**Dictating the Message**. Before you dictate the actual message, always dictate instructions to the person who will transcribe the message. If you are using a centralized dictation system, you will need to identify yourself, your department, and your telephone number. This step is important because word-processing centers using centralized dictation systems may have a large number of both full-time and part-time employees transcribing messages for many departments.

Following your identification, indicate the following information:

1. The date
2. The type of message—a letter, a memo, minutes, a report
3. The format to be used—a blocked letter, open punctuation, a bound report, etc.
4. The type of transcription—a rough draft, a revision, or a final copy
5. Any special stationery to be used
6. The number of copies needed
7. The priority of the items—routine, rush, etc.
8. Any special mailing instructions, such as registered, certified, express mail, etc.
9. The need for enclosures and what they are
10. The name and address (spelled) of the receiver if this information is not already available to the transcriber

Throughout the remainder of the dictation, use good dictation techniques to make your job and the transcriber's job easy. The following list includes helpful dictation techniques:

1. *Speak clearly and spell all unusual words, names, and words that sound similar*. The following examples include words that may be easily confused:

|  |  |
|---|---|
| affect | effect |
| personnel | personal |
| brake | break |
| principal | principle |
| disburse | disperse |
| than | then |
| higher | hire |
| your | you're |

2. *Talk at an even rate to separate words clearly*. The best pace for dictation is a little slower than normal conversation. Avoid distractions such as smoking, background music or other noises, speaking with your hands in front of your mouth, chewing gum, eating, or pacing back and forth.
3. *Dictate unusual punctuation*. Specifying all punctuation marks is not necessary when dictating to a skilled transcriber. Use voice inflection and pauses to indicate standard punctuation such as commas, periods, semicolons, and question marks. However, specify other punctuation such as dashes, parentheses, and exclamation points.
4. *Indicate other instructions*. Other instructions should include indicating such items as paragraphs, underlining, indentions, listings, columns, capitalization, and quotations.

5. *Avoid extraneous remarks.* Statements that are not part of the message only tend to confuse the transcriber. Such comments as "I think that is correct" or "Check that figure" should be avoided unless they are part of the dictated message. If extraneous remarks are necessary, preface these comments by saying "Transcriber, please check that figure" or use the individual's name, "Terri, please check that figure."

6. *Indicate corrections.* If corrections are necessary, simply say "Correction," and then dictate the change.

7. *Avoid lengthy pauses.* If you are interrupted, turn off the dictating machine. When you resume, rewind the machine to hear what you dictated last.

8. *Play back a recorded message.* To ensure that it has been recorded clearly, replay the entire message and listen to it.

9. *Indicate closing information.* Closing information includes your title and department, enclosures to be included, how copies are to be distributed, any other special instructions, and a statement such as "End of letter" to indicate the end of the message.

10. *Thank the transcriber.* Your courtesy to those who transcribe your messages is important for maintaining good working relationships.

**Checking the Transcribed Message.** The person who originated a message, not the person who transcribed it, is responsible for its accuracy. Therefore, proofread all transcribed messages carefully before signing or approving them for distribution. If only minor corrections such as a missing comma are necessary, insert the corrections neatly with a black pen. However, if major corrections are needed, indicate them with proofreader's marks (specified in Appendix A) and return the document to the appropriate individual for corrections.

## SUMMARY

Many of the principles of written communication apply to oral presentations. Unlike written messages, however, effective oral presentations involve control of the audience, immediate feedback, and visual cues such as the speaker's facial expression and gestures. A speaker's credibility and analysis of the audience are essential for successful presentations.

Steps in preparation include determining the specific objective, researching the subject, considering the time allotment, outlining the presentation, using transitional aids, planning the use of audiovisual aids, controlling nervousness, and rehearsing the presentation. The presentation outline includes three parts — the introduction, the body, and the conclusion. Finally, the delivery of the presentation includes considerations on different modes of delivery, visual and vocal cues, and audience feedback.

The use of dictation rather than longhand to originate messages can save a business both time and money. Two methods of dictation — live or machine—may be used, depending on the type of message, the equipment, and the available office staff. Effective dictators must plan and organize, use good dictation techniques, and carefully check the transcribed message. Mastery of appropriate dictation skills can improve the overall efficiency of preparing written messages.

## CHAPTER REVIEW

1.  List and briefly explain three differences between written messages and oral presentations.
2.  List five reasons for giving oral presentations.
3.  What is the ultimate goal of oral presentations?
4.  Give an example of a situation that might damage a speaker's credibility.
5.  Why are *demographics* and *size* important in analyzing an audience?
6.  Describe the eight steps in preparing for an oral presentation.
7.  List the parts of a presentation outline.
8.  Define "supporting evidence" and list four types of supporting evidence.
9.  Describe how you would rehearse for an oral presentation.
10. Discuss the advantages and disadvantages of the following modes of delivery: *unplanned*, *memorized*, *textual*, and *extemporaneous*.
11. Explain why dictating saves time and money in comparison to producing messages in longhand.
12. Identify the two methods of dictation; discuss how they are used and identify the major differences between them.
13. List four steps in preparing to dictate.
14. List the items that should be included in the instructions to the transcriber before dictating the actual message.
15. React to this statement: The transcriber is responsible for the accuracy of the transcribed message.

## APPLICATIONS

1.  In a current business periodical such as *BARRON'S*, *Forbes*, or *Business Week* find an article that discusses a controversial business issue or a new business development. Prepare a 3-5 minute oral presentation about that article. Use at least one visual aid as part of your presentation.

2.  If possible, have your presentation in No. 1 videotaped. Critique your presentation for content, preparation, and delivery.

3.  Analyze an oral presentation that is either live or on television. Write a short description of the purpose of the presentation, the credibility of the speaker, and the delivery techniques. Analyze the parts of the presentation, including the introduction, the supporting evidence used within the body, and the conclusion.

4. Create a fictitious new product for an imaginary company. Prepare a persuasive sales presentation about that product. Your instructor will determine the length of the presentation and other details.

5. Using an example of a letter or memo you wrote previously for this class, dictate that same letter using available dictation equipment.

6. Choose a letter or memo given as an example in Chapter 5, 6, or 7 and dictate a response to that example using available dictation equipment.

7. If your school has shorthand or machine-transcription classes, dictate a message either to a shorthand student or to a machine for transcription. Ask the person who transcribes to evaluate your dictation. Then evaluate the transcribed document.

## CASE STUDY

Carolyn Darner, manager of the sales division of a large computer firm, was in a hurry. She had just returned from a week-long conference, and now she needed to return a number of phone calls and answer several letters.

As a first step, Carolyn decided to dictate a few letters that had to go out right away. She called Vicki Garcia to her office to take dictation.

"Now, where is that letter I was going to answer?" Carolyn asked, leafing through the papers on her desk. Vicki sat quietly while Carolyn looked for the letter. "Okay, here it is. Now, let's see . . . ." Carolyn skimmed over the letter and began dictating.

"'Dear Paul,' no—let's start out, 'Dear Mr. Sareko. I want to thank you.' Sorry, Vicki, let's start over. 'Dear Mr. Sareko, Thank you for your letter.' No, Vicki, make it, 'Thank you for your inquiry about our services.' Change that to 'products and services.'"

Carolyn stopped. "You know," she said to Vicki, "maybe I'd better answer this other letter first, as it's more urgent. Let's start out, 'Dear Ms. Riley, We are pleased to inform you about'—no, Vicki, sorry, let's make it, 'We are pleased to tell you about our new portable computer.' Oh, great, look at this! A note from the vice president about a meeting today, of all times. Can you find the file I'll need for the meeting?"

Vicki left Carolyn's office to find the file. She sighed heavily as she left the room.

Carolyn sorted through the papers on her desk again. "Vicki just isn't keeping up with my workload," she thought to herself. "I'll have to talk with her about it when I have time."

1. Why was the dictation session unproductive? Explain your answer.
2. What advice would you give Ms. Darner about how to dictate more effectively?

## REFERENCES

Natalie H. Rogers, *Talk-Power—How to Speak Without Fear, A Systematic Training Program* (New York: Dodd, Mead and Company, 1982), 17.

## SUGGESTED READINGS

Bates, Jefferson D. *Dictating Effectively—A Time-Saving Manual*. Washington, D.C.: Acropolis Books Ltd., 1981.

Kenny, Michael. *Presenting Yourself*. New York: John Wiley & Sons, Inc., 1982.

Leech, Thomas. *How to Prepare, Stage, and Deliver Winning Presentations*. New York: American Management Associations, 1982.

Linver, Sandy. *Speak and Get Results—The Complete Guide to Presentations and Speeches that Work in any Business Situation*. New York: Summit Books, 1983.

Smith, Terry C. *Making Successful Presentations—A Self-Teaching Guide*. New York: John Wiley & Sons, Inc., 1984.

# BUSINESS MEETINGS

## CHAPTER 18

After a business meeting, the following conversation may be typical:

Alice: "What did you think of today's department meeting, Juan?"
Juan: "That meeting really dragged on. How boring!"
Alice: "That's for sure! The same few people did all the talking, and most people didn't talk at all."
Juan: "After all that hot air, no final decisions were made anyway. I still don't know what we are supposed to do next."
Alice: "Me neither! We seem to have a meeting every Tuesday whether we need one or not."

Business meetings should be more productive than the one that Alice and Juan attended. As a form of nonwritten communication, meetings can be an effective way for people to accomplish common goals within an organization.

A meeting takes place whenever three or more people work together face to face to (1) present information or create new ideas, (2) report facts and opinions and receive feedback, or (3) solve problems and make decisions. This chapter discusses the following topics as they relate to this definition of meetings:

- Importance of meetings
- Policy for meetings
- Planning meetings
- Duties of the leader
- Role of the participant
- Follow-up activities

## IMPORTANCE OF MEETINGS

Why hold a meeting? What are some of the positive aspects of meetings?

One of the major advantages of meetings is that a group can solve a complex problem more easily than an individual can. The experience and knowledge of a group of people can provide many more new solutions and alternatives than that of one person. A second advantage of meetings is that a number of people with a common interest can hear a message at one time rather than individually. This collective presentation will reduce communication problems because participants can ask questions for clarification and receive immediate feedback. A third advantage is that participants who are involved in the decision-making process generally experience a firm commitment to the results. Therefore, employees' morale may improve because of their participation in meetings.

## POLICY FOR MEETINGS

For meetings to be productive, a company should have a policy about meetings and adhere to that policy. The subject matter and the purpose of the meeting, the participants, the structure of the meeting, and the minutes should all be part of a company's policy.

Meetings may be called for one or more of the following reasons:

1. To create (or generate) new ideas
2. To disseminate facts or to state opinions
3. To provide instructions
4. To solve a problem or to make a decision

Give participants advance notice of each meeting so that they are prepared to participate. Use an action verb, such as "study," "adopt," "plan," or "identify" within announcements to communicate clearly the purpose of each meeting. Define topics to be considered as part of a meeting so that participants will know what they are supposed to accomplish in the meeting. An example of a notification for a meeting is shown in Figure 18.1.

### Participants at a Meeting

Various types of meetings differ in number and composition. If the group is too small, participants may not have enough collective knowledge to make a decision about an action to be taken. On the other hand, too many participants may generate unwieldy numbers of facts and opinions. Consider the following factors in determining how many individuals should attend a meeting:

1. The nature of the group involved; for example, department meetings generally involve all department members
2. The purpose of the meeting; for example, for a board meeting, the number of members may be set by a company's constitution or bylaws

## FIGURE 18.1 SAMPLE MEETING NOTIFICATION

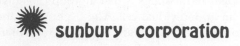 **sunbury corporation**          INTEROFFICE COMMUNICATION

      TO:    Sue Kato
              Maria Lopez
              Joe Morgan
              Bill Smith

   FROM:    Frank Torres, Sales Manager

   DATE:    April 19, 19--

SUBJECT:    Purpose of Next Week's Departmental Meeting

The Sales Department will meet next Tuesday, April 26, promptly
at 2 p.m. in the Conference Room to discuss the possible
purchase and installation of a new computer inventory system.

Please review and bring the attached documents about this new
system.  Consider how you might use this system on a daily or
weekly basis.  Be prepared to name what you consider to be the
advantages and disadvantages of this new system.  Each member's
opinion is vital to this decision.

sa

Attachment

3. The time available for accomplishing the purpose of the meeting; if time is short, appoint only a few members to a committee, as small groups tend to be more efficient than large ones

Weigh the following additional criteria in selecting participants. People who satisfy one or more of these criteria may be included as participants in meetings:

1. Individuals whose positions require their attendance; for example, a sales manager at a weekly sales meeting
2. Individuals who need to know what will occur during the meeting; for example, people whose jobs are directly affected by the outcome of the meeting
3. Individuals who will have to carry out the decisions made at the meeting; for example, the head of the purchasing department should attend a management meeting in which "purchase of 500 microcomputers" is the main item on the agenda
4. Individuals whose technical knowledge can serve as a resource; for example, a computer systems analyst, when a company is considering a new computer system (Hays, 1969, 157)

## Structure of a Meeting

An agenda or a list of items to be discussed helps provide **structure** to the meeting. The agenda may be informal—oral comments, a note, a reference in a memo or letter, or a brief written announcement. A formal agenda should contain the following items:

1. Specific topics that are to be covered, listed in order from high priority to low priority
2. Reference to accompanying reports or other information that might pertain to agenda topics; attach these materials to the agenda
3. An identification of the person(s) responsible for each topic
4. An estimation of time allocation for each topic

A formal agenda is shown in Figure 18.2.

# PLANNING MEETINGS

A few fundamental areas to consider when you plan a meeting are *preparing and distributing materials*, *choosing the location and seating arrangement*, and determining whether to use *formal or informal procedures* in conducting the meeting.

## Preparing and Distributing Materials

Three problems sometimes occur in the distribution of materials for meetings—(1) the participants at a meeting may receive too much reading mate-

FIGURE 18.2 SAMPLE FORMAL AGENDA

AGENDA

XYZ Corporation

Monthly Board of Directors Meeting

Wednesday, September 15, 19--, 1:30 p.m.

Conference Room

| Time | Item | Presenter |
|---|---|---|
| 1:30 p.m. | Call to Order<br>Approval of August 15<br>　　Minutes | Evelyn Jones, Chair<br>Robert Cheng, Executive Secretary |
| 1:35 p.m. | Financial Report (Mailed<br>　　August 30) | David Goldberg,<br>　　Vice President of<br>　　Accounting |
| 1:40 p.m. | CEO Report<br>　　(Summary attached) | Samuel Garcia, Chief<br>　　Executive Officer |
| 2:00 p.m. | Unfinished Business: | |
| | Resolution regarding<br>　　purchase of computer<br>　　conferencing equipment<br>　　(Copy attached) | Marian Brown,<br>　　Director of<br>　　Communications |
| 2:15 p.m. | New Business: | |
| | Approval of new net-<br>　　working system | Sylvia Lopez,<br>　　Director of Data<br>　　Processing |
| | Other Business | Evelyn Jones |
| 3:00 p.m. | Announcements<br>Adjournment | Evelyn Jones<br>Evelyn Jones |

rial in advance and generally be tardy in studying it thoroughly, (2) a stack of handouts may be piled on the chairs when participants arrive at a meeting, with no time to read the materials; or (3) participants may not receive any information in advance. To help eliminate these problems, follow these guidelines:

- Distribute *only* those materials that are essential for the purpose of the meeting.
- Provide condensed versions of long documents for quick review and make available entire documents for further examination as necessary.
- Distribute materials for meetings one to two weeks in advance. If distributed much earlier, the materials will be forgotten or misplaced. If materials are distributed much later, participants may not have enough time to study them.

## Choosing the Location and Seating Arrangement

The location is an essential consideration in planning a meeting. Large meetings (i.e., stockholders meetings of large corporations or meetings of trade associations) are held in auditoriums. The location of a smaller meeting may convey to participants whether the meeting is important or urgent. For example, having a meeting in the CEO's private conference room may indicate to participants the importance of the meeting.

The location of a meeting does, however, involve more than the obvious duties of choosing a room of adequate size. Providing comfortable chairs, adequate ventilation, lighting, and acoustics; or acquiring necessary audiovisual equipment are important considerations. If participants are required to travel to a meeting, arrange to hold it at a central location if possible.

Another factor in selecting a location is the relationship of the participants. For example, a meeting between a superior and subordinate will more than likely be held in the superior's office. Meetings between same-level employees may be held in someone's office or in a nearby meeting room. If a business is a service organization, meetings are often held at the office of a customer or client.

In important meetings where individuals involved are of equal or near-equal status, a neutral location may be best. For example, division vice presidents might meet in a neutral place rather than in anyone's office to avoid the impression that one participant is superior to another. A similar situation may occur in adversary meetings such as contract negotiations or employee grievances. A neutral meeting location outside of either party's territory may be better to avoid the impression that some one has an unfair advantage. The most important consideration is to choose a location compatible with the objectives of the meeting.

The seating arrangement within a meeting room may be even more important to the effectiveness of the meeting than the room itself. One of four basic arrangements is used for most meetings—rectangular, circular, U-shaped, and semicircular arrangement. The four arrangements are illustrated in Figure 18.3.

## FIGURE 18.3 SEATING ARRANGEMENTS

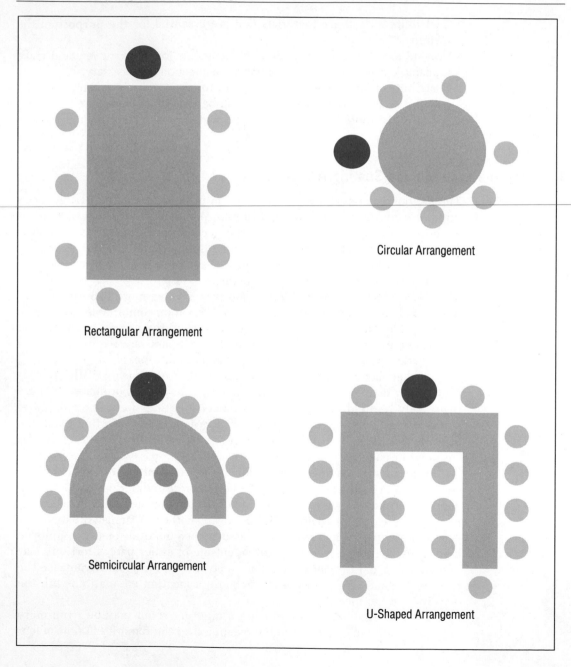

Rectangular Arrangement

Circular Arrangement

Semicircular Arrangement

U-Shaped Arrangement

The rectangular arrangement allows the leader to have excellent control of the meeting because all communication is directed toward the head of the table. This type of arrangement is particularly effective for formal meetings. For discussion purposes, the rectangular arrangement is advantageous because individuals seated opposite each other are more likely to talk to each other. However, if the table is too long, some of the participants might be out of the sight of the head of the table. This type of arrangement will make communication difficult because nonverbal cues such as eye contact, facial expression, and body movement will not be apparent to either the leader or participants.

The circular arrangement is particularly effective for informal meetings and for minimizing status positions. In a circle, the leader has less control than in any other arrangement. Because participants are seated side by side around a table or in a circle, communication channels are fairly equal among all members—no one has a dominant position. Use this type of arrangement for brainstorming for new ideas and for arriving at a decision when input from all participants is desired.

The U-shaped arrangement and the semicircular arrangement are particularly good for groups ranging from six to twelve members. In these two configurations, the leader has moderate control over the meeting. Visual contact and oral communication remain fairly good except for participants seated adjacent to the leader. This type of arrangement is desirable for semiformal meetings.

## Determining Formal or Informal Procedures

The purpose of a meeting determines the degree of formality that is appropriate. Using highly structured procedures may not be appropriate for department meetings, small committee meetings, informational and/or educational meetings, and the like. However, allowing discussions to ramble aimlessly without some structure may ensue with little or no effective results.

The term **parliamentary law** was the name given many years ago to the customs and rules used in carrying out business in the English Parliament. The term **parliamentary procedure** refers to parliamentary law, along with whatever other rules of order an organization may adopt. Formal rules and regulations for conducting a meeting (the *Pocket Manual of Rules of Order for Deliberative Assemblies*) were developed by General Henry M. Robert of the United States Army in 1867 (1970, xxi). Modern organizations needing a formal set of rules and regulations for conducting orderly meetings generally use *Robert's Rules of Order Newly Revised* as a reference.

Use parliamentary procedure as a regulator of formal meetings—as a means to ensure control of a meeting—particularly when a large number of people having a wide range of beliefs and values are involved in making decisions. For example, parliamentary procedure might be appropriate at a meeting of the board of directors of a large corporation or at an annual business meeting for a professional organization.

Too much emphasis on rules, however, can hamper the flow of communication if participants become too involved in the process of conducting the meeting rather than focusing on the issues at hand. Therefore, a meeting leader should be somewhat flexible in using parliamentary procedure.

Some of the basic vocabulary for parliamentary procedure is shown in Figure 18.4. Remember, though, that initially parliamentary procedure may seem very complex to participants who are unfamiliar with it. Facilitate communication by modifying parliamentary procedures appropriately for the participants of a meeting. Although a thorough understanding of parliamentary procedure is beyond the scope of this text, an awareness of some of the basics of parliamentary procedure may enhance your own participation as either a meeting leader or a participant.

## FIGURE 18.4 PARLIAMENTARY PROCEDURE TERMINOLOGY

PARLIAMENTARY PROCEDURE TERMINOLOGY

ADOPT: to approve a motion or amendment

AMEND: to change a motion by adding, deleting, or substituting words

CARRIED: to approve a motion or amendment by the necessary affirmative vote of the group

CLOSE DEBATE: to stop all discussion about a motion and to take a vote about it immediately

CONSIDERATION: to deliberate on a subject before taking a vote

DEBATE: to discuss a motion or an amendment pending before a group

DIVISION OF A GROUP: to take a vote by counting members, either by rising or by a show of hands, to verify a voice vote

FLOOR: the formal recognition by the chair allowing a member to speak

GERMANE: to pertain to or relate directly to in reference to the relationship of amendments to motions

LIMIT DEBATE: to restrict the amount of time for discussion or the number of speakers per question

MAIN MOTION: a motion presenting a subject to a group for discussion and decision

OBJECT TO CONSIDERATION: to oppose discussion and decision of a main motion

OUT OF ORDER: a matter of business that is inappropriate at that particular time according to proper order of business

POINT OF ORDER: to bring some error to the attention of the chair and other members for correction

POSTPONE INDEFINITELY: to kill a motion by deferring consideration indefinitely

PRECEDENCE: the order or priority of consideration of motions

PREVIOUS QUESTION: a motion to close debate and force an immediate vote (also known as "question")

QUORUM: the minimum number of members that must be present at a meeting for business to be transacted legally

RECONSIDER: a motion to cancel the effect of a vote so that the question may be reviewed and redecided

RESCIND: to cancel or nullify a motion from a previous meeting

SECOND: an indication of approval of consideration of a proposed motion without indicating favor for the motion

SUSPEND THE RULES: to set aside temporarily the rules of an organization to consider a particular question that normally would be out of order

TABLE: to postpone a motion until an undetermined time

TAKE FROM THE TABLE: a motion to consider a motion that had been previously tabled (postponed)

UNFINISHED BUSINESS: refers to business that was incomplete when the previous meeting adjourned (incorrectly called "old business")

WITHDRAW: a motion by a member to remove her or his motion from consideration

---

## DUTIES OF THE LEADER

The duties of the meeting leader include planning the meeting, notifying participants, developing an agenda, and choosing a location. As a rule, the meeting leader should not *lead* or dominate the meeting but rather should serve as a catalyst or stimulator for the meeting. He or she should stimulate discussion among participants to help achieve the goals of the meeting. Specific responsibilities of the meeting leader include *managing the meeting time, encouraging and controlling discussion*, and *summarizing and concluding the discussion*.

### Managing Time

If participants at a meeting are to realize the importance of punctuality, the leader must start the meeting on time. However, if a key participant such as a prospective customer is not on time, some flexibility may be necessary.

The agenda is the controlling device used during a meeting, and following it is necessary for managing time. The leader should try to keep within the allotted time for each individual item on the agenda. However, cutting off discussion for the sake of adhering to specific time limits may cause negative reactions and may even result in failure to fulfill the purpose of the meeting. The judgment of the leader is critical in permitting adequate time for discussion, in avoiding unnecessary repetition and details, and in modifying the agenda as needed.

Starting each meeting with a clear statement of the objective or purpose of the meeting will help in following the agenda. This early clarification of purpose sets the tone for the meeting. If participants get off the subject during a meeting, redirect discussion by a simple reference back to the appropriate item on the agenda.

Finishing on time is as important as starting on time. Meetings that do not progress evoke negative reactions from participants because time is an important resource in most organizations.

## Encouraging and Controlling Participants

Silent members at meetings can be just as much of a problem as overly talkative members. Meeting leaders should try to determine the reason for nonparticipation. Are individuals shy, insecure, or bored? Perhaps the nonparticipants have just as much to offer as participating members but need to be drawn into the discussion. Three effective ways of encouraging participation are as follows:

1. Provide positive reinforcement to nonparticipants both before and after they speak; for example, "To reach a decision today, input from all members is important. Mary, your comments last week were helpful. What do you think about this topic?" or "Very good, Mary. No one has mentioned that idea yet."
2. Ask for nonparticipants' views or direct to them carefully worded questions that are simple and nonthreatening; for example, "What are your views about this topic, Bob?" or "Bob, do you agree with the last speaker?"
3. If possible, seat previously noticed nonparticipants toward the middle of the meeting room where most of the activity takes place rather than on the edges where they can remain unresponsive.

Encourage members to participate by using positive feedback and thought-provoking questions. Give positive nonverbal feedback such as nodding your head in agreement and smiling. Also provide verbal feedback such as "Your suggestion is just what we were looking for!" Thought-provoking questions such as "What do you think of that idea?" or "Did we miss anything?" or "Does anyone else agree or disagree with that suggestion and why?" are all examples of questions that will help to make individuals contribute to the group discussion.

Dealing with the overly talkative participant can be very challenging to a meeting leader. Individuals should never be cut off as long as they are making useful contributions to the discussion. However, if they get off the subject, overly dominate the discussion, bring up useless information, or repeat themselves, the meeting leader needs to control these individuals.

The leader can control overly talkative participants in an indirect manner in several ways. Some of the ways are by giving the floor to others ("Ray, your comments are good, but we need to hear what other individuals have to say. Let's move on to Carol."), by summarizing for the individual and moving on to the next topic ("Overall, Joyce, you and others feel that cost is the most important factor for our consideration. Let's now take a vote on it."), or by acknowledging her or his remarks but redirecting the discussion to the topic at hand ("That may be a consideration for later, Hector, but let's continue our present discussion about which system we want to buy."). More direct approaches for controlling too-dominant participants are by actually stopping unwarranted comments ("I'm sorry but that is not the topic we are discussing now . . . .") or by not giving them the floor.

## Summarizing and Concluding Discussion

When discussion about a particular topic appears to have ended or participants have reached agreement, take a vote on the item or simply summarize and move on to the next item on the agenda. However, if such factors as lack of information or a need for additional research prevent the group from reaching an agreement, conclude the meeting until the necessary information is available.

Once all items on the agenda have been covered, summarize final key points, including necessary actions to be taken. If an additional meeting is needed, outline the items to be discussed and determine a time and place for that meeting. *All* participants should leave a meeting feeling that their time was well spent and that each made a unique contribution to the success of the meeting. Both the leader and the participants share this responsibility.

# ROLE OF THE PARTICIPANT

The success or failure of a meeting does not rest solely with the meeting leader. Participants also have responsibilities before, during, and after a meeting.

## Participant Responsibility Before a Meeting

Before a meeting, participants have the responsibility to become adequately prepared to make an informed contribution. Along with the meeting agenda that is sent to each participant, participants may receive additional materials as background information. When preparing for a meeting, study these materials thoroughly and keep in mind the purpose of the meeting during your review. Write down a few suggestions, comments, or questions formulated from your study. This notetaking is a signal that you are adequately prepared for a meeting. If you do your homework before a meeting, you will avoid wasting time during the actual meeting.

## Participant Responsibility During a Meeting

Participants have the responsibility of arriving at a scheduled meeting on time. In addition, they have several other responsibilities during the meeting. Participants basically need to come to the meeting with a good attitude for discussion, to follow the agenda, to participate in but not dominate the discussion, and to listen effectively.

A good discussion attitude includes being open minded and respectful of the rights of both the leader and other participants. When presenting your own views, be objective and open to other views that may be different from your own. You should be willing to compromise or to consider alternative solutions.

Although following the agenda may seem inflexible, participants should not bring up items that are not part of the agenda. All discussion should be relevant to the goals and purposes of the meeting. A member should participate only when he or she has something meaningful to contribute. Not dominating the conversation and allowing others to express their viewpoints will lead to productive results.

Finally, effective listening is necessary. Listening involves holding back a response until a complete understanding of the speaker's message is obtained. Any member has a right to express opinions without interruption by other participants. In addition, effective listening means giving full attention to the meeting—not doing other work or daydreaming during meetings. Other principles of effective listening are outlined in Chapter 16.

## Participant Responsibility After a Meeting

At the conclusion of a meeting, participants may express the following feelings: "Boy, am I glad that's over! I've put in my time. Now I can get back to work." "Putting in your time" may not be where your responsibility as a participant stops. Meeting discussion may end with your being appointed to a committee or your need to take some action. Participants have a responsibility to fulfill these obligations after a meeting has concluded.

## FOLLOW-UP ACTIVITIES

Follow-up activities, which can be as important as planning and conducting a meeting, involve both leaders and participants. These activities include *follow-up memorandums, distribution of minutes, and evaluations of meetings*.

## Follow-Up Memorandums

Results of a productive meeting generally lead to actions and decisions that need to be carried out by various participants. The leader may send a **follow-up memorandum** confirming decisions reached and reminding participants of actions to be taken. In addition, this memo can serve as informal minutes of the meeting to inform absent members or other interested individuals of the results of a meeting.

Although a follow-up memorandum generally is the responsibility of the leader, it may be assigned to a participant. The memo simply reflects the decisions reached or actions taken, the person or persons responsible for carrying them out, and dates when the actions are due. An example of a brief follow-up memo is shown in Figure 18.5.

## FIGURE 18.5 SAMPLE MEETING FOLLOW-UP MEMORANDUM

**sunbury corporation**    INTEROFFICE COMMUNICATION

TO:    Sue Kato
Maria Lopez
Joe Morgan
Bill Smith

FROM:    Frank Torres, Sales Manager

DATE:    April 27, 19--

SUBJECT:    Report of April 26 Departmental Meeting

The following decisions and actions were determined at yesterday's meeting:

1.    The new computer inventory system will be purchased and installed the first of next month.

2.    Bill Smith and Sue Kato will attend a training seminar about the inventory system on April 29. They should call my secretary about the time and location.

I believe our mutual decision to adopt this inventory system will greatly increase our sales potential.

sa

## Distribution of Minutes

For most meetings, a follow-up memorandum is sufficient. However, sometimes more formal minutes are necessary.

**Who Should Take the Minutes?** The responsibilities of a meeting secretary are often underrated. However, the person recording the minutes actually has one of the most important responsibilities at a meeting. The minutes should accurately reflect what took place at a meeting. The person selected to record the minutes should have an understanding of the subject area so that he or she can organize the key points rather than merely record the events.

The latter generally occurs when a novice takes the minutes. Finally, the individual chosen to record the minutes should do so objectively without bias or interpretation.

**What Is Included in the Minutes?** The content and format of minutes vary from one organization to another. However, the following items are standard information to be included in the minutes of any business meeting:

1. The first paragraph should indicate the kind of meeting (regular, special, monthly, etc.); the name of the group; the date, time, and meeting place, if not always the same; the presence of the chair or leader, or the name of the substitute; and whether the minutes of the previous meeting were reviewed and approved or corrected. The first paragraph may also include a list of members present and absent.

2. The body of the minutes should contain any reports, summaries, or motions made, and actions taken under various topics on the agenda. Important motions should be worded verbatim and should include the name of the person making the motion. Summarize debate and list amendments. State decisions about motions (passed, tabled, etc.). In addition, include any assignments of committees or other actions to be taken, along with due dates and the individuals responsible.

3. The last paragraph should include the time of adjournment. Other optional items that may be included in the final paragraph are announcements and the date, time, and place of the next meeting if the group does not meet regularly.

4. The signature of the secretary for the group should be included at the end of the minutes. The signature of the chair is optional. The words "respectfully submitted" before a signature are traditional but are now often omitted from minutes.

An example of formal minutes is shown in Figure 18.6.

## FIGURE 18.6 SAMPLE FORMAL MINUTES

MINUTES

The monthly board meeting of the XYZ Corporation took place on Wednesday, September 15, 19--, at 1:30 p.m. in the Conference Room of the main office building, Evelyn Jones presiding. The Board approved the minutes of the previous meeting as corrected.

David Goldberg placed the financial report for the fiscal year ending June 30, 19--, on file for audit. Samuel Garcia presented the CEO report, which was placed on file.

Under unfinished business, the resolution about purchasing computer conferencing equipment was taken from the table. After amendment and debate, the Board adopted the following resolution: "Resolved, that the Communications Department purchase state-of-the-art computer conferencing equipment not to exceed $50,000."

Under new business, Bill Taylor moved "that the XYZ Corporation approve the purchase of a new networking system." Liwen Tang moved to amend the motion by inserting the words "not to exceed $75,000" at the end of the main motion. Susan Morgan moved that the main motion and pending amendment be referred to a committee of three. The Chair appointed Sylvia Lopez, Bill Taylor, and Susan Morgan to the committee with instructions to report their findings next month.

Also under new business, Thomas Green moved "that the Corporation look into upgrading the liability insurance package." The motion was tabled.

No other new business or announcements were presented. The meeting was adjourned at 3:00 p.m.

(signature)

Robert Cheng
Executive Secretary

---

**When Are Minutes Needed?** Whether formal as shown in the previous section or informal (such as a follow-up memorandum listing the results of a meeting), minutes of a meeting are recommended when the following conditions exist:

1. When members are to report and/or are held accountable for meeting results to a higher level within an organization
2. When members meet often and a record is necessary because their activities are continuous
3. When members are instructed at the meeting to carry out specific actions
4. When members are making decisions that will affect a large number of people
5. When members are discussing and acting upon several topics and need a summary of each

**When Are Minutes Distributed?** The chair or leader should edit the minutes of a meeting if possible. Ideally, the secretary should prepare and distribute the minutes within 48 hours of a meeting. This prompt delivery of the minutes serves as a reminder to those who must take follow-up action. Nonparticipants who are interested in the results of a meeting may also receive a copy of the minutes.

Distributing the minutes eliminates the need to read them aloud before approving them at the next meeting. In addition, if some discrepancies are discovered, these errors can be corrected. Finally, the minutes can become part of a permanent record. Members who attended the meeting and those who were absent can later review the minutes at their leisure or as necessary.

## Evaluation of a Meeting

The leader can receive feedback from participants by asking them to answer the following questions at the end of a meeting:

1. What did this meeting accomplish?
2. Did this meeting fulfill its purpose?
3. Does anything need to be handled differently to improve the next meeting?

If evaluation is not to be part of a regular routine, look for the following symptoms of poor meetings:

- Participants tell the leader or chair either directly or indirectly that the meeting was a waste of time.
- The leader senses "bad vibes," receives little praise for the meeting, experiences a low level of energy at the meeting, or sees nonverbal cues suggesting dissention.
- The leader finds that issues that appeared to be resolved during or immediately after the meeting may reappear later (Dunsing, 1978, 73).

Some organizations require formal evaluations which include not only an evaluation of the actual meeting session but also an evaluation of other factors such as meeting purpose, notification, planning, participation, and follow up. Formal evaluation forms should be short and simple. The most important considerations in designing an evaluation form are (1) what is to be evaluated?, (2) why is it to be evaluated?, and (3) what changes will be made as a result of this evaluation? A sample evaluation form is shown in Figure 18.7.

## FIGURE 18.7 SAMPLE FORMAL EVALUATION FORM FOR MEETINGS

### MEETING EVALUATION

|  | Yes | No |
|---|---|---|
| 1. Was the purpose of the meeting clear? | —— | —— |
| 2. Was sufficient advance notice of the meeting given? | —— | —— |
| 3. Was the agenda well prepared? | —— | —— |
| 4. Was the meeting location convenient? | —— | —— |
| 5. Was the meeting room arrangement satisfactory? | —— | —— |
| 6. Did the leader have control of the meeting? | —— | —— |
| 7. Did the proper participants attend the meeting? | —— | —— |
| 8. Were participants involved in discussion? | —— | —— |
| 9. Were decisions made and actions to be taken summarized? | —— | —— |
| 10. Was the purpose of the meeting accomplished? | —— | —— |

Please indicate any additional comments you wish to make on the back of this form.

Thank you

## SUMMARY

A specific company policy about meetings can help business meetings to be more productive. The meeting policy should specify the subject matter and purposes of meetings, participants of meetings, structure—formal versus informal—of meetings; and, if necessary, the format for minutes. Preparing and distributing materials, choosing the location and seating arrangement, and determining formal or informal procedures are all functions of a meeting planner. Both the leader and participants have equally important duties and roles that can determine the success or failure of a meeting. The leader is responsible for managing the meeting time, controlling participants, and concluding the discussion. Participants also have specific responsibilities before, during, and after a meeting. Follow-up activities include follow-up memorandums, distribution of minutes, and evaluation of meetings.

## CHAPTER REVIEW

1. React to this statement: "Meetings serve no purpose and are always a waste of time." Defend your answer.
2. List four criteria for selecting meeting participants.
3. What information should be contained in a *formal agenda*?
4. What type of seating arrangement would you recommend for a meeting that thirty participants attend? Why?
5. What type of seating arrangement would you recommend for a democratic meeting with five participants? Why?
6. List the three specific responsibilities of the meeting leader and briefly discuss each.
7. What rules should regulate formal meetings? What source should the chair of a formal meeting use as a reference for formal procedures?
8. When are *formal* and *informal procedures* appropriate for meetings?
9. How can the role of the participant cause success or failure of a meeting?
10. Should meetings be evaluated? Defend your answer.

## APPLICATIONS

1. Assume that you are the chair of a committee set up to voice needed changes on campus about students' concerns. Write a memorandum notifying committee members of your first meeting. Include an agenda of that meeting.

2. Attend an open public meeting within your community. Write an analysis of that meeting. Your analysis should include discussion about the purpose of the meeting, the agenda, the physical location and seating arrangement, the formal or informal procedures used, the roles of the leader and participants, and your overall evaluation of the meeting.

3. Divide the class into groups of approximately five to six members and hold a mock meeting of a business-related or student-related organization. Conduct a 15-minute meeting from beginning to end. Submit a set of minutes of your meeting to your instructor. Have other class members evaluate your meeting.

4. If possible, have your meeting in No. 3 tape recorded or videotaped. Then replay and critique the tape.

5. Assume that you are the vice president of the Elton Company, a manufacturer of women's sportswear. You are concerned that the weekly department meetings are unproductive. Formulate a specific plan of action and include it in a memorandum directed to all the department heads.

## CASE STUDY

"Fridays are terrible!" growled Pat Merritt to the rest of the group working out in the athletic club weight room. "Sometimes I wonder why we bother having a weekly management meeting. Most people don't prepare before they show up—*if* they show up. We waste *hours* on things that don't matter, and we never seem to have time for important issues!"

Exchanging knowing looks with the rest of the group present, the group listened to Pat's tirade against meetings in general and, in particular, against the required weekly plant management meeting at Tildon, Inc. Pat, the general manager of plant No. 2, had been with Tildon for 15 years.

"The meeting this morning was a disaster! We needed to prepare a schedule for the Board's annual plant visit. Headquarters is expecting the schedule by Tuesday—and we never got to it at this morning's meeting! I'm going to have to plan the whole thing myself so that it gets done on time, and then everyone will complain that they should have had input into the planning. Well, I put the schedule on the agenda and sent it out at the beginning of the week. They just didn't come prepared!"

"First, we took 25 minutes to get started because Sones from Marketing was sitting in the cafeteria waiting for us while we were waiting for him in the new training building. Then, because all of the furniture isn't unpacked yet, we had to meet around the desks in the main office because that was the only place where we could sit. By the time we got started, Chuck Moritz was in a real huff because he'd been there since 9:30 a.m.—even though he knows we always meet at 10 a.m., unless we have to use the cafeteria. He can be very uncooperative when he's upset."

"We took until 11 to plan out Miriam Miller's retirement party, so we were running behind schedule anyway. Then Joe Marx decided to present his master plan for repaving all of the roads at the plant. He had charts and graphs and stacks of vendor evaluations. I finally asked him why he was bringing up all this stuff now. He said, 'Well, it was on the agenda.' I explained to him that the traffic problem item on the agenda was a brief report on getting the city to put a traffic light at our parking lot exit. Then he lost his temper! Well, it's not my fault he couldn't read the agenda."

"Then on top of everything else, Coacher and Siegel—those two young management trainees we hired last fall—wanted to talk about promotion policies and career paths. 'The agenda did say we were going to discuss headquarters' assignments,' they said. So, I explained to them that the item was to be a discussion of parking lot assignments in the new lot east of headquarters. If they had just read the agenda, we would have saved some time."

"Anyway, we took until after noon to get the parking lot arranged. Now I'm stuck doing the Board visit by myself. Why does every Friday have to be like this one?"

Pat had sent out this agenda at the beginning of the week:

```
                        MEMORANDUM


       DATE:     February 1, 19--

       TO:       Plant #2 Management

       FROM:     Pat Merritt, Plant Manager

       SUBJECT:  Friday's Meeting

       This week's management meeting will be held in
       T & D classroom No. 3.  If the painters aren't
       finished in there by Friday, we'll meet in the
       cafeteria again at 9:30.  Please come prepared
       to discuss the following agenda items:

            1.  Miriam Miller's retirement
            2.  Traffic problems
            3.  New HQ assignments
            4.  Priorities for using space in the
                new T & D facility
            5.  Board's annual plant visit

       dk
```

1. Why did Pat's meeting accomplish so little?
2. Who is responsible for these unproductive Friday meetings? Why?
3. What suggestions would you make to increase the efficiency and productivity of the Friday meeting?

# REFERENCES

Richard J. Dunsing, *You and I Have Simply Got to Stop Meeting this Way: How to Run Better Meetings in Business and Industry, Government, Education, Religion, Health Care, Your Community* (New York: American Management Associations, 1978).

Robert Hays, *Practically Speaking—In Business, Industry, and Government* (Reading, MA: Addison-Wesley Publishing Company, 1969).

General Henry M. Robert, *Robert's Rules of Order* (Glenview, IL: Scott, Foresman and Company, 1970).

## SUGGESTED READINGS

Auger, B. Y. *How to Run Better Business Meetings: An Executive's Guide to Meetings that Get Things Done*. 8th ed. Minneapolis, MN: Minnesota Mining and Manufacturing Company, 1979.

Callanan, Joseph A. *Communicating—How to Organize Meetings and Presentations*. New York: Franklin Watts, 1984.

Jorgensen, James D., Ivan H. Scheier, and Timothy F. Fautsko. *Solving Problems in Meetings*. Chicago: Nelson-Hall, 1981.

Palmer, Barbara C. and Kenneth R. Palmer. *The Successful Meeting Master Guide for Business and Professional People*. Englewood Cliffs, NJ: Prentice-Hall, 1983.

Tropman, John E. and Gersh Morningstar. *Meetings—How to Make Them Work for You*. New York: Van Nostrand Reinhold Company Inc., 1985.

Wheeler, Mary Bray, ed. *The Basic Meeting Manual: For Offices and Members of Any Organization*. Nashville, TN: Thomas Nelson Publishers, 1986.

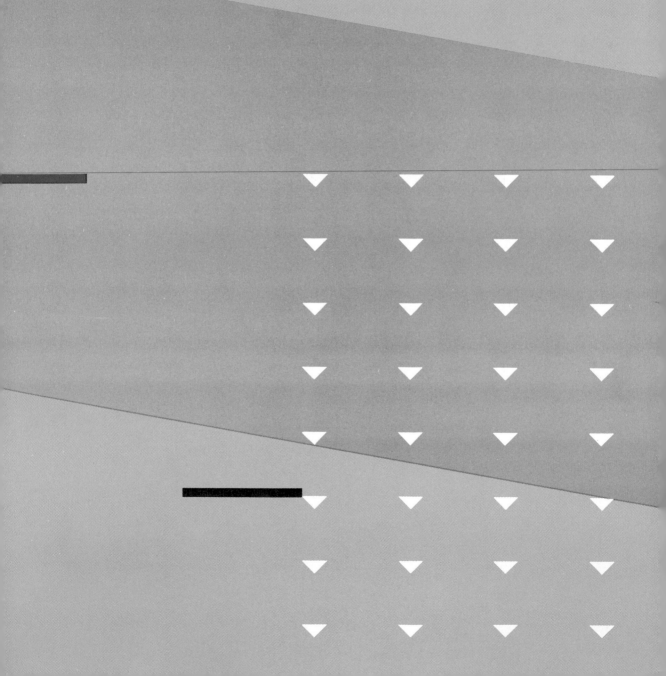

# COMMUNICATION THROUGHOUT THE ORGANIZATION

## PART 7

The increase in size and complexity of business organizations today, together with the need for improved productivity, is creating a demand for better management of communication. Today's corporate executives realize that managing the information explosion is much more complicated than merely acquiring a larger computer.

Technological developments in telecommunications, office information, and information processing are continuing to improve the quantity, accuracy, timeliness, and accessibility of information that executives and managers need for making business decisions. However, the more data an organization produces, the more difficult communication becomes. In the future, the success of a company increasingly will depend upon the company's ability to manage information and communication systems effectively throughout the organization.

# COMMUNICATION TECHNOLOGY

## CHAPTER 19

Ken Peters, the sales manager of Astro Electronics, arrives at work, turns on his workstation, and checks the electronic mail service. He quickly reads and deletes those "pieces" of mail that are not necessary to save. Others he files electronically for later reference. He responds immediately to one memo by sending an electronic message to a sales rep in a different state. He responds to another memo with a short voice message.

Next he resumes working on a sales forecast that he needs by mid-afternoon. Ken retrieves the forecast from a hard-disk drive file, which is part of his workstation. After making a number of revisions and additions, he saves the forecast on the hard-disk drive.

Then he writes a sales report with graphs and charts reflecting the new forecast. While writing this report, Ken accesses several database files in the memory of the company's main computer for some information that he needs.

Finally, Ken electronically sends the sales forecast and the report to a laser printer. Within minutes, a letter-quality copy is delivered to his office. All these tasks are completed without leaving his desk.

Ken Peters' use of computer technology to send and receive information is commonplace in business offices today. Instead of obtaining business information from paper, many executives and managers are turning to computer video-display monitors to access data. The trend toward electronic storing, retrieving, and sending of information has been called an "information revolution" or the "communications revolution" (Williams, 1983).

This chapter provides an overview of the following topics:

- The "communications revolution" and its impact on management
- The processing of data through the basic data-flow pattern
- The integration of networking systems
- Business applications software
- Components and features of the new technology
- Developments related to artificial intelligence
- Computer security

## THE COMMUNICATIONS REVOLUTION

As a result of technological innovations in the early 1980's, the computer and communication industries began to merge (Copithorne, 1980, 68). The integrated technology in large computer systems began to be used in microcomputers, low-cost data storage and retrieval systems, and high-speed communication facilities that link systems together. Companies now routinely use computer terminals as the primary means to send and store information. The ability of computer systems to communicate with one another has enabled business firms to use these systems for electronic mail, teleconferencing, and other purposes. Just as the industrial revolution brought automation to the factory, the communications revolution has brought automation to business offices.

Futurist Alvin Toffler (1980, 207) predicted in his book *The Third Wave* that vice presidents, other executives, and managers would soon be manipulating computer keyboards rather than shuffling papers as a part of their daily work routine. Trinet, an information and marketing services subsidiary of Control Data Corporation, in a survey of managers in 1,500 corporations, discovered that more than half of the managers were personally using computers in their offices (Betts, 1985, 72).

In the 1960's, computer technology was concerned primarily with mainframe computers. Data were taken to the computer room via punched cards or tape and processed on a **mainframe** (*central*) **computer**, as shown in Illustration A in the color insert found between pages 486 and 487. (All of the illustrations referred to in this chapter are found in the color insert.) With the advent of remote terminals in the 1970's, however, data processing began to decentralize from mainframe computers. When *microcomputers* became popular in business offices in the 1980's, computer technology began a trend toward **functional integration**—the bringing together of data processing, word processing, and other forms of data communication into an information system through the process of networking. **Networking** makes possible the sharing of peripheral resources such as printers, modems, and storage devices. In addition, shared **databases** (*files*) and other information expedite the flow of information through an organization.

The communications revolution has increased the productivity of managers and executives by giving them direct access to integrated information systems that can assist them in decision making. Various components of integrated information systems also make more time available for decision making by reducing the amount of time managers must spend on routine tasks.

Many integrated information systems do not require users to have an in-depth knowledge of computer technology. However, for users to comprehend the capabilities of an integrated information system, they must first understand the basic concepts of electronic data processing and networking.

## ELECTRONIC DATA PROCESSING

The purpose of **data processing** is to change raw data into information that can be used for decision making. Raw data, which consist of various pieces of unorganized information, must be processed and organized to become information that managers and executives can use. To be useful, raw data must follow the basic data-flow pattern of *input*, *processing*, and *output* (see Figure 19.1).

### FIGURE 19.1 DATA-FLOW PATTERN

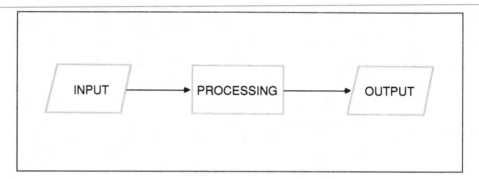

### Input

In the basic data-flow pattern, **input** (the *data-entry step*) must occur before any raw data can be processed. Data entry is often the weakest link in the basic data-flow pattern because of problems such as keyboarding errors. You may have heard the expression "GIGO—Garbage In, Garbage Out!" This expression simply means that inaccurate data (input) will produce inaccurate results (output).

**Input Media**. Data must be entered into the computer in a form that the computer can read, such as magnetic tape and various types of magnetic disks (see Illustration B). These media are used for data storage as well as data input.

**Optical disks** (see Illustration C) store and retrieve data by means of laser (light) technology. The advantage of optical disks is that data may be in the form of video, audio, text, computer images, or any combination of these types of data.

**CRT Keyboards**. The most popular method of data entry is keyboarding at a **cathode ray tube (CRT) terminal** (sometimes called *VDT* for *video-display terminal*; see Illustration D). A CRT terminal uses a television-like screen or monitor that displays data as the user keys it or retrieves it from an electronic file within a computer. The keyboard is usually arranged in the same format as a standard typewriter keyboard, with additional function keys to the left and/or right of the main keyboard. Some keyboards also have separate numeric keypads to the right of the main keyboard for more rapid entering of numeric data or as extra function keys (see Illustration E).

Computer terminals may be of two basic types — "dumb" or "intelligent." A **dumb terminal**, which is not programmed to perform processing functions, is specifically used for entering data into a larger computer system. Because dumb terminals are connected to a main computer, they are referred to as being *online*.

An **intelligent terminal** contains a microprocessor (a tiny silicon or integrated circuit chip) that can perform processing functions *offline* (without being connected to a mainframe computer). Because they can be programmed, intelligent terminals have many more applications than dumb terminals. Microcomputers (personal computers), which are discussed later in this chapter, can be used as terminals to a mainframe computer in addition to being used as intelligent stand-alone systems.

**Optical-Character Recognition (OCR)**. OCR technology is used to enter data into a computer without keyboarding. **Optical-character readers** are machines that scan printed information and convert the information into digital form that a computer can process. Optical-character recognition input can be produced by sales registers, typewriters, accounting machines, adding machines, and computer printers. For example, the specially designed and printed numbers at the bottom of checks are optical characters used by check-sorting machines in banks. As another example, point-of-sale (POS) terminal scanning devices are used at grocery stores with Universal Product Codes (UPC), or bar codes, printed on grocery items (see Illustration F).

Hand-held and desk-top optical-character scanners are used for typed documents (see Illustration G). These devices eliminate the need to rekey typewritten documents by scanning their contents directly into a computer. Some of these OCR devices can read handwritten characters.

**Source-Data Automation**. Traditional methods of data entry at a centralized location are relatively expensive and time consuming. A newer and more efficient method of data entry is called **source-data automation**, which is also known as *transaction-oriented processing*. With this method of data input, information is entered directly into the computer for immediate processing when and where a transaction takes place. For example, an airline ticket agent places a reservation directly into a computer system for processing simply by keying in the data as the customer waits, or a cashier uses a wand-like device to read the price of an item that a customer purchases in a department store (see Illustrations H and I). From a tag on the article, the price and inventory number are "read" directly into the computer for accounting and inventory control.

**Other Data-Entry Methods**. Other means of entering data include touchscreens, mice (hand-held input devices discussed in Chapter 10), light pens, and speech-recognition systems. **Touchscreens** are special computer screens that receive data input when a user touches a word, picture, or number on the screen. Some companies use touchscreen technology to market their products in convenience stores, where a touchscreen terminal using videodiscs becomes an electronic catalog showroom. A shopper simply touches defined areas of the screen and selects a department to "shop" in and progressively narrows the selection to a particular product (see Illustration J). After choosing a product, the customer obtains shipping and billing information by inserting a credit card into a reader. Later the product is shipped to the customer's home.

**Light pens** are input devices for creating computer graphics. By touching a light pen to a computer screen, a user can draw lines, erase lines, and move lines from one point to another (see Illustration K).

**Speech recognition** is the translation of human speech into a form that a computer can recognize. A user dictates into a voice-recognition unit, and a computer translates the information into print that appears on a CRT screen for immediate formatting or editing. Most speech-recognition devices are "speaker dependent"; that is, they require the user to dictate words and/or phrases into a microphone several times to train the system to recognize her or his voice patterns. With these types of systems, the user's voice commands can move cursors, open files, and print documents. The ultimate goal for voice technology is to allow an executive or manager to dictate directly into a computer documents to be transformed into printed text. This technology is available on an experimental basis and in the future probably will be available for commercial use.

## Processing

Once data enter an electronic processor, whether the processor is part of a main computer or is a microprocessor, the data must be manipulated to produce output. This manipulation is called **processing**, the second phase of the basic data-flow pattern.

Most users do not need to have a complete understanding of the internal workings of a computer. The processing of data occurs within the electronic circuitry of the **central processing unit** (**CPU**), which contains a computer's logic and memory. The CPU interprets the directions of a computer program (a set of instructions), communicates with input/output devices, holds data in memory, manipulates data (including performing arithmetic functions), and transfers data to and from the computer memory.

Whenever the amount of data or a set of programs exceeds the capacity of the computer memory, the computer must use devices such as magnetic tapes, hard disks, floppy disks, and optical disks for auxiliary (secondary) storage.

## Output

Useful **output** is the end result of data processing. For years, printed reports from high-speed printers were the main means of obtaining output from a computer. Today a variety of output devices includes *printers*, *CRT screens*, *plotters*, and *voice-response systems*.

Various types of printers include dot matrix, daisy wheel, jet, thermal, laser, and ion deposition. A **dot-matrix printer** has tiny metal rods that produce closely packed dots to form characters. A **daisy-wheel printer** prints letter-quality characters on impact with a ribbon. A **jet-printer** shoots a fine stream of ink and actually paints characters on the paper. **Thermal printers** use a heated printing element to etch images onto special paper. **Laser printers** use electrical impulses or light to print. **Ion-deposition printers** form characters and graphic images by depositing electronic particles on a drum, then transferring them electronically (without impact) to paper.

**Plotters** have mechanical arms that draw illustrations on paper with pens (see Illustration L). Although slower than printers, plotters can produce a wider range of colors than printers and produce drawings for use on an overhead projector. A newer development, called a **robot plotter**, is unconstrained by traditional margins and has a drawing vehicle that can extend to the edge of a three-foot square sheet of paper.

**Voice response** (*voice communication output*) uses "speech synthesis," a process that converts data within a computer into output in the form of intelligible speech. Some computerized sales-register systems use voice response to inform customers of purchase amounts and correct change. Special *talking computers* for vision-impaired users also employ speech synthesis for voice output.

## NETWORKING

A **network** is a combination of software and hardware that links computers and computer devices. Networks allow workstations to communicate with one another as well as with an organization's central computer, share peripheral devices, and transmit information over long and short distances. Networks allow computers to send data very rapidly by integrating the following technologies: satellite communications, large-scale integrated circuits, high-level communication software, light-wave technology, and digital communications. Local-area networks, switch-and-access networks, and wide-area networks link systems that collect, store, display, move, and manipulate information as needed.

A **local-area network (LAN)** links computers and other compatible devices within a building or nearby buildings. A LAN allows different departments of an organization to share various capabilities such as data processing, word processing, and electronic mail. Local-area networks also can be expanded to distant locations by linking with wide-area networks.

A **switch-and-access network** connects local networks with either a public (such as AT&T) or private wide-area network that uses digital, light-wave, or microwave equipment (see Illustration M). In **wide-area networks**, a private network is often linked to a public network through telephone lines. A special switch determines the most cost-effective route.

By using various types of networks, business organizations eliminate the duplication of computer hardware, software, and databases at various locations. Thus, networking enables companies to gain efficiencies and improvements in their communication capabilities.

## SOFTWARE

Computer application packages, or **software**, are sets of programs that perform specific tasks such as word processing, spreadsheet analysis, or database management. Word-processing software may include special features such as spelling, punctuation, and style checkers. Some sophisticated packages offer proportional spacing, footnoting, and indexing features. The footnoting feature allows a user to key a footnote beside the cited material; and when printed, the footnote will appear either at the bottom of the page or at the end of the document. An indexing function permits every word of a document to appear in an alphabetical index automatically.

**Computer-generated graphics**, discussed in Chapter 10, are used to create graphic aids such as pie charts, bar charts, or even animated displays (see Illustration N). Some graphics software allows the user to change the data by increments or decrements. For example, by changing the data used to develop a vertical bar chart, the user can watch the relative size of the bars increase or decrease.

**Integrated business software** includes several tasks—for example, word processing, database management, graphics, spreadsheet, and communications—all in one package. Some integrated packages allow more than one application program to run at a time without reloading. Other software can send data between a personal computer and a mainframe system.

Many business tasks require looking at several documents at once or creating a new document based on existing ones. **Windowing** allows the display of more than one document or item on the computer screen at a time for simultaneous review (see Illustration O). Windowing also may allow the user to work on more than one task at a time. For example, a manager could be working on figures on a spreadsheet, take information from the spreadsheet and add it to a report in another window, and then go back to the spreadsheet.

# THE "NEW" TECHNOLOGY

As you are reading this textbook, additional innovations in telecommunication and other automated communication equipment are being developed. The components of information systems discussed separately in this chapter may overlap in actual use because one device may have some of the same capabilities as another. The ideal business environment is to have all components linked into one information system through networking. Therefore, an ideal integrated information system would have the following features:

- Personal or microcomputers
- Multi-function workstations
- Telecommunication, including electronic telephones, electronic mail, voice mail, and teleconferencing
- Micrographics
- Reprographics

## Personal or Microcomputers

**Personal computers** (*microcomputers*), independently or in a network, are used for word processing, spreadsheet analysis, and other business-related functions. The basic personal computer consists of a memory microprocessor, a keyboard, one or two disk drives, a display screen, and usually a printer. The trend is for these computers to have more power and increased memory capacity for running larger, more complex programs at faster speeds, and to have easier-to-use software.

Today portable or "lap-top" models are becoming more popular (see Illustration P). The TV-like monitors of personal computers are being replaced with portable flat-panel displays. *Electroluminescent* and *gas-plasma displays* will soon replace the *liquid-crystal display (LCD)* screens presently used in portable models. Lighter, smaller, and rechargeable battery packs will run these models for longer periods.

Features such as icons on touchscreens have made personal computers easier to use. **Icons** are symbols or pictures on a computer screen that represent computer commands. Examples include a picture of a file folder or file cabinet to represent filing and a picture of a wastebasket to represent deleting. Rather than keying a chain of commands, users can simply point to the appropriate icon on a touchscreen and press the return or "go" on the keyboard.

Since personal computers are user friendly, managers and executives themselves can compose messages on a keyboard faster than by conventional methods of originating documents. Composing at a keyboard eliminates the inefficient sequence of dictation-type-proofread-retype-proofread. Using personal computers can result in increased speed and decreased costs of written communication.

## Multi-Function Workstations

A **multi-function** (or *executive*) **workstation** is a data/voice terminal used mainly to access information that is important to executive decision making. Each workstation in an organization is linked to the corporate network. A multi-function workstation eliminates the need for a separate personal computer, telephone, and modem, as well as appointment calendar, calculator, message pad, and many other desk-top items. Workstations make computer processing and data-storage resources instantly available for compiling, interpreting, and analyzing information for decision support (see Illustration Q).

Usual functions of executive workstations include personal computer applications; electronic mail; data communication; and simultaneous communication in text, graphics, voice, and image. Specific functions may include the following capabilities:

- Text editing with sophisticated word-processing packages
- Spelling, grammatical, and mathematical checks
- Electronic mail via built-in modems
- Teleconferencing and video conferencing through telephone lines
- Graphics production on peripheral printers
- Telephone directories and automatic redialing
- Two-line capability allowing voice and data messages to be received at the same time
- Computer security through a password system
- Multi-function operation allowing more than one application at a time
- Share mode allowing two or more users to view the same information simultaneously
- Electronic scheduling and calendaring
- Database management and indexing
- Information tracking

For the **electronic scheduling** and **calendaring** function, managers' and other employees' schedules are held in computer memory. Employees can access one another's schedules to determine when individuals are available for meetings, etc. Master and individual calendars of meetings, appointments, and the like can be accessed; and employees can receive audible or visual reminders of such events. The **database management** and **indexing** functions enable users to retrieve and display specific documents such as memos and reports on the workstation CRT screen. Both incoming and outgoing correspondence can be indexed automatically and filed by using a touchscreen or function keys. **Information tracking** involves automatic reminders of upcoming events and tasks, as well as quick checks into the status of requests for information.

Again, the key to the multi-function workstation and the entire integrated information system is a linking of components through networking. These components may include voice, graphics, document preparation, and data-communication systems.

# Telecommunication

**Telecommunication** refers to advanced electronic means of transmitting information over distances. Communication within a company and between companies can use various transmission media.

Although a discussion of all types of transmission media is beyond the scope of this text, one will be discussed briefly—communication satellites. Basically, to communicate between two points with a **communication satellite**, an "earth station" sends a microwave radio signal to an orbiting satellite. Once the satellite receives the signal, it rebroadcasts the signal toward another earth station (see Illustration R). The key advantage of this system is that the cost of transmitting a message is unaffected by its distance. For example, the cost of sending a signal from New York to San Francisco is the same as sending a signal from New York to Boston.

Satellite communication systems handle three fundamental modes of communication. These three modes—data, voice, and image transmission—may be used either separately or as a combination of electronic telephones, electronic mail, voice mail, and teleconferencing.

**Electronic Telephones.** **Cellular** (*mobile*) **telephones**, which have been used in cars for some time, are also being carried in briefcases. **Photophones** can be used to send and receive quality black-and-white still pictures over regular telephone lines (see Illustration S). **Videophones** transmit and receive live video images over dial-up telephone lines.

Cooperative ventures between the computer and communication industries will continue to establish international standards that will enable homes, offices, and other services to tie into one network. This combined technology will enable, for example, an American investor to negotiate in English with a foreign investor in that person's native language by a computer that translates the two languages.

Another innovation is **voice messaging** or *phone mail*, which uses advanced recording and routing features. A caller may hear a previously recorded message or leave a message with such options as replaying the message, erasing it, adding to it, sending it by normal or urgent delivery, or switching the call to another line. Business applications include voice-recorded daily updates of sales and/or inventories, daily work schedules, and hourly changes in competitive prices. Users of voice messaging can dial their "mailboxes" any time, regardless of time zones.

**Electronic Mail.** As stated in Chapter 1, electronic mail is the transmission of messages at high speeds over local or long-distance telecommunication networks. One electronic mail service ("Global Communications," 1985, 35) claims that personal computer users can, for less than the price of a hamburger, send an electronic letter from Los Angeles to Paris through international telephone networks. International businesses have difficulty calling clients overseas because of time differences. Electronic mail solves this problem.

Other features of electronic mail include **mail notification**, which lets the user know when a message has been sent; **receipt notification**, which tells the sender that the message has been received; **multidestination delivery**, which allows the user to create and use distribution lists; and **priority levels**, which allow the sending of messages when system use is low, such as overnight.

**Voice Mail**. **Voice-mail** messaging combines the following three items of communication equipment: a telephone, a computer, and a recording device. Because of its simplicity and similarity to the telephone, voice mail requires little new learning.

A user receives access to a voice-mail system by entering a code on a dial or touch telephone. Then a prerecorded message tells the sender to dial the voice-mail address of the receiver. The dictated message is then converted into digital data and delivered. If the message cannot be delivered, the computer files the message in its memory. Later, when the receiver dials into the system to receive "mail," the system reconstructs the sender's message with a synthesized voice.

**Teleconferencing**. Meeting people face to face, establishing rapport with clients, and seeing nonverbal cues are all advantages of traditional meetings and conferences. However, transportation, lodging, meals, and other related travel costs are expensive. Modern telecommunication provides an alternative to traveling to business meetings. A meeting can be held electronically in a manager's or executive's office or a company's conference room by *audio teleconferencing*, *computer teleconferencing*, or *video teleconferencing*.

**Audio teleconferencing** uses speaker phones from participants' own desks. **Speaker phones**, which provide hands-free communication by amplifying voices, allow a number of participants to speak on the same line (see Illustration T). Because no visual input of participants is provided, facsimile (image) equipment is often used for transmitting graphic materials during audio teleconferences.

Also for visual input, messages can be written on an **electronic blackboard** (see Illustration U). When a manager or executive writes on a pressure-sensitive surface, the words or diagrams are instantly converted to electronic signals that are quickly transmitted over telephone or other communication lines. The receivers can not only hear the discussion or report but also see what is written on the blackboard via a video screen at their locations. Changes and additions to the visual input can be made by using a special blackboard eraser.

**Computer teleconferencing** enables meeting participants to "talk" through computer terminals linked by telephone lines to a communication network. Computer teleconferences enable a continuing dialogue by storing participants' questions, answers, and other comments in computer memory. Several participants can "talk" simultaneously by keying their questions or responses online. In addition, participants can remain anonymous or take part at their convenience by accessing a shared database for later reaction.

ILLUSTRATION A   LARGE MAINFRAME COMPUTERS PLAY A CENTRAL ROLE IN THE "INFORMATION REVOLUTION."

ILLUSTRATION B   DATA ARE STORED ON MAGNETIC TAPES AND COMPUTER DISKS.

ILLUSTRATION C   OPTICAL DISKS STORE AND RETRIEVE DATA WITH THE USE OF LASER TECHNOLOGY.

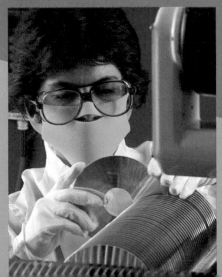

ILLUSTRATION D   A CRT TERMINAL USES A TELEVISION-LIKE MONITOR THAT DISPLAYS DATA.

ILLUSTRATION E   NUMERIC KEYPADS PERMIT RAPID ENTRY OF NUMERIC DATA.

ILLUSTRATION F   POINT-OF-SALE (POS) TECHNOLOGY ALLOWS IMMEDIATE PROCESSING OF DATA.

ILLUSTRATION G   DESK-TOP OPTICAL SCANNERS "READ" THE CONTENTS OF TYPEWRITTEN DOCUMENTS DIRECTLY INTO A COMPUTER.

ILLUSTRATION H   SOURCE-DATA AUTOMATION ENABLES INFORMATION TO BE PROCESSED WHEN AND WHERE A TRANSACTION TAKES PLACE.

ILLUSTRATION I   FROM A TAG ON THE ARTICLE, THE PRICE AND INVENTORY NUMBER ARE "READ" DIRECTLY INTO THE COMPUTER.

ILLUSTRATION J   TOUCHSCREENS RECEIVE DATA INPUT WHEN A USER TOUCHES A WORD, PICTURE, OR NUMBER ON THE COMPUTER SCREEN.

ILLUSTRATION K   LIGHT PENS ARE INPUT DEVICES FOR CREATING COMPUTER GRAPHICS.

ILLUSTRATION L   PLOTTERS CAN PRODUCE
DRAWINGS FOR VISUAL PRESENTATIONS.

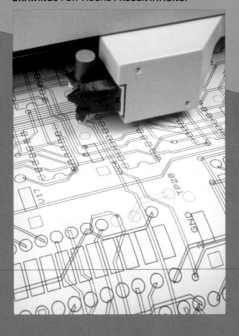

ILLUSTRATION M   A PRIVATE WIDE-AREA
NETWORK USES MICROWAVE (AS SHOWN),
DIGITAL, OR LIGHT-WAVE EQUIPMENT.

ILLUSTRATION N   A COMPUTER PROJECTOR CAN DISPLAY GRAPHIC AIDS
SUCH AS PIE CHARTS, BAR CHARTS, OR ANIMATED FIGURES.

ILLUSTRATION O "WINDOWS" ALLOW THE DISPLAY OF MORE THAN ONE ITEM ON THE COMPUTER SCREEN FOR SIMULTANEOUS REVIEW.

ILLUSTRATION P PORTABLE OR LAP-TOP COMPUTERS ARE BECOMING POPULAR.

ILLUSTRATION Q A MULTI-FUNCTION WORKSTATION ELIMINATES THE NEED FOR A SEPARATE PERSONAL COMPUTER, TELEPHONE, AND APPOINTMENT CALENDAR.

ILLUSTRATION R   THE COST OF TRANSMITTING A MESSAGE BY MEANS OF A COMMUNICATION SATELLITE IS UNAFFECTED BY THE DISTANCE.

ILLUSTRATION S   PHOTOPHONES SEND AND RECEIVE BLACK-AND-WHITE STILL PICTURES OVER TELEPHONE LINES.

ILLUSTRATION T   SPEAKERPHONES PROVIDE HANDS-FREE COMMUNICATION BY AMPLIFYING VOICES.

ILLUSTRATION U    AN ELECTRONIC BLACKBOARD CONVERTS WORDS OR DIAGRAMS INTO ELECTRONIC SIGNALS THAT CAN BE TRANSMITTED OVER TELEPHONE LINES.

ILLUSTRATION V    INDIVIDUALS AND GROUPS SEE AND HEAR EACH OTHER ON TELEVISION-LIKE MONITORS DURING A VIDEO TELECONFERENCE.

ILLUSTRATION W    VIDEO-CONFERENCING TECHNOLOGY HAS BECOME QUITE SOPHISTICATED.

ILLUSTRATION X  THE PRODUCTION OF
MICROFORMS REQUIRES A SPECIAL
CAMERA THAT TAKES MINIATURE PICTURES
OF DOCUMENTS.

ILLUSTRATION Y  A COPY BOARD IS AN ELECTRONIC
BLACKBOARD FROM WHICH COPIES CAN BE MADE.

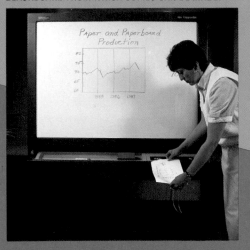

ILLUSTRATION Z  ROBOTICS TECHNOLOGY INVOLVES MACHINES THAT CAN MOVE AND PERFORM
REPETITIVE TASKS.

**Video teleconferencing** combines both the audio and visual components of communication. Presently, most video teleconferencing takes place in specially equipped rooms (see Illustration V). Individuals and groups see and hear each other on television-like monitors in either full-motion or still-frame (nonmoving) reception. Again, diagrams, printed text, and other graphics can be transmitted and viewed on video screens. Facsimile equipment can be used for hard-copy documents. Users can prepare copies of still frames and make videotapes or videodiscs of moving pictures for later reference.

Newer developments include the integration of full-motion color video and voice communication with a personal computer. These systems include a color monitor and camera, a viewfinder, and a speakerphone (see Illustration W). Two or more individuals can use a speakerphone; changes in images are activated by changes in voices. Some units have two-color monitors that allow users to view people and documents simultaneously.

## Micrographics

**Micrographics** replaces paper filing for large volumes of information. Keeping unnecessary records online (within the central processing unit of a computer) can waste valuable memory and reduce response time, but micrographics eliminates this problem.

The production of materials in microform requires a special camera or microfilmer that takes miniature pictures of documents. A **microfilm processor** converts the tiny photographs into either *microfilm* or *microfiche* (a film sheet), and the pictured documents are indexed for later retrieval (see Illustration X). In the retrieval step, a microfilm reader magnifies the microform for viewing. A micro-reader-printer may be used to reproduce full-sized hard copies. Managers or executives can use microfiche outside the office by carrying it in a briefcase fitted with a viewer that projects recorded information onto a curved screen built into the cover of the case.

Microforms also can be produced directly from computers as **computer-output microfilm (COM)**. The COM process eliminates paper printouts. In some cases, the output is recorded on magnetic tape that is then reproduced on microfilm. In other systems, the COM equipment displays output on a computer screen.

**Computer-aided retrieval (CAR)** permits rapid access to stored microform records. With a CAR system, records and documents may be filmed in any order. No matter where a record is located, the CAR will find the record immediately.

## Reprographics

In its broadest definition, **reprographics** is the reproducing or copying of information. Today, however, reprographics primarily refers to computer typesetters and intelligent communicating copiers.

In **computer typesetting**, a typesetting machine is connected to a computer. The output is film or tape to be used to prepare page layouts for documents such as brochures, newspapers, magazines, and books. The type is set automatically from the text stored in the computer's memory. Special codes indicate various typefaces such as boldface or italics and space for inserting photographs.

**Intelligent communicating copiers** use a variety of paper stock and sizes; perform high-quality, rapid printing and sorting; produce in color; enlarge and reduce copies; and copy on both sides of a sheet. To eliminate rekeying of information, computers can be connected to intelligent communicating copiers for volume printing. In addition, copies can be prepared from data sent by computers without first making an original.

A newer development in reprographics is a **copy board**, an electronic blackboard with a white enameled surface from which copies can be made (see Illustration Y). Colored water-based, felt-tipped pens are used to write on the electronic board, from which letter-size copies can be produced in a matter of seconds.

## ARTIFICIAL INTELLIGENCE

Computer processing of knowledge (similar to thinking) is referred to as **artificial intelligence (AI)**. The goal of artificial intelligence is to imitate electronically the human thought processes of recognition, reasoning, and learning.

Four basic areas of AI research are being conducted in the business field—*voice and visual recognition*, *natural language processing*, *robotics*, *expert systems*. **Voice and visual recognition systems** are machines that have the ability to see, to understand what is seen, and to react either manually or verbally to the environment. **Natural language processing** enables computer users to communicate with computers in ordinary English rather than in programming language. **Robotics** research is geared toward developing machines that can move and perform repetitive tasks such as "working" on an assembly line (see Illustration Z). An **expert system** utilizes software that imitates a human expert's thought processes in a narrow specialty or problem area and "teaches" a machine to solve problems and make decisions.

Of these four areas, the expert system area of AI has had the most applications. In the field of medicine, an expert system can be used to diagnose diseases. Expert systems are also being used for aerospace designs, for diagnosing engine trouble, and for control systems in oil refineries. Specific business applications include programs for advising division managers on purchasing database management systems, locating faulty circuit boards in computer systems, training personnel in international banking services, and altering computer equipment according to customers' specifications.

Essentially, an expert system consists of a knowledge base or sets of facts as well as sets of "IF . . . THEN" rules. These "IF . . . THEN" rules are the expert's heuristic knowledge (rules of thumb) used in solving problems and reaching conclusions. Basically, an expert system lays out a set of contingencies or searches for a way to reach a particular goal after it is given an initial set of circumstances and constraints. Generally, most expert systems do not make independent decisions without human input. Most systems are used as consulting tools along with human input.

Artificial intelligence is just beginning to emerge in various areas of business. However, with a continuing increase in computer power and decrease in cost, artificial intelligence will play an important role in many more areas of business in the future.

## COMPUTER SECURITY

Business organizations use various security procedures to prevent unauthorized people from using their computer systems. Many companies require employees to receive a security clearance before they are provided with an account number and password to access certain files.

Many organizations also require employees to have a security clearance before they are permitted to enter "classified" areas containing computer equipment and confidential information such as product formulas, payroll records, and personnel files. Some computer systems use a "smart" identification card that incorporates an integrated circuit containing the owner's digitized fingerprint. A person wanting access to a controlled area simply inserts the card into a computer terminal and places a finger on a glass plate. The machine scans the finger and compares it with the "print" on the card; and if it matches, permits the employee to enter the area.

## SUMMARY

A communications revolution is underway as a result of technological innovations that are merging the computer and communication industries. Developments in telecommunication and other automated equipment continue to improve the timeliness and quality of the information available to managers. Additionally, the technology reduces the time required for routine activities, leaving more time for decision making.

Electronic processing of data — input, processing, and output — converts raw data into information that managers can use. Advances in data-input equipment include optical-character recognition, source-data automation, and devices such as touchscreens, mice, light pens, and speech recognition systems. Output devices include printers, CRT screens, plotters, and voice-response systems.

Integrated information systems use the process of networking to combine computers and telecommunication systems. By networking, multi-function workstations communicate with one another and transmit data over distances. Integrated information systems involve such features as electronic telephones, electronic mail, voice mail, teleconferencing, micrographics, and reprographics.

Through artificial intelligence, computer technology can imitate human thought processes. Business applications of AI include voice and visual recognition, natural language processing, robotics, and expert systems.

Organizations employ various types of computer-security systems to prohibit unauthorized access to computer hardware, software, and files. Security measures include security clearance checks, passwords, identification cards, and digitized fingerprinting.

## CHAPTER REVIEW

1. Identify and explain the purpose of business automation as it relates to managers and executives.
2. Define *icons* and *windowing* and explain how they are used.
3. Identify the components of the *data-flow pattern* and give an example of each part.
4. List the components of an ideal integrated information system and give an example of each component.
5. What is the main advantage of a manager or executive using a computer versus using conventional methods such as pen and paper, "live" dictation, or a calculator?
6. Explain the differences among the three types of teleconferencing outlined in the chapter.
7. Define *optical-character recognition* and discuss its importance.
8. Name the advantages of *micrographics* over conventional filing.
9. Define *networking* and state its advantages.
10. Define *artificial intelligence* and describe related research being conducted in the business area.

## APPLICATIONS

1. Survey two or three local computer software stores to determine the five top-selling business application software packages available. Describe in a memo report or oral presentation (as outlined by your instructor) how these software packages are used in business.

2. Find a current article about one of the seven innovations discussed in this chapter under the heading "The 'New' Technology" and write a one-page summary of the article. Predict the eventual impact on management of the technology described in the article. Include complete documentation of the article.

3. Find a current article about each type of teleconferencing (audio, computer, and video). Write a one-page summary of each article. Infer ways in which each form of teleconference could increase the productivity of managers. Include complete documentation for each article.

4. Visit a local company that uses electronic or voice mail and report orally to your class how and when company employees use this type of mail.

5. Visit a local company that uses teleconferencing and report orally to your class the type of equipment that is used, and when and how.

6. Arrange to have a local vendor demonstrate to your class the latest equipment in optical-character recognition, micrographics, computer-generated graphics, or reprographics.

7. Write a short report about networking applications, costs, and examples.

8. Write a short report about the latest developments in artificial intelligence as they relate to business. Use sources published within the past two years.

## CASE STUDY

"We have a chance—a *good* chance—to land the Worldwide, Inc., account; but I need your help!" exclaimed George Minor, as he burst into the outer office of Markets Unlimited, an up-and-coming advertising agency.

George had been working on the Worldwide account for six months, and everyone in the office was excited by the possibility of his capturing this $4,000,000 account for the agency. The office staff stood poised, like an army ready to move, waiting for George's instructions.

"Here's what we're up against," George began. "Monday—that's four days from now—Worldwide wants us to present our campaign to their board at their national headquarters in London. Then, on Thursday—a week from today—they want us to repeat the presentation to their Asian affiliate in Tokyo. If both groups like the campaign, the account is ours!"

The general excitement was interrupted by a question from Marian Flint, President of Markets Unlimited, "Can we do it? Can we get everything we need for the presentations to London in four days and to Tokyo just three days later?"

After considerable discussion, everyone agreed that the following materials were necessary for both presentations to be effective:

1. Complete files of all cost data, indicating how all media costs were calculated
2. Complete files on the media that were considered and how the proposed media were selected
3. Storyboards (pictorial summaries) for all television ads
4. Samples of all print media ads
5. Tapes of all radio ads
6. Graphic presentations of estimated benefits of the campaign
7. Extensive backup research data to answer questions that have not been anticipated specifically

As the discussion ended, Marian asked again, "Can we do it? Can we get everything we need for the presentations to London in four days and to Tokyo just three days later?"

George went over the list carefully. "We already have all the media samples, but we don't have time to ship them—and I can't carry that much with me on the plane. Although the cost and media selection information still needs some work, it could be ready to present by Saturday. The benefits package is ready now, and we have a ton of background data. But how are we going to get it there?"

"Don't panic," said Mason Jenson, the head of MU's new technical communications section. "I may be able to solve most of your problems with our new equipment."

1.  If you were in Jenson's shoes, what equipment would you need to compile the cost and the media-selection data? Explain your answer.
2.  What type of equipment could make the media samples easier to get to the overseas presentations? Explain your answer.
3.  What alternatives are available in getting the bulky background data to the meetings? Which would you recommend, and why?

## REFERENCES

Kellyn S. Betts, "PCs Are Getting Down to Business," *Modern Office Technology* (November 1985): 66-74.

David Copithorne, "The 'Compunications' Revolution," *Dun's Review* (August 1980): 68.

"Global Communications Field Has New Competitor," *Modern Office Technology* (January 1985): 35-37.

Alvin Toffler, *The Third Wave* (New York: William Morrow and Company, Inc.), 1980.

Frederick Williams, *The Communications Revolution* (New York: New American Library), 1983.

## SUGGESTED READINGS

Athey, Thomas H. and Robert W. Zmud. *Introduction to Computers and Information Systems*. Glenview, IL: Scott, Foresman and Company, 1986.

Cross, Thomas B. and Marjorie B. Raizman. *Networking: An Electronic Mail Handbook*. Glenview, IL: Scott, Foresman and Company, 1986.

Kelleher, Kathleen and Thomas B. Cross. *Teleconferencing: Linking People Together Electronically*. Englewood Cliffs, NJ: Prentice-Hall, 1985.

Meadow, Charles T. and Albert S. Tedesco. *Telecommunications for Management*. New York: McGraw-Hill, 1985.

Sanders, D. H. *Computers Today*, 2nd ed. New York: McGraw-Hill, 1985.

Smith, Allen N., Wilma Jean Alexander, and Donald B. Medley. *Advanced Office Systems*. Cincinnati: South-Western Publishing Co., 1986.

# MANAGING ORGANIZATIONAL COMMUNICATION

## CHAPTER 20

"What did Mr. Warren tell you about the firm?" Al Torres asked Penny Bates. Penny had just been hired to work on Al's audit team at Warren, Jamison, and Knutsen, a local public accounting firm.

Penny replied, "He told me that the partners believe in participative management and that all the decisions are made democratically at a weekly staff meeting."

"He thinks the meetings are democratic," said Al, "because we vote on everything."

He laughed and added, "Mr. Warren always says 'Everyone in favor say aye' when he makes a decision, but we know he really means 'Everyone opposed, resign.'"

As Penny discovered, managers and employees sometimes have different perceptions and attitudes toward organizational factors such as management styles, formal and informal channels, decision processes, and information systems. These factors are all components of organizational communication, which affects every member and all activities of an organization.

This chapter discusses organizational communication and its management, including the following topics:

• Organizational systems
• Communication networks in organizations

- Communication management functions—planning, organizing, directing, and controlling
- Design and management of information systems
- Communication audits

# ORGANIZATIONAL COMMUNICATION

**Organizational communication** is the internal and external flow of information within and from an organization. Through organizational communication, individuals transmit information outward, upward, downward, and across the organizational structure.

The various facets of organizational communication include human relationships, written and oral media, and various types of hardware. These ingredients all contribute to the primary goal of organizational communication, which is to support the management process in achieving the objectives of an organization.

Organizational communication involves both internal and external messages in various forms, for example:

1. *Oral messages*, including face-to-face conversations, meetings, phone calls, informal complaints and grievances, and negotiations
2. *Written messages*, including memos, letters, policy and procedure manuals, company publications, official notices, directives, reports, formal complaints and grievances, news releases, and other messages relating to publicity
3. *Graphic or pictorial messages*, including computer graphics, printed charts and graphs, bulletin boards, and photographs
4. *Other organizational variables* that affect communication, such as communication "climate," management styles, interpersonal relationships, position titles and roles, office layout, and organizational image

Organizational communication is concerned with not only the intended and perceived content of messages but also with the origin and destination of messages, the message channels, and the relationships among the channels. In addition, the attitudes and feelings of personnel toward the organization's communication processes also play an important role. A discussion of organizational communication must take into account the many events, processes, and behaviors that cause a company's personnel to perceive meaning from the information they receive.

Through organizational communication, executives manage the entire company and coordinate its units. These organizational units include all the various levels of a company's divisions and departments.

## ORGANIZATIONAL SYSTEMS

A **system** is a network of related components or activities that interact to accomplish a particular goal. In organizations, the various systems are divided into smaller units or **subsystems** that exist to accomplish specific functions or tasks. Business organizations generally are composed of systems such as production, marketing, and finance. Marketing systems, for example, typically contain subsystems such as sales, marketing research, and advertising.

The larger and more complex the organization, the more coordination is needed among the various systems and subsystems as they work together to accomplish the goals of the organization. To coordinate information needs, *information systems* specialize in acquiring, processing, storing, retrieving, and transmitting information throughout the organization.

Organizational communication may be classified according to the following system levels (Farace et al., 1977, 50):

1. *Individuals* who send information to and receive information from the organization as a whole
2. *Dyads* consisting of two-person units such as a pair of coworkers or a superior and a subordinate
3. *Groups* composed of three or more persons linked by a working relationship (for example, members of a department or "teams" within a department)
4. *The entire organization* interacting with other organizations

The four system levels of organizational communication are linked together in a set of interdependent relationships called *networks*.

## COMMUNICATION NETWORKS IN ORGANIZATIONS

As discussed in Chapter 2, *communication networks* are the paths along which messages travel from one person to another or among groups. People occupy different roles at various system levels within an organization; networks allow people in those various roles to interact with one another in accomplishing the work of the organization.

Basically, networks are determined by who communicates with whom and for what purpose. Some group members function in special network roles such as *gatekeepers* who control the flow of information (Allen, 1977, 83), *liaisons* who serve as a link between networks, and *isolates* who are isolated from the flow of information (Farace et al., 1977, 185-191). Managers often serve as gatekeepers because they have access to important information and are in a position to control it. Liaisons generally are leaders who communicate with and often coordinate activities of several networks. Isolates are individuals who do not receive information because they are physically separated from the group, work on a different shift, or for some other reason do not belong to a network.

*Formal networks* follow the lines of authority prescribed in a formal organization chart; *informal networks* follow various patterns of informal relationships. Managers and executives primarily rely on formal networks to transmit information in an orderly way. When formal networks receive inadequate flows of information within an organization, "bottlenecks" are formed that are often bypassed by informal networks — the grapevine (Wofford et al., 1977, 361-362). Informal networks, which tend to emerge whenever the formal network system does not meet people's needs for information, may develop in any direction (upward, downward, laterally, or even diagonally across the formal structure of the organization). Disseminating adequate, timely information through formal networks is usually a more effective means of managing organizational communication than relying on the grapevine, moreover, because the grapevine is difficult to control.

Formal networks, however, often tend to be rigid and less flexible than informal networks. Rigid patterns such as scheduling meetings and preparing reports at set times rather than when they are actually needed may result in wasted time and resources, low morale, and failure to adapt to change.

The systems and subsystems within an organization ideally do not function independently of one another. The various components of an organization depend upon one another for the distribution of information about their activities. That information is disseminated through network *channels* (such as meetings, memorandums, and computer printouts), which are discussed in Chapter 2.

In a typical manufacturing firm, the sales and production departments depend upon each other for accurate and timely information about orders for their products. For example, when a salesperson receives an order from a customer for a particular product, he or she goes to a computer terminal and "pulls" up information about that product from the finished goods inventory file in the product database. If the available quantity of that product is adequate, the salesperson accepts the order. If the product inventory is insufficient for filling the order, the salesperson calls the production department to find out how long the order must be delayed and then relays that information to the customer. The production department personnel, in turn, depend upon the sales staff to inform them about customers' orders and to give them feedback from customers about the product. If bottlenecks develop in the communication network between the two departments, the company is likely to lose customers.

The communication network linking the people in two or more departments is determined by factors such as the structure of the organization, purpose and quantity of information to be transmitted, physical distance between individuals, social relationships between people, and available technology. The network between the two departments also may be affected by other networks; for example, the marketing department might receive certain production information from the information systems department rather than directly from the production department.

Communication systems, networks, and hardware must be managed effectively if an organization is to function efficiently. Communication management is a complex task that involves coordinating all the various components of organizational communication.

## COMMUNICATION MANAGEMENT

As organizations have become more complex, communication processes have become increasingly complicated and important. Increased organizational size, complexity, and the technology explosion, together with the need for greater efficiency and effectiveness have created a constant demand for better organizational communication. Ineffective communication often has been blamed for everything from poor morale and personnel problems to increased costs, declining sales, and low productivity. On the other hand, improved communication may be credited with improving managerial effectiveness and increasing the effectiveness of an entire organization.

Many organizations experience problems related to the information explosion. Executives find themselves buried in administrative communication. The more data the organization produces, the more difficult communication is to manage. An overload of information can cause problems just as easily as insufficient information. To function efficiently, a company's organizational policies and information systems must eliminate communication bottlenecks and at the same time avoid information overloads by eliminating unnecessary paperwork and meetings.

In many organizations, communication problems have reached critical proportions. Typical communication problems may include the following issues:*

1. Employees do not receive all the information they would like to have, particularly information relating to the goals and concerns of the organization as a whole.
2. Information bottlenecks occur due to poor interpersonal relationships, lack of cooperation, and personality clashes.
3. In large organizations, employees tend to feel isolated from the bulk of information flow and may not receive adequate information needed to perform their jobs well.
4. Employees are dissatisfied with top management as communicators.
5. Horizontal communication between work groups is often poor; this situation creates conflict between departments and competition for resources.
6. Supervisors frequently misuse authority by showing favoritism, discriminating against certain employees, and failing to follow correct communication procedures.
7. Employees receive inadequate feedback about their performance and become dissatisfied with the reward system.

*Adapted from Norman K. Perrill and Martha H. Rader, "The Communication Audit: An Ounce of Prevention," *Arizona Business*, 26, no. 7 (August/September 1979), 15-16.

8. Although opportunities may exist for employees to communicate upward, management often fails to respond adequately, particularly to negative information about the performance of supervisory personnel.
9. The overall communication climate is frequently more negative than positive; this condition is associated with distrust, the lack of openness, and poor morale.

Because organizational communication involves so many complex factors and problems, managing organizational communication is not an easy task. Managers have difficulty grasping what is happening in terms of the flow of information, where it is occurring, how it is affecting the organization, and which procedures might improve the situation. Managing such a large number of variables in so many complex relationships is an enormous task that requires major commitments of time and energy from top executives as well as middle managers.

In its broadest sense, communication management includes not only the transmission of information but also the collection, processing, storage, retrieval, use, and destruction of information. To be effective, these activities must be managed appropriately throughout an organization rather than handled haphazardly.

**Communication management** involves the application of management techniques to organizational communication. Management consists of the following four functions: *planning*, *organizing*, *directing*, and *controlling*. Effective communication management depends upon all four of these functions.

## Planning

**Planning** is the process of deciding what an organization should do in the future. In particular, planning means setting comprehensive long-range goals and objectives for the organization and determining when and how those goals and objectives should be met. Planning also involves collecting the necessary information on which to base those decisions, anticipating technological and other changes, and selecting appropriate strategies in response to those changes.

Effective planning requires the support of top management in formulating goals and developing policies. If top management does not participate in the planning process, the resulting plans likely will not be carried out.

Personnel are more apt to accept change if they are involved in the planning process. Therefore, planning the information and communication needs of a business organization should include the use of internal planning committees. These committees should be composed of knowledgeable representatives at various levels and from different divisions and/or departments. The planning process, which may be directed by a professional information manager, may also include the use of outside consultants. The task of the planning committee should be to collect information, develop strategy and policy, recommend projects to implement policy, and set priorities.

The information to be collected should begin with a review and assessment of current information policies and communication activities. This information may be obtained by conducting a communication audit discussed on page 505. Other helpful information includes industry norms as well as projections of future information needs for the industry, the total organization, and its component parts.

**Strategic planning** refers to developing organizational **strategy** (courses of action designed to achieve overall organizational goals). Companies generally specify organizational strategy in terms of management policies. A **policy** is a written statement that describes organizational strategy and guidelines for achieving that strategy. Communication policy should include topics such as what information should be available to whom, who is responsible for various communication activities, and how confidentiality will be maintained.

Strategy and policy are supported by various projects and procedures. A **project** is a set of activities designed to achieve a specific objective, and a **procedure** is a particular way to accomplish that objective. For example, an organization might formulate a strategy to improve office productivity by reducing paperwork. The policy would set objectives for supporting that strategy, including specifying timetables, percentages, and costs. Particular projects for achieving the objectives might include installing electronic mail, redesigning office forms, and reducing the number and frequency of routine reports. Various procedures would specify how and by whom these projects would be accomplished.

Additional planning activities include *setting priorities*, *establishing timetables*, and *budgeting resources*. Setting priorities involves evaluating various projects and ranking them in terms of importance—in other words, which should be accomplished first. Timetables specify when projects will be undertaken and when they are scheduled to be completed. Finally, budgets allocate resources such as funds for hiring additional personnel and purchasing new equipment needed for implementing various communication projects in the future.

## Organizing

**Organizing** is the process of determining the means by which plans are to be carried out. Organizing involves structuring activities designed to accomplish the objectives that were established in the planning stage. Various components of organizing include structuring various projects and tasks within those projects, determining how to allocate the work among organizational systems, and defining the relationships among systems and subsystems.

Many companies employ an *information systems approach* to organizing communication activities. The **information systems approach** centrally integrates and coordinates various information resources—people, services, hardware, software, and information flow—that will help carry out the policies developed through corporate planning. Developing an integrated information system is an efficient alternative to managing information piecemeal in different departments.

The design of information systems may involve the following general issues:

1. Should the company have a single information systems/resource department?
2. To what degree should computers and other office equipment be centralized?
3. How should control over office automation be distributed between an information systems department and user departments?
4. How will new technology be integrated into the existing information base consisting of office information and management information systems?

The implementation of an information system may include the following specific issues:

1. When, where, and in what form should information be created?
2. When and where should the various phases of data and information processing take place?
3. In what format and media will information be the most useful?
4. Where and when is the information needed? Who should have it?
5. By and to whom, and how should the information be transmitted?
6. What technology should be used in producing, processing, transmitting, and storing the information?
7. Who is responsible for the security of the information?
8. What information should be stored and for how long?
9. Who is responsible for the storage and retrieval of the information?
10. How, when, and by whom should the information be destroyed?

Information systems can be organized in one of the following four ways (Smith et al., 1985, 372):

**Centralized Information Systems**. In a **centralized information system**, all resources for that particular system, including people and equipment, are together in one location. For example, when data entry is centralized, all data-entry equipment and the personnel who use it are located together in a large data-entry center. Advantages of a centralized system include lower expenditures for equipment, closer supervision of employees, and better conformity to work standards than with a decentralized system. However, disadvantages may include slow turnaround time and employee dissatisfaction with bureaucratic procedures.

**Clustered Information Systems**. A **clustered information system** consists of several system centers located throughout an organization. The clustered arrangement has the advantage of being closer to the users than a centralized system. However, a clustered system is generally more expensive than a centralized system because it requires duplication of equipment and personnel.

**Distributed Information Systems**. A **distributed information system** employs the ideal "state of the art" in communication technology. A distributed system is composed of an information center linked with other parts of the organization by an electronic network. A typical distributed system consists of a centralized mainframe computer linked with smaller computers (minicomputers and microcomputers) located throughout the organization. A distributed information system allows strong centralized control over the network and also permits employees to access the system easily, no matter where their offices are located.

**Decentralized Information Systems**. In a **decentralized information system**, each organizational component is independently responsible for its own information and communication activities, including collecting, processing, transmitting, storing, and retrieving information. Decentralized systems are becoming less prevalent than in the past because of inherent inefficiencies such as duplication of activities and equipment, hardware incompatibility, and lack of standardization of components.

To function efficiently within the framework of the overall information system, the various components (including computer hardware, other office equipment, software, and procedures) must be compatible with one another. Component processes include document creation, reproduction, transmission, storage, retrieval, and destruction. All of these processes should function together in a well-organized, integrated information system with well-defined policies and procedures.

## Directing

**Directing**, or the human factor in management, is the process of leading the members of an organization. The directing function includes activities such as staffing, delegating, supervising, training, motivating, coordinating, and communicating with subordinates. Managers carry out the organizational plan by delegating various components of the plan to subordinates, communicating information about expected tasks and job performance standards, and providing feedback about performance.

*Leadership*, which is the process of influencing others to achieve specified goals, is perhaps the most important factor in directing the work of subordinates. Effective leadership occurs when subordinates behave in a specified manner and, through their efforts, the organizational system achieves its goals and objectives. Although management literature describes many characteristics and styles of leadership, the following communication variables are essential attributes of effective management:

1. *An open communication climate*. Communication channels ideally should encourage free flow of information in a climate of trust and mutual respect. Employees should be able to trust their supervisors, who in turn, should support, respect, and trust their subordinates. Everyone

should know what is going on and what is planned for the future. Methods of achieving an open communication climate include meetings of individuals and departments, memorandums, employee newsletters, and notices posted on bulletin boards.

2. *Participative decision making*. A democratic rather than authoritative style of management is characterized by participative decision making. Those who are affected most by a decision should have an opportunity to help make that decision. For example, users of office equipment should be involved in selecting equipment and deciding how it should be used and maintained.

3. *Clearly defined policies and procedures*. In many organizations, employees do not understand management policies or how those policies affect their jobs. Often employees and their supervisors have different expectations about their roles and responsibilities. Clear and up-to-date policy and procedures manuals, organization charts, and job descriptions should be provided to all personnel.

4. *Specific performance standards*. Performance standards should be clearly communicated to employees, who ideally should participate in developing performance criteria and standards for the tasks they perform. Performance appraisal standards should specify what constitutes an "average" performance and differentiate between "average" and other performance levels, such as outstanding, good, poor, and unsatisfactory.

5. *Adequate feedback*. Positive feedback is usually a better motivator than negative feedback. When employees receive recognition for doing a good job, they become motivated to do even better. In contrast, criticism and punishment often discourage and demoralize employees rather than motivate them to improve their performance. Employee feedback, which should be handled through informal meetings as well as through a formal appraisal system, should be as positive and constructive as possible.

6. *Advancement opportunities*. Managers should provide opportunities for subordinates to learn new skills and to advance in the organization. People who are in dead-end jobs are likely to lose their enthusiasm and become unproductive. Opportunities for advancement can motivate employees to reach their potential in the organization. Supervisors should identify employees who have the potential to advance and provide them with additional responsibilities and/or training.

## Controlling

The **controlling** function of management emphasizes identification of and evaluation of accomplishments within an organization. When a manager controls an organizational unit, he or she evaluates what tasks have been accomplished and how well. Managerial control involves collecting information about quantity, quality, and costs of work output and then comparing these factors with performance objectives and budgets. If actual output is less or of lower quality than planned or if costs exceed budgeted amounts, a manager must determine the cause and take appropriate corrective action.

For example, standards for the credit and collection department may specify that no more than 10 percent of the company's accounts receivable may be past due at any time. If the accounts receivable begin to exceed that percentage, then management must determine why the problem has occurred and take steps to stop the trend. Perhaps the computerized system is malfunctioning and customers are not receiving reminder notices and collection messages, or perhaps the credit-evaluation system has established credit standards that are too low. Whatever the cause or combination of causes, corrective measures must be implemented.

Managerial control entails measuring, comparing, and correcting. All of these processes require effective communication among the people who are involved. A manager must provide feedback, in particular, to the units and individuals who can actually implement the needed corrections.

Managerial control processes are categorized as *work measurement*, *comparison to standards*, and *corrective measures*.

**Work Measurement**. The quantity, quality, timeliness, and costs of written communication generally can be measured fairly easily. To measure accurately the amount of output, a manager must use a standard unit of measurement such as pages of typewritten copy, number of form letters mailed, number of envelopes, or reams of duplicating paper. Units for measuring quantity of oral communication output may include the number of local or long-distance telephone calls, number of interviews, and number of meetings and conferences.

The quality of written communication output may be measured in units such as the number of errors, number of complaints received, or number of pages returned for correction. The quality of both written and oral communication also can be measured by having information receivers or users fill out evaluation forms regularly or periodically.

Timeliness can be measured in turnaround time (hours or days) to complete a specified unit of work (for example, keying a letter or writing a report). Costs are measured by the amount of expenditures for items such as purchase and repair of equipment, office supplies, long-distance telephone calls, postage, and overtime wages for hourly employees.

**Comparison to Standards**. Work should be evaluated by using standards as a basis for comparison. Standards (for example, keyboarding at a rate of 60 words per minute with 95 percent accuracy) are used to determine if work quantity and quality are satisfactory. Therefore, standards ought to be based on average rather than outstanding performance. In large organizations, standards are set by professional *work evaluators* from the personnel or human resources department. Standards need to be written clearly and reviewed periodically to ensure that they are current. Standards may be included in job descriptions, personnel manuals, or departmental procedures manuals.

Communication costs should be evaluated by using *budgets* as a standard for comparision. Budgets are based on previous costs as well as projected increases or decreases in future costs due to changes in factors such as technology and workload. Sources of cost information for budgeting purposes include accounting reports (such as accounts payable and payroll records), departmental requests, and estimates from vendors.

Communication costs are controlled by comparing actual expenditures with budgeted amounts for *labor*, *overhead*, *equipment*, and *material costs*. Labor costs include salaries, wages, and fringe benefits of office employees. Overhead costs include items such as building rental or depreciation, utilities, and costs of leasing telecommunication systems. Equipment costs include purchase and leasing expenditures, maintenance, and repair of items such as computer and office equipment, computer software, filing cabinets, and office furniture. Material costs include expenditures for office supplies such as computer disks, paper, office forms, letterheads, envelopes, file folders, microfilm, and postage.

Controlling costs should be a continuous rather than an occasional process. For cost controls to be effective, all employees, not just managers, must cooperate in controlling costs. Suggestion systems and bonus systems are two popular techniques many organizations use to encourage employees to help control costs.

**Corrective Measures**. When quantity, quality, timeliness, and costs of work output meet or exceed standards, corrective measures are unnecessary. When one or more of these factors are below the standard, however, some type of corrective action is required. An analysis of the situation, which should include feedback from employees who are closest to the problem, ought to indicate what type of corrective measures are needed. For example, insufficient quantity of output, or a backlog of work, may indicate that additional personnel should be hired. Poor quality of work output might be corrected by providing training for employees or supervising employees more closely. Failure to meet deadlines may be corrected by purchasing more up-to-date equipment or hiring temporary workers during particularly busy times. Budget overruns may be corrected by various methods such as requiring all purchases over a certain amount to be approved by top management; by eliminating or combining services; by reducing or deferring expenditures for equipment and supplies; or as a last resort, by reducing staff.

**Communication Audits**. An increasingly popular method of controlling organizational communication is to conduct a *communication audit*. Just as a periodic financial audit provides information about the financial condition of a firm, a **communication audit** is a diagnostic examination of the communication processes operating within an organization. A communication audit provides an objective analysis of the organization's communication processes, procedures, and effectiveness. Just as a company uses the results of a financial audit to control finances and prevent financial crises from occurring, the purpose of a communication audit is to furnish management with information that may be used to prevent or correct potential communication problems. By getting an objective assessment of communication strengths and weaknesses, managers can plan intelligently and implement training programs. In addition, early diagnosis of communication problems can enable management to take remedial action before minor problems develop into major ones. Finally, measuring communication activities after implementing remedial action can serve as a follow-up assessment of the effectiveness of intervention actions. Various methods of auditing organizational communication include *information-flow studies*, *message studies*, and *perceptual/attitudinal studies*, as follows:*

1.  *Information-flow studies* (network analyses) determine the structure and functions of communication networks in organizations. Such studies may include directionality of messages (who initiates communication with whom), channels (formal and informal), and identification of communication systems and subsystems. Network analyses usually involve written surveys of employees.
2.  *Message studies* evaluate the content of messages, including factors such as purpose, appropriateness, accuracy, timeliness, distortions, overload, underload, and credibility. Message studies typically use data collected by surveys, content analysis, diaries (logs of messages sent and received), or oral and written descriptions of critical incidents (major communication problems).
3.  *Perceptual/attitudinal studies* assess individuals' perceptions and attitudes about communication practices and climate in an organization. Interviews and questionnaires are often used to collect this type of information.

A comprehensive communication audit consists of two phases: (1) a *descriptive stage*, which involves studying the organizational communication system to determine the communication activities that take place and (2) an *analysis* of the effectiveness of the communication system, which entails relating communication data to measures of organizational effectiveness (such as employee morale, productivity, turnover, absenteeism, complaints, etc.) and the achievement of organizational objectives.

In a typical communication audit, employees fill out questionnaires that elicit information relating to the current status of the communication system as well as their perceptions of the desired or ideal system. For example, an employee would indicate (on a scale of 1 to 5) the amount of information he or she currently receives about such topics as job duties, pay and benefits, evaluation procedures, and advancement opportunities. Each respondent also would indicate on a similar scale the amount of information *needed* about each of these topics. When the data from these scales are analyzed, a comparison of the amount of information received with the amount needed may reveal a

---

*This section is taken from "The Communication Audit: An Ounce of Prevention," 10-16 (with adaptation).

number of potential trouble spots. For example, if the amount of information needed is found to be significantly greater than the amount being received, the employee may not be getting enough information on a specific topic to accomplish expected work tasks, or may at the very least feel cut off from essential communication channels.

Similar questions elicit additional information about timeliness and accuracy of messages, employee job satisfaction, and relationships with others. Questions about timeliness are concerned with whether the employee gets information when it is needed—from sources such as the immediate supervisor, middle or top management, and subordinates. Questions about relationships ask respondents to indicate, for example, how much they trust various sources of information (coworkers, supervisors, top management, etc.). Employees also rate the following factors: (1) the extent to which supervisors listen to them and allow them to participate in decisions affecting their jobs, (2) how free they are to disagree or tell a supervisor when things are going wrong, and (3) how they feel about various relationships that directly affect the achievement of organizational goals.

Although managers often give lip service to the need to improve communication, they often are unable to follow through with steps to improve communication because they are unable to evaluate the adequacy of the organization's communication policies and practices. A communication audit can provide management with just such concrete information on which to base enlightened decisions.

## SUMMARY

Organizational communication is the flow of information within and from the system and subsystems of an organization. Simply stated, organizational communication encompasses every member and activity of an organization, as information travels from person to person and group to group along both formal and informal networks.

As an organization grows in complexity and size, it produces more and more information. This increase in information makes communication more difficult to manage. Paradoxically, the growth in a company demands more effective communication, which in turn requires more effective management of organizational communication.

Communication management involves applying the primary management functions—planning, organizing, directing, and controlling—to the improvement of a company's information system. Planning entails collecting information, developing policy and strategy, recommending projects, and setting priorities. Organizing involves structuring and assigning the projects and defining the relationships among different components. In particular, organizing involves determining whether a company's information system should be centralized, clustered, distributed, or decentralized. Directing deals with supervising and leading personnel. Controlling involves collecting information about output, comparing it with standards, and acting to correct major discrepancies between actual output and objectives.

Control techniques used by communication managers include measuring work in relation to performance standards and conducting communication audits. To round out the information systems approach to communication management, executives use the results of communication audits and other "controls" in future planning, organizing, and directing.

## CHAPTER REVIEW

1. Define *organizational communication* and describe its goal.
2. Who uses *communication networks* in business organizations? For what purpose?
3. Define the following terms and provide an example of each:
   a. *Organizational system*
   b. *Organizational subsystem*
   c. *Information system*
4. List and describe three *communication network* roles.
5. Identify and describe the two classifications of communication networks. What factors determine the pattern of communication networks?
6. What is *communication management*? What information-related activities are included in managing organizational communication?
7. List and briefly describe the four primary managerial functions.
8. React to the following statement and discuss why it is true or false: "Determining organizational strategy is part of the control function of management."
9. List and describe four ways that information systems may be organized.
10. What is the purpose of a *communication audit*? Describe the two components of a communication audit.
11. Some managers believe that employees should participate in making decisions that affect them. If managers have more education and experience than the employees they supervise, then shouldn't the managers make the decisions? Why or why not?
12. "Communication costs are skyrocketing out of control." What evidence would a communication manager need to support this statement?

## APPLICATIONS

1. Interview an information manager at a local organization that processes a large volume of information (for example, a large bank, insurance company, or government agency). From your interview, determine the network or path that a typical document such as a loan application or life-insurance policy application follows within the organization. Write a one- or two-page report describing the route the document follows from one department to another and from one individual to another. Include a diagram or flow chart.

2. Assume that you are manager of the information systems department at Rad-kur Manufacturing Company. Recently Jacqueline King, the personnel director, revealed at a management meeting that the company has been experiencing a number of personnel problems, including several incidents related to poor communication between employees and their supervisors, as well as between departments. Jacqueline stated that she was not sure what the root of these problems was, and she asked for suggestions. After thinking it over, you decide to suggest a communication audit. Write a persuasive memo to Jacqueline, who has probably never heard of a communication audit. Your memo should "sell" the advantages of a communication audit, which could be conducted by a management consulting firm called Management Pros. Be sure to follow the outline for a persuasive message (see Chapter 7, page 148).

3. You are communication manager at Telles Electronics Company. Yesterday the company president showed you a stack of letters that company sales representatives had written to customers. "These letters are an embarrassment to the company," he said. "I've never seen such poor writing and so many errors. You'll have to do something about it." On the basis of the four management functions discussed in this chapter, write a short outline of the steps you would take to implement a writing-improvement program.

4. You are vice president of administration at Allison Insurance Underwriters, a firm with approximately a hundred employees. You receive a request from Hal O'Steen, supervisor of the insurance adjusting department, to purchase a $2,000 copying machine for his department. His memo states that having a copier in his department would be more efficient than continuing to use the machines in the copy center. Identify and discuss the issues that are involved in making this decision.

5. Visit a local company and interview a manager or supervisor in the management information systems department. Find out how data processing, word processing, records management, and reprographics services are organized (centralized, decentralized, distributed, or clustered). Present to the class a short oral report of your findings.

## CASE STUDY

Brad Warren, manager of the Westex Metals Products plant in Denver, pounded on the table. "We *really* need a minicomputer," he shouted, "it's *not* a frill!"

"Now don't get ruffled," said Alice Turner, the vice president of finance. "Why do you need one?" she inquired.

The group, which was attempting to discuss budget proposals at the quarterly executive planning meeting, had become embroiled in an argument over whether the information system should decentralize or remain centralized.

"By the time we receive customer orders and inventory reports from L.A.," Brad replied, "they're already out of date. If we had our own minicomputer, we could process our own information without having to go through the L.A. office."

Vivianne Allen added, "We need one in Kansas City, too. The sales staff could process orders online, and we could get information to our customers much faster."

Alice turned to Harry Schwartz, the corporate director of Management Information Systems, and asked, "What do you think, Harry?"

"I think it's a good idea," he replied, "but it's not practical. It would duplicate services and equipment and create a lot of problems with two different databases."

1. Who is right, Harry or Brad?
2. What other solutions could you suggest, and why?

## REFERENCES

Richard K. Allen, *Organizational Management Through Communication* (New York: Harper and Row, 1977).

Richard V. Farace, Peter R. Monge, and Hamish M. Russell, *Communicating and Organizing* (Reading, MA: Addison-Wesley, 1977).

Harold T. Smith et al., *Automated Office Systems Management* (New York: John Wiley and Sons, 1985).

Jerry C. Wofford, Edwin A. Gerloff, and Robert C. Cummins, *Organizational Communication: The Keystone to Managerial Effectiveness* (New York: McGraw-Hill, 1977).

## SUGGESTED READINGS

Allen, Richard K. *Organizational Management Through Communication*. New York: Harper and Row, 1977.

Diebold, John. *Managing Information: The Challenge and the Opportunity*. New York: American Management Associations, 1985.

Goldhaber, Gerald M. *Organizational Communication*, 4th ed. Dubuque, IA: William C. Brown, 1986.

Goldhaber, Gerald M. and Donald P. Rogers. *Auditing Organizational Communication Systems: The ICA Communication Audit*. Dubuque, IA: Kendall-Hunt, 1979.

Stallard, John J. and George R. Terry. *Office Systems Management*, 9th ed. Homewood, IL: Richard D. Irwin, 1984.

# GRAMMAR AND MECHANICS

## APPENDIX A

Correct grammar and mechanics are essential for effective business communication. Grammatical, punctuation, spelling, and other errors create negative impressions, distract readers, and lessen the effectiveness of business messages. Appendix A provides a review of English grammar and mechanics. Consult a reference manual or textbook (such as *Harbrace College Handbook* or *Effective English for Colleges*) for a comprehensive listing of rules and guidelines.

## GRAMMAR

**Grammar** is the study of words, their function, and relationship to each other in sentences. Grammatical rules provide the foundation on which communication stands. Good communication relies on the correct use of grammar; therefore, learning and mastering grammatical rules is a necessity.

### Parts of Speech

Words are generally grouped under seven major parts of speech: *nouns*, *pronouns*, *verbs*, *adjectives*, *adverbs*, *prepositions*, and *conjunctions*.

**Nouns.** Nouns are words that name persons, places, things, qualities, and concepts.

NOUNS:   Jim Evans, Mary, California, room, tree, chair, sorrow, fatigue, self

Nouns can be classified as *common*, *proper*, *collective*, *compound*, and *concrete or abstract* nouns.

1. *Common Nouns*. A **common noun** names a person, group of persons, place, thing, quality, or concept.

PERSON:   doctor, woman

GROUP OF PERSONS:   board of directors, senators

PLACE:   street, country

THING:   book, hotel

QUALITY:   happiness, determination

CONCEPT:   identity, belief

Common nouns are generally not capitalized unless they are used as part of a proper noun.

EXAMPLES:   the Gramm-Rudman *Bill*
Martin Luther King *Avenue*
Bell *Laboratories*

2. *Proper Nouns*. A **proper noun** names a particular person, place, or thing. Proper nouns are always capitalized.

PERSON:   Ronald Reagan, Georgia O'Keefe

PLACE:   London, United States of America

THING:   the Constitution, the Stars and Stripes

3. *Collective Nouns*. A **collective noun** names a group of persons, animals, or things.

PERSONS:   committee, jury, group

ANIMALS:   school, pack, herd

THINGS:   batch, collection, set

4. *Compound Nouns*. A **compound noun** is made up of two or more words used as a single noun. Some compound nouns are combined into one word, some consist of two separate words, and some are hyphenated.

EXAMPLES:   timetable      life cycle      eye-opener
eyewitness      trade name      half-truth
chairperson      sales agent      father-in-law

5. *Concrete or Abstract Nouns*. **Concrete nouns** name what our physical senses can perceive; **abstract nouns** identify what our physical senses cannot perceive.

CONCRETE NOUNS:   chair, song, fragrance

ABSTRACT NOUNS:   ambition, enthusiasm, honor

Nouns function in sentences as *subjects*, *direct and indirect objects*, *objects of preposition*, *appositives*, and *predicate nominatives*.

SUBJECT:   *Jim Evans* moved to California.
           The *tree* was struck by lightning.

DIRECT OBJECT:   Mary composed a *letter*.
                 Harry went *home*.

INDIRECT OBJECT:   Mary wrote *Harry* a letter.
                   The personnel manager offered the *employees* a raise.

OBJECT OF PREPOSITION:   Carol Andrews lives in *Toronto*.
                         The orders came from *management*.

APPOSITIVE:   Diane Williams, the *anchorperson*, is both articulate and analytical.
              He ordered filet mignon, the most expensive *item* on the menu.

PREDICATE NOMINATIVE:   Frank Aquino is our firm's *controller*.
                        Careful planning is a *necessity*.

**Pronouns**. Pronouns are words that replace nouns in sentences. A pronoun refers to the noun, once the noun has been identified.

PRONOUNS:   I, me, myself, you, yourself, they, them, their, he, she, her, him, it, who, whom

A pronoun should agree with its antecedent (the noun it replaces) in number. A singular antecedent requires a singular pronoun, and a plural antecedent requires a plural pronoun.

SINGULAR PRONOUN:   Harry answered *his* electronic mail.

PLURAL PRONOUN:   The employees answered *their* electronic mail.

Compound antecedents are two or more singular antecedents that are joined by *and* and require a plural pronoun.

PLURAL PRONOUN:   Mary and Dori answered *their* electronic mail.
                  Ben and the other employees submitted *their* resignations.

Pronoun *case* indicates whether the pronoun is used as a subject (*subjective* or *nominative* case), an object (*objective* case), or possessive (*possessive* case).

SUBJECTIVE:   I, we, you, he, she, they, who, it

OBJECTIVE:   me, us, you, her, him, them, whom, it

POSSESSIVE:   my, our, your, her, his, their, whose, its

1. *Subjective Case*. When a pronoun is the subject of a sentence or clause, use the **subjective case**.

SUBJECTIVE CASE:   *She* attended the meeting. (subject of the sentence)
When Marty was traveling on business, *he* called his family every day. (subject of the clause)

Use *who* as the subject of a clause or sentence.

EXAMPLES:   *Who* left a message? (subject of the sentence)
May I ask *who* is calling? (subject of the noun clause)

2. *Objective Case*. Use the **objective case** when a pronoun is used as the direct or indirect object of a verb or the object of a preposition.

OBJECTIVE CASE:   Frank's joke embarrassed Mary and *me*. (direct object)
Marvin sent *us* a message. (indirect object)
Last evening I spoke with Della and *him*. (object of preposition)
The supervisor sent an evaluation form to *him*. (object of preposition)

Use *whom* as a direct or indirect object or object of preposition.

EXAMPLES:   *Whom* do you trust? (direct object)
You gave *whom* the report? (indirect object)
To *whom* did you wish to speak? (object of preposition)

The case of a pronoun following *than* or *as* may be either subjective or objective, depending upon whether the pronoun is the subject or object of the following verb (which may be stated or implied).

SUBJECTIVE CASE:   Kathy has been with the company longer than *we* (have). (subject of verb)
The boss criticizes him more than (he criticizes) *me*. (object of verb)

3. *Possessive Case*. Use the **possessive case** before a noun or gerund (verb used as a noun), also before a noun to indicate possession.

POSSESSIVE CASE:   The supervisor approved *her* travel request. (possessive used before a noun)
Trina appreciated *his* moving the furniture. (possessive used before a gerund)
The Sheltons had a party at *their* house. (possessive denoting possession)

Possessive pronouns should not be confused with contractions that sound like possessive pronouns.

POSSESSIVE PRONOUNS:    its
                        their
                        theirs
                        your

CONTRACTIONS:    it's (it is, it has)
                 they're (they are)
                 there's (there is, there has)
                 you're (you are)

POSSESSIVE CASE:    The employees fought for *their* union.

CONTRACTION:    *They're* requesting a 10 percent salary increase.

## EXERCISE 1

In the following sentences, select the correct pronouns.

1. The manager delegated the task to Helen and (I, me).

2. Mr. Anderson called Linda and (I, me) to his office.

3. I appreciated (him, his) redecorating my office.

4. Susan is unaware of (him, his) offering a promotion to you and (I, me).

5. Frank and (I, me) objected to (our, us) buying the machine because of (it's, its) noise.

6. Wayne Hunter, (who, whom) recently joined the firm, has more management experience than (I, me).

7. The firm is paying Andres a higher salary than (I, me).

8. May I have an appointment with (whoever, whomever) is in charge of this department.

9. From (who, whom) did you receive the information about (them, they)?

10. The sales representative offered a special deal to (he and I) (him and me).

**Verbs.** Verbs are words that express action or state of being. Verbs function as *predicates* of sentences and clauses. Other verb forms are *gerunds*, *participles*, and *infinitives*.

VERBS:    speak, speaks, is speaking, are speaking, has spoken, had spoken, is, am, are, was, were, had been

1. *Predicates.* The main verb of a sentence or clause functions as a predicate. The **predicate** is a part of a sentence that says something about the subject.

PREDICATE:     Marie *is laughing*.
                 Jack *will help*.

2. *Gerunds*. Verb forms called **gerunds** end in *-ing* and function as nouns.

GERUND:     *Running* for political office is against company policy.
              *Paying* promptly is necessary for *establishing* good credit.

3. *Participles*. Verb forms called **participles** function in sentences as adjectives. Participles often end in *-ing*, *-ed*, and *-n*. A participial phrase should clearly refer to the word it modifies which should be placed next to it in the sentence.

PARTICIPLE:     We saw Joe *sitting* in the reception area. (modifies "Joe")
                *Sitting* in the reception area, we saw Joe. (modifies "we")

4. *Infinitives*. Verb forms called **infinitives** are composed of a verb preceded by "to." Infinitives usually function in sentences as nouns. Avoid "splitting" an infinitive (placing a modifier between "to" and the verb that follows).

INFINITIVE:     The professor plans *to dismiss* class early.
               When the fire alarm sounded, the security guard told everyone *to leave* the building quickly. (*not* "to quickly leave")

A verb should agree with its subject in *number*. Use a singular verb with a singular subject and a plural verb with a plural subject.

SINGULAR SUBJECT:     Jerry *is* our newest account executive.

PLURAL SUBJECT:     Account executives *are* well paid.

Use a plural verb with a compound subject.

COMPOUND SUBJECT:     The supervisor and the construction manager *are* at the job.
                         The new computer and the old printer *were* incompatible.

Modifiers and parenthetical words between the subject and verb do not affect the verb number.

EXAMPLES:     Mr. Henderson, not the secretaries, *is* responsible for the error.
             The two accidents, not the citation, *are* why the insurance rates increased.
             The negligence of drivers *is* responsible.
             Determination, as well as intelligence, *is* necessary for success.

Verbs may be classified as *transitive* or *intransitive*. A **transitive verb** must have an object to complete its meaning; however, an **intransitive verb** does not require an object. Avoid confusing the transitive verbs *set* and *lay* with the intransitive verbs *sit* and *lie*.

TRANSITIVE:   set, setting, lay, laid, laying

INTRANSITIVE:   sit, sat, sitting, lay, lain, lying

TRANSITIVE:   Joe *set* the stack of letters in the basket.
              Mary *laid* the report on my desk.

INTRANSITIVE:   Carolyn should *sit* down and rest.
                I have a headache and need to *lie* down.

When expressing contrary-to-fact conditions and formal motions, recommendations, commands, and demands, use the **subjunctive mood**. The subjunctive mood uses the verbs *be* (present tense) and *were* (past tense) with both singular and plural subjects.

SUBJUNCTIVE MOOD:   If today *were* Friday, Jack would be in California.
                    I move that the minutes *be* approved.
                    He recommends that the first alternative *be* adopted.

## EXERCISE 2

In the following sentences, select the correct verb.

1. The audit report recommended that the procedures (are, be) revised.

2. The collection department, not the sales clerks, (are, is) at fault.

3. The reputation of our accountants (are, is) excellent.

4. Ellen White and Miriam Oakes (has, have) the most experience.

5. The company plans (to rapidly expand, to expand rapidly).

6. One of the personal computers (are, is) broken.

7. If I (was, were) Jack, I would use the new computer.

8. The employees and the new supervisor (was, were) in a meeting.

9. The judge ordered that the money (be, is) held in escrow.

10. Marylin (sit, sat) down and (laid, lay) her briefcase on the table.

**Adjectives and Adverbs.** Adjectives are words that modify nouns and pronouns; adverbs are words that modify verbs, adjectives, and other adverbs. Adjectives have various endings, while adverbs often end in *-ly*.

ADJECTIVE:   Henry is a *fast* typist. (modifying "typist")

ADVERB:   Jan ran *quickly* to answer the phone. (modifying "ran")

Use the appropriate forms of comparison called *positive*, *comparative*, and *superlative* to indicate various degrees of adjectives and adverbs. Use the **comparative degree** when referring to two people or things and the **superlative degree** for three or more. The comparative degree of most adjectives is formed by adding *-r* or *-er*, and the superlative degree usually is formed by adding *-est*. The comparative or superlative degree of adverbs usually is formed by adding the word *more*, *most*, *less*, or *least* before the adverb. Some adjectives and adverbs have irregular comparison forms.

| Positive | Comparative | Superlative |
|---|---|---|
| short | shorter | shortest |
| fast | faster | fastest |
| little | less | least |
| nicely | more nicely | most nicely |
| good, well | better | best |
| bad, badly | worse | worst |
| appealing | less appealing | least appealing |

1. *Predicate Adjective and Linking Verb*. **Predicate adjectives** (not adverbs) modify the subject of a sentence.

    **Transitive linking verbs** such as various forms of *be*, *seem*, *appear*, and *become* and verbs of the senses (*feel*, *look*, or *sound*) are needed to connect the subject of a sentence with the predicate adjective.

PREDICATE ADJECTIVE:   Jack felt *apprehensive*.
                       The paint job looks *good*.
                       The exchange rate *appeared* exorbitant.

2. *Adverbs*. **Adverbs** usually follow a verb and refer to the action of a verb.

ADVERB:   The organization finished that project *quickly*.
          The speaker enunciated very *distinctly*.
          The young man acted *courageously* at the scene of the accident.

## EXERCISE 3

In the following sentences, select the correct adjective or adverb.

1. The discount pet store sells pet food (cheaper, more cheaply) than the grocery store.

2. John doesn't think they are (real, really) interested in our offer.

3. That offer was our (lowest, most lowest) price.

4. The advertising layout looks (good, well).

5. Jack worked (real, really) (quick, quickly) to meet the deadline.

6. Of the three accountants, Jack was the (more, most) experienced.

7. The first bid was the (lower, lowest) of the two we received.

8. The credit department (sure, surely) received the check.

9. Jane was (real, really) disappointed.

10. I feel (positive, positively) about the outcome.

**Prepositions**. Prepositions are words that relate a noun or a pronoun to another word called its *object*. A *prepositional phrase* consists of a preposition and its object and modifiers.

PREPOSITIONS:   among, as, at, before, between, by, for, from, in, of, on, over, through, under, up, with

*Prepositional Phrase*. Prepositional phrases should be placed near the word they clearly modify.

PREPOSITIONAL PHRASE:   The professor advised us to study hard for the quiz *on Monday*. (The quiz was on Monday.)
*On Monday* the professor advised us to study hard for the quiz. (The professor told us on Monday.)

Avoid ending sentences with prepositions.

INCORRECT:   Where is the company getting the money to pay the note with?

CORRECT:   Where is the company getting the money to pay the note?

Avoid confusing *between* and *among*. Use *between* when referring to only two items, and use *among* to refer to three or more items.

BETWEEN:   We divided the work *between* the two of us.

AMONG:   We divided the work *among* the three secretaries.

**Conjunctions**. Coordinate conjunctions are words that connect equal words, phrases, and clauses. Subordinate conjunctions connect dependent clauses with independent clauses. Correlative conjunctions are pairs of words that connect two words, phrases, or clauses.

COORDINATE CONJUNCTIONS:   and, but, or, nor, yet

SUBORDINATE CONJUNCTIONS:   after, although, as, because, if, since, when, where

CORRELATIVE CONJUNCTIONS:   both/and, either/or, neither/nor, not only/but also

COORDINATE CONJUNCTION:   Marty *and* I went to the open house.

SUBORDINATE CONJUNCTION:   I plan to return to upstate New York *when* I graduate.

CORRELATIVE CONJUNCTION:   *Either* the U.S. dollar *or* the Mexican peso are acceptable as currency.

## EXERCISE 4

In the following sentences, correct any errors in usage and sentence construction.

1. The construction plans were shared between the three development companies.

2. What reason does he need that information for?

3. With ten errors in it, Jeff gave us the printout.

4. Where did you file that report at?

5. Where is the new parking lot located at?

6. The recruiter greeted the applicant with a friendly smile.

7. She put a note on my desk from John.

8. Neither the computer or the printer is working properly.

9. Hal Brooks is a successful stockbroker and who is starting his own company.

10. That information is confidential between you and me.

## Sentences, Phrases, and Clauses

**Sentences** are independent units of expression with a subject and a predicate. Avoid **sentence fragments**, which are incomplete sentences.

SENTENCE FRAGMENTS:   When I heard about the new job. Decided to apply for it.

COMPLETE SENTENCE:   When I heard about the new job, I decided to apply for it.

**Phrases** are composed of two or more words — without subject and predicate — that function together as one part of a sentence. Various types of phrases include *noun phrases, verb phrases, prepositional phrases, infinitive phrases, gerund phrases,* and *participial phrases*.

NOUN PHRASE:   A new *quality-control supervisor* joined the firm.

VERB PHRASE:   Grace *should have been* with us today.

PREPOSITIONAL PHRASE:   She saw Jim *with the CEO*.

INFINITIVE PHRASE:   His ambition is *to be department head*.

GERUND PHRASE:   *Operating the machine* is hard work. (gerund functions as a noun)

PARTICIPIAL PHRASE:   *Noticing my agitation*, Jack asked what was wrong. (participle ends in "-ing" and functions as an adjective)

**Clauses** are groups of words containing a subject and a predicate and functioning together as part of a sentence. Clauses may be *independent* or *dependent* (subordinate). An independent clause can stand alone as a simple sentence, but a dependent clause cannot. Dependent clauses include noun, adjective, and adverb clauses.

INDEPENDENT CLAUSE:   *Frank received the message*, and *he returned the call*.

DEPENDENT CLAUSE:   *When Frank received the message*, he returned the call.

# MECHANICS

Business communication students need to master the **mechanics** of the English language, which include the rules governing *punctuation*, *capitalization*, *abbreviation*, *number style*, *spelling*, *word division*, and *proofreaders' marks*.

## Punctuation

**Punctuation marks** help clarify sentences. Punctuation marks include *periods*, *commas*, *semicolons*, *colons*, *question marks*, *exclamation points*, *quotation marks*, *hyphens*, and *apostrophes*.

**Periods**. Periods serve several functions. Some of its uses are discussed below.

1. *Period Ending Sentences*. Use periods at the end of sentences that are statements, mild commands, indirect questions, or courteous requests.

STATEMENT:   Today we ordered ten new computers.

COMMAND:   Order ten new computers right away.

INDIRECT QUESTION:   I asked him if he ordered the new computers.

COURTEOUS REQUEST:   Will you please place the order today.

2. *Period after Abbreviation*. Use periods after most abbreviations (see page 531).

EXAMPLES:   Mr.     (Mister)
            Ph.D.   (Doctor of Philosophy)
            N.W.    (northwest)
            c.o.d.  (cash on delivery)

3. *Spacing Conventions for Keyboarding—Period.*

|  | | Before | After |
|---|---|:---:|:---:|
| a. | Normal use at the end of sentence | 0 | 2 |
| b. | After an abbreviation | 0 | 1 |
| c. | After an enumeration | 0 | 2 |
| d. | When followed by another punctuation mark | 0 | 0 |
| e. | As a decimal | 0 | 0 |

**Comma.** Commas indicate a pause. Use a comma where the structure of the sentence requires it.

1. *Comma Before a Coordinate Conjunction.* Use a comma before a coordinate conjunction (*and, but, for, nor, or, so,* and *yet*) joining two independent clauses. The comma may be omitted if the clauses are very short.

COORDINATE CONJUNCTION:    Tom will purchase the tickets, and Maria will plan the itinerary.
Interest rates are rising, but the price of gold is steady.

2. *Comma after an Introductory Element, Dependent Clause, or an Introductory Phrase.* Place a comma after an introductory element that consists of one or more words, a dependent clause, or a long (over five words) introductory phrase.

ONE WORD:    Consequently, we will have to cancel our travel plans.

DEPENDENT CLAUSE:    When Jack calls about the contract, I will notify you.

LONG PHRASE:    In light of the alarming situation, we canceled all afternoon meetings.

Note that transitional words within a sentence should have a comma following them.

TRANSITIONAL WORD:    Dallas had a snowstorm; consequently, all flights were canceled.

3. *Comma after Items in a Series.* Place a comma after each item in a series (three or more parallel items). (Some writers omit the comma before the conjunction.)

SERIES:    We need to order folders, envelopes, and paper clips.
I read the mail, answered three letters, and returned two phone calls.

4. *Commas Around Parenthetical (Nonessential, Interrupting) Expressions.* Place commas around parenthetical expressions.

PARENTHETICAL EXPRESSIONS:    The stock market, as you know, has declined recently.
The Governor, as we have seen, has lost credibility among voters.

5. *Commas Around Appositives*. Place commas around nonessential appositives. (An *appositive* is a noun or pronoun that renames another noun or pronoun beside it.) Essential appositives do not require commas.

APPOSITIVES:    He introduced Dan, *the research assistant*.
Margaret Levene, *the psychologist*, is our advertising consultant.

6. *Comma Between Independent Adjectives*. Place a comma between two or more independent adjectives modifying the same noun. (The adjectives are independent if you can insert "and" between them without changing the meaning.) If the first adjective modifies both the second adjective and noun together, a comma is not required.

INDEPENDENT ADJECTIVE:    Wendy is a fast, accurate typist. (fast *and* accurate typist)
I need a new file cabinet. (*new* modifies *file cabinet*)

7. *Commas to Separate Months, Days, and Years*. Use commas to separate months or days from years. In sentences, place an additional comma after the year, unless it is at the end of the sentence.

EXAMPLES:    On July 15, 1988, our company was incorporated.
The paperback edition reached bookstores in February, 1988.
Harry plans to retire on December 31, 1992.

8. *Comma to Separate City and State*. Use a comma to separate the name of a city and state. In sentences, place a comma after the state also, unless it comes at the end of the sentence.

EXAMPLES:    I lived in Denver, Colorado, before moving to Oakland, California.

9. *Commas to Set Off Dependent Phrases and Clauses*. Use commas to set off nonrestrictive (nonessential) dependent phrases and clauses. Restrictive (essential) dependent phrases and clauses are not set off with commas.

NONRESTRICTIVE CLAUSE:    Jack Henderson, *who is very well organized*, is in charge.

NONRESTRICTIVE PHRASE:    He laughed loudly, *grating on our nerves*.

RESTRICTIVE CLAUSE:    The agency has two accounts *that are inactive*.

RESTRICTIVE PHRASE:    Chris has a daughter *named after me*.

10. *Comma to Set Off Direct Quotation*. Use commas to set off a direct quotation from the rest of the sentence.

DIRECT QUOTATION:   Jack asked, "Do you plan to attend the meeting?"
Mary said, "I agree;" but did not elaborate.

11. *Spacing Conventions for Keyboarding — Comma*.

|  |  | Before | After |
|---|---|---|---|
| a. | Normal use within a sentence | 0 | 1 |
| b. | Followed by a closing quotation mark | 0 | 0 |
| c. | Used in numbers | 0 | 0 |

**Semicolon**. The semicolon has various uses. Some of its major uses are described below.

1. *Semicolon Between Two Independent Clauses and in Sentences with Transitional Expressions*. Place a semicolon between two independent clauses not joined by a coordinate conjunction.

INDEPENDENT CLAUSES:   The conference is next week; Fred and I are attending.
The surgery was successful; Mary will go home next week.

Place a semicolon between two independent clauses separated by transitional expressions such as *accordingly*, *consequently*, and *therefore*.

EXAMPLE:   The shipment has been delayed; consequently, our stock is low.

2. *Semicolon Between Items in a Series*. Place semicolons between items in a series if one or more of the items contains internal commas.

EXAMPLE:   We visited Beaumont, Texas; Tulsa, Oklahoma; and Little Rock, Arkansas.

3. *Spacing Conventions for Keyboarding — Semicolon*.

|  | Before | After |
|---|---|---|
| All uses | 0 | 1 |

**Colon**. Use the colon to call attention to what follows. Guidelines for the use of the colon are provided below.

1. *Colon after an Independent Clause*. Place a colon after an independent clause introducing a formal listing or enumeration of items.

EXAMPLES:   The following TV stations broadcast in stereo: KWET, KODL, KNET, and KTTL.

We had several reasons for canceling our trip to Southern Europe: (1) The weather was chilly, (2) The exchange rate was prohibitive, (3) The political climate was unstable.

2. *Colon Between Hours and Minutes.* Use a colon between hours and minutes when expressing time.

EXAMPLES:    3:00 p.m.
             7:15 a.m.

3. *Colon after the Salutation.* Place a colon after the salutation in a business letter when using the mixed style of punctuation.

EXAMPLES:    Dear Mr. Green:
             Ladies and Gentlemen:

4. *Spacing Conventions for Keyboarding — Colon.*

|     |                               | Before | After |
|-----|-------------------------------|--------|-------|
| a.  | Normal use within a sentence  | 0      | 2     |
| b.  | Used in time of day, ratio    | 0      | 0     |

**Question Mark.** The question mark is used most frequently after direct questions. Guidelines for its use are provided below.

1. *Question Mark Ending a Direct Question.* Use a question mark after a sentence that is a direct question and after a quotation that contains a question.

DIRECT QUESTION:    Where is your new office?

QUOTATION WITH A QUESTION:    John asked, "Does the company pay overtime?"

2. *Spacing Conventions for Keyboarding — Question Mark.*

|     |                                                              | Before | After |
|-----|--------------------------------------------------------------|--------|-------|
| a.  | Normal use at the end of a sentence                          | 0      | 2     |
| b.  | In a parenthetical question                                  | 0      | 0     |
| c.  | Within a sentence, not followed directly by another punctuation mark | 0      | 1     |
| d.  | Within a sentence, followed directly by another punctuation mark | 0      | 0     |

**Exclamation Point.** The exclamation point is used to express surprise, disbelief, or other strong emotion. Guidelines for its uses are provided below.

1. *Exclamation Point after an Emphatic Interjection.* Use an exclamation point after a sharp command, statement, or expression of protest or complaint. Use exclamation points sparingly in business writing.

SHARP COMMAND:   Go now!

EMPHATIC STATEMENT:   Oh no! My car has a flat tire!
You're fired!

EXPRESSION OF COMPLAINT:   That chair is killing my back!

2. *Spacing Conventions for Keyboarding—Exclamation Point.*

|  |  | Before | After |
|---|---|---|---|
| a. | Normal use at the end of a sentence | 0 | 2 |
| b. | For information in parentheses | 0 | 0 |
| c. | Within a sentence; followed directly by another punctuation mark | 0 | 0 |
| d. | Within a sentence; not followed directly by another punctuation mark | 0 | 1 |

**Quotation Marks.** Use quotation marks for direct quotations and for words requiring emphasis. Guidelines for its use are provided below.

1. *Quotation Marks Around Direct Quotations.* Place quotation marks around a direct quotation. Place a comma or period inside the ending quotation mark. Note that quotation marks are not required for indirect quotations.

EXAMPLES:   Mr. Johnson said, "We are planning to remodel the plant."
"I am pleased to announce," said the plant manager, "that we are recalling all furloughed employees."
I told Mary and Connie that I would meet them at the restaurant.

2. *Single Quotation Marks.* Use single quotation marks around a quotation within a quotation.

EXAMPLE:   Frank said, "I told her 'No deal.' "

3. *Long Quotations.* For direct quotations longer than three lines, quotation marks are not required. Instead, create a separate paragraph, indent five spaces from the right and left margins, and single-space the paragraph.

4. *Quotation Marks for Published Works.* Quotation marks are used for any section (chapter, unit, article, etc.) of a published work (book, magazine, play, etc.). Note that titles of published works are underscored or keyed in all capital letters.

EXAMPLES:   The third chapter of her book is entitled "The New Tax Laws."
THE WALL STREET JOURNAL had an interesting article titled "Lee Iacocca: His Management Success."

5. *Quotation Marks for Unpublished Works*. Use quotation marks for the title of an unpublished work.

EXAMPLE:    Stanford University's "A Study of Third World Debtor Nations" is revealing. (unpublished work)
The keynote address entitled "A Symphony of Software" was well received at the data-processing convention. (unpublished speech)

6. *Quotation Marks for Emphasis*. Use quotation marks for special emphasis in definitions. The word defined is underscored or capitalized.

EXAMPLE:    <u>Cybernetics</u> is "a self-regulating control system."

7. *Spacing Conventions for Keyboarding—Quotation Marks*.

### Opening Quotation Mark

|     |                                    | Before | After |
|-----|------------------------------------|--------|-------|
| a.  | At the beginning of a sentence     | 0      | 0     |
| b.  | Following a colon                  | 2      | 0     |
| c.  | Following a dash                   | 0      | 0     |
| d.  | Following an opening parenthesis   | 0      | 0     |
| e.  | All other uses                     | 1      | 0     |

### Closing Quotation Mark

|     |                                    | Before | After |
|-----|------------------------------------|--------|-------|
| a.  | At the end of a sentence           | 0      | 2     |
| b.  | Preceding another punctuation mark | 0      | 0     |
| c.  | All other uses                     | 0      | 0     |

**Hyphen**. Hyphenate words to avoid ambiguity. Guidelines for using hyphens are provided below.

1. *Hyphen in Compound Adjectives*. Use a hyphen between two or more words serving as a compound adjective before a noun.

EXAMPLES:    up-to-date report
well-known brand
chocolate-covered peanuts
three-day weekend

2. *Hyphen in End-of-a-Line Word Division*. Use a hyphen when dividing a word at the end of a line. See *Word Division* on page 538.

3. *Hyphen in Fractions and Compound Numbers*. Hyphenate fractions and spelled-out compound numbers from twenty-one to ninety-nine.

EXAMPLES:    two-thirds
thirty-three

4. *Hyphen after Prefixes*. Hyphenate words containing prefixes such as *ex-*, *self-*, and *all-*.

EXAMPLES:   ex-husband
self-made
all-American

5. *Spacing Conventions for Keyboarding — Hyphen*.

|  |  | Before | After |
|---|---|---|---|
| a. | Normal use within a sentence | 0 | 0 |
| b. | In numbers | 0 | 0 |

**Apostrophe**. Use the apostrophe to indicate the possessive case, in contractions, and to mark the plural form of letters and figures. Guidelines for using the apostrophe are listed below.

1. *Apostrophe in Possession*. Use an apostrophe with a noun to indicate possession. In singular nouns, the apostrophe usually appears between the noun and the "s" at the end, unless the noun ends in an *s* or *z* sound.

EXAMPLES:   Mary's desk
the company's wage scale
Bess' telephone

In plural nouns, the apostrophe always appears at the end of the plural noun.

EXAMPLES:   seven hours' work
the Jones' rental property
the associates' offices

2. *Apostrophe in Contractions*. Use an apostrophe in a contraction to mark omitted letters.

EXAMPLES:   she'll
isn't
won't
can't

3. *Apostrophe in Forming Plural Abbreviations*. Use an apostrophe and *s* to form the plural of abbreviations followed by periods and the plural of letters and numerals.

EXAMPLES:   C.P.A.'s
A's and B's
2's and 3's

4. *Spacing Conventions for Keyboarding—Apostrophe.*

|  |  | Before | After |
|---|---|---|---|
| a. | Following a word, abbreviation, etc., within a sentence | 0 | 1 |
| b. | Other uses | 0 | 0 |

## EXERCISE 5

In the following sentences, add appropriate punctuation marks.

1. Terri Andrews our research assistant has a computer but she seldom uses it

2. Jim said I quit but did not sign a resignation form

3. Mr. James who is our sales manager ordered some fresh new merchandise

4. Employees who use illegal drugs will be fired from this company

5. The company has subsidiaries in the following cities Madison Wisconsin Detroit Michigan and Cleveland Ohio

6. Jack Cordova requested a budget increase however management did not approve Jacks request

7. Mary our new accountant is a persistent hard working employee

8. Twenty three obsolete computers were auctioned but no one bid on them

9. He started the business on May 1 1986 and has already become a millionaire

10. Bob asked Have you seen Carols new office

## Capitalization

Capital (uppercase) letters are used for emphasizing important words. Guidelines governing the rules of capitalization are provided below.

Capitalize the first word of a sentence, quoted sentence, and item in an outline.

SENTENCE:    *The* wholesale price index is rising.

QUOTED SENTENCE:    She replied, "*We* will be glad to help."

ITEM IN AN OUTLINE:    A. *Production* costs
　　　　　　　　　　　　　　1. *Raw* materials
　　　　　　　　　　　　　　2. *Wages* and salaries
　　　　　　　　　　　　　B. *Marketing* expenses

1. *Capitalize Proper Nouns.* Capitalize proper nouns, including the names of individuals, organizations, places, geographic locations, streets, build-

ings, holidays, days of the week, months, brands and trademarks, publications, and academic courses (subject areas that are not proper nouns are not capitalized).

EXAMPLES:    *Marylin* is going to a convention in *Las Vegas* next *Monday*.
The *January* edition of *Motor News* has an article about *Lang* computers.
The *Westex Bank* has reserved the *Grand Ballroom* at the *Palace Hotel* for a *Christmas* party.
I am taking three courses in economics this fall; but they are not as challenging as *Economics* 302 that I took last semester.

2. *Indirect Quotations or Seasons*. Do not capitalize indirect quotations or seasons of the year.

EXAMPLES:    He said *we* should sign the guest register.
The manager told us that the store would be having *fall* and *winter* sales.

3. *Capitalize a Formal Statement after a Colon*. Capitalize the first word after a colon that introduces a complete formal statement. Do not capitalize the first word after a colon introducing a clause or a listing that is dependent upon the preceding clause.

EXAMPLES:    This policy is effective immediately: *Employees* may not drive company cars for personal business.
The new policy will affect the following employees: *sales* representatives, managers, and production supervisors.

4. *Capitalize Professional or Family Titles*. Capitalize a professional or family title written in front of an individual's name, unless the title is preceded by a possessive pronoun. A professional or family title that follows the name usually is not capitalized unless the individual is a high-ranking government official. (Exception: Titles are always capitalized in the address and typewritten signature of business letters.)

EXAMPLES:    The keynote speaker is Frank Weston, *president* of Union Chemical Company.
My *brother* John introduced *President Weston*.
Yesterday *Uncle Harry* announced his retirement.
Sandra Day O'Connor, *Justice* of the Supreme Court, presented the graduation address.

5. *Capitalize Salutations and Complimentary Closings*. Capitalize the first word of a salutation and complimentary closing.

EXAMPLES:    *Dear* Mrs. Green
*Cordially* yours

6. *Capitalize Nouns Followed by Numbers or Letters*. Nouns preceding numbers or letters and denoting sequence should be capitalized.

EXAMPLES:    The policy in *Appendix B* applies to all employees.
The clause in *Article 4* indicates that plaintiffs have a right to object to unfair questioning.
The bar chart in *Fig. 6* is not accurate.

## EXERCISE 6

Correct any capitalization errors in the following sentences.

1. Frank said that We should get a raise next Fall.

2. All Marketing majors are required to take Advertising 411.

3. My Uncle Andy leaves for europe next wednesday.

4. Apex company manufactures the following automotive products: Transmission seals, brake shoes, and mufflers.

5. An Insurance Company announced the following policy: One moving violation will result in an automatic rate increase.

6. The Administrative Assistant left a message that aunt mary called to invite us to thanksgiving dinner.

7. She was born on may 1, 1965, in san antonio, texas.

8. Mary Anderson, vice president of finance, will be the next Chief Executive Officer of the Company.

9. The Newscaster announced that Bill Jamison, mayor of dallas, has decided not to run for re-election in the fall.

10. The discussion is in chapter 10 on page 233.

## Abbreviation

**Abbreviations** are the shortened forms of words. Guidelines for abbreviating words are provided below.

1. *Abbreviate Courtesy and Academic Titles*. Abbreviate courtesy and academic titles (except "Miss") that accompany names. The use of the comma in personal or business names followed by abbreviations or numerals is optional.

EXAMPLES:    *Mrs.* Anna Willingham          Randy Tchai, *M.D.*
*Mr.* John Penn, *Sr.*              *Ms.* Lynne McCoy
Juan Cordova, *Ph.D.*           Andrew Thompson *III*

2. *Abbreviate Names of States.* Use the official two-letter abbreviation for the name of a state, district, or territory in a letter address. Note that the two-letter abbreviations are written without periods, in all capital letters.

| STATE NAME | TWO-LETTER ABBREVIATION | STATE NAME | TWO-LETTER ABBREVIATION |
|---|---|---|---|
| Alabama | AL | Montana | MT |
| Alaska | AK | Nebraska | NE |
| American Samoa | AS | Nevada | NV |
| Arizona | AZ | New Hampshire | NH |
| Arkansas | AR | New Jersey | NJ |
| California | CA | New Mexico | NM |
| Colorado | CO | New York | NY |
| Connecticut | CT | North Carolina | NC |
| Delaware | DE | North Dakota | ND |
| District of Columbia | DC | Northern Mariana | |
| Federated States of | | Islands | CM |
| Micronesia | TT | Ohio | OH |
| Florida | FL | Oklahoma | OK |
| Georgia | GA | Oregon | OR |
| Guam | GU | Palau | TT |
| Hawaii | HI | Pennsylvania | PA |
| Idaho | ID | Puerto Rico | PR |
| Illinois | IL | Rhode Island | RI |
| Indiana | IN | South Carolina | SC |
| Iowa | IA | South Dakota | SD |
| Kansas | KS | Tennessee | TN |
| Kentucky | KY | Texas | TX |
| Louisiana | LA | Utah | UT |
| Maine | ME | Vermont | VT |
| Marshall Islands | TT | Virgin Islands | VI |
| Maryland | MD | Virginia | VA |
| Massachusetts | MA | Washington | WA |
| Michigan | MI | West Virginia | WV |
| Minnesota | MN | Wisconsin | WI |
| Mississippi | MS | Wyoming | WY |
| Missouri | MO | | |

3. *Abbreviate Addresses and Directions.* Do not abbreviate parts of addresses such as *Street*, *Avenue*, and *Road* or directions such as *North* and *South*. Compound directions such as *N.W.* are abbreviated if written after the name of the street.

EXAMPLES:    305 East Pecan Avenue
1032 Peachtree Street, N.E.

4. *Abbreviate Well-Known Agencies, Companies, and Organizations*. The names of well-known government agencies, companies, and other organizations may be abbreviated. Such abbreviations should be capitalized and written without periods or spaces between the letters.

EXAMPLES:   GE        UN
            IBM       NAACP
            FAA       NEA
            FDIC      AAUP
            AMA       UCLA
            MIT       AFL-CIO

5. *Abbreviate Titles of Organizations*. Abbreviate *company*, *incorporated*, *corporation*, *association*, or any other part of the name of an organization *if the organization uses the abbreviation in its official letterhead*.

EXAMPLES:   Smithson, Inc.
            Duskin & Duskin, P.A.
            Weatherly Co.

6. *Acronyms*. An **acronym** is an abbreviation derived from the initial letters of the complete term. Acronyms are usually written in all capitals, without periods, and pronounced like words.

EXAMPLES:   FIFO — First *in*, first *out*
            NOW — *N*ational *O*rganization for *W*omen
            ZIP — *Z*one *I*mprovement *P*lan

7. *Shortened Forms of Words*. Some shortened forms of words are not abbreviations and should not be followed by periods.

EXAMPLES:   stereo    memo      photo
            TV        ad        auto

8. *Dates, Days, and Months*. Do not abbreviate dates, including months and days.

EXAMPLES:   January 15, 1988
            Saturday, November 12

9. *Expressions of Time*. When expressing time, write a.m. (before noon) and p.m. (after noon) in lowercase letters without a space.

EXAMPLES:   11 a.m.
            3:30 p.m.

10. *Measurements*. Do not abbreviate measurements such as feet, inches, weight, and miles, except in graphic aids and tabulations.

EXAMPLES:   45 miles      130 pounds
            16 feet       32 inches

Do not use abbreviation symbols for percent (%), number (#), or measurements such as inches (") and minutes ('), except in graphic aids and tabulations.

EXAMPLES:   93 percent
            15 minutes
            5 feet 9 inches

## EXERCISE 7

Correct any abbreviation errors in the following sentences.

1. Our Burbank, Calif., store received two bad checks from a Dr. James Wood, Junior, 309 W. Elmwood Ave., L.A., Calif. 90046-1729.

2. She is leaving Fri., Oct. 14, on TWA flight #444.

3. Nearly 30 % of Americans are at least 20 lbs. overweight.

4. I have an appointment with the Internal Revenue Service auditor tomorrow at 9:30 AM.

5. Our Metropolis Ins. policy expired on 5/15 of last year.

6. Our advertising co. was bought by a larger corp.

7. Mister Kent is a Certified Public Accountant.

8. The contractor ordered 480 yds. of blue acrylic carpet from Baldwin Carpets, Inc.

9. We are expecting to receive a shipment of 500 gallons of paint by next Monday.

10. His temporary address is 1402 Buckhead Road, Northeast, Atlanta, Ga. 30305-5317.

## Number Style

The rules for writing numbers are listed below in the order of general to specific; specific rules take precedence over general rules.

1. *Basic Number Rule*. Express numbers one through ten in words (unless another rule applies); express numbers 11 and over in figures.

EXAMPLES:   The firm hired *six* new accountants.
            The company owns *23* department stores.

2. *Figures*. Express the following in figures: money amounts of a dollar or more, amounts of money less than a dollar followed by the word "cents," and money amounts of a dollar or less with the "$" sign preceding it.

EXAMPLES:   Marian earned *$35,000* this year.
            The telecommunication system costs *$2,423.25* per month.
            The sales tax on the purchase is *33 cents*.
            I spent *$6.06* on gas, *$21.66* on groceries, and *$.49* on fast food today.

Large amounts of money (millions and billions) may be written as follows:

EXAMPLES:   $30 million
            $5.5 billion
            $58.3 billion

Indefinite money amounts and approximate money amounts should be spelled out.

EXAMPLES:   many millions of dollars
            several thousand Swiss francs
            approximately five hundred dollars
            less than fifty cents

3. *Percentages*. Express percentages in figures followed by the word "percent," except at the beginning of a sentence. (A percent sign (%) should be used in graphic aids.)

EXAMPLES:   Total sales increased *52 percent*.
            The union contract provides only a *2 percent* raise.
            *Seventy percent* of voters surveyed said they would vote for Marcianni.

4. *Weights and Measurements*. Express weights and measurements (feet, inches, pounds, miles) in figures.

EXAMPLES:   The lot measures *102* by *55* feet.
            The express package weighed *9* ounces.
            The baby weighed *9* pounds *11* ounces at birth.

5. *Decimals*. Always express decimals in figures. (When a period is used as a decimal, do not leave a space before or after it.)

EXAMPLES:   2.27
            $32.81
            $101.88

6. *Fractions*. Fractions should be spelled out unless they are part of a mixed number.

EXAMPLES:    three-fifths
one-third
The length of the board is *2 1/2* feet.

7. *Ratios and Proportions*. Ratios and proportions should be written in figures.

EXAMPLES:    5 to 1
1:2
73-84

8. *Years and Days of the Month*. Express years and days of the month in figures. Use the "th" or "nd" in dates only when the day precedes the month (avoid this usage).

EXAMPLES:    Bill's birthday is October *8*.
The contract was signed on January *15, 1988*.
The closing on the house was set for the *24th* of September.

9. *Ordinal Numbers*. Ordinal numbers that can be written in one or two words are spelled out. Other ordinals are written in figures, except in formal writing.

EXAMPLES:    the *thirty-fifth* anniversary of the republic
the *150th* anniversary of the company

10. *Street Numbers*. When the name of a street is a number, express "First Street" through "Tenth Street" in words; express streets named 11 or higher in figures ("th" or "nd" are optional).

EXAMPLES:    121 *Third* Avenue
5227 South *52* Street
911 *89th* Avenue

11. *Parts of Addresses*. Express house numbers, apartment numbers, suite numbers, route numbers, and post office box numbers in figures.

EXAMPLES:    *422* Pecan Street, Apartment *12*
Commerce Title Building, Suite *37*
P.O. Box *905*
Route *1*

12. *ZIP Codes*. Express ZIP Codes in figures and key them one or two spaces after the state abbreviation. Separate "ZIP + 4" numbers from the first five digits by a hyphen, no spaces.

EXAMPLES:    Warrensburg, MO *64093*
Denver, CO *80220-1005*

13. *Time Expressions*. Use figures in writing time followed by a.m. and p.m. When "o'clock" is spelled out, the time may be written in either figures or words.

EXAMPLES:    The meeting is scheduled for *10* a.m.
Flight 103 leaves at *5:36* p.m.
I'll call you at *ten* o'clock (or *10* o'clock).

14. *Numbers in the Same Category*. Consistency should be maintained in expressing numbers in the same category. Words and figures may be used to keep categories apart.

EXAMPLE:    The purchasing manager ordered *35* new Lang computers for the *eleven* advertising departments, *14* for the *fourteen* quality control departments, and *8* for management use.

Adjacent numbers should be expressed similarly—in words or in figures—with a comma separating them.

EXAMPLES:    We noticed that Highways 126, 32, and 42 converged on the outskirts of Morrow.
The Springers have three children aged two, four, and sixteen years.

15. *Beginning Sentences*. Spell out numbers at the beginning of a sentence (or rearrange the sentence).

EXAMPLES:    *Fifty* customers complained about the poor service.
*Twenty-two* employees joined the new credit union.

## Spelling

Misspelled words create a poor impression. Every business writer should consult a dictionary or pocket speller if in doubt about the correct spelling of a word. Some word-processing software contains spelling checkers that can "flag" or highlight words that may be misspelled. The most efficient way to avoid misspelled words, however, is to become familiar with the correct spelling of words you use frequently.

The following words occur often in business writing. Memorize and test yourself on the correct spelling and usage of these words.

## FREQUENTLY MISSPELLED WORDS
### (list of 100 most frequently misspelled words in alphabetical order)

| | | | |
|---|---|---|---|
| absence | decision | maintenance | questions |
| account | division | management | receipt |
| activities | during | material | receive |
| addition | education | mortgage | received |
| additional | employee | necessary | receiving |
| appreciate | employees | office | recommendations |
| appropriate | equipment | opportunity | required |
| approval | established | other | requirements |
| approximately | experience | our | schedule |
| area | facilities | paid | scheduled |
| audit | faculty | per | section |
| available | financial | personnel | service |
| balance | first | please | services |
| basis | following | policy | subject |
| because | further | position | support |
| benefits | general | possible | system |
| business | immediately | premium | than |
| commission | important | present | their |
| committee | industrial | prior | there |
| completed | information | procedure | through |
| contract | installation | procedures | upon |
| control | insurance | production | well |
| corporate | interest | property | whether |
| currently | international | proposal | which |
| customer | its | provided | with |

Courtesy of Dr. Scot Ober and the Delta Pi Epsilon Research Foundation, Inc.

# Word Division

Divide words only as necessary to prevent an extremely uneven right margin. Include enough of a word on the first line to give the reader a clue to the entire word. Avoid leaving only one or two letters of a divided word on a line. Avoid dividing the last word in a sentence, especially if it is the last word in a paragraph. Finally, divide hyphenated words at the hyphen.

1. *Basic Word Division*. Divide words between syllables. One-syllable words should not be divided.

EXAMPLES:    frag/ment    plea/sure
                con/signee   moun/tain
                helped       eighth
                head         deer

2. *Word Division in Words with Six or Fewer Letters*. Avoid dividing words that contain six or fewer letters.

EXAMPLES:    awakes     finger     letter     floppy
                among      apple      report    optic

3. *Word Division in Compound Words*. Divide compound words between the elements of the compound.

EXAMPLES:    head/ache    anchor/person
                book/keeper   check/book

## Proofreaders' Marks

Use the symbols on page 540 when marking correspondence, reports, and other documents for revising and editing. These symbols also may be used when editing copy for typesetting.

## EXERCISE 8

Use appropriate proofreaders' marks to correct typographical errors in the following passage.

Data were first obtained by following both stocks porformance on the New yourk Stock Exchang (NYSE for a nine day period. Current financail
inform ation came from a Variety of compputer and business perodicals. Computter publicataions provvided insite in to the companies inovations and prodduct changes Bussiness publicatons showed how these changes effected company incomeand growth potentiale.

| Proofreaders' Marks | Examples |
|---|---|
| Capitalize | 112 Broad street |
| Center the line | *ctr.* ] Recommendations [ |
| Delete | to rapidly acquire |
| Delete space | with in the company |
| Do not change | *stet* The forseeable future |
| Double space | *ds* → To:   Hal Winter<br>From:  Lee Irwin |
| Hyphenate | up=to=date material |
| Insert a character | recive |
| Insert punctuation | Dr Bill Wood |
| Insert a space | (#) LaQuinta Apartments |
| Italicize | *ital.* Call today. |
| Lowercase letter(s) | *lc* Mary Shea, the Accountant |
| Move down | ⌐Cordially⌐ |
| Move left | ⌐ Cordially |
| Move right | Cordially |
| Move up | ⌐Cordially⌐ |
| Paragraph | ¶ Please call on Monday. |
| No paragraph | *No*¶ Please call on Monday. |
| Single space | Please call on Monday, as we have<br>*ss* → the information. |
| Transpose | *tr* We recieved the merchandise. |

# DOCUMENT FORMATS

## APPENDIX B

Most business documents such as letters, memorandums, and reports are arranged in one of several generally accepted formats. Companies frequently adopt a particular style of each type of document as the standard for all company uses.

## LETTERS

A letter format consists of the parts of the document and the arrangement of the parts on a page. The three basic letter formats that are described in the paragraphs below and illustrated on pages 546 to 548 include several standard parts and may include one or more optional parts.

## Standard Letter Parts

The following parts are standard in most business letters: *dateline*, *letter address*, *salutation*, *body*, *complimentary close*, and *signature and title*.

1. *Dateline*. Include the month (spelled out in full), day, and year; for example, May 1, 1988. Place the dateline approximately 2 inches from the top edge of the paper. If you are using letterhead stationery, the date should be at least two line spaces below the printed letterhead. If not, place the date immediately below the typewritten return address (see Figures B.1 to B.3 on pages 546 to 548).

2. *Letter Address*. Include the name and title of the addressee, company (department optional), street address, city, state abbreviation, and ZIP

Code or ZIP + 4 Code (see pages 546 to 548). Include an appropriate courtesy or professional title (Mr., Ms., Mrs., Dr., etc.) before the addressee's name.

3. *Salutation*. Use a greeting such as *Dear Ms. Green*, or if you are on a first-name basis with the addressee, "Dear Jan." When addressing a letter to a company in general, use "Ladies and Gentlemen." If you are using the *mixed* style of punctuation, place a colon after the salutation (see Figure B.2 on page 547). In the AMS Simplified style, a salutation is omitted (see Figure B.3 on page 548).

4. *Body*. The body (message) should be single spaced, with a double space between paragraphs.

5. *Complimentary Close*. Place a complimentary closing such as *Cordially* or *Sincerely* a double space below the body of the letter. If the mixed style of punctuation is used, place a comma after the complimentary close (see Figure B.2 on page 547). In the AMS Simplified style, a complimentary close is omitted (see Figure B.3 on page 548).

6. *Signature and Title*. Key your name four line spaces below the complimentary close. (Leave three blank lines for the handwritten signature.) Place your official title on the next line. If your name and title are short, they may appear on the same line, with a comma after the name.

## Optional Letter Parts

In addition to the standard parts, business letters may contain one or more of the following parts as needed: *return address, mailing notation, attention line, subject line, second-page heading, typewritten company name, reference initials, enclosure notation, copy notation,* and *postscript*.

1. *Return Address*. When preparing a letter on plain paper rather than on printed letterhead stationery, include your address (street address, city and state abbreviation, and ZIP Code) above the date, about 2 inches from the top of the page. Place the street address on the first line; the city, state, and ZIP Code on the next line; and the date on the third line (see Figure B.2 on page 547).

2. *Mailing Notation*. If sending a letter by special means such as certified, registered, or express mail, you may include a special mailing notation. The mailing notation appears in all capital letters, a double space below the dateline.

3. *Attention Line*. An attention line may be used to direct the letter to an individual or department when the letter is addressed to the company in

general. Although an attention line facilitates transmitting the letter to a particular person, the letter may be opened by someone else in the company. Disregard the attention line when selecting an appropriate salutation for a letter. For example, in a letter addressed to "Acme Company" with "Attention Mr. Robert Holland," the salutation would be "Ladies and Gentlemen" because the letter is addressed to the company, not to Mr. Holland. Place an attention line on the second line of a letter address. Some companies prefer the attention line placed a double space below the letter address.

4. *Subject Line*. The subject line indicates the topic of the letter. Key the subject line a double space below the salutation, in either all-capital or capital and lower-case letters. Some companies prefer the word "Subject" or "Reference" preceding the subject line. In the AMS Simplified format letters, a subject line is required and should be keyed in all capital letters without the word "Subject."

5. *Second-page Heading*. For letters that are longer than one page, the second page and additional pages, which are keyed on plain paper, should include a heading containing the following information: first line of the letter address (addressee's name or company name), page number, and date. The second-page heading appears one inch from the top of the page and may be arranged horizontally or vertically, as follows:

```
Mrs. Alma Ellis                2                May 1, 19—
```

or:

```
Mrs. Alma Ellis
page 2
May 1, 19—
```

The body of the letter is continued a double space below the heading.

6. *Typewritten Company Name*. The company name may be placed in all capital letters a double space below the complimentary close, with the sender's name keyed four line spaces below it.

```
                    Cordially,

                    VINEY RIDGE COMPANY




                    H. B. Heidelberg, Manager
```

Use of the company name in the closing lines is recommended especially for letters that resemble a legal agreement, though it may be used in any business letter.

7. *Reference Initials*. The initials of the keyboard operator who prepared the letter — if not the same individual who composed the letter — are keyed in lower-case letters a double space below the sender's name and/or official title. The initials of the letter writer may be included — and should be if the letter is signed by someone other than the writer. If the reference initials include the writer's initials, a colon or slash mark should separate the writer's initials (which are always capitalized) from those of the typist.

```
cs (typist's initials)

RH/cs (writer's and typist's initials)
```

8. *Enclosure Notation*. Use an enclosure notation to indicate that attachments accompany the letter. If more than one item is enclosed, use the plural word *Enclosures*, which may be followed by the number of items or a listing of the actual items that are enclosed. Place the enclosure notation a double space below the reference initials.

9. *Copy Notation*. The copy notation indicates the names of those who are receiving copies of a letter. Use the lower-case letter *c* to indicate *copy*, followed by a list of those individuals who will receive the letter. Key the copy notation a double space below the enclosure notation (if any) or reference initials.

10. *Postscript*. Place a postscript at the end of a letter to add comments that update or reinforce information contained in the body of the letter. The abbreviation *P.S.* is optional. The postscript should be separated from the preceding letter part by a double space.

## Letter Formats

Three basic letter formats include *block*, *modified block*, and *AMS Simplified* style. Most companies use one of these letter styles or adapt it to the needs of the organization. Technological factors such as types of computer printers and word-processing capabilities often influence the selection of a letter style.

In many companies, the side margins of all letters are a width that coincide with the default margins on the electronic typewriter or word-processing software used. Left and right margins of 1 1/2 inches and 1 inch are common. Otherwise, the width of the side margins may vary depending upon the length of the body of the letter: 2 inches for short letters; 1 1/2 inches for average (most) letters; and 1 inch for long letters.

**Punctuation style** is a term that refers to the punctuation after the salutation and complimentary close. Some companies use a colon after the salutation and a comma after the complimentary close; this style is called **mixed punctuation**. Other companies omit punctuation marks after the salutation and complimentary close; this style is called **open punctuation**.

1. *Block*. In the **block** (*full-block*) format, all parts of the letter begin flush with the left margin, and paragraphs are not indented. The punctuation style may be either *open* or *mixed*. An example of a block letter is shown in Figure B.1 on page 546.

2. *Modified Block*. In the **modified-block** format, the dateline (and return address, if included), complimentary close, signature line, and sender's title begin at the center of the page. Five-space paragraph indentions are optional. Although either style of punctuation is appropriate, mixed punctuation is recommended in modified-block letters. An example of the modified-block format is shown in Figure B.2 on page 547.

3. *AMS Simplified Letter*. The **AMS Simplified** style, a special adaptation of the block-format letter, was developed by the Administrative Management Society. In the AMS Simplified format, use a subject line and omit the salutation and complimentary close. Key the sender's name and title in all capital letters and on the same line regardless of length. An example of an AMS Simplified letter is shown in Figure B.3 on page 548.

4. *Envelopes*. Envelopes for business letters should be the same color and quality of paper as the enclosed letter. The No. 10 envelope (10 inches in length) is the most common size for business letters; sometimes No. 6 3/4 envelopes are used. The sender's name and address are preprinted or typewritten in the upper left corner of the envelope.

On both sizes of envelopes, start keying the letter address at approximately the horizontal and vertical center of the envelope, with all lines blocked at the left. To facilitate mail sorting, the postal service recommends addressing envelopes in all capital letters, without punctuation (see Figure B.4 on page 549), and with the ZIP + 4 Code. However, traditional capital and lower-case letters with punctuation marks and 5-digit ZIP Code also are acceptable. (See Figure B.5 on page 549.)

Notations, such as PERSONAL or PLEASE FORWARD, appear four lines below the return address. Place an attention line in this position if it is not included as the second line of the letter address.

## FIGURE B.1 BLOCK-FORMAT LETTER WITH OPEN PUNCTUATION

**-O-O-I- Office Automation, Inc.**    P. O. Box 905
Alexandria, VA  22307-7534        (703) 234-5555

Dateline
May 29, 19--
                    4 line spaces
                    (3 blank lines)

Letter
address
Ms. Miriam Hansen
Office Manager
Nuttall Advertising Company
1832 Lakeshore Drive
Akron, OH  44301-7811

Salutation
Dear Ms. Hansen

Subject line
BLOCK FORMAT LETTER

Body
We are glad to answer your questions about block format letters.  The block style, which is very popular in business
offices today, is compatible with your company's electronic
office equipment.

This letter is an example of the block format.  As you can
see, all parts (including the dateline, letter address,
salutation, body, complimentary close, signature lines, and
optional letter parts) begin at the left margin.  Paragraphs
are also blocked.

The enclosed booklet describes several ways to improve your
communication productivity.  If you have any questions,
please call me at 703-234-5557.

Complimentary
close
Cordially
                            4 line spaces
*M. J. Hamilton*            (3 blank lines)

Sender's
name
Official title
M. J. Hamilton
Director of Public Relations

Reference
initials
rbc

Enclosure
notation
Enclosure

## FIGURE B.2 MODIFIED-BLOCK LETTER WITH MIXED PUNCTUATION

Return address

Dateline

                                               101 North Seventh Avenue
                                               Northport, AL  35476-4281
                                               October 10, 19--

                             4 line spaces
                             (3 blank lines)

Letter
address

    Mr. M. J. Hamilton
    Director of Public Relations
    Office Automation, Inc.
    P.O. Box 905
    Alexandria, VA  22307-7534

Salutation       Dear Mr. Hamilton:

Body             Your keynote speech at our Southeast Office Automation Conference was excellent.  Thank you for sharing your ideas on
office productivity and offering to answer our questions.

             Which letter style do you recommend for computer-generated
form letters?  Which format do you recommend for individually keyboarded letters?

             I will appreciate this information, which is needed for a
research project for a business communication class at the
University of Alabama.

Complimentary
close

                          Sincerely,

                          *Arlene Morgan*   4 line spaces
                                               (3 blank lines)

Sender's name                    └──────▶ Arlene Morgan

                    Businesswomen who prefer to be addressed
                    "Miss" or "Mrs.," rather than "Ms.,"
                    should include the preferred title here.

## FIGURE B.3 AMS SIMPLIFIED LETTER

**Office Automation, Inc.**
P. O. Box 905
Alexandria, VA  22307-7534　　(703) 234-5555

Dateline　　October 15, 19--

4 line spaces
(3 blank lines)

Letter　　Ms. Arlene Morgan
address　　101 North Seventh Avenue
Northport, AL  35476-4281

Subject line　　AMS SIMPLIFIED LETTER STYLE

Body　　Our firm recommends the AMS Simplified letter style for all
types of letters, including computer-generated form letters.
This letter style can be keyed in less time and with lower
risk of error--because of fewer letter parts--than most
other letter styles.  Thus the AMS Simplified format reduces
the cost of producing business letters.

When keying a letter in the AMS style, follow these procedures:

1.  Block all parts of the letter with the left margin.

2.  Omit the salutation and complimentary close.

3.  Place a subject line in all capital letters a triple
space below the letter address; triple-space below the
subject line, before the first line of the body.

4.  Key the sender's name and title in all capital letters,
four spaces after the last line of the body.

Best wishes and good luck with your research paper.

*M. J. Hamilton*　　4 line spaces
(3 blank lines)

Sender's name　　M. J. HAMILTON, DIRECTOR OF PUBLIC RELATIONS
and title
Reference　　ab
initials
Copy　　c  J. Hepworth
notation

## FIGURE B.4 NO. 10 ADDRESSED ENVELOPE

M. J. Hamilton

**OAI** Office Automation, Inc.    P. O. Box 905
Alexandria, VA 22307-7534

MS ARLENE MORGAN
101 NORTH SEVENTH STREET
NORTHPORT AL  35476-4281

## FIGURE B.5 NO. 6 3/4 ADDRESSED ENVELOPE

A. Morgan
101 North Seventh Street
Northport, AL  35476-4281

Mr. M. J. Hamilton
Director of Public Relations
Office Automation, Inc.
P.O. Box 905
Alexandria, VA  22307-7534

# MEMORANDUMS

Memorandums may be typewritten on preprinted memorandum forms, letterhead stationery, or plain paper (see Figure B.6 and B.7). Preprinted memorandum forms contain these headings: **To, From, Date,** and **Subject.** The subject line may be filled in either in all capital letters or with only the first and important words capitalized. On letterhead stationery or plain paper, the word MEMORANDUM may be centered on the page about 1 1/2 inches from the top. Key the headings in all capital letters, approximately 2 inches from the top of the page.

The body of a memorandum should be single spaced, with a double space between paragraphs. Memorandums rarely contain paragraph indentions. Optional parts similar to those in letters may include reference initials, enclosure or attachment notation, copy notation, and postscript.

## FIGURE B.6 PRINTED MEMO FORM

OAI  Office Automation, Inc.

INTEROFFICE MEMO

TO: Cindy Cho

FROM: J. D. Webster

DATE: November 7, 19--

SUBJECT: United Children's Fund

Would you be willing to represent our company by serving with me on the local United Children's Fund committee this year?

The assignment would involve attending four or five meetings and helping with our fund-raising drive in March.  Please let me know your decision by next week.

## FIGURE B.7 MEMO ON PLAIN PAPER

```
                          MEMORANDUM


       TO:        Martin Clark

       FROM:      Jane Henderson

       DATE:      March 17, 19--

       SUBJECT:   WEEKLY STAFF MEETING

       Because of the trade show in New Orleans next week, our
       usual staff meeting is canceled.  Please notify your staff
       about the change in plans.

       The following week we will have our usual meeting on
       Tuesday, March 28, at 9 a.m.  An agenda for the meeting is
       attached.

       abr

       Attachment
```

# FORMAL REPORTS

Formal business reports are often single-spaced, with a double space between paragraphs, as shown in the example of a report in Chapter 11. However, formal academic reports are formatted in **manuscript style** (double-spaced, with paragraph indentions, see Figure B.8 on pages 552 to 556). Major report parts include *title page*, *table of contents*, *body*, and *references* or *bibliography page*. Additional report parts are discussed in Chapter 11.

The top margin should be 1 inch, except the first page of each report part including the body, which should have a top margin of 1 1/2 or 2 inches. The bottom margin should be approximately 1 inch on all pages. The side margins should be at least 1 inch, except on reports to be bound at the left; leftbound reports should have at least a 1 1/2 inch left margin and a 1-inch right margin.

## FIGURE B.8 MANUSCRIPT-STYLE FORMAL REPORT—TITLE PAGE

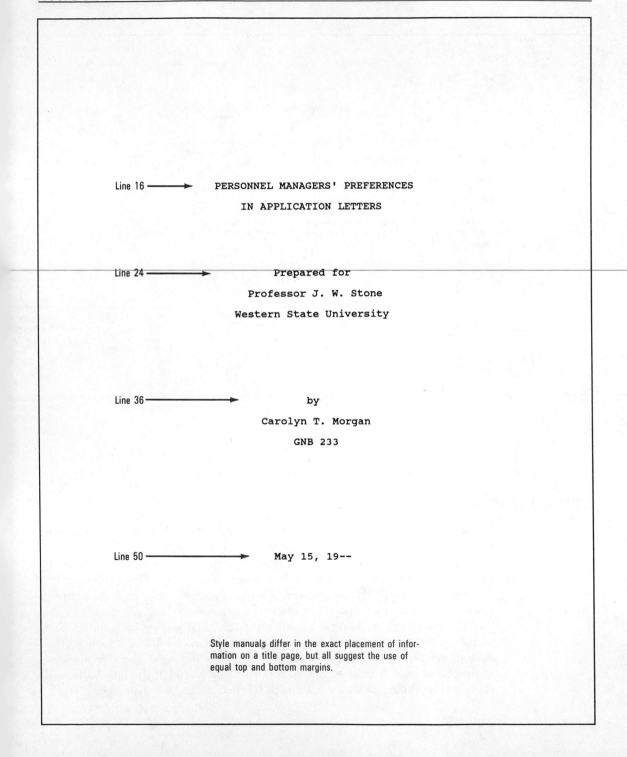

Line 16 ⟶          PERSONNEL MANAGERS' PREFERENCES

IN APPLICATION LETTERS

Line 24 ⟶          Prepared for

Professor J. W. Stone

Western State University

Line 36 ⟶                  by

Carolyn T. Morgan

GNB 233

Line 50 ⟶          May 15, 19--

Style manuals differ in the exact placement of information on a title page, but all suggest the use of
equal top and bottom margins.

## MANUSCRIPT-STYLE FORMAL REPORT — CONTENTS PAGE

Line 10 ——————————————➤    **CONTENTS**
4 line spaces
(3 blank lines)

## MANUSCRIPT-STYLE FORMAL REPORT—FIRST PAGE OF REPORT BODY

Line 10 ——————————→   PERSONNEL MANAGERS' PREFERENCES

IN APPLICATION LETTERS

4 line spaces
(3 blank lines)

Application letters are letters that sell a product (the writer's services) to a buyer (a prospective employer) for value received.[1]  An application letter is the opening step in an applicant's campaign to get a job.  If the letter fulfills its purpose, the job seeker is successful in obtaining a job interview.

The purpose of the study was to determine what information personnel managers prefer to see in application letters from college students.  An additional objective of the study was to determine what information personnel managers actually receive from job applicants.

Data were obtained from both primary and secondary sources.  Primary research consisted of a survey of 100 personnel managers in Phoenix, Arizona, which received a 70 percent return.  Secondary research consisted of a computer literature search and review of relevant books and periodicals.

_____

[1]Walter S. Henderson, _Writing for Business and Industry_ (New York:  Richardson Publishing Co., 1987), 33.

Line 60 ——————————→   1

## MANUSCRIPT-STYLE FORMAL REPORT—SECOND PAGE OF REPORT BODY

Line 6 ————————————————————————————→    2

Line 8 ——————————→    <u>Importance of Application Letters</u>

Although job applicants often submit only a data sheet, the study revealed that personnel managers prefer to receive an application letter as well.  Eighty-five percent of the respondents rated the application letter as "important" or "very important," as shown in Table I.

Personnel managers rated application letters as less important than resumes.  However, 53 percent of the respondents indicated that they would not consider an applicant who submitted a resume without an accompanying letter of application (see Figure 1).

<u>Application Letter Components</u>

Application letter components commonly include information also contained in the resume, such as job objective, education, experience, personal information, and extracurricular activities.[2]  Respondents indicated that job objective was the most important of these factors.  Specific concerns included correct grammar and mechanics, writing style, and persuasiveness.

<u>Correct Grammar and Mechanics</u>

The most serious problem area was correct grammar and mechanics.  The survey revealed that 95 percent of the respondents viewed errors in grammar and mechanics as "very serious."  Spelling errors were reported as the most common

————————————————

[2]Mary C. Becker, "Application Letters Revisited," <u>Personnel Communication</u> 11, (December 1987):  14.

## MANUSCRIPT-STYLE FORMAL REPORT — BIBLIOGRAPHY PAGE

Line 10 ⟶ **BIBLIOGRAPHY**
4 line spaces
(3 blank lines)

Becker, Mary C.  "Application Letters Revisited."  <u>Personnel</u>
    <u>Communication</u> 11, (December 1987):  12-18.

Carr, J. W.  "The Application Letter."  <u>Personnel</u> <u>Management</u>
    <u>Journal</u> 22, (January 1988):  123-130.

_____.  <u>Job</u> <u>Application</u> <u>Methods</u>.  Chicago:  Listermann
    Publishing Co., 1984.

Ferguson, M. R.  <u>How</u> <u>To</u> <u>Get</u> <u>a</u> <u>Job</u>.  Chicago:  Listermann
    Publishing Co., 1987.

Henderson, Walter S.  <u>Writing</u> <u>for</u> <u>Business</u> <u>and</u> <u>Industry</u>.
    New York:  Richardson Publishing Co., 1987.

Johnson, Marvin J.  "Job-Application Techniques That Work."
    <u>Business</u> <u>Executive</u> 14, (January 1988):  33-39.

<u>Occupational</u> <u>Outlook</u> <u>Handbook</u>.  Washington, D.C.:  U.S.
    Government Printing Office, 1986.

West, Carolyn.  <u>Effective</u> <u>Job</u> <u>Application</u> <u>Procedures</u>.  New
    York:  Sanford Publishing Co., 1987.

Zinky, M. J.  Interview by writer, 15 January 1988, Los
    Angeles.

In the third entry above, the use of a line indicates a publication by the author named in the
preceding entry.

Either solid underscores or titles in all capital
letters are also acceptable.

8

# GLOSSARY OF COMPUTER TERMS

## APPENDIX C

**access**  The process of locating data.

**backup copy**  A duplicate of a disk or other data storage medium for use in case of loss or destruction of original data.

**batch processing**  The accumulation of similar items of information or transactions to be processed all at one time.

**baud**  The rate of speed (referred to as baud rate) at which information is sent between two computer devices, for example, when sending files to serial printers or across modems.

**bit**  A binary digit, the smallest storage unit for data in a computer.

**block move/copy**  A word-processing software capability that consists of moving or copying a portion of text (block) within a document or to another document.

**boilerplate**  A collection of stored data that may be combined with new data to create a document.

**boot**  The process of loading an operating system into a computer memory.

**buffer**  A temporary memory storage area that holds data during data flow between input/output devices.

**byte**  An unit used for storage of data and consisting of eight bits.

**cathode ray tube (CRT)**  A television-like screen that displays information as the user keys it or retrieves it from a file within a computer.

**centering, automatic**    A word-processing software capability that allows users to center copy between margins by means of a single command.

**central processing unit (CPU)**    The component of a computer that interprets the directions of a computer program and executes instructions.

**comment line**    The instructions that appear on the screen but are not printed.

**computer conferencing**    The linking of several computers in various locations for conducting long-distance online or offline conferences between two or more individuals.

**computer graphics**    A type of software used to create visual displays of various kinds.

**computer literacy**    The condition of developing familiarity with computers.

**computereze**    Jargon used in the computer field.

**control key**    A special key on a computer keyboard that is used simultaneously with certain other keys to initiate special functions.

**cursor**    A movable marker on a display screen that indicates the position at which data can be entered.

**daisy-wheel printer**    An output device that prints letter-quality characters on impact with a ribbon.

**data processing**    The process by which raw data are organized into meaningful information.

**database**    An organized collection of related information that is stored in computer-readable form.

**default**    The option that a computer system uses when no other option is selected by the operator; for example, the line-spacing default in most word-processing software is single spacing.

**delimiter**    A character marking the beginning and end of a text segment to find, save, or load.

**disk operating system (DOS)**    A software capability that processes commands to allow users to manage information and hardware resources.

**dot matrix printer**    An output device that has tiny metal rods that produce small dots to print characters.

**double-sided diskette**    A computer diskette designed so that data can be recorded on and read from both sides.

**dumb terminal**    A terminal used specifically for entering data into a larger computer system, and not programmed to perform processing functions.

**editing**   The rearranging, revising, and/or correcting of text to create an updated document.

**electronic calendar**   A software feature that keeps track of daily schedules in a computer.

**electronic mail**   The transmission of computerized information by telecommunication systems.

**external storage**   The data stored on media such as magnetic tapes, disks, and drums outside the CPU memory.

**field**   A group of related characters entered as a unit within a data record.

**file**   A group of related records — e.g., payroll file, inventory file.

**first-generation software**   The early versions of word-processing programs used mainly by secretarial personnel.

**floppy disk**   A flexible oxide-coated plastic disk (diskette) used with microcomputers for storing data, software, and operating systems.

**flowchart**   A diagram consisting of symbols to represent a solution to a problem or step-by-step progression through a procedure or system.

**footnoting, automatic**   A word-processing software feature that allows notes of reference or explanations to be placed simply and easily below text material on printed pages.

**format**   The process by which a new disk is prepared to accept data.

**function keys**   The keys on a computer keyboard that can be programmed to perform specific tasks.

**global find and replace**   The ability of word-processing software to go through records in search of a certain word or phrase and at each incidence replace it with another word or phrase.

**hard copy**   The computer output printed on paper; a document.

**hardware**   The physical equipment of a computer system.

**highlighting**   The indications such as inverse video, blinking, or high and low intensity image on a display screen showing that affected text can be moved, copied, inserted, or deleted.

**icon**   A pictorial representation of a function to be performed on a computer.

**incremental printing**   A word-processing feature that moves the paper and the printhead in very small increments and uses microspacing to justify, to vary line heights, and to offset subscripts and superscripts by a partial line height.

**indexing function**   A word-processing software feature that permits every word of a document to appear in an alphabetical index automatically.

**ink-jet printer**   An output device that shoots a fine stream of ink and "paints" characters on the paper.

**input**   The entry of data with a keyboard or other external device into a computer for processing.

**integrated business software**   The collection of data processing, word processing, and other forms of data communication into a single software package.

**intelligent terminal**   A programmable display terminal with built-in processing capabilities.

**interactive processing**   An online operation in which users communicate (interact) with computers and other equipment throughout the data-flow process.

**ion-deposition printer**   An output device that forms characters and graphic images by depositing electronic particles on a drum, then transferring them electronically (without impact) to paper.

**justification**   A word-processing software capability that produces output with even right margins.

**keyboarding**   The entry of data by means of a computer keyboard.

**laser printer**   An output device that uses electrical impulses or light to print.

**letter-quality printer**   An output device that prints documents as legibly as a typewriter.

**line printers**   A high-speed output device that prints lines of information as a unit, rather than character by character.

**mail merge**   The process by which documents are merged with mailing lists.

**mainframe**   A large computer with extensive processing and storage capabilities.

**memory**   A basic computer component that stores information.

**menu**   A list of options on a display screen from which a user can choose and initiate a function by selecting an option.

**merge printing**   The process of inserting information into a document while it is being printed.

**microcomputer**   A small computer (also called a personal computer) having less speed and memory capacity than a mainframe or minicomputer.

**minicomputer**   A computer that is smaller and less capable than a mainframe but larger and more capable than a microcomputer.

**modem**  A device that changes digital data to an analog signal (**MO**dulates) for transmission over communication channels and changes analog data into digital data on the receiving end of the transmission (**DEM**odulates).

**mouse**  A hand-held puck used in controlling the movement of a cursor.

**natural language processing**  A process that enables computer users to communicate with computers in ordinary English rather than in programming language.

**network**  A linking of computers and/or peripheral devices at different locations so that information may be shared among these devices.

**null modem**  A one-way device that connects two computers for the purpose of transferring data from one computer to the other.

**offline**  A term denoting (1) equipment that is not connected to the central processing unit of a computer, and (2) information that is not immediately accessible to computer users.

**online**  A term denoting (1) equipment that is connected to the central processing unit of a computer for interactive processing or computer conferencing, and (2) information that is accessible to computer users without their having to load the data into the system.

**output**  The end result of information processing in a readable form.

**pagination, automatic**  A word-processing software capability that allows users to set desired page length (number of printed lines per page).

**password**  A "confidential" word or number that allows users access to a computer system; a security feature.

**peripheral devices**  An input/output device or auxiliary storage equipment connected to a central processing unit.

**place markers**  A word-processing command that allows users to find their place in long files and to move the cursor quickly to that spot.

**printer port**  A connector on a computer for plugging in (interfacing) a printer cable.

**prompt**  A short message on screen to assist users in performing a task.

**proportional spacing**  A word-processing feature that allocates space to each character that is proportional to the character's actual width.

**random access memory (RAM)**  The area of computer memory that the microprocessor can "write" to or "read" from.

**read only memory (ROM)**  The area of computer memory that is used to store permanently the information vital to computer operation; users cannot "write" to this memory.

**record**    A collection of related data fields; one item in a data file.

**scrolling**    A software feature that enables users to see all their files one screen at a time.

**soft copy**    A nonpermanent image displayed on a terminal screen.

**software**    The programs used to instruct (run) a computer system.

**spreadsheet, electronic**    A type of software used to manipulate data (usually financial) in columns and rows and especially to analyze effects on data of hypothetical (what-if) situations.

**standalone word processing system**    Word-processing equipment that functions independently of a central computer.

**status line**    The top line of the display that provides text information such as page number, line number, and position of the cursor.

**strikeover**    A word-processing feature that allows corrections to be made by keying over what already appears on the screen.

**technophobia**    A fear of technology.

**telecommunication**    The transmission of data, text, voice, or image electronically over communication networks.

**terminal**    An input/output device used to send and receive data.

**thermal printer**    An output device that uses a heated printing element to etch images onto special paper.

**touchscreen**    A special computer screen that receives data input when a user touches a word, picture, or number on the screen.

**user-friendly software**    A computer program that is easy to use.

**window**    A portion of a terminal screen used to display information separate from the display area.

**word processing**    A system involving the use of computers, software, and peripherals to create, edit, store, retrieve, and print text.

**wordwrap**    A word-processing software feature that automatically places characters onto the next line when a line is filled.

**workstation**    A desk-top terminal or personal computer within a network for performing data/word processing, database management, graphics, telecommunications, and other support functions in an individual's work area.

# INDEX

# G

gas-plasma display, 483
gatekeepers, defined, 496
geographical organization, 68
gerunds, defined, 516
Goldhaber, 20, 22
goodwill messages, 384-393
goodwill and personnel
    messages, 384-409
Goss, 419
government publication
    indexes, 169
grammar, 511-521
    defined, 511
    mechanics and, 511-540
grammatical construction, 74-75
grapevine, defined, 21
graphic aids, comparison of
    common, 233-234
graphic communication, 214-255
graphic or pictorial messages,
    495
graphics
    computer, 7, 240-249
    defined, 215
    documentation in, 218-219
    footnotes in, 219
    interpretation of, 219
    introduction to, 215-219
    numbering and titles in,
        217-218
    placement in reports,
        215-216
    size of, 216-217
    source acknowledgments in,
        218-219
graphs
    component-part line,
        231-232
    line, 230-234
    multiple line, 231
    single line, 230-231
*Guidance Information System
    (GIS)*, 300
Gunning, 41
Gunning Fog Index, 40

# H

halo effect, defined, 401
Hays, 455

headings, 75
    defined, 265
headings and tabulations, 75
horizontal communication,
    defined, 21
horizontal reports, defined, 165
*How to Take the Fog Out of
    Writing*, 42
human messages, defined, 20
human relations, 21-23
    communication and, 22-23
    computers and, 23
human resources, 22
Hunt, 415
Hutchinson, Kevin L., 222
hyphen, 527-528
hypotheses, 262
hypothetical questions in
    interviews, 347-348

# I

icons, defined, 483
ion-deposition printer, defined,
    481
implicit language, explicit or, 75
importance, organization by, 68
impressive words, 35
impromptu delivery. *See*
    unplanned presentation
    delivery
*Index to U.S. Government
    Periodicals*, 169
indexes
    book, 168
    government publication, 169
    periodical, 168-169
indexing, defined, 484
indirect and direct questions in
    interviews, 347
indirect organization, 66-67
indirect question, defined, 347
inductive order in formal
    reports, 259
inductive plan of organization,
    defined, 259
industrial relations, defined, 22
industry directories, corporate
    and, 170-171
infinitives, defined, 516
informal invitations, 390-391
informal listening. *See*
    interactive listening

informal networks, 497
    defined, 21
informal reports, 256-258
    abbreviated and concise
        layout in, 258
    deductive order in, 257
    defined, 166, 256
    few or no preliminary and
        supplementary parts in,
        257-258
    structure of, 257-258
informal tables, 219-220
informal writing style, defined,
    257
information
    defined, 15
    denying requests for,
        114-115
    identifying, in research
        plan, 179
    sources of business, 167-177
    sources of other, 171
informational reports, defined,
    166
information and communication
    theory, 15-18
information explosion, 4
information-flow study, 506
information load, defined, 27
information overload, defined,
    27
information reply, additional,
    340-341
information systems
    centralized, 501
    clustered, 501
    decentralized, 502
    distributed, 501
information systems approach,
    defined, 500
information underload, defined,
    27
input, 478-480
    defined, 478
input devices, 245-247
input media, 478
integrated business software,
    defined, 482
integrity, 52
intelligent communicating
    copiers, defined, 488
interactive listening, defined,
    414

# PHOTO CREDITS

## Chapter 1

Illustration A: Courtesy of Radio Shack, A Division of Tandy Corporation; Illustration C: Courtesy of Hewlett-Packard Company; Illustration D: Courtesy of Hewlett-Packard Company; Illustration F: Courtesy of Hewlett-Packard Company; Illustration G: Courtesy of The Stock Market/Brownie Harris; Illustration H: Courtesy of Hewlett-Packard Company; Illustration J: Courtesy of Hewlett-Packard Company; Illustration P: Courtesy of GTE Corporation.

## Chapter 19

Illustration A: Courtesy of Sperry Corporation; Illustration C: Courtesy of ALCOA; Illustration F: Courtesy of NCR Corporation; Illustration H: Courtesy of Delta Airlines; Illustration I: Courtesy of IBM Corporation; Illustration J: Courtesy of NCR Corporation; Illustration K: Courtesy of Hewlett-Packard Company; Illustration L: Courtesy of Hewlett-Packard Company; Illustration M: Courtesy of Satellite Business Systems; Illustration O: Courtesy of Radio Shack, A Division of Tandy Corporation; Illustration P: Courtesy of Radio Shack, A Division of Tandy Corporation; Illustration Q: Courtesy of NCR Corporation; Illustration S: Courtesy of Mitsubishi Electric Sales America, Inc.; Illustration U: Courtesy of AT & T; Illustration V: Courtesy of The Stock Market/Gabe Palmer, MUG SHOTS 1987; Illustration W: Courtesy of WIDCOM INC.; Illustration X: Courtesy of Bell & Howell Business Equipment Group; Illustration Z: Courtesy of General Motors Corporation.